S0-AYP-573

HUMAN BEHAVIOR
FOR SOCIAL WORK PRACTICE

Also available from Lyceum Books, Inc.

Advisory Editor: Thomas M. Meenaghan, *New York University*

Complex Systems and Human Behavior
by Christopher Hudson

Social Work with HIV and AIDS: A Practice-Based Guide
by Diana Rowan and Contributors

Diversity in Family Constellations: Implications for Practice
edited by Krishna L. Guadalupe and Debra L. Welkley

The Costs of Courage: Combat Stress, Warriors, and Family Survival
by Josephine G. Price, Col. David H. Price, and Kimberly K. Shackleford

Lesbian and Gay Couples: Lives, Issues, and Practice
by Ski Hunter

Citizenship Social Work with Older People
by Malcolm Payne

Character Formation and Identity in Adolescence
by Randolph L. Lucente

Surviving Disaster: The Role of Social Networks
edited by Robin L. Ersing and Kathleen A. Kost

Social Work Practice with Latinos: Key Issues and Emerging Themes
edited by Rich Furman and Nalini Negi

Raise Up a Child: Human Development in an African-American Family
by Edith V. P. Hudley, Wendy L. Haight, and Peggy Miller

HUMAN BEHAVIOR
FOR SOCIAL WORK PRACTICE
A Developmental-Ecological Framework

Second Edition

Wendy L. Haight
University of Minnesota, Twin Cities

Edward H. Taylor
University of British Columbia, Okanagan Campus

LYCEUM
BOOKS, INC.

5758 South Blackstone Avenue
Chicago, Illinois 60637

© 2013 by Lyceum Books, Inc.

Published by

LYCEUM BOOKS, INC.
5758 S. Blackstone Ave.
Chicago, Illinois 60637
773+643-1903 fax
773+643-1902 phone
lyceum@lyceumbooks.com
www.lyceumbooks.com

All rights reserved under International and Pan-American Copyright Conventions. No part of the publication may be reproduced, stored in a retrieval system, copied, or transmitted in any form or by any means without written permission from the publisher.

6 5 4 3 2 1   13 14 15 16

ISBN 978-1-935871-25-5

Cover art by Richard Hull.

Printed in the United States of America.

Library of Congress Cataloging-in-Publication Data
Haight, Wendy L., 1958–
    Human behavior for social work practice : a developmental-ecological framework / Wendy Haight, Edward Taylor.—2nd ed.
        p. cm.
    ISBN 978-1-935871-25-5 (pbk.: alk. paper)
    1. Social service—Philosophy. 2. Social service—Methodology. 3. Social service—Research. I. Taylor, Edward H. II. Title.
    HV40.H22   2013
    361.3'2—dc23
                                                                                2012020332

We are grateful to Mary Whalen and Dawn D'Amico for permission to use their photographs.

For my parents, Richard L. Haight and Donna V. Boitano Haight

For my children, Dominique and Marisa Taylor

Contents

Preface to the Second Edition

Since its publication in 2007, we have had the opportunity to teach with the first edition of *Human Behavior for Social Work Practice* and to receive feedback from our students and colleagues. As a result of these experiences, we have added content and modified the organization to strengthen the second edition. First, we have included a chapter on using social science evidence to understand human behavior in the social environment, and to enhance social work practice. We have found that it is important for students to be exposed to characteristics of research (e.g., longitudinal designs) that have been central to the study of human development, as well as to learn to discriminate those studies with strong validity from those whose claims are based on weaker arguments. We also find that discussions of evidence-informed practice are best integrated throughout the social work curriculum, and not isolated in research-methods classes.

The second edition also includes separate chapters on infants and young children. This change allowed us to include more developmental material to describe the rapid changes occurring during these early years. The new chapter on infancy, written with Susan Cole, highlights preventive interventions. The new early childhood chapter retains its focus on attachment and the child welfare system, but includes enhanced coverage of play. Developmental theorists from Freud to Piaget to Vygotsky agree that play is a central developmental function in early childhood. Yet many early childhood programs, especially those for vulnerable children, increasingly focus on adult-led, academically oriented activities. This focus decreases young children's opportunities to participate with peers in play, an important "zone of proximal development."

We also include a chapter with reflections on race, racism, and resistance in the United States, written with Jane Marshall. Diversity content is infused throughout the text, but we believe it is also important to explicitly address issues surrounding race in greater depth. Furthermore, many of the issues that other chapters focus on, such as attachment, spirituality, mentoring, and depression, occur in various forms throughout the life span. By departing from our developmental structure, the race, racism, and resistance chapter allows us to present important developmental issues across the life span.

The second edition also includes a chapter with reflections on women and gender written with Kathleen Reutter. Similar to the chapter on race, racism, and resistance, this chapter discusses important developmental issues as they are manifested throughout the life span. The chapters on gender and race also integrate important sociological concepts of intersectionality with developmental research.

In this edition, we also include a short, introductory chapter on the brain, tailored to social work students. This chapter includes brief sections on the history of neuroscience, the anatomy of the cerebral cortex, the neurological bases of memory and anxiety, brain development, and plasticity. We also explain ways in which the brain is scientifically and medically studied. Our focus is on procedures that students may encounter as part of multidisciplinary teams, especially in medical social work such as positron-emission tomography (PET) and functional magnetic resonance imaging (fMRI).

The organization of this edition has been modified so that presentation of developmental material is paused at key points. The chapter on race, racism, and resistance in the United States follows the developmental chapters on adolescence and early adulthood. The chapter on women and gender follows the developmental chapters on middle and later adulthood.

Despite these and other changes, the second edition of *Human Behavior for Social Work Practice: A Developmental-Ecological Framework* maintains its focus on presenting students with a coherent, conceptual framework for applying social science content on human behavior in the social environment to social work practice. Although the second edition is expanded, it continues to reflect our commitment to providing a "core" HBSE 1 text, one that is neither a "supplementary" nor a "comprehensive" text. It is not supplementary because it aims to deliver a coherent and complete argument regarding the centrality of human development to social work practice through in-depth exemplars of the use of developmental knowledge in social work practice throughout the life span. It is not comprehensive because the scholarship in the area of human behavior in the social environment is vast, and there are many excellent human development textbooks. Our aim is not to duplicate these textbooks, but to focus on a set of key developmental concepts and their connection to social work practice. By maintaining this focused approach, the book allows instructors to supplement and expand upon the text as they choose, and students will receive a taste of what it is like to think developmentally in their social work practice.

Acknowledgments

Many people had a hand bringing the second edition of this book to fruition, and it is a pleasure to acknowledge them here. The social work students in Wendy's and Ed's HBSE classes energetically provided thoughtful and comprehensive critiques. John Orwat, Loyola University–Chicago; Shelagh Larkin, Xavier University; Melody Loya, West Texas A&M University; David Kondrat, University of South Florida; John Doherty, University of North Carolina–Charlotte; Brian Masciadrelli, State University of New York–Fredonia; Tim Page, Louisiana State University; and Carole Olson, Morehead State University, reviewed the manuscript, and their commentary was invaluable.

We greatly appreciate Susan Cole's, Kathleen Reutter's, and Jane Marshall's help in writing chapters of this book. They have been true collaborators and thoughtful coauthors.

Our family members, Susan Wells, and James, Matthew, and Camilla Black, provided support and advice. Susan was particularly helpful with the sections on child welfare, and Jim advised on brain development.

We also thank David Follmer for his innovative and interdisciplinary approach to publishing social work texts. Thanks also to Joann Hoy, who provided thoughtful and thorough text editing.

In the United States, African Americans and the elderly are at increased risk of living in poverty. This older man is purchasing used winter clothing.

Thinking Developmentally about Social Work Practice

Social workers are committed to enhancing the welfare of vulnerable people through direct services to individuals in need and through social and political action. These commitments to social justice are a legacy from the nineteenth-century progressive era, with its "friendly visitors," volunteers, and paraprofessionals who provided assistance to those who were impoverished. Today, social work is a profession requiring undergraduate and, increasingly, graduate degrees. Contemporary social workers practice in a wide variety of contexts, including public schools, child welfare agencies, health and mental health settings, nonprofit agencies, and colleges and universities. Given the complexity of modern social problems, the challenges facing social workers are enormous. Students of social work may ask: How do social workers approach such complex and diverse issues as child maltreatment, poverty, unemployment, oppression, violence, mental illness, and end-of-life care? What unifies "social work" practice across such varied contexts as inner-city schools and rural nursing homes with individuals of different ages, ethnicities, and socioeconomic status?

Clearly, there are no simple answers. Social work draws upon a rich knowledge base built primarily upon the social and biological sciences, as interpreted from the perspective of social work values such as service, social justice, the dignity and worth of each individual, and the centrality of human relationships. The interdisciplinary stance of social work may be one of its greatest strengths. It may also be its greatest challenge, as social workers struggle to formulate and apply a consistent analytic framework for approaching diverse social problems. The goal of this book is to present and illustrate a coherent, interdisciplinary framework for social work practice: a **developmental, ecological-systems** framework.[1] This framework is compatible with the **bio-psycho-social-spiritual** framework common in social work texts. It elaborates upon this approach through a focus on developmental change across individual lives within particular cultural and historical contexts. An example of a nineteenth-century forebear of modern social work, Clara Brown, illustrates the developmental, ecological-systems framework.

---

[1] For the purposes of this book, we use the terms "framework" and "theory" interchangeably.

In the 1800s, Central City was the capital of the Colorado Territory and a growing, wealthy mining town. Discovery of gold and silver had helped turn a miners' camp into an economic and cultural center. An elegant opera house and East Coast–style hotel were built. Operas and stage productions were routinely brought in from New York and the West Coast. The town was also the home of several stone churches with colorful stained-glass windows. As in many towns and cities, the wealthy and upper-middle class of Central City lived on one side of a mountain stream, and the working-class people and poor lived on the other side. Racial segregation existed in both law and practice, but slavery was not allowed, and a free African American could find gainful employment. Voting rights for women had not yet been seriously considered, and laws and customs impeded women's acquisition of wealth or power.

Within this historical and cultural context, an African-American woman, Clara Brown, won financial stability and exercised considerable leadership for approximately twenty years. Mrs. Brown spent her first fifty years of life as a slave in Kentucky, suffering not only physical hardship but, most significantly, the loss of her four children and husband, who were sold away from her. Upon the death of her slave owner, she was granted her freedom, and because the laws of Kentucky required that freed slaves leave the state within a year, she eventually joined a wagon train headed for the Colorado gold rush. After settling in Central City, Mrs. Brown began taking in laundry and doing odd jobs for wealthy miners and landowners. Within a short time, she began investing in land and developed considerable wealth, which she used to give back to her community. Mrs. Brown started the first Sunday school in Central City, and nurtured it into the city's first permanent church. In addition, she opened her home as an informal settlement house for people of all races. At the age of sixty, Mrs. Brown organized a wagon train to rescue approximately thirty-four African Americans endangered by racial violence in Kentucky and Tennessee at the end of the Civil War. For the remainder of her life, Mrs. Brown gave financial help to every church in Central City, supported antipoverty causes, and worked to end segregation in public schools. In her late seventies, the governor appointed Mrs. Brown to represent Colorado in assisting former slaves fleeing the South's brutality and racism. At the end of her life, dignitaries from across the state attended Mrs. Brown's funeral. Today, people visiting Colorado's state capital in Denver can see a stained-glass window honoring this courageous pioneer who overcame so many odds, traveled so far, and gave so much (Baker, 2003).

How can we account for the remarkable leadership of Clara Brown, who lived when African Americans were regarded by the larger society as sub-human, and women as both intellectually and morally inferior to men? What role might biology, psychology, social context, and sociocultural-historical factors have played in shaping her into a leader who influenced public policy, won the confidence of powerful male politicians, and became a recognized spiritual and ethical leader for a predominantly white community? The developmental, ecological-systems framework presented in this text will provide you with an analytic framework, or set of intellectual problem-solving tools, to systematically consider the development of complex individuals such as Clara Brown, their families, communities, and times, as well as to address challenging issues facing social workers in the twenty-first century.

A developmental, ecological-systems framework draws upon the fields of **human development**, **ecology**, and **systems theory** to consider the ways in which human beings shape, and are shaped within, complex and dynamic sociocultural and historical contexts. Human development examines the loosely coordinated ensemble of biological, psychological, and social changes that humans undergo throughout the life span, as well as the process (or causes) of change (Lightfoot, Cole, & Cole, 2009). Such changes may be universal to all humans, or they may vary in content and timing across cultural and historical contexts. Ecology is a branch of science that deals with the interrelationships of organisms with their environment (Bronfenbrenner, 1995; Germain & Gitterman, 1996). Systems are collections of interrelated parts that typically function as a unit and change in concert. They exist at multiple levels, including the biological, psychological, familial, bureaucratic, political, and cultural (Hudson, 2010). Thus, a developmental, ecological-systems analysis of Clara Brown would consider her biological, psychological, and social characteristics as they change over time in relation to her particular cultural and historical context. This analysis of Clara Brown might consider

- the strength provided by lifelong physical and mental health;
- an ability to learn without formal training;
- persistence and commitment to hard work and service;
- Kentucky's law forcing freed slaves to leave the state;
- the lack of organization and need for leadership on America's frontier;
- the existence of a community where one could prosper financially and socially; and
- the problems of racism, sexism, and poverty within nineteenth-century American society.

Thus, to understand Clara Brown, we must consider not only her resiliency, talent, and drive, but also the social systems, culture, and group needs in nineteenth-century Central City. Together, health, personal skills, and ecological factors created a unique set of opportunities and challenges. Mrs. Brown thrived, in part, because she successfully created a fit within the particular social context of Central City. Without her internal personal strengths interacting within a particular ecological context, Mrs. Brown's story would have unfolded differently. Much of human development is profoundly intertwined with social systems, time, place, and space. It is impossible to understand human actions removed from their cultural and historical contexts. Had Mrs. Brown arrived earlier or later in Colorado, or not gone to Colorado, her development and destiny would have been different: perhaps, also, the destiny of Colorado City.

THE HISTORICAL CONTEXT OF SOCIAL WORK IN THE UNITED STATES

Understanding societal responses to social problems such as those tackled by Clara Brown requires understanding of the historical and cultural contexts in which those responses are embedded. According to the National Association of Social Workers' (NASW) **code of ethics**, "The primary mission of the social work profession is to enhance human well-being and help meet the basic needs of all people, with particular attention to the needs and empowerment of people who are vulnerable, oppressed, and living in poverty" (p. 1). The emergence of the social work profession illustrates, however, that perceptions of what those basic needs are, who is in need, and how to address those needs have varied widely. Unlike law, medicine, and education, which can trace their roots back to classical Greece and Rome, social work is a relatively new profession. It emerged in the nineteenth century during a time of social crisis and change brought about by industrialization and urbanization. Social work originated in volunteer efforts to address issues resulting from the paradox of increasing poverty in the increasingly productive and prosperous economies of Europe and North America. That prosperity, a result of industrial economies and urbanization, contributed to pressing social problems such as unemployment, child neglect and maltreatment, chronic disability, and poverty in the midst of unprecedented wealth (Stuart, 2008).

In the early 1800s, volunteers primarily carried out services to impoverished individuals. These "friendly visitors" mainly were middle-class women steeped in Victorian morality. They acquired their knowledge and skills through apprenticeship, and did not necessarily have an in-depth knowledge of the conditions facing the individuals they were trying to help. They took a moralistic approach, stressing religious values based on love to save "the miserable from the sin of poverty" (Brieland, 1995, p. 2248). According to Lubove (1965, as cited in Brieland, 1995, p. 2248), "the visitor saw in her client less an equal or potential equal than an object of character reformation whose unfortunate and lowly condition resulted from ignorance or deviation from middle-class values and patterns of life-organization: temperance, industriousness, family cohesiveness, frugality, foresight, and moral restraint."

In the late nineteenth century, most large American cities established charity organization societies (COSs) to coordinate the efforts of various voluntary charity groups in providing assistance to the poor. The goal was to provide relief on a rational basis. COSs sought to save cities from the evils of pauperism, reduce the cost of charity, and deal with the antagonism created by social-class differences. District agents, paid COS employees, interviewed applicants for relief, determined appropriate assistance, and arranged for friendly visits from volunteers. The visitors were to provide good advice and an example of caring, while the district agents were to curb potential abuse. COSs stressed the moral imperative for material aid only to the worthy, summarily rejecting the "sturdy beggar, the alcoholic, the womanizer and the prostitute." Only decades later would environmental and social structural conditions be recognized as causes of poverty and illness (Stuart, 2008).

The late nineteenth century also saw the settlement house movement, which embodied a somewhat distinct philosophy and approach from the COSs. Jane Addams and Ellen Starr established the most famous settlement house in the United States, Hull House, in Chicago. Settlement workers were middle-class and affluent volunteers who "settled" in immigrant neighborhoods. Addams believed that the settlement houses provided a service both to the volunteer residents, who needed a purpose in life, and to an increasingly stratified society at large by building bridges between social classes. The philosophy of the settlement house movement is captured, in part, in Addams's (1902) critique of the "friendly" visiting of charity workers:

> A most striking incongruity, at once apparent, is the difference between the emotional kindness with which relief is given by one poor neighbor to another poor neighbor, and the guarded care with which relief is given by a charity visitor to a charity recipient. The neighborhood mind is at once confronted not only by the difference of method, but by an absolute clashing of two ethical standards.
> ...When they [COS clients] see the delay and caution with which relief is given, these do not appear to them cautious scruples, but the cold and calculating action of the selfish man. (as cited in Brieland, 1995, p. 2248)

By 1900, working for social betterment had become an occupation, a separate occupational status existed for charity workers, and schools of charity and philanthropy provided training in a number of cities. Social work emerged as a profession by the 1930s as a result of efforts to conceptualize social work method, expand social work education programs, and develop a stable funding base for voluntary social service programs. Currently, social work is a major profession with graduate education and a common framework of practice that addresses a wide range of social problems (Stuart, 2008).

DEVELOPMENTAL, ECOLOGICAL-SYSTEMS ANALYSIS OF SOCIAL WORK ISSUES

An adequate understanding of the life of Clara Brown, as well as societal responses to the issues she tackled, clearly requires consideration of a large amount of information. Similarly, practicing social workers must respond to an enormous volume of complex information on a daily basis as they advocate for and support their clients. Systematic consideration of biological, psychological, and social factors as they change over time within particular sociocultural-historical contexts is critical to adequate assessment and effective intervention.

One way in which human beings deal with complex social information is through informal **folk theories** of human behavior and development. Such folk theories include commonly held values, beliefs, and explanations for how the social world works. In general, folk theories are effective for dealing with everyday life within our particular families and communities, for example, interacting with our neighbors and parenting our children. Folk theories are less useful, however, when we are confronted with problems that are difficult or unusual for us, or that occur within cultural communities with which we are not familiar. For example, implementing an effective intervention for a child struggling in school may be especially challenging when that child comes from an immigrant family with folk theories of child development that diverge from those of the social workers. Reliance on folk theories in such situations can result in misunderstandings and poor communication because they often are implicit and unexamined, and may include stereotypes, superstitions, and inaccuracies.

Historically, social workers have served as leaders in supporting individuals struggling with poverty.

Like folk theories, **social science theories** are frameworks that help us understand, explain, and predict the social world. In contrast to folk theories, social science theories are explicit regarding, for example, the nature of human development, and must be supported by logic and empirical research. They are open to critical evaluation and may be challenged on the basis of their accuracy, breadth, and coherence. Most importantly, they may be revised as new knowledge and perspectives emerge.

According to the philosopher of science Karl Popper (1902–1994), scientific theories are attempted explanations, approximations of the "truth." They are not self-evident, taken-for-granted, or cherished perspectives. Ideally, they are treated as intellectual objects that can be put on the metaphorical table for scrutiny. By vigorously and actively criticizing our theories, we uncover incorrect assumptions, inconsistencies, narrowness, and errors, thereby moving toward a more adequate understanding of the social world (Popper, 1999).

Social work draws upon a wide variety of social science theories, from those exploring individual development to those focusing on community development. There is no single, comprehensive theory that adequately portrays the complexities of human development. There are a variety of different theories that contribute to our understanding of the complex interaction of biological, psychological, and social factors that shape human development within particular historical and cultural contexts. For the purposes of analysis in this book, we will discuss these aspects of development separately. In reality, however, they interact in mutually influential and complex ways. For example, as infants develop the physical strength and coordination necessary to crawl and toddle independently, their spatial knowledge expands. In addition, their social relationships change. For example, babies may be physically capable of independent locomotion before they have the judgment necessary to do so safely, resulting in new restrictions and conflicts with caregivers. Thus, changes in one area of development have ramifications for other areas of development, and development may be uneven. Furthermore, social and cultural contexts vary in the ways in which development is supported. For example, the extent to which babies are allowed to move about independently varies. Some families in the United States allow young babies to career around in baby walkers, while in some hunter-gatherer groups, even older infants are carried attached to the mother for much of the day. These different experiences may shape not just early physical development, but social and emotional development as well.

USING THIS TEXT

The primary goal of this text is to help social work students "think developmentally" in approaching their practice. It attempts to establish a bridge between comprehensive undergraduate courses in developmental psychology or human development and social work practice courses—in other words, to help social work students understand and practice a developmental approach to effective social work practice. It establishes and illustrates a conceptual framework for approaching social work practice, developmentally.

This text does not attempt to replicate the many excellent texts on human development available and widely used in courses on developmental psychology, human development, and life-span development. Students should plan on referring to any number of excellent texts by developmental scholars such as Laura Berk; Mavis Hetherington and Ross Parke; Cynthia Lightfoot, Michael Cole, and Sheila Cole; and Lawrence Steinberg throughout their careers. They also should become familiar with the *Handbook of Child Psychology* and *The Child: An Encyclopedic Companion,* to name just two professional references regularly updated by experts in the dynamic field of human development.

ORGANIZATION OF THE TEXT

The book is divided into several parts. The introduction is a series of chapters describing the developmental, ecological-systems framework, introducing human brain development and function, and discussing how social science evidence is used to understand development and enhance social work practice (evidence-based practice). The second major section illustrates and teaches developmental thinking in social work practice with infants, young children, children in middle childhood, adolescents, and young adults. It is followed by a reflection on race, racism, and resistance in the United States. The next section focuses on developmental thinking in social work practice with midlife and older adults. It is followed by a reflection on women and gender throughout the life span. The last chapter integrates major themes presented throughout the text. In addition, we present in text boxes a set of perennial issues encountered by social workers that affect individuals throughout the life span. These text boxes appear throughout the chapters and include topics such as violence, poverty, and substance misuse. Other text boxes introduce selected topics such as international social work.

SUMMARY

American social work has evolved within the complex social and historical forces of the nineteenth and twentieth centuries. With roots in nineteenth-century charity organization societies and philanthropy, social work emerged largely in response to problems associated with industrialization and urbanization. Historically, social workers have been committed to enhancing the welfare of people who encounter problems related to poverty, mental health, health care, employment, shelter and housing, and abuse. As it evolved, social work developed a dual focus on the needs of individual clients and the ways in which the community and society respond to those needs. Social workers are concerned both with individuals' well-being and with the environmental and social structural factors that affect them. Social workers support those in acute need, and encourage those in positions of power to use their resources to meet those needs.

Understanding human development and thinking developmentally are central to social work, or any profession whose goal is to enhance the well-being of vulnerable individuals. The developmental, ecological-systems framework in social work, described in chapter 2, reflects an interdisciplinary integration of theory and empirical research in the social and biological sciences.

References

Addams, J. (1902). *Democracy and social ethics*. New York: Macmillan.

Baker, R. (2003). *Clara: An ex-slave in gold rush Colorado*. Central City, CO: Black Hawk Publishing.

Brieland, D. (1995). Social work practice: History and evolution. In *Encyclopedia of social work* (19th ed., Vol. 3, pp. 2247–2254). Washington, DC: NASW Press.

Bronfenbrenner, U. (1995). Developmental ecology through space and time. In P. Moen, G. H. Elder Jr., & K. Luscher (Eds.), *Examining lives in context: Perspectives on the ecology of human development* (pp. 619–648). Washington, DC: American Psychological Association.

Germain, C. B., & Gitterman, A. (1996). *The life model of social work practice* (2nd ed.). New York: Columbia University Press.

Hudson, C. (2010). *Complex systems and human behavior*. Chicago: Lyceum Books.

Lightfoot, C., Cole, M., & Cole, S. (2009). *The development of children* (6th ed.). New York: Worth Publishers.

National Association of Social Workers. (2008). *NASW code of ethics: Guide to the everyday professional conduct of social workers*. Washington, DC: Author.

Popper, K. (1999). *All life is problem solving*. New York: Routledge.

Stuart, P. (2008). Social work profession: History. In T. Mizrahi & L. Davis (Eds.), *Encyclopedia of social work* (20th ed., Vol. 4, pp. 157–164). Washington, DC: NASW Press.

2

The Developmental, Ecological-Systems Framework
A Brief Historical Overview of Theories

Understanding human development is central to social work, or any profession whose goal is to enhance the well-being of vulnerable individuals. The developmental, ecological-systems framework in social work reflects an interdisciplinary integration of theory and empirical research in the social and biological sciences. Conceptual frameworks clearly are necessary, given the volume of complex information to which social workers must respond on a daily basis. Systematic consideration of biological, psychological, and social factors as they change over time within particular sociocultural-historical systems is critical to adequate social work assessment and effective intervention. This chapter presents a brief historical overview of the intellectual forebears and core concepts of the developmental, ecological-systems perspective.

BIOLOGICAL THEORIES

Biology plays a fundamental role in the developmental process. Biological theories of human development traditionally have focused on genetic factors underlying developmental change—changes in behavior were seen as resulting primarily from changes in biology. The major cause of development was viewed as maturation, that is, genetically determined patterns of change that unfolded with age. Individual differences in human development were attributed primarily to differences in genetic inheritance (see Lightfoot, Cole, & Cole, 2009). In the early part of the twentieth century, relatively little attention was given to the role of environment in human development. Arnold Gesell (1880–1961), an influential pediatrician, attributed children's behavioral development primarily to inherent, maturational mechanisms, with the environment playing a relatively minor role (Gesell, 1940).

Recent research from a biological perspective typically attributes a stronger and more complex role to the environment. It addresses the myriad ways in which biology and environment interact, including in brain development throughout the life course. A now classic experimental paradigm involves the postmortem comparison of the biological development of young rats raised in a complex, or "enriched," environment, with that of rats raised under standard laboratory conditions, an "impoverished environment."[1] The rats raised in the enriched environment have many other rats with which to interact and objects to explore. The rats raised in the impoverished conditions are reared in social isolation in standard laboratory cages. William Greenough and colleagues demonstrated that rearing in a socially and intellectually enriched environment has dramatic effects on rats' brain anatomy, endocrine systems, physical growth, and behavior. Complex social and cognitive experiences result in improved social skills and greater control over stress responses (Black, Jones, Nelson, & Greenough, 1998). These brain changes are distributed over several neural systems and involve a gross enlargement of the brain, as well as the formation of new **neurons** (brain cells) and **synapses** (connections between neurons; Wallace, Kilman, Withers, & Greenough, 1992).

In addition to illustrating the flexibility of the mammalian brain, neurodevelopmental research also illustrates that there are limits to the influence of environment. For example, older rats display neural plasticity, but even when placed in enriched environments, they do not display the same degree of plasticity as young rats (Greenough, Black, & Wallace, 1987). The development of the mammalian brain appears to be shaped by environment and experience throughout the life span, but particularly in early life.

Human neurological development also reflects the complex interaction of genes and environment. The developmental milestones of the first several years of life are remarkably universal. Unless they experience significant deprivation, children reared in different cultures learn to walk, talk, manipulate objects, and interact socially at similar rates. **Experience-expectant developmental processes** (see Black et al., 1998) develop as an interaction of innate neural wiring with experiences that are universally present in any human environment. For example, typically developing infants in all cultures experience visual stimulation. Deviation from this universally expected experience, for example, early and prolonged visual deprivation, can result in a permanent inability to see. Similarly, typically developing infants in all cultures experience social interactions. Children who experience severe social deprivation may have permanent impairments to their social and language development (Sharpe & Trauner, 2009).

In contrast with relatively universal developmental process, **experience-dependent developmental processes** are more variable. They emerge as

---

[1]Because of ethical considerations, some developmental research uses animal models. Findings may be relevant to humans to the extent that systems (e.g., mammalian brains) share relevant characteristics.

an interaction of genes and unique environmental conditions. They allow for flexibility and plasticity throughout the life span. In later childhood and adolescence, the effects of cultural variation and within-cultural differences in education and other experiences become more apparent. For example, whether a child learns to care for sheep or to play the piano depends on culturally available opportunities.

Modern biological research is important to social work, in part, because it draws our attention to the complex ways in which our genetic and cultural heritages interact. For example, the use of mood- and mind-altering substances has a long history in human cultures, but some genetically predisposed individuals may become dependent (see boxes 2.1–2.3). Modern research into the biological bases of behavior and development also

---

BOX 2.1 SUBSTANCE MISUSE ACROSS THE LIFE SPAN

Defining Substance Dependence

Substance dependence has been viewed from moral, cultural, public health, and scientific perspectives. From a social work perspective, substance dependence may have a biological component resulting in intense physical cravings and illness. In addition, substance dependence can be thought of as a compulsion motivating the individual to seek and use a substance at all costs, even when there are severe consequences. A compulsion is a behavior that cannot simply be stopped. It must be performed even when the person understands that it makes no logical sense, and may even be harmful to oneself or others. Serious compulsions are caused by an injured brain and are seldom cured by self-motivation, knowledge, or awareness of the destructive behavior alone.

The National Institute of Drug Abuse identifies substance dependence as present if three or more of the following have been experienced or exhibited during the previous year:

- difficulties in controlling substance-taking behavior in terms of its onset, termination, or levels of use
- a strong desire or sense of compulsion to take the substance
- progressive neglect of alternative pleasures or interests because of psychoactive substance use
- increased amount of time necessary to obtain or take the substance or to recover from its effects
- persisting with substance use despite clear evidence of overtly harmful consequences, depressed mood states consequent to heavy use, or drug impairment of cognitive functioning
- evidence of tolerance, so that higher doses of the psychoactive substance are required to achieve effects originally produced by lower doses

- a physiological withdrawal state when substance use has ceased or been reduced, as evidenced by the characteristic withdrawal syndrome for the substance, or use of the same (or closely related) substance with the intention of relieving or avoiding withdrawal symptoms.

———
Source: Barlow & Durand, 2005.

BOX 2.2 SUBSTANCE MISUSE ACROSS THE LIFE SPAN

Substance Use in the United States

Alcohol and other substances are widely misused throughout the United States. Here are some data from the National Survey on Drug Use and Drug Health:

- In 2008, 47 percent of the general population reported having used an illegal substance in their lifetime.
- In 2009, approximately 8.7 percent of the general population reported having used an illegal drug in the past twelve months.
- In 2009, marijuana (4.3 million people), pain relievers (1.9 million), and cocaine (1.1 million) had high levels of past-year dependence or misuse.
- In 2009, 22.5 million people (8.9 percent of the population age twelve or older) were classified with substance dependence or misuse in the past year, based on criteria specified in the *Diagnostic and Statistical Manual of Mental Disorders*, 4th edition (*DSM-IV*). Of these, 3.2 million depended on or misused both alcohol and illicit drugs, 3.9 million depended on or misused illicit drugs but not alcohol, and 15.4 million depended on or misused alcohol but not illicit drugs.
- In 2009, adults age twenty-one or older who had first used alcohol at age fourteen or younger were more than six times as likely to be classified with alcohol dependence or misuse as adults who had their first drink at age twenty-one or older (16.5 percent versus 2.5 percent).
- In 2009, 23.7 percent of people age twelve or older participated in binge drinking. Binge drinking is defined as having five or more drinks on the same occasion on at least one day in the thirty days prior to the survey.
- In 2009, heavy drinking was reported by 6.8 percent of the population aged twelve or older, or 17.1 million people. Heavy drinking is defined as binge drinking on at least five days in the past thirty days.

———
Sources: Substance Abuse and Mental Health Services Administration, 2009, 2010.

> ### BOX 2.3 SUBSTANCE MISUSE ACROSS THE LIFE SPAN
> #### Risk Factors for Substance Dependence
>
> Race, ethnicity, and living in city/urban environments are not good predictors of who will become dependent or misuse a substance. However, higher rates of addiction are found in people who have lower levels of education and income. And men are at greater risk for developing dependency on alcohol than women: lifetime alcohol dependence for men is 21.4 percent, and for women 9.2 percent.
>
> ---
>
> Source: Barlow & Durand, 2005; Schuckit, 2009.

addresses a variety of issues central to social work policy and practice, including **learning differences** (disabilities), **autism spectrum disorders**, and serious neuropsychiatric disorders such as **schizophrenia** or **bipolar disorder (manic depression)** (e.g., Goodwin & Jamison, 1990; Gottesman, 1991; McNeil et al., 1994; E. H. Taylor, 1987, 1997, 2006; Torrey, Bowler, Taylor, & Gottesman, 1994).

Understanding the biological origins of a behavior or disorder and how it interacts within particular sociocultural-historical contexts can have profound implications for the development of effective social work interventions. For example, understanding the neurological bases of autism as a developmental disability, as well as the ways in which early intervention can and cannot affect its course, has shifted the focus of interventions. In the first half of the twentieth century, interventions focused on modifying presumably pathological family interactions. Today, social workers recognize autism as a neurodevelopmental disability, provide support to families of autistic children, and identify appropriate early-intervention resources within the community (see Cash & Hallahan, 2009; Schreibman & Koegel, 1996).

PSYCHOLOGICAL AND SOCIAL PSYCHOLOGICAL THEORIES

Psychoanalytic Theories

Psychological and social factors also play important roles in human development. Psychoanalytic theory, based on the work of Sigmund Freud (1856–1939) and his followers, influenced psychological and social theories of development throughout the twentieth century. Freud was trained as a neurologist and was heavily influenced by Charles Darwin's theory of evolution. He treated patients experiencing extreme fear, emotional trauma, and problems in dealing with everyday life by tracing these problems back to traumatic, unresolved experiences in early childhood.

On the basis of clinical data, Freud constructed a theory of personality development that emphasized the way in which children satisfy basic drives that guarantee survival. These drives, mental pressures to relieve physical needs such as hunger and sex, create the tension (libido) that propels development. Freud reasoned that the goal of all biological drives is survival and propagation of the species. Since reproduction of the species is accomplished through sexual intercourse, Freud reasoned that all drives must ultimately serve the fundamental sex drive.

According to Freud, development occurs as children progress through a series of stages. Although gratification remains sexual in nature throughout the life course, the forms of that gratification change, for example, oral gratification in infancy and genital gratification in adolescence. Conflicts that individuals encounter in each stage of development determine their later personality.

One important concept in Freudian theory is the unconscious. According to Freud, behavior emerges as a result of psychodynamics, movement and interaction in the mind. Some of these thought processes are hidden from conscious awareness; that is, they are the unconscious (Freud, 1905/1953, 1920/1955, 1933/1964; for overviews, see Lightfoot, Cole, & Cole, 2009; Wood, 1971; Yelloly, 1980). Identifying and exploring such thought processes are important components of contemporary psychodynamic therapies.

Erik Erikson (1902–1994) built on many of Freud's ideas of development, including the importance of early childhood in the formation of the personality and the existence of unconscious drives. Erikson, however, considered social and cultural interaction, not just biological drives, as central mechanisms of development. He also viewed development as continuing throughout the life course, not as ending with sexual maturity in adolescence. According to Erikson, the personality continues to undergo changes as individuals experience varying contact with social institutions and cultural practices throughout the life span. Erikson viewed the main challenge of life not simply as biological survival, but as the search for identity. At each stage of life, the person must accomplish a major task, which Erikson referred to as a crisis. The individual's sense of identity is formed at the resolution of these crises. For example, in infancy, babies learn to trust or mistrust others to meet their basic needs. In adolescence, individuals establish a sense of their personal identity as part of their social group, or they become confused about who they are and what they want in life. In later adulthood, individuals make sense of their prior experiences and feel that their lives have been meaningful, or they despair over unachieved goals and ill-spent lives. Broadly conceived, at each stage of life, people ask themselves, "Who am I?" and at each stage they arrive at somewhat different answers (Erikson, 1963, 1968a, 1968b; for an excellent overview, see Lightfoot, Cole, & Cole, 2009).

Various contemporary psychological theories trace their roots back to the psychodynamic theories of Freud and Erikson. For example, Freud's emphasis on the mother-infant relationship and Erikson's ideas that treating the child with love and sensitivity will allow her to develop a sense of trust in herself and her caregiver set the stage for John Bowlby's theory of attachment (discussed in chapter 5). Today, attachment theory continues to generate a highly active and influential body of empirical research (see Mangelsdorf & Brown, 2009).

Until the end of the 1960s, psychodynamic perspectives reflected the dominant theoretical approach in social work to understanding human behavior. Social work has drawn upon the rich and complex developmental ideas of psychodynamic theory to consider how emotion from past relationships and experiences affects individuals' present behavior (Irvine, 1956), as well as to consider challenges and changes in identity throughout the life course. Other positive contributions of psychodynamic perspectives to social work include an emphasis on feelings and an open listening relationship in clinical practice (Wallen, 1982).

Although psychodynamic theory has left an important legacy, today it is widely contested as an adequate social science theory of human development. One of the requirements of a scientific theory is that it must be possible to disprove it empirically. Yet virtually any human behavioral response can be posited to result from psychodynamic processes. The often unconscious thought processes that undergird psychodynamic approaches are difficult to assess empirically. From a more pragmatic perspective, an increasing reliance on empirical research in social work, as well as pressure from managed care in the United States, has directed models of explanation away from the interpretive and metaphorical accounts of behavior provided by psychodynamic theory.

Learning Theory

In contrast to psychoanalytic approaches, some psychological theories focused on observable behaviors and environmental factors underlying developmental change. According to **learning theory**, development is an incremental process that occurs as a result of experiencing the consequences of behavior, as well as observing and imitating others. Systematic studies of learning emerged in the late nineteenth and early twentieth centuries. Edward Thorndike's (1874–1949) experiments with trial-and-error learning in cats led to the law of effect. The basic idea is that responses followed by satisfying outcomes are strengthened, while those followed by negative consequences are weakened (see Thorndike, 1898, 1911, 1921). By 1927, Ivan Pavlov (1849–1936) had published his famous experiments of **classical conditioning**, that is, learning in which previously existing behaviors come to be elicited by new stimuli. For example, Pavlov taught dogs to salivate when presented with a light, by pairing presentations of food and light until the dogs came to associate the light with food (Pavlov, 1927).

In the first half of the twentieth century, John B. Watson (1878–1958) and then B. F. Skinner (1904–1990) extended the classical-conditioning paradigm into a more comprehensive theory that explained how learning also results from an individual's active, operant responses to the environment (Watson, 1913). **Operant conditioning** occurs when changes in behavior are shaped by the consequences of that behavior. **Reinforcement** (rewards) and **punishment** shape and give rise to new and more complex behaviors (see Novak, 2009). As a result of reinforcement, the occurrence of a behavior can be increased in frequency or elaborated. For example, messages from friends can be a reinforcement that results in an increase in the frequency with which one checks e-mail and social-media sites. Negative instructor responses to student papers can be a punishment that leads to students' avoidance of writing.

Beginning in the 1960s and 1970s, our understanding of learning was further expanded by **social learning theory**. Social learning theorists retained the earlier behaviorists' empirical commitment, but they also sought to incorporate distinctly human cognitive and social processes into the science of human behavior. Albert Bandura and his colleagues presented a "sociobehavioral" approach. They focused on the social nature of human behavior, arguing that human learning occurs not only through reinforcement and punishment, but also through observation and imitation of others (Bandura, Grusec, & Menlove, 1967; Bandura & Walters, 1963). Internalization of societal standards emerges as individuals come to judge their own actions based on observational and direct learning. Children, for instance, select from the conflicting information they receive to establish their own standards of behavior. Their selection depends on a variety of factors, including identification with particular models and the degree to which behavior is seen to arise from their own efforts rather than events over which they have no control (Bugental & Grusec, 2006).

Research conducted from learning theory perspectives has led to the development of a variety of effective interventions used in social work today. **Behavior therapy** (i.e., the use of learning theory principles to change behavior) continues to be used with clients, including those who are intellectually disabled, harm themselves, harm others, or have autism spectrum disorders (Courchesne & Pierce, 2005; Spiegler & Guevremont, 1998; Vance & Pumariega, 2001). Research has found that therapies based on learning theory, particularly when combined with other approaches, also have some positive effects on clients struggling with mental health, mental retardation, and substance misuse issues (DePaulo, 2002; Spiegler & Guevremont, 1998; E. H. Taylor, 2002; Vance & Pumariega, 2001).

Despite their successes, behavioral therapies also have limitations, for example, with the treatment of depression. Beginning in the 1960s, behavior therapy expanded as it was integrated with cognitive therapies. Albert Ellis and Aaron Beck focused on enhancing clients' rationality, that is, the extent to which conclusions about the self and the world are based on objective, external evidence (Beck, 1976, 1995; Ellis, 1962; Ellis & McLaren, 1998). Beck's insight was that irrational thoughts often precede negative emotions; in other words, cognitions can cause emotions. Cognitive behavioral therapy (CBT) integrates cognitive and behavioral therapies to enhance client functioning by systematically modifying thoughts and their related behavior. For example, in working with an individual struggling with depressed mood due to social isolation, the clinician might first examine the client's thinking that precedes social withdrawal (e.g., other people do not like him, or he is unlovable) and then might draw upon a combination of cognitive and behavioral strategies to modify these maladaptive thoughts and the accompanying behaviors. CBTs typically are focused and time limited and have been empirically shown to be generally effective for a variety of problems including mood, anxiety, personality, eating, and substance misuse disorders (e.g., Butler, Chapman, Forman, & Beck, 2006).

Some scholars and practitioners criticize cognitive behavioral methods as constraining client freedom, focusing on individual deficits rather than unfavorable or unjust environments that cause the problems, and frequently ignoring the socioeconomic and cultural contexts in which the targeted behaviors occur. A contemporary social worker and professor, Mary Eamon (2008), has responded to such criticisms with a source book on the use of cognitive behavioral interventions to facilitate the empowerment of vulnerable groups.

Information Processing

In the 1980s, our understanding of learning was influenced by **information-processing** research. Information-processing theory uses a computer metaphor to examine how humans receive, store, retrieve, and process information (Seifert, Hoffnung, & Hoffnung, 2000). For example, Robert Sternberg (2009) used information-processing theory to posit a triarchic model of intelligence. This model challenges the Wechsler intelligence scales, which were developed around the concept of intelligence as a single general type (Osterlind, 2006). In contrast, Sternberg views intelligence as consisting of three specific neuroprocessing elements involving the ability to (1) receive and analyze information in an efficient manner (componential elements), (2) easily and efficiently compare new information with stored knowledge and experience (experiential elements), and (3) solve everyday, real-life problems (contextual elements).

Alternative ways of framing intelligence such as those offered by Sternberg offer social workers tools for assessing, advocating, and documenting client skills and strengths that often go unnoticed; for example, the intelligence required to survive in a dangerous community is rarely measured, discussed, or labeled. In his theory of multiple intelligences, Howard Gardner

(1983/2011, 1993) argues that human beings have a variety of ways of learning and processing information. This diversity is reflected not in one "general intelligence," but in multiple intelligences, including linguistic, logical, musical, interpersonal, and kinesthetic, that are not necessarily correlated with one another. For example, an individual with high interpersonal intelligence may not have high musical or logical intelligence. An individual with high logical intelligence may not have high kinesthetic intelligence, and so on.

Constructivist Theories of Human Development

Many modern developmental scholars emphasize that human beings are complex biological beings who actively contribute to their own development by interpreting, finding meaning, and responding creatively to the world. From the perspective of **constructivist theories of human development**, individuals are seen as shaping or constructing their own reality. By actively striving to master their environments, individuals construct higher levels of knowledge from elements contributed by both biological maturation and environment. Indeed, both biological heritage and environment are viewed as equally important to development. The individual's acquisition of knowledge, however, is not a simple process of copying reality. The knowledge we acquire results from the ways in which we actively understand, modify, and transform reality (Lightfoot, Cole, & Cole, 2009).

The constructivist perspective of human development is perhaps best exemplified by the theory and research of Jean Piaget (1896–1980), a brilliant Swiss scholar often cited as the father of modern developmental psychology. Piaget's work focuses on **cognitive development**, particularly the development of logical, scientific reasoning (e.g., see Voneche & Bennour, 2009). He observed that children's logical thinking develops through a series of qualitatively different stages over the course of childhood and adolescence. Beginning with the sensorimotor stage (birth to approximately age two), children base their thought in actions, focusing on what they can perceive and do. As they acquire the ability to use symbols, as evidenced, for example, through their use of language and pretend play, they enter the preoperational stage (approximately ages two to six). During this stage, children can mentally represent people, objects, and actions in their minds. As children develop more effective skills for manipulating these representations, they enter the stage of concrete operations, the logic of concrete statements. During this stage they can mentally coordinate several concrete characteristics of people and objects. For example, they know that their mothers play several roles including mother, wife, surgeon, friend, and so forth. As children move into adolescence, their thinking may become increasingly abstract as they enter into the stage of formal operations. This final stage of cognitive development is marked by the ability to engage in hypothetical, scientific thinking (Fischer & Lindsey, 2009; Furth, 1969; Piaget & Inhelder, 1966).

Piagetian theory has generated literally thousands of empirical studies and sustained theoretical debate for nearly ninety years. It has been challenged on many grounds, including assumptions regarding the universality of developmental stages. For example, cross-cultural research indicates that formal operational reasoning is more prevalent in societies with widespread secondary and higher education (Hollos & Richards, 1993; Segall, Dasen, Berry, & Poortinga, 1999), suggesting that there may be multiple pathways to intellectual competence in adulthood. Yet Piaget's careful and insightful observations of infants and children and his focus on the active process of development have made a lasting impact on our understanding of the process of human development, even beyond cognitive development.

The active, creative efforts of the individual that are central to the constructivist perspective can also be illustrated in other areas of human development; for example, Roger Brown's (1973) classic research on children's early language development illustrates constructivist perspectives. For example, one of the author's children, twenty-two-month-old Sharon, told a story about the family cat, concluding with the observation, "Midnight ran." A few weeks later, she commented, "Midnight runned." This comment is remarkable for Sharon's creative attempt to apply her newly acquired linguistic rules for past-tense markers. Eventually, Sharon returned to the conventional grammatical construction, "Midnight ran," suggesting that she now understood the rule and its exceptions. This order of acquisition in which the child first produces the irregular form correctly, then incorrectly, and then correctly again has been observed in other children for a variety of grammatical forms (e.g., see Brown, 1973). How do we account for these patterns? From a constructivist perspective, children's rapid acquisition of a highly complex native language, in part, reflects our human genetic potential. In addition, the environment clearly plays a role: Sharon's family spoke English at home, and so she was learning English grammar. She was not passive in this learning process, however, but actively constructed an understanding of language from innate human ability and input from the environment. When children first use an irregular form correctly, they may be simply imitating others. When they subsequently come to understand the underlying grammatical rule, they may creatively overapply it to the irregular form. From this perspective, Sharon's use of the word *runned* actually reflected a higher level of knowledge than her earlier version of *ran*. Finally, children become aware of the exceptions to the rule, and once again produce the irregular form, correctly. In addition, Sharon's communication occurred within a social and emotional context. She was motivated by her desire to express herself to family members about a beloved pet.

Human development research conducted from a constructivist perspective has many implications for social work. Most importantly, it draws our attention to the role of meaning in human behavior and development. Social workers intervene with clients with diverse experiences from a wide range of backgrounds. Effective social work interventions go beyond simple biological or environmental manipulations to consider how clients will understand, interpret, and, ultimately, respond to change.

An example of a constructivist approach to social work is a parenting class for African-American grandparents. Many social workers are called upon to conduct parenting classes for parents with children in Head Start, prospective adoptive parents, parents and foster parents involved in the child welfare system, and parents of children with special needs. To be effective, however, parenting classes must go beyond the simple "training." From a constructivist perspective, effective classes also consider how parents understand and interpret new skills and techniques. For example, are generally effective behavioral techniques for managing children's difficult behaviors consistent with views of appropriate discipline commonly held within these particular parents' community? In a parenting class for African-American grandparents fostering their grandchildren, several grandmothers expressed serious reservations about the use of "time-out." From their perspective, placing a young child in social isolation following a misdeed, even for a short time, was unkind, had the potential to be abusive, and was ineffective. One grandmother expressed the opinion that when a small child misbehaves, the appropriate and effective action is to draw that child closer to you. She advocated a brief spanking immediately following serious misbehavior, accompanied by an explanation and expression of love and concern. The social worker presenting this class had effectively taught the skill of time-out in the sense that the grandmothers responded to questions on a postgroup assessment in a manner desired by the social worker. The meaning attached to this behavior by class members, however, made it highly unlikely that they would ever use it. Because this social worker went beyond "training" to consider "meaning," she encouraged the class to actively discuss the appropriate and inappropriate use of spanking, the actual disciplinary technique traditionally used in these grandmothers' cultural community.

In general, attention to psychological and social factors in human development is important to social work, in part because it draws our attention to the various ways in which individuals respond. For example, U.S. society is among the most violent of the industrialized world. Understanding why particular individuals behave aggressively requires an understanding not only of possible biological vulnerabilities, but of individual psychological characteristics (e.g., poor impulse control), and social context (e.g., being raised in a physically abusive family or violent neighborhood; see boxes 2.4 and 2.5).

BOX 2.4 VIOLENCE ACROSS THE LIFE SPAN
Severe Violence

A single factor cannot explain the continuation of chronic aggressive behavior in adolescence and adulthood. Rather, there is growing agreement that violence from repeat offenders results from multiple interacting elements. Researchers hypothesize that combinations of the following environmental and biological factors increase the risk of violent behaviors:

- abuse during childhood or during adolescent years
- poor parenting and inappropriate punishment
- witnessing violence in the family, community, and media
- living in a culture that promotes aggression and violence
- genetic predispositions
- trauma to the central nervous system and neurobiological abnormalities
- childhood temperament, attention, and impulse-control problems
- childhood aggressive behavior
- abnormal hormonal levels
- being male

Growing up in an environment that reinforces violent behavior significantly increases the risk for chronic aggressive behavior across the life span. Children living in a violent household or community learn to respond aggressively to perceived dangers in the environment. Risk for violent behavior also increases greatly when a person has a genetic predisposition for aggression, or neurobiological abnormalities.

Sources: Boxer et al., 2005; Bushman & Huesmann, 2006; Guerra, Huesmann, & Spindler, 2003; Huesmann, 1998; Huesmann, Dubow, & Boxer, 2009.

SOCIOCULTURAL AND HISTORICAL THEORIES

Society, culture, and history critically impact human development. **Sociocultural-historical theories of human development** are very compatible with constructivist theories, for example, in their emphasis on individuals' active contributions to their own development. Michael Cole and colleagues (Lightfoot, Cole, & Cole, 2009), however, point out that sociocultural-historical theories elaborate on constructivist theories in two important ways. First, a sociocultural-historical perspective views cultural and historical context as a critical third factor in development, through

BOX 2.5 VIOLENCE ACROSS THE LIFE SPAN
Neighborhood and Crime

Violence is particularly pronounced in certain neighborhoods, but typically violence and related crimes are committed by a small number of people. A study of a high-crime neighborhood in Washington, DC, found the following:

- Age is a factor in crime. Younger children are less delinquent than older adolescents, who are more likely to commit street crimes than midlife adults.

- Only 7 percent of the adolescent boys in the studied neighborhoods committed robbery, but these same teenagers were responsible for 36.2 percent of reported delinquent acts.

- The 7 percent of youth involved in robberies also committed 20.5 percent of all juvenile assaults.

- Each adolescent involved in robbery physically assaulted an average of approximately twelve people each year.

- The same 7 percent who participated in robbery committed 44 percent of all drug deals in the neighborhood.

- Most adolescents involved in selling drugs, but not robbery or other major criminal activities, were less violent.

- Having a job does not appear to prevent delinquency. The most seriously delinquent boys were the most likely to have a paying job.

- Social isolation appears to be a major factor for adolescent boys who get in trouble with the legal system. Seventy-seven percent of the adolescent boys who were involved in robbery identified that they most often keep to themselves, and that they are different than their peers.

- Only 15 percent of the adolescent boys in the most violent neighborhoods reported having gang connections.

Source: U.S. Department of Justice, 2000.

which biology and experience interact. **Culture** involves the physical objects, activities, patterns of living and meaning, and social structures that are shaped by the experiences of earlier generations and elaborated by later generations. All human beings are born into a community with a variety of rich sociocultural resources, and these resources, including medicine, language, music, mathematics, and economic and health-care systems profoundly shape development. Each generation does not remake itself from scratch. From the moment we are conceived, our development is profoundly shaped by our sociocultural and historical context, for example, by the adequacy of our mother's prenatal care. As we develop, we act on our world using a particular set of cultural tools, and we view our world through a particular cultural lens. For example, language is a critical tool for negotiating our social world, but language also shapes the very way we view that social world—even such basic concepts as how we understand ourselves and others. Our development also is constrained or enhanced by how we are positioned within larger social structures by virtue, for instance, of our gender, ethnicity, or socioeconomic status.

The second way in which the sociocultural-historical perspective elaborates upon the constructivist perspective is that it assumes that both less experienced individuals (e.g., children, students, and new social workers) and more experienced individuals (e.g., parents, teachers, and supervisors) are active collaborators in the process of development. The individual is not the "lone scientist" out to discover the world on his or her own. For example, parents, teachers, and even peers are active in shaping the individual's development; that is, development is "co-constructed" (Lightfoot, Cole, & Cole, 2009). Parents, for instance, directly support children's development in many ways, such as by helping them with homework. They also shape the environments in which their children develop, perhaps arranging for a child to attend church-sponsored day care, join scouts, play on a sports team, or enroll in the public high school. Children, of course, are not passive, but may take any variety of stances toward the particular socialization messages they encounter. A little girl may embrace, reject, challenge, or ignore her mother's efforts to encourage her active and assertive interactions with boys. Furthermore, the process of negotiating issues such as gender roles may impact the development of both the mother and her little girl.

As these examples suggest, the processes through which new generations acquire and elaborate culture are complex. From a sociocultural-historical perspective, development occurs throughout the life span through the complex, dialectical (interactive) processes of **socialization** and **acquisition**. In brief, socialization is the process by which more experienced individuals structure the social environment and display patterned meanings for the novice. Socialization may be direct and intentional, as when a professor assigns students to read the *NASW Code of Ethics*, or indirect and unintentional, as when a student observes a field supervisor grappling with a complex, real-life ethical dilemma. Acquisition is the process through which novices interpret, respond to, and ultimately ignore, reject, embrace, or elaborate upon the social patterns to which they are exposed (e.g., Haight, 2002; Wentworth, 1980).

These processes of socialization and acquisition are mutually influential. Excellent field supervisors alter the content and structure of their socialization practices in relation to social work interns' various backgrounds, and students adjust their own understanding and behavior in relation to their field supervisors' guidance. A school social work supervisor, for example, might provide extra support to a student with relatively little background working with young adolescents, before allowing her to actively participate in a **social developmental study** involving a middle school student. For her part, the student may spend extra time reading about development in early adolescence, and interacting with middle school students, their teachers, and families in preparation for participating in a social developmental study. From this dialectical perspective, professional development occurs as students actively read, reflect, observe, discuss, and participate with teachers, field supervisors, and peers in the everyday practices through which the culture of social work is maintained and elaborated.

Lev Vygotsky (1896–1934), a Russian psychologist, had a profound impact on sociocultural-historical theories of human development (Vygotsky, 1962; Wertsch, 1985). He viewed the mind as developing "in" society. For Vygotsky, all development proceeds from interpersonal processes to intrapersonal processes. For example, children develop more complex and adequate forms of thought first while interacting with those with more experience and competence. During interpersonal interactions, these experts can scaffold, or support, children in developing new and more complex ways of thinking. These interactions create a **zone of proximal development** in which children function at a higher level with the support of a more experienced individual than they could function independently. Eventually, these new forms of thought are internalized, and children can use them independently of the expert.

Many contemporary scholars of human development have elaborated upon Vygotsky's work. The developmental psychologist Barbara Rogoff has spent over twenty years studying children's learning in a variety of cultural contexts, including Guatemala and the United States (1990, 2003; Rogoff, Turkanis, & Bartlett, 2001). In the Mayan community she studied, children's learning occurred primarily during informal, apprenticeship-like everyday interactions. Children learned to complete chores, weave, farm, and care for younger children from observing and joining everyday activities, and from the nonverbal guidance of those with more experience. In the middle-class, European-American community Rogoff studied, an important context for children's learning was formal classroom settings where instruction occurred primarily through verbal instruction. Children learned to complete household chores, read, write, and do arithmetic often during deliberate, verbal, face-to-face interactions. Although the content and contexts of learning in Mayan and U.S. middle-class communities varied, nearly all children grew to be successful members of their diverse communities.

Sociocultural-historical theories of human development are highly relevant to social work because they underscore human diversity, especially the rich variety of developmental pathways that lead to healthy adaptation in various contexts. Sociocultural-historical perspectives do not assume that there is one developmental pathway, but consider that development may vary in relation to context, including the individuals' opportunities, and the requirements and values of successful functioning in particular communities. Hence, there is not one universal "best" way to develop. Similarly there cannot be one "best practice" for social work intervention that applies across sociocultural and historical contexts.

Knowledge of cultural and historical diversity is essential to appropriate and effective social work intervention. It allows social workers to understand the challenges clients may face in particular settings, as well as how they may interpret these challenges and the resources they may bring to bear in meeting them. For example, many Mayan immigrant kindergartners entering the Los Angeles public school system for the first time have been socialized into a very different social role than that of most middle-class, European-American children. The Mayan immigrant child, for example, may be used to interacting in mixed-age settings, and taking significant responsibility for her own care as well as that of younger siblings. How will this particular child understand and respond to the new context of school in the United States? What individual psychological resources, as well as external social resources, can be rallied to meet the new challenge of starting school in the United States? Establishing ongoing communication with the child's family or other community members can help the school social worker identify issues that may facilitate or hinder the child's success in school, including her responses to interaction in a large group of same-age peers.

Although the sociocultural-historical context, to some extent, shapes the challenges and resources encountered at various ages, a narrow focus on variation *across* cultural groups can lead to the development of stereotypes. Sociocultural-historical perspectives also draw our attention to variation *within* human communities. For example, communities across the United States comprising individuals from the same ethnic group can reflect diversity due to differing historical conditions and current challenges and resources. The evolution and adaptation of African-American communities in Salt Lake City and New York City, for example, may be similar due to common historical contexts, but different due to the various challenges and resources present in the broader sociocultural-historical contexts of Utah and New York. Furthermore, the individuals within all communities display a wide range of variation in personality, intelligence, and sociability. As social workers, we need to be sensitive to diversity that occurs within as well as across cultural communities to avoid stereotyping.

One source of intracultural diversity results from how individuals are positioned within larger social structures. For example, the African-American child growing up in a middle-class family and suburb will have different opportunities and obstacles than her cousin growing up in an impoverished inner-city neighborhood. From its inception, social work has been concerned with the devastating effects of poverty on human development. Boxes 2.6 through 2.8 summarize poverty in the United States by age and race, and worldwide.

BOX 2.6 POVERTY ACROSS THE LIFE SPAN
U.S. Official Poverty Rate

Poverty is increasing significantly in the United States, especially for children. In 2009, 45.6 million people (14.3 percent of the population) were considered poor by the U.S. government, an increase of 1.3 million people from 2002. Children experienced the highest poverty rates. The percentage of American children living in poverty (20.7 percent) was higher than any other age group. In 2003, the poverty rate for adults age eighteen to sixty-four was approximately 12.9 percent, and for seniors sixty-five and older was 8.9 percent. Furthermore, the number of children in poverty rose from 12.1 million in 2002 to 15.3 million in 2009.

Source: DeNavas-Walt, Proctor, & Mills, 2010.

BOX 2.7 POVERTY ACROSS THE LIFE SPAN
U.S. Poverty Rate by Race, 2008–2009

Racial or minority identity	Percentage living at or below the poverty line
Blacks	25.8
Hispanics	25.3
Asians	12.5
Whites	9.4
Native Hawaiians & other Pacific Islanders	Not listed
American Indians & Alaska Natives	Not listed

Note: Rates reflect those who reported themselves as representing only one racial or minority group. Therefore, the rates do not include people who claimed membership in two or more racial or minority groups.

Source: DeNavas-Walt, Proctor, & Mills, 2010.

BOX 2.8 POVERTY ACROSS THE LIFE SPAN

Worldwide Poverty

According to the World Bank, approximately 1.9 billion people in 1981 and 1.8 billion in 1990 lived in extreme poverty, "defined as average daily consumption of $1.25 or less and . . . living on the edge of subsistence." In 2009, 1.4 billion people were estimated as living in extreme poverty. The number of people living in extreme poverty has been decreasing over the past three decades. The largest reduction has occurred in East Asia and the Pacific region, where China has made great improvements. Regions with the highest extreme-poverty rates include equatorial and sub-Saharan Africa, Southeast Asia, eastern Europe, and Central and South America. The time has come for social work advocacy to focus beyond the borders of this country, and insist on a global perspective of human development and welfare. We can no longer stand by and allow 1.5 billion people across the globe to lose their potential for personal growth and their very lives because of poverty.

Sources: World Bank, 2010, n.d.a, n.d.b.

ECOLOGICAL THEORIES

Sociocultural-historical theories of human development consider development to be intimately intertwined with the contexts in which it emerges. In order to fully use this insight in social work practice, however, it is useful to add specificity to the concept of context in relation to human development. What are the critical characteristics of contexts that we expect to affect and be affected by human development? How do the multiple contexts (e.g., family, school, work) that we all occupy interact? To address these and other issues, we consider ecological-systems perspectives.

Physical Ecology

Ecology concerns the interrelationships of organisms with their environment. Those characteristics of the **physical ecology** relevant to human development include the climate, plant and animal life, and human artifacts. The physical ecology clearly has been shaped by human culture, affecting the nature and quantity of our food and shelter, as well as planet temperatures. Artifacts are human-made products such as tools, toys, books, and musical instruments. They emerge over generations, reflecting our complex human history. They shape and are shaped by current generations.

The physical ecology is an important consideration for social work policy and practice. The forebears of modern social workers from charity organization societies and settlement houses provided assistance to those who were impoverished (Brieland, 1995). And inadequate physical resources remain a central issue for social workers today. Debates in child welfare have included criteria for identifying and intervening in cases of child neglect. What constitutes adequate food, shelter, and sanitation? Are homeless and destitute parents who are unable to provide adequate food and shelter for themselves and their children guilty of "child neglect," and should these families be separated?

Social Ecology

Characteristics of the **social ecology** relevant to human development include the people with whom we interact, what we do together, how we interact, and the dynamics of the social groups in which we live. Like the physical ecology, the social ecology has been shaped by generations, and it shapes and will be shaped by current and future generations. For example, all human infants require protection and care, but how, what, and by whom such care is provided ranges widely from stay-at-home mothers in middle-class suburban United States, to sibling care in Mayan communities in Mexico, to group care in Israeli kibbutzim. The composition, activities, and interactions that we experience within the social ecology also change over development.

Social Composition. Social composition refers to the people who are available to interact with us. For a young child, the composition of the social ecology may include parents, siblings, extended family members, and neighbors. For an adult in midlife, the social ecology may be much expanded to include adult children, bosses, and coworkers. Awareness of the composition of the social ecology can be extremely important to social work practice. For example, to support the child's developing ability to form close relationships with others, child welfare workers are careful that infants and toddlers in foster care are moved around as little as possible, so that they can interact over time with a consistent primary caregiver.

Social Activities. The activities in which we routinely engage with others is another dimension of the social ecology relevant to development. The everyday, routine social activities the young child engages in with parents or older siblings may include chores, book reading, storytelling, bath and mealtimes, and play. These activities may support intellectual and social development, language learning, and literacy. The social activities of an adolescent might include formal lessons on a musical instrument, organized sports, or paid work. These social activities may impact development in adolescence. Analysis of social activities also is relevant to social work policy and practice. A school social worker contributing to the assessment of a school-age child with a suspected learning disability will consider whether the child has had the opportunity to participate with more experienced others at home in everyday routines, such as book reading and storytelling, that support emerging literacy skills.

Social Interactions. The ways in which we interact with others is another characteristic of our social ecology that is critical for understanding development. To return to our example of the infant in foster care, the child's developing ability to form close relationships with other people depends on having not only a relatively constant caregiver, but a caregiver who interacts with the baby in a consistent, supportive, and responsive manner. The protective function of social interaction for older adults who are vulnerable to depression presumably also depends on the support and warmth experienced during those exchanges.

Social Climate. In considering physical and social ecologies, it is important to remember that they are not separate, but interacting, parts of our environment, and that we imbue both our physical and social surroundings with meaning. Rudolf Moos (e.g., Timko & Moos, 1991) applied the term "social climate" to refer to a setting's "personality." Moos views characteristics of the social climate and individuals participating in the setting as separate, but interacting. In other words, social climate can influence individuals and groups, and people's actions can alter a setting's social climate. Concrete elements of the social climate include a setting's physical characteristics, such as size or space, lighting, colors, temperature, objects, decorations, tools, state of repair, neatness or clutter within the space, and so forth. More abstract elements are the explicit and implicit rules, boundaries, roles, goals, and other expectations placed on individuals participating within the setting. Together a setting's concrete and abstract elements create a social climate. For example, fast-food restaurants use clowns and identifiable play areas to concretely communicate that children are welcomed, and that the abstract rules tolerate a wide range of behaviors. On the other hand, a library uses physical characteristics to announce that individuals of all ages are expected not only to modulate their voices, movement, and activities, but also to acknowledge the importance of written and recorded information. Understanding the concept of social climate helps social workers assess a client's goodness of fit within and across environmental settings. For example, a home visit from a child welfare caseworker might be a better fit for a quiet child who prefers order and routine than a trip to the fast-food restaurant.

SOCIAL SYSTEMS THEORIES

The dynamics of the social ecology also are important to understanding development. The social ecology can be thought of as a system. A system is a regularly interacting or interdependent group of parts forming a unified and bounded whole. Depending on the purposes of our social work assessment or intervention, we might define a system as a family, classroom, mental health facility, school, community, or nation. Such social systems have a number of related characteristics that are important to highlight when thinking about social work assessment and intervention.

First, social systems are composed of parts, or subsystems, which interact and can influence one another. Consider a family as a system consisting of several members, including a child suspected of being depressed. Social work assessment of the child requires not only knowledge of the child's functioning, but knowledge of the family system in which that child is embedded. Pertinent information includes marital, sibling, and parent-child relationships because these relationships can powerfully affect and be affected by the child's depression (E. H. Taylor, 2002). For example, an ill child can place enormous strain on parents, which can erode the quality of the marital relationship, affect the quality of parenting, and lead to resentment among the siblings.

Second, social systems tend toward "self-preservation," and not all subsystems have equal power to impact other parts of the system. Lasting, meaningful system change often requires multiple interacting factors. Consider the system of slavery in the United States. Despite their centrality to the system, African Americans were virtually powerless to effect lasting and meaningful change in their social, health, or economic situation. Regardless of their intelligence, talent, hard work, artistry, obedience, defiance, or intimacy with whites, African Americans were virtually powerless to meaningfully affect the slave system. Minor improvements in living conditions were given and taken away, but dismantling the slave system required not only changes in regional and national economics, manufacturing methods, transportation, federal policy, and time, but also a long, bloody civil war.

Next, systems vary in their stability. Family therapists have noticed that in some families, change in one subsystem can cause a ripple effect of change throughout the family or system. Medical intervention and therapy may result in the lessening of a child's depression that, in turn, may result in improved marital, parent-child, and sibling relationships. In other families, however, patterns of behavior and interaction are less responsive to change. Treatment of a child's depression may have little or no impact on how his family members respond to him or to one another. Stability may or may not be desirable, depending on whether the existing patterns of interaction are satisfactory.

Further, systems are complex, and their changes over time are not necessarily predictable in any simple fashion. Complex systems theory assumes that systems are dynamic: change is universal and typically irreversible. Furthermore, **chaos theory** demonstrates the impossibility of predicting the long-term evolution of complex systems, given that very small differences in initial conditions can result in widely divergent outcomes (Hudson, 2010).

Finally, at any given point in time, we all participate within multiple social systems, such as home, school, work, neighborhood, community, and nation. These various systems can influence one another. For example, family systems can affect and be affected by school systems. Morning and afternoon routines of families may be structured around school beginning and dismissal times. On the other hand, families may influence schools through social and political pressure. Systems vary in how open they are to influence from other systems. For example, some public school administrators welcome and act upon input from families, while others are highly resistant.

Urie Bronfenbrenner (1917–2005), a developmental psychologist, described five interacting, embedded levels of social context critical to human development: the microsystem, mesosystem, exosystem, macrosystem (Bronfenbrenner, 1979, 1995), and macrochronological system (Bronfenbrenner & Morris, 2006). To this framework, Dolores Norton (n.d.) adds the focal system. The **focal system** is our analytic vantage point. It is the perspective from which we view related systems. Depending on the nature and purpose of our social work assessment and intervention, the focal system might be an individual person, family, or community. For the purposes of the following discussion, however, we will consider that the focal system is the individual person. Relevant characteristics of the individual as a focal system include biological, psychological, and social factors. These characteristics are embedded within all five levels of system.

The first level of context is the **microsystem**. It encompasses the immediate social environment, the day-to-day reality of the focal system (in this case, a person). It usually includes those settings in which we have face-to-face, sustained, and significant relationships with others, for example, our families, peer groups, schools, workplaces, and churches. Microsystems change with the individual's development, and they change across sociocultural-historical contexts. A young girl's microsystems may include relationships with family, friends, and teachers. As she grows, they may include relationships with a husband and professional colleagues. In the twenty-first century, middle-class North American women's microsystems commonly include professional colleagues, but such microsystems were rare at earlier points in history and remain rare in some cultural communities. If major microsystems are missing or are in conflict, the social worker might anticipate that developmental problems could result. For example, a foster child who does not have a permanent family may experience emotional, social, and learning difficulties.

The second level of context is the **mesosystem**. Mesosystems encompass the set of interrelationships between two or more of the person's microsystems. For example, a child's parent takes her to kindergarten on the first day of school and meets the teacher, thereby forming a new home-school mesosystem. A more complex mesosystem can involve a variety of distinct microsystems, for example, the home, school, church, and neighborhood. The composition and complexity of mesosystems also vary with development and sociocultural-historical context.

Analysis of the similarities and differences across the microsystems in an individual's mesosystems can help the social worker anticipate challenges and resources for development. Children whose mesosystems comprise microsystems with homogeneous beliefs and practices experience a world very different from those experienced by children whose mesosystems comprise more diverse or conflicting microsystems. If family, neighborhood, and school are all dominated by a particular religion, for example, then the child's values, beliefs, and identity may be reinforced within multiple homogeneous mesosystems, and there may be little stress during childhood. On the other hand, there may be considerable stress in adolescence if the focal system is in conflict with homogeneous mesosystems. For example, the young Mormon teenager living in Utah who comes to understand he is gay may feel condemned by multiple homogeneous mesosystems comprising his family, neighborhood, school, and church. He may have nowhere to turn for support.

On the other hand, individuals whose mesosystems comprise diverse, even conflicting microsystems may experience more stress during childhood and less in adulthood. A multiethnic child with a European-American, Jewish mother and an African-American, Baptist father, who lives in a midwestern, working-class suburb, may experience more conflict and stress within her various heterogeneous mesosystems than the typical Mormon child growing up in Utah. Conflict and stress, however, are not necessarily detrimental, and can even facilitate development. If the African-American, Jewish child receives the support she needs to develop effective coping strategies, then as an adult she may display considerable resiliency and the ability to establish ties to diverse groups, thereby enhancing her social resources.

The third level of context is the **exosystem**. It encompasses settings that do not involve the person as an active participant, but in which events occur that do affect the person. A husband may have no contact with his wife's workplace, but the chronic and consistent stress she experiences there may affect her ability to relate to him within their marriage. Other examples of exosystems include the local school board of a child who is attending public school, and the local zoning board of a family whose house is in the path of urban renewal. Exosystems also vary across individual development and sociocultural-historical contexts. Analysis of a client's exosystems can help social workers identify sources of stress and support that exist outside of the client's immediate relationships, but that do affect those relationships.

The fourth level of context is the **macrosystem**. It includes the cultural patterns of the larger society that pervade all of the other systems. Macrosystems include widespread societal values such as individual freedom, major institutions such as government and education, and economic structure. They also include the diverse belief systems and practices of subcultures, which may vary in terms of ethnicity, income, education, age, ability/disability, urban/rural locale, sexual orientation, and so forth.

Analysis of macrosystems also can help the social worker identify potential sources of support and stress. In a homogeneous world, the macrosystem values and culture closely mirror those of the micro-, meso-, and exosystems, creating little stress on the focal system. In a pluralistic society, the individual's subcultural values, beliefs, and practices may differ from those of the general society, and may even be incongruent with that of the societal macrosystem. For example, Jill McLean Taylor (1996) studied the relationships of adolescent Latina and Portuguese girls with their mothers. Some of these dyads described considerable tension resulting, essentially, from the conflicting values and behaviors of the U.S. mainstream and Hispanic or Portuguese families. In school, the girls were socialized toward independence and self-assertion. In contrast, socialization in the family focused on showing respect to elders and remaining interdependent with the family.

The fifth level of context is the **macrochronological system**. Individual development is embedded in and shaped by the historical times and events experienced over a lifetime. For example, the experience of the Great Depression impacted the development of a generation. Furthermore, the age at which the individual experienced this historic event moderated its impact on development. Younger children, especially boys, were most adversely affected by economic stresses of the economic collapse (see Elder & Shanahan, 2006).

LIFE-SPAN DEVELOPMENTAL THEORIES

It is important to underscore that the developmental, ecological-systems framework encompasses a life-span developmental perspective. There are a number of contemporary scholars who have examined life-span development, including Glen Elder, Warner Schaie, and Paul and Margaret Baltes. Human development does not end in childhood or adolescence; rather, it extends from conception to death. Each age period of the life span presents unique opportunities and challenges, which can shape the developmental trajectory from birth to death. The concept of development from a life-span perspective includes not just growth in the sense of maturation and advancement, but lifelong adaptive processes that evolve over time. For example, biological resources such as physical strength decline over the life span, but cultural resources, such as wisdom, can increase, giving rise to new, adaptive processes. Furthermore, how individuals respond and adapt even to biological facts such as birth, puberty, death, illness, and disability depends on their meanings in the life course: in other words, how they are embedded within particular sociocultural and historical contexts (Baltes, Lindenberger, & Staudinger, 2006; Elder & Shanahan, 2006).

One goal for social workers is to promote healthy development across the life span. Understanding the developmental trajectory—what has occurred before and what is anticipated in the future—can enhance understanding of issues at any given point in time. For example, a midlife adult's problematic responses to the death of a loved one may be related to prior traumatic experiences with death and to fears of his own future death. The social worker's efforts to support him, at a particular point in time, can be enhanced by understanding his responses as embedded within a life span of actual and anticipated experiences.

Evolving lifetime processes of adaptation, as well as the significance of how we interpret biological facts within particular social and historical contexts, can be illustrated by Donald T. He was the first person diagnosed with autism, in a 1943 medical article by the child psychiatrist Leo Kanner. Donald displayed some of the classic signs of autism, a biologically based, neurodevelopmental disability. In his article, Kanner presented eleven cases, describing a complex set of behaviors including a lack of interest in and ability to relate to other people, problems in communication, fascination with objects, and need for sameness, which he labeled autism. Donald was first examined at Johns Hopkins University in the 1930s when, at the age of five, he appeared indifferent to people, including his parents for whom he displayed no obvious affection; was generally unresponsive when his name was called; spoke very little; spent hours spinning objects; had intense dislikes, including for any changes in routine; and when interrupted, threw intense temper tantrums. He also had isolated, splinter skills; for example, by the age of two, he could recite the twenty-third psalm and had memorized twenty-five questions and answers from the Presbyterian catechism.

Throughout his life, Donald developed and adapted in a small town, Forest, Mississippi, where people largely accepted him as eccentric, but one of their own. This social construction of Donald's autism may have been supported by his family's circumstances as influential community insiders. His parents were well educated, financially well-off, and respected. Donald's father was a successful lawyer, and his mother cared for him in Forest for fifty-two years, until her death. He attended the local public school through high school, and then a small college in Mississippi, where he majored in French. He was teased a little in school, but was generally regarded as eccentric and even "brilliant"; for example, as a child he could multiply double-digit numbers in his head. Donald continued to develop and adapt within the context of his hometown throughout adulthood. He worked in the family bank as a teller, and his family established an irrevocable trust fund that continues to pay his bills. At the age of twenty-three, he learned to golf. At twenty-seven, he learned to drive. And at thirty-six, he learned to travel. At the age of seventy-seven, Donald lives alone in the home where his parents raised him. He has traveled to thirty-six foreign countries, and twenty-eight U.S. states. He remains distant from others and awkward in conversation

(Donvan & Zucker, 2010). Yet he has a niche where he is accepted. In one of her later letters to Leo Kanner (1971, pp. 121–122), Donald's mother wrote that "Don is now 36 years old, a bachelor living with us . . . He takes very little part in social conversation and shows no interest in the opposite sex . . . While Don is not completely normal, he has taken his place in society very well, so much better than we ever hoped for. If he can maintain status quo, I think he has adjusted sufficiently to take care of himself. For this much progress we are truly grateful."

SUMMARY AND DISCUSSION

The developmental, ecological-systems framework elaborated in this book portrays human development across the life span as resulting from the complex interaction of biological, psychological, and social characteristics of the individual, embedded within, and interacting with, particular sociocultural-historical contexts. These contexts include micro-, meso-, exo-, macro-, and macrochronological systems. This dynamic framework underscores the fact that all of us are positioned in complex and changing ways within multiple social systems, such as family, school, work, and community. This is true for the white, middle-class adult male, as well as the Latina, inner-city, high school student. We all develop multiple perspectives and frameworks for understanding and operating within diverse systems. For example, our language changes in predictable and systematic ways when we move from speaking to clients, to speaking with supervisors, to speaking with family members. Furthermore, our positions within these diverse, interacting systems can vary tremendously over time and place. For example, culturally based differences between home and school in adult expectations of child behavior may be particularly stressful to the beginning kindergartner, but less so as the child becomes familiar with the demands of school and moves on to elementary school. On the other hand, racial/ethnic differences between home and school may be relatively benign in kindergarten peer groups, but become a source of stress in elementary school.

By merging insights from human development research with ecological-systems concepts, social workers can better understand and support their clients. A developmental, ecological-systems approach suggests specific issues to which social workers must attend when assessing problems and planning interventions: focal system characteristics, physical ecology, social ecology, and social climate.

1. *Focal system characteristics*. What are the characteristics of the focal system? In the case of the individual, what are his/her bio-psycho-social characteristics at this point in development? How does the client understand and respond to the issue at hand? How might the client's interpretations and reactions, strengths, and vul-

nerabilities relate to problems (e.g., intimate partner violence) and possible solutions at this point in time and later in development?

2. *Physical ecology.* What are the characteristics of the physical ecology in which the client is embedded? For example, what are the client's available physical resources (food, shelter, human artifacts)? Are they adequate for continued development?

3. *Social ecology.* What are the characteristics of the social ecology in which the client is embedded?

   a. *Social composition.* Who is present and available for interaction with the client? What is the nature of these relationships? How might these relationships contribute to problems and possible solutions?

   b. *Social activities.* What is the client doing with others? Are these activities supportive of continued development and adaptation?

   c. *Social interaction.* How are the client and others interacting? Are these interactions supportive of continued development and adaptation; for example, are they mutually respectful?

   d. *Social structure.* How are various levels (micro-, meso-, exo-, macro-, and macrochronological systems) of the client's social ecology related? How does this social structure relate to problems (e.g., lack of communication between a child's home and school microsystems) and possible solutions (e.g., outreach by school social workers)?

   e. *Social system dynamics.* What are the characteristics of the social system? For example, who has the power to change the system? How does this system interact with other systems? How do system characteristics impact the issue at hand?

4. *Social climate.* What is the goodness of fit between the client and the "personality" of his or her environment?

Study and Discussion Questions

1. What is a developmental, ecological-systems framework? To what extent is this conceptual framework relevant to social work? Why?

2. From the perspective of social work, what are the contributions and limitations of theories or conceptual frameworks of human development that focus on biological, psychological, social, or ecological factors?

3. Summarize Bronfenbrenner's descriptions of the micro-, meso-, exo-, macro-, and macrochronological systems. Write down an example of a social work issue. How might Bronfenbrenner's characterization of social context be used to facilitate analysis of this issue?

4. Write down one example of how social work intervention or policy might be approached or impacted from a developmental, ecological-systems framework.

5. We all have folk theories of human behavior and development: values, beliefs, and explanations for how the world works that we've acquired within our families and communities. In general, folk theories are very effective for dealing with everyday life within our particular communities. What are the limitations of folk theories? How do theories within social science (e.g., the developmental, ecological-systems perspective) differ from folk theories?

Resources

There are a number of influential works to which interested students may turn to enhance their understanding of a developmental, ecological-systems framework. They include Vygotsky (1962, 1978; see also Wertsch, 1985) as well as modern works by Bruner (1990), Rogoff (1990, 2003), Bronfenbrenner (1979, 1995), Bronfenbrenner and Morris (2006), Gibson (1979), Wertsch (1991), Germain (1991), and Lightfoot, Cole, and Cole (2009).

Interested students can supplement this chapter through a number of excellent web-based resources.

Cornell University's College of Human Ecology has been a constant leader in studies focused on improving the human condition through national policy changes, improved nutrition, innovative housing and clothing, health care, and legal resources. Available at http://www.human.cornell.edu/.

For a brief overview of different personality, social, emotional, and evolutionary/sociobiological development theories, including those of Freud, Piaget, Erikson, Vygotsky, and Kohlberg, go to http://classweb.gmu.edu/awinsler/ordp/theory.html#vygotsky.

References

Baltes, P., Lindenberger, U., & Staudinger, U. (2006). Life span theory in developmental psychology. In W. Damon & R. M. Lerner (Eds.), *Handbook of child psychology:* Vol. 1, *Theoretical models of human development* (6th ed., pp. 565–664). Hoboken, NJ: Wiley.

Bandura, A., Grusec, J. E., & Menlove, F. L. (1967). Vicarious extinction of avoidance behavior. *Journal of Personality and Social Psychology, 5*, 16–23.

Bandura, A., & Walters, R. (1963). *Social learning theory and personality development*. New York: Holt, Rinehart & Winston.

Barlow, D. H., & Durand, V. M. (2005). *Abnormal psychology: An integrative approach*. Belmont, CA: Thomson Wadsworth.

Beck, A. T. (1976). *Cognitive therapy and the emotional disorders*. New York: International Universities Press.

Beck, A. T. (1995). *Cognitive therapy: Basics and beyond*. New York: Guilford.

Black, J. E., Jones, T. A., Nelson, C. A., & Greenough, W. T. (1998). Neural plasticity. In N. Alessi (Ed.) & J. T. Coyle (Section Ed.), *Handbook of child and adolescent psychiatry:* Vol. 4, *Varieties of development, Section I. Developmental neuroscience* (pp. 31-51). New York: Wiley.

Boxer, P., Guerra, N. G., Huesmann, L. R., & Morales, J. (2005). Proximal peer-level effects of a small-group selected prevention on aggression in elementary school children: An investigation of the peer contagion hypothesis. *Journal of Abnormal Psychology, 33*(3), 325-338.

Brieland, D. (1995). Social work practice: History and evolution. In *Encyclopedia of social work* (19th ed., Vol. 3, pp. 2247-2254). Washington, DC: NASW Press.

Bronfenbrenner, U. (1979). *The ecology of human development*. Cambridge, MA: Harvard University Press.

Bronfenbrenner, U. (1995). Developmental ecology through space and time. In P. Moen, G. H. Elder Jr., & K. Luscher (Eds.), *Examining lives in context: Perspectives on the ecology of human development* (pp. 619-648). Washington, DC: American Psychological Association.

Bronfenbrenner, U., & Morris, P. A. (2006). The bioecological model of human development. In W. Damon & R. M. Lerner (Eds.), *Handbook of child psychology:* Vol. 1, *Theoretical models of human development* (6th ed., pp. 793-828). New York: Wiley.

Brown, R. (1973). *A first language: The early stages*. Cambridge, MA: Harvard University Press.

Bruner, J. (1990). *Acts of meaning*. Cambridge, MA: Harvard University Press.

Bugental, D., & Grusec, J. (2006). Socialization processes. In W. Damon & R. M. Lerner (Eds.), *Handbook of child psychology:* Vol. 3, *Social, emotional, and personality development* (5th ed., pp. 366-428). New York: Wiley.

Bushman, B. J., & Huesmann, L. R. (2006). Short-term and long-term effects of violent media on aggression in children and adults. *Archives of Pediatrics & Adolescent Medicine, 160*(4), 348-352.

Butler, A., Chapman, J., Forman, E., & Beck, A. (2006). The empirical status of cognitive-behavioral therapy: A review of meta-analyses. *Clinical Psychology Review, 26*(1), 17-31.

Cash, D., & Hallahan, D. (2009). Education of children with autism spectrum disorders. In R. Shweder (Ed.), *The child: An encyclopedic companion* (pp. 90-91). Chicago: University of Chicago Press.

Courchesne, E., & Pierce, K. (2005). Brain overgrowth in autism during a critical time in development: Implications for frontal pyramidal neuron and interneuron development and connectivity. *International Journal of Developmental Neuroscience, 23*(2-3), 153-170.

DeNavas-Walt, C., Proctor, B. D., & Mills, R. J. (2010). *Income, poverty, and health insurance coverage in the United States* (U.S. Census Bureau, Current Population Reports, Publication No. P60-238). Washington, DC: U.S. Government Printing Office. Retrieved from http://www.census.gov/prod/2010pubs/p60-238.pdf

DePaulo, J. R. (2002). *Understanding depression: What we know and what you can do about it*. New York: Wiley.

Donvan, J., & Zucker, C. (2010). Autism's first child. *Atlantic,* October, 78-90.

Eamon, M. K. (2008). *Empowering vulnerable populations: Cognitive-behavioral intervention*. Chicago: Lyceum Books.

Elder, G., & Shanahan, M. (2006). The life course and human development. In W. Damon & R. M. Lerner (Eds.), *Handbook of child psychology:* Vol. 1, *Theoretical models of human development* (6th ed., pp. 665–707). Hoboken, NJ: Wiley.

Ellis. A. (1962). *Reason and emotion in psychotherapy*. New York: Stuart.

Ellis, A., & McLaren, C. (1998). *Rational emotive behavior therapy: A therapist's guide* (Vol. 2). Atascadero, CA: Impact Publishers.

Engel, R., & Schutt, R. (2010). *Fundamentals of social work research*. Los Angeles: Sage.

Erikson, E. (1963) *Childhood and society* (2nd ed.). New York: Norton.

Erikson, E. (1968a). *Identity: Youth and crisis*. New York.

Erikson, E. (1968b). Life cycle. In D. Sills (Ed.), *International encyclopedia of the social sciences* (Vol. 9, pp. 286–292). New York: Crowell, Collier.

Fischer, K., & Lindsey, R. (2009). Cognitive theories. In R. Shweder (Ed.), *The child: An encyclopedic companion* (pp. 262–264). Chicago: University of Chicago Press.

Freud, S. (1905/1953). Three essays on the theory of sexuality. In J. Strachey (Ed.), *The standard edition of the complete psychological works of Sigmund Freud* (Vol. 7, pp. 135–171). London: Hogarth Press.

Freud, S. (1920/1955). Beyond the pleasure principle. In J. Strachey (Ed.), *The standard edition of the complete psychological works of Sigmund Freud* (Vol. 18, pp. 145–221). London: Hogarth Press.

Freud, S. (1933/1964). *New introductory lectures in psychoanalysis*. New York: W. W. Norton.

Furth, H. (1969). *Piaget and knowledge: Theoretical foundations*. Englewood Cliffs, NJ: Prentice-Hall.

Gardner, H. (1983/2011). *Frames of mind: The theory of multiple intelligences*. New York: Basic Books.

Gardner, H. (1993). *Multiple intelligences: New horizons*. New York: Basic Books.

Germain, C. B. (1991). *Human behavior in the social environment: An ecological view*. New York: Columbia University Press.

Gesell, A. (1940). *The first five years of life* (9th ed.). New York: Harper & Row.

Gibson, J. J. (1979). *The ecological approach to visual perception*. Boston: Houghton Mifflin.

Goodwin, F. K., & Jamison, K. R. (1990). *Manic-depressive illness*. New York: Oxford University Press.

Gottesman, I. I. (1991). *Schizophrenia genetics: The origins of madness*. New York: W. H. Freeman.

Greenough, W. T., Black, J. E., & Wallace, C. S. (1987). Experience and brain development. *Child Development, 58*(3), 539–559.

Guerra, N. G., Huesmann, L. R., & Spindler, A. (2003). Community violence exposure, social cognition, and aggression among urban elementary school children. *Child Development, 74*(5), 1561–1576.

Haight, W. (2002). *African-American children at church: A sociocultural perspective*. New York: Cambridge University Press.

Hollos, M., & Richards, F. (1993). Gender-associated development of formal operations in Nigerian adolescents. *Ethos, 21*, 24–52.

Hudson, C. (2010). *Complex systems and human behavior*. Chicago: Lyceum Books.

Huesmann, L. R. (1998). Aggression and the self: High self-esteem, low self-control, and ego threat. In R. G. Geen & E. Donnerstein (Eds.), *Human aggression: Theories, research, and implications for social policy* (pp. 73–109). San Diego, CA: Academic Press.

Huesmann, L. R., Dubow, E. F., & Boxer, P. (2009). Continuity of aggression from childhood to early adulthood as a predictor of life outcomes: Implications for the adolescent-limited and life-course-persistent models. *Aggressive Behavior, 35,* 136–149.

Irvine, E. E. (1956). Transference and reality in the casework relationship. *British Journal of Psychiatric Social Work, 3*(4), 1–10.

Kanner, L. (1971). Follow-up study of eleven autistic children originally reported in 1943. *Journal of Autism and Childhood Schizophrenia, 1*(2), 119–145.

Lightfoot, C., Cole, M., & Cole, S. (2009). *The development of children* (6th ed.). New York: Worth Publishers.

Mangelsdorf, S., & Brown, G. (2009). Infant attachment. In R. Shweder (Ed.), *The child: An encyclopedic companion* (pp. 73–76). Chicago: University of Chicago Press.

McNeil, T. F., Cantor-Graae, E., Torrey, E., Sjöström, K., Bowler, A., Taylor, E., . . . Higgins, E. (1994). Obstetric complications in histories of monozygotic twins discordant and concordant for schizophrenia. *Acta Psychiatrica Scandinavica, 89,* 196–204.

Norton, D. (n.d.). *Ecology and plurality: An ecological systems framework for a pluralistic curriculum: Beyond the dual perspective.* Unpublished manuscript.

Novak, G. (2009). Behavioral theories. In R. Shweder (Ed.), *The child: An encyclopedic companion* (pp. 260–261). Chicago: University of Chicago Press.

Osterlind, S. J. (2006). *Modern measurement: Theory, principles and applications of mental appraisal.* Upper Saddle River, NJ: Prentice Hall.

Pavlov, I. P. (1927). *Conditional reflexes.* Oxford: Oxford University Press.

Piaget, J., & Inhelder, B. (1966). *The psychology of the child.* New York: Basic Books.

Rogoff, B. (1990). *Apprenticeship in thinking: Cognitive development in social context.* New York: Oxford University Press.

Rogoff, B. (2003). *The cultural nature of human development.* New York: Oxford University Press.

Rogoff, B., Turkanis, C., & Bartlett, L. (Eds.). (2001). *Learning together: Children and adults in a school community.* New York: Oxford University Press.

Schreibman, L., & Koegel, R. L. (1996). Fostering self-management: Parent-delivered pivotal response training for children with autistic disorder. In E. D. Hibbs & P. S. Jensen (Eds.), *Psychosocial treatment for child and adolescent disorders: Empirically based strategies for clinical practice* (pp. 525–553). Washington, DC: American Psychological Association.

Schuckit, M. (2009). Alcohol use disorders. *Lancet, 373*(9662), 7–13.

Segall, M., Dasen, P., Berry, J., & Poortinga, Y. (1999). *Human behavior in global perspective: An introduction to cross-cultural psychology* (2nd ed.). Needham Heights, MA: Allyn & Bacon.

Seifert, K. L., Hoffnung, R. J., & Hoffnung, M. (2000). *Life span development* (2nd ed.). Boston: Houghton Mifflin.

Sharpe, C., & Trauner, D. (2009). Neurological and brain development. In R. Shweder (Ed.), *The child: An encyclopedic companion* (pp. 677–681). Chicago: University of Chicago Press.

Spiegler, M. D., & Guevremont, D. C. (1998). *Contemporary behavior therapy* (3rd ed.). Pacific Grove, CA: Brooks/Cole.

Sternberg, R. (2009). Intelligence. In R. Shweder (Ed.), *The child: An encyclopedic companion* (pp. 509–512). Chicago: University of Chicago Press.

Substance Abuse and Mental Health Services Administration. (2009). *Results from the 2008 national survey on drug use and health: National findings detailed tables* (Office of Applied Studies). Rockville, MD. Retrieved from http://www.oas.samhsa.gov/NSDUH/2K8NSDUH/tabs/Sect1peTabs1to46.htm#Tab1.1B

Substance Abuse and Mental Health Services Administration. (2010). *Results from the 2009 national survey on drug use and health:* Vol. 1, *Summary of national findings* (Office of Applied Studies, NSDUH Series H-38A, HHS Publication No. SMA 10-4586Findings). Rockville, MD. Retrieved from http://oas.samhsa.gov/NSDUH/2k9NSDUH/2k9ResultsP.pdf

Taylor, E. H. (1987). The biological basis of schizophrenia. *Social Work, 32,* 115–121.

Taylor, E. H. (1997). Serious mental illness: A biopsychosocial perspective. In R. L. Edwards (Ed.), *Encyclopedia of social work* (19th ed., Supplement, pp. 263–273). Washington, DC: NASW Press.

Taylor, E. H. (2002). Manic-depressive illness. In V. S. Ramachandran (Ed.), *Encyclopedia of the human brain* (Vol. 2, pp. 745–758). San Diego, CA: Academic Press.

Taylor, E. H. (2006). *Atlas of bipolar disorders.* London: Taylor & Francis.

Taylor, J. M. (1996). Cultural stories: Latina and Portuguese daughters and mothers. In B. J. Ross Leadbeater & N. Way (Eds.), *Urban girls: Resisting stereotypes, creating identities* (pp. 117–131). New York: New York University Press.

Thorndike, E. L. (1898). Animal intelligence: An experimental study of the associative processes in animals. *Psychological Review Monograph Supplement, 2*(8).

Thorndike, E. L. (1911). *Individuality* (Riverside Educational Monographs). Boston: Houghton Mifflin.

Thorndike, E. L. (1921). *The psychology of learning.* New York: Teacher's College Columbia University.

Timko, C., & Moos, R. (1991). A typology of social climates in group residential facilities for older people. *Journal of Gerontology, 46*(3), S160–S169.

Torrey, E. F., Bowler, A. E., Taylor, E. H., & Gottesman, I. I. (1994). *Schizophrenia and manic depressive disorder: The biological roots of mental illness as revealed by the landmark study of identical twins.* New York: Basic Books.

U.S. Department of Justice, Office of Justice Programs, Office of Juvenile Justice and Delinquency Prevention. (2000, March). Violent neighborhoods, violent kids. *Juvenile Justice Bulletin* (NCJ Publication No. 178248), 1–15.

Vance, H. B., & Pumariega, A. (Eds.). (2001). *Clinical assessment of child and adolescent behavior.* New York: Wiley.

Voneche, J., & Bennour, M. (2009). Piaget, Jean. In R. Shweder (Ed.), *The child: An encyclopedic companion* (pp. 738–740). Chicago: University of Chicago Press.

Vygotsky, L. S. (1962). *Thought and language.* Cambridge, MA: MIT Press.

Vygotsky, L. S. (1978). *Mind in society: The development of higher mental processes.* Cambridge, MA: Harvard University Press.

Wallace, C. S., Kilman, V. L., Withers, G. S., & Greenough, W. T. (1992). Increases in dendritic length in occipital cortex after 4 days of differential housing in weanling rats. *Behavioral and Neural Biology, 58*(1), 64–68.

Wallen, J. (1982). Listening to the unconscious in case material: Robert Langs' theory applied. *Smith College Studies in Social Work, 52*(3), 203–233.

Watson, J. B. (1913). Psychology as the behaviorist views it. *Psychological Review, 20*, 158–177.

Wentworth, W. M. (1980). *Context and understanding: An inquiry into socialization theory*. New York: Elsevier.

Wertsch, J. V. (1985). *Vygotsky and the social formation of mind*. Cambridge, MA: Harvard University Press.

Wertsch, J. V. (1991). *Voices of the mind: A sociocultural approach to mediated action*. Cambridge, MA: Harvard University Press.

Wood, K. M. (1971). The contribution of psychoanalysis and ego psychology to social work. In H. S. Strean (Ed.), *Social casework: Theories in action* (pp. 45–122). Metuchen, NJ: Scarecrow Press.

World Bank. (2010, June 2). *Extreme poverty rates continue to fall*. Retrieved from http://data.worldbank.org/news/extreme-poverty-rates-continue-to-fall

World Bank. (n.d.a). *Millennium Development Goals*. Retrieved from http://ddpext .worldbank.org/ext/GMIS/gdmis.do?siteId=2&goalId=5&menuId=LNAV01 GOAL1

World Bank. (n.d.b). *Poverty*. Retrieved from http://data.worldbank.org/topic/poverty

Yelloly, M. A. (1980). *Social work theory and psychoanalysis*. New York: Van Nostrand Reinhold; Cambridge, MA: Harvard University Press.

3

Brain Function and Development

This chapter presents a brief overview of the human brain for social work students. Prior to the 1990s, neurobiological systems were seldom included in our social work textbooks, classroom teaching, and practice interventions. Indeed, very few social work professors had been educated in basic neuroscience concepts. Today, social workers are publishing books and articles on how the brain and environment interact to shape the human experience (Farmer, 2009; Johnson, 2004; Taylor, 2002, 2006). We now appreciate that understanding clients' behavior depends not only on an assessment of their bio-psycho-social-spiritual perspective, but also on their neurobiological functioning as well. We also understand more about neuroplasticity, including the interaction of brain function and development within sociocultural contexts.

Social workers are not expected to become neuroscientists. We do, however, need to understand enough neuroscience to provide evidence-based education to clients suffering from health, developmental, and mental disorders, and to their families. We play important roles, for example, on treatment teams that include physicians and other professionals, in communicating neurobiological information to clients and their families. For example, certain mental disorders manifesting in late adolescence and early adulthood may be related to viruses attacking a fetus's developing brain, delivery problems, high fevers occurring at critical periods of brain development, and head injuries during the first two years of life (Taylor, 2006, in press; Torrey, Bowler, Taylor, & Gottesman, 1994). Social workers may be called upon to help families understand how neurodevelopmental and mental disorders can appear in a previously symptom-free person. A basic knowledge of the brain and human development within an ecological context is fundamental to fulfilling this role.

Brain development exemplifies the complex transactions of biological, physical, social, and cultural contexts from our earliest development. For example, infants born to mothers in poverty who do not receive proper nutrition are at risk neurodevelopmentally. During prenatal development, the brain needs adequate nourishment for normal growth. During periods of rapid brain growth, inadequate nutrition can result in profound negative physiological changes (Georgiefe & Rao, 2001). During the first twelve weeks following conception, for example, deficiencies in iodine, selenium, folate, and vitamin A can trigger changes in brain development, some of which will cause persistent problems even if adequate nutrition is restored (Georgiefe & Rao, 2001). These biological processes can also be profoundly impacted by political, economic, and macrocultural contexts that affect women's access to prenatal care, and the availability and quality of food.

HISTORICAL OVERVIEW

Throughout history, beliefs about the brain have not simply emerged from scientific findings, but also from existential, religious, and even political concerns. The prehistoric practice of drilling holes into the skull to release demons and evil spirits disappeared and reappeared across cultures until the late Middle Ages, even as scientific knowledge of the brain emerged. We no longer open a person's skull to release evil, but some contemporary religious groups teach that mental illness occurs from demonic possession and sin. From the earliest of times, there have also been periods of enlightenment and scientific inquiry. Hippocrates, the Greek medical doctor and teacher, believed that mental disorders resulted from disease and head injuries. He described what we now call schizophrenia as a brain disorder that has some similarities with **dementia**. Hippocrates was also one of the first to teach that the mind is an intangible element created by the brain (Taylor, in press). Plato agreed with Hippocrates's theory of mind, but Aristotle declared that feelings and thought stemmed from one's heart. Interestingly, today we continue to talk about emotions of love, hate, charity, and selfishness as flowing from a person's heart (Taylor, in press).

Throughout the Middle Ages, mental illness was mostly viewed from a religious perspective. The mentally ill were seen either as possessed by demons or as being punished for their sins. Banishment, exorcism, confinement, and sometimes torture and death were often the prescribed treatments. In the 1800s, however, attention was once again focused on science, and brain studies flourished. For example, Emil Kraepelin, a German psychiatrist, conducted research and taught that schizophrenia, bipolar disorders, and dementia were disorders of the brain and that those suffering from them deserved humane, professional treatment. The early 1900s ushered in psychoanalytic theory, which framed mental illness as an internal emotional conflict rather than as a disease of the brain. Sigmund Freud built a sweeping theory for explaining mental illness, based on Western philosophy and limited clinical observations. Although his theory made a number of psychological contributions, it placed the blame for mental illness on mothers, fathers, and free will (Taylor, 2006, in press) and targeted exploration of the unconscious (Barlow, Durand, & Stewart, 2009). There is no empirical evidence that targeting unconscious, unresolved crises cures mental illness (Gassaniga & Heatherton, 2009; Taylor, in press). While modern neuro-science has again moved the focus of mental disorders back to the brain, aspects of psychoanalytic theory and some religious beliefs continue to stig-matize the mentally ill and their families.

THE CEREBRAL CORTEX IN BRIEF

The adult human brain may be one of the most complex structures in the universe. At a microscopic level, it contains approximately 100–500 tril-lion synapses, or connections between neurons. Neurons are brain cells that receive, process, and transmit information. Neurons communicate across synapses through neurotransmitters and related molecules (Gassaniga & Heatherton, 2009; O'Rourke, Weiler, Micheva, & Smith, 2012) and electrical impulses (Rayport & Kriegstein, 1997). A single neuron can have several hundred thousand synapses. The neuronal **axon** is an elongated fiber that projects from the body of the neuron and splits into smaller branches and

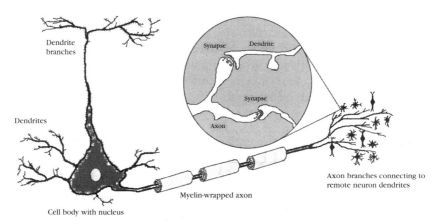

Simplified schematic of one neuron connecting to neurons at a distant location. In the foreground, a local neuron has many dendrite branches, each with numerous synaptic connections receiving sig-nals from other neurons. The local neuron sends out signals on its one axon. The long axon is insu-lated in a myelin sheath. At the remote location, the axon can branch many times before terminating in synapses. The close-up shows the two axon terminals connecting to the remote neuron dendrites. The synapse connections are complex, often with vesicles containing neurotransmitters (shown as small bubbles), and the dendritic side has a complex structure (shaded dark gray) with receptors for the neurotransmitters as well as complex molecular cascades. The synapse communicates with DNA in the cell nucleus as well as transmitting electrical impulses. The gray background in the close-up denotes a complex mesh of dendrites, axons, synapses, glia, and blood vessels. Not shown are com-plex structures inside the axons, dendrites, and cell bodies, which include a molecular skeleton, sig-naling cascades, transport systems, and mitochondria for energy.

twigs. **Myelination** is a process where myelin sheaths insulate longer axons, which when bundled together form "white matter" tracts connecting remote brain areas. Myelin is a fatty substance that both protects and assists electrical impulses to propagate rapidly along the axon (Gassaniga & Heatherton, 2009; Lenroot & Giedd, 2007). The sheer number of neurons, synaptic connections, and interconnections of brain regions produces an information network that is extremely complex.

In terms of gross anatomy, the brain is divided into two connected hemispheres. The outer layer of the brain is the **cerebral cortex**. The cerebral cortex is like a wrinkled cap covering and connected to important, phylogenetically older structures. This folded, grooved, outer layer of neural tissue is sometimes referred to as the "gray matter." Every cubic millimeter of cerebral cortex contains roughly a billion synapses (Squire, Bloom, & Spitzer, 2008). The cerebral cortex plays a key role in many of the basic functions that contribute to our sense of self, including memory, thought, language, perception, emotion, and consciousness. For purposes of discussion, we will describe various regions of the cerebral cortex as having discrete functions. It is important to remember, however, that these various, complex structures are interconnected and interacting.

The cerebral cortex can be grossly divided into the frontal, temporal, parietal, and occipital lobes. The **frontal lobes** are involved in planning, movement, and some memory. Impairment in this region can cause numerous difficulties, depending on the part of the lobe that is injured. A lesion in one area can cause difficulty retrieving words, while injury to other areas result in problems with social conduct, planning, judgment, and decision making (Tranel, 1997).

The **temporal lobes** are located behind the frontal lobes in the lower region of the cerebral cortex. They contain a complex group of structures that process auditory information, store and activate memory, and influence emotion. They are connected to structures in the limbic system, including the **amygdala**, which is involved in producing and controlling emotion, and the **hippocampus**, which is involved in forming short-term memories and determining which environmental events or cues require immediate attention. Damage occurring to the temporal lobes can result in problems with both long-term and short-term memory. In some cases, clients with temporal lobe injuries can fail to have or show emotions and appear fearless when facing obvious danger (Nolte, 2002).

The **parietal lobes** are located behind the frontal lobes and above the temporal lobes. This area controls language comprehension, spatial orientation and perception, and the sense of touch. Moving through the world constantly requires an ability to interpret spatial relationships between ourself, other people, and all types of objects. Individuals who have a stroke in the right parietal lobe fail to notice items on their left side. Even when looking

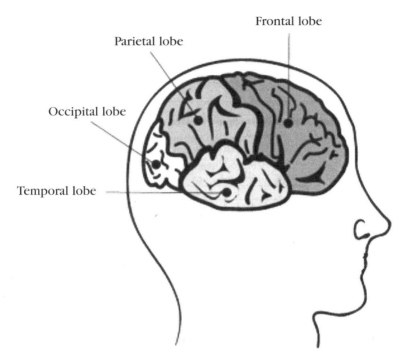

A very simplified diagram of the cerebral cortex and its major lobes (regions): frontal, parietal, temporal, and occipital. The frontal lobe sits over the eyes, and the occipital is at the back of the head. The right and left sides of the cerebral cortex are largely symmetric, although most people have their language areas on the left. Dense white-matter tracts underneath the cortex connect different cortical regions and both sides. The cerebral cortex in humans is large and sits like a cap over many complex subcortical brain structures (not shown).

in a mirror, they will see only their right side. As a result, people with a stroke in the right parietal lobe may shave or apply makeup to a single side of their face (Gassaniga & Heatherton, 2009). Damage to the parietal lobes can also cause agnosias and apraxias. When people have agnosias, they lose the ability to use one or more of their senses for object recognition, even though the required sense has not been damaged. If vision is affected, for example, the person is unable to recognize common objects by sight, even though nothing is wrong with his or her eyes or ability to recognize objects by touch. Apraxias refer to a person's inability to *deliberately* perform an action of which he or she is physically capable. For example, an individual who can't mimic on command the physician's standing on one foot in the doctor's office, may spontaneously accomplish the same balancing movement at home. The problem is not in the person's physical abilities, but rather a parietal-lobe lesion (Nolte, 2002).

The **occipital lobes** sit toward the back of the brain. They are primarily responsible for vision and visual associations. Any damage to this area results in complete or partial loss of conscious visual awareness.

MEMORY AND ANXIETY

Memory and anxiety serve as excellent examples of how complex, interacting brain structures and environments shape our experiences. Development of anxiety disorders such as obsessive compulsive disorder (OCD) and post-traumatic stress disorder (PTSD) involves numerous interacting and overactive brain areas that contribute to ongoing, negative life experiences. Difficult environmental situations, when repeated, result in learning and memories. Negative memories can trigger expectations and fears of the future.

Consider, for example, OCD. The brain's primary anxiety circuits consist of the orbitofrontal-limbic-basal ganglia areas (orbitofrontal is a region of the frontal lobes, and basal ganglia are subcortical structures involved in movement and other complex functions). Overactivity in this area can result in unrealistic emphasis on cleanliness, fears of behaving inappropriately, increased general social worries, and unexplained feelings of guilt. Underactivity of the prefrontal-orbital cortex is associated with a lack of feelings of inhibition and guilt. When the amygdala is hypersensitive and gives overreactive emotional responses, the hippocampus develops memories and passes forward signals that fail to match the realities of the environment. Additionally, a frontal cortex area called the cingulate gyrus allows us to shift our attention to appropriate environmental cues, employ cognitive flexibility, and accept the environment. Overactivity in this brain section results in a lack of flexibility, obsessions, compulsions, worries, and an inability to let go of fearful thoughts (Taylor, in press).

Consider also PTSD. The basal ganglia, a group of nuclei strongly connected to the cerebral cortex and other brain areas, serve many purposes. In anxiety, they are responsible for integrating feelings and movement, and they suppress unwanted fine-motor behaviors. Motivation is also supported by the basal ganglia. Panic attacks, muscle tension, and reduced motivation are associated with overactive basal ganglia. Moreover, the caudate nucleus, which is part of the basal ganglia, is extremely important for understanding anxiety. The caudate nucleus filters signals coming from other brain sections, and manages or controls unwanted repetitive behaviors. Unfortunately, if the caudate nucleus is overactive, the emotion signals pass unfiltered to the frontal cortex, our brain's center of judgment and reasoning. When functioning correctly, the frontal cortex reviews the overstated emotions and slows the entire process down. However, overactivity in the frontal cortex can block our ability to apply judgment, reasoning, and abstract thinking. Therefore, we can think of anxiety as like a fast-acting, encapsulated, and unprocessed cognition that, through practice, becomes embedded in long-term memory as automatic beliefs.

BRAIN DEVELOPMENT

Brain development starts almost at conception and continues throughout the life span. It is especially rapid through early childhood. By the age of two, a child's brain weighs about 80 percent of its potential adult mass. Over the next three years, it will increase by another 10 percent, and reach adult weight and appearance by about ten years of age (Lenroot & Giedd, 2007).

Within three to four weeks of gestation, the neural tube that will form the central nervous system develops. If abnormalities caused by malnutrition or toxins occur during the formation of the neural tube, a child can be born with spina bifida (damaged spinal cord) or anencephaly (lack of brain).

During the first trimester of gestation, the forebrain is formed in an intricate, genetically programmed choreography. At the end of the first trimester and start of the second trimester, neurons proliferate. During this early development, the brain produces many more neurons than needed in a programmed sequence, and between the end of the second trimester and one month following birth, approximately 50 percent of these neurons rapidly die. This is a normal process called apoptosis (Lenroot & Giedd, 2007; Pinel, 2006). This process of neuron overproduction and pruning continues between the ages of four months and four years (Lenroot & Giedd, 2007). In addition, near the end of the third trimester of pregnancy and through the child's early postnatal years, the developing brain is rapidly organizing synaptic connections (Lenroot & Giedd, 2007).

Part of the choreography of brain development is that neurons form in clusters; then they sequentially migrate to specific locations. This migration is guided in part by a temporary network of glial cells (Pinel, 2006). The glial cells are the "glue" that surrounds, supports, and buffers the neurons. They continue developing throughout the first year of life (Lenroot & Giedd, 2007) and play an ongoing role in structure, metabolism, and protection of neurons and synaptic connections.

The brain's cortex consists of six layers. Each layer develops at a different time and requires six separate neuronal migrations. This means that many neurons must move through already existing layers of cortex to reach their target. After reaching the correct location, the neurons aggregate, or align themselves with other neurons in the area, and form nervous system structures (Pinel, 2006). If the migration process is disrupted, future development can be altered. For example, prenatal alcohol, genetic disorders, malnutrition, and toxins have well-documented adverse effects on brain development. Also, the risk for adult-onset schizophrenia is increased if a virus infects the fetal brain during the second trimester and disrupts neuron migration (Torrey et al., 1994).

BRAIN PLASTICITY

Of course, brain development does not end in childhood or adolescence. Brain changes occur throughout the life span. New synaptic connections, for example, continue to emerge as we learn from new experiences across the life span. **Plasticity** refers to brain changes over time from social, educational, and treatment experiences. At times the phenomenon of plasticity has been both overstated and underappreciated. Some motivational speakers claim that anyone can change their brain and become whatever they want. Others see change as impossible and life situations as rigid and genetically dictated. Neither belief is factual or healthy.

Learning disorders illustrate both plasticity and its limits. Only about 15 percent of reading problems in North America, for example, stem from poor schooling, mental retardation, or other problems. The remaining 85 percent have a biologically based learning disorder (Grigorenko, 2007). Furthermore, these disorders appear to be highly inheritable. The neurobiological bases for reading and other learning disorders are well established. Individuals with a variety of learning disorders generally have less integrated neural structures in the left hemisphere. People with reading disorders often demonstrate difficulty with phoneme awareness, language-processing skills, speech perception, vocabulary, and phonological representation (Mann, 2002).

While learning disorders are genetically based, they are also environmentally sensitive. Neither genetics nor environment completely dictates the outcome. That is, through experience focused on left hemispheric exercises and learning, the brain develops new pathways. With continued educational practice and increased engagement of the left hemisphere, reading mastery often increases. Biologically based reading disorders are also influenced by a child's environment. The ability to remediate a learning disorder improves if the child lives in a secure home, gets more schooling, receives education from teachers trained in direct reading methods and phonemic awareness, resides in a literacy-enriched home, and receives an adequate diet (Grigorenko, 2007).

It is important to understand that environmental factors can at best interact and moderate reading and other learning disorders. As with other neurobiological disorders, environments do not always have the power to completely correct the problems. A child may live in an enriched home environment, never want for food, receive the best of instruction, always have support, and continue to have severe reading problems (Taylor, in press). It is important to remind ourselves that there are limits to plasticity. Furthermore, remediation may be slow and requires continuous work and maintenance.

The brain can most certainly change. Nonetheless, we cannot neuro-engineer our development. There is, for example, no evidence that having infants and toddlers listen to classical music will enhance their intellectual skills. We know that there are few critical periods, and that positive brain development can occur across the life span (Thompson & Nelson, 2001). Finally, it is essential for social workers to keep in mind that neurological development and maturation is uneven and that every child, adult, and senior citizen has a unique brain.

STUDYING THE BRAIN

Social workers may have clients who turn to them for information and guidance about neurological assessments. Listening and understanding medical information while at a crowded clinic is difficult. Additionally, some clients need time to consider treatment proposals before they are emotionally ready to receive new information. Regaining access to medical professionals is often challenging, and turning to the social worker can feel less threatening or tiring. Therefore, it is important for social workers to have at least a minimal understanding of the instruments used for studying the brain.

Positron-emission tomography (PET) and functional magnetic resonance imaging (fMRI) allow medical personnel and neuroscientists to observe which areas of the brain are active when a person is resting or performing a specific task. For example, when healthy individuals mentally solve a problem, the frontal cortex will become more active than other brain sections. PET scans and fMRI, however, indicate that people with schizophrenia have reduced functioning in the frontal cortex. Individuals experiencing anxiety show increased activity in the emotional areas of the brain, such as the amygdala (Phelps & LaBar, 2006; Price, Noppeney, & Friston, 2006).

PET scans provide computerized illustrations of how actively the brain is working within and across structures. More specifically, they measure the amount of oxygen and glucose metabolized simultaneously throughout the brain. To stay alive and work, the brain must have oxygen and glucose. As the brain functions, specialized areas accelerate their rate of metabolism, and the body rushes more glucose and oxygen to these working areas. The PET scan requires the person to either breathe or be injected with a low dose of radioactive substance. As the chemical enters the brain, gamma rays are emitted and detected by sensors. Gamma rays occur at a faster and greater rate in brain areas that are metabolizing more glucose. The computer is able to track where the gamma rays are emitted and create a color map of where and how much the brain is working (Taylor, 2006). Because this method exposes the person to radiation, it is seldom used with children and adolescents.

Like the PET scan, **functional magnetic resonance imaging** (fMRI) and **magnetic resonance imaging** (MRI) capture brain functioning, but these tests do not emit any radiation. An extremely strong magnet housed in the MRI equipment measures the response of hydrogen nuclei when they are exposed to changes in magnetic fields. Hydrogen atoms are found throughout the body. Hydrogen nuclei actively respond and move when a magnetic field is introduced. As the nuclei react, a computer measures changes in the amount of energy absorbed and emitted and produces a three-dimensional picture of the brain or any internal organ (Song, Huettel, & McCarthy, 2006). The fact that a person is not exposed to any radiation has allowed doctors and scientists to use MRI and fMRI to study the brain across the life span.

In addition to investigating how the human brain functions, it is also important to study the relative size and shape of neurostructures. The shape and size of brain areas are measured using **computerized axial tomography** (CAT scan) and MRI-created images. A CAT scan (also called a CT scan) is created by a computer that turns multiple X-ray images of a selected body area into high-contrast pictures. CAT scans provide much sharper resolution of soft tissue than routine X-rays. Until the CAT scan was invented, brain images were impossible. Standard X-rays of the head show the skull, but little or no brain tissue. The CAT scan rotates 180 degrees around the person, creating numerous X-ray photos. This allows the doctor or scientist to view the selected tissue area as a single picture, or as numerous thin slices.

The MRI was developed after the CAT scan, and has been used internationally for studying the brain. While both technologies continue to be used, the MRI has two major advantages over the CAT scan: an MRI scan does not expose individuals to radiation, and it can make clearer images of structures deep within the brain. Until the MRI was perfected, for example, neuroscientists were uncertain whether antipsychotic medications damaged the brain. They also discovered that people with schizophrenia, as a group, have larger ventricles than individuals who have no history of psychosis. (Ventricles are cavities in the brain that produce and circulate cerebrospinal fluid.) Because CAT scans emit radiation, however, ethical problems and a lack of volunteers prevented studying medication-free individuals who were experiencing their first psychotic break. Understandably, clients and families did not want to participate in a study that had radiation exposure and offered little or no diagnostic information. Evidence for ventricular enlargement came almost entirely from imaging patients already receiving medications. Thus, it was unclear if ventricular enlargement was a characteristic of people who develop schizophrenia, or if medication was damaging their brains.

Once MRI was available, barriers for scanning medication-free clients disappeared. With no radiation risk, people could have a free brain scan and confirm that the psychosis was not triggered by a hidden brain tumor. The drug-free psychosis studies strongly associated enlarged ventricles with schizophrenia rather than medication-induced brain damage (Taylor, in press). This discovery enabled countless clients to accept medication treatment for their schizophrenia. The fear that medications would change brain structures was now reduced, and families gained confidence in their support of drug treatment.

The electroencephalogram (EEG) provides another method for studying the brain. Rather than producing an image, the EEG measures and graphs the brain's electrical activities. A normally functioning brain produces a set pattern of recordable brain waves. The electrical impulses emitted from the brain are picked up from sensors placed on the head and fed into a computer. A trained person can identify unusual wave patterns that signal abnormal electrical activity. The EEG is often used for assessing, diagnosing, and monitoring seizures and sleep disorders. Also, a head-trauma victim may receive a series of EEGs to assess and monitor wave pattern changes.

Families with mentally ill members sometimes question whether a correct diagnosis has been given. The Internet and books are filled with photos of brain scans showing abnormal functioning or structural formations for almost every mental disorder. This creates a desire in some to have a brain scan as a means to validate or discredit their current diagnosis. For most clients and families, it is important to counsel against taking a scan in an assessment for mental illness. Imaging is primarily a research tool for studying the brain, but it cannot inform individual clients (Taylor, 2006). Findings from neuroimaging research are based on group data, and may not represent any one person. While variation in group patterns of glucose metabolism and cellular structure size and shapes exist for most disorders, there is no standard for determining individual diagnoses. Furthermore, most clients have not had a preillness brain scan that can be used as a baseline. The case of a leading schizophrenia researcher illustrates why brain scans cannot be used diagnostically. This individual has no personal or family history of mental disorders. When imaged, however, his brain's ventricles are larger than those in most people who suffer with schizophrenia. We have used his scan in numerous diagnostic workshops. Trained neuroscientists are given scans of people with and without schizophrenia. They are then asked to select the images they think are of clients who have a major psychotic disorder. Our friend, the scientist, is almost always labeled as having schizophrenia.

Medical-imaging studies are expensive and seldom answer mental health diagnostic or treatment questions. In most cases, medical insurance will not cover the cost of an MRI, fMRI, or CAT scan to rule out or verify a mental disorder. Therefore, until imaging becomes a proven assessment process for mental health, little or no benefit will be gained from an expensive brain scan. This is not true, however, if the mentally ill client shows symptoms of having had a stroke, brain tumor, head trauma, high fevers, or other complicating neurological problems. Brain scanning is also used to rule out disorders such as **Alzheimer's disease** and multiple sclerosis. We must always keep in mind that clients can develop life-threatening neurological disorders *and* have an active mental health problem. Whenever symptoms or any indicator signals a possible neurological problem beyond the known mental disorder, a medical consultation is immediately needed. As social workers, we do not make medical decisions, conduct medical assessments, give medical advice, or prescribe or even suggest medications.

SUMMARY

The biological brain and the mystical mind are intrinsically bound together. Nonetheless, it is the mind, and not the brain, that social workers most often contemplate. One way of understanding the mind is to consider it the reality we have trained our brain to produce (Gassaniga & Heatherton, 2009). Without the countless interactions among brain functioning, memory, and the sociocultural context, there is no mind (Gassaniga & Heatherton, 2009). In the same way that the brain cannot be separated from the environment, the concept of mind is inseparable from the biological brain. To help clients understand neurological testing, learning, and brain disorders, and to contribute to multidisciplinary teams serving individuals suffering from mental illnesses, contemporary social workers require a basic understanding of the brain, and how it relates to that elusive concept of the mind.

Study and Discussion Questions

1. Discuss three reasons why it is important for you as a social worker to have a basic understanding of the brain.

2. Provide an example of how brain development exemplifies the complex transaction of bio-psycho-social contexts.

3. Summarize some ways in which our concepts of the brain have changed throughout history. To what extent do you see evidence of contemporary scientific understandings reflected in earlier times? To what extent do you see earlier religiously based perspectives reflected in contemporary society?

4. Describe the gross anatomy of the cerebral cortex and summarize its major functions.

5. Describe the major categories of brain cells and their functions.

6. Describe the role of apoptosis and cell migration in brain development.

7. Summarize the ways in which neurons receive and transmit information.

8. Consider how the phenomenon of brain plasticity might be of relevance to your future social work practice.

9. Describe the major ways in which the brain is studied. What are some contexts in which knowledge of these procedures would be important for you as a social worker?

References

Barlow, D. H., Durand, V. M., & Stewart, S. H. (2009). *Abnormal psychology: An integrative approach* (2nd Canadian ed.). Toronto: Nelson Education.

Farmer, R. L. (2009). *Neuroscience and social work practice: The missing link.* Thousand Oaks, CA: Sage.

Gassaniga, M., & Heatherton, T. F. (2009). *Psychological science.* New York: W. W. Norton.

Georgiefe, M. K., & Rao, R. (2001). The role of nutrition in cognitive development. In C. A. Nelson & M. Luciana (Eds.), *Handbook of developmental cognitive neuroscience* (pp. 491–504). Cambridge, MA: MIT Press.

Grigorenko, E. L. (2007). Triangulating developmental dyslexia. In D. Coch, G. Dawson, & K. W. Fischer (Eds.), *Human behavior, learning, and the developing brain: Atypical development* (pp. 117–144). New York: Guilford.

Johnson, H. C. (2004). *Psyche and synapse expanding worlds: The role of neurobiology in emotions, behavior, thinking, and addiction for non-scientists* (2nd ed.). Greenfield, MA: Deerfield Valley Publishing.

Lenroot, R. K., & Giedd, J. N. (2007). The structural development of the human brain as measured longitudinally with magnetic resonance imaging. In D. Coch, K. W. Fischer, & G. Dawson (Eds.), *Human behavior, learning, and the developing brain: Typical development* (pp. 50–73). New York: Guilford.

Mann, V. A. (2002). Reading disorders, developmental. In V. S. Ramachandran (Ed.), *Encyclopedia of the human brain* (Vol. 4, pp. 141–154). San Diego: Academic Press.

Nolte, J. (2002). *The human brain: An introduction to its functional anatomy* (5 ed.). St. Louis: Mosby.

O'Rourke, N. A., Weiler, N. C., Micheva, K. D., & Smith, S. J. (2012). Deep molecular diversity of mammalian synapses: Why it matters and how to measure it. *Nature Reviews Neuroscience 13*, 365–379.

Phelps, E. A., & LaBar, K. S. (2006). Functional neuroimaging of emotion and social cognition. In R. Cabeza & A. Kingstone (Eds.), *Handbook of functional neuroimaging of cognition* (2nd ed., pp. 421–454). Cambridge, MA: MIT Press.

Pinel, J. P. J. (2006). *Biopsychology.* Boston: Pearson Education.

Price, C. J., Noppeney, U., & Friston, K. J. (2006). Functional neuroimaging of neuropsychologically impaired patients. In R. Cabeza & A. Kingstone (Eds.), *Handbook of functional neuroimaging of cognition* (2nd ed., pp. 455–480). Cambridge, MA: MIT Press.

Rayport, S., & Kriegstein, A. R. (1997). Cellular and molecular biology of the neuron. In S. C. Yudofsky & R. E. Hales (Eds.), *The American Psychiatric Press textbook of neuropsychiatry* (3rd ed., pp. 3–34). Washington, DC: American Psychiatric Press.

Song, A. W., Huettel, S. A., & McCarthy, G. (2006). Functional neuroimaging: Basic principles of functional MRI. In R. Cabeza & A. Kingstone (Eds.), *Handbook of functional neuroimaging of cognition* (2nd ed., pp. 21–52). Cambridge, MA: MIT Press.

Squire, L. R., Bloom, F., & Spitzer, N. (2008). *Fundamental neuroscience*. Burlington, MA: Academic Press.

Taylor, E. H. (2002). Manic-depressive illness. In V. S. Ramachandran (Ed.), *Encyclopedia of the human brain* (Vol. 2, pp. 745–758). San Diego: Academic Press.

Taylor, E. H. (2006). *Atlas of bipolar disorders*. London: Taylor & Francis Group.

Taylor, E. H. (in press). *Assessing, diagnosing, and treating mental disorders: A bioecological perspective*. New York: Oxford University Press.

Thompson, R. A., & Nelson, C. A. (2001). Developmental science and the media. *American Psychologist, 56*(1), 5–15.

Torrey, E. F., Bowler, A. E., Taylor, E. H., & Gottesman, I. I. (1994). *Schizophrenia and manic depressive disorder: The biological roots of mental illness as revealed by the landmark study of identical twins*. New York: Basic Books.

Tranel, D. (1997). Functional neuroanatomy. In S. C. Yudofsky & R. E. Hales (Eds.), *The American Psychiatric Press textbook of neuropsychiatry* (3rd ed., pp. 77–118). Washington, DC: American Psychiatric Press.

4

Using Social Science Evidence to Understand Human Development and Enhance Social Work Practice

This chapter discusses the role of research in understanding human development and enhancing social work practice. We all have folk theories of human behavior and development. As discussed earlier, these folk theories typically stand us in good stead in our daily lives, interacting with family and friends. They often contain gaps and misinformation that can be problematic, however, especially in dealing with individuals from diverse backgrounds or in unusual situations. It is important to distinguish folk theories from an understanding of human development derived from social science research. Thus, it is important to consider the diverse histories, goals, and methods of the social science research on which this book is based.

One of the distinguishing features of modern social work as a profession is the use of social science research to guide practice and policy. Social science evidence can increase social work's effectiveness, efficiency, and accountability. Research helps us understand complex issues, identify effective interventions, and eliminate ineffective or harmful approaches. Evidence-based practice, however, is complex and not uncontroversial. We do not take a "key to the universe" stance on evidence-based practice; rather, we recognize its limitations and the many challenges to its implementation. The final sections of this chapter illustrate how practicing social workers used social science evidence in a research program addressing drug use in rural families.

THE ROLE OF RESEARCH IN CONTEMPORARY SOCIAL WORK

A significant challenge for early social workers in the late nineteenth and early twentieth centuries was to find their distinctive niche, to distinguish their work from the domains of the church and clergy, and from political and social advocates. The clergy ministered to the individual needs of the poor, disabled, and dispossessed, while political activists rallied for collective social justice and reform. As an aspiring profession, social work sought a modern grounding distinct from religion and political activism. For this purpose, social work followed the pathway taken by medicine and adopted the rubric of science (Parton & Kirk, 2010).

Today, social work research can be broadly defined as original investigation undertaken to gain knowledge and understanding in order to address social issues. It uses a range of research methods, primarily from the social sciences, which include psychology, sociology, anthropology, economics, and policy analysis. A common denominator in this diverse research is a concern with social inclusion, justice, and change (Shaw, Briar-Lawson, Orme, & Ruckdeschel, 2010). The general goals of social work research include understanding complex problems that include human behavior and development in the social environment, improving and evaluating social work interventions (Gredig & Marsh, 2010), providing evidence for decision making and public accountability (Boaz & Blewett, 2010), and developing theory and knowledge about social problems to enhance policy development (Orme & Briar-Lawson, 2010). In addition, utilization of research findings enhances the credibility of social work as a profession.

One illustration of the importance of basing interventions on social science evidence is the Scared Straight programs that originated in the 1970s. Youth who have committed, or who are at risk of committing, delinquent acts visit prisons where convicted felons present them with the realities of prison life. They "scare them straight" through presentations and interactive discussions that are sometimes harsh and intimidating. These innovative programs flourished around the country in response to increasing rates of juvenile delinquency. They have received glowing testimonials from convicts, who described a newfound purpose in life, using their experiences to encourage youth to take a more positive path. Youth and their parents have also provided glowing testimonials of how participation in this program changed the youth's perspectives and behavior. Developers of Scared Straight are fully committed to helping youth, and passionately believe in their program. Today, Scared Straight programs remain popular and are found throughout the United States as well as abroad in Australia, the United Kingdom, Norway, and Germany.

Yet objective social science research on the impact of Scared Straight programs tells a rather different story. Empirical research comparing youth randomly assigned to a Scared Straight program or to no intervention indicate that these programs are not just generally ineffective at preventing crime, they may be harmful to some youth. Indeed, youth exposed to Scared Straight are at increased odds of committing delinquent offenses compared with youth randomly assigned to a control group (Petrosino, Turpin-Petrosino, & Buehler, 2003). How can these counterintuitive findings be explained? Scared Straight has unintended negative effects, including that some youth come to identify with and want to be like the prisoners, and that they experience traumatic stress from realistic and frightening encounters with the adult prisoners.

Evidence-Based Practice

Broadly conceived, **evidence-based practice** is the use of current empirical evidence to make practice and policy decisions. In social work, Eileen Gambrill (2006) explains that evidence from empirical research is integrated with professional understanding of the sociocultural context, including individual clients' beliefs, values, and behaviors as a guide to intervention. According to David Sackett (Sackett, Strauss, Richardson, Rosenberg, & Haynes, 2000, p. 1), evidence-based practice is the "integration of best research evidence with clinical expertise and [client] values." It first appeared in the medical profession to help physicians select effective treatment for their patients. Evidence-based practice helped move medicine from long-standing reliance on authority-based decision-making processes, to those that take account of empirical evidence. Evidence-based practice is used today in a wide variety of disciplines from education to policing (Sherman, 1998).

In the past decade, evidence-based practice has received a great deal of attention in social work. Knowledge of empirical research is essential for the modern social worker to address questions such as, Do we understand the origins and contributing factors to this complex human problem? Did the intervention produce the desired results? Did a well-intentioned intervention cause unintended harm? Could scarce resources be better spent elsewhere? Such questions are scrutinized through applied social science research combined with practice experience with particular individuals and communities. The alternatives to evidence-based practice, including appealing to religious (or other) authority, personal experience, or popular opinion, are simply unacceptable to professional practice in our complex, pluralistic society. Ethical practice necessitates a rigorous assessment of social work practice and policy (Gambrill, 2000).

Evidence-based practice relies on and encourages habits of critical thinking. According to Eileen Gambrill (2000, p. 43), "Critical thinking is the careful appraisal of beliefs and actions to arrive at well-reasoned ones that maximize the likelihood of helping clients and avoiding harm. It involves reasonable and reflective thinking focused on deciding what to believe or do . . . Viewed broadly the process is part of problem solving. It requires clarity of expression, critical appraisal of evidence and reasons, and the consideration of alternative points of view. Critical thinkers question what others take for granted. They challenge accepted beliefs and ways of acting." Critical-thinking skills can help social workers avoid questionable grounds for accepting practice-related claims, for example, about the effectiveness of particular interventions. Such claims may be based on authority, tradition, popularity, newness, intuition, and attractive presentation. Such claims may also be false. Critical thinking requires a careful examination of the evidence, and consideration of alternative views and practices, even when they conflict with our own personal preferences. It leads to well-reasoned practice decisions based on related research findings, and to full disclosure to clients about the risks and benefits of recommended services, as well as alternatives. Critical thinking helps social workers choose wisely among options, discover alternative views, and avoid false prophets (Gambrill, 2000).

In one influential variant, the process of evidence-based practice is broken down into five structured steps (Sackett et al., 2000). First, the practitioner converts practical information needs into questions that can be answered through empirical research. For example, a social worker observes that a group of young men in an eating disorders clinic is not showing the same treatment gains as the young women. The social worker then asks a question that can be answered empirically: What clinical techniques are generally effective with young men suffering from eating disorders? Once the social worker has posed the question, the next step is to locate the evidence to address the question. This process involves searching professional journals, books, published lists of effective programs by federal entities and research centers, and published guidelines that offer treatment protocols based on empirical evidence. The next step is to appraise the evidence. Many reports will contain valuable recommendations that have the potential to strengthen practice and policy. Other reports, however, are based on weak research methods and may contradict reports with firmer empirical foundations. It is essential for social workers to develop the critical-thinking skills necessary to evaluate the empirical evidence on which recommendations for practice and policy are based (Gambrill, 2000). Step four applies evidence to practice and policy decisions. In this step, the social worker must integrate professional judgment, as well as knowledge of the sociocultural context and specific client, with the empirical research. For example, interventions generally effective for young men with eating disorders in urban communities may need to be modified for implementation with a particular urban adolescent, or group of rural adolescents. The final step in evidence-based practice is to evaluate the process, that is, to conduct an ongoing evaluation and reflection on one's knowledge of current literature, familiarity with electronic databases, and skills in drawing conclusions based on methodological rigor.

Despite its importance, adequately addressing issues of concern to social work from an evidence-based perspective is a daunting task requiring integration of professional experience with a burgeoning empirical literature that is increasingly complex and interdisciplinary. Not surprisingly, there is some evidence that use of research by social workers is infrequent and sporadic, and that many frontline practitioners currently have a limited sense of how to implement evidence-based practice (Gray, Plath, & Webb, 2009; Yunong & Fengzhi, 2009).

A number of strategies have been employed to facilitate social workers' use of social science evidence in their practices. First, researchers must make greater efforts to synthesize large bodies of complex research for practitioners; that is, they must translate research findings into usable information. For example, there are research organizations and centers that generate systematic reviews of empirical research, including the Cochrane and Campbell Collaborations. Second, social service organizations must provide social workers with the time and resources necessary to access such information. Third, educators must clearly show that empirical research is used in conjunction with, not as a substitute for, practitioner judgment, knowledge of the practice context, and client goals and values. Finally, practitioners and researchers must be willing to work together to establish partnerships for developing knowledge relevant to social work practice (Yunong & Fengzhi, 2009).

Professional social workers obtain and present information on current applied social science research through a variety of sources, including professional journals. A few of these social work journals that students may wish to peruse include *Social Work, Social Work Research, Research on Social Work Practice, Social Service Review, Journal of the Society for Social Work and Research, Social Work Education, Child Welfare, Children and Youth Services Review,* and *Affilia: Journal of Women and Social Work.* Research published in these journals has undergone critical peer review by social work scholars, which enhances its credibility. Interpreting this research, however, is complex. Certain findings may contradict other findings, or be suspect because of methodological weaknesses. To develop the critical-thinking skills necessary to appraise and use this literature, it is necessary first to consider the aims and assumptions of various types of social science evidence, the multiple roles such evidence may play in social work practice and policy, and the strengths and limitations of some commonly employed social science methods and designs.

AIMS AND ASSUMPTIONS OF VARIOUS TYPES OF SOCIAL SCIENCE EVIDENCE

"There has been considerable debate over the last several centuries over what the purposes of science should be, and how it should be conducted. Moreover, modern times have not brought an end to this controversy. Many divergent views about the nature of science and its methods have been voiced . . . Philosophers of science continue to explore questions such as 'what are the aims of science?,' 'what types of information does science yield?' and 'how should science be conducted?' " (Ladd, 1992, p. 1).

All social science research rests upon basic philosophical assumptions about the social world that are not empirically verifiable, but that critically guide empirical research. Modern social science encompasses a variety of philosophical perspectives with related research aims, methods, and interpretations. Much research consumed by social workers from the late twentieth century reflects **postpositivist** perspectives of **critical realism** with an emphasis on quantitative methods. From a postpositivist perspective, there is an objective social world, including social work interventions, that exists independently of our minds. Critical realism, however, underscores that our biased perspectives limit our ability to perceive that reality. For example, our sincere desire to help clients may blind us to the shortcomings of our interventions. Despite these human imperfections, it is necessary to move toward a relatively objective assessment of the extent to which our social work interventions contributed to the desired changes.

From a postpositivist perspective, the aim of social science research is to develop methods to minimize subjective data and to capture data that are "really real." Hence, the methodological emphasis is on controlling extraneous variables, bias, and human subjectivity (e.g., see Shadish, Cook, & Campbell, 2002). Within the postpositivist tradition, studies employing experimental designs and large samples randomly selected from the population, such as those seen in pharmaceutical research, are considered the gold standard of evidence. The basic idea is to rigorously examine social work interventions and policy. Those shown to be effective and not harmful should be widely employed by ethical professionals.

Other research of relevance to social workers reflects **interpretive perspectives** with an emphasis on **qualitative research**. According to interpretive perspectives, there are multiple legitimate perspectives from which to understand the social world. Interpretive theorists emphasize the necessity of examining beliefs, values, meaning, and cultural context in understanding human beings. Clifford Geertz (2003, p. 173), an influential anthropologist, articulated: "Believing, with Max Weber, that man is an animal suspended in webs of significance he himself has spun, I take culture to be those webs, and the analysis of it to be therefore not an experimental science in search of law but an interpretive one in search of meaning." According to Geertz, social science data are our constructions of other people's constructions of their social world. This is appropriate as, in most instances, human behavior is symbolic action. Culture, an interworked system of construable signs and symbols, is the context within which social behaviors, events, institutions, and processes can be intelligibly—that is, "thickly"—described from participants' perspectives. As Geertz so vividly argues, "It is not in our interest to bleach human behavior of the very properties that interest us before we begin to examine it" (p. 184).

Many interpretive researchers ask questions that are appropriately addressed through qualitative methods. Qualitative methods have been contributing to knowledge about human development for a very long time. Indeed, **ethnography** and field observations were around a century before the twentieth-century rise of quantification with its emphasis on measurement and statistical analysis, and have become commonplace in social work research (Padgett, 2009). The basic assumption of qualitative research, implicit in Geertz's discussion, is that there is no single "really real" social world that exists independently of our representations or interpretations of it (e.g., Denzin & Lincoln, 2003; Shweder, 1996). Human beings are qualitative beings with feelings, beliefs, goals, values, desires, and thoughts that critically affect the ways in which they respond, including to social work interventions. There are multiple legitimate interpretations of complex social phenomenon, including client responses to social work interventions and policy. Applied social science research that does not attend to human context, culture, and subjectivity is incomplete and limited in its practical utility. Empirical research can enhance our understanding and empathy for clients with life experiences and cultural contexts different from our own by articulating their experiences and perspectives, including negative responses to generally effective intervention strategies.

Hence, the methodological emphasis in qualitative research is on sustained, in-depth study of complex sociocultural contexts through qualitative designs. Studies that provide a richly contextualized analysis of social phenomenon through practices such as sustained engagement and use of multiple methods, including direct observations, in-depth interviewing, and record reviews, are considered the gold standard in this tradition. The basic idea is that rigorous empirical research that interprets clients' diverse experiences and perceptions in sociocultural-historical context is essential for ethical social work practice and policy.

Although it is important to understand the aims and assumptions of various types of applied social science research, distinctions should not be too sharply drawn. **Mixed-method research** deliberately combines quantitative and qualitative research traditions in a single study. According to Charles Teddlie and Abbas Tashakkori (2003), the purpose is threefold. First, mixed-method research addresses questions other methods do not; it might demonstrate relationships between two variables such as participation in an intervention and positive outcomes, and explore how that relationship actually comes about through participants' experiences of the intervention. Second, mixed-method research can provide better, stronger inferences by combining methods that have complementary strengths and nonoverlapping weaknesses, such as case studies plus surveys to explore a phenomenon in depth and with breadth. Third, mixed-method research can present a diversity of views; for example, if quantitative and qualitative components lead to different conclusions, the divergent findings can lead to the reexamination of the conceptual framework and underlying assumptions of each component. According to Jennifer Greene and Valerie Caracelli (1997, p. 7): "Mixed method inquiry intentionally combines different methods— that is, methods meant to gather different kinds of information . . . The underlying premise of mixed method inquiry is to understand more fully, to generate deeper and broader insights, to develop important knowledge claims that respect a wider range of interests and perspectives."

THE MULTIPLE ROLES OF EMPIRICAL EVIDENCE IN SOCIAL WORK

The variety of aims and methods in applied social science research suggests that it can play a range of roles in social work practice and policy. Evidence-based practice in social work is complex because there is no single research tradition, set of methods, or design that represents a gold standard of evidence. Indeed, "best practice" for any complex social work intervention or policy requires attention to different kinds of evidence obtained through diverse social science traditions. To fully utilize the potential of applied social science research, it is necessary to reflect upon the multiple roles it may play in informing practice.

One role for social science research in practice and policy is to assess the extent to which intervention goals have been met for particular clients, or whether an intervention approach generally is effective in meeting its goals and is not harmful. Postpositivist research using quantitative methods and experimental designs can help identify generally effective interventions, and eliminate the use of harmful or ineffective interventions. A good example of postpositivist research is the experimental studies used to evaluate the impact of Scared Straight programs (see Petrosino et al., 2003).

Another role for applied social science research is to explore the experience and perspectives of those for whom generally effective interventions are problematic. For example, research drawing on interpretist perspectives and using qualitative methods can enhance understanding of the ways in which cultural contexts interact with interventions, resulting in diverse outcomes. In her research, Kayama (2010) examined cultural beliefs about disability and strategies for special education intervention in Japan and the United States. She describes similar difficulties experienced by parents of children with disabilities in both countries, including establishing a trusting relationship with service providers, but culturally diverse expectations regarding those relationships, including how respect is shown for the parent and the roles of parents and teachers in rearing children. Those culturally based expectations are linked in complex ways to parents' engagement in services for their children with disabilities and, indirectly, to children's developmental outcomes.

Another important role for applied social science research is to introduce new concepts to social work policy and practice. These concepts can contribute insights and creative new ways of thinking about persistent problems. Through interpretive research using qualitative methods, Bamba

(2010; Bamba & Haight, 2011) explored the experiences and perspectives of Japanese child welfare workers and maltreated children living in state care. A primary goal and persistent problem for child welfare professionals in Japan, the United States, and other countries is to enhance children's social and psychological well-being. The ways in which well-being is understood, however, vary widely, as do interventions to achieve this goal. Bamba introduces the Japanese concepts of *Ibasho* and *mimamori*. In brief, Ibasho is a place one makes for oneself where peace of mind, reassurance, security, acceptance, and belonging are experienced. Japanese child welfare workers value children's creation of their Ibasho as important to their well-being. One of the ways in which they facilitate maltreated children's Ibasho creation is through *mimamori*, a practice of watching affectionately over children to ensure their safety, while avoiding direct or excessive adult interference that would inhibit their free exploration and developing sense of autonomy and responsibility. Qualitative social science research as exemplified by Kayama's and Bamba's research provides us with opportunities to step outside what we take for granted, to consider creatively the various ways we might serve clients within our own pluralistic practices and societies. Another role for empirical research in social work is to articulate the experience and perspectives of clients, especially those who lack access to certain systems of power. The issue of power is never simple, but within the United States, asymmetries clearly exist by virtue of class, gender, ethnicity, disability, illness, and so forth. A broader, deeper understanding of clients' perspectives, particularly those whose voices are hidden, is an important contribution of applied social science research. For example, Momper (2010) explores the complex issue of gambling among Native Americans. She begins by considering increases in problem and pathological gambling concurrent with the rapid appearance of casinos in Native American tribal communities. The complexities of this issue are brought to the fore when Momper considers the positive effects of casinos on socioeconomic development from the perspectives of Native American community members. This more complex portrait has implications for more adequate policy responses to gambling on Native American reservations.

ELEMENTS OF SOCIAL SCIENCE RESEARCH

In addition to considering the aims, assumptions, and roles of social science research, students of human behavior in the social environment and all social workers must be aware of the basic elements of such research. The social science research literature is vast, and not all studies are equally rigorous with equally valid implications for our understanding of human development and social work. There are several elements that the professional social worker should consider when separating the empirical wheat from the chaff.

Relevance of the Research Question or Hypothesis

Regardless of a study's methodological rigor, its significance will be quite limited if the research question is trivial. A good research question should contribute to understanding a significant conceptual, practice, or policy issue. Many research hypotheses are important to confirming and expanding existing theory. Other research questions are more open and intended to allow theoretical insights to emerge from the data. Strong research questions in applied social science research will have implications for practice and policy. Examples of good research questions include What is the incidence of eating disorders in adolescent boys in the United States? What types of eating disorders do adolescent boys display? How are these disorders experienced and understood by the boys and their families? What factors contribute to the development of eating disorders in adolescent boys? What are the general effects of cognitive-behavioral and psychodynamically oriented therapies on the maintenance of healthy weight in young men with eating disorders? What are the perspectives of adolescent boys with eating disorders regarding helpful interventions? What are the challenges of implementing particular interventions within specific sociocultural contexts?

Adequacy of the Sampling Methods

Sampling methods are important in critically evaluating empirical research. Who was sampled from the larger group under study, and how were they sampled in relation to the research question? If the research question attempts to generalize to a larger population, for instance, a national group or members of a particular community, then it is important that the sample is representative of the population from which it was selected, in all respects potentially relevant to the study. The distribution of relevant characteristics such as gender, ethnicity, and age among those sampled should be the same as the distribution of those characteristics among the population to which the researcher wishes to generalize. To obtain such a **representative sample**, research might use some form of **probability sampling** method, which relies on a random or chance selection of individuals, each of whom has a known probability of inclusion.

Not all research questions attempt to generalize findings to a larger population. Some qualitative research questions might focus on in-depth understanding of a particular phenomenon, community, or group of individuals. For these research questions, there are a variety of **nonprobability sampling** methods. For example, in **purposive sampling**, key individuals are selected for a purpose, perhaps because they reflect a variety of different experiences or are particularly knowledgeable about the issues under study (Chambliss & Schutt, 2010). The issue of whether findings from such qualitative research studies *transfer* to other groups and individuals is considered an open empirical issue for further research. The role of the researcher is to provide enough rich, in-depth description so that others can consider the extent to which various aspects of the findings are likely to transfer to other settings.

Adequacy of the Research Methods

In evaluating a study's methodology, it also is necessary to consider the types of information collected and how that information was collected. A variety of methods are used in social science and social work research, each with inherent strengths and limitations. An informal perusal of social work journals suggests that **self-report** is perhaps the most common method in social work research. Self-report involves the systematic collection of individuals' own reports of their behavior or psychological processes. For example, a group of battered mothers involved in the public child welfare system provide information about how they protected their children from harm during incidents of domestic violence. The information may be provided through face-to-face individual or group interviews, mailed questionnaires, or standardized assessments. The questions may range from highly unstructured (e.g., Tell me about your relationship with your husband or boyfriend) to highly structured (e.g., How many times has your partner struck you with his fist?). All of these varying characteristics of self-report affect the type of data collected.

One consideration for professional social workers deciding whether to adopt the recommendations of the research is the inherent strengths and limitations of self-report methods. Strengths include detailed accounts of people's lives that might not otherwise be available (e.g., domestic violence), and a glimpse into the beliefs that motivate behavior (e.g., the belief that viewing domestic violence is not itself harmful to children, and the failure to shield the child from exposure to domestic violence). Limitations include inaccurate or biased reporting that can result from selective recall (e.g., a woman is motivated to maintain a positive view of her partner and therefore denies or represses memories of abuse), from coping strategies such as emotional blunting and minimization, or from the desire to make a favorable impression on the researcher.

Systematic observations of behavior are another method used in social work research. This method involves the direct observation of the behavior of interest, for example, parenting practices. Data may be collected through videotaping, audiotaping, and paper-and-pencil notes. Data may be collected by the researcher or another person (e.g., a teacher). Direct observations may be highly structured and occur in a laboratory setting, or less intrusive, unstructured observations of everyday life. Again, all of these characteristics have implications for the type and quality of information that is collected. Strengths of observations include the ability to directly observe the behavior of interest, sometimes as it occurs within real-world settings in participants' everyday lives. Limitations include any effects caused by the presence of an observer, and the cost, including extensive amounts of time.

Some of the strongest social science research combines methods. Using multiple methods can lead to the most comprehensive and rigorous understanding, by including methods that provide different types of information, and by combining methods so that they compensate for each method's limitations. Ethnography is one tradition in which multiple methods are used. It has its roots in anthropology but is increasingly appreciated in social work research. The aim of ethnography is to illuminate the unique beliefs, values, and practices of a particular social or cultural group. It is characterized by extended contact within a community and the use of multiple methods such as interviews, direct observations, and review of historical records in an attempt to provide a "thick description" of social practices in context, including what those practices mean to the participants. Important strengths of the ethnographic method include its rich description and lack of superficiality, and cultural relevance. It is, however, expensive and time consuming. In addition, the goal is to understand human behavior within a particular community, and so the applicability of findings to other settings is an open empirical question.

Recent trends in research go beyond multimethod approaches to create **transdisciplinary research teams**, in which scholars from the biological and the social sciences work together to address complex problems. These scientists create teams with high levels of communication to develop a shared language; pooled bodies of knowledge; and jointly developed research questions, methods, analyses, and interpretations (Gehlert, 2005). For example, a transdisciplinary research team comprising biologists, psychologists, social workers, and others addressed the problem of racial disparities in breast cancer. Although European-American women are more likely to get breast cancer, African-American women are more likely to die of the disease. Working with a complex multilevel model encompassing "genes to geography and back again," these researchers discovered that African-American women living in neighborhoods with high crime and poverty rates display high levels of stress, which inhibit DNA repair of cell mutations (see McClintock, Conzen, Gehlert, Masi, & Olopade, 2005). Social work researchers, expert in dealing with communities, familiar with holistic approaches, and accustomed to working on teams are well suited to participate in such transdisciplinary efforts to creatively tackle some of our most perplexing and persistent social problems.

Adequacy of the Research Design

The research design is the way in which various elements of the research project are organized to address the research question or hypothesis. There is no single best design; rather, the design chosen should be sufficient to address the research question or hypothesis.

Observational research designs do not involve active manipulation of variables. These designs are excellent for answering descriptive questions about the nature of a particular social work issue, incidence of a particular disorder within a community or population, the experience and perspective of clients receiving a particular social work intervention, the need for particular social work services in a rural community, and the fidelity with which particular interventions or policies are implemented. These designs can be used in relatively simple studies, such as surveys of client satisfaction with social work services, or in highly complex ethnographic research involving in-depth interviewing, extended observations, and document reviews conducted over a period of years.

Experimental designs involve the deliberate manipulation of variables to observe their effects—that is, to test causal hypotheses. Experimental designs use research methods such as measures of behaviors and attitudes to make inferences, or test hypotheses, about causality. For example, experimental designs allow us to infer that it was the social work intervention, and not some other environmental events or characteristics of individuals, that actually caused any change in client behavior.

There are several necessary characteristics of experimental designs. First, experimental designs have at least two comparison groups. For example, an experimental group of individuals who receive the new social work intervention is compared with a control group of individuals who do not receive the intervention (they may receive the standard intervention or the new intervention after the experiment is concluded). Group differences are then examined to determine if exposure to the social work intervention is associated with the desired change. Second, there must be random assignment of individuals to the comparison groups through a process such as a flip of the coin or random numbers table. If participants are assigned to an experimental group and control group by chance, then the two groups will be probabilistically similar to one another, on average. Those extraneous variables that could impact outcome are as likely to occur in the control group as in the experimental group. If individuals are not randomly sorted into groups, but allowed, for example, to volunteer for experimental or control groups, then any association between group membership and outcome might be attributed to other differences between the groups, such as individuals' motivation to change, and not to the social work intervention. Finally, experimental designs establish time order. Pre- and posttest assessments can establish that any change in client behavior occurred after the intervention was introduced (see Engel & Schutt, 2010).

In real-life settings, it is not always possible to use experimental designs to test the effectiveness of our interventions or policies. For example, the researcher may not be able to control who is assigned to receive the treatment and who will serve as the comparison group, due to scheduling difficulties or other real-world complexities. **Quasi-experimental designs** also aim to test causal hypotheses, but they lack random assignment to experimental and control groups. Instead a number of other design features are used to rule out plausible alternative explanations for any observed differences between groups. For example, if we are unable to randomly assign clients to the social work intervention, then we might create a comparison group of clients matched to clients receiving the intervention, based on characteristics that are likely to be relevant, such as age, gender, and income. Although we might be able to make an argument about the effectiveness, or lack thereof, of the intervention, this argument will not be as strong as one made from an experimental design. Other relevant client characteristics such as education level might be unmatched and differ across comparison groups. It may be these unanticipated initial group differences, and not the intervention, that account for any observed group differences over time. Other design elements used in quasi-experimental designs include multiple pre- and posttests to observe change over time, and the use of multiple comparison groups, some of which receive alternative treatments to eliminate alternative explanations for any observed changes not due to the treatment (see Shadish et al., 2002).

Questions of ethics often emerge in discussions of experimental designs. For example, is it ethical to withhold treatment to participants in the control group who might be helped by the intervention under study? One strategy for addressing this concern is to use a wait-list control design. In these studies, participants initially assigned to the control group are offered the intervention at the end of the study. These individuals can benefit from the experience of the researchers in implementing the intervention with the experimental group. Another strategy is to employ as participants those who are already receiving traditional interventions, such as traditional child welfare interventions, and add the treatment under study, such as a mental health intervention, to that existing treatment. That way, traditional intervention is not withheld from control-group participants. It is important to consider risk to the experimental group. The intervention under study is not necessarily effective, and may even have unintended negative side effects. Informed consent is critical; that is, participants must fully understand and be willing to endure any risks of participation. It is also important to remember that, as professionals, we are ethically obligated to employ interventions that have a reasonable chance of helping clients, and minimal chance of harming them. Experimental designs provide rigorous tests of such effectiveness.

Research designs focused on human development can be described in terms of temporal characteristics. **Longitudinal designs**, which follow the same individuals over time, are especially important for developmental research. Within social work, longitudinal designs are particularly appropriate for tracking client growth and development over time, for example, a child's progress in school or a couple's acquisition of strategies for nonviolent resolution of marital disputes. Following the same individuals over time provides the strongest inferences regarding changes in human behavior due to development. For example, researchers interested in changes in children's understanding about drug and alcohol use may follow the same group of children from elementary school through high school.

There are many challenges to implementing longitudinal designs. **Attrition** may limit the confidence researchers have in the inferences they draw. In the hypothetical drug and alcohol study, children who drop out might have attitudes and experiences that differ in systematic and important ways from those who remain in the study from elementary school through high school. In some cases, the children who drop out might be those from substance-involved families who were placed in foster care and moved to another school. The developmental trajectories of these children in relation to substance use may differ from those who did not move, and these differences can impact the apparent effectiveness of the intervention.

Cross-sectional designs also make inferences about developmental change in human behavior, but do so through examining different individuals of varying ages at one particular point in time. In this design, researchers interested in changes in children's understanding of drug and alcohol use might focus on three different groups of children, in elementary school, middle school, and high school. Cross-sectional designs are less expensive to implement than longitudinal designs. They provide less strong inferences about developmental change than longitudinal designs, however, because they confound individual and age-group (cohort) differences. For example, researchers employing a cross-sectional design to consider developmental changes in attitudes about the military in adulthood would face the challenge of distinguishing developmental change from **cohort effects**. Consider a hypothetical study in which younger adults have more positive attitudes toward the military than do older adults. On one hand, the findings might suggest developmental changes in the extent to which individuals find violent resolutions to conflicts acceptable. On the other hand, they might reflect cohort effects. Younger adults might be relatively more influenced by the events of 9/11, and older adults by those of the Vietnam War.

Research designs can also be distinguished in terms of their use of single (quantitative or qualitative approaches) or mixed (quantitative and qualitative approaches) methodologies. We would argue that the complexities of social work practice, especially their micro- and macrodimensions, can be understood only by using the full social science repertoire. The combined use of multiple methods in social inquiry—that is, mixed-methods social inquiry—has seen an explosion of interest and development over the past fifteen to twenty years (see Greene, Sommerfeld, & Haight, 2010).

Appropriateness of the Interpretation of the Data and Recommendations

The social worker must carefully evaluate the conclusions and implications of research reports. Have the authors considered and eliminated alternative explanations for their empirical findings? Are their recommendations drawn from their empirical data versus just restating traditional or favored practice methods and policies? Have the authors used their data to draw out new insights for practice and policy?

One relatively common weakness in the interpretation of social work research is treating data that establish empirical associations as if they established causality. Consider a hypothetical study in which adolescent girls who avoid teen pregnancies are more likely than those who do not to graduate from high school; that is, there is an association between their educational attainment and adolescent pregnancy. The authors recommend pregnancy-prevention programs to enhance educational attainment. This recommendation implies that the authors have established a causal relationship between pregnancy and education, which they have not. It could be that the same conditions that leave girls vulnerable to pregnancy, such as inadequate support and monitoring by adults, also leave them vulnerable to educational failure. In other words, pregnancy is not causal in educational failure. Both pregnancy and educational failure are caused by another set of factors. Reducing adolescent pregnancies, which may be a laudable goal for many other reasons, would have no effect on educational attainment because the true reasons for educational failure (e.g., inadequate adult support and monitoring) have not been addressed by the intervention.

ETHICS IN SOCIAL SCIENCE RESEARCH

The ethical treatment of human participants in social science research is a central issue for both researchers and consumers of research. Scientific research unquestionably has produced many substantial social benefits. It has also raised troubling ethical issues. During the Nuremberg war crime trials, horrific biomedical experimentation by Nazi physicians and scientists on concentration camp prisoners was made public. Other examples of ethically troubling research include the Tuskegee syphilis research. From 1932 to 1972, the U.S. Public Health Service conducted an experiment with over 400 male, African-American sharecroppers with syphilis. The purpose of the research was to observe the development of the disease. The men were not told that they had syphilis, warned of its effects, or given medical treatment. At the end of forty years, more than one hundred men had died from syphilis or related complications, despite the fact that new drugs had become available to combat the disease (Jones, 1993).

In 1974, the National Research Act (PL 93-348) was signed into law. The act created the National Commission for the Protection of Human Subjects of Biomedical and Behavioral Research. One of the charges of the commission was to identify the basic ethical principles that should underlie all biomedical and behavioral research involving human participants, and to develop guidelines to ensure that research is conducted in an ethical manner. *The Belmont Report* (U.S. Department of Health and Human Services, 1979) summarizes three basic ethical principles identified by the commission, as well as its implications for ethical practice.

1. Respect for persons. Participants in research must be treated as autonomous individuals capable of making their own decisions about participation. Individuals with diminished autonomy, for example children or those with mental disabilities, must be afforded special protection. In practice, this principle means that researchers must inform individuals, or their guardians, that their participation in a particular research project is entirely voluntary; that they can withdraw from the study at any time; what their participation will entail, including any risks to their health or well-being; and that their individual responses will be confidential. They must give potential participants all the information they need to provide **informed consent**. Informed consent clearly was lacking in the Tuskegee syphilis study. In order to continue the study, the researchers did not inform these men when effective treatment for their disease became available.

2. Beneficence. Ordinarily, *beneficence* refers to acts of kindness or charity that go beyond strict obligation. In research, beneficence is an obligation. In practice, this means that researchers not only must avoid harming participants, but also must maximize possible benefits to participating in the research. For example, individuals participating in research may benefit from the educational opportunity to discuss with an interested and informed interviewer issues of importance to their lives. Society as a whole may benefit from the knowledge gained from the research. The Tuskegee study exemplifies the absence of beneficence. Some participants reportedly assumed that because they were seeing a doctor, they were being treated for their disease: that is, they incorrectly assumed the researchers were beneficent.

3. Justice. Those who bear the burdens of the research should also receive its benefits. In practice, this means that researchers may not use individuals as participants because they are convenient or can be manipulated. For example, research with individuals who are in hospitals, incarcerated, public schools, and so forth, may occur only if research questions and findings are directly relevant to individuals in those settings. Questions arose in the Tuskegee syphilis study as to why rural, African-American sharecroppers were chosen to bear the burden of the research when syphilis obviously affected the population at large.

Federal regulations require that every institution seeking federal funding for biomedical or behavioral research using human participants must have an institutional review board (IRB). IRBs at universities and other institutions review and approve research proposals. These review boards, comprising a diverse group of researchers and practitioners, ensure that the ethical standards in research are upheld. If members of the IRB have questions, they may ask for clarification, request changes in the treatment of participants, or even decline to approve the research. In addition, ethical standards outlined in *The Belmont Report* may be expanded by professional organizations. The *NASW Code of Ethics* (2008), for instance, requires that social workers engaged in research should take steps to ensure that participants have access to appropriate supportive services.

A MIXED-METHOD RESEARCH PROGRAM INVESTIGATING RURAL, DRUG-INVOLVED FAMILIES

In this section, we provide a more extended example of social work research from one of our own research programs. It is rare that any single method, design, or study can fully address complex social issues. More commonly, issues are addressed through multiple studies using various methods and designs. The following example addresses the thorny problem of rural drug-involved families through a series of studies employing various methods and designs. Each of these studies underwent an especially rigorous review by the university IRB, because of the vulnerability of the participant families and children. For example, researchers had to think through and develop strategies for handling any instances of child maltreatment that might come to light during the research. The solution was to inform parents that researchers would report any instances of child maltreatment, and allow them to decide for themselves whether to take that risk by participating.

The problem of rural drug misuse became particularly apparent during the opening years of this century. The misuse of methamphetamine, a powerful central nervous system stimulant and neurotoxin, emerged as a persistent and urgent problem in public health, criminal justice, and child welfare across the United States, especially in rural areas. Here, mom-and-pop drug labs flourished, and law enforcement and social service resources were limited. Many individuals who misuse methamphetamine experience long-lasting psychiatric symptoms such as psychosis, depression, intense paranoia, visual and auditory hallucinations, and suicidal behavior; repetitive behavior; rapid mood changes; irritability; and out-of-control rages and violent behavior (see Haight et al., 2005). This problem of methamphetamine misuse affects not just individuals, however, but entire families and communities. Rural law enforcement officers and health, mental health, and child welfare professionals encounter children living in homes where methamphetamine is produced and misused.

The problem of methamphetamine misuse came to our attention in 2002. Two social workers from the Illinois Department of Children and Family Services approached professors at the University of Illinois–Urbana-Champaign. They sought information on the impact of parental methamphetamine misuse on children's psychological development and mental health functioning. They were practicing in a rural area hard hit by methamphetamine production and misuse, and were experiencing an influx of children from methamphetamine-involved families. Their informal observations suggested that many of these children had more serious needs than did most other children on their caseloads. They felt a need for empirical evidence to guide their practice with these children. A thorough review of the existing literature identified a number of studies examining the impact of exposure to the toxins from methamphetamine production on children's physical health, but no systematic study of the impact of exposure to the lifestyle associated with parents' methamphetamine involvement on children's psychosocial development.

We formed a research team comprising child welfare workers and university professors and initiated a mixed-methods program of research to supply information needed by these child welfare professionals. Informed by our experience of child welfare practice in rural Illinois and by the existing literature, we developed several general research questions: (1) What are the contexts in which rural, school-age children from methamphetamine-involved families are reared? (2) What is their psychosocial functioning? (3) What distinguishes children who are developing relatively well from those children who are struggling? (4) What are the basic components of a culturally appropriate mental health intervention tailored to the contexts and needs of these children? (5) How effective is this intervention? We adapted our research methods and designs to appropriately address each of these questions through a three-phase, mixed-methods research program.

Understanding the Contexts in Which Children from Methamphetamine-Involved Families Are Reared and Their Psychosocial Functioning

Phase 1 of the research program provided an in-depth description of the problem of parental methamphetamine misuse in rural Illinois from 2003 to 2006 (Haight et al., 2005; Haight, Ostler, Black, & Kingery, 2009). We used ethnographic and developmental methods to describe children's experiences and psychological functioning (Haight, Ostler, Black, Sheridan, & Kingery, 2007; Ostler et al., 2007). Access to the community was made possible by our collaborator, a child protection worker with deep roots in the community and generally excellent relations with other professionals as well as clients. We began our study with extensive participant observation, including attendance at Illinois state methamphetamine task force meetings, drug court, and over ninety hours of shadowing child welfare investigators. Systematic field notes recorded our conversations, community reactions and responses to the methamphetamine problem, and the living conditions of rural families involved with methamphetamine.

In addition, we conducted in-depth, audiotaped, individual interviews with participants occupying diverse social vantage points in relation to methamphetamine misuse. We interviewed professionals who deal with the problem of methamphetamine misuse on a regular basis (child welfare professionals, law enforcement professionals, educators, substance misuse treatment providers, and counselors), and foster caregivers of children from methamphetamine-involved families. They discussed their experiences with families involved with methamphetamine, beliefs about the effects of parental methamphetamine misuse on children, and appropriate strategies for intervention. We also conducted oral histories with recovering mothers with children in foster care because of their methamphetamine misuse. Mothers described their experiences of methamphetamine addiction and recovery. They described their own experiences growing up, how they became involved with methamphetamine, the experience of addiction, and its impact on their lives and children (Haight, Carter-Black, & Sheridan, 2009).

We also visited the children from methamphetamine-involved families in and around their homes and communities. As part of individual, semi-structured interviews, we engaged with children in a variety of leisure and play activities, or just talked, during which time we invited them to respond to several questions. We began with some fairly open-ended probes. These included "Who is in your family? Tell me about a time in your family that was happy. Tell me about a time in your family that was sad or scary." Then we moved on to more specific probes about methamphetamine. These included "Sometimes adults use meth. How does it make them act?" In addition, we conducted a variety of standardized assessments of children's development and mental health. These assessments included the Peabody Picture Vocabulary Test (Dunn & Dunn, 1997). This instrument requires children to define words by pointing to pictures. It was used to screen for any language or intellectual difficulties, which could impact children's participation. The Child Behavior Checklist (Achenbach & Rescorla, 2001) allows parents or other caregivers to report various child behaviors such as aggression or withdrawal. The Trauma Symptom Checklist for Children Revised (Briere, 1997) allows children to self-report symptoms of trauma.

We first examined the contexts in which children from methamphetamine-involved families were reared. Our participant observation and interviews indicated that many children from rural, methamphetamine-involved families were growing up in conditions of marked poverty and substandard housing. Many were exposed to adult polysubstance misuse, violence, and criminality. In addition, many were exposed to environmental dangers associated with methamphetamine production, chaotic home lives, neglect, abuse, loss, and isolation (Haight et al., 2005; Haight et al., 2009).

We next considered children's mental health functioning. We found that the majority of children showed significant symptoms of dissociation and post-traumatic stress typically associated with exposure to trauma (Ostler et al., 2007). These problems included attention problems, anxiety, and nightmares. Perhaps most strikingly, 50 percent of children scored in the clinical range (98th percentile or higher) on the externalizing (delinquent and aggressive behavior) scale and 26 percent on the aggression subscale of the Childhood Behavior Checklist (Haight, Marshall, Hans, Black, & Sheridan, 2010). If untreated, these problems could result in long-term mental health problems, as well as the continuation of substance misuse into future generations.

Of course, not all children were exposed to the same level of environmental risk, nor did they all suffer from mental health problems. When invited during semistructured interviews to talk about their families, approximately half of the children spontaneously described socially and emotionally supportive relationships with healthy grandparents. Children's reports of support from grandparents were associated with lower scores on externalizing and aggressive behaviors. Interestingly, when asked to talk about their families, more than half of methamphetamine-involved parents spontaneously described the support their children received from grandparents, and more than a quarter also described the support that they had received from their own grandparents. Children's and parents' descriptions of grandparent support suggest how grandparents may protect children from the development of aggressive and other externalizing behavior problems. First, grandparents may prevent obstacles to healthy development by providing their grandchildren with safe shelter and basic child care when parents are incapacitated from substance misuse. Second, they may promote their grandchildren's positive social-emotional development through supportive relationships. Third, they may promote social competence through enjoyable leisure activities with healthy adults and nondelinquent peers (Sheridan, Haight, & Cleeland, 2011).

Designing and Implementing a Culturally Sensitive Intervention

In phase 2 of our research program, we considered how to adapt and deliver an evidence-based mental health intervention to children from rural methamphetamine-involved families in a way that is acceptable and makes sense to their families, and is sustainable in rural communities with limited access to mental health facilities. We integrated findings from phase 1 with evidence-based clinical research and practice experience to develop a narrative- and relationship-based mental health intervention. Life Story Intervention is adapted for individual rural children (age seven to seventeen) affected by parental methamphetamine misuse, by a transdisciplinary team including a child clinical psychologist, counselor, psychiatrist, developmental psychologist, child welfare professional, and social worker. Life Story Intervention is evidence-based. It draws upon empirical research from phase 1 of our study, narrative traditions, and the treatment of trauma in children who have experienced family violence (e.g., Lieberman & Van Horn, 2005). It also draws upon the American Academy of Child and Adolescent Psychiatry (Cohen, 1998) guidelines for intervention with children who have experienced trauma, and the considerable locally based clinical experience of team members with traumatized children in foster care who are affected by parental substance misuse.

The conceptual bases and implementation of Life Story Intervention have been described in detail elsewhere (Haight, Ostler, et al., 2009). In summary, it is a narrative- and relationship-based intervention administered in and around the children's homes by community-based clinicians, typically educators and child welfare workers. Over approximately seven months, children meet individually for hour-long weekly sessions with community-based clinicians. The clinicians receive weekly training and supportive supervision via Skype or in a small-group setting with other community clinicians and a PhD-level clinical psychologist or psychiatrist experienced in working with traumatized children and drug-involved families.

The first phase of the intervention lasts approximately two months. During this time, clinicians focus on establishing an emotionally supportive relationship with the children, most of whom have histories of maltreatment and disrupted relationships with caregivers and other adults. During this time, the clinician and child may engage in activities of the child's choosing similar to those of children and grandparents such as walking in the woods, eating at a fast-food restaurant, and playing with pets.

The co-construction of personal narratives is the focus of the next five months. Children are invited, but never pressured, to talk about their lives in familiar surroundings in and around the home, while engaged in activities such as swinging, drawing, reading children's books, pretending with puppets or a dollhouse, or just talking. Narratives of personal experience are a central component of a wide range of therapies (e.g., Coles, 1989; Holmes, 2001). Therapists working within a narrative framework emphasize the importance of creating stories as a way to help children interpret and gain a feeling of control and continuity in their lives, rethink views of themselves and others, and begin to alter problematic beliefs (e.g., Hanney & Kozlowska, 2002).

In the context of children's own stories, clinicians also introduce information and correct misinformation on substance misuse, a necessary component of any intervention for children affected by parental substance misuse. As part of the intervention, we drew on existing preventive research and clinical techniques to address the negative behavior that can result from substance misuse and prevention of addiction (see Haight, Ostler, et al., 2009). Given the emotionally sensitive nature of this topic for many of the children in our study, as well as the socialization messages they may have received from parents prohibiting the discussion of such information with family outsiders, our approach to substance misuse education is flexibly adapted to the child's tolerance.

Any intervention for children from methamphetamine-involved families also must address trauma. There are a variety of approaches to therapeutic intervention with children who have experienced trauma. Cognitive behavioral therapies (Cohen, 1998) and psychodynamically based therapies (Lieberman & Van Horn, 2005) deal with the psychological sequelae of trauma and family violence in various ways. Although there is considerable debate within the field, there also is some convergence across diverse perspectives on key components (see Hanney & Kozlowska, 2002), which we incorporate in Life Story Intervention: (1) Establishing a trusting relationship with a supportive adult is the focus of the first two months of Life Story Intervention and is emphasized throughout. (2) Life Story Intervention focuses on children's understanding of and emotional reactions to trauma through the co-construction of personal narratives. Clinicians do address traumatic events, an approach shown to be more effective than nondirective treatments (e.g., Cohen & Mannarino, 1996; Deblinger, McLeer, & Henry, 1990), but with careful attention to the child's tolerance. (3) Life Story Intervention is designed to support a sense of mastery over traumatic events, an approach that has been shown to be more effective than techniques designed to merely help children express their feelings (e.g., Corder & Haizlip, 1989; Galante & Foa, 1986; Shelby, 2000). To encourage perspective taking, Life Story Intervention focuses on the meaning of traumatic events within the context of the child's life. The focus is not on the development of a "trauma narrative," but of a life story, which includes traumatic as well as other events, and the child's mature and adaptive responses to difficult situations, as well as problematic responses.

Termination issues are the focus in the final month of Life Story Intervention. During this time, the end of the intervention is discussed with children, mementos are created (e.g., pictures, stories, and other artwork), and children are helped to identify a trustworthy, supportive adult in their existing social network (e.g., a grandparent), who can provide ongoing emotional support. In the final sessions, clinicians meet with these "natural mentors" and the children to review progress, share the mementos, and say good-bye.

Evaluating the Intervention

In phase 3 of our research program, we evaluated the intervention, using an experimental design with qualitative elaboration to describe children's functioning over a period of approximately two years (Haight et al., 2010).

Participants were rural children age seven to fifteen from methamphetamine-involved homes who were in foster care. As a group, the children ($N = 15$) showed problematic levels of Child Behavior Checklist externalizing behaviors (e.g., aggressive and delinquent behaviors), total problem behaviors, and symptoms of **post-traumatic stress disorder** and **dissociation** on the pre- and posttests.

Children were randomly assigned to an experimental group who received the intervention ($n = 8$) or a wait-list control group ($n = 7$) who received the intervention at the end of the study. In contrast to the wait-list control group, most children receiving the intervention showed modest improvement over a seven-month period. In particular, children in the experimental group showed less externalizing problems over time, and children in the control group showed more externalizing behaviors. Gains made by the experimental group were maintained at the seven-month follow-up tests. (Children in the wait-list control received the intervention between the posttest and follow-up.)

Comparative case studies and individual qualitative interviews and open-ended questionnaires with experimental-group children, their caregivers, and the community clinicians who administered the intervention provided rich elaboration of participants' experiences of the intervention, including corroboration and elaboration of its modest effects. Most children were able to form supportive relationships with community clinicians through which they began to discuss their past experiences through personal narratives. The qualitative component also illuminated the complexities and challenges of implementing and participating in the intervention, including maintaining professional boundaries with emotionally vulnerable children in informal settings, and termination with children whose histories included multiple traumatic disruptions of relationships with adults.

The findings from our research program are provisional. This research program is still in its early phases. In the future, it will be important to examine the extent to which findings from rural Illinois transfer to other settings. It also will be important to strengthen the intervention, for example, to elaborate the component of substance misuse prevention. Also important is evaluating the intervention using a larger number of children for purposes of replication, so that more subtle effects of the intervention, such as effects on trauma, can be detected.

SUMMARY

An important characteristic of modern, professional social work emphasized throughout this book is the use of empirical social science research to assess theory and to inform practice and policy. Knowledge of empirical research is essential for the contemporary social worker. The alternatives, including appealing to religious (or other) authority, tradition, personal experience, or popular opinion, are simply unacceptable to professionals practicing in our complex, pluralistic society. Ethical practice necessitates a rigorous assessment of social work interventions to ensure that vulnerable individuals receive the best possible support. The social worker is professionally obligated to practice based on the best social science evidence, not unsubstantiated opinion, the views of noted authorities, fads, or some other type of information, in lieu of credible research findings.

In addition to the ethical practice of social work, there are practical reasons for social workers to maintain up-to-date knowledge of empirical research. As Thyer and Kazi (2004) articulate, social resources are finite, but social needs are complex and changing. Empirical research on program effectiveness is one way to make social programs accountable, and to enable politicians, agencies, and practitioners to make hard choices in the allocation of scarce resources. Social workers have a challenging task: to demonstrate that clients with various difficulties who receive professional social work services do indeed get better, and then to demonstrate that they improve more than they would have done simply through the passage of time, from placebos, or at the hands of nonprofessionals. "Without credible evidence that social worker–provided services help to solve client and societal problems, why should the public and private sectors support the expensive social welfare empires currently found in mental health, health care, child welfare, and so on?" (Thyer & Kazi, 2004, p. 17).

In this chapter, we have attempted to convey both the complexity of modern social science research and its potential for enhancing social work practice and policy. Awareness of the diverse roles that applied social science research from a variety of traditions can play in evidence-informed practice will allow us to utilize it to its full potential. Attention to research evidence from diverse traditions can encourage both critical and creative thinking about complex social issues and interventions.

Study and Discussion Questions

1. What is evidence-based practice? Why is it necessary? What are the challenges to its implementation? How can these challenges be overcome?

2. What are some aims and assumptions of social science research?

3. What are the various roles of empirical research in social work?

4. Critique the research program on rural methamphetamine-involved families, considering the relevance of the research question, adequacy of sampling methods, adequacy of research methods, adequacy of the design, appropriateness of the data interpretations and recommendations, and ethics.

5. How did contemporary IRBs evolve, and what is their significance?

Resources

Students interested in an overview of social work research are directed to Engel and Schutt (2010) and Shaw, Briar-Lawson, Orme, & Ruckdeschel (2010). Those interested in more in-depth treatment of various research methods are directed to Denzin and Lincoln (2003) for a discussion of qualitative methods, Teddlie and Tashakkori (2003) for an overview of mixed methods, and Shadish et al. (2002) for a discussion of quantitative research designs.

Interested students can supplement this chapter through a number of excellent web-based resources.

For further information on issues in the history and philosophy of science, see the *Stanford Encyclopedia of Philosophy*, http://plato.stanford.edu/entries/, especially entries on Thomas Kuhn and Karl Popper.

For further information on evidence-based practice in the arena of intervention and prevention of domestic violence, substance misuse, mental health, child welfare, and much more, refer to the Social Work Policy Institute's website. Available at http://www.socialworkpolicy.org/research/evidence-based-practice-2.html.

You are familiar now with evidence-based practice, but what about practice-based evidence, or PBE? Terry Cross, executive director of the National Indian Child Welfare Association, advocates PBE because much of the research lacks evidence pertaining to minorities, including First Nations Americans. Therefore, evidence-based practice cannot be used in such cases. PBE uses information and observations garnered from practice to inform the evidence or knowledge base. An exemplary research project that illustrates the benefits of PBE can be found in Cross and colleagues' PBE research proposal. Available at http://www.d.umn.edu/sw/snydersfiles/AdvCW/week1/practice-based_evidence.pdf.

References

Achenbach, T., & Rescorla, L. (2001). *Manual for the ASEBA school-age forms & profiles*. Burlington, VT: Achenbach System of Empirically Based Assessment (ASEBA).

Bamba, S. (2010). The experiences and perspectives of Japanese substitute caregivers and maltreated children: A cultural-developmental approach to child welfare practice. *Social Work, 55*(2), 127–138.

Bamba, S., & Haight, W. (2011). *Child welfare and development: A Japanese case study*. New York: Cambridge University Press.

Boaz, A., & Blewett, J. (2010). Providing objective, impartial evidence for decision making and public accountability. In I. Shaw, K. Briar-Lawson, J. Orme, & R. Ruckdeschel (Eds.), *The Sage handbook of social work research* (pp. 37–48). London: Sage.

Briere, J. (1997). *Psychological assessment of adult posttraumatic states*. Washington, DC: American Psychological Association.

Chambliss, D., & Schutt, R. (2010). *Making sense of the social world: Methods of investigation* (3rd ed.). Los Angeles: Pine Forge Press.

Cohen, J. A. (1998). Practice parameters for the assessment and treatment of children and adolescents with posttraumatic stress disorder. *Journal of the American Academy of Child and Adolescent Psychiatry, 36* (Supplement 10), 4–26.

Cohen, J. A., & Mannarino, A. (1996). Factors that mediate treatment outcome of sexually abused preschool children. *Journal of the American Academy of Child and Adolescent Psychiatry, 34*(10), 1402–1410.

Coles, R. (1989). *The call of stories: Teaching and the moral imagination.* Boston: Houghton Mifflin.

Corder, B., & Haizlip, T. (1989). The role of mastery experiences in therapeutic interventions for children dealing with acute trauma: Some implications for the treatment of sexual abuse. *Psychiatric Forum, 15*(1), 57–63.

Deblinger, E., McLeer, S. V., & Henry, D. (1990). Cognitive behavioral treatment for sexually abused children suffering post-traumatic stress: Preliminary findings. *Journal of the American Academy of Child and Adolescent Psychiatry, 29,* 747–752.

Denzin, N., & Lincoln, Y. (2003). Introduction: The discipline and practice of qualitative research. In N. Denzin & Y. Lincoln (Eds.), *The landscape of qualitative research: Theories and issues* (2nd ed., pp. 1–46). London: Sage.

Dunn, L. M., & Dunn, L. M. (1997). *Peabody Picture Vocabulary Test* (3rd ed.). Circle Pines, MN: American Guidance Service.

Engel, R., & Schutt, R. (2010). *Fundamentals of social work research.* Thousand Oaks, CA: Sage.

Galante, R., & Foa, D. (1986). An epidemiological study of psychic trauma and treatment effectiveness for children after a natural disaster. *Journal of the American Academy of Child Psychiatry, 25,* 357–363.

Gambrill, E. (2000). The role of critical thinking in evidence-based social work. In P. Allen-Meares & C. Garvin (Eds.), *The handbook of social work direct practice* (pp. 43–46). Thousand Oaks, CA: Sage.

Gambrill, E. (2006). Evidence-based practice and policy: Choices ahead. *Research on Social Work Practice, 16*(3), 338–357.

Geertz, C. (2003). Thick description: Toward an interpretive theory of culture. In C. Jenks (Ed.), *Critical concepts in sociology* (pp. 173–196). New York: Routledge.

Gehlert, S. (2005). *Health disparities and doctoral education in social work.* Keynote address at the annual meeting of the Group for Advancement of Doctoral Education, University of Alabama.

Gray, M., Plath, D., & Webb, S. (2009). *Evidence-based social work: A critical stance.* New York: Routledge/Taylor & Francis Group.

Gredig, D., & Marsh, J. (2010). Improving intervention and practice. In I. Shaw, K. Briar-Lawson, J. Orme, & R. Ruckdeschel (Eds.), *The Sage handbook of social work research* (pp. 64–82). London: Sage.

Greene, J., Sommerfeld, P., & Haight, W. (2010). Mixing methods in social work research. In I. Shaw, B. Briar-Lawson, J. Orme, & R. Ruckdeschel (Eds.), *The Sage handbook of social work research* (pp. 315–331). London: Sage.

Greene, J. C., & Caracelli, V. J. (1997). Defining and describing the paradigm issue in mixed-method evaluation. In J. C. Greene & V. J. Caracelli (Eds.), *Advances in mixed method evaluation: The challenges and benefits of integrating diverse paradigms* (New Directions for Evaluation, No. 74, pp. 5-17). San Francisco: Jossey-Bass.

Haight, W., Black, J., & Sheridan, K. (2010). A mental health intervention for rural, foster children from methamphetamine-involved families: Experimental assessment with qualitative elaboration. *Children and Youth Services Review, 32*(10), 1446-1457.

Haight, W., Carter-Black, J., & Sheridan, K. (2009) Mothers' experience of methamphetamine addiction: A case-based analysis of rural, midwestern women. *Children and Youth Services Review, 31*, 71-77.

Haight, W., Jacobsen, T., Black, J. E., Kingery, L., Sheridan, K., & Mulder, C. (2005). In these bleak days: Parent methamphetamine abuse and child welfare in the rural Midwest. *Children and Youth Services Review, 27*, 949-971.

Haight, W., Marshall, J., Hans, S., Black, J., & Sheridan, K. (2010). "They mess with me, I mess with them": Understanding physical aggression in rural girls and boys from methamphetamine-involved families. *Children and Youth Services Review, 32*(10), 1223-1234.

Haight, W., Ostler, T., Black, J., & Kingery, L. (2009). *Children of methamphetamine-involved families: The case of rural Illinois.* New York: Oxford University Press.

Haight, W., Ostler, T., Black, J., Sheridan, K., & Kingery, L. (2007). A child's eye view of parent methamphetamine abuse: Implications for helping foster families to succeed. *Children and Youth Services Review, 29*(1), 1-15.

Hanney, L., & Kozlowska, K. (2002). Healing traumatized children: Creating illustrated storybooks in family therapy. *Family Process, 41*(1), 37-65.

Holmes, J. (2001). *The search for the secure base: Attachment theory and psychotherapy.* Hove, UK: Brunner-Routledge.

Jones, J. (1993). *Bad blood: The Tuskegee syphilis experiment.* New York: Free Press.

Kayama, M. (2010). Parental experiences of children's disabilities and special education in the United States and Japan: Implications for school social work. *Social Work, 55*(2), 97-192.

Ladd, G. (1992). Perspectives on the aims, assumptions, and activities of human science: An historical overview. In R. D. Parke & G. W. Ladd (Eds.), *Family-peer relations: Modes of linkage* (pp. 1-36). Hillside, NJ: Erlbaum.

Lieberman, A. F., & Van Horn, P. (2005). *Don't hit my mommy! A manual for child-parent psychotherapy with young witnesses of family violence.* Washington, DC: Zero to Three Press.

McClintock, M., Conzen, S., Gehlert, S., Masi, C., & Olopade, F. (2005). Mammary cancer and social interactions: Identifying multiple environments that regulate gene expression throughout the lifespan. *Journals of Gerontology, 60B*, 32-41.

Momper, S. (2010). Implications of American Indian gambling for social work research and practice. *Social Work, 55*(2), 139-146.

National Association of Social Workers. (2008). *NASW code of ethics: Guide to the everyday professional conduct of social workers.* Washington, DC: Author.

Orme, J., & Briar-Lawson, K. (2010). Theory and knowledge about social problems to enhance policy development. In I. Shaw, K. Briar-Lawson, J. Orme, & R. Ruckdeschel (Eds.), *The Sage handbook of social work research* (pp. 49-63). London: Sage.

Ostler, T., Haight, W., Black, J., Choi, G., Kingery, L., & Sheridan, K. (2007). Mental health outcomes and perspectives of rural children raised by parents who abuse methamphetamine. *Journal of American Academy of Child and Adolescent Psychiatry, 46*(4), 500–507.

Padgett, D. (2009). Qualitative and mixed methods in social work knowledge development. *Social Work, 54*(2), 101–106.

Parton, N., & Kirk, S. (2010). The nature and purposes of social work. In I. Shaw, K. Briar-Lawson, J. Orme, & R. Ruckdeschel (Eds.), *The Sage handbook of social work research* (pp. 23–36). London: Sage.

Petrosino, A., Turpin-Petrosino, C., & Buehler, J. (2003). Scared straight and other juvenile awareness programs for preventing juvenile delinquency: A systematic review of the randomized experimental evidence. *Annals of the American Academy of Political and Social Science, 589*, 41–62.

Sackett, D., Strauss, S., Richardson, W., Rosenberg, W., & Haynes, R. (2000). *Evidence-based medicine: How to practice and teach EBM* (2nd ed.). New York: Churchill Livingstone.

Shadish, W., Cook, T., & Campbell, D. (2002). *Experimental and quasi-experimental designs for generalized causal inference*. Boston: Houghton Mifflin.

Shaw, I., Briar-Lawson, K., Orme, J., & Ruckdeschel, R. (Eds.). (2010). *The Sage handbook of social work research*. London: Sage.

Shelby, J. S. (2000). Brief therapy with traumatized children: A developmental perspective. In H. G. Kaduson & C. E. Schaefer (Eds.), *Short-term play therapy for children* (pp. 69–104). New York: Guilford.

Sheridan, K., Haight, W., & Cleeland, L. (2011). The role of grandparents in preventing aggressive and other externalizing behavior problems in children from rural, methamphetamine-involved families. *Children and Youth Services Review, 33*, 1583–1591.

Sherman, L. (1998). Evidence-based policing. In *Ideas in American Policing*. Washington, DC: Police Foundation. Retrieved from http://www.policefoundation.org/potf/sherman.pdf

Shweder, R. A. (1996). Quanta and qualia: What is the "object" of ethnographic method? In R. Jessor, A. Colby, & R. A. Shweder (Eds.), *Ethnography and human development: Context and meaning in social inquiry*. Chicago: University of Chicago Press.

Teddlie, C., & Tashakkori, A. (2003). Major issues and controversies in the use of mixed methods in the social and behavioral sciences. In A. Tashakkori & C. Teddlie (Eds.), *Handbook of mixed methods in social and behavioral research*. Thousand Oaks, CA: Sage.

Thyer, B., & Kazi, M. (2004). An overview of evidence-based practice in social work. In B. Thyer & M. Kazi (Eds.), *International perspectives on evidence-based practice in social work* (pp. 9–22). Birmingham, UK: Venture Press.

U.S. Department of Health and Human Services (1979). *Belmont Report*. Retrieved from http://www.hhs.gov/ohrp/humansubjects/guidance/belmont.html

Yunong, H., & Fengzhi, M. (2009). A reflection on reasons, preconditions, and effects of implementing evidence-based practice in social work. *Social Work, 54*(2), 177–181.

5

Social Work with Infants
Preventive Interventions to Support Attachment Relationships in the Family

Susan A. Cole, Wendy L. Haight, and Edward H. Taylor

The focal system in this chapter is the infant and the rapid changes that occur during the first two years of life. As you read, think about the infant's developing biological, psychological, and social competencies, as well as the physical and social ecologies in which these achievements emerge. The microsystems and mesosystems that influence infant development in the first year of life may include infants' family members (caregivers, siblings), extended family members, and unrelated caregivers (such as child-care providers and family friends). During infancy, the quality of relationships with the primary caregivers is crucial, especially to the development of attachment relationships, which impact all domains of infant development. As you read, consider the quality of infants' attachment relationships, what factors affect how these relationships emerge, and their implications for the child's future development. Social workers may be involved in delivering preventive interventions that support the child-caregiver relationship. As you read, consider how preventative interventions can support positive infant-caregiver relationships that lead to the best development outcomes.

The need for high-quality preventive interventions is especially acute during infancy. Infants undergo dramatic growth and development of their bodies and brains in the first two years of life. They physically change in size and shape, lay the foundation for the acquisition of their first language, actively explore the physical and social world, develop play and humor, and form complex relationships. Given their rapid development, infants are

Portions of this chapter draw upon, expand, and update "Understanding and Supporting Parent-Child Relationships during Foster Care Visits: Attachment Theory and Research," by W. Haight, J. Kagle, and J. Black, 2003, *Social Work, 48*(2), 195–208.

especially vulnerable to developmental delays due to illness, maltreatment, poverty, and extended separations from their primary caregivers (Shonkoff & Phillips, 2001). Unlike older children, infants cannot care for their own basic needs, escape abusive relationships, or seek supportive adults and peers outside of their families. Dependent on others for their very survival, they are more likely to suffer long-term or permanent disabilities because of abuse or neglect than are older children. Yet infants' very dependence and rapid cognitive, physical, psychological, and social growth also offer an important window of opportunity to intervene when they experience risks to their development due to illness, disability, accidents, neglect, or abuse.

The attachment relationship between a primary caregiver and the infant is an important aspect of infant development to consider when designing and delivering interventions to prevent the emergence of problems in development, or to prevent existing problems from becoming more serious. **Attachment** is defined as the close, enduring, affective bonds that develop throughout life (Ainsworth, 1973). Over three decades of empirical research have confirmed what diverse theoretical perspectives have predicted: adequate attachment relationships are necessary for children's healthy development in all domains—cognitive, physical, and psychological (Mangelsdorf & Brown, 2009; Shonkoff & Phillips, 2001; Zeanah, Boris, & Larrieu 1997). Early attachment relationships can influence a child's basic sense of himself or herself as lovable and worthy of attention, of others as trustworthy and reliable, and of the world as a basically safe and interesting place. Such concepts of self and other can influence children's expectations for, and responses to, subsequent interpersonal relationships in self-perpetuating ways (Carlson, 1998; Crittenden & Ainsworth, 1989). Infants who experience poor support from their caregivers, or are uncertain of their caregivers' responses, are less apt than infants in supportive relationships to engage in the active exploration of physical and social environments that is optimal for all aspects of development (Cicchetti, 2002).

Infant-parent attachment relationships do not emerge in isolation, but are embedded within complex sociocultural contexts, which can critically impact those relationships. At the macrosystem level, the availability of affordable child care can reduce caregiver stress and promote more positive caregiver-child interactions. At the mesosystem level, the relationship between parents can impact the developing child. As described in box 5.1, for instance, the development and well-being of infants is affected by witnessing **domestic violence** within the family.

PREVENTIVE INTERVENTIONS

Social work with infants is challenging both because they are so vulnerable and because they experience rapid and complex developmental

> ## BOX 5.1 VIOLENCE ACROSS THE LIFE SPAN
> ### The Impact of Domestic Violence on Infants
>
> Intimate partner violence (domestic violence) is abuse within close, loving, romantic relationships. It is witnessed by an estimated 3.3 to 10 million children annually in the United States. Witnessing domestic violence is a form of traumatic stress that may threaten children's well-being and development. Traumatic stress involves experiencing or witnessing actual or threatened physical injury to the self or other person, especially a family member, accompanied by fear, helplessness, horror, and, in children, disorganized or agitated behavior. Traumatic stress that results from intentional human design, particularly that caused by parents or other attachment figures, is especially challenging for children. There is extensive empirical evidence that witnessing angry and violent exchanges between adults has detrimental effects on children, even if they themselves are not the targets of abuse. Decades of research testify to the relations between family discord and children's maladjustment. Clear associations have been found between exposure to violence and post-traumatic symptoms and disorders even in infants and toddlers. Infants in violent homes may have difficulty eating and sleeping, and may cry excessively or very little. Toddlers and preschoolers may show language delays, regress to infantlike behavior, or act out aggressively. In addition, traumatic stress may disturb children's emerging concepts of self and other, safety, and protection, and interfere with the development of affect regulation.
>
> _____
>
> American Psychiatric Association, 2000; Osofsky, 1995a, 1995b; Parens, 1991; Pynoos, Steinberg, & Goenjian, 1996; Stephans, 1999.

changes. Illness, neglect, and abuse experienced even for short periods of time can derail these developmental processes and result in significant delays. Social workers can play important roles in advocating for and delivering preventive interventions to infants and their families. Preventive interventions can occur at many points in time relative to the emergence of problems. In this chapter, we focus on primary and secondary prevention. Primary prevention refers to actions taken to prevent predictable problems from emerging, to protect existing healthy development, and to promote positive development (Bloom & Gullotta, 2008). Examples of primary preventive programs include supportive services for pregnant and parenting teens. Secondary prevention refers to early intervention into existing problems to prevent more serious conditions from emerging. Examples of secondary preventive programs are crisis nurseries that provide respite care when parents are temporarily unable to care for their infants due to stress or trauma resulting, for instance, from homelessness, medical emergencies, or domestic violence. When problems do arise for infants, promptly addressing their medical needs or changing the caregiving environment can support their rapid recovery and developmental catching up.

The Japanese child welfare system is one excellent exemplar of an extensive, national system of primary and secondary prevention for children and their families. One of the problems facing Japanese society is a declining birth rate. Partly as a consequence, Japanese society has chosen to invest heavily in a broad array of preventative programs to ensure that its children are healthy and safe, and develop to their fullest. Preventative programs include a child allowance program that provides financial support for approximately 90 percent of families with children under age twelve, and universal child and maternal health care from the prenatal years through preschool. Additional support is provided for vulnerable families. For example, the government provides subsidies to day-care centers offering extended hours for working parents of infants and preschool children. Respite nursery care also is provided for parents who are ill or fatigued from child care. In addition, a variety of programs are aimed specifically at single parents, including additional financial aid granted until children are approximately eighteen years old; loans, including for parents' higher education; services, including child-rearing and living assistance (e.g., shelters and daily life support); and employment support. Additional preventive services are designed to promote the well-being of children with physical or mental disabilities, such as home-helpers to assist parents with routine child care and additional financial support (see Bamba & Haight, 2011).

Although not as extensive or widespread as in Japan, there has been an increasing interest in preventive interventions for U.S. infants and their families over the past two decades. This interest emerged, in part, from evidence of the impact of early experiences on brain, socioemotional, and cognitive development, as well as the increasing number of mothers of infants entering the labor force. In particular, the onset of welfare reform with its stringent requirements for parents to engage in paid work has pushed unprecedented numbers of children from low-income families into the child-care system (see Azzi-Lessing, 2010).

Early intervention is one of the major systems through which preventive services are delivered to infants and their families. These services are provided to children from birth through age five who have significant developmental disabilities or who are at risk for developmental problems. These services are aimed at reducing or preventing problems in the first few years of life and include comprehensive, family-based services for children from birth to age three. These programs are authorized by the federal Individuals with Disabilities Education Improvement Act of 2004 (PL 108-446; Azzi-Lessing, 2010).

A variety of early intervention programs to support optimal development for infants have been established in local communities. One such program is Parents Interacting with Infants (PIWI), developed at the Early Childhood Special Education Department, College of Education, University of Illinois at Urbana-Champaign, by Jeanette McCollum and her team of culturally diverse early-childhood experts and worldwide early-childhood consultants. PIWI was developed for infants with developmental and physical disabilities such as **Down syndrome** and **cerebral palsy** and their parents. It is based, in part, on attachment research that shows the importance of the parent-child relationship for children with disabilities (see Spiker, Boyce, & Boyce, 2002, for a summary; McCollum, 1984). The primary goal of PIWI is to help parents and infants develop positive ways of interacting with each other, and support parents in fostering their babies' development. Small groups comprising parents with special-needs infants and those with typically developing infants meet weekly in playgroups. The playgroups are hosted by early-childhood interventionists who provide developmentally appropriate toys and activities for parents and infants to explore, as well as information on a range of topics. Parents also serve as resources for one another as they form supportive relationships that may continue outside of PIWI.

Early Head Start is another major system through which comprehensive, preventive services are delivered to children from the prenatal period to age three and their families. It encourages young, pregnant women to enroll, so that service delivery can begin before the baby is born. Individualized services are delivered in the families' homes, and in early child-care and education programs. The overarching goal is to give infants and toddlers from low-income families the best possible start by strengthening child development, parent empowerment, and overall family well-being. Early Head Start was launched in 1995 as an outgrowth of Head Start. Early Head Start has undergone rigorous national evaluation, and the results indicate that participating children have better developmental outcomes at age three, and their parents score higher on a range of parenting and self-sufficiency measures, than do their counterparts in control groups (see Azzi-Lessing, 2010).

A variety of other preventive programs focus more narrowly on providing positive coaching and support to struggling parents who have an inadequate understanding of infant development (Paradis, Montes, & Szilagyi, 2008). Limitations in parents' knowledge of their infants' development can lead to inappropriate expectations of the infants (Bornstein & Cote, 2004). Inappropriate expectations can be especially prevalent in adolescent parents. Although emotionally committed to their infants, some adolescents' limited knowledge of infant development can lead to frustration that adversely affects emerging attachment relationships (Clewell, Brooks-Gunn, & Benasich, 1989; Long, 2009). In addition, they may fail to recognize any emergent developmental problems. Children in at-risk families whose parents receive education about the typical cognitive, physical, and social development of infants and young children, coupled with coaching on parenting skills, fare better than children whose parents do not receive such support (McFarlane, Dodge, Crowne, Cheng, & Duggan, 2010). Social workers who practice with parents of infants need accurate information about infant development and also need to interact with parents about their cultural views of infancy.

During a family crisis, one of the ways in which social workers support parents and their infants and young children to prevent more serious problems from emerging is through **crisis nurseries services**. Historically, crisis nurseries in the United States developed from a grassroots movement in the 1960s to provide respite to parents experiencing stress and to prevent child abuse and neglect. Today, crisis nursery services, sometimes called "respite services," provide twenty-four-hour, temporary emergency care for infants and young children whose families are experiencing a wide range of challenges from medical emergencies (e.g., an automobile accident or surgery), to unexpected stressful home situations (e.g., domestic violence and homelessness), to risks of abuse and neglect (e.g., a stressed single parent without support). Although crisis nurseries vary in the services they offer to families, many provide initial crisis assessment and intervention services, after-crisis interventions, follow-up care, and/or referral to other community services (e.g., domestic violence, shelter, food, etc.).

A core service for all crisis nurseries is the substitute care they provide to infants and young children. Infants and young children may not understand what is happening during crises, but they perceive the emotionality of the situation and respond to it. Furthermore, their primary caregivers may be unavailable physically or psychologically to meet their needs. When the family environment is chaotic, dangerous, and uncertain, infants and young children need the support of people who understand their needs and can provide appropriate interventions until their primary caregivers are available. Indeed, both the infants and their caregivers need timely interventions in a safe place where the workers are trained to understand how crisis affects each member of the family. Social workers who work in crisis nurseries are experts in ameliorating the effects of the trauma on infants and young children, and helping their families negotiate the immediate crisis and its aftereffects.

Empirical research indicates that crisis nurseries can be effective in meeting their goals. Subramanian (1985) found that parents experienced a decrease in parenting stress after accessing crisis nursery services. This effect did not depend on what the stressors were; they included child-care difficulties, financial problems, current living situation (e.g., homelessness or domestic violence), and child-care responsibilities (e.g., difficult behaviors). Some research suggests that those who use crisis nursery services perceive them as safe places for children (Dougherty, Yu, Edgar, Day, & Wade, 2002). Postcrisis services can support the development of positive family relationships that enhance secure attachment (Cole, Wehrmann, Dewar, & Swinford, 2005). Crisis nursery support also can alleviate the need for longer-term foster-care placement, or other separations of the primary caregiver from the infant or young child (Subramanian, 1985).

The following case excerpt illustrates the role of preventive interventions in keeping a vulnerable family together.

> Six-month-old Sally Smith was diagnosed with failure to thrive and hospitalized by the family doctor. Below the 5th percentile for weight, Sally weighed only ten pounds. Her ribs showed, and she was listless. In less than twenty-fours hours of hospitalization, she had gained eight ounces and was responding to her mother with smiling and cooing.
>
> Sally's family consists of two sisters, ages three and four, and two parents. Her mother is developmentally disabled with an IQ of 54. Her father is higher functioning with an IQ of 90. The family resides in a small midwestern town where both parents were born and raised. They are well liked by neighbors and community social service and medical providers. Everyone seems to agree that the parents have "good hearts," are "nice people," and "love their children." No one wants to see this family separated, but it is clear that secondary preventive efforts are necessary if the children are to live safely with their parents. The family has an excellent relationship with their doctor, who learned that the mother was mixing the baby's powdered formula incorrectly in an effort to make it last longer. He has arranged for a nurse to visit the home weekly to monitor feeding of the children, including canned formula for the baby. Child Protective Services has enrolled the family in an intensive family preservation program where someone will visit the home daily for six months to help the parents learn to more adequately care for the children. In addition, the older children are enrolled in an early-intervention program during the day, and upon release from the hospital, Sally will begin attending day care. In the morning, the father and mother will get the children off to school and day care, and put them to bed in the evening. In addition, people in the community have stepped forward to help, most notably the family's pastor and church members. The long-term goal is to preserve this family with professional and community support, and to continue monitoring as new challenges emerge.

The Smith family faces many challenges, including developmental disability and poverty. Yet the parents love their children and are highly motivated to parent. With significant help from community members and professionals, they may succeed. Yet decisions regarding how to support this family are complex. The infant clearly is developing an attachment relationship with her mother, and disrupting this process through temporary foster-care placement would create additional risks. On the other hand, her health and safety are paramount concerns.

HIGHLIGHTS OF DEVELOPMENT DURING INFANCY

Social workers who provide services to parents and infants need accurate information about the rapid, complex developmental changes of infancy. Newborns are entirely dependent on others for their survival and will remain so for several years. This period of dependency results not only in vulnerability but also provides rich and extensive opportunities for learning. During the first two years of life, infants' abilities to communicate, understand the world, and interact socially undergo dramatic transformations.

Even before birth, tremendous biological and psychological development occurs. By five months after conception, the higher brain regions have begun to develop. The fetus's senses develop relatively early in prenatal development. The fetus responds to sounds about five or six months after conception, and to light at about six months. Furthermore, the uterine environment provides rich sensory experiences. Sounds from outside the mother's body such as loud noises and voices can be heard by the fetus, as can sounds from within the mother's body such as her heartbeat and digestion. Given this sensory-rich prenatal environment and the relatively early development of the senses, it is not surprising that some rudimentary learning occurs in utero. Neonates show a preference for their mother's voice over the voices of other women (Fifer & Moon, 1995) and for the mother's native language over other languages (Moon, Cooper, & Fifer, 1993). In contrast to William James's (1890) description of the newborn as occupying a world of impenetrable confusion, we now know that newborns arrive with relatively developed sensory, behavioral, and reflex systems. Full-term, healthy newborns are ready to interact, learn, and form attachment relationships (see Lightfoot, Cole, & Cole, 2009 for a review).

During the prenatal period, the developing child is vulnerable to **teratogens**, which are environmental agents that cause deviations from normal development and lead to abnormalities or death. They include certain viruses, drugs, and pollutants. The use of substances such as alcohol, cocaine, and tobacco during pregnancy can have teratogenic effects on the fetus, resulting, for example, in an infant with reduced brain size (Malanga & Kosofsky, 2004) or other abnormalities. Boxes 5.2 and 5.3 describe the effects of alcohol misuse during pregnancy.

During infancy, remarkable physical, verbal, and cognitive developmental changes occur. Physical growth is dramatic, and by the end of the second year of life, babies typically reach 30–34 inches and 22–27 pounds. They begin crawling at around 8–9 months and walking around 1 year. They begin to recognize common words and expressions by 6–9 months, babble by about 7 months, and speak their first words at around 1 year. Bones begin to ossify, body proportions change (e.g., the head becomes proportionally smaller relative to body length), and muscle strength increases. Brain development also is dramatic. Areas of the cerebral cortex develop, including language and the prefrontal cortex, which is important for the development of

---

BOX 5.2 SUBSTANCE MISUSE ACROSS THE LIFE SPAN

Prenatal Exposure to Alcohol

Fetal alcohol spectrum disorders (FASDs) is an umbrella term that includes several disorders caused by prenatal exposure to alcohol. The estimated rates of children with FASDs range from 0.2 to 2 children per 1,000 live births, but these rates are most likely underestimated. There is no known amount of alcohol that is safe to drink while pregnant. There is also no safe time to drink during pregnancy and no safe kind of alcohol to drink while pregnant. Fetal alcohol syndrome (FAS) represents the most severe outcome of FASD.

A child is considered to have FAS if these signs are observed: abnormal facial features (e.g., smooth ridge between nose and upper lip); lower-than-average height, weight, or both; problems with the central nervous system (e.g., small head size, problems with attention and hyperactivity, poor coordination).

Adults who were born with FAS often have lifelong cognitive, socialization, and communication deficits. For example, 50 to 60 percent have disruptive school experiences, trouble with the law, and/or inappropriate sexual behaviors, and 35 percent have alcohol/drug problems.

Other types of FASDs are alcohol-related neurodevelopmental disorders, whose symptoms include behavior and learning problems, and alcohol-related birth defects.

Sources: Centers for Disease Control and Prevention, n.d.; Malanga & Kosofsky, 2004; Riley, Mattson, & Thomas, 2009; Streissguth et al., 2004.

---

voluntary behaviors. Increased myelination, the formation of an insulating sheath of fatty cells around a nerve fiber, speeds transmission of nerve impulses from one neuron (brain cell) to the next, including neurons in language-related areas and those linking various areas of the brain. In conjunction with these brain changes, by the end of infancy babies' behaviors are increasingly intentional; they mentally represent objects and experiences, understand cause-effect relationships, and classify objects. In addition, their memory improves and their ability to control and sustain attention increases, as does the speed with which they process information (see Lightfoot, Cole, & Cole, 2009).

Babies also exhibit rapid psychosocial development from birth to age three. Erikson (1963) identifies the psychosocial stage of the first year of life as resolving the crisis or conflict of trust versus mistrust, largely through experiences of caregivers' reliability. The psychosocial stage of the second to third year of life involves resolution of the crisis of autonomy versus shame or doubt as the child explores the world (Erikson, 1963).

....

**BOX 5.3 POVERTY AND SUBSTANCE MISUSE
ACROSS THE LIFE SPAN**

Alcohol Misuse during Pregnancy and in Poverty

In the United States, a child born to a mother who has a middle or higher income is at significantly less risk for FAS than children born to low-income mothers. Lower socioeconomic status is associated with ten times more risk for FAS. As a social worker, consider how clustering low-income housing, limiting prenatal care and addiction rehabilitation centers, and living in a culture that encourages the use of substances for escaping stress could play a major role in pregnant women's misusing drugs and alcohol. For the purposes of discussion, what other macro- and microsystems issues can be identified that increase the probability that low-income pregnant women will misuse a substance? What policy issues may help prevent pregnant women from using addictive substances?

––––––––––
Source: Malanga & Kosofsky, 2004.

....

A variety of sociocultural factors can enhance or impede development in infancy. Poverty is a serious risk to development during the prenatal period and infancy. Each year, hundreds of thousands of infants are born into U.S. families who are living below the poverty level or struggling to maintain economic viability (Knitzer & Perry, 2009). Risks to development associated with poverty include poor health care for the mother and baby. Boxes 5.4 through 5.7 discuss infant and maternal mortality rates in the United States and internationally, as well as the relatively low rate of immunization in the United States. In addition, parents with limited time and money may struggle to provide the tools (e.g., attention, objects to explore such as toys and books) and environment (e.g., good-quality day care) to ensure their babies' optimum development. The added stress of economic survival also affects the emotional well-being of parents and is another risk factor in infant development. Some programs such as the Harlem Children's Zone (Tough, 2008) are helping caregivers who are struggling financially, to support their children's optimal development from infancy through adolescence and, hopefully, to break the cycle of family poverty.

When considering the individual person as the focal system, it is important to remember that although we may focus on biological, psychological, and social factors separately for the purposes of discussion, in fact they are interrelated. Children's increasing competence during infancy is made possible by a complex ensemble of interrelated biological, psychological, and social developments supported within particular sociocultural-historical contexts (Lightfoot, Cole, & Cole, 2009). Children's increasing ability to

---

BOX 5.4 POVERTY ACROSS THE LIFE SPAN

The Developmental Link between Focal Systems and Macrosystems

Healthy development of a fetus is enhanced when a pregnant woman

- is physically and mentally healthy before becoming pregnant;
- receives good prenatal care throughout the pregnancy;
- avoids alcohol, street drugs, and tobacco during the pregnancy;
- avoids certain prescription drugs that can be toxic to the fetus;
- avoids certain foods, such as fish high in mercury;
- follows health-care directives;
- regularly eats well-balanced meals, including foods rich in folic acid;
- routinely gets a complete night's rest;
- reduces emotional and physical stress; and
- is emotionally supported by family, employer, community, and friends.

This list illustrates the partnership that must exist between the expecting mother and the macrosystem. Unless the national government provides health care, education, and nutritional help, many women living in poverty are unable to properly care for their bodies and the developing fetus. On the other hand, mothers must be willing to use available facilities and educational opportunities. In some cases, this means overcoming personal and community beliefs regarding, for example, the trustworthiness of helping professionals.

Source: "CDC Pregnancy Gateway," n.d.; Kids Health, n.d.

---

move around during infancy provides one example. During the first few months of life, motor areas of the cortex develop rapidly. In the second half of the first year, physical changes in strength and coordination allow mobility. Different cultural and historical contexts, however, provide different opportunities for the development of mobility. During the nineteenth century, many European-American babies spent the first years of life restrained within wagons as their families moved west. Today, the descendents of these babies may careen around in walkers in their baby-proofed playrooms. The experience of mobility, in turn, allows for the development of children's understandings of spatial relationships, such as how objects are positioned relative to one another and various routes through the familiar environment. Mobility also leads to changes in social relationships as caregivers become concerned with the newly mobile infant's safety. Yet it is not until

BOX 5.5 POVERTY ACROSS THE LIFE SPAN

Infant Mortality Rates in the United States and Internationally

Infant mortality rates are declining in the United States. In 2007, however, the death rate for African-American infants was 2.3 times higher than for European-American infants. The neonatal mortality rate for African Americans in 2007 was 8.65 per 1,000 live births compared to 3.7 per 1,000 live births for European-American infants. During the postneonatal period (twenty-eight days to one year), African-American infants died at a rate of 4.59 per 1,000 live births compared to 1.94 for European-American infants.

The United States ranks only twenty-ninth in the world in prevention of infant deaths. This is a strong indication that the United States does not provide the quality, availability, and accessibility of primary care that women need during pregnancy and the medical attention that both the child and mother require during the infant's first year of life.

Worldwide, reasons for infant mortality include poor nutrition and famine during gestation and infancy, toxins in the environment, limited social and health services, and sudden infant death syndrome (SIDS).

Sources: MacDorman & Mathews, 2008; Xu, Kochanek, Murphy, & Tejada-Vera, 2010.

BOX 5.6 POVERTY ACROSS THE LIFE SPAN

Maternal Mortality Rates

Ethnic differences in poverty rates impact maternal as well as infant mortality. Not only do African-American infants die at a greater rate than European-American infants, but African-American women die giving birth 2.7 times more often than European-American women. The maternal mortality rate for African-American mothers is 26.5 per 100,000 live births compared to 10 maternal deaths per 100,000 for European-American women.

Source: Xu, Kochanek, Murphy, & Tejada-Vera, 2010.

the second and third years of life that children's rapid acquisition of fluency in their native languages allows verbal communication and negotiation with the caregiver around issues of safety and separations.

The rapid, complex developmental changes that occur during infancy are mediated through relationships with other people, especially primary

BOX 5.7 POVERTY ACROSS THE LIFE SPAN

Immunization

In 2007, only 77 percent of children in the United States received all of the recommended preventive immunizations. Poverty can play a role in a child not getting immunizations for these reasons:

- Parents may work at low-paying jobs that are at a distance from the clinic.
- Taking off from work for well-baby care may reduce the parent's pay check.
- Parents have difficulty receiving health information and determining the truth of rumors and immunization myths.
- Parents have no regular medical care provider, and primarily use hospital emergency rooms for medical attention.

Source: U.S. Department of Health and Human Services, 2009.

caregivers (van Ijzendoorn & Sagi, 1999). Other people provide food, shelter, and a safe and adequate physical environment for the infant. Other people also provide emotional comfort, access to language, and intellectual stimulation. Again, different cultural and historical contexts allow for different opportunities for social interaction. In some families and communities, infants and young children are rarely separated from their mothers even when they sleep at night; in others, young infants are put into their own rooms to sleep at night; in others, they are cared for by a variety of individuals, including older siblings, grandparents, and neighbors, and are rarely separated from human contact. Because of the complex developmental changes in social relationships during the first year of life, infants are vulnerable to disturbances in their relationships, such as foster-care placement.

DEVELOPMENT AND ORGANIZATION OF ATTACHMENT RELATIONSHIPS

Attachment research focuses on relationships. Before considering the details of this research, it is important to underscore that children can and do develop attachment relationships with more than one individual and within diverse family forms. Children can develop healthy attachment relationships with fathers, mothers, siblings, grandparents and other extended family members, substitute care providers, and others. They also develop healthy attachment relationships in families headed by single parents, and with gay and lesbian parents. Quality of relationships, not family role or family structure, is critical to developing attachment relationships.

This migrant worker is providing her infant son with the kind of positive, responsive parenting that facilitates secure attachment relationships.

Understanding how attachment relationships develop is critical to providing preventive services that are appropriate to infants and their families and that support the emergence of attachment relationships. For example, when serious problems occur and infants must enter foster care, they lose the opportunity for extensive daily interaction with their parents. If they move from foster home to foster home, they lose the ability to interact with those caregivers as well. Frequent and consistent contact with a primary caregiver is necessary for the development of adequate attachment relationships during the first few years of life when the organization of these relationships changes dramatically (e.g., Ainsworth, 1973; Bowlby, 1969/ 1982; Thompson, 1998).

There are several important developmental changes in infants' early attachment behavior. At birth, infants display innate attachment behaviors, such as crying, that draw caregivers near, but they do not have a specific relationship with a caregiver. In this "preattachment" phase, lasting from birth to approximately six weeks, infants do not become upset when left with an unfamiliar caregiver. In the "attachment-in-the-making" phase, lasting from approximately six weeks to six to eight months of age, infants begin to show signs of wariness when confronted with unfamiliar people. Infants placed in foster care early in life may respond with wariness to their birth parents. Their foster or other substitute caregivers have become their primary attachment figures. In reunions with their birth parents, infants may display behavior that reflects their perceptions that these parents are unfamiliar; for example, they may stiffen and turn away when their parents pick them up. The reaction of the infant may make it difficult for the birth parent to continue to engage the infant in order to establish a more secure relationship.

At approximately seven months, infants will display "clear-cut attachment" behaviors. Infants from all over the world become overtly distressed when their primary caregiver is not available in unfamiliar situations, or with strangers. As children become more mobile (twelve to eighteen months), they may use their caregivers as "secure bases" from which to freely explore, checking in with the caregiver if they feel frightened or anxious. By twenty-four months of age, as the child becomes more mobile and communicatively competent and spends more time away from the caregiver, the dyad enters a phase of "reciprocal relationships" in which they share responsibility for maintaining closeness as needed. By three years of age, the child enters a more sophisticated phase of attachment, which Bowlby (1969/1982) termed "goal-corrected partnership." During this phase, caregivers and children communicate and negotiate differences in plans and reach mutual agreement. For example, when leaving the child with a substitute caregiver, parents can explain where they are going, why, and when they will return. The child's sense of security no longer depends so much on the actual presence of the caregivers as on mutual trust and understanding. These developmental changes are supported by children's emerging abilities to communicate and understand others' perspectives, motivations, and feelings (see Lightfoot, Cole, & Cole, 2009).

Given the significance and complexity of rapidly changing caregiver-child relationships in infancy, preventive interventions are important to avoid disruptions of these relationships. The potential harm due to an inadequate home environment must be weighed against the potential harm due to the disruption of caregiver-child relationships, for example, during foster-care placement. Whenever possible, primary and secondary preventive services support children and families at home, to avoid out-of-home placement, with the inherent disruption of emerging attachment relationships. When foster placement is necessary, placing an infant with a relative may facilitate the development of existing attachment relationships that can continue after the child returns home. Whether or not the substitute caregiver is related to the child, however, does not seem to be significant if she or he is providing adequate care and meeting the basic physical and relational needs of the child (Cole, 2006). When an infant is placed at birth with a foster caregiver, the disruption may be experienced at the reunion with the birth parent, or in placement within an unfamiliar adoptive home (Cole, 2005).

A developmental, ecological-systems analysis of attachment relationships provides a framework to assess and support emerging caregiver-infant attachment relationships. It draws our attention to the development of attachment relationships as they emerge within particular physical and social ecologies. We consider the interaction of biological, psychological, and social factors as they shape and are shaped within particular sociocultural-historical contexts.

Biological Factors

When thinking about attachment relationships in infancy, it is important to understand that the formation of attachment relationships appears to be part of our primate heritage. In all human social groups, infants and their primary caregivers develop affective bonds and organized behaviors in order to relate in times of stress. These relationships emerge over time, and in conjunction with children's and caregivers' experiences. Bowlby (1969/1982, 1973, 1980) argues that such attachment relationships evolved because they enhance our potential for survival. As infants achieve mobility, they are still unable to care for themselves, and the world can be a dangerous place. The attachment relationship between infants and their caregivers provides the basis for a balance of exploration necessary for learning, and proximity-seeking behavior necessary for safety. Infants explore until they begin to feel mild discomfort and then seek the security of their caregivers by going to them or by visually checking in with them over a distance. When the perceived danger diminishes, infants again begin to explore. If the infant experiences the caregiver's response as consistently available for protection in times of perceived danger, the infant is free to explore the physical and social environments, knowing that the caregiver will sensitively respond and provide any needed protection. This confident exploration forms the basis for physical, cognitive, social, and emotional development.

Recent neuroscience research supports Bowlby's theoretical arguments that attachment relationships have universal, biologically based origins. Like many mammals, human infants appear to have some biologically based behaviors that assist caretaking (e.g., clinging and nursing), as well as other behaviors that make them more attractive (e.g., smiling and cooing; Shonkoff & Phillips, 2001; Stevenson-Hinde, 1994). Neural processes in neonates and mothers establish behaviors that promote survival and serve as the foundation for later emotional and social development. Human neonates and mothers recognize and prefer one another's unique smell. In mammals, specific brain regions and neurotransmitters (chemicals that communicate between brain cells) have been identified that mediate early olfactory learning (e.g., Leon, 1992).

Neuroscience research extends Bowlby's theoretical arguments regarding the importance of experience in the development of universal, biologically based processes. Biologically based attachment and other processes require enriched and structured experience for their development (Black, Jones, Nelson, & Greenough, 1998). There are extended periods of neural plasticity in childhood during which experiences affect brain structure. In their classic paper, Black and Greenough (1986) categorized these processes as either developmentally scheduled for all species members (termed "experience-expectant") or idiosyncratic learning and memory that is unique in timing and content (termed "experience-dependent").

Experience-expectant developmental processes appear to have evolved to make adaptive use of experience that could be "expected" at a particular time and of adequate quality for nearly all juveniles of a species (e.g., close and sustained early contact with older caregivers). For experience-expectant neural plasticity, experience that is impoverished or distorted may have lasting effects on brain development. It appears that humans and other mammals have developmentally scheduled neural processes for incorporating and using early emotional and social experience relevant to attachment relationships (see Black et al., 1998; Francis & Meaney, 1999). The disruption of these processes by inadequate or grossly distorted experience can have lasting adverse consequences. Indeed, child abuse and severe neglect can affect both brain anatomy and physiology (see Cicchetti, 2002; Kaufman & Charney, 1999), which may account for findings that child abuse can result in lifelong vulnerability to depression and personality disorders (Jacobsen, Miller, & Kirkwood, 1997; Weiss, Longhurst, & Mazure, 1999). Severe neglect, as in the example of institutionalized Romanian orphans, can substantially impair emotional and cognitive development (Zeanah, Smyke, Koga, Carlson, & Bucharest Early Intervention Core Group, 2005).

Experience-dependent developmental processes, on the other hand, encompass several forms of lifelong neural plasticity that allow for some modification of earlier brain development. Experience-dependent processes are flexible in their developmental timing and nature of information storage. These processes appear to make new synaptic connections between neurons on demand (e.g., learning of particular vocabulary, spatial information, and social relationships). The presence of experience-dependent processes suggests that positive experiences such as the development of a secure attachment relationship with a foster parent, or therapy, may partially correct the effects of early neglect or trauma. Attachment theory and research indicate that expectations and patterns of attachment behaviors in children with histories of problematic attachment relationships may gradually change if subsequent relationships develop in more positive and stable ways (Ainsworth, 1989; Ainsworth & Marvin, 1995; Main, Kaplan, & Cassidy, 1985; Sroufe, Carlson, Levy, & Egeland, 2003).

Social and Psychological factors

Mary Ainsworth conducted the first empirical research on attachment relationships. She conducted extensive naturalistic observations of polygamous families in Uganda and middle-class, European-American families in Baltimore, Maryland (Ainsworth, 1967; Ainsworth, Blehar, Waters, & Wall, 1978). In both groups, she observed some consistent differences in the ways in which caregivers and children organized their attachment relationships. To facilitate study of the causes and consequences of this variation in apparently adequately functioning families, she developed a laboratory procedure referred to as the **strange situation** (Ainsworth et al., 1978). The strange situation allows observation of parent-child interaction during gradually escalating, low-level, relatively common, and nontraumatic stressors. During this procedure, the twelve- to thirty-six-month-old child and the caregiver enter a playroom. Then a female stranger enters the room. Next the child remains in the playroom while the primary caregiver and the stranger alternately leave and return.

Several broad categories of attachment relationships have been identified through the strange situation and naturalistic observations (see Thompson, 1998, for review). Across cultures, the majority of attachment relationships are classified as **securely attached** (van Ijzendoorn, Goldberg, Kroonenberg, & Frenkel, 1992), and parents generally express a preference for secure attachment (van Ijzendoorn & Sagi, 1999). During the strange situation, children in securely attached relationships use their caregivers as a safe base from which to explore their physical and social worlds. They move away from their caregivers easily but also monitor their physical locations and periodically reestablish contact with them, especially if they become distressed. The child is upset when the caregiver leaves and is unlikely to be comforted by the stranger. When the caregiver reappears, the child establishes physical contact, quickly calms down, and resumes playing (see Lightfoot, Cole, & Cole, 2009).

However, a substantial proportion (approximately 35 percent in the United States) of parent-child relationships in middle-class, intact families fall into one of two subcategories of insecure attachment. During the strange situation, children in **insecure/avoidant attachment** relationships are relatively indifferent to their caregivers' physical locations, and may or may not cry if their caregivers leave the room. If they do cry, they are as likely to be comforted by the stranger as by their caregivers. When their caregivers return after brief separations, children may look away instead of approaching their caregivers (Lightfoot, Cole, & Cole, 2009). These children display fewer attachment behaviors and remain more distant from their caregivers during periods of stress than do securely attached children. Rather than going to the caregiver, they may self-comfort, for example, by playing with a toy (Carlson, Cicchetti, Barnett, & Braunwald, 1989).

During the strange situation, children in **insecure/resistant attachment** relationships generally cling to their caregivers and appear upset even when the caregiver is near. They are distressed when their caregivers leave, but are not comforted when they return. Instead, they simultaneously seek contact with their caregivers and protest their efforts to comfort them. They may cry angrily to be picked up but after being picked up immediately struggle to climb down. Children in insecure/resistant relationships do not readily resume play after their caregivers return (see Lightfoot, Cole, & Cole, 2009). In contrast to children in securely attached relationships, they expend relatively more time and energy monitoring the whereabouts of their caregivers and seeking comfort from them, and less time in independent play and exploration (Carlson et al., 1989).

In many family and cultural contexts, secure attachment emerges, in part, from sensitive parenting (van Ijzendoorn & Sagi, 1999). Sensitivity refers to the caregiver's ability to perceive the child's verbal and nonverbal communications accurately, and to respond to these signals promptly and appropriately (Ainsworth & Bell, 1969; De Wolff & van Ijzendoorn, 1997). Caregivers in insecurely attached relationships tend to be less accessible and responsive to their children than those in securely attached relationships. These caregivers are more likely than those in securely attached relationships to have difficulty interpreting children's communications and may respond inappropriately to children's behavioral cues by overstimulating, intruding, or otherwise ignoring children's desires. Caregivers in insecure/avoidant relationships tend to express more anger and rejection, and to withhold physical contact more often than do caregivers in securely attached relationships (Lightfoot, Cole, & Cole, 2009).

Caregivers' sensitivity to the children in their care is related, in part, to their early attachment experiences with their own caregivers. Human (Main & Hesse, 1990) and primate (Suomi, 1999) studies indicate that parenting behavior is strongly associated with the caregiver's own experience of being parented. Humans' experiences of being parented result in **working models**, or mental representations of attachment experiences: their characteristics, values, and meanings. These mental models influence parenting behavior and hence the quality of parents' relationships with their own children. This process is referred to as the "intergenerational transmission" of attachment (Bowlby, 1969/1982). Indeed, the security of parents' mental representations of attachment is associated with the security of their attachment relationships with their own children (Main & Hesse, 1990). Parents who represent their relationships with their own parents as secure tend to have securely attached children, and those who represent their relationships with their own parents as insecure tend to have insecurely attached children (see van Ijzendoorn, 1995, for review).

Although moderately stable over infancy and early childhood, the organization of attachment behavior may vary, for example, with parents' fluctuating levels of stress. Parents who are preoccupied with financial, job, or marital problems; family illness; or other common stressors within micro-, meso- and exosystems, may be less sensitive in their responses to their infants and young children (Belsky, 2005). Infants from intact families show some instability in attachment behaviors when their parents are experiencing stress (Cole, 2005; Thompson, 1998). For example, a previously secure infant may display insecure patterns of attachment behaviors when her parents are experiencing financial or marital difficulties.

Cross-cultural data, although not extensive, indicate that secure attachment typically increases the likelihood of better social competence in the future (van Ijzendoorn & Sagi, 1999). Stable, secure caregiver-child attachment in infancy is associated with positive relationships with parents, peers, and teachers, and enhanced development and self-confidence in childhood (Belsky & Pasco Fearon, 2002). Children with insecure caregiver-child relationships in infancy are more likely to experience subsequent behavioral problems, conflicts with caregivers, low self-esteem, and impaired peer relationships (see Lightfoot, Cole, & Cole, 2009).

Researchers studying children with developmental and social risk factors have identified another problematic pattern, **disorganized attachment** relationship. Children in disorganized attachment relationships do not use their caregivers as a secure base, or employ any other coherent behavioral strategy to cope with stress. Rather, they show a range of complex responses to the strange situation, atypical of children in secure or insecure attachment relationships (see Barnett & Vondra, 1999). Children with disorganized attachment relationships may display disorganized strategies involving interrupted, confused, or undirected behaviors that are unsuccessful in gaining comfort from their caregivers. They may respond to their caregivers with rapidly cycling, contradictory behaviors, such as inappropriate laughter when the caregiver departs, followed by an emotional collapse. Upon reunion, their behavior may alternate between seeking proximity and fleeing, simultaneously avoiding the caregiver and crying. They may attempt to escape the situation even when the caregiver is present. Some children also show disorientation through glazed expressions, mistimed movements, freezing, and anomalous postures. Some children also show severe apprehension in the presence of the caregiver by head banging, wetting, or huddling on the floor; through asymmetrical or mistimed approaches to the caregiver; or by freezing when the caregiver enters the room (Crittenden & Ainsworth, 1989; Main & Solomon, 1990). Such disorganized attachment relationships are relatively rare in presumably well-functioning families (Carlson et al., 1989).

The pathways to disorganized attachment responses are multiple. Certain behaviors associated with disorganized attachment relationships (e.g., incomplete strategies for obtaining proximity or anomalous posturing) may reflect symptoms of neurological impairments. A significantly higher percentage of disorganized behaviors appears in samples of children with diagnoses of autism and Down syndrome (35 percent), premature children (25 percent), and children whose mothers misused alcohol and drugs (43 percent), but not in samples of children who have severe physical problems that do not involve neurological functioning (see Pipp-Siegel, Seigel, & Dean, 1999). Children who have experienced abuse or neglect are much more likely to demonstrate disorganized attachment behaviors than those who have not (Barnett, Ganiban, & Cicchetti, 1999; Lyons-Ruth, Bronfman, & Parsons, 1999; Vondra, Hommerding, & Shaw, 1999). Carlson et al. (1989) analyzed data from forty-three mother-infant pairs: twenty-two from families receiving protective services for child abuse or neglect, and twenty-one from demographically matched comparison families who had no history of abuse or neglect. Of the children who were maltreated, 82 percent met the criteria for disorganized attachment relationships. In contrast, only 19 percent of the children in the comparison group exhibited disorganized attachment behaviors.

Disorganized patterns of attachment behavior also are associated with a history of parental psychopathology (Greenberg, Speltz, & DeKlyen, 1993) such as maternal depression (van Ijzendoorn et al., 1992), and parents' own traumatic and unresolved loss of an attachment figure (Main, 1996). The characteristic that these parents may share with maltreating parents is behavior that may alarm a young child. Disorganized attachment behavior in neurologically normal children is a response to frightened or frightening caregiver behavior, such as helplessness, distress, or abusiveness (Main & Hesse, 1990).

Disorganized attachment relationships in early childhood have been associated with persistent atypical attachment behavior as children develop. During the preschool years, when the strange situation is no longer stressful for most children, some children who were in disorganized attachment relationships with caregivers in infancy continue to display signs of distress (Crittenden & Ainsworth, 1989). Other children who showed disorganized attachment behaviors in infancy rely on controlling behavior toward the parent (Main & Cassidy, 1988). These children no longer organize their attachment behaviors around their own need for comfort and protection. Instead, they maintain engagement with the parent on the parent's terms, becoming either punitive or caregiving in response to the hostile or helpless parent (Zeanah, Mammen, & Lieberman, 1993). The development of adaptive responses to alarming parental behavior may predispose children to difficulties in other relationships (Crittenden, 1995; Schneider-Rosen, Braunwald, Carlson, & Cicchetti, 1985). For example, a child who is preoccupied with caring for a parent may seek proximity to the parent to avoid punishment, but may have relatively little energy to devote to developing relationships with peers.

It is not surprising that disorganized attachment relationships in infancy place children at risk for developing psychosocial disorders (e.g., Greenberg et al., 1993; Main, 1996) and psychopathology (Carlson, 1998). Disorganized attachment relationships in infancy are linked to such problems as aggressive and hostile behavior toward peers (Lyons-Ruth, Alpern, & Repacholi, 1993), poor overall school adjustment, behavior problems in preschool and elementary school (Lyons-Ruth, Easterbrooks, & Cibelli, 1997), and dissociative disorders and psychopathology in adolescence (Carlson, 1998).

Sociocultural-Historical Context

Caregiver-child attachment relationships in infancy do not exist in isolation. They are embedded within particular families, communities, and cultures at particular points in history. Bowlby's evolutionary perspective on attachment relationships allows for universally adaptive behavioral propensities to be realized in specific ways, depending on the niche in which the child must survive. If across cultures all infants used the same fixed strategies to deal with attachment challenges, there would be no room for adaptation to changes in the environment, and to various constraints imposed by particular social and physical contexts. For example, the exploration of Hausa infants in Nigeria is restricted because of environmental hazards. Hausa infants, like their U.S. counterparts, use their caregivers as secure bases from which to explore the environment, but Hausa infants' exploration is more visual, and done only in close proximity with a caregiver (Marvin, VanDevender, Iwanaga, LeVine, & LeVine, 1977).

Critiques of attachment theory from the perspective of family systems theory (Cowan, 1997) and cultural psychology (Harwood, Miller, & Irizarry, 1995; Shweder et al., 1998) emphasize the relative neglect of sociocultural-historical context in attachment research. The cross-cultural database is relatively small and includes only a few studies of non-Western cultures, or families of low socioeconomic status (Tomlinson, Cooper, & Murray, 2005; van Ijzendoorn & Sagi, 1999). Available cross-cultural studies on attachment relationships in Israel (Sagi et al., 1985), Japan (Miyake, Chen, & Campos, 1985), and Germany (Grossmann & Grossmann, 1981; Grossmann, Grossmann, Spangler, Suess, & Unzer, 1985) suggest how socioeconomic context can shape attachment behaviors.

Sociocultural-historical context may shape attachment behaviors through specific beliefs and related child-rearing practices. The Grossmanns, who studied a nonclinical group of families in northern Germany, found that 49 percent of twelve-month-olds were classified as insecure/avoidant during the strange situation, almost double the proportion usually found in European-American samples. Observations of parent-child interactions within German homes, however, did not indicate that German mothers generally were insensitive to their children. Rather, these mothers endorsed a broader cultural belief system emphasizing independence. They believed that babies should be weaned from body contact with their mothers as soon as they became mobile. These cultural beliefs were translated into socialization practices that affected the organization of mother-infant attachment relationships. These mothers maintained a relatively large interpersonal distance from their young children, they sometimes pushed their babies away, and they left them alone more often than do middle-class mothers in the United States.

Sociocultural-historical context also may shape attachment behaviors through the social ecologies in which children are reared. For example, in some Israeli kibbutzim, infants' collective rearing includes sleeping away from their parents in a children's house. During the night, and for significant portions of the day, they are cared for in groups by child-care workers (*metapelet*). Infants form attachment relationships with child-care workers as well as family members (Sagi et al., 1985). Furthermore, consideration of the quality of attachment relationships across this extended attachment network predicts social competence at age five more strongly than any single attachment relationship even to the mother (see van Ijzendoorn & Sagi, 1999). Attachment research in the United States has focused on the dyadic, primary caregiver-child relationship. This cross-cultural research illustrates the importance of examining the wider social networks in which children develop (Harkness & Super, 1996; Thompson, 1998), including those in the United States.

Attachment behaviors also may be influenced by physical ecology. Comparative studies of attachment relationships across diverse groups within the United States suggest that some attachment behaviors are influenced by factors associated with families' socioeconomic status. For example, a meta-analysis of eighteen studies using middle-income samples and eight studies using lower-income samples revealed that maternal sensitivity was more strongly associated with parent-child attachment in middle-income groups than in lower-income groups (De Wolff & van Ijzendoorn, 1997). Sensitive middle-income mothers were more likely to have a securely attached child than sensitive lower-income mothers. In some families, environmental factors associated with lower socioeconomic status, such as inadequate food and shelter and dangerous neighborhoods, may override maternal sensitivity. Despite maternal sensitivity, a child from a lower-income family may adopt an insecure pattern of attachment behaviors. Furthermore, these behaviors may actually be adaptive in the sense of maximizing the child's vigilance and safety in environments beyond the parent-child relationship.

Sociocultural-historical and socioeconomic factors may also interact in complex ways to influence attachment behaviors. Mothers of toddlers were asked to comment on scenarios of toddlers' behaviors in the waiting room of a doctor's office (Harwood et al., 1995). Mothers were middle- and lower-income Anglo, and middle- and lower-income Puerto Rican. Each scenario was a strange situation analogue, and portrayed a child demonstrating behaviors associated with a different attachment classification (e.g., secure, insecure/resistant, insecure/avoidant). In general, mothers' responses varied both with their socioeconomic status and their culture. In discussing what they did or did not like about the toddlers' behaviors, European-American mothers were more likely to discuss "self-maximization" (i.e., self-confidence, independence, and development as an individual), and Puerto Rican mothers were more likely to discuss "proper demeanor" (i.e., the child's manners, behavior, cooperativeness, and acceptance by the larger community). However, within each cultural community, middle-income mothers were more likely to mention self-maximization, and lower-income mothers were more likely to mention proper demeanor.

IMPLICATIONS FOR PREVENTIVE INTERVENTIONS

A developmental, ecological-systems analysis of attachment relationships has important implications for social workers providing preventive interventions for infants and their families.

1. Preventive interventions with infants must include attention to the caregiver-child attachment relationship. Attachment relationships impact all aspects of infant development. Securely attached infants freely explore their social and physical worlds, optimizing their learning and emotional well-being. To be successful, even narrowly focused preventive interventions designed to enhance cognitive development and eventual school readiness need to support the infant's attachment relationships.

2. When families with infants face challenges, a basic issue for social workers should be the maintenance and development of infants' attachment relationships. When professionals intervene to help parents experiencing stress or trauma (e.g., due to substance misuse, violence, health and mental health problems, and poverty), they should prioritize programs that result in minimal disruption to infants' attachment relationships. For example, some substance rehabilitation facilities allow parents to keep their infants on site. When parents and infants must be separated, facilities such as crisis nurseries, where the relational needs of infants are understood, should be utilized, and frequent visits between parent and infant arranged.

3. Social workers can serve as effective advocates for funding preventive interventions for infants and their families. Although there is increased recognition of the need for preventive services, funding needed for these systems is lagging. Social workers can team with other

professionals such as early interventionists to lobby for prevention interventions for infants and their families (Azzi-Lessing, 2010).

4. Social workers can increase their participation in early-childhood preventive interventions. Social workers have been underrepresented in many early-childhood programs. Yet social workers' abilities to partner with struggling families and to navigate complex systems are vital, given the multiple challenges faced by many families. Social workers also can help ensure that preventive interventions for infants and their families are comprehensive and holistic (Azzi-Lessing, 2010).

SUMMARY

Social work with infants during the first two years of life is an exciting field with opportunities for social workers. Secure attachment relationships with caregivers are crucial during this period of rapid, complex developmental changes. A developmental, ecological-systems analysis of the infant's attachment relationships provides a framework for thoughtful social work practice that explores ways to support vulnerable infants and their families. Attachment relationships, part of our biological heritage, are necessary to adequate development. Consideration of biological, psychological, social, and sociocultural-historical dimensions of attachment relationships allows social workers to flexibly and creatively support the emergence and elaboration of attachment relationships in the safest environment possible. Box 5.8 contains practice stories and advice from Laura S., a social worker who directs a crisis nursery.

BOX 5.8 PRACTICE STORY AND ADVICE

Laura S., crisis nursery social worker: "You don't just do A, B, and C and get your results. It doesn't happen that way. It's messy work and important work. It's beautiful work and shouldn't be taken lightly."

Laura S., MSW, has worked with children from birth to adolescence. She began working at a crisis nursery in 1997 as a children's worker. In 2003 she became the nursery's program director and supervises the nursery's two programs: the Safe Children program, which shelters up to twelve children from birth to five years old, and the Strong Families program, which offers support groups, home visiting programs, parenting skills, and family bond strengthening. Laura is extremely passionate about the necessity of respecting and maintaining the attachment relations between the child and family and has worked hard to develop this component in the nursery.

Practice Story

[When I was younger], children never fascinated me. I received my bachelor's in psychology. I was driving home from a meaningless job, a retail store job, and got a vision of a circle of children, where kids were holding hands. I know it sounds weird. I felt I had to pursue that vision. A friend who I had shared my vision with told me about a job at a local inpatient mental health facility. My interview there didn't go so well, and I had no experience working with children. I [persisted and] asked to meet with the director anyhow, just to introduce myself and explain how interested I was in working with the kids. I got the job then and there. This job was so hard on the first day because of seeing child abuse, such as burns all over this one boy from his father. I didn't know how I'd go back the next day, but thought that if I was sad, how sad the children must be.

[But] I had problems leaving work at work and drawing boundaries. I had psych nurses say, "The children all want Laura's time and energy because she gives them all her time and energy" . . . A child who had been abused by his grandma had scars all the way down his back where she had dragged him across the gravel driveway. He would say, "Grandma was sick and tired of my bullshit." It was heartbreaking . . . He pushed me to where I wanted to lose my patience or yell at him, or tell him something he's heard before. This links to the families I work with now [at the crisis nursery] . . . I will not judge them if they say, "I feel like hitting my child." Everyone needs to know that I know how that feels, especially since I don't have children of my own. They have to know that I've been pushed to that place before. If I judge them for being pushed or losing patience, then they won't reach out and ask for help. I didn't lose my patience [with the boy] because I felt like he deserved a different answer from the world. When he was shouting out and looking for a response, hopefully I gave him a response that he will remember, which was kindness and compassion and love that he deserved from the world.

Some kids spit, hit, kick. I threw my back out. You stay calm and open, and my job as another human being is to be there for the child and to make it as safe as possible in the midst of the storm. [The important thing] for a child having a meltdown or a breakdown is to show how you understand that they're angry and every feeling deserves space. Validate their feelings. You don't want to tell a child in crisis everything is going to be okay, because it might not be okay. What you can say is, "I'm going to sit here with you, and I'm going to make space for every tear that falls and for every feeling that you have. I'm going to make space for that, and I'm going to be here. In this moment you're safe."

I wanted to go back to school [and find a place to work] where I would want to leave my own children, and [I] wanted to influence policy and practice and knew I couldn't do that with a bachelor's. So I left town to find myself and figure out what I wanted to do. I went to Athens, Greece, to teach English to children for one year. When I came back, that's when I found the job at the crisis nursery. I couldn't stay sane working with kids at the [mental health facility] because I felt so powerless and the children were so damaged.

Advice

You need to respect that bond between parent and child. You can't tell a parent what to do. What's most important is what happens in the bond between the child and parent. Confidence, competence, and mutual respect are components necessary for work between children and parents. A parent is the most important person in a child's life. Point out to the parent what is happening, and that they do know what they are doing, that they are the experts on their child, that they do a lot of things right. I don't think a lot of parents hear what they do right very often. It's always what they're doing wrong and why it's their fault. If you can, focus on the positives and strengths to build the bond.

Family bonds are very important. They go deeper than you'll ever understand as a social worker. You have to respect the family and the bond between the parent and the child because I think it's so easy to want to go in and just fix it and you can't, nor should you. You need to remember that you are working for the parent and the child. You're honestly not there to teach them or change them.

[If parents are having problems parenting,] we use triadic strategies (work between parent, child, and child-care worker) to try to bring to their awareness what it is that they're doing and strengthen the bond, for example, pointing out [to the parent] that the child is looking at them with a loving gaze. It brings attention to the child and reminds parents that they are so important to the child. Dysfunction is something that is so deep-rooted that it needs to be addressed gently. Families have their own will, and you're not going to change that, and you shouldn't be burnt out by that. I think a lot of times social work and evidenced-based practice and models that you're going to apply to help families are not clean or neat. They don't just happen. You don't just do A, B, and C and get your results. It doesn't happen that way. It's messy work and important work. It's beautiful work and shouldn't be taken lightly. If you're in it to get something directly for yourself, like a result . . . you may never see results. And that's okay. If you know you're doing your work selflessly and for the parent and child, that's the most important work you can do. But you may never see an outcome that you want to see. You need to constantly remind yourself, what outcome does the parent want? The outcome is really driven by the family.

[Work with children and families] is going to get in and affect you. If something's affecting you, it's important to you. If it's not affecting you, it doesn't mean you should go find a different job, because sometimes we're not affected. Social workers are human. You need to take care of yourself. [Still, it is important] to find what does make [you] feel. [You] need to find what [you] are passionate about, what matters to [you]! This is important because this is where [you] will do [your] best work.

I see a lot of judging. Everyone judges because we're human. But if you can suspend those judgments and keep them at bay for a while in order to be surprised, or to learn more information, it can be really helpful and really useful in your work with children and families. You never know until you're in their shoes.

I felt hopeless working with the families at the [mental health facility], like, "Oh, this is what awaits the child. Oh, this is why the child is like that. Oh, I'm not going to be able to keep this child safe forever." So all these things we would teach on the [mental health] unit, like being a good friend, taking care of yourself, being respectful of others—all these things we want people to see in the world didn't apply to those children's lives. No one else was going to be a good friend when he went home. It wasn't going to translate. And so it quickly brought to mind the reality that being a good friend wasn't going to work in their lives. When they'd look at me, like "What do you mean be a good friend? That's ridiculous!" I could still teach them what that was like, but I needed to hear from them that that wasn't going to work. Or I needed to see that that wasn't going to work in their lives, when they left the [facility], and that was the reality, and still find a way I was going to be with them and help them look at some of their maladaptive behaviors that were probably going to get reinforced when they went home. But to know that I've done something—when you work with the whole [family] system and you do something for that system, so that it works better for them, then you've done your job, but you're not going to change them or the whole [family]. I'm glad I didn't give up because it was really difficult.

. . . I renewed myself by working with children in a different atmosphere, and came back knowing that I wanted to come at it in a different way, which is how I found the [crisis] nursery. Also some research work I did [as an MSW student] on domestic violence really opened my eyes to the fact that this is not something that just happened yesterday. This event has happened before, and increased my compassion for mothers . . . this event has been going on for a long time . . . Don't try to fix it all because we can't. What we can do is meet people on their paths and we can be with them in that moment and that's really important. If you make it bigger than that, it can be kind of overwhelming.

Seeing families and parents and seeing that they really do want to be good moms and dads. It's really difficult and really expensive to be poor. Just because you are poor and don't have resources at your fingertips does not mean you don't want your children to be in a safe place or that you just leave your children anywhere. How scary and how much trust must the parents have to leave their children [at the crisis nursery]. I would feel comfortable leaving my [own] child with any one of the staff persons here. We are mandated reporters, so if anything happens or is said we have to report, but I'm doing that hopefully with the family and not to the family. So I let them know we saw this or your child said [abuse or neglect happened], we have to report this. This is scary so let's do this, make it happen together.

Study and Discussion Questions

1. What is attachment?

2. How do caregivers and children vary in the quality or organization of their attachment relationships?

3. What experiences are associated with various types of attachment relationships?

4. What are the consequences of various types of attachment relationships to the child's development?

5. How do we interpret variation in attachment behavior within and across cultural communities?

6. Describe problematic aspects of attachment relationships, the experiences associated with them, and their impact on children's development.

7. Describe several preventive interventions for infants and their families.

8. What roles can social workers play in preventive interventions?

9. Some say the best way to support infants is to support their caregivers. What do you think?

10. Consider the Smith family. What are the risks and benefits of preventive interventions that allow Sally's parents to continue caring for her?

Resources

Interested students may supplement this chapter through a number of excellent web-based resources.

The American Academy of Family Physicians has an excellent article, "Primary Care of Infants and Young Children with Down Syndrome," at http://www.aafp.org/afp/990115ap/381.html.

The Centers for Disease Control and Prevention provides safety tips for protecting infants and young children around domestic pets, at http://www.cdc.gov/healthypets/child.htm.

The United Nations' World Health Organization provides an online booklet dedicated to issues of feeding and nutrition of infants and young children. The emphasis is on specific problems and solutions faced by families in countries that were formally part of the Soviet Union, and are currently economically struggling. Available at http://www.euro.who.int/__data/assets/pdf_file/0004/98302/WS_115_2000FE.pdf.

Infants & Young Children is an interdisciplinary journal aimed primarily at medical health professionals. The journal's core focus is on the clinical management of infants and young children with, or at risk for, developmental disabilities. The articles provide research, educational methods, diagnostic and treatment techniques, and therapeutic steps for supporting families. Available at http://journals.lww.com/iycjournal/pages/default.aspx.

The United Nations' World Health Organization provides an excellent international overview of the importance and methods for preventing HIV transmission to infants. Available at http://www.who.int/hiv/topics/mtct/en/index.html.

Autism and other pervasive developmental disorders strike the very young and last a lifetime. The Autism Society of America is the leading voice for the entire autism community and provides resources and support. Available at http://www.autism-society.org.

For students interested in cultural variation, we recommend the documentary film *Babies*, which chronicles development during the first year of life of four infants from around the world.

References

Ainsworth, M. (1967). *Infancy in Uganda: Infant care and the growth of love.* Baltimore: Johns Hopkins University Press.

Ainsworth, M. (1973). The development of infant-mother attachment. In B. M. Caldwell & H. N. Ricciuti (Eds.), *Review of child development research* (Vol. 3, pp. 1–94). Chicago: University of Chicago Press.

Ainsworth, M. (1989). Attachments beyond infancy. *American Psychologist, 44,* 709–716.

Ainsworth, M., & Bell, S. (1969). Some contemporary patterns of mother-infant interaction in the feeding situation. In A. Ambrose (Ed.), *Stimulation in early infancy* (pp. 133–163). New York: Academic Press.

Ainsworth, M., Blehar, M., Waters, E., & Wall, S. (1978) *Patterns of attachment*. Hillsdale, NJ: Erlbaum.

Ainsworth, M., & Marvin, R. (1995). On the shaping of attachment theory and research: An interview with Mary D. S. Ainsworth (Fall 1994). *Monographs of the Society for Research in Child Development, 60*(2–3, Serial No. 245), 3–21.

American Psychiatric Association. (2000). *Diagnostic and statistical manual of mental disorders* (4th ed., text revision). Washington, DC: Author.

Azzi-Lessing, L. (2010). Growing together: Expanding roles for social work practice in early childhood settings. *Social Work, 55*(3), 255–263.

Bamba, S., & Haight, W. (2011). *Child welfare and development: A Japanese case study*. New York: Cambridge University Press.

Barnett, D., Ganiban, J., & Cicchetti, D. (1999). Maltreatment, negative expressivity, and the development of Type D attachments from 12 to 24 months. In J. Vondra & D. Barnett (Eds.), Atypical attachment in infancy and early childhood among children at developmental risk. *Monographs of the Society for Research in Child Development, 64*(3), 97–118.

Barnett, D., & Vondra, J. (1999). Atypical patterns of early attachment: Theory, research and current directions. In J. Vondra & D. Barnett (Eds.), Atypical attachment in infancy and early childhood among children at developmental risk. *Monographs of the Society for Research in Child Development, 64*(3), 1–24.

Belsky, J. (2005). Attachment theory and research in ecological perspective: Insights from the Pennsylvania Infant and Family Development Project and the NICHD Study of Early Child Care. In K. E. Grossmann, K. Grossmann, & E. Waters (Eds.), *Attachment from infancy to adulthood: The major longitudinal studies* (pp. 71–97). New York: Guilford.

Belsky, J., & Pasco Fearon, R. M. (2002). Early attachment security, subsequent maternal sensitivity, and later child development: Does continuity in development depend upon continuity of caregiving? *Attachment and Human Development, 4*, 361–387.

Black, J., & Greenough, W. (1986). Induction of pattern in neural structure by experience: Implications for cognitive development. In M. E. Lamb, A. L. Brown, & B. Rogoff (Eds.), *Advances in developmental psychology* (Vol. 4, pp. 1–50). Hillsdale, NJ: Erlbaum.

Black, J. E., Jones, T. A., Nelson, C. A., & Greenough, W. T. (1998). Neural plasticity. In N. Alessi (Ed.) & J. T. Coyle (Section Ed.), *Handbook of child and adolescent psychiatry*: Vol. 4, *Varieties of development: Section I, Developmental neuroscience* (pp. 31–51). New York: Wiley.

Bloom, M., & Gullotta, T. (2008). Prevention. In T. Mizrahi & L. Davis (Eds.), *Encyclopedia of social work* (20th ed., Vol. 3, pp. 398–405). Washington, DC: NASW Press; New York: Oxford University Press.

Bornstein, M. A., & Cote, L. R. (2004). "Who is sitting across from me?" Immigrant mothers' knowledge of parenting and children's development. *Pediatrics, 114*, 557–564.

Bowlby, J. (1969/1982). *Attachment and loss:* Vol. 1, *Attachment*. New York: Basic Books.

Bowlby, J. (1973). *Attachment and loss: Separation:* Vol. 2, *Anxiety and anger*. New York: Basic Books.

Bowlby, J. (1980). *Attachment and loss:* Vol. 3, *Sadness and depression*. New York: Basic Books.

Carlson, E. (1998). A prospective longitudinal study of attachment disorganization/ disorientation. *Child Development, 69,* 1107–1128.

Carlson, V., Cicchetti, D., Barnett, D., & Braunwald, K. (1989). Finding order in disorganization: Lessons from research on maltreated infants' attachments to their caregivers. In D. Cicchetti & V. Carlson (Eds.), *Child maltreatment: Theory and research on the causes and consequences of child abuse and neglect* (pp. 494–528). New York: Cambridge University Press.

CDC Pregnancy Gateway. (n.d.). Retrieved from http://www.cdc.gov/ncbddd/ pregnancy_gateway/index.html

Centers for Disease Control and Prevention. (n.d.). *Fetal alcohol spectrum disorders.* Retrieved from CDC.gov/ncbddd/fasd/facts.html

Cicchetti, D. (2002). How a child builds a brain: Insights from normality and psychopathology. In W. Hartup & R. Weinberg (Eds.), *Minnesota Symposia on Child Psychology:* Vol. 35, *Child psychology in retrospect* (pp. 23–71). Mahwah, NJ: Erlbaum.

Clewell, B., Brooks-Gunn, J., & Benasich, A. (1989). Evaluating child-related outcomes of teenage parenting programs. *Family Relations, 38*(2), 201–209.

Cole, S. A. (2005). Infants in foster care: Relational and environmental factors affecting attachment. *Journal of Reproductive and Infant Psychology, 23,* 43–61.

Cole, S. A. (2006). Building secure relationships: Attachment in kin and unrelated foster caregiver-infant relationships. *Families in Society, 87,* 497–508.

Cole, S. A., Wehrmann, K. C., Dewar, G., & Swinford, L. (2005). Crises nurseries: Important services in a system of care for families and children. *Children and Youth Services Reviews, 27,* 995–1010.

Cowan, P. (1997). Beyond meta-analysis: A plea for a family systems view of attachment. *Child Development, 68,* 601–603.

Crittenden, P. (1995). Attachment and risk for psychopathology: The early years. *Developmental and Behavioral Pediatrics, 16,* 12–16.

Crittenden, P., & Ainsworth, M. (1989). Child maltreatment and attachment theory. In D. Cicchetti & V. Carlson (Eds.), *Child maltreatment: Theory and research on the causes and consequences of child abuse and neglect* (pp. 432–463). New York: Cambridge University Press.

De Wolff, M., & van Ijzendoorn, M. (1997). Sensitivity and attachment: A meta-analysis on parental antecedents of infant attachment. *Child Development, 68,* 571–591.

Dougherty, S., Yu, E., Edgar, M., Day, P., & Wade, C. (2002). *Planned and crisis respite for families with children: Results of a collaborative study.* Chapel Hill, NC: ARCH National Respite Network and Resource Center.

Erikson, E. (1963). *Childhood and society* (2nd ed.). New York: Norton.

Fifer, W., & Moon, C. (1995). The effects of fetal experience with sound. In J. Lecanuet, W. Fifer, N. Krasnegor, & W. Smotherman (Eds.), *Fetal development: A psychobiological perspective* (pp. 351–368). Mahwah, NJ: Erlbaum.

Francis, D., & Meaney, M. (1999). Maternal care and the development of stress responses. *Current Opinion in Neurobiology, 9,* 128–134.

Greenberg, M., Speltz, M., & DeKlyen, M. (1993). The role of attachment in the early development of disruptive behavior problems. *Development and Psychopathology, 5,* 191–213.

Grossmann, K., & Grossmann, K. E. (1981). Parent–infant attachment relationships in Bielefeld. In K. Immelman, G. Barlow, L. Petrovich, & M. Main (Eds.), *Behavioral development: The Bielefeld interdisciplinary project* (pp. 694–699). New York: Cambridge University Press.

Grossmann, K., Grossmann, K. E., Spangler, G., Suess, G., & Unzer, L. (1985). Maternal sensitivity and newborns' orientation responses as related to quality of attachment in northern Germany. In I. Bretherton & E. Waters (Eds.), Growing points of attachment theory and research. *Monographs of the Society for Research in Child Development, 50*(1–2), 233–256.

Haight, W., Kagle, J., & Black, J. (2003). Understanding and supporting parent-child relationships during foster care visits: Attachment theory and research. *Social Work, 48*(2), 195–208.

Harkness, S., & Super, C. (1996). Introduction. In S. Harkness & C. Super (Eds.), *Parents' cultural belief systems: Their origins, expressions, and consequences.* New York: Guilford.

Harwood, R., Miller, J., & Irizarry, N. (1995). *Culture and attachment: Perceptions of the child in context.* New York: Guilford.

Jacobsen, T., Miller, L. J., & Kirkwood, K. P. (1997). Assessing parenting competency in individuals with severe mental illness: A comprehensive service. *Journal of Mental Health Administration, 24*, 189–199.

James, W. T. (1890). *The principles of psychology.* New York: Holt, Rinehart & Winston.

Kaufman, J., & Charney, D. S. (1999). Neurobiological correlates of child abuse. *Biological Psychiatry, 45*, 1235–1236.

Kids Health. (n.d.). *Staying healthy during pregnancy.* Retrieved from http://kids health.org/parent/pregnancy_center/your_pregnancy/preg_health.html#

Knitzer, J., & Perry, D. F. (2009). Poverty and infant toddler development. In C. H. Zeanah Jr. (Ed.), *Handbook of infant mental health* (3rd ed., pp. 135–152). New York: Guilford.

Leon, M. (1992). The neurobiology of filial learning. *Annual Review of Psychology, 43*, 377–398.

Lightfoot, C., Cole, M., & Cole, S. (2009). *The development of children* (6th ed.). New York: Worth Publishers.

Long, M. S. (2009). Disorganized attachment relationships in infants of adolescent mothers and factors that may augment outcomes. *Adolescence, 44*, 621–633.

Lyons-Ruth, K., Alpern, L., & Repacholi, B. (1993). Disorganized infant attachment classification and maternal psychosocial problems as predictors of hostile-aggressive behavior in the preschool classroom. *Child Development, 64*, 572–585.

Lyons-Ruth, K., Bronfman, J., & Parsons, E. (1999). Maternal frightened, frightening, or atypical behavior and disorganized infant attachment patterns. In J. Vondra & D. Barnett (Eds.), Atypical attachment in infancy and early childhood among children at developmental risk. *Monographs of the Society for Research in Child Development, 64*(3), 67–96.

Lyons-Ruth, K., Easterbrooks, M., & Cibelli, C. (1997). Infant attachment strategies, infant mental lag, and maternal depressive symptoms: Predictors of internalizing and externalizing problems at age 7. *Developmental Psychology, 33*, 681–692.

MacDorman, M. F., & Mathews, T. J. (2008). *Recent trends in infant mortality in the United States* (NCHS data brief, No. 9). Hyattsville, MD: National Center for Health Statistics. Retrieved from http://www.cdc.gov/nchs/data/databriefs/db09.htm#arethere

Main, M. (1996). Introduction to the special section on attachment and psychopathology: 2, Overview of the field of attachment. *Journal of Consulting and Clinical Psychology, 64*, 237–243.

Main, M., & Cassidy, J. (1988). Categories of response to reunion with the parent at age six: Predicted from infant attachment classifications and stable over a one-month period. *Developmental Psychology, 24*, 415–426.

Main, M., & Hesse, E. (1990). Parents' unresolved traumatic experiences are related to infant disorganized attachment states: Is frightened or frightening parental behavior the linking mechanism? In M. Greenberg, D. Cichetti, & M. Cummings (Eds.), *Attachment in the preschool years* (pp. 161–182). Chicago: University of Chicago Press.

Main, M., Kaplan, N., & Cassidy, J. (1985). Security in infancy, childhood, and adulthood: A move to the level of representation. In I. Bretherton & E. Waters (Eds.), Growing points of attachment theory and research. *Monographs of the Society for Research in Child Development, 50*(1–2), 66–104.

Main, M., & Solomon, J. (1990). Procedures for identifying infants as disorganized/disoriented during the Ainsworth strange situation. In M. Greenberg, D. Cichetti, & N. Cummings (Eds.), *Attachment in the preschool years: Theory, research, and intervention* (pp. 676–678). Chicago: University of Chicago Press.

Malanga, C. J., & Kosofsky, B. E. (2004). Effects of drugs of abuse on brain development. In D. S. Charney & E. J. Nestler (Eds.), *Neurobiology of mental illness* (2nd ed.). New York: Oxford University Press.

Mangelsdorf, S., & Brown, G. (2009). Infant attachment. In R. Shweder (Ed.), *The child: An encyclopedic companion* (pp. 73–76). Chicago: University of Chicago Press.

Marvin, R. S., VanDevender, T., Iwanaga, M., LeVine, S., & LeVine, R. (1977). Infant-caregiver attachment among the Hausa of Nigeria. In H. McGurk (Ed.), *Ecological factors in human development* (pp. 247–259). Amsterdam: North-Holland.

McCollum, J. (1984). Social interaction between parents and babies: Validation of an intervention procedure. *Child: Care, Health and Development, 10*, 301–315.

McFarlane, E., Dodge, R. A. D., Crowne, R., Cheng, T. L., & Duggan, A. K. (2010). The importance of early parenting in at-risk families and children's social-emotional adaptation to school. *Academic Pediatrics, 10*, 330–337.

Miyake, K., Chen, S., & Campos, J. (1985). Infant temperament, mother's mode of interaction, and attachment in Japan: An interim report. In I. Bretherton & E. Waters (Eds.), Growing points of attachment theory and research. *Monographs of the Society for Research in Child Development, 50*(1–2), 276–297.

Moon, C., Cooper, R., & Fifer, W. (1993). Two-day-olds prefer their native language. *Infant Behavior Development, 16*, 495–500.

Osofsky, J. (1995a). Children who witness domestic violence: The invisible victims. *Social Policy Report, 9*(3), 1–16.

Osofsky, J. (1995b). The effects of violence exposure on young children. *American Psychologist, 50*, 782–788.

Paradis, H., Montes, G., & Szilagyi, P. G. (2008, May). *A national perspective on parents' knowledge of child development, its relation to parent-child interaction, and associated parenting characteristics.* Paper presented at Pediatric Academic Society, Honolulu, HI.

Parens, H. (1991). A view of the development of hostility in early life. *Journal of the American Psychoanalytic Association, 39* (Supplement), 75–108.

Pipp-Siegel, S., Siegel, C., & Dean, J. (1999). Neurological aspects of the disorganized/disoriented attachment classification system: Differentiating quality of the attachment relationship from neurological impairment. In J. Vondra & D. Barnett

(Eds.), Atypical attachment in infancy and early childhood among children at developmental risk. *Monographs of the Society for Research in Child Development, 64*(3), 25–44.

Pynoos, R., Steinberg, A., & Goenjian, A. (1996). Traumatic stress in childhood and adolescence: Recent developments and current controversies. In B. Van der Kolk, A. McFarlane, & L. Weisaeth (Eds.), *Traumatic stress: The effects of overwhelming experience on mind, body and society* (pp. 331–358). New York: Guilford.

Riley, E. P., Mattson, S. N., & Thomas, J. D. (2009). Fetal alcohol syndrome. In L. R. Squire (Ed.), *Encyclopedia of neuroscience* (Vol. 4, pp. 213–220). Oxford: Academic Press.

Sagi, A., Lamb, M., Lewkowicz, K., Shoham, R., Dvir, R., & Estes, D. (1985). Security of infant-mother, -father, and -metapelet attachments among kibbutz reared Israeli children. In I. Bretherton & E. Waters (Eds.), Growing points of attachment theory and research. *Monographs of the Society for Research in Child Development, 50*(1–2), 257–275.

Schneider-Rosen, K., Braunwald, K., Carlson, V., & Cicchetti, D. (1985). Current perspectives in attachment theory: Illustration from the study of maltreated infants. In I. Bretherton & E. Waters (Eds.), Growing points of attachment theory and research. *Monographs of the Society for Research in Child Development, 50*(1–2), 194–210.

Shonkoff, J. P., & Philips, D. A. (2001) *From neurons to neighborhoods: The science of early childhood development.* Washington, DC: National Academy Press.

Shweder, R., Goodnow, J., Hatano, G., LeVine, R., Markus, H., & Miller, P. (1998). The cultural psychology of development: One mind, many mentalities. In W. Damon & R. M. Lerner (Eds.), *Handbook of child psychology:* Vol. 1, *Theoretical models of human development* (5th ed., pp. 865–938). New York: Wiley.

Spiker, D., Boyce, G. C., & Boyce, L. K. (2002). Parent-child interactions when young children have disabilities. *International Review of Mental Retardation, 25*, 35–70.

Sroufe, L. A., Carlson, E. A., Levy, A. K., & Egeland, B. (2003). Implications of attachment theory for developmental psychopathology. In M. E. Hertzig & E. A. Farber (Eds.), *Annual progress in child psychiatry and child development: 2000–2001* (pp. 43–61). New York: Brunner-Routledge.

Stephans, D. (1999). Battered women's views of their children. *Journal of Interpersonal Violence, 14*(7), 731–746.

Stevenson-Hinde, J. (1994). An ethological perspective. *Psychological Inquiry, 5*, 62–65.

Streissguth, A. P., Bookstein, F. L., Barr, H. M., Sampson, P. D., O'Malley, K., & Young, J. K. (2004). Risk factors for adverse life outcomes in fetal alcohol syndrome and fetal alcohol effects. *Journal of Developmental and Behavioral Pediatrics, 25*(4), 228–238.

Subramanian, K. (1985). Reducing child abuse through respite center intervention. *Child Welfare, 64*, 501–509.

Suomi, S. J. (1999). Attachment in rhesus monkeys. In J. Cassidy & P. R. Shaver (Eds.), *Handbook of attachment: Theory, research, and clinical implications* (pp. 181–197). New York: Guilford.

Thompson, R. (1998). Early sociopersonality development. In W. Damon & R. M. Lerner (Eds.), *Handbook of child psychology:* Vol. 3, *Social, emotional and personality development* (5th ed., pp. 25–104). New York: Wiley.

Tomlinson, M., Cooper, P., & Murray, L. (2005). The mother-infant relationship and infant attachment in a South African peri-urban settlement. *Child Development, 76,* 1044–1054.

Tough, P. (2008). *Whatever it takes: Geoffrey Canada's quest to change Harlem and America.* New York: Houghton Mifflin.

U.S. Department of Health and Human Services, Health Resources and Services Administration, Maternal and Child Health Bureau. (2009). *Child health USA 2008–2009.* Rockville, MD: U.S. Department of Health and Human Services. Retrieved from http://mchb.hrsa.gov/chusa08/pdfs/c08.pdf

van Ijzendoorn, M. H. (1995). Adult attachment representations, parental responsiveness, and infant attachment: A meta-analysis on the predictive validity of the adult attachment interview. *Psychological Bulletin, 117,* 387–403.

van Ijzendoorn, M. H., Goldberg, S., Kroonenberg, P. M., & Frenkel, O. J. (1992). The relative effects of maternal and child problems on the quality of attachment: A meta-analysis of attachment in clinical samples. *Child Development, 63,* 840–858.

van Ijzendoorn, M. H., & Sagi, A. (1999). Cross-cultural patterns of attachment: Universal and contextual dimensions. In J. Cassidy & P. R. Shaver (Eds.), *Handbook of attachment: Theory, research, and clinical applications* (pp. 713–734). New York: Guilford.

Vondra, J., Hommerding, K., & Shaw, D. (1999). Stability and change in infant attachment in a low-income sample. In J. Vondra & D. Barnett (Eds.), Atypical attachment in infancy and early childhood among children at developmental risk. *Monographs of the Society for Research in Child Development, 64*(3), 119–144.

Weiss, E., Longhurst, J., & Mazure, C. (1999). Childhood sexual abuse as a risk factor for depression in women: Psychosocial and neurobiological correlates. *American Journal of Psychiatry, 156,* 816–828.

Xu, J., Kochanek, K. D., Murphy, S. L., & Tejada-Vera, B. (2010). Deaths: Final data for 2007. *CDC national vital statistics reports, 58*(19). Retrieved from http://www.cdc.gov/nchs/data/nvsr/nvsr58/nvsr58_19.pdf

Zeanah, C. H., Boris, N. W., & Larrieu, J. A. (1997). Infant development and developmental risk: A review of the past 10 years. *Journal of the Academy of Child and Adolescent Psychiatry, 36,* 165–178.

Zeanah, C. H., Mammen, O., & Lieberman, A. (1993). Disorders of attachment. In C. Zeanah (Ed.), *Handbook of infant mental health* (pp. 332–349). New York: Guilford.

Zeanah, C. H., Smyke, A. T., Koga, S. F., Carlson, E., & Bucharest Early Intervention Core Group. (2005). Attachment in institutionalized and community children in Romania. *Child Development, 76,* 1015–1028.

6

Social Work with Young Children
Expanding Relationships and Developmental Contexts

This chapter considers the young child as the focal system and the rapid changes that occur during the course of early childhood. As you read, think about the young child's developing biological, psychological, and social competencies, as well as the physical and social ecologies in which these achievements emerge. This chapter highlights microsystems that influence development from the age of two and a half to six. Young children typically participate in relationships that include parents, siblings, peers, child-care providers, and extended family members. These interactions take place in an expanding array of developmental contexts, including home, peer groups, and child care. Despite their impressive developmental accomplishments, young children remain dependent on their caregivers. If problems emerge, social workers in the field of child welfare may intervene. These professionals are called upon to make complex decisions about the safety of the child, and interventions to support the caregiver's ability to provide for the child's basic physical and psychological needs. As you read, consider how interventions that may be necessary for the young child's safety, for example, temporary out-of-home placement in foster care, can affect children's development. What are the unintended consequences of child welfare interventions?

By the age of two and a half to three, typically developing children are clearly no longer babies. They grow taller and lose their baby fat, use the toilet, ride tricycles, communicate well in their native languages, develop elaborate forms of play and humor, and form complex relationships with a widening array of individuals. Despite their impressive achievements, young children still need help from caregivers with most aspects of daily living, including basic hygiene (e.g., bathing, tying shoes), meals, and safety (e.g., crossing a busy street, dressing appropriately for the weather). They understand relatively little about the wider world, and have minimal control over many aspects of their daily lives. When problems arise in their families over which young children have no control, their development and well-being may be affected. For instance, box 6.1 describes the impact of witnessing domestic violence on young children.

BOX 6.1 VIOLENCE ACROSS THE LIFE SPAN

The Impact of Domestic Violence on Young Children

Domestic violence (intimate-partner violence) is abuse within close, loving, romantic relationships. It is witnessed annually by an estimated 9.8 percent of children in the United States. Exposure to violence can have damaging consequences for the physical and mental health of children and for their long-term functioning and well-being as adults. Although caretakers frequently believe they are protecting their children from witnessing their abuse, children living in these homes report differently. Researchers have found that 80–90 percent of children in homes where domestic violence occurs can provide detailed accounts of the violence in their homes. The effects of domestic violence on children include these problems:

- Behavioral, social, and emotional problems—higher levels of aggression, anger, hostility, oppositional behavior, and disobedience; fear, anxiety, withdrawal, and depression; poor peer, sibling, and social relationships; low self-esteem.

- Cognitive and attitudinal problems—lower cognitive functioning, poor school performance, lack of conflict-resolution skills, limited problem-solving skills, acceptance of violent behaviors and attitudes, belief in rigid gender stereotypes and male privilege.

- Long-term problems—higher levels of adult depression and trauma symptoms, increased tolerance for and use of violence in adult relationships.

Children also display specific problems unique to their physical, psychological, and social development. For example, infants exposed to violence may have difficulty developing attachments with their caregivers and in extreme cases suffer from "failure to thrive." Preschool children may regress developmentally or suffer from eating and sleep disturbances. School-age children may struggle with peer relationships, academic performance, and emotional stability. Adolescents are at a higher risk for either perpetrating or becoming victims of teen dating violence. Reports from adults who repeatedly witnessed domestic violence as children show that many suffer from trauma-related symptoms, depression, and low self-esteem.

Here are some possible symptoms in children exposed to domestic violence:

- sleeplessness, fears of going to sleep, nightmares, dreams of danger

- physical symptoms such as headaches or stomachaches

- hypervigilance to danger or being hurt
- fighting with others, hurting other children or animals
- temper tantrums or defiant behavior
- withdrawal from people or typical activities
- listlessness, depression, low energy
- feelings of loneliness and isolation
- current or subsequent substance misuse
- suicide attempts or engaging in dangerous behavior
- poor school performance
- difficulties concentrating and paying attention
- fears of being separated from the nonabusing parent
- feeling that his or her best is not good enough
- taking on adult or parental responsibilities
- excessive worrying
- bed-wetting or regression to earlier developmental stages
- dissociation
- identifying with or mirroring behaviors of the abuser

Children's risk levels and reactions to domestic violence exist on a continuum where some children demonstrate enormous resiliency while others show signs of significant maladaptive adjustment. Protective factors include social competence, intelligence, high self-esteem, outgoing temperament, strong sibling and peer relationships, a supportive relationship with an adult, nature of the violence (children who see adults resolve the conflict experience better outcomes), and being older (younger children may not possess the cognitive skills necessary to make sense of witnessing violence).

—————
Sources: Bragg, 2003; Finkelhor, Turner, Ormrod, Hamby, & Kracke, 2009.

CHILD WELFARE WITH YOUNG CHILDREN

Given their greater vulnerability, infants and young children are a special concern of social workers in **child welfare** practice. Child welfare is the government-organized, formal service-delivery system designed to assist children from birth through adolescence who have been abused or neglected, or whose well-being is at risk. In the United States, child welfare services are the responsibility of each state, and vary in organization from statewide systems to loosely networked county-by-county systems (Downs, Costin, & McFadden, 1996). In many states with "statewide" child welfare systems, the state contracts with private agencies such as Children's Home and Aid, Catholic Charities, and Lutheran Social Services to provide child welfare services to families in or near their own communities. Because of the high demand for child welfare services and the limited pool of trained personnel, some staff may not have social work training, and the turnover rate is often high. In Illinois, practitioners who provide child welfare services receive training prescribed by the Department of Children and Family Services to ensure that they have adequate skills and knowledge.

Federal government policy supports a range of services provided by state governments and private agencies to vulnerable children and families. Services include in-home support for children and their struggling families, treatment for parents' substance misuse or mental health problems, and if need be, out-of-home, foster-care placement for children. Recent legislation (Fostering Connections to Success and Increasing Adoptions Act of 2008, PL 110-351) provides support for children to be placed with relative caregivers, or in permanent adoptive homes. Through networking with other service providers, child welfare agencies also attempt to find services that address the social conditions that negatively affect children and families, such as inadequate housing, poverty, substance misuse, domestic violence, and lack of access to adequate health and mental health services (Liederman, 1995).

In the United States, children under one year of age have the highest incidence of placement in foster care (Wulczyn & Brunner, 2000), and infants three months and younger are most at risk for foster-care placement (Wulczyn, Hislop, & Harden, 2002). The rate of placement for children younger than one year is more than double the rate of children age one through three, and more than four times that of children age four through seventeen. Infants in urban areas (primarily African Americans) are at the highest risk, with 1.5 percent of all urban children younger than one year entering foster care (Wulczyn & Brunner, 2000). Although foster care may protect children's physical safety, it does put their emerging attachment relationships with family members at risk. In addition, when infants and young children experience multiple foster-care placements, their subsequent abilities to form attachment relationships may be impaired (Dozier et al., 2001).

When infants and young children enter foster care, it is essential for foster parents to establish attachment relationships with them. This task can be especially challenging because infants and young children in foster care are at special risk, and many have multiple, complex needs (Berrick, Needell, Barth, & Jonson-Reid, 1998). They may enter foster care substance-exposed, neglected, and with developmental delays and medical problems (Leslie et al., 2005). Overall, infants and young children in foster care have three to seven times more chronic emotional disorders and chronic medical conditions than children of similar socioeconomic backgrounds who remain at home (Blatt & Simms, 1997), and they experience disproportionate rates of developmental delays (Cicchetti & Toth, 1995).

Child welfare systems vary around the world, reflecting social and cultural beliefs regarding the causes and consequences of maltreatment. How child abuse and neglect are defined and understood, including interpretations for why caregivers abuse their children and the consequences of maltreatment, vary throughout the world. For example, in middle-class families in the United States, it is common and often seen as preferable for infants and young children to have their own bedrooms away from parents and other siblings. In Micronesia, this same practice of having the infant and young child sleep apart from other family members is considered neglect (Le, 2000).

Cultural and subcultural variation also exists in perspectives on appropriate societal responses to child maltreatment. What are the moral and pragmatic obligations of society, for example, to provide resources to support vulnerable families and to maintain infants and young children within their birth families? Some cultures place these responsibilities with the extended family, others with religious organizations, and some with the government (Ippen, 2009). The U.S. child welfare system is but one possible response among many to the inappropriate treatment of children. Examination of child welfare in other societies can provide an important vantage point from which to consider our own assumptions about maltreatment, and the quality of our own practices. Box 6.2 describes aspects of child welfare in Japan.

BOX 6.2 INTERNATIONAL PERSPECTIVES
Child Welfare in Japan

In Japan, parental social isolation is viewed as a primary risk factor in maltreatment, addressed more often than poverty. In an urbanized society, where interpersonal relationships are highly valued, an individual who lacks a sense of community and informal, mutual support systems can feel "socially dead." In their stress and frustration, these parents may maltreat their children. For example, it was argued during the Hyogo Prefecture Child Maltreatment Prevention Professionals' Meeting that child maltreatment is likely to occur when parents live in a "stifling" situation, isolated from the community and relatives. The goal, then, is to create a support system where each parent and child can find their own Ibasho, that is, a "place" where they can feel peace, stability, belonging, and security to fully express themselves. Developing interpersonal relationships that are accepting and supportive, where one feels valued, typically is central to finding one's Ibasho.

Source: Bamba & Haight, 2011.

In this chapter, we elaborate upon how a developmental, ecological-systems analysis can inform one important issue in child welfare practice: supporting the attachment relationships of infants and young children who are in foster care. We begin with a case illustrating the complexity of this task.

In the following excerpt, two-and-a-half-year-old Sharon and Priscilla, her mother, are briefly reunited for a visit following a month-long separation. Priscilla, who is addicted to heroin, was charged with child neglect several months earlier when Sharon and her three-and-a-half-year-old sister were found wandering, unsupervised, near a busy intersection. Following an investigation by social workers specializing in child welfare, they were placed in foster care with their elderly great-grandmother.

> Sharon (with hair carefully braided and dressed in a beautiful, immaculate Sunday dress) arrived at the playroom before her mother and stood, quietly examining the xylophone mallet. When Priscilla arrived, she and Sharon did not immediately greet one another. Priscilla stood near the door, holding her coat, and Sharon stood across the room looking down at the mallet in her hands. Priscilla did not bend down or move toward Sharon. She looked over Sharon's head and appeared tense. Sharon initiated the first interaction by holding the mallet out to Priscilla. Priscilla asked if Sharon wanted her to sing, but Sharon made no response. Priscilla then greeted her, "Hi, Sharon," and "Hi, how you doing?" but Sharon did not respond or acknowledge these greetings. Then Priscilla, still standing upright, reached out for the mallet, and Sharon handed it to her. They both stood still for a moment, and then Sharon turned away, pulled out a chair and sat, quietly, facing away from Priscilla . . . Thirteen minutes into the visit, Priscilla drew Sharon to her for a hug. Sharon initially was stiff and unresponsive, but then relaxed, laid her head on her mother's shoulder, and cried softly. Priscilla kissed her and asked, "What's wrong? . . . Your mommy love you" (Haight, Black, Workman, & Tata, 2001, p. 330).

Social workers practicing in child welfare settings routinely make complex and difficult decisions regarding the best interests of vulnerable children like Sharon. What are the risks to Sharon of placing her in foster care, particularly to her developing attachment relationships with her birth family? How does one determine when the home environment is safe and, if necessary, with whom an infant or young child should be placed: an elderly relative who, like Sharon's great-grandmother, the child knows but who may develop health problems necessitating another move, or a foster family, perhaps one pursuing adoption?

The decisions that child welfare professionals make regarding children's safety and permanency are especially complex when parents suffer from addiction, other mental illnesses, or major disabilities. Some parents are able to recover from substance misuse or other mental illnesses and go on to successfully care for their children. Others develop strategies for parenting despite developmental disabilities or while suffering with chronic physical or mental illnesses. In Illinois, a parenting assessment team comprising social workers, psychologists, and psychiatrists worked together to develop and apply criteria for assessing the competency of parents with severe mental illnesses who are involved with the public child welfare system (Jacobsen, Miller, & Kirkwood, 1997). Although severe mental illness typically disrupts parenting, some parents are able to parent adequately, given appropriate support. Rather than automatically removing infants and young children from their mentally ill parents' care and thus disrupting the developing attachment relationships, the parenting assessment team designed comprehensive evaluative techniques to determine when it was safe for an infant or young child to remain in the care of, or return to the care of, a parent with a major mental illness. These assessments include a complete psychiatric evaluation of the parent and developmental screening of the child, videotaped observations of parent-child interaction to assess attachment and parental behaviors that are associated with maltreatment, parents' responses to a variety of questionnaires, parents' understanding of the child and the parent-child relationship, interviews with parents, an appraisal of the home environment, interviews with collateral historians such as health and day-care providers to obtain additional information on families, and a review of pertinent records. These data are then used to make well-informed decisions about the safety and placement of children. Given the shortage of adoptive homes for children of color, older children, and children with special needs, the recovery or development of their parents may be the best chance that many children like Sharon have for a stable attachment relationship and permanent home.

To provide perspective on child welfare in early childhood, we will begin with a brief overview of the rapid developmental changes that occur during this time. Then we examine child welfare practices that support attachment relationships in early childhood.

HIGHLIGHTS OF DEVELOPMENT DURING EARLY CHILDHOOD

By early childhood (approximately two and a half to six years of age), children clearly are no longer babies. They can communicate through language, understand their everyday physical and social worlds, and participate in their own basic care. Their increasing abilities to communicate, think, and play provide them with opportunities for interacting with a range of adults and children in a variety of contexts. Typically developing, healthy young children may ride tricycles with siblings, join in the pretend play of neighborhood friends, express their opinions forcefully to caregivers, interact with nonkin adults while out with caregivers in the community, and participate in preschool or day care.

Physical milestones of development in early childhood include an increasing ability to control the body. Typical gross motor developments include running, kicking, climbing, throwing, and skipping. Fine motor developments include unbuttoning, using eating utensils, pouring liquid into a glass, and coloring within the lines. During early childhood, the brain grows to 90 percent of its full weight, with myelination (the insulating sheath of tissue around a nerve fiber) and neuronal branching continuing in the frontal cortex and other regions that are important to advanced intellectual functions, such as regulating behavior (Lightfoot, Cole, & Cole, 2009). Sociocultural context can have an important impact on physical and psychological development of young children. For instance, box 6.3 describes the impact of poverty on children's health.

BOX 6.3 POVERTY ACROSS THE LIFE SPAN
Poverty and Children's Health

Poverty impacts children's health in a variety of ways, including access to routine health care. Nationally, over 8 million American children (11 percent) are without health insurance. Despite the recommendation of the American Academy of Pediatrics that children see a doctor at least annually, in 2007 almost 21 percent of children between ten and fourteen and 22 percent of youth age fifteen to seventeen did not see a medical doctor. Moreover, approximately 12 percent of all children under eighteen years of age had no doctor visits within the past year. Hispanic children were the least likely to visit a medical doctor.

Source: U.S. Department of Health and Human Services, 2009.

Psychological milestones of early childhood include significant cognitive and socioemotional development. During early childhood, children's memory increases, as does their basic knowledge of physical laws and properties of objects, such as gravity and inertia. They also develop coherent theories about mental life and activity. Nonetheless, they still tend to confuse appearance with reality, have difficulty taking the perspective of others, and have limited cause-effect reasoning. Young children become fluent in their native language, perhaps the most intellectually complex task any of us will ever encounter in our lifetime. They also begin to understand the concepts of boy and girl, and ethnicity. They display an increased ability to regulate their emotions and actions, and to feel empathy toward others (Lightfoot, Cole, & Cole, 2009). Erikson describes a major psychosocial crisis of early childhood as initiative versus guilt, as children gain the ability to accomplish basic tasks such as dressing on their own (Erikson, 1963). Most young children also spend considerable amounts of time in increasingly complex forms of play.

Play

Play is an important activity of early childhood that exemplifies how sociocultural contexts interact with children's bio-psycho-social development. It is one of the important ways in which young children interact with and make sense of their social, emotional, and physical worlds. Play, in its many forms, is a universal activity of early childhood. Around the world

Play is central to development in early childhood. This young mother is taking her young children to visit and play with friends.

young children may roughhouse; sing and tease; build creations with mud, sticks, clay, or blocks; and pretend. Play is part of our genetic heritage and is important for healthy development. Yet how much children play, the way that they play, and with whom they play is fundamentally shaped by their sociocultural contexts.

Pretending is one form of play in early childhood that has received a great deal of attention. During **pretend play**, actions, objects, and persons are transformed or treated nonliterally. For example, a child may use a stick as a magic wand, gesture as if sleeping, or take on the role of parent while coordinating a complex plot with several friends. Virtually all major developmental theorists from Freud to Piaget to Vygotsky stress the importance of play. Freud (1961) was interested in the role of play in emotional well-being. For him, play is a repetition compulsion, a therapeutic activity in which children relive painful past experiences in order to work through the feelings caused by the experiences. Piaget (1962) was interested in children's intellectual development. For him, play reflects and consolidates development. Children play for the pleasure of exercising their newly developed competencies, for example, their abilities to use symbols. Play may consolidate developmental achievements, but does not actually facilitate new development.

In contrast to Piaget, Vygotsky (1962, 1978) was interested in the role of the sociocultural context in development. He viewed play as the leading activity of development. He referred to play as the zone of proximal development in which the imagined situation allows children to function beyond their existing level of competence. As children enact the familiar roles and daily activities that reflect cultural norms and values, they come to better understand implicit rules of social behavior. Vygotsky provided a memorable example of two sisters "pretending" to be sisters. To successfully enact the role of "sister," these children had to make explicit those social roles that previously were implicit in their daily lives. For example, they exaggerated their similarities to one another vis-à-vis others. Vygotsky also emphasized pretend play as a mechanism in language development. He claimed that the ability to represent an experience (e.g., feeding a baby) through a symbolic means (e.g., putting a stick in a doll's mouth) enables children to grasp the notion that words can be used to represent the meaning of experience (Goncu, Tuermer, Jain, & Johnson, 1999).

A number of more recent scholars have emphasized play as a sociocultural activity (e.g., Goncu, 1999; Goncu & Gaskins, 2006). One challenge is to understand those aspects of play that are universal, a product of our common human heritage, and how play is shaped within particular sociocultural-historical contexts. In one study, European-American families from Chicago and Taiwanese families from Taipei were followed longitudinally from the time their children were two and a half until they were four years of age (Haight, Wang, Fung, Williams, & Mintz, 1999). Consistent with Vygotskian theory, children's play in Chicago and Taipei was fundamentally social, moving from the interpersonal as children initially played with more experienced partners to the intrapersonal as their ability to sustain and elaborate play independently grew. As the following case excerpts of Angu and Nancy illustrate, however, the content of this play and the ways in which it was socially structured varied in relation to its sociocultural contexts. In the following excerpt, two-and-a-half-year-old Angu and her caregiver are playing school in the living room of their compact apartment in Taipei (Haight, 1999, p. 128, translated from the Mandarin).

> CAREGIVER, *smiling*: Stand up, bow, sit down, Teacher is going to deliver a lesson. *[Angu, smiling, moves closer to her caregiver.]*
>
> CAREGIVER: Teacher is coming to the classroom. What should the class monitor say?
>
> ANGU: Stand up!
>
> CAREGIVER: OK. Stand up. *[Angu stands up and bows.]*
>
> CAREGIVER: Sit down . . . *[They read a story.]*
>
> CAREGIVER: We have finished the story. *[She claps her hands.]* . . . Before we dismiss the class, the class monitor should say: "Stand up! Bow! Sit down!" Stand up. *[Angu stands up.]*
>
> CAREGIVER: Bow! *[Angu bows.]*
>
> CAREGIVER: Class is dismissed. Go play on the slide *[indicates imaginary sliding board in the living room]*. Class is dismissed and you are happy.

Halfway around the world, three-year-old Nancy and her caregiver also are pretending together in their house in Chicago. Nancy's mother is preparing decorations for a Halloween party when Nancy begins to show signs of boredom. Her mother suggests that she drive her car (Haight & Miller, 1993, p.1).

> Nancy retrieves a child-size, red plastic dashboard with steering wheel and seatbelt, and positions herself for driving. "Be sure to fasten your seatbelt, right?" reminds her mother, "Buckle up for safety!" Nancy fastens her seat belt, turns the steering wheel, and pushes the horn. To her mother's queries, "Where are you going? Are you taking a trip?" Nancy replies, "To Havana" . . . Nancy continues to steer the car while demonstrating how to drive. "You drive a car like this. Like this. OK?" She explains that Havana is far away and discusses with her mother how many stops will be needed en route, and how old one must be to get a driver's license.

Angu, Nancy, and their caregivers display a variety of similarities in their interactions. Both Angu and Nancy frequently engage in pretend play with their caregivers, and both children develop into skillful pretenders. Furthermore, both caregivers encourage their children's pretending within such everyday contexts as caregiving, cooking, and cleaning. Sometimes they even use their children's interests in pretending to encourage cooperation or to teach. For example, Nancy's mother is able to complete her Halloween preparations by simultaneously alleviating her daughter's boredom with a pretend game. She even manages to insert a safety lesson ("Be sure to fasten your seatbelt, right? . . . Buckle up for safety!").

Despite their similarities, there are also substantial variations in the ways in which Angu and Nancy interact with their caregivers, and the apparent social functions of those interactions. In contrast to Nancy's caregiver, Angu's caregiver frequently uses her child's interest in pretending to rehearse appropriate conduct such as formal interactions with a teacher ("Before we dismiss the class, the class monitor should say: 'Stand up! Bow! Sit down!'") Furthermore, she leads the interaction throughout the play, introducing topics, and providing instructions. Nancy's caregiver also initiates the play, but then she allows her daughter to lead the interaction, supporting and elaborating Nancy's ideas.

How can one understand these intercultural similarities and differences? The styles of interaction and functions of caregiver-child pretend play in Angu's and Nancy's homes seem to reflect caregivers' sensitivities both to young children's development and to broader, culturally specific socialization beliefs and goals. Angu's caregiver is concerned with teaching her child proper conduct during hierarchically organized adult-child interactions. Nancy's caregiver is concerned with supporting her child's individuality and self-expression. Both caregivers apparently use caregiver-child pretend play to support their children's development of culturally valued characteristics, and they do so through developmentally and culturally appropriate communicative practices (Haight, 1999).

Through pretend play, young children can express and communicate their emerging concerns and interpretations of the social and cultural world. As an interpretive activity, pretend play allows children to explore, practice, and critique emotions they have observed or experienced (Haight, 2006). Pretend play offers children an important outlet to express negative emotions that are inherent in increasing demands to follow social rules, everyday stresses, and more serious trauma in a context with no real-world consequences. In a study of children experiencing chronic illness (diabetes and asthma), Cindy Dell Clark (2003) described the pervasive and spontaneous use of pretend play by chronically ill children as a means of coping with the vicissitudes of illness and treatment. These children engaged in pretend play to reassure themselves about painful treatments and worrisome symptoms, and to compensate for vulnerable feelings related to their illness and treatment. Through pretend play they transformed threatening, painful, or frightening events into occasions for mastery or even celebration.

In addition to facilitating children's learning about emotions, pretend play facilitates adults' learning about children, and children's and adults' learning together. In the words of a young mother of a two-and-a-half-year-old: "I have a tendency of watching how she's pretending . . . to see if she is having any anxieties or worries or, you know, happiness that she wants to share with me that maybe she, at her age, isn't able to come right out and say, 'I'm scared about this' . . . It's important for me to *see* what's on her mind" (Haight, Parke, & Black, 1997).

When children and adults pretend together, they may spontaneously co-construct an interpretation of the social and cultural world as issues naturally emerge in the contexts of their everyday lives. Such communications may be particularly important when young children experience highly stressful or traumatic events. Indeed, pretend play has been used extensively by play therapists to facilitate children's recovery from trauma (see Webb, 2002).

Despite the centrality of play to development in early childhood, busy adults may devalue this activity. Parents, eager to support their young children's success in life, may fill children's days with structured activities such as group music classes for tots, gymnastics classes for preschoolers, and school learning activities at home. In day-care centers, preschools, and kindergartens, academic content is introduced to children at younger and younger ages. In contrast to traditional play-based curriculums, many preschools focus on teaching letters and numbers and other academic skills that are traditionally taught in kindergarten or even first grade. These trends have been the subject of much criticism from experts in early-childhood development (Hirsh-Pasek & Golinkoff, 2003; Zigler, Singer, & Bishop-Josef, 2004). Social workers, particularly those who are consultants to preschool programs and who participate in early intervention, can have an important role in advocating the importance of young children's play.

Supporting Young Children's Development through Parent-Child Visitation

Play is a fundamental way in which young children express and communicate their feelings, learn, and relate to their environments. Yet play may be suppressed under conditions of stress. When young children are placed in foster care, the stress they experience, both from the maltreatment that led to child welfare involvement and the subsequent separation from their parents and placement in another family, may disrupt their development through suppressing play as well as disrupting attachment relationships.

The scheduled, face-to-face contact between parents and their children in foster care is the primary child welfare intervention for supporting the development of adequate attachment relationships while children are in foster care. Regular visits are considered so critical to the effort to reunite families that the Adoption Assistance and Child Welfare Act of 1980 (PL 96-272) requires inclusion of regular visits in family preservation efforts. Ideally, parent-child visits occur frequently and in a comfortable, homelike setting in which parent and child can interact in various ways, including through play. In reality, however, the environment in which children and parents visit may be less than ideal: a sterile office with no toys or other amenities, and under the watchful eyes of foster parents, social workers, or other outsiders.

Not surprisingly, existing research suggests that visits often fall short of meeting their goals. Indeed, parents, foster parents, social workers, and adolescents in care report a range of emotional and behavioral responses to visits. Sometimes visits evoke painful feelings about separation, and the child's behavior worsens following the visit (see Haight, Kagle, & Black, 2003). Sometimes parent-child interaction clearly is supportive of the development of positive relationships—the parent and child are responsive and positive toward each other—and sometimes more problematic aspects of interaction emerge (see Haight et al., 2001; Haight et al., 2005).

In a study of parents' visits with their young children that occurred in a comfortable, homelike, and child-friendly setting, pretend play was a common parent-child activity (Haight et al., 2001). Much of the pretend play revolved around everyday routines such as talking on the telephone, eating, and caring for babies. Mothers typically encouraged children to behave in ways appropriate to the larger sociocultural context (e.g., to feed and hold the baby gently), and they typically pretended around themes embraced by the child. In some instances, pretend play became a venue through which mothers reminded young children of the mundane, everyday routines they had shared when the children were at home. In the following example of pretend play, Susan reminded two-and-a-half-year-old Anna of their shared dinner and bedtime routines.

Susan and Anna are pretending with a dollhouse. They have chosen dolls to represent Susan, Anna, and Anna's older sister, Melinda, who is not at the visit.

> SUSAN: You want to sit at the table with Melinda? *[Susan places the Anna doll in a chair at the table.]* You know how we used to do it at home? Do you have another chair so Mommy can sit at the table? *[They place the Susan doll at the table.]* . . . What do we do at home? We put you in the highchair, right? *[They change the Anna doll to the highchair, and the dinner play continues.]* . . .
>
> ANNA: That's you! *[Referring to the Susan doll.]*
>
> SUSAN: Are you talking to the Mama Susan? Hmm?
>
> ANNA: That you.
>
> SUSAN: Yeah.

ANNA: Yeah.

SUSAN: Does Mama Susan read books to you when you go to bed at night?

ANNA: Yeah . . .

In this play episode, Susan connects with her daughter emotionally and reminds her of their shared lives together and her commitment to their remaining together. By reminding Anna of the daily routines they had shared, Susan reminded Anna that she was her mother and was there to help her. For a young child who is experiencing the trauma of a prolonged and forced separation from a caregiver, this is critical information that may help to sustain the parent-child attachment relationship (Haight, Black, Ostler, & Sheridan, 2006).

Although mother-child pretend play typically was supportive of children's prosocial behavior and well-being, there was considerable diversity in its content and the ways in which it was socially conducted during visits. As illustrated by the following excerpt of Shareese and three-year-old Robert's visit, pretend play occasionally may include antisocial themes or be resisted by the child. Before their involvement with child protective services, Shareese and Robert had lived together in a public housing facility notorious for its violence. Before and after participation in this visit, Robert visited Shareese in jail where she was serving time for selling drugs.

> SHAREESE: Look. I'm gonna handcuff you. *[Picking up play handcuffs. Smiling, she takes Robert by the arm and tries to lead him back to the chair. He whimpers and resists.]*
>
> SHAREESE: C'mere. *[Robert whines. Shareese frowns.]* Gun—C'mere! C'mere! *[She pulls Robert back to the chair, sits in the chair, and stands Robert in front of her.]*
>
> SHAREESE: C'mere. Turn around. Put your hands behind your back. *[Shareese puts a toy gun in her lap and handcuffs Robert.]* OK, we're gonna take you to jail. We're gonna shoot you. *[Shareese takes a toy gun and puts it to Robert's chest and pulls the trigger.]* Pow! *[Robert starts to shake and whine.]*
>
> SHAREESE: Break out! *[Robert shakes his hands to free his wrists from the handcuffs. Shareese holds the gun near Robert's head and pulls the trigger. He whines.]*
>
> SHAREESE: OK. Here. *[She holds the gun out for Robert to take. Robert takes the gun and stands watching as Shareese takes another toy gun. She puts a holster on her waist and returns to the chair.]*
>
> SHAREESE: You want it?
>
> ROBERT: No *[whining]*.

SHAREESE: C'mere. *[She points her gun at Robert and shoots twice. Then, smiling, she hands it to Robert, pointing it at herself.]* Shoot it. Shoot it.

SHAREESE: OK. Give me your knife. I'm gonna stab you. *[Shareese pretends to stab Robert. The play continues and, eventually, Robert joins in as a willing partner, pretending to shoot and stab his mother.]*

Shareese's interactions with Robert were complex. There was a sense of warmth and playfulness in their interactions. On the other hand, Shareese did not create a sense of safety for Robert during their shared play. Her behaviors sometimes frightened her son, and her comments may have inculcated antisocial behavior by teaching him to respond with aggression (Ostler & Haight, 2011).

IMPLICATIONS FOR SUPPORTING YOUNG CHILDREN'S DEVELOPMENT DURING FOSTER-CARE PLACEMENT

A developmental, ecological-systems analysis of development in early childhood has important implications for how social workers in child welfare may support young children in foster care.

Removing a young child from his or her birth home or foster home must be done with full awareness of the emotional distress and unintended effects on development that may result from such an intervention. Two-and-a-half-year-old Sharon's mother is addicted to heroin and unable to adequately care for her. Placement in foster care clearly was necessary for Sharon's physical survival. Sharon was, however, in her mother's care for her first twenty-four months of life. During this time they did develop an attachment relationship, however troubled. When separated, both experienced considerable emotional pain and distress. Sharon's foster caregiver, a relative, noticed regression in Sharon's development and a lack of interest in play.

In contrast, three-year-old George was placed with his foster mother when his birth mother left him at the hospital where he was born. George has been with his foster mother since he was a week old. They have developed a close and caring relationship. The foster mother is hoping to adopt George, but in attempting to release George for adoption, the child welfare agency has found a cousin who is willing to adopt George.

Regardless of the safety and permanency plans, a basic issue for child welfare professionals should be how to best support the young child's attachment relationships and overall development. Many families, even those who presumably are well-functioning, sometimes need support in caring for children. Families with social and financial resources may draw upon family and friends for advice or hire respite child care. Because she was seriously ill and did not have such informal social support or financial resources, Sharon's mother might have benefited from a substance misuse treatment center that could accommodate both her and her daughters, or a foster-care provider who would work with her to support her relationship with Sharon in a positive way while she recovered from her addiction. Perhaps George's foster mother and relatives also need support in developing a lifelong plan for George that would incorporate into his life all of the people who have concern for him, including his foster parents. At the very least, these situations call for a supportive transition to any new environments into which Sharon and George may be placed while in the child welfare system.

If removing the infant or young child from the home is necessary, the development of an adequate relationship between the child and the foster parent must be a priority. Supporting the attachment relationships of infants and young children with their foster families is an important aspect of supporting optimal development for infants and young children entering care. A significant number of infants are placed with foster caregivers within the first three months of life and may be eventually adopted by their foster caregivers. Clearly, for these families to be successful, adequate attachment relationships between children and their foster families must be supported (Dozier & Albus, 2000; Dozier, Higley, Albus, & Nutter, 2002; Stovall & Dozier, 1998, 2000). In supportive families, foster caregivers and their infants and young children can and do develop securely attached relationships (Cole, 2006).

Even if the foster placement is temporary, the development of an adequate attachment relationship with a foster-care provider will allow the infant or young child the security to continue exploring, playing, and learning from the physical and social world, thus minimizing developmental delays. Also, having a responsive caregiver provides the model for subsequent responsive intimate relationships. In Sharon's case, her great-grandmother was able to provide foster care. Sharon had an existing attachment with her because she and her mother lived close by and she had taken care of Sharon when her mother was not home or unable to respond. We know that children like Sharon and George can develop multiple secure relationships with sensitive caregivers. Sharon's social worker focused on providing her great-grandmother with the resources she needed to care for a young child without exhausting her modest physical and economic resources.

The goal for most children in foster care is to return the child home. For this goal to succeed, the attachment relationship with the parent must be supported throughout the child's stay in foster care. Social workers may advocate developmentally appropriate plans for parent-child visitation conducive to the maintenance and development of adequate attachment relationships. Research on developmental aspects of attachment relationships points to the need for tailoring visits to children's and parents' changing developmental needs. Regular and frequent visits are especially important during infancy and early childhood. These visits should occur in homelike settings that allow parents to respond to the children's needs through routine care such as feeding and changing, and to interact and play comfortably with them.

Assessments of "secure" versus "insecure" attachment relationships between children and the parents from whom they are separated through foster care are of limited value. Many otherwise secure infants and young children respond to their parents in "insecure" ways after separations much briefer and less traumatic than foster-care placement. However, the observation of any problematic aspects of attachment relationships (e.g., disorganized relationships) always warrants further investigation, including medical and psychosocial assessments. In cases of problematic attachment relationships, visits typically should be coordinated with other intensive services, and may require professional supervision.

When the child welfare intervention is successful and the child returns home, care must be taken with the transition. If the young child was removed soon after birth, the only caregivers that child knows are the foster caregivers who acted as surrogate parents. Time with the birth parent is very limited in comparison to the amount of time the child is with the foster caregiver. The primary relationship becomes the child–foster caregiver dyad. The reunion process can be very traumatic for both the child and the birth parent. The birth parent feels love and the desire to parent well. The child literally does not know the birth parent and mourns the loss of her known parent—the foster caregiver. It is important in both the transition from the birth parent to the foster parent or from the foster parent to the birth parent to consider the child's attachment relationships, and to give the child time to establish new attachment relationships.

SUMMARY

Social work with young children from two and a half to six years of age has the potential to significantly support children's positive development. Box 6.4 contains practice stories and advice from Linda K., a social worker practicing in child welfare. Secure attachment relationships with caregivers remain important during this period of development, but children's relationships and contexts of develop expand considerably. Play is an increasingly important way in which children interact with their social and physical environments. Pretend play appears to be a human universal, but its development is shaped in relation to particular sociocultural-historical contexts. When children must be placed in foster homes, care must be taken to support their attachment relationships and play.

BOX 6.4 PRACTICE STORY AND ADVICE

Linda K., rural social worker: "How would you want to be treated if someone came to your home to social work you?"

Linda K. has twenty-five years of experience in social work with families and children in rural communities. An MSW, she particularly enjoys crisis intervention where she can assist whole families in getting services to meet their needs better. A natural storyteller, Linda describes some of her experiences as a child welfare worker in rural Illinois. She also offers some words of advice to social workers considering child welfare work.

Practice Story

When you are working in child welfare, in a rural area, you will find yourself in a position where you are out in the middle of nowhere, cell phones don't reach, and you have no protection. I know they train us in child protection very thoroughly about how to protect yourself, the things that you should and should not do when there is, or looks like there is going to be, a physical altercation. A couple Fridays ago, I called the deputy, which is protocol. I was going to the middle of nowhere. I didn't know the family. I called the sheriff's office, said, "Tell me how to get to this house." The deputy said, "Oh, go over the hill and turn left on Coon Chase Road. When you get to Coon Chase Road, you are going to go just about a mile along, and you look over there at the right and you'll see his big ole brown house. Just a little heads up," he said. "This guy is a little odd." I said, "Okay. Thanks, Joe, for all your help." And I just go out there, oblivious to what I am walking into. Get out there and this midsixties grandma greets me. I tell her that I am there because I am investigating her daughter, who has reportedly put bruises on the back of her thirteen-year-old child when they got into a physical fight. So grandma and I are sitting there visiting, and I am telling her who I am and she has hummingbirds and I have commented on the hummingbirds, and she is telling me about her little farm there. And I said, "Would you care if I went ahead and saw your granddaughter?" And she said, "Well, I'd rather you wouldn't 'till my daughter gets here." She said she was at the Wal-Mart, and she'd be back in a little. So, we visit a little bit more . . . I was 25 minutes from the highway. I really didn't know where I was. I had taken a lot of twists and turns, talked to the deputy, got directions. I really didn't know where I was, and about that time I heard this car screech. This truck screeched into the driveway, gravel flying everywhere, and this older gentleman, probably sixties, got out, "What the *hell* is going on here!"

And he just came right for me. I stood up to shake his hand, and I said, "Hi, I am Linda K. . . ." and he wouldn't let me get it out. His face was blood red, "You get off my goddamn property! I don't want any of you sons of bitches around here! You aren't going to come here and tell me how to raise my family!" And I put my hands up like this—one of the things that we are taught in training is very important: You keep a low tone of voice, and make direct eye contact. Don't divert your eyes, like you are scared, just make direct eye contact, keep a low voice, and try to deescalate the situation. So I said, "Now, sir, I am not clear as to why exactly you are upset, but if you can just let me have a minute . . ." Then he started flaying his arms around, "You guys were out here before, you sent out some faggot fucker . . . and you are not going to come out here and treat me that way on my property again." And I said, "Sir, you will have no problem with me." And I said to him, "Sir, this is your property and if you tell me to leave I will be gone, because this is your home, this is your family." And he said, "Yeah, you will just leave and go get some goddamned cop and bring him out here." And I said, "Well, I do have to ensure the safety of your granddaughter, but I will leave if that's what you want." And then he was just so irate that he slid around the corner of the house, like back in this garage-type thing. I told you, I had just worked this investigation a week before where there were gunshots involved, so I was very nervous. He slipped around the corner and I said to his wife, I said, "Please have your husband step back around here. That's making me nervous." She goes, "Oh, honey, you don't want him back around here, he is going to hurt you." I said, "No, I'd rather have him back around here where I can see him." So she went and got him, and he came back and they got in an argument, and he pushed her aside and got right up in my space and he was flaying, cussing me and telling me what he was going to do. I started to back towards my car, but he wasn't having any part of that. He just continued to kind of corner me, and then his wife, thank God, stepped in between us and she said, "Now Sam, back off!" And he just pushed her aside and said, "You don't fuck with me, woman, when I am getting in a fight." And she said, "Sam, you are not going to fight this woman." And I continued to try to talk to him and he just went off to the camper. By that time, the daughter and the granddaughter were there. I stood there and talked to them. I talked to the thirteen-year-old and said, "Do you have any bruises now?" And she said, "No." I asked her if she was afraid, kind of quickly assessed the safety, and I said, "I think it would be best if we assessed this in my office." And mom was willing. She was undergoing mental health treatment. She signed a release to talk to her mental health counselor, and when I called her mental health counselor, the mental health counselor assured me that the girls would be safe there. Mom was not violent, and so I left while he was still in the camper. I left there, I cried half the way into (town), because it was one of the most frightening situations I have ever been in. All I could think of was that my cell phone was dead. I mean it was gone. There was no reception. I was out in the middle of nowhere. Had he walked out of there with a gun, there was absolutely no way I'd be protecting myself. I found out later that he was a chronic alcoholic, and he was just out of it. His grandkids asked me when I interviewed them later, "Were you scared when Grandpa was so mad at you?" "Well," I said, "actually, I was." And they said, "That's the maddest he's been—reddest we have seen his face—since he pulled the shotgun on the neighbor."

But most of the time people are very friendly, very hospitable. Seems to be the rural culture . . . Almost all people say, "You need something to drink?" I have had so many people say, "Can I get you a glass of water or glass of tea?" I've had experiences with people I was investigating—they have gone above and beyond to make sure that I found their place. I've had people, I was leaving, will say, "Where you going? Because it might be easier if you go this way."

Advice

The most important thing, I think, is to remember that there are no such things as problem people. There are only people with problems. And every person that you work with is just like you, except that we all get different cards dealt to us. I think it's so easy when you first start into social work—my thinking was to help people be better. Now after over 20 years in the field, my goal is to help Joe [client], with whatever Joe wants help with. In social work we get this mentality that we want everybody to be like us, or at least like what our definition of a successful life is and, the truth is, Joe's life isn't what I would want for my life, but it's what Joe has chosen for his life and I have to respect that. I just think the most important thing is to recognize that clients are people just like you are—a person. How would you want to be treated if someone came to your home to social work you? Would you want somebody to see your life, figure out what it is that you need to change? I wouldn't. If *I* said that this is a need that I have, then I would be very grateful for help. But I wouldn't want you to tell me what my needs are. I remember all the years in my own life that I have been in therapy, had counseling for the traumatic childhood I went through, the most important thing that all those people did in my life was help me on my journey, to get where I wanted to go. And I think that's what I can do for Joe. Ultimately it is his life.

The other thing, you have to recognize that when you first start, really, you don't know . . . You know something. You have some skills You have some natural and some learned skills, but most importantly you are beginning as a new social worker on a path where the most important teachers are the clients you serve. Every single person that I have come in contact with in doing social work has taught me something. And so, never put yourself on that level that, "I am the social worker and because I have a blah-blah degree, and I know these things, I will come into your home and I will share all my wonderful insights with you and then you, ta-da!, can become as I would want you to be!" Really we should be learning the things that we learn about culture from people—not only different ethnicities, but the culture of poverty or rural culture. We learn that as we serve in these communities.

Also, relationships are the most important thing in social work: relationships with your colleagues, relationships with community members, relationships with, most importantly, the clients. But if you are not a people person, if you can't build relationships, I don't see how you can function in this field. Especially in rural areas where there really is—I hate to call it—but that neighborly, good-old-boy network. And if you are not part of that, it's hard to get in. I've been working G. county for over a year. Just last week, I felt that the G. county police department really stepped over into accepting me as part of them. We were doing a court case together, and it actually came down that the defendant was accusing them of conducting an interview in a less than professional manner. And since I was present for the interview, I had to testify as to their integrity. They weren't in there to hear me testify, but they knew why I was there. And I am telling you once I did that, when I walked out, in fact, Chief J. gave me a high five. Part of that was because the attorney had said to me when I was on the stand, "So when you went in this interview with the police, you knew that the goal was to get my client to admit to [sexual abuse]." I said, "No." I said, "To be honest with you, no I didn't have that in mind." He smiled at me, the attorney smiled at me, and he said, "So you went into that interview with the police not knowing what the police were looking for?" I said, "I went into the interview with the assumption that the police were looking for the same thing I was, and that was an accurate account of what had happened from the perpetrator's standpoint." Then the attorney started laughing and said, "Mrs. K., do you really expect this court to believe that you go into an interview with an alleged perpetrator such as my client and you have his best interests in mind?" And, because it is the foundation of my practice, and because it's the heartbeat of what I do, that quickly I was able to respond, "Absolutely, sir. I am a child protection services worker. My responsibility is first to ensure the safety of children, but also to offer assistance to any family member who should need help. And, absolutely, I have your client's best interests in mind as well as the child's." And the smile went from his face, and he went right on. When we got outside and the state's attorney's assistant, Tammy, was telling the cops about it. That's when J. [police chief] gave me a high five and he was just praising me, and he doesn't generally do that. I have often thought about the importance of your integrity, your honesty and being who you say you are. Nothing will hurt you more in a courtroom than for you to be a different person on that witness stand than you are when you work with your clients, because not only does the client see it, the attorneys see it, and no one respects that. I mean, they expect if you say you advocate for your clients, then you should behave that way, no matter where you are at, because if you don't, then it just shows poorly. And I know that we have these humorous conversations and we make light of certain situations just to survive, but the thrust of your practice always has to be the ever genuine concern for the client, because if you don't have that, then you shouldn't be doing this.

Study and Discussion Questions

1. Describe some milestones of development in early childhood, with particular attention to the widening array of relationships and developmental contexts.

2. What are the various roles of play in early development? Why is play considered to be an important development process? What are possible universal features of play, and how is play shaped within particular sociocultural-historical contexts?

3. What is the child welfare system?

4. What are some of the moral and ethical dilemmas faced by child welfare professionals in considering the placement of young children in foster care?

5. What is the role of parent-child visits in supporting the development of young children placed in foster care? How can social workers in child welfare optimize the effectiveness of parent-child visits in supporting attachment relationships and play?

Resources

Interested students can supplement this chapter through a number of excellent web-based resources.

Kids Count of the Annie E. Casey Foundation is a national and state-by-state effort to track the status of children in the United States. Data, publications, and information on social policies related to key indicators of child well-being are available at http://www.aecf.org/MajorInitiatives/kidscount.aspx.

The Child Development Institute provides information and tools intended to help parents develop a positive parenting style that leads to young children's healthy development and socialization. Available at http://www.childdevelopmentinfo.com/.

The Children's Welfare Gateway of the U.S. Department of Health and Human Services' Administration for Children and Families is a resource for practitioners and researchers. This website includes rates and demographics on maltreatment, foster care, and adoption. Available at http://www.child welfare.gov/.

Play and creativity are essential for young children's healthy emotional development and learning. More information can be found at http://help guide.org/life/creative_play_fun_games.htm.

The Public Broadcasting System offers an educational resource guide on the benefits of play and creativity. Creativity and play can nurture children's emotional health by aiding the development of young children's coping, problem solving, and interpersonal relationship skills. Available at http://www.pbs.org/wholechild/providers/play.html.

References

Adoption Assistance and Child Welfare Act of 1980. (1980). Pub. L. No. 96-272, 94 Stat. 500.

Bamba, S., & Haight, W. (2011). *Child welfare and development: A Japanese case study*. New York: Cambridge University Press.

Berrick, J. D., Needell, B., Barth, R. P., & Jonson-Reid, M. (1998). *The tender years*. New York: Oxford University Press.

Blatt, S., & Simms, M. (1997, April). Foster care: Special children, special needs. *Contemporary Pediatrics, 113*(14), pp. 109–129.

Bragg, H. L. (2003). The overlap between child maltreatment and domestic violence. In U.S. Department of Health and Human Services (Ed.), *Child protection in families experiencing domestic violence* (pp. 7–13). Washington, DC: USDHHS Administration for Children, Youth, and Families: Retrieved from http://www.childwelfare.gov/pubs/usermanuals/domesticviolence/domesticviolence.pdf

Cicchetti, D., & Toth, S. L. (1995). Developmental psychopathology perspective on child-abuse and neglect. *Journal of the American Academy of Child and Adolescent Psychiatry, 34*(5), 541–565.

Clark, C. D. (2003). *In sickness and in play: Children coping with chronic illness*. New Brunswick, NJ: Rutgers University Press.

Cole, S. A. (2006). Building secure relationships: Attachment in kin and unrelated foster caregiver-infant relationships. *Families in Society, 87*, 497–508.

Downs, S., Costin, L., & McFadden, E. (1996). *Child welfare and family services: Policies and practice* (5th ed.). White Plains, NY: Longman.

Dozier, M., & Albus, K. E. (2000). Attachment issues for infants in foster care. In R. Barth, M. Freundlich, & D. Brodzinsky (Eds.), *Adoption and prenatal alcohol and drug exposure: The research, policy, and practice challenges* (pp. 171-197). Washington, DC: Child Welfare League of America Press.

Dozier, M., Higley, E., Albus, K. E., & Nutter, A. (2002). Intervening with foster infants' caregivers: Targeting three critical needs. *Infant Mental Health Journal, 23*, 541-554.

Dozier, M., Stovall, K. C., Albus, K. E., & Bates, B. (2001). Attachment for infants in foster care: The role of caregiver state of mind. *Child Development, 72*, 1467-1477.

Erikson, E. (1963) *Childhood and society* (2nd ed.). New York: Norton.

Finkelhor, D., Turner, H., Ormrod, R., Hamby, S., & Kracke, K. (2009). *Children's exposure to violence: A comprehensive national survey* (Juvenile Justice Bulletin, OJJDP). Retrieved from http://www.ncjrs.gov/pdffiles1/ojjdp/227744.pdf

Freud, S. (1961). *Beyond the pleasure principle*. New York: Norton.

Goncu, A. (Ed.). (1999). *Children's engagement in the world: Sociocultural perspectives*. New York: Cambridge University Press.

Goncu, A., & Gaskins, S. (Eds.). (2006). *Play and development: Evolutionary, sociocultural, and functional perspectives*. Mahwah, NJ: Erlbaum.

Goncu, A., Tuermer, U., Jain, J., & Johnson, D. (1999). Children's play as cultural activity. In A. Goncu (Ed.), *Children's engagement in the world: Sociocultural perspectives* (pp. 148-170). New York: Cambridge University Press.

Haight, W. (1999). The pragmatics of caregiver-child pretending at home: Understanding culturally specific socialization practices. In A. Goncu (Ed.), *Children's engagement in the world: Sociocultural perspectives* (pp. 128-147). New York: Cambridge University Press.

Haight, W. (2006). A sociocultural perspective of parent-child pretend play. In D. Fromberg & D. Bergen (Eds.), *Play from birth to twelve: Contexts, perspectives, and meaning* (2nd ed., pp. 309-314). New York: Garland Press.

Haight, W., Black, J., Ostler, T., & Sheridan, K. (2006). Pretend play and emotion learning in traumatized mothers and children. In D. Singer, R. Golinkoff, & K. Hirsh-Pasek (Eds.), *Play = learning: How play motivates and enhances children's cognitive and social-emotional growth* (pp. 209-230). New York: Oxford University Press.

Haight, W., Black, J., Workman, C., & Tata, L. (2001). Parent-child interaction during foster care visits: Implications for practice. *Social Work, 46*, 325-340.

Haight, W., Kagle, J., & Black, J. (2003). Understanding and supporting parent-child relationships during foster care visits: Attachment theory and research. *Social Work, 48*(2), 195-207.

Haight, W., Mangelsdorf, S., Black, J., Szewczyk, M., Schoppe, S., Giorgio, G., Madrigal, K., & Tata, L. (2005). Enhancing parent-child interaction during foster care visits: Experimental assessment of an intervention. *Child Welfare, 84*, 459-481.

Haight, W., & Miller, P. (1993). *Pretending at home: Early development in a sociocultural context*. Albany: State University of New York Press.

Haight, W., Parke, R., & Black, J. (1997). Mothers' and fathers' beliefs about and participation in their toddlers' pretend play. *Merrill-Palmer Quarterly, 43*, 271-290.

Haight, W., Wang, X., Fung, H., Williams, K., & Mintz, J. (1999). Universal, developmental and variable aspects of young children's play: A cross-cultural comparison of pretending at home. *Child Development, 70*(6), 1477–1488.

Hirsh-Pasek, K., & Golinkoff, R. (2003). *Einstein never used flash cards.* New York: Rodale.

Ippen, C. M. G. (2009). The sociocultural context of infant mental health: Towards contextually congruent interventions. In C. H. Zeanah Jr. (Ed.), *Handbook of infant mental health* (3rd ed., pp. 104–119). New York: Guilford.

Jacobsen, T., Miller, L. J., & Kirkwood, K. P. (1997). Assessing parenting competency in individuals with severe mental illness: A comprehensive service. *Journal of Mental Health Administration, 24*, 189–199.

Le, H. N. (2000). Never leave your little one alone: Raising an Ifaluk child. In J. DeLoache & A. Gottlieb (Eds.), *A world of babies* (pp. 199–220). New York: Cambridge University Press.

Leslie, L., Gordon, J., Meneken, L., Premiji, K., Michelmore, K., & Granger, W. (2005). The physical, developmental, and mental health needs of young children in child welfare. *Journal of Developmental and Behavioral Pediatrics, 26*, 177–185.

Liederman, D. S. (1995). Child welfare overview. In R. Edwards & J. Hopps (Eds.), *Encyclopedia of social work* (19th ed., Vol. 1, pp. 424–433). Washington, DC: NASW Press.

Lightfoot, C., Cole, M., & Cole, S. (2009). *The development of children* (6th ed.). New York: Worth Publishers.

Ostler, T., & Haight, W. (2011). Viewing young foster children's responses to visits through the lens of maternal containment: Implications for attachment disorganization. In J. Solomon & C. George (Eds.), *Disorganized attachment and caregiving* (pp. 269–291). New York: Guilford.

Piaget, J. (1962). *Play, dreams and imitation in childhood.* New York: Norton.

Stovall, K. C., & Dozier, M. (1998). Infants in foster care: An attachment theory perspective. *Adoption Quarterly, 2*, 55–88.

Stovall, K. C., & Dozier, M. (2000). The development of attachment in new relationships: Single subject analyses for 10 foster infants. *Developmental Psychopathology, 12*, 133–156.

U.S. Department of Health and Human Services, Health Resources and Services Administration, Maternal and Child Health Bureau. (2009). *Child health USA 2008–2009.* Rockville, MD: U.S. Department of Health and Human Services. Retrieved from http://mchb.hrsa.gov/chusa08/pdfs/c08.pdf

Vygotsky, L. S. (1962). *Thought and language.* Cambridge, MA: MIT Press.

Vygotsky, L. S. (1978). *Mind in society: The development of higher mental processes.* Cambridge, MA: Harvard University Press.

Webb, N. (2002). *Helping the bereaved child: A handbook for practitioners* (2nd ed.). New York: Guilford.

Wulczyn, F. H., & Brunner, K. (2000). Infants and toddlers in foster care. *Protecting Children, 16*, 4–12.

Wulczyn, F., Hislop, K. B., & Harden, B. J. (2002). The placement of infants in foster care. *Infant Mental Health Journal, 23*, 454–475.

Zigler, E., Singer, D., & Bishop-Josef, S. (Eds.). (2004). *Children's play: The roots of reading.* Washington, DC: Zero to Three Press.

7

Social Work with Children in Middle Childhood
Spiritual Development in the Community

*The focal system in this chapter is the six- to eleven-year-old child. As you read, think about the child's developing biological, psychological, and social competencies as they emerge within physical and social ecologies. The focus of this chapter is the macrosystem as it affects the focal system. Our exemplar is the cultural beliefs and practices within an African-American community as they affect children's spiritual development. This chapter highlights an ethnographic study and an **oral history** of spiritual development conducted in Salt Lake City, Utah. This research discusses children's emerging spiritual development as a factor that counteracts their exposure to racism. As you read, consider what is to be learned from these ethnographic and case-based approaches to social work scholarship. Also consider the socialization of cultural beliefs and practices pertaining to spirituality and racism within microsystems of adult and child relationships; mesosystems formed through connections between the church and home, or the church and university; and exosystems, such as the impact of decisions made by church boards on resources available for children's Sunday school. Social workers practicing in community contexts such as church-based after-school programs, boys and girls clubs, and mentoring programs can play a vital role in supporting the development of children through middle childhood.*

Middle childhood, broadly the period from age six to twelve, is an exciting time of change, ushering in many new experiences and roles. While

---

This chapter draws upon and elaborates *African-American Children at Church: A Sociocultural Perspective*, by W. Haight (New York: Cambridge University Press, 2007); "His Eye Is on the Sparrow: Teaching and Learning in an African American Church," by W. Haight and J. Carter-Black, in E. Gregory, S. Long, and D. Volk (Eds.), *Many Pathways to Literacy: Young Children Learning with Siblings, Grandparents, Peers and Communities*, pp. 195–207 (New York: Routledge Falmer, 2004); and *Raise Up a Child: Human Development in an African-American Family*, by E. Hudley, W. Haight, and P. Miller (Chicago: Lyceum Books, 2003/2009).

family ties remain central, children's increased intellectual and social competencies allow their independent participation in widening social contexts of neighborhood peer groups, school, and community organizations. Some of these contexts, such as scouting and elementary school, may provide new experiences and relationships. Other contexts, such as church and family, may be familiar, but school-age children begin to take on new roles, for example, watching over younger siblings at home in the afternoon or actively participating as ushers in church.

Social workers encounter school-age children in a wide variety of community contexts. The following case summary illustrates the way in which a social worker, in charge of a church-based after-school program that provides homework assistance and recreational activities for children in middle childhood, advocated for and supported a struggling child.

> Every day after school, Mitchell, a bright, outgoing, and intelligent eight-year-old, attended an after-school program at his church. Although he was an active and enthusiastic participant in this program, for some perplexing reason he had developed an active dislike of school. The social worker in charge of Mitchell's after-school program approached his parents. They, too, were concerned about Mitchell. They had read to Mitchell on a regular basis since he was a toddler, an activity he loved and still requested frequently, and could not understand why, by the third grade, Mitchell had failed to learn to read independently. The social worker helped Mitchell's parents request from their local public school an assessment of Mitchell for a possible learning disorder. A thorough neuropsychological assessment revealed that Mitchell had a perceptually based learning disorder. He had difficulties in discriminating letters, for example, *M* from *W*, and "seeing" punctuation at a neurological level. This disorder is not something that Mitchell would "outgrow," but, like blindness or other more obvious physical disabilities, he could learn to compensate. With intervention to support his reading, as well as the use of assistive technology including books on tape and voice-activated software, Mitchell was able to succeed in school.
>
> Regaining his confidence and love of learning, however, required more than academic intervention. Psychosocial support was an important part of the intervention for Mitchell. Supported by the social worker in his after-school program, Mitchell used the Internet to research dyslexia. He then provided education for his peers at school through a science presentation on the brain and dyslexia, including famous scientists with this disorder. Mitchell's emotional recovery was also supported in his church community. An important belief in this community is the inherent worth of each individual as a child of God. This resistance to a definition of self-worth based upon external achievements proved to be enormously comforting and, ultimately, quite motivating to Mitchell. Eventually, he graduated from university.

Regardless of the context in which they encounter school-age children like Mitchell, social workers consider biological, psychosocial, and cultural dimensions of experience. In addition, religion and spirituality may play an

After-school tutoring programs can support children's understanding of basic concepts and teach them good study habits.

increasing role in the experiences of children in middle childhood, and many social workers argue for the inclusion of spirituality in social work assessment and intervention. Mitchell had a biologically based disorder that impacted his cognitive and psychosocial development in a cultural context (school) in which literacy and achievement are highly prized and expectations of African-American males too often are low. Religiously based beliefs within his African-American, Baptist church were comforting and provided an interpretation of his learning disorder that helped Mitchell persist in the face of these difficulties.

HIGHLIGHTS OF DEVELOPMENT DURING MIDDLE CHILDHOOD

In contrast to the rapid and dramatic changes that occur in infancy, early childhood, and adolescence, development in middle childhood is slower and less dramatic. Nevertheless, considerable interrelated changes in physical, cognitive, social, and emotional development do occur between the ages of six and twelve. By the end of middle childhood, most typically developing children have made remarkable progress toward acquiring many of the complex skills and attitudes necessary to participate in an increasing variety of everyday activities within their cultural communities. Erikson (1963) describes a major psychosocial crisis of middle childhood as industry versus inferiority, as children come to recognize disparities in their own abilities relative to other children. In the United States, most children have mastered basic literacy skills and successfully negotiate increasingly complex social relationships with peers. These achievements allow them to participate in physical work and chores around the home and community; to enjoy recreational activities such as organized sports; and to develop culturally valued skills such as dance and playing a musical instrument. (See Lightfoot, Cole, & Cole's [2009] excellent overview of development in middle childhood, which we draw upon here.)

In a wide variety of cultures, middle childhood is marked by increased independence and responsibilities. By five to seven years of age, children from around the world are expected by adults to monitor their own behavior and well-being, and to take on increased responsibilities (Sameroff & Haith, 1996). Children are no longer restricted to home settings where they are carefully supervised by adults. Among the Mayan people in highland Guatemala, boys assume responsibility for gathering wood, an important chore that takes them beyond the supervision of adults (Rogoff, 2003). In the United States, children spend hours in school and in the company of peers. The increased responsibility and autonomy of children in middle childhood are made possible by important biological and cognitive developments, and are supported by widening social opportunities (Lightfoot, Cole, & Cole, 2009).

During middle childhood, children's brains continue to develop. Neural maturation makes possible more complex thinking. Increased myelination, the formation of an insulating sheath of tissue around a nerve fiber, speeds up the transmission of nerve impulses in the **prefrontal cortex**. The prefrontal cortex coordinates the activities of other brain centers in more complex ways, enabling children increasingly to control their attention, form explicit plans, and engage in self reflection (Lightfoot, Cole, & Cole, 2009).

During middle childhood, children become physically stronger and more agile. In the United States and around the world, however, poverty continues to threaten children's physical development and well-being. Box 7.1 describes the impact of poverty on children's access to dental care in the United States.

:···:
:
: ## BOX 7.1 POVERTY ACROSS THE LIFE SPAN
: ### Access to Dental Care
:
:   Children living in poverty have limited access to dental care. In
: 2006, only 28 percent of children from low-income families eligible
: for dental services under Medicaid's Early and Preventive Screening,
: Diagnosis, and Treatment (EPSDT) program received preventive dental
: care. In 2007, approximately 27 percent of low-income children had
: not had a dental checkup in the past year. This represents a macro- and
: microproblem that needs to be addressed by social workers.
:   Something is wrong when the macrosystem provides a means for
: low-income children to receive preventive dental care, but families fail
: to take advantage of the program. This may represent a lack of under-
: standing by parents that preventive dentistry is important, or a sign
: that the program's benefits are not understood. It may also occur
: because parents have difficulty taking off from work, or finding a den-
: tist who accepts Medicaid payments. Dentists and doctors are not
: required to take Medicaid insurance. As a result, finding an available
: dentist who does not have an extremely long wait list can be difficult.
: It may be impossible for parents to accurately predict whether they
: will be able to take a child to an appointment that is months away.
: Changes in work requirements, parental or child health, transporta-
: tion, and other problems may force the most well-meaning and orga-
: nized parent to cancel an approaching appointment made months in
: advance.
: _____
:   Source: U.S. Department of Health and Human Services, 2009.
:···:

Among the cognitive competencies made possible by increased brain development are the ability to reason more logically, follow through on a problem, keep track of more than one aspect of a situation at a time (see classic research by Piaget, 1928), and reflect on thinking (Flavell, Green, & Flavell, 1995). On a given afternoon, an eleven-year-old child might travel independently home from school, complete homework (e.g., construct a logical argument to explain a multistep word problem in math, and employ mnemonic devices to recall the spelling of vocabulary words), supervise a younger sibling, and set the table for dinner.

As suggested by the above list of competencies, planning is a hallmark of cognitive development in middle childhood. "Planning is the deliberate organization of a sequence of actions oriented toward achieving a specific goal" (Gauvain, 1999, p. 176). Planning is necessary for children to successfully meet increased adult demands for responsible behavior. By the end of middle childhood, the planning abilities of many children in the United States are sufficient to allow them to keep track of, complete, and hand in class assignments from multiple teachers as they transition into middle school.

The cognitive abilities that underlie planning include the ability to set goals, and identify and coordinate actions to reach those goals. Children learn about planning through the course of everyday activities, especially as they interact with more experienced planners, for example, parents and older siblings at home. Planning in a social context involves collaboration as participants coordinate and direct their future activities to satisfy mutual interests and needs, such as planning a meal or weekend trip. As children's abilities to plan expand, adults gradually transfer responsibility to them for planning their everyday activities. By the end of middle childhood, children show increasing competence in devising a range of elaborate and effective plans. For example, they may independently deliver newspapers and Girl Scout cookies, plan birthday parties, finish chores, and complete homework (Gauvain, 2009).

In many parts of the world, the increased biological and cognitive competencies of middle childhood are supported by participation in school. An important challenge to children entering middle childhood is to master learning in school. School is a formal and specialized context for learning that differs in a variety of ways from learning in informal, everyday contexts. Unlike the informal learning environment of the home, in school children are expected to learn and demonstrate their learning primarily through symbols: spoken and written language, and mathematical notations. School learning typically is led by one adult supervising a large group of same-age children. It often involves developing skills learned out of context, whose significance is not immediately clear. It may be unclear to a child individually completing a worksheet of division problems at her school desk why this skill is important. On the way home from school, however, this same child may eagerly cooperate with friends to determine how many packs of gum they can purchase with their pooled allowances.

If formal learning in school initially presents challenges to children from majority communities, it can be even more daunting for children unfamiliar with the European-American, middle-class culture that dominates public schools. In the United States, public schools include children from an increasing variety of cultural communities. Many of these otherwise competent children struggle to succeed in school. For example, Suina and Smolkin (1994) describe the experience of Pueblo children and their European-American teachers. The Pueblos of the southwestern United States have their own languages, governments, social patterns, and other cultural components. Pueblo children experienced uncertainty and confusion in response to common practices of their European-American teachers, such as asking children to introduce themselves individually to a class visitor, or asking them to vote in the absence of group consensus. Although the European-American teachers viewed these practices as innocuous, they were in conflict with traditional Pueblo culture. To successfully engage and teach Pueblo children, European-American teachers not only had to incorporate appropriate content from the Pueblo community; they also had to learn culturally appropriate ways of teaching that content.

Formal learning in school also presents challenges to approximately 5 percent of children in the United States who, like Mitchell in our opening case study, have learning disorders (also termed *learning disabilities* or *learning differences*). Children are diagnosed with cognitive learning disorders when their academic skills in reading, mathematics, or written expression are significantly below what is expected for their overall intelligence, age, and experience (see American Psychiatric Association, 2000; Hale & Fiorello, 2004; Lavoie, 2005). The challenges experienced by a child with a learning disorder are not the result of mental retardation, cultural differences, deprivation, medical illness, lack of school attendance, trauma, hearing or visual problems, or mental disorders. Learning disorders result from neurologically based differences in information processing, for example, how the child discriminates sounds, comprehends visual information, recalls factual information, and communicates with others. If not addressed, learning disorders can lead to frustration in school, stigmatization, and other negative feedback from adults and peers. These experiences can lead to social, behavioral, and mental health problems. With adequate support, however, children with learning disorders can succeed in school and beyond. Box 7.2 provides examples of how some children with learning disorders have found their way as adults.

BOX 7.2 ADULT OUTCOMES FOR CHILDREN WITH LEARNING DISORDERS

People with learning disorders often can excel academically, once they are helped to compensate for specific deficits. For example, Richard Jed Wyatt, MD, an internationally known expert in molecular biology, neuropsychiatric interventions, psychiatric medications, and advocacy for people suffering with mental illness, was in special-education programs throughout his school experience, including medical school, because of a learning disorder. Even as a senior psychiatrist and researcher, his reading skills remained so poor that important professional articles and chapters had to be read into a tape recorder for him by others. Yet before his death in 2002, he was the director of an internationally recognized neuropsychiatry research program. Wyatt was a modern pioneer in mental health research who found time to volunteer at homeless shelters, where he provided psychiatric care and researched homelessness and mental illness. Although reading and organizing material was always difficult for him, he still managed to develop educational materials designed to help people understand depression, bipolar disorders, and schizophrenia.

It is important to recognize that Wyatt's accomplishments required the interaction of social systems and personal motivation. Without social support for discovering how to learn and live with a learning disorder, and personal motivation, sacrifice, and unwillingness to accept academic defeats, Wyatt's talent for scientific inquiry would not have blossomed. Unfortunately, far too many children with learning disorders do not receive the level of educational and social support needed to help them find their potential skills.

Compensating for a learning disorder, however, is more than discovering alternative ways to succeed academically. The child needs assistance to discover that she or he can be competent. An older adult interviewed by the authors illustrates the importance of social validation and the value of help in discovering one's talents. This person secretly feared that he was mildly mentally retarded throughout his childhood, adolescence, and early adulthood. He believed others had simply tried to be kind and not confront him with his retardation. The man was aware that in school he was unable to learn academic subjects, and that his reading and writing skills remained far below those of others. He believed he was passed from grade to grade and given a high school diploma as a consolation prize for not dropping out. He was unable to give up the fear of being mentally retarded until he was drafted into the army. To his surprise, the U.S. Army identified him as a potential leader, sent him to Officer Candidates School (OCS), and then commissioned him as a second lieutenant. The self-efficacy gained from completing OCS, becoming a military officer, and successfully leading combat troops in Vietnam convinced him that he must not be mentally retarded. Without successes across major ecological systems, people with learning disorders can have great difficulty freeing themselves of self-destructive beliefs. Once the above individual accepted that he was "normal," but had to learn differently than others, he completed a college degree. With this further validation, he entered graduate school and successfully completed a master's degree and PhD.

Sources: American Psychiatric Association, 2000; Hale & Fiorello, 2004; Lavoie, 2005.

Children in low-income neighborhoods may also face challenges because of the quality of the public schools that they attend. The physical and social resources available to children for learning in public schools in the United States vary widely. These inequalities have emerged, at least in part, because of the ways in which the public schools are funded. Local control over educational funding has been an enduring value in the United States. The U.S. federal government provides relatively little funding to public schools compared to the centralized government funding typical of many European, Asian, and developing nations. School funding from local property taxes helps finance elementary and secondary schools in the United States. The federal government provides categorical grants that earmark money for specific purposes, for example, special education services for children with disabilities under the Individuals with Disabilities Education Act. States also provide modestly funded "foundation plans" intended to ensure that all children receive at least basic educational resources. These plans, however, have failed to keep up with the rising costs of educating children, particularly those who need additional resources to overcome the challenges of poverty. The result of modest state contributions and minimal federal efforts has been a continuing differential between property-wealthy and property-poor communities. The opportunities available to children attending public schools in affluent, suburban communities stand in stark contrast to those available to children attending public schools in high-poverty, urban communities (Koski, 2009).

Attending school provides children in middle childhood increasing amounts of time with peers. In the United States, children between the ages of six and twelve spend approximately 40 percent of their waking time with peers (Lightfoot, Cole, & Cole, 2009). Positive relationships with peers are important for children's well-being and development. Children who are popular with their peers generally are good at initiating and maintaining positive social relationships, compromising, and negotiating (e.g., see Rubin, Bukowski, & Parker, 1998). Good relationships with peers can provide a feeling of belonging, and opportunities for exploring social relationships and developing moral understanding and personal identity. In the United States, many children in middle childhood also spend increasing amounts of time in the community participating in boys and girls clubs, after-school programs sponsored by churches, scouting, and sports.

Children may experience problems in peer interactions for a variety of reasons, including poor social skills or even physical appearance. Children who are actively rejected by peers are at risk for school failure and mental health problems (e.g., see Rubin et al., 1998). Such experiences can have a profound impact on a child's sense of self, as illustrated in Lucy Grealy's (1994) first-person account, *Autobiography of a Face*. After being smacked on the jaw at school during a game of dodge ball, the obviously bright, outgoing, and socially skilled nine-year-old Lucy was diagnosed with Ewing's sarcoma, a virulent form of cancer with a 5 percent survival rate. Her treatment included removal of part of her jawbone. As a result of the discomfort that others felt with her changed face, as well as the cruel taunting she experienced from other children, Lucy felt set apart from her peers, guilty, and ashamed. Although she survived the cancer, she subsequently endured years of painful and unsuccessful plastic surgeries in an attempt to change her appearance to gain, and feel worthy of, others' love and acceptance.

Despite their increased autonomy and time spent with peers, most children in middle childhood remain closely connected with their parents. Their relationships, however, may undergo changes. There may be a decrease in overt affection, an increase in parental expectations for competent and appropriate behavior, and an increased concern with school performance. In addition, there may be changes in control strategies, with parents increasingly relying on reasoning to keep children safe when not under direct adult supervision (Lightfoot, Cole, & Cole, 2009).

Unfortunately, many children do not experience the benefits of a supportive relationship with a parent. Child abuse remains a significant risk factor for development in middle childhood. Box 7.3 describes poverty as a macrolevel risk factor for child abuse. Most parents struggling with poverty do not abuse their children. Nevertheless, poverty places enormous stress on adults. Effective, long-term prevention of child abuse must address macrolevel factors such as poverty.

BOX 7.3 VIOLENCE ACROSS THE LIFE SPAN
Child Abuse and Poverty

National surveys indicate that child abuse increases the farther a family falls below the poverty line. Poverty places parents under enormous stress, and some lash out at their children. Social workers working at the level of the macrosystem can possibly help prevent child abuse by

- working to eliminate poverty through affordable housing and living wages;
- providing supportive case management to people under a set income;
- providing systematic high-quality day care, after school care, and evening child care, because parents need time for work and rest away from children.

Source: Myers, 2011.

The intellectual competencies and social and emotional maturity displayed by children in middle childhood are significantly more advanced than those of children in early childhood. It is important to remember, however, that despite the impressive developmental advances of children in middle childhood, they still need considerable adult supervision and support. Although they reason logically about concrete objects and events, their ability to reason abstractly and hypothetically is limited. They have made great strides in their ability to plan daily activities, but may need considerable support in planning for the more distant future; for example, they may be quite competent at completing nightly homework assignments, but need considerable adult supervision to complete long-term projects. They spend increasing amounts of time in peer groups, but peers can be difficult, and adults may need to intervene to discourage bullying and other aggressive behavior, as well as to provide emotional support and comfort.

Unfortunately, there are children who for various reasons do not receive adequate adult support and supervision. Parental substance misuse, for example, can result in inconsistent parental discipline and inadequate monitoring of children's activities (Dishion & McMahon, 1998). Box 7.4 describes some of the challenges to children growing up in homes where parents misuse substances.

BOX 7.4 SUBSTANCE MISUSE ACROSS THE LIFE SPAN

Problems Found in Families with a Substance-Misusing Parent

Addiction and substance misuse changes the family system and can impact each of the members. Children from a family living with addiction have a higher probability for experiencing several problems:

- alcohol and other substance misuse beginning in late childhood or early adolescence
- severe family problems over extended time periods
- inconsistent family involvement, and fragmented and unhealthy coalitions between family members
- reduced or poor school achievement
- increased social and behavioral problems while attending school
- increased antisocial behavior and child conduct problems across community and home settings

Source: Mack, Franklin, & Frances, 2003.

Children in middle childhood are increasingly autonomous, but still need adult monitoring and supervision because they can be misled or tricked by potential abusers. In addition, the ways in which child abuse is understood varies widely and has implications for societal-level responses. For example, child sexual abuse has emerged as an issue of great concern in both the United States and Kenya. In the United States, child sexual abuse is framed as a child protection and criminal justice issue and is generally considered the result of individual pathology divorced from larger societal problems. The U.S. system often views child victims as passive and powerless and in need of assistance from adults. Researchers, activists, and healthcare providers have amassed a tremendous amount of evidence on the prevalence of child sexual abuse, its consequences, how to prevent it, and how to treat survivors. Ideally, perpetrators are incarcerated, and children are removed from homes deemed unsafe. Unfortunately, a dearth of child protection workers and resources means that some families and children receive inadequate attention and interventions.

The Kenyan government views child sexual abuse as a child welfare and children's rights issue that is deeply connected to broader societal concerns like poverty, the AIDS pandemic, and commercial sex trafficking of children. Children who are detached from their families and communities are considered especially vulnerable. The Kenyan children's rights approach has included children in discussions of sexual abuse and how to respond to it, a method that may empower survivors and encourage children to speak up against child sexual abuse. Yet its focus on the family as the remedy results in relatively little attention paid to child sexual abuse perpetrated by caregivers.

Understanding various strategies for preventing and treating child sexual abuse may broaden our perspectives and suggest ways of strengthening approaches in any given cultural context. For example, the United States might consider community-based approaches that empower children to be their own advocates. Kenyans might address sexual abuse within families (Mildred & Plummer, 2009).

DEVELOPMENTAL, ECOLOGICAL-SYSTEMS ANALYSIS OF SPIRITUAL DEVELOPMENT IN MIDDLE CHILDHOOD

The religious and spiritual experiences of children in middle childhood often have remarkable emotional depth, and can be drawn upon to cope with life challenges. Before elaborating these processes, however, it is important to reflect upon the diversity of religious experiences, and the complexities of their role in social work practice.

Religious Pluralism

Hundreds of research studies of children's religious development have been conducted worldwide, spanning the twentieth century and a variety of faith traditions. The vast majority of this research, however, represents Western cultures: primarily the United Kingdom, Europe, United States, and Scandinavia, with most concentrating on white, Judeo-Christian beliefs (Ratcliff & Nye, 2006). In this section, we will begin by discussing the diversity of religious and spiritual experiences both within the United States and worldwide, using an African-American Baptist community and religion in Japan as contrasting case examples.

Religion is a fundamental force in development for most of the world's population. In most cultures, religion has been an integral part of life for thousands of years. Worldwide, approximately 86 percent of people report that they identify with a particular religious group. The largest religions are

Christianity (approximately 32 percent of the world's population), Islam (19 percent), and Hinduism (13 percent), but there are at least sixteen other major religious groups that can be divided into at least 270 denominations or sects. There is also significant variation in religion within particular countries. In the United States, for example, most people (76 percent) consider themselves to be Christian, but there are numerous Christian denominations as well as Jews, Muslims, Buddhists, Hindus, members of nondenominational congregations, and so forth. Of course, religion does not have a uniform impact on human development, as religions vary in beliefs and practices, and individuals vary in their adherence to the beliefs and practices of their religious tradition (Holden & Vittrup, 2010).

Given variability in religions, merely defining *religion, spirituality*, or *religiosity* is challenging. Many definitions used in research and practice are problematic because basic elements, such as concepts of God or humans' relations to the spiritual, are drawn from a specific, predominantly Judeo-Christian framework not necessarily appropriate to other religions (Hyman & Handal, 2006; Traphagan, 2005). For example, elite forms of Confucianism and Taoism have been characterized as "godless" religions. They conceive of an underlying force or principle governing life, but unlike Christianity, it is impersonal, remote, lacking consciousness, and not a being or God (e.g., Stark, Hamberg, & Miller, 2005). In Japan, for example, religious and ritual behavior is primarily conceptualized in terms of an interconnection with other humans, not with God, and "religious experience" is as much a matter of family or community as it is of the individual (Traphagan, 2005). Further, Japan's two major, traditional faiths—Buddhism and Shintoism—do not sustain congregations. Their priests perform a variety of rites, such as funeral services and the pacification of spirits, on a fee-for-service basis. There is no emphasis on regular participation, nor do these faiths seek to impose a particular set of beliefs, although each sustains a full-time priesthood that does embrace a creed. Like the laity, both Buddhist and Shinto priests assume that individuals will combine a variety of religious traditions to meet their own needs (Stark et al., 2005). This mixture may include aspects of Christianity, which was first introduced to Japan in 1550 (e.g., Earhart, 1997). Indeed, many Japanese claim several affiliations, with Shintoism and Buddhism being the most common combination (Stark et al., 2005).

To encompass such pluralism, *religion, spirituality*, and *religiosity* must be broadly defined. **Religion** refers to the institutionalization of beliefs about spirituality and any related codes of behavior and rituals. Considered a human universal, **spirituality** refers to a subjective experience of connection to something greater than the self that yields a sense of coherence, purpose, security, peace, and guidance (e.g., Coles, 1990; Hay & Nye, 2006; Hyman & Handal, 2006; King & Benson, 2006; Ratcliff & May, 2004). Spirituality may emerge within or outside of the context of religion (Oser, Scarlett, & Bucher, 2006). **Religiosity** refers to spiritual and/or religious involvement.

Understanding complex religious landscapes in the United States and elsewhere requires careful attention to cultural and historical contexts. In the United States, significant numbers of adults and children value religion, endorse religious beliefs, and participate in formal religious organizations. In 2007, national survey results indicated that 82 percent of U.S. adults viewed religion as very important or fairly important in their own lives, 78 percent believed in God, 61 percent reported membership at a church or synagogue, and 59 percent indicated that religion can answer all or most of today's problems (Gallup, n.d.). Likewise, national survey results indicated a high rate of religiosity in youth. Among U.S. adolescents age thirteen to seventeen, 84 percent reported that they believe in God, 51 percent stated that religious faith was very important in shaping daily life, 78 percent reported praying alone at least once a month, and 40 percent reported attending a religious service at least once a month (Smith & Denton, 2005).

There is also within-group variation in religiosity. The diverse histories and experiences of groups in the United States, such as African-American and European-American, result in various uses of religion and interpretations of common faiths such as Christianity (Haight, 2002). It also results in variation in the valuing of religion. For example, 88 percent of African-American adults reported that religion was very important in their lives, in contrast to 56 percent of whites and 44 percent of Asians (Newport, 2006).

The importance of attending to sociocultural-historical context also is apparent when examining the complex religious landscapes of other countries, for example, Japan. Available data suggest that relatively few Japanese adults (5 percent) reported that they are active in church, and most indicated that they were not raised "religiously" and do not consider themselves to be "religious" (77 percent and 72 percent, respectively; World Values Survey, 1993). In a large interview study of adults, most (72 percent) reported that they do not believe in any religion (*Yomiui Shinbun*, 2008). Similarly, surveys of Japanese college students reveal that relatively few (approximately 10 percent) reported specific religious affiliations (Inoue, 2008).

The relatively few Japanese adults indicating involvement in religion can be understood within the context of a complex national history. This history has resulted in a widespread and deeply felt belief that religion is strictly a private matter and in suspicion of organized religion. In brief, from the Meiji Restoration in 1868 to the end of World War II, the Japanese government attempted to establish a strong, centralized nation-state, in part, by restoring the emperor as a central divine figure and manipulating and regulating religion. Eventually, freedom of religion was guaranteed conditionally (by the Constitution of the Empire of Japan, 1890–1947) as long as its *social* expression was restricted. More recently (1995), an incident in which members of a religious cult spread sarin gas in the Tokyo subway, killing twelve and injuring more than 5,000, reinforced for many Japanese that religion should remain private and not be expressed in public (Ama, 2005). Interestingly, many Japanese college students have indicated both that religions are or possibly are dangerous (63 percent), and that they are or possibly are necessary for human beings (61 percent; Inoue, 2008).

Although Japanese typically do not identify with organized religion, spiritual beliefs and ritual practices are common in private, everyday life. Available data indicate that most Japanese adults (87 percent) believe that it is important to have spiritual beliefs and that there is a power beyond humans in nature (56 percent; *Yomiui Shinbun*, 2008). In addition, the majority of Japanese (55 percent) report a belief in the "supernatural," that rivers and mountains have spirits (59 percent), and that humans have souls (63 percent). Most Japanese (75 percent) regularly visit their family grave site, and few (26 percent) doubt that a person's spirit remains with the family after death (Stark et al., 2005). The majority of Japanese households maintain Buddhist and/or Shinto altars (estimates range from 62 percent to 88 percent; Stark et al., 2005). Many Japanese perform frequent rituals before Buddhist altars or Shinto shrines, and offer gifts, including food, to the ancestors. Most Japanese adults (94 percent) report ancestor worship (*Yomiui Shinbun*, 2008). Most (74–78 percent) report visiting graves during Obon, a festival to honor and express gratitude to the spirits of one's ancestors, and shrines and temples at the New Year (73–76 percent; *Yomiui Shinbun*, 2008). Other rituals are performed outside of the home, for example, to bless a new vehicle, purify the land before building a new home, or appease the spirit of a tree before cutting it down (Stark et al., 2005).

Large-scale surveys of Japanese college students also indicate spiritual beliefs and ritual practices. In 2007, many college students (64 percent) reported a belief that spirits or souls do or possibly do exist after death. More specifically, many Japanese college students (50 percent) report belief in the presence of *kami* (spirits of nature) or *hotoke* (Buddha), and in the presence of *rei* (the soul and spirits; 60 percent). Most (57 percent) reported New Year visits to shrines or temples, and to family graves during Obon (55 percent; Inoue, 2008).

Religion and Social Work

During the past twenty years, the field of social work has seen a resurgence of interest in religion and spirituality (e.g., see Bullis, 1996; Canda, 1997; Canda & Furman, 1999; Garland, 2008; Haight, 1998; Pinderhughes, 1989; Sheridan, Bullis, Adcock, Berlin, & Miller, 1992). The concern of contemporary social workers with religion and spirituality is not surprising, given social work's origins in nineteenth-century sectarian ideologies regarding charity and community service, and institutions such as the charity organization society, the settlement house movement for immigrants, and Jewish communal services. During the twentieth century, however, as social work became increasingly professionalized, serious concerns arose with sectarian approaches. Critical questions focused on issues of moralistic judgments about the "deserving" and "undeserving" poor, combining prose-lytizing with the provision of social services, and the increasing religious diversity of the United States. Social work shifted from a sectarian to an aca-demic approach drawing upon social science theories, assessments, and intervention (Canda, 1997).

At first blush, the focus of some contemporary social workers on reli-gion and spirituality may seem regressive. An important distinction, how-ever, should be made between proselytizing (i.e., advocating one's personal spiritual and religious beliefs and practices) and the attempts of contempo-rary social workers to fully understand an important component of clients' diverse worldviews and resources. For many individuals, spirituality is the legacy into which they are born, spiritual experiences form the grid on which other life events are located, religious beliefs form the foundation for interpretation and evaluation of one's life, and a church "family" provides critical support in times of need (Haight, 2002; Hudley, Haight, & Miller, 2003/2009). If social workers ignore such fundamental belief systems, they may also fail to understand their client's worldview, making effective, pro-fessional intervention impossible.

Consideration of religion and spirituality is not necessarily incompati-ble with modern, "scientific" approaches to social work—it can provide a more complete understanding of clients' worldviews, and can suggest potential sources of stress and coping in times of crisis. Attention to religion and spirituality is compatible with **strengths-based practice** (e.g., Salee-bey, 2003). For some, religious teachings and spirituality are a strength and protective factor. They are a source of joy, comfort, meaning, and interpreta-tion of life's trials. There is a growing awareness that spirituality may illumi-nate the quality of **resilience** (Garmezy, 1985; Masten, Best, & Garmezy, 1990). People who are resilient are able to find meaning in their lives even in the face of extraordinary hardship. Robert Coles provides a memorable example, quoting the words of an eight-year-old girl who helped desegre-gate a North Carolina school in 1962: "I was all alone, and those people [segregationists] were screaming, and suddenly I saw God smiling, and I smiled . . . A woman was standing there (near the school door), and she shouted at me, 'Hey, you little nigger, what are you smiling at?' I looked right at her face and I said, 'At God.' Then she looked up at the sky, and then she looked at me, and she didn't call me any more names" (Coles, 1990, pp. 19–20).

Religion and Coping in Middle Childhood

As this quotation suggests, the spiritual and religious experiences of middle childhood often have remarkable emotional depth. Religion and spirituality play an increasing role in the experiences of some children in middle childhood, and many social workers argue for the inclusion of spirituality in social work assessment and intervention. Tamminen's (1991, 1994) studies of Finnish children and adolescents found that spiritual experiences are relatively common in middle childhood and adolescence. The percentage of individuals who reported experiencing "God's nearness," however, was greatest during middle childhood, prior to a period of questioning and analysis during adolescence. During their discussions of morality and political issues, Robert Coles (1990) was so impressed with children's spontaneous use and elaborations of their religious beliefs that he embarked on an exploration of the spiritual life of children. He found that spirituality was central to the lives of many children of Jewish, Muslim, and Christian traditions. Sarah Moskovitz (1983) concluded from her study of child survivors of the Nazi holocaust that a sense of hope rooted in religious faith enabled some children to love and behave compassionately toward others in spite of the atrocities they had experienced. Recent collections that describe the religious and spiritual experiences of children include works by Karl Rosengren and colleagues (Rosengren, Johnson, & Harris, 2000), Donald Ratcliff (Ratcliff, 2004), and Eugene Roehlkepartain and colleagues (Roehlkepartain, King, Wagener, & Benson, 2006). In her oral history, *Raise Up a Child*, Edith Hudley (Hudley et al., 2003/2009) describes human development in a rural African-American community as rooted in spirituality. Scholarship within African-American studies portrays spirituality as a common cultural value and as an agent of socialization (e.g., see Haight, 2002).

One of the ways in which spirituality may support children's resilience is through religious coping. Religious coping uses religion and spirituality to interpret and respond to life problems. It is the intersection of the construct of religiosity and diverse forms of coping. Pargament and Brant (1998) describe several forms of religious coping: self-directed coping, when individuals use religious resources to individually solve their own problems; deferred coping, when individuals, especially in hopeless situations, give up control to a higher power or God; and collaborative coping, when individuals conceive of God as a helping partner.

Developmental research has focused on age-related changes in thinking about religion and spiritual experience (e.g., Oser & Gmunder, 1991; Rosengren et al., 2000; Tamminen, 1994), with relatively less attention to how children and youth *use* their religion and spirituality in everyday life, including in their response to challenges (Oser et al., 2006). Yet the possibility that religious coping is a protective process for children is suggested by a growing body of Western, large-scale, primarily survey research that indicates an inverse relationship between religiosity and risk behaviors, and a positive association with healthy behaviors (for reviews see King & Benson, 2006; Oser et al., 2006). Children and youth who are involved in religion and spirituality are less likely to engage in unsafe behavior (e.g., carrying weapons), misuse substances, engage in early or risky sexual behavior, engage in violent or other delinquent acts, or display internalizing behaviors such as depression. On the other hand, religiosity is positively linked to adolescents' self-esteem and emotional health (for reviews see King & Benson, 2006), healthy lifestyle (e.g., good dietary habits, seat-belt use, exercise, and sleep), prosocial values and behavior, and academic success (for review see Crawford, Wright, & Masten, 2006).

The apparent value of religiosity extends to children experiencing risks to development. For example, adolescent religiosity served as a protective process for those exposed to parental alcohol misuse and sexual abuse (Chandy, Blum, & Resnick, 1996). Church attendance of children living in high-risk neighborhoods contributed to their academic progress (Regnerus, 2003). For adolescents in foster care in Missouri, attendance at religious services was associated with reduced odds of recent engagement in sexual behavior and current use of cigarettes. Religious beliefs were associated with reduced odds of children's recent use of alcohol and current use of cigarettes (Scott, Munson, McMillen, & Ollie, 2006)

Religion and spirituality offer a variety of coping methods to children in times of stress (Pargament, 2003). Religious coping can occur through social support. For vulnerable children in the United States, involvement in church may inhibit risk-taking behavior and promote healthful behaviors by providing guidelines for behavior and problem solving, reinforced by an intergenerational community of supportive elders and peers (e.g., King & Benson, 2006). For example, throughout its history, the African-American church has played a significant role in social support (e.g., Franklin, 1969; Moore, 1991), and strong involvement in churches has long been one of the means through which African-American families have coped with adversity (e.g., McAdoo & Crawford, 1991). A related feature of African-American religion is an emphasis on community. Community is central to African-American culture (e.g., Stack, 1974). This emphasis on community has religious underpinnings. For example, a common theme in spirituals is that loneliness and despair threaten to disrupt the community of faith (Hale-Benson, 1987). In Japan, where the major religions (Buddhism and Shintoism) do not sustain congregations, youth may draw on social support less directly, for example, through feelings of inclusion in a larger Japanese community during participation in Obon and New Year visits to shrines and temples.

Religious coping may also occur through protective beliefs which provide meaning and purpose in life. Religiously based beliefs such as in the interconnection of human beings may allow children to experience the self as embedded within a larger context that encourages care and compassion and motivates them to contribute to something greater than themselves (King & Benson, 2006). Religiously based beliefs such as hope, gratitude, and forgiveness can allow release from pain, resentment, and anger, and reframe difficult experiences (Crawford et al., 2006). For example, religious beliefs can be central to the healthy psychological development of African-American youth experiencing racism (Haight, 2002; Hudley et al., 2003/2009).

For more than 200 years, the African-American church has been a context in which an oppressed people have maintained and developed a non-racist, culturally distinct, alternative identity and view of reality (e.g., Becker, 1997; Ellison, 1997; Frazier, 1964; Fulop & Raboteau, 1997; Lincoln, 1999; Long, 1997; McAdoo & Crawford, 1991; Smitherman, 1977; Wills, 1997). This alternative system of beliefs is not a simple imitation or derivation of European-American Christianity (Long, 1997), but evolved in relation to a distinct African heritage, shaped by unique experiences in North America (Becker, 1997; Hale-Benson, 1987; Long, 1997; Smitherman, 1977; Wills, 1997). Cornerstones of contemporary African-American theology (see Mitchell, 1986; Hale-Benson, 1987) that may promote the resilience of at-risk youth include belief in the inherent dignity and worth of each individual as a child of God (Hale-Benson, 1987), and in the centrality of community (Hale-Benson, 1987), especially with regards to the survival of children (Mitchell, 1986). The belief that God recognizes African Americans as equal to European Americans—each is one of his children—has given many the inner resolve to "keep on keeping on" (Hale-Benson, 1987).

Religious coping also may occur through rituals (Traphagan, 2005). Religious coping involving rituals may promote stress reduction and feelings of peace and social connection. Ritual can be defined as controlled repetition that controls the self and others and expresses solidarity (e.g., Garvey, 1990). Religious rituals can provide order, structure, predictability, and connection to a larger community, experiences often lacking in the lives of maltreated children in state care. In situations when predictability and control (central to stress reduction) are limited, certain religious rituals such as prayer and meditation can elicit a relaxation response, an integrated physiological reaction that opposes the stress response (e.g., Fetzer Institute, 1999).

In Japan, most individuals do not receive formal religious instruction, and the major religions (Buddhism and Shintoism) do not impose a particular set of beliefs. It is assumed that individuals will integrate religious beliefs from a variety of sources, and a range of beliefs is tolerated. It is expected, however, that individuals will participate in ancestor worship and rituals such as Obon and New Year celebrations. Furthermore, ritual practice associated with religious institutions is a central frame through which people express concern about health and well-being, for example, trips to shrines to collect good-luck tokens for an ill loved one. Whether at home or at a temple or shrine, rituals associated with health and well-being tend to be performed in contexts permeated by religious symbolism.

Social workers also must be aware that religion can introduce risk. Involvement with religious cults or negative religious mentors, exposure to abuse by those in positions of authority, intolerance toward religious differences, and belief in a condemning higher power may lead to increased health-risk behaviors in vulnerable youth. Some vulnerable youth report feeling forsaken and neglected by God and conventional religion. Such feelings and experiences may lead to a decrease in religiosity and an increase in risky behavior. Clearly, any study of religious coping and health-risk behaviors in vulnerable children must consider possible negative influences (Crawford et al., 2006).

A CASE OF SPIRITUAL DEVELOPMENT IN AN AFRICAN-AMERICAN COMMUNITY

To illustrate the role of the macrosystem in children's spiritual development, we provide an in-depth discussion of First Baptist Church (a pseudonym). The research began with the collection of developmental and ethnographic materials over a four-year period in the late twentieth century within an African-American, Baptist community in Salt Lake City, Utah. The goal was to understand, in depth, the coherence and diversity of adults' spiritual socialization beliefs and practices, and children's emerging participation within this specific cultural context. In the long run, the complex, differentiated portrait emerging from this case-based strategy provided a basis for meaningful comparisons with other communities. In the short run, it highlighted and perhaps challenged culturally based assumptions about educational practices and social service interventions with children and families.

First Baptist Church is an important case for at least two reasons. First, the African-American community in Utah is similar to African-American communities in other parts of the United States. Many African-American Utahns experience racial discrimination in employment, housing, education, and everyday social interactions (Coleman, 1981). The developmental literature, however, is virtually silent with respect to the impact of racism on children's development (Fisher, Jackson, & Villarruel, 1998), or protective processes such as spirituality that allow children to develop well despite such stressors. Second, the African-American Utahn community has characteristics distinct from many other African-American communities. For example, the overwhelming majority of African-American Utahns find themselves in the religious as well as the racial minority. In contrast to the predominantly Baptist African-American community, most of the population of the state of Utah belong to the Church of Jesus Christ of Latter Day Saints (whose members are commonly known as Mormons). Despite the diversity present across African-American communities, there remains an unfortunate tendency in some developmental, educational, and social service literature to minimize such complexities. This case provides an important illustration of adaptation and development within a particular African-American community in relation to a geographically and culturally distinct larger community.

This study focused on socialization practices, including storytelling, verbal conflict, and role-playing, through which adults and children constructed personal meanings from an important cultural resource, the Bible, and applied those lessons to coping positively with the challenges in their own lives. These observations focused on Sunday school. A total of forty Sunday school classes for children ranging in age from three to sixteen were audiotaped and their contexts described in field notes. From these materials, detailed verbatim transcripts of Sunday school classes, and descriptions of nonverbal contexts, were reconstructed. These observations were contextualized by multiple, in-depth, semistructured interviews with the pastor, Sunday school superintendent, and Sunday school teachers. These interviews were also audiotaped and transcribed. Practices and beliefs associated with Sunday school were further contextualized through systematic observations of yearly events such as vacation Bible school, monthly events such as youth emphasis day, weekly events such as the pastor's sermons for children, a variety of other special occasions focusing on children, adult Sunday school classes, and weekly Sunday school teachers' meetings. Observations and interviews were further contextualized through historical and social background information obtained from a variety of sources including local newspaper articles, historical documents, and church publications.

Mother Edith Hudley's Oral History

A "mother" and deaconess of First Baptist Church, and master storyteller, Edith Hudley deepened our understanding of the socioculturalhistorical context of children's spiritual socialization and development, through her in-depth oral history (Hudley et al., 2003/2009). Mrs. Hudley was born in 1920 on a small family farm in Kennard, Texas. The sixth of eight surviving children, Edith was her mother's helper and apprentice. Before she attended an all black, segregated school, which began when children were seven years old, Edith was taught at home by her mother. Her mother taught her to cook, sew, and care for infants. Edith described feelings of great pride and self-worth at her increasing ability to help her family in such concrete ways. By the time she was ten and her mother died from complications of childbirth, Edith was able to perform these tasks independently. The family's burdens were lessened through their close community ties, especially to the church. When Edith brought her father questions that he found inappropriate for a father to answer, he sought out his older sister, cousins, and other female community members. He also encouraged Edith to form relationships with the "mothers of the church," the ones with experience who would keep her to the right path. In turn, Mrs. Hudley became a mother of First Baptist Church, mentoring and teaching the children.

Mrs. Hudley recounted her life story during several days in the fall of 1998 and the winter of 1999. Although she had never narrated so much of her life story in a single sitting, her stories had a shape that had been honed over multiple tellings. Her collaborators (Wendy Haight and Peggy Miller) respected the integrity of her tellings by not interrupting or redirecting her talk. Twenty-three hours of audio recordings were transcribed verbatim, yielding 346 typed, single-spaced pages. The transcripts were edited to retain the essence of Mrs. Hudley and the conviction of her telling (see Hudley et al., 2003/2009, for a further description of methods).

There is a growing awareness that children cannot be understood apart from the cultural and historical contexts that shape their lives. This is true of all children, but because African-American children and other children of color have been underrepresented in studies of child development, the need to imagine the contexts of their lives is especially urgent. Edith Hudley's story stimulates our imaginations, and prompts us to question, enlarge, or reaffirm certain assumptions about child rearing. For example, Mrs. Hudley's strong opinions about child rearing were grounded in the messages that she received from the family and community into which she was born: religious faith is the most important force in life, the compass by which all conduct is oriented.

The Macrosystem: Spiritual Development at First Baptist Church

Adults like Mrs. Hudley were central to the spiritual socialization of children at First Baptist Church. Complex cultural beliefs and practices were conveyed to the children during church activities through interactions with adults and other children. Several key cultural concepts and socialization practices emerged from the ethnography and oral history.

Spirituality Is a Lifeline. At First Baptist Church, religious beliefs— such as the inherent worth of each individual, and the value of freedom, justice, and forgiveness—were viewed as lifelines both to healthy spiritual development and to coping positively with the challenges of everyday life. The primary goal of Sunday school teachers was to "bring the child to God" for spiritual salvation. In addition, they argued that children must be familiar with religious beliefs so that they may reach for them in times of need. In the words of one Sunday school teacher, children must know how to "put on the armor of God." This protection can be carried inside of each child to school, to work, and in the community (Haight, 2002).

Consistent with this emphasis on spiritual protection, Mrs. Hudley provided numerous illustrations of how her faith provided her with a coherent framework for coping with life's challenges, including racism, poverty, violence, and, in the following excerpt, death.

> I was a little girl and they was building a chimney . . . And Mama had this baby. It was a pretty baby, and I was in the house . . . they let me stay in the kitchen, and Mama was in the room when the baby was born. That was the prettiest baby. It had a full head of hair. And the baby died . . .
>
> And I went and I was lookin at the baby, and Papa had to stop buildin the chimney to build a little box to go bury the baby. And I was just lookin for the baby to say somethin. And I said, "Mama, the baby ain't sayin nothin!" I was listenin for the baby to cry. And Mama said, "Well the baby won't be sayin anything. The baby's goin back to Jesus," she said. That's the way she told me the baby's dead. (Hudley et al., 2003/2009, p. 11)

Meaningful Involvement in Community. Consistent with the literature in African-American studies, a key finding from the ethnographic research and the oral history was the emphasis on community. The significance of community as it relates to the African-American church was exemplified in the common reference to one's "church home," indicating membership in a particular church. At First Baptist Church, children were valued members of a cultural community stretching back in time and including members of the church who were highly esteemed for their wisdom and spirituality. Each child participated in meaningful ways beside these esteemed community members, for example, ushering worship services, leading devotions, singing in the choir, or providing service to families in need. In describing her own participation as a child with adults at church, Sister Irma noted, "I gathered my spirit from them. I saw what they did. I saw them pray. I saw them read the Bible. I saw them sing, and they would sing joyously" (Haight, 2002, p. 69).

Adults also described the necessity of knowing the child's family and community in order to teach effectively. During Sunday school, teachers often referred to individuals and events that class members knew. When Davon misbehaved, Sister Justine reminded him of their mutual connection to his rather stern grandmother. A sense of community also was fostered during the "Children's Story," a part of the regular Sunday morning worship services, when the pastor or other church leaders would tell the children stories relating biblical concepts to the lives of famous African Americans or to African or African-American folktales. These stories encouraged a sense of pride in being African American and connected the child to a broader African or African-American heritage.

Community ties also were seen as central to survival. When Mrs. Hudley told the story of her home burning down when she was a child, it was neighbors and community members who provided the family with the shelter, food, and clothing necessary for survival (Hudley et al., 2003/2009).

Inherent Worth of Each Individual: Love and Respect. Another key concept to emerge from this research program was the inherent worth of each individual. This worth exists independently of material success and social status. In the words of a popular hymn, each individual is a "child of the King" with unique, God-given gifts. As such, each child is entitled to love and respect, and with opportunity and effort will go far. As elaborated in the stories told in Sunday school, vacation Bible school, and other church contexts, however, the journey will be difficult. Just as many were blind to Jesus—a powerful, personal role model for many African-American children—many will not see the black child's inner resources and strengths. Just as the Egyptians enslaved and oppressed Moses' people, some will attempt to oppress the black child. These and other stories told to children, however, also stress that through faith, effort, and community, they too, like the Hebrew people, can prevail. The challenge is to remain a loving and moral person throughout the journey, and to maintain a deep optimism in the ultimate rewards of a successful journey.

The following excerpt from Mrs. Hudley's narrative of her experiences walking to segregated school as a seven-year-old illustrates how religious beliefs can aid children in a successful journey despite racism. "The whites would be walking one way. And we'd be walking the other. They'd yell at us, 'You dirty, black niggers! We hate you! We hate you!' I'd go to Mama and ask her, 'Why do they hate us?' She'd always take me to the Bible. She taught me that God loves us all. God is the judge. She taught me not to take hate inside of myself" (Haight, 1998, p. 213). Mrs. Hudley went on to explain that when we hate, we destroy that part of God which he left inside each of us when he created us. From Mrs. Hudley's perspective, the black children were not the victims of this story; rather, their taunters were.

The inherent worth of children also was communicated through the love that adults showed them. Indeed, a love for children pervaded the narratives collected in this research program as well as the practices observed. For example, when asked what made a good Sunday school teacher, adults at First Baptist Church did not refer to intellectual qualities or professional achievement. A good Sunday school teacher loves children. In describing her life's work, Mrs. Hudley repeatedly emphasized, "I love children, period." This love provided a basis for a relationship that was viewed as prerequisite to effective socialization.

A respect for children also pervaded adults' beliefs and practices. At First Baptist Church, children were seen as the hope of the future, but also respected as models for spiritual salvation. The pastor exhorted the congregation to "learn to be more childlike," that is, to trust and have faith in God. Furthermore, children's spiritual experiences were taken seriously. For example, ten-year-old Edith repeatedly interacted with visions of her dead mother. These visions were interpreted by her father and pastor as legitimate spiritual experiences. Mrs. Hudley's belief that the dead remain connected to the living was introduced and reinforced through relationships in middle childhood with these adults.

Appropriate Adult-Child Relationships. Love and respect for the child and the child's spiritual experiences, however, did not lead to dissolution of generational boundaries. Haight (2002) described the nature of adult-child relationships at First Baptist Church as "child-sensitive and growth-oriented." Sunday school teachers and Mrs. Hudley clearly were sensitive to children's emotional, social, and cognitive immaturity. On the other hand, they demanded respect and took very seriously their charge to pass down spiritual lifelines to children. In a narrative relating a conversation with her son, Mrs. Hudley emphasized, "Honor your mother and father that your days may be longer . . . God gave y'all to me to raise, and if I fail to raise you, I have failed God. And I have to suffer the consequences" (Hudley et al., 2003/2009, p. 158).

Adults' leadership roles, however, did not result in children's passivity. Sunday school classes clearly were led by the teachers, who initiated narratives, posed questions, and made demands on children's behavior and performance. Children actively contributed by responding to questions, debating issues, and putting forth their own interpretations, for example, of how scriptures related to their own lives.

Storytelling. Another key finding from this research program was the importance of storytelling to relating new and complex concepts to children's own lives and experiences. Helping children to understand and then to apply biblical concepts in their everyday lives was described by every informant as a central goal of Sunday school. When asked how they accomplished their goals, adults consistently discussed storytelling. For example, Pastor Daniels explained: "We are convinced that it is out of life that the best applications of any kind of principles can be found. And, certainly if you're going to make sense of it, you have to relate it to life. And, when we tell our own personal stories, there's almost an immediate connection with the youngsters" (Haight, 2002, p. 83).

Observations of Sunday school classes revealed that storytelling was a central part of lessons. Children's formal Sunday school lessons included reading extended excerpts from the King James Bible, which children struggled to understand. It was through the stories that accompanied or followed these texts that the ideas really came to life. These stories had several characteristics. First, these stories frequently contained comments that explicitly linked the biblical texts to children's everyday lives. For example, Sunday school teachers routinely concluded a story with challenges such as, "And how is this lesson relevant to our lives today?" Such stories sometimes contained deeply personal, spiritual meanings. In her oral history, Mrs. Hudley related numerous stories told to her by her own parents more than seventy-five years ago that have provided guidance during difficult times, and remain a touchstone for her life.

Second, narratives related a variety of types of events. Consistent with adults' emphasis on the significance of biblical text, many narratives involved retelling the biblical text. Stories also related personal experiences and elaborated hypothetical events. These stories always followed the biblical text and were used by teachers to illustrate and elaborate key points from the text. Sister Irma ended a particularly dramatic story from her own life with the explicit comments, "Now I share that with you not that you need to be worried about it . . . but that's something that happened to me that's in line with today's lesson" (Haight, 2002, p. 96).

Typically, adults used stories of personal experience to communicate to children how biblical principles are important to their own lives. After discussing with her class several examples from the New Testament of storms at sea, Sister Justine challenged the eight- to twelve-year-old children to understand the metaphorical meaning of "storm." Embedded within this discussion was Sister Justine's personal story of recovery from alcoholism, the "major storm" in her life "calmed by Jesus."

Although stories of personal experience can be very powerful, they also have limitations. First, teachers were concerned about keeping children focused on the biblical text—and children's own personal experiences could be highly distracting to them. Second, teachers were concerned with respecting the privacy of families, and children were not always discreet in relating their stories. On the other hand, teachers also needed to check children's ability to apply the lesson to their own lives. Hypothetical talk referring to temporally sequenced, hypothetical events within narratives was common in Sunday school. Like stories of personal experience, hypothetical stories provided children with concrete instances of how biblical concepts relate to modern, everyday experiences, and elaborated upon biblical text. Sister Justine routinely asked the eight- to ten-year-olds, "If Jesus was walking with us today, what would he want you to do?" Unlike personal narratives, however, they frequently cast a child in the role of protagonist. By middle childhood, some children began to initiate hypothetical narratives. The following excerpt involves nine-year-old Latasha and Sister Justine (Haight, 2002, p. 99):

> LATASHA: If, if you were good and—say you were really good.
>
> SJ: Ahha.
>
> LATASHA: And an angel when you were a child, but you got up and when you got grown up you were just mean in a gang—but then turned back over to God and then when you die—say you were shot by a gang member . . . So where would they go then? Because their sins were there?
>
> SJ: All you have to do is ask for forgiveness! You're saying this person went to church, came back hard-headed, then came back to church, and then got accidentally killed in the line of fire of a gang member? . . . All it takes is believing.
>
> LATASHA [interrupting]: Yeah, but you believe yes and you believe no.
>
> SJ: You can't waiver in your faith.

Social Work Intervention. Information and insights gained from Mrs. Hudley and from the ethnography were used to inform the development of an intervention for children in collaboration with community members. This intervention had two goals. First, community members identified computer literacy as a weak area in the education of many children who had little access to computers either at home or in their relatively poorly funded public schools. As the pastor said, adults worried that children would be "behind the eight ball" (they would be at a disadvantage academically to other children) in their secondary school education and beyond if they did not receive some meaningful computer experience. Second, community members identified multicultural education as a relatively weak area of preparation at the local university. Experience at First Baptist Church could provide a context for white, middle-class students, especially those who intended to become teachers, social workers, or other helping professionals, to learn from the local African-American community.

In collaboration with community members, we developed a computer club for children age three to eighteen. Computers were donated from the local university and housed in the church basement. The computer club operated on Thursday evenings and Saturdays. It was staffed by university students taking a child development class. These students were made aware of research findings regarding spiritual socialization and adult-child interaction in church. They were supervised in their interactions with the children by university staff and church community members (see Haight, 2002, for further discussion of the computer club).

IMPLICATIONS FOR SOCIAL WORK WITH SCHOOL-AGE CHILDREN AND THEIR FAMILIES

Within the United States and other industrialized societies, school is a central context of development in middle childhood. Despite the strong value African-American communities historically have placed on academic achievement and educational attainment (e.g., see Comer, 1988), educational underachievement in public schools remains a sad reality for many African-American children and youth. Yet the context of the African-American church appears to facilitate competence and motivation in children, even those who experience difficulty in the public school setting. The findings presented below, in conjunction with those of Robin Jarrett (1995), Jan Carter-Black (2001), and others, provide several clues for social workers concerned with supporting children's development, especially in school (see Haight & Carter-Black, 2004).

Respect the Inherent Worth of Each Individual

The Sunday school teachers at First Baptist Church taught the children to believe in the inherent dignity and worth of each individual. Regardless of racism and other indignities in the world, they are always "children of the King." Crucial to the development of African-American children are curriculums, programs, and services that incorporate strategies for dealing with racism in ways that diminish the experience as a risk factor. Adults must display beliefs and practices that promote children's healthy racial identity, and awareness of and constructive responses to racism, without promoting hatred or discrimination toward members of other racial groups (Sanders, 1997).

Gain Familiarity with Culturally Normative Styles of Adult-Child Interactions

Adult-child interactions at First Baptist Church were described as "child-sensitive and growth-oriented" (Haight, 2002). Adults prioritized their relationships with children and their families, and they held very high standards for conduct and achievement. As is not uncommon for Sunday school teachers in African-American churches, teachers at First Baptist Church presented in a manner that conveyed strong conviction, absolute authority, and clear generational boundaries. While these teaching techniques may vary from the norm of middle-class white strategies, social workers from other ethnic groups must realize that the meaning African-American children and their families attach to diverse teaching strategies may in fact be quite different from their own. Within the African-American community, teachers who love children and feel a personal calling to teach are easily identified. European-American social workers may respond negatively to tone of voice, volume, cadence of speech, and relatively authoritarian demeanor and affect. African-American children and their families, however, are more likely to pay attention to the teacher's motivation and intentions. Does she care about the children? Is she able to convey that caring? Is she willing to be nurturing and encourage children to be strong, competent, and ambitious, yet conform to church community and parental values and goals? Does she love the children?

Recognize the Centrality of Spirituality for Some Children and Families

Spirituality was the central value at First Baptist Church and a lifeline for Mrs. Hudley. Certain values expressed in public schools, however, may be in conflict with the strong spiritual orientation of many African-American families (e.g., Jarrett, 1995). Awareness by school social workers of a family's spiritual orientation may minimize misunderstanding and facilitate home-school relations. For example, many adults at First Baptist Church seemed less concerned with concepts such as individuality, competition, and personal achievement—considerations more reflective of the analytical learning environment in schools—and more concerned about instilling in children the importance of placing God first in their lives.

Understand Community

At First Baptist Church, children participated as valued members of the community. School social workers need to be cognizant of the meaning of *community* as programs and services are being developed that will enhance the resilience in African-American children. The inclusion of members of a child's extended kinship system, including fictive kin, in planning and decision making resonates with the construction of "family" within the African-American church and larger social community.

Use Storytelling to Engage Children in Learning

Storytelling is a historically and culturally prescribed strategy for passing along lessons for living to children, from which social workers may draw. Mrs. Hudley and teachers in Sunday school used stories to bring biblical meanings to life and to relate central concepts to everyday life. Stories provide a venue for engaging children's imaginations. The use of stories including hypothetical talk keeps children focused on the lesson and minimizes opportunities for childish indiscretions. Furthermore, stories provide powerful and coherent frameworks for interpreting even the most difficult experiences.

SUMMARY

Development in middle childhood, although not as dramatic as that in infancy and adolescence, nonetheless reflects significant biological, psychological, and social growth. As with other periods of development, growth is intertwined with sociocultural-historical contexts. Unfortunately, many children in middle childhood continue to experience risk due to poverty, maltreatment, parental substance misuse, and racial discrimination. Social workers address such issues through direct practice and through policy. Box 7.5 contains practice stories and advice from a social worker who has spent a significant part of his career working to change policy.

By middle childhood, spirituality has become, for many individuals, an important part of their experience and a tool for coping with adversity. Social workers and those engaged in community-based youth programs who have some knowledge of the ethos and principles of the African-American church will understand how the church, especially Sunday

··

**BOX 7.5 PRACTICE STORY AND ADVICE
FROM THE FIELD**

**Steve A., social work professor and policy expert:
"You don't develop coalitions overnight."**

*After completing his MSW, Steve A. worked for ten years for the
Michigan state legislature. He then completed a PhD in political science and currently is a social work professor. He conducts research
on social policy and teaches students in MSW and doctoral social
work programs. In this interview, he discusses the ways in which
social workers are involved in policy, relates a practice story, and
offers some advice for students interested in policy work.*

*What are some of the contexts in which social workers interested in
social policy might work?*

There is a huge need for advocacy, and there are a lot of social
advocacy organizations out there. They can play an important role in
the political process, and in policy development. And I mean anything
from local community organization advocacy, to the state-level associations and federal associations, like Children's Defense and the Center
on Budget and Policy Priorities. There are a lot of social service-
oriented think tanks. But there are a lot of possibilities at the local,
state, and federal level for some types of advocacy-oriented positions.

Another route for those who come out of policy is to go into government. For example, I had a couple of [MSW] policy students who
did their placements down there at the Illinois Department of Human
Services and then got hired at either the local or state offices, to keep
working. So they could do a number of things. Some of them go into
management, in terms of running a local office; others go into state
evaluation units, which would be closer to the work that I did in the
House. So there are a lot of different opportunities along the government lines.

You know I never went this route [local agency] myself, but I did
some research in aging and I got to be friends with a guy who is running an area agency on aging. I saw the types of things that he could
do in terms of just developing service networks, and his role was very
interesting. It was a role of management, because he had to manage
programs, but also he had to be out, advocating on behalf of seniors in
his region. He became very familiar with government funding sources
and what it is that they advocate, so I thought it was a very rich world.
I thought of going that way for a while: heading a local agency.

One of our graduates went in kind of at the ground level of the
agency, and she has moved up to program director. And I have no
doubt that some day she will be the director of the agency . . . You

··

know, you can start out in practice and move up, or you start out in policy and move up more as a manager type, and I have seen it happen both ways. Those are interesting jobs, running a local agency or even being a program director in a local agency, where you have a lot of say in what direction the agency might go in terms of initiatives, and how they go about coming up with the money to do that, or convincing the public it's a good thing to do. Those are all viable roles I have seen our students take.

What were some people or experiences that helped you to understand policy?

The guy that I mentioned before, who was my subcommittee chair, the thing that I always admired about him was he was just dogged. He had that perspective. He knew that things didn't change very quickly, and I think a lot of times the staff would have given up, but every year he had his little tick list of things that he was going to bring up again. He was the author of the mandatory seat-belt law in Michigan. When I got there [state legislature], he had already proposed the seat-belt legislation about ten times. Finally got it passed in its sixteenth year. And I talked to him about that. When I first got there, he was still a lot of votes short. He said, "I'm going to get this sooner or later. I get a few votes every year, and I go back and I work more people every year. And every year it's gone up, but sooner or later I am going to get this passed." When I got there I was a little skeptical, but you know fifteen or sixteen years out he got it passed, and it was because he did it every year. He worked somebody every year, and he kept making these little gains, and he finally got it changed. And it's not the biggest change in the world, but it's a fairly major change in that state. But it couldn't have happened without somebody just pushing and pushing every year and building coalitions and not getting too frustrated by getting beaten every year . . . You have to be very persistent and recognize the complexity of things, and the resistance to change, and the importance of going at it year in and year out.

What advice do you have for social workers interested in going into policy?

Respect diverse views. In legislature you have people who are all over the board. We had 110 members, and you had some really right-wing people, and you had some very liberal people . . . One of the problems I see with some of our students—and I try and work with them on this because I was that way—social workers tend to come in having pretty strong views about things. When you go into a legislature, or even a bureaucracy that's focused just on social services, you get a range of views that are quite a bit different from your own—

often quite a bit more conservative than your own. And if you come on too strong, and don't learn to respect those views and don't really put quite an effort into understanding them, it compromises your ability to be effective . . . I mean, I have heard members and legislators say the same thing, just what an experience it is of broadening your perspectives on what people think. Because you have to. I think in general for our students that's a real important thing, if they go into that kind of broader arena where there are a lot of conflicting interest groups wanting things. It's just a way of thinking about things that most people don't have when they start out.

Understand that most change is incremental. Unless you are really lucky, changes that are big don't happen very often—it's just the nature of things. Most changes tend to be small and incremental and a lot of times that flusters people, because they are in this partially because they think big changes are needed, or they would have gone and done something else in the first place. So then you get into the environment, and first of all you find out that it's much more complex than you thought, and there are a lot of people who don't think like you. So you have to be pretty patient in terms of learning the players and learning how things actually work. But then you also have to be persistent in terms of long-term perspective on change. You might get lucky and you might see a big change right away. But usually that doesn't happen, and most successful change efforts that I have seen have been the combination of long periods of work by a lot of different people. So it is really important to know people and form coalitions with them, which again has something to do with being able to work with people who don't think quite like you. But also realizing that things don't happen very quickly and a lot of times it's a small change. If you keep making small changes every year, they accumulate over time into something that makes a lot of sense.

Make a time commitment. You have to make a little bit of a time commitment, and I mean you have to stay several years so that you learn the actors. You don't develop coalitions overnight. You have to meet people. They have to trust you, and you have to develop working relationships. People who end up being most effective in my mind, in terms of advocacy change efforts, usually have been around a while. You know, it's almost like an industry. You have to do the legwork and the development, because credentials really become important. I mean, we tend to be seen as specialists—you are not asked to talk about every area. You are asked to talk about an area where you are seen as having credibility, and that credibility tends to come with time, and being tested.

school, functions as a significant context for children's socialization. This increased knowledge can be called upon as a guide in the development of various community-based youth programs that support rather than conflict with the characteristics of an African-American, alternative system of beliefs. Programs designed to reach children and youth might even consider modeling effective child development strategies employed by the church as they seek to develop culturally appropriate programs that are tailored to specific communities. Similarly, academic and extramural school-based programs that reflect dimensions of the relationships and interactions between African-American children and their Sunday school teachers, pastors, mothers' boards, and other significant church leaders may find that children exhibit competencies where previously they were struggling. Such strategies are examples of strengths-based practice.

Study and Discussion Questions

1. Considering the global diversity of religious and spiritual beliefs, how would you define religion and spirituality? How might you recognize such orientations in your social work clients?

2. When and how is it appropriate for social workers to discuss spiritual issues with their clients? How might these discussions differ from proselytizing?

3. How might your own spirituality or religion affect your future work (both positively and negatively) not only with children, but with clients across the life span?

4. How might the relationships that children formed at First Baptist Church serve as protective factors in public school?

5. What might social workers learn from the interactions of teachers at First Baptist Church with school-age children?

6. Considering development in middle childhood, how do you explain Tamminen's finding that children in middle childhood are especially moved or responsive to spiritual experiences?

7. What are some of the risks to development in middle childhood, and how might these risks be addressed by social workers through direct practice and policy?

8. Consider Mitchell. How might his undiagnosed, biologically based learning disorder have impacted the ways in which adults and peers responded to him, as well as his perceptions of himself? What interventions might be appropriate for Mitchell's family members and peers? How might religiously based beliefs, such as the inherent worth of each individual, serve as protective factors for Mitchell?

Resources

Interested students can supplement this chapter through a number of excellent web-based resources.

The MacArthur Network on Successful Pathways through Middle Childhood systematically studies the course of development during middle childhood. Additionally, the program explores how typical developmental experiences are similar and different within and across cultural and racial groups. Available at http://childhood.isr.umich.edu/mission/index.html.

The Centers for Disease Control and Prevention outlines physical and psychosocial changes that parents and professionals can expect to observe as a child advances to middle childhood. Available at http://www.cdc.gov/ncbddd/child/middlechildhood.htm.

The MacArthur Network on Successful Pathways through Middle Childhood offers parents and professionals access to comprehensive bibliographies, and research reports. Available at http://childhood.isr.umich.edu/.

Lois Melina offers thoughts about the impact of adoption on the child during middle childhood. The website also provides links to other adoption sites. Melina is the editor of *Adopted Child* newsletter and on the Evan B. Donaldson Adoption Institute's (EBDAI) board. EBDAI is dedicated to improving information about adoption and advocating for practice and policy change in the field. Available at http://www.ivillage.com/talking-about-adoption-your-elementary-school-age-child/6-a-128133.

The Children, Youth, and Family Consortium at the University of Minnesota provides information on normal and abnormal development for children and teens. The consortium also provides links and academic information on family development. A brief overview of middle childhood development is available at http://www.cyfc.umn.edu/watch/watc_connections.html.

The U.S. Department of Education's National Center for Education Statistics has prepared a sixty-seven-page working paper, *Measures of Socio-emotional Development in Middle Childhood*. The paper is available at http://nces.ed.gov/pubs2001/200103.pdf.

References

Ama, T. (2005). *Why are the Japanese non-religious? Japanese spirituality: Being non-religious in a religious culture*. New York: University Press of America.

American Psychiatric Association. (2000). Disorders usually first diagnosed in infancy, childhood, or adolescence. In *Diagnostic and statistical manual of mental disorders* (4th ed., text revision, pp. 94–51). Washington, DC: Author.

Becker, W. H. (1997). The black church: Manhood and mission. In T. Fulop & A. Raboteau (Eds.), *African American religion: Interpretive essays in history and culture*. New York: Routledge.

Bullis, R. (1996). *Spirituality in social work practice*. Washington, DC: Taylor & Francis.

Canda, E. R. (1997). Spirituality. In R. Edwards (Ed.), *Encyclopedia of social work* (19th ed., Supplement, pp. 299–309). Washington, DC: NASW Press.

Canda, E. R., & Furman, L. D. (1999). *Spiritual diversity in social work practice: The heart of helping*. New York: Free Press.

Carter-Black, J. (2001). The myth of "the tangle of pathology": Resilience strategies employed by middle-class African-American families. *Journal of Family Social Work, 6*(4), 75–100.

Chandy, J. M., Blum, R. W., & Resnick, M. D. (1996). Gender-specific outcomes for sexually abused adolescents. *Child Abuse & Neglect, 20*(12), 1219–1231.

Coleman, R. (1981). Blacks in Utah history: An unknown legacy. In H. Z. Papanikolas (Ed.), *The peoples of Utah*. Salt Lake City: Utah Historical Society.

Coles, R. (1990). *The spiritual life of children*. Boston: Houghton Mifflin.

Comer, J. P. (1988). *Maggie's American dream: The life and times of a black family*. New York: New American Library.

Crawford, E., Wright, M., & Masten, A. (2006). Resilience and spirituality in youth. In E. Roehlkepartain, P. E. King, L. Wagener, & P. Benson (Eds.), *The handbook of spiritual development in childhood and adolescence* (pp. 355–370). Thousand Oaks, CA: Sage.

Dishion, T. J., & McMahon, R. J. (1998). Parental monitoring and the prevention of child and adolescent problem behavior: A conceptual and empirical formulation. *Clinical Child and Family Psychology Review, 1*, 61–75.

Earhart, H. B. (1997). *Religion in the Japanese experience: Sources and interpretations* (2nd ed.). Belmont, CA: Wadsworth Publishing.

Ellison, C. (1997). Contemporary African American religion: What have we learned from NSBA? *African American Research Perspectives, 3*, 30–39.

Erikson, E. (1963) *Childhood and society* (2nd ed.). New York: Norton.

Fetzer Institute/National Institute on Aging Working Group. (1999). *Multidimensional measurement of religiousness/spirituality for use in health research: A report of the Fetzer Institute/National Institute on Aging Working Group*. Kalamazoo, MI: Fetzer Institute.

Fisher, C. B., Jackson, J. F., & Villarruel, F. A. (1998). The study of African-American and Latin American youth. In W. Damon & R. M. Lerner (Eds.), *Handbook of child psychology: Vol. 1, Theoretical models of human development* (5th ed., pp. 1145–1207). New York: Wiley.

Flavell, J. H., Green, F. L., & Flavell, E. R. (1995). Young children's knowledge about thinking. *Monographs of the Society for Research in Child Development, 60* (1, Serial No. 243), 1–95.

Frankin, J. H. (1969). *From slavery to freedom: A history of American Negros* (3rd ed.). New York: Vintage Books.

Frazier, E. F. (1964). *The Negro church in America*. New York: Schocken Books.

Fulop, T., & Raboteau, A. (Eds.). (1997). *African American religion: Interpretive essays in history and culture*. New York: Routledge.

Gallup Poll survey results on religion in the U.S. (n.d.). Retrieved from http://www .gallup.com/poll/1690/Religion.aspx

Garland, D. (2008). Christian social services. In T. Mizrahi & L. Davis (Eds.), *Encyclopedia of social work* (20th ed., Vol. 1, pp. 282–288). Washington, DC: NASW Press; New York: Oxford University Press.

Garmezy, N. (1985). Stress-resistant children: The search for protective factors. In *Journal of Child Psychology and Psychiatry, Book Supplement 4* (pp. 213–233). Oxford: Pergamon Press.

Garvey, C. (1990). *Play*. Cambridge, MA: Harvard University Press.

Gauvain, M. (1999). Everyday opportunities for the development of planning skills: Sociocultural and family influences. In A. Goncu (Ed.), *Children's engagement in the world: Sociocultural perspective* (pp. 173–201). New York: Cambridge University Press.

Gauvain, M. (2009). Planning. In R. Shweder (Ed.), *The child: An encyclopedic companion* (pp. 740–741). Chicago: University of Chicago Press.

Grealy, L. (1994). *Autobiography of a face*. New York: Houghton Mifflin

Haight, W. (1998). "Gathering the spirit" at First Baptist Church: Spirituality as a protective factor in the lives of African American children. *Social Work, 43*, 213–221.

Haight, W. (2002). *African-American children at church: A sociocultural perspective*. New York: Cambridge University Press.

Haight, W., & Carter-Black, J. (2004). His eye is on the sparrow: Teaching and learning in an African American church. In E. Gregory, S. Long, & D. Volk (Eds.), *Many pathways to literacy: Young children learning with siblings, grandparents, peers and communities* (pp. 195–207). New York: Routledge Falmer.

Hale, J. B., & Fiorello, C. A. (2004). *School neuropsychology. A practitioner's handbook*. New York: Guilford.

Hale-Benson, J. (1987). The transmission of faith to young black children. Paper presented at the Conference on Faith Development in Early Childhood, Henderson, NC.

Hay, D., & Nye, R. (2006). *The spirit of the child*. London: Jessica Kingsley Publishers.

Holden, G., & Vittrup, J. (2010). *Handbook of cultural and developmental science*. M. Bornstein (Ed.). New York: Psychology Press.

Hudley, E., Haight, W., & Miller, P. (2003/2009). *Raise up a child: Human development in an African-American family*. Chicago: Lyceum Books.

Hyman, C., & Handal, P. (2006). Definitions and evaluation of religion and spirituality items by religious professionals: A pilot study. *Journal of Religion and Health, 45*(2), 264–282.

Inoue, Y. (Ed.). (2008). *The 4th research report on college students' perceptions of religions in Japan and Korea*. Tokyo: Kokugakuin University.

Jarrett, R. L. (1995). Growing up poor: The family experiences of socially mobile youth in low-income African-American neighborhoods. *Journal of Adolescent Research, 1*(1), 111–135.

King, P., & Benson, P. (2006). Spiritual development and adolescent well-being and thriving. In E. Roehlkepartain, P. E. King, L. Wagener, & P. Benson (Eds.), *The handbook of spiritual development in childhood and adolescence* (pp. 384–398). Thousand Oaks, CA: Sage.

Koski, W. (2009). School funding. In R. Shweder (Ed.), *The child: An encyclopedic companion* (pp. 859–860). Chicago: University of Chicago Press.

Lavoie, R. (2005). *It's so much work to be your friend*. New York: Simon & Schuster.

Lightfoot, C., Cole, M., & Cole, S. (2009). *The development of children* (6th ed.). New York: Worth Publishers.

Lincoln, C. E. (1999). *Race, religion, and the continuing American dilemma*. New York: Hill & Wang.

Long, C. H. (1997). Perspective for the study of African-American religion in the United States. In E. Fulop & A. Raboteau (Eds.), *African-American religion: Interpretive essays in history and culture* (pp. 21–36). New York: Routledge.

Mack, A. H., Franklin, J. E., Jr., & Frances, R. J. (2003). Substance use disorders. In R. E. Hales & S. C. Yudofsky (Eds.), *The American Psychiatric Publishing textbook of clinical psychiatry* (4th ed., p. 365). Washington, DC: American Psychiatric Publishing.

Masten, A. S., Best, K. M., & Garmezy, N. (1990). Resilience and development: Contributions from the study of children who overcome adversity. *Development and Psychopathology, 2*, 425–444.

McAdoo, H., & Crawford, V. (1991). The Black church and family support programs. *Prevention in Human Services, 9*, 193–203.

Mildred, J., & Plummer, C. A. (2009). Responding to child sexual abuse in the United States and Kenya: Child protection and children's rights. *Children & Youth Services Review, 31*(6), 601–608.

Mitchell, E. P. (1986). Oral tradition: Legacy of faith for the black church. *Religious Education, 81*, 93–112.

Moore, T. (1991). The African-American church: A source of empowerment, mutual help and social change. *Prevention in Human Services, 10*, 147–167.

Moskovitz, S. (1983). *Love despite hate: Child survivors of the Holocaust and their adult lives*. New York: Schocken Books.

Myers, J. E. B. (Ed.). (2011). *APSAC handbook on child maltreatment*. Thousand Oaks, CA: Sage.

Newport, F. (2006). Religion most important to blacks, women, and older Americans. Gallup News Service. Retrieved from http://www.gallup.com/poll/25585/Religion-Most-Important-Blacks-Women-Older%20-Americans.aspx

Oser, F., & Gmunder, P. (1991). *Religious judgment: A developmental perspective*. Birmingham, AL: Religious Education Press.

Oser, F., Scarlett, G., & Bucher, A. (2006). Religious and spiritual development throughout the life span. In W. Damon & R. M. Lerner (Eds.), *Handbook of child psychology: Vol. 1, Theoretical models of human development* (pp. 942–998). Hoboken, NJ: Wiley.

Pargament, K. (2003). Religious/spiritual coping. In *Multidimensional measurement of religiousness/spirituality for use in health research: A report of the Fetzer Institute/National Institute on Aging Working Group* (pp. 43–56). Kalamazoo, MI: Fetzer Institute.

Pargament, K., & Brant, C. (1998). Religion and coping. In H. Koenig (Ed.), *Handbook of religion and mental health* (pp. 112–129). Boston: Academic Press.

Piaget, J. (1928). *Judgement and reasoning in the child*. London: Routledge & Kegan Paul.

Pinderhughes, E. (1989). *Understanding race, ethnicity, and power: The key to efficacy in clinical practice*. New York: Free Press.

Ratcliff, D. (Ed.). (2004). *Children's spirituality: Christian perspectives, research, and applications*. Eugene, OR: Cascade Books.

Ratcliff, D., & May, S. (2004). Identifying children's spirituality, Walter Wangerin's perspectives, and an overview of the book. In D. Ratcliff (Ed.), *Children's spirituality: Christian perspectives, research, and applications* (pp. 473–483). Eugene, OR: Cascade Books.

Ratcliff, D., & Nye, R. E. (2006). Childhood spirituality: Strengthening the research foundation. In E. C. Roehlkepartain, P. E. King, L. Wagener, & P. Benson (Eds.), *The handbook of spiritual development in childhood and adolescence* (pp. 473–483). Thousand Oaks, CA: Sage.

Regnerus, M. D. (2003). Religion and positive developmental outcomes: A review of research and theory. *Review of Religion Research, 44*(4), 394–413.

Roehlkepartain, E. C., King, P. E., Wagener, L., & Benson, P. (Eds.). (2006). *The handbook of spiritual development in childhood and adolescence.* Thousand Oaks, CA: Sage.

Rogoff, B. (2003). *The cultural nature of human development.* New York: Oxford University Press.

Rosengren, K. S., Johnson, C. N., & Harris, P. L. (2000). *Imagining the impossible: Magical, scientific, and religious thinking in children.* New York: Cambridge University Press.

Rubin, K., Bukowski, W., & Parker, J. (1998). Peer interactions, relationships, and groups. In W. Damon & R. M. Lerner (Eds.), *Handbook of child psychology:* Vol. 3, *Social, emotional, and personality development* (5th ed., pp. 571–645). New York: Wiley.

Saleebey, D. (2003). Strengths-based practice. In R. English (Ed.), *Encyclopedia of social work* (19th ed., Supplement, pp. 150–162). Washington, DC: NASW Press.

Sameroff, A. J., & Haith, M. M. (1996). *The five to seven year shift: The age of reason and responsibility.* Chicago: University of Chicago Press.

Sanders, M. G. (1997). Overcoming obstacles: Academic achievement as a response to racism and discrimination. *Journal of Negro Education, 66*(1), 83–93.

Scott, L., Munson, M., McMillen, J., & Ollie, M. (2006). Religious involvement and its association to risk behaviors among older youth in foster care. *American Journal of Community Psychology, 38*, 223–236.

Sheridan, M., Bullis, R., Adcock, C., Berlin, S., & Miller, P. C. (1992). Practitioners' personal and professional attitudes and behaviors toward religion and spirituality: Issues for education and practice. *Journal of Social Work in Education, 28*, 190–203.

Smith, C., & Denton, M. L. (2005). *Soul searching: The religious and spiritual lives of American teenagers.* New York: Oxford University Press.

Smitherman, G. (1977). *Talkin and testifyin: The language of black America.* Boston: Houghton Mifflin.

Stack, C. B. (1974). *All our kin: Strategies for survival in a black community.* New York: Harper & Row.

Stark, R., Hamberg, E., & Miller, A. (2005). Exploring spirituality and unchurched religions in America, Sweden, and Japan. *Journal of Contemporary Religion, 20*(1), 3–23.

Suina, J., & Smolkin, L. (1994). From natal culture to school culture to dominant society culture: Supporting transitions for Pueblo Indian students. In P. Greenfield & R. Cocking (Eds.), *Cross-cultural roots of minority child development* (pp. 115–130). Hillsdale, NJ: Erlbaum.

Tamminen, K. (1991). *Religious development in childhood and youth: An empirical study.* Helsinki: Suomalainen Tiedeakatemia.

Tamminen, K. (1994). Religious experiences in childhood and adolescence: A viewpoint of religious development between the ages of 7 and 20. *International Journal for the Psychology of Religion, 4*(2), 61-85.

Traphagan, J. (2005). Multidimensional measurement of religiousness/spirituality for use in health research in cross-cultural perspective. *Research on Aging, 27*(4), 387-419.

U.S. Department of Health and Human Services, Health Resources and Services Administration, Maternal and Child Health Bureau. (2009). *Child health USA 2008-2009*. Rockville, MD: U.S. Department of Health and Human Services. Retrieved from http://mchb.hrsa.gov/chusa08/pdfs/c08.pdf

Wills, D. W. (1997). The central themes of American religious history: Pluralism, puritanism, and the encounter of black and white. In T. Fulop & A. Raboteau (Eds.), *African American religion: Interpretive essays in history and culture* (pp. 7-20). New York: Routledge.

World Values Survey. (1993). Dearborn, MI: Inter-University Consortium for Political and Social Research, University of Michigan.

Yomiui Shinbun, 2008. [Japanese newspaper article.]

8

Social Work with Adolescents
Mentoring in Schools

Susan A. Cole, Wendy L. Haight, and Edward Taylor

The focal system in this chapter is the adolescent. As you read, consider the rapidly changing biological, psychological, and social characteristics of people eleven to twenty-two years old. In the United States and other industrialized societies, school remains an important context for development for many individuals throughout adolescence. Social workers have a central role in delivering school-based services to adolescents. Mentoring programs have been shown to be effective for adolescents as they transition into adulthood and, increasingly, are based in school settings. As you read, consider the mesosystems created between microsystems formed at school, home, and the community through school-based mentoring programs. How might such mesosystems affect and be affected by the developing adolescent?

Adolescence is a time of dramatic physical, psychological, and social development. The rapid changes young people experience can be challenging for them, their parents, and their caregivers. Stanley Hall (1904) described adolescence as a period of storm and stress characterized by mood disruptions, conflict with parents, and risky behaviors. For some individuals, however, adolescence is no more stressful than childhood. As they enter adolescence, individuals vary in the skills they have developed during childhood, as well as their experiences in home, school, and community, which can affect their functioning in adolescence. Indeed, adolescents display a wide range of responses to pubertal and other changes, from pride and enjoyment of new roles, to more cautious or even negative responses. Nevertheless, adolescents remain one of the most stereotyped groups in contemporary society, widely portrayed in the media as delinquent, overly sexual, foolish, irresponsible, and troubled (Steinberg, 2011).

Although most contemporary scholars would disagree with such stereotypes, they agree that adolescence is a time of rapid development. From approximately eleven to twenty-two years of age, adolescents negotiate biological, psychological, social, and economic transitions as they prepare to assume adult roles. The expectations of adults for how and when adolescents make the transition to adulthood, and what roles and responsibilities are appropriate for them, vary by culture. The acquisition of new roles is shaped within an expanding array of diverse social contexts, including family, school, peer groups, work, leisure activities, and community organizations. For many individuals, especially in the United States and other industrialized nations, school remains a central context of development throughout adolescence. The mentoring interventions that are the focus of the school social work interventions described in this chapter can provide crucial support for adolescents negotiating the transition from childhood to adulthood.

SCHOOL SOCIAL WORK WITH ADOLESCENTS

School social work blends the fields of education and social work to support the well-being and academic achievement of children in school. School social work is an active and growing profession, with approximately 27,000 social workers providing services in schools throughout the United States (U.S. Department of Education, 2007). Like other social work specializations, school social work applies intervention strategies that are evidence based (Franklin, Harris, & Lagana-Riordan, 2010). School social work emerged at the beginning of the twentieth century from a concern for children and youth whose school learning was impeded by poverty or family issues. School social workers, called "visiting teachers," went to the homes of immigrant children to develop links between families and schools. A primary role of contemporary school social workers remains that of home-school-community liaison.

School social workers have a variety of roles. First, they provide direct interventions to children and families. For example, they may lead social skills groups or mediate disputes between students. Second, they link children and families to community services not available at the school. For example, they may provide referrals for children identified with possible **depression** or **attention deficit with hyperactivity disorder**, or identify support for children whose families are homeless. Third, school social workers also advocate for children to make schools more responsive to their needs. For example, they may advocate that schools adopt positive approaches to discipline, or meet the needs of young people with developmental disabilities. One important context in which school social workers function in all three roles is multidisciplinary teams. Multidisciplinary teams convene to evaluate and plan interventions for children who are struggling in school, for example, those who may have a learning or behavioral disorder. They may comprise parents, psychologists, teachers, principals, and other relevant school staff members. Following a thorough assessment, the teams develop **individual education plans** (IEPs), formal plans to assist students' learning and functioning in the school setting. The school social worker might meet with the parents and child to evaluate the child's social and developmental history, help the parent understand and participate in the team, and advocate services for the child.

How school social workers support and advocate for children varies by state and by school district. In some areas, school social workers primarily do assessment and referral to community resources for therapeutic interventions. In other areas, the school social worker actually engages the student and family in therapeutic interventions. Providing immediate, direct interventions for adolescent problems is becoming more important as funding limitations have shrunk other community resources. The availability of a school social worker is especially important for students in rural school districts, where the school social worker may be the only resource for mental health screening, assessment, intervention, and referral. Some rural districts have so few social workers that they rely on teachers to provide functions usually provided by social workers (Cole, 1993).

The typical daily schedule for a school social worker encompasses a diverse array of activities. On any given day in Illinois, for instance, a school social worker might facilitate groups for students experiencing grief, struggling with their parents' divorces, or negotiating pregnancy and parenting. (Box 8.1 describes some of the challenges faced by pregnant and parenting

---

BOX 8.1 TEEN PREGNANCY

Between 1992 and 2005, adolescent pregnancy rates declined by 45 percent for African-American girls, 50 percent for European-American girls, and 26 percent for Hispanic girls. In 2006, however, adolescent pregnancy rates increased for all three ethnic groups. The national pregnancy rate for all young women fifteen to nineteen years of age was 71.5 pregnancies per 1,000 women, which was about 4 percent higher than in 2005. These numbers indicate that in 2006, 750,000 women under twenty years of age (7 percent) became pregnant.

Pregnancy is an important risk factor for healthy development in adolescence. Teen mothers and their babies face increased physical health risks and decreased future opportunities. With proper support, adolescent mothers can finish their educations, sustain lasting romantic and other interpersonal relationships, and successfully parent their children. As a group, however, they face more economic, health, and developmental difficulties than other young women. Young women need our support in these areas:

- understanding the emotional and social factors that may sustain adolescent pregnancy choices
- programs that help prevent teen pregnancy

- a gateway for physical, emotional, and educational support early in the pregnancy
- assistance in making an informed choice on whether to carry the fetus to term
- assistance in making an informed choice on whether to parent the child upon delivery or to place the child in an adoptive home
- ensuring that those who choose to parent know how to care for a baby, are in a safe environment, and have the necessary financial and emotional support
- intervention to minimize the risk of becoming pregnant again soon, thereby overwhelming the mother and her social support system
- finding productive ways to ensure that the father provides financial, physical, and emotional support for the child

A challenge for social workers is to discover interventions and educational methods that increase sexual responsibility in both adolescent boys and girls. Teenage boys are often left out of the psychosocial equation once the girl is pregnant. This not only penalizes the girl, but may also stand in the way of the teenage male's emotional and social growth. That is, the boy is not challenged to develop sexual responsibility before or after the pregnancy. In addition to understanding the dangers of unprotected sex, adolescent boys need help comprehending that once pregnancy occurs, they have moral responsibilities to the mother, developing baby, and society. The goal is not to prevent or delay sexuality by threatening adolescents, but rather to improve and increase their abstract thinking skills, empathy, and understanding of moral-social responsibilities.

Source: Kost, Henshaw, & Carlin, 2010.

teens.) The school social worker might then meet with a group of community volunteers to educate them for working as mentors for middle school children. The social worker might collaborate with teachers, school administrators, and community leaders to develop school policies for responding to the increasing cultural diversity of our public schools, or to the unique needs of homeless families with youth trying to stay in school. Later, the social worker might meet with parents in their home to discuss the development and functioning of a child referred for assessment of a possible learning disorder.

As this overview suggests, school social workers apply developmental, ecological-systems thinking. Ecological perspectives in school social work emphasize the relations of the child, family, school, and community that can affect educational outcomes (Germain, 1999; Kutash, Duchnowski, Robbins, & Keenan, 2008; Monkman, 1999). Understanding children's development alerts the school social worker to potential problems and suggests intervention strategies (Haight, Carpenter, & Tata, 1999). For example, understanding adolescent development may help a school social worker distinguish depression from normative stress and decide whether a referral to a therapist, community psychiatrist, or school mentoring program is most appropriate. It also alerts school social workers to potential mismatches between children's developmental needs and the demands of the school system (Allen-Meares et al., 2000). For example, puberty is a universal, socially significant developmental transition that occurs at about the same time that many young adolescents move from small, personal, elementary school classrooms to large middle schools with multiple teachers and new peers (Germain, 1999). School social workers, anticipating the stress that may emerge as a result of the mismatch between large school systems and children's developmental needs for support during early adolescence, may advocate change in the school system, such as elementary-style education to extend through eighth grade, small homeroom cohorts, or school-within-a-school models (see Dewees, 2009). In addition, they may develop preventive interventions such as school-based mentoring programs to establish personal, trusting relationships for children with an adult, to compensate for the impersonal nature of an existing middle school system.

The following excerpt describes the mentoring relationship of a young adolescent in foster care and a worker who has retired from child protective service.

> Jeremy is a thirteen-year-old child living in the rural Midwest. He is in foster care following his parents' arrest for crimes associated with their drug addiction. His parents are now serving prison sentences, and Jeremy is facing an adolescence in long-term foster care. Fortunately, Jeremy has been placed with loving foster parents who genuinely care for and support him. He is thriving in a home with structure: regular meals, bedtimes, school attendance, and leisure activities, and, most of all, available parents. Nevertheless, Jeremy is aware of the stigma associated with drug misuse in his small community, and feels pressure to be a "perfect child" for his foster parents. In addition, he feels great ambivalence about distancing himself from the parents he loves. He also feels tremendous rage at being separated from them.
>
> Shortly after entering foster care, Jeremy was matched through a mentoring program with a retired child protection worker who lives in his community. Lydia picks Jeremy up from school every Thursday, and they go to "their restaurant" for a treat and to talk. Because she lives in the same small town as Jeremy, Lydia has even been able to attend some of Jeremy's baseball games. Jeremy treasures his time with Lydia, in part because it makes him feel special. As a child who experienced neglect in his birth home and is one of seven foster children, Jeremy has received precious little one-on-one time with adults. As their relationship has deepened, Lydia has proven to be an

invaluable sounding board for Jeremy to express his anger and grief. By listening, providing an adult perspective, and communicating her unconditional positive regard, Lydia has become a major source of support for Jeremy.

In this excerpt, the term **mentor** is used to refer to a relationship between an older, more experienced adult and an unrelated younger person, in which the adult provides ongoing support, encouragement, and guidance. Over time, the mentor and young person may develop a special bond of mutual commitment, respect, identification, and loyalty. This relationship supports the adolescent's well-being and development, and facilitates the transition into adulthood (Rhodes, 2002).

A positive, supportive relationship with an adult such as a mentor is a protective factor for young teens. This thirteen-year-old girl is enjoying a visit with her grandmother, a retired middle school teacher.

Research suggests that informal relationships with caring adults such as Lydia can make an important difference in the lives of vulnerable children and adolescents (Garmezy, 1985; Robins & Rutter, 1990; Werner & Smith, 1982). Adolescents who grew up under extremely difficult circumstances yet somehow succeeded often credit their success to the influence of an informal role model or mentor (Fisher & Rivas, 2001; Freedman, 1995; Lefkowitz, 1986; Levine & Nidiffer, 1996). Support from natural mentors— more experienced people with whom the adolescent has established an informal, supportive relationship—is associated with improvements in the psychological, social, academic, and career functioning of at-risk adolescents (McLearn, Colasanto, & Schoen, 1998; Rhodes & Davis, 1996). Adolescents with natural mentors are less likely to smoke marijuana or engage in delinquent activities (Zimmermann, Bingenheimer, & Notaro, 2002). Unfortunately, relatively few adolescents spontaneously develop such relationships with natural mentors (Rhodes & Davis, 1996). Even for those adolescents predisposed to do so, families, schools, and communities have changed in ways that have dramatically reduced the availability of caring adults. Families are increasingly mobile, and isolated from family members and other safe adults who could serve as mentors. In addition, some parents who live in high-crime neighborhoods sequester their children at home, which protects them from danger but also restricts their opportunities for contact with any supportive, caring, adult neighbors (Rhodes, Bogat, Roffman, Edelman, & Galasso, 2002).

One approach to intervention with adolescents has been to develop formal mentoring programs, which pair supportive adults with vulnerable adolescents. In recent years, thousands of mentoring programs have emerged. These efforts have included a wide range of youth (e.g., gay, lesbian, and questioning youth; pregnant girls; African-American boys) and volunteers (e.g., teachers, community members, executives, and elderly people; McLearn et al., 1998). Research suggests that, beyond their intuitive appeal, mentors assigned through more formal volunteer programs can positively affect youth outcomes through a combination of emotional support, practical assistance, and role modeling (Rhodes, 2002). Formal mentors can promote social and emotional development, promote school achievement, provide critical support to pregnant and parenting teenagers, and reduce delinquent behavior and substance misuse (Grossman & Tierney, 1998; Morrow & Styles, 1995; Rhodes, 2002; Rhodes, Contreras, & Mangelsdorf, 1994; Sipe, 2002; Tierney, Grossman, & Resch, 1995). In general, mentoring relationships that are of longer duration, have more frequent and consistent meetings, and are associated with strong emotional bonds are associated with better youth outcomes (Rhodes & Du Bois, 2006).

A recent trend in mentoring is school-based programs, which make up approximately 28 percent of mentoring programs (Wheeler, Keller, & Du

Although adolescent pregnancy is a significant risk factor, with adequate support, teen mothers may go on to raise healthy children and enjoy productive lives.

Bois, 2010). Although a rarity fifteen years ago, school-based mentoring is the fastest-growing form of mentoring, serving hundreds of thousands of vulnerable students across the country. In a typical school-based program, children and mentors meet regularly, for example, weekly throughout the school year, to engage in a variety of activities such as homework, talking, or participating in games, arts and crafts, or other activities (e.g., Portwood, Ayers, Kinnison, Waris, & Wise, 2005). These programs can capitalize on the knowledge, referrals, supervision, and support of the many adults who are already in the setting (Rhodes, 2002). They may reach more youth because of the reduced requirements for parental involvement, pose fewer safety risks, and more efficiently monitor the relationships. On the other hand, meetings between youth and mentors typically are limited to the school setting. Relationships tend to be less emotionally intense and of shorter duration than community-based programs (Wheeler et al., 2010).

Research indicates that school-based mentoring programs can be modestly effective in improving support from nonfamilial adults, peer support, perceptions of scholastic efficacy, school-related misconduct, absenteeism, and truancy (Wheeler et al., 2010), as well as improving relationships with teachers (Curtis & Hansen-Schwoebel, 1999; Herrera, 1999; see Rhodes, 2002). They seem to be less effective at improving academic achievement. The programs that yield the best results use volunteers who were well trained, monitored, and supervised. The mentors also continued with the children over time to develop a consistent ongoing relationship. Although not a magic bullet for all problems in adolescence, high-quality, school-based mentoring programs can be helpful preventive interventions for which school social workers may advocate, support, and provide services.

HIGHLIGHTS OF DEVELOPMENT DURING ADOLESCENCE

Mentoring is an intervention particularly well-suited to adolescence, a time of life when young people increasingly explore relationships outside of the family. Roughly speaking, adolescence is the second decade of life. Although at one time adolescence was synonymous with the teenage years (thirteen to nineteen), the adolescent period has lengthened in the United States in the past century, both because young people mature physically earlier and because so many older adolescents and young adults remain economically dependent on their parents into their twenties. Because of the vast changes that occur between ages ten to twenty-two, developmental psychologists find it useful to divide adolescence into three periods: early adolescence (ten to thirteen years), middle adolescence (fourteen to eighteen years), and late adolescence or youth (nineteen to twenty-two years). For those who remain in school, these periods roughly correspond to the middle school, high school, and college years (Steinberg, 2011).

An analysis of 175 societies around the world indicates that adolescence is a widespread, if not universal, social stage (Schlegel & Barry, 1991). Adolescents master the skills necessary for economic survival, learn the appropriate social roles associated with adult status, develop emotional independence from parents and other adults, acquire a deeper understanding of their culture's values and ethical system, and learn to behave in a socially responsible fashion as defined by their culture (Grotevant, 1998). For some adolescents, this developmental period is cut short because of poverty or victimization, and the young person may struggle throughout life to acquire the skills necessary to participate in mainstream society. Box 8.2 describes research by a Taiwanese social worker involved in an intervention designed to help aboriginal girls who had been victimized by prostitution to develop the values and vocational skills necessary to function in mainstream society.

The length of adolescence and the degree to which it is associated with social and psychological disruptions varies greatly across societies. In the United States and other industrialized societies, a gap of seven to nine years typically separates biological changes that mark the onset of sexual maturity from the social changes that confer adult status, such as the right to vote or to marry without parental consent. This lengthy adolescent period has developed in mainstream society in the United States because

BOX 8.2 INTERNATIONAL PERSPECTIVES
Juvenile Prostitution in Taiwan

As in other parts of the world, juvenile prostitution is a serious issue in Taiwan. The government has responded by creating and supporting residential vocational centers to protect and counsel adolescent girls arrested because of prostitution. Such institutions provide young women with a safe home, opportunities to develop alternative means of self-support, and role models. Sadly, a number of the teenagers return to prostitution after leaving the vocational centers.

In an effort to better understand the problem of juvenile prostitution in Taiwan and strengthen intervention programs, Mary Ku, a Taiwanese social worker, researched the risk and protective factors for juvenile prostitution. She found that children's experiences of crushing poverty, domestic violence and maltreatment in their homes, identification as a "bad girl," and sexual abuse were among the risk factors for entry into prostitution. Protective factors that facilitated adolescents' reentry into a conventional lifestyle included cutting ties with previous boyfriends, changes in attitudes toward sexuality, negative experiences in prostitution such as rape and other forms of violence, successful substance misuse rehabilitation, and a positive relationship with a family member.

Source: Ku, 2003.

of the time required to acquire the knowledge and skills necessary to be independent and to perpetuate society (Lightfoot, Cole, & Cole, 2009). It also is linked to a lengthy life expectancy and to limited training and economic opportunities for older adolescents outside of the educational track (Boonstra, 2002).

By contrast, in some societies there is a relatively brief delay between the beginning of sexual maturity and the beginning of adulthood. These are usually societies in which biological maturity occurs late by Western standards and in which the level of technology is relatively low. By the time biological reproduction becomes possible, at about fifteen years of age in many nonindustrial societies, young people already know how to perform the basic tasks of their culture such as farming, weaving cloth, preparing food, and caring for children (Lightfoot, Cole, & Cole, 2009). Because of the variation across time and place in the age of onset and length of adolescence, many developmental psychologists prefer to define adolescence as a series of intertwined biological, psychological, social, and economic transitions from immaturity to maturity (Steinberg, 2011).

Latino culture is preserved in this *quinceañera* (fifteenth birthday) celebration in a rural farming community.

Biological Factors

The biological transition known as **puberty** results in dramatic changes in the adolescent's physical appearance and capability for sexual reproduction. During puberty, the child develops secondary sex characteristics. These characteristics distinguish males and females but are not directly part of the reproductive system, for example, the appearance of body hair, and the development of breasts in females and facial hair in males. Secondary sex characteristics can be distinguished from primary sex characteristics, the sexual organs that are necessary for reproduction. The development of secondary sex characteristics is triggered by hormonal changes resulting in rapid maturation of the gonads (ovaries in girls and testicles in boys; Tanner, 1962). One of the first visible signs of puberty is the adolescent growth spurt. People grow more quickly during this spurt than at any other time of life except infancy. In the span of two to three years, boys may grow as much as nine inches, and girls as much as six or seven inches. Muscle tissue and fat also increase dramatically (Lightfoot, Cole, & Cole, 2009). The magnitude and rate of physical changes experienced during puberty may be more significant than those of infancy, because of their psychological effects as the adolescent reflects upon and interprets those changes. As described in box 8.3, the physical development and health of adolescents in the United States may be threatened by inadequate access to health care due to poverty. Initiating programs such as school-based health clinics often increases adolescents' access to health-care services and accurate information about health-care risks (Kisker & Brown, 1996). Indeed, there are clear links between the access to health and mental health care in the school and enhanced school performance, especially for at-risk youth (Dilley, 2009).

BOX 8.3 POVERTY ACROSS THE LIFE SPAN

Hospitalization

Many low-income families in the United States either have no health insurance or have policies that fail to adequately cover pregnancies and mental disorders. Yet the leading cause of hospitalization for children age ten through fourteen years is mental disorders. For individuals age fifteen through twenty-one years, pregnancy and childbirth account for the largest number of inpatient admissions, with mental disorders being the second highest cause of hospitalization. With adequate, ongoing mental health care, many youth experiencing mental health problems could avoid hospitalization. Likewise, with adequate prenatal care, many problems of pregnancy and childbirth could be reduced.

Source: U.S. Department of Health and Human Services, 2009.

There is wide variation in the age at which puberty begins and its duration. The first pubertal changes (growth of testes and scrotal sac for boys, and growth of breasts for girls) typically occurs between seven and nine and a half years of age for girls, and nine and a half and thirteen for boys (Steinberg, 2011). The age at which puberty begins depends on complex interactions of genetic and environmental factors, such as caloric intake, health, nutrition, and stress. Perhaps because of changes in living standards, there have been striking historical changes in the onset of puberty. In the 1840s, the average age of menarche among women of European descent was between fourteen and fifteen years, whereas today it is between twelve and thirteen years (Steinberg, 2011).

Mentors can provide support and reassurance to young adolescents experiencing puberty. Many parents and young adolescents find discussing pubertal changes to be awkward and uncomfortable. Mentors can serve as resources, helping young people interpret and respond to the psychological and social implications of physical maturity by supporting the young person in maintaining a positive body image, critiquing body image and sexual norms presented in the media, and coaching him or her about developing positive interpersonal relationships.

During puberty, many individuals also experience a consolidation of their sexual orientation as heterosexual, bisexual, or homosexual that will remain largely stable throughout their lives (Zucker, Bradley, & Notaro, 2004). There is growing evidence that sexual orientation is biologically based, a result of interactions of multiple genes, not a lifestyle choice (Gladue, 1994). There is also some evidence that differences in brain structure and hormone production may relate to sexual orientation (Berenbaum & Snyder, 1995; LeVay, 1993). As would be predicted from a biological model, a higher rate of joint homosexuality is found in identical twins than in fraternal and nontwin siblings (LeVay, 1993). Environmental factors may delay or suppress the expression of a gay, lesbian, or bisexual identity, but research on sexual orientation has largely discredited theories that posit a causal role to family relationships (Freud, 1922/1959) and social learning (Isay, 1990).

Adolescents who find themselves in the sexual minority face real and significant challenges. Throughout modern history, sexual minorities have been penalized and labeled as deviant. Hitler placed gay men and lesbian women in concentration camps, religions demonized them, early psychiatric diagnostic manuals called them disordered and in need of treatment, and public laws stripped away their civil rights. While progress has been made, stigma remains. In part this occurs because of the popular belief that one becomes homosexual by choice—a position not supported by modern research.

Mentors can play an important role in the lives of children who are in sexual minorities. Often family members respond insensitively to young people, because of personal religious values, confusion, or loss of their own dreams for the young person (Longres & Etnyre, 2004). Youth who "come out" during adolescence may be at risk for homelessness, victimization (Jucovy, 2000; Rivers & D'Augelli, 2001), sexual exploitation (Graber & Archibald, 2001), and suicide (Hershberger & D'Augelli, 2001; Proctor & Groze, 1994). Mentors can provide such youth with perspective, psychological support, affirmation, and advocacy.

Psychological Factors

The psychosocial transitions of adolescence are also dramatic. Erikson viewed adolescence as a period revolving around the identity crisis (identity versus role confusion), a conflict that is affected both by pubertal changes and by society's demands that young people make decisions about their futures. The challenge of adolescence is to emerge with a coherent sense of who one is and where one is headed (Erikson, 1968).

The psychosocial changes of adolescence interact with changes in brain regions associated with impulse control, decision making, and the ability to multitask (Lightfoot, Cole, & Cole, 2009). Psychological development in adolescence includes changes in thinking (Inhelder & Piaget, 1958). Compared to children, adolescents are better able to think about hypothetical situations and abstract concepts such as friendship, democracy, and morality. These changes have far-reaching effects on the adolescent's ability to plan ahead, reason scientifically, and consider moral dilemmas. Adolescents can begin to think in logical ways about what their lives will be like in the future, about their relationships with friends and family, and about politics, religion, and philosophy (see Steinberg, 2011; Lightfoot, Cole, & Cole, 2009). These changes in thinking are facilitated by school attendance. Unfortunately, poverty forces too many adolescents in the United States out of school (see box 8.4).

BOX 8.4 POVERTY ACROSS THE LIFE SPAN
High School Dropouts

Individuals who do not complete high school report worse health outcomes than their peers who did complete high school, as well as reduced access to medical care and higher rates of uninsurance. Between 2005 and 2006, approximately 407,000 youth dropped out of high school in the United States. Teens living in poverty or near poverty are 4.5 times more likely to drop out of school than teens from higher-income families. Youth living in poverty may experience hunger, lack of clothing, the need to work to help support their families, illness, multiple family moves, safety concerns, and lack of academic support.

Since 1972, Hispanic youth have had the highest dropout rate. Of youth who dropped out of school in 2006, 30.4 percent were foreign-born Hispanic youth; 12.9 percent of these youth were first-generation Hispanic youth, and 6.5 percent were second-generation Hispanic youth.

Sources: Laird, Cataldi, Kewal Ramani, & Chapman, 2008; National Center for Health Statistics, 2006.

Mentors can facilitate psychological development, including intellectual changes, in their protégés through social interaction. The twentieth-century Russian psychologist Lev Vygotsky described development as proceeding from the interpersonal to the intrapersonal (Wertsch, 1985). When interacting with a more experienced person who scaffolds and supports the developing person's emerging competencies, the developing person functions at a higher level (interpersonal processes). For example, the mentor scaffolds the youth's emerging abilities to think in more abstract ways about the self in relation to others, by elaborating the youth's understanding of others' motivations. As a result of this support, the adolescent's competence increases, and she or he gradually acquires the ability to engage in such abstract thought independently of the mentor (intrapersonal processes).

Social Factors

As the changes in physical, cognitive, and social abilities emerge throughout adolescence, social relations are reconstructed. Relationships with peers remain central, but now may include sexual and romantic components. In early adolescence, peers begin to socialize in mixed-gender groups, perhaps going to the movies or the mall with a group of boys and girls, and attending parties. Later in adolescence, individuals may pair off and begin dating (see Steinberg, 2011).

Relationships with parents also remain central. The changes in responsibilities and social roles that occur during adolescence, however, cause some friction as adolescents and their parents renegotiate their social relations (Lightfoot, Cole, & Cole, 2009). This may be especially difficult for young people who mature into adults different from the ones imagined or planned for by their parents; these differences may be due to physical or mental disabilities, gender identification, or career pathways. As youth remain dependent on their parents for longer and longer periods of time to obtain greater levels of education or as an economic strategy, such negotiations may occur repeatedly.

These important social transitions in relationships may be disrupted when adolescents must live and learn in violent peer groups, schools, and communities. Violence not only threatens the physical well-being of adolescents, but also affects the development of their relationships with adults and with peers (see boxes 8.5 through 8.8).

The transitions of adolescence inevitably result in profound shifts in an adolescent's sense of self and understanding of others: parents, teachers, siblings, and peers. Changes in social status permit young people to try new

---

BOX 8.5   VIOLENCE ACROSS THE LIFE SPAN

Teens and Guns

Thousands of adolescents are killed annually by firearms. In 2006 there were 2,809 teenagers age fifteen through nineteen years killed by guns. Of these deaths, 70 percent were murders, 25 percent were suicides, and 5 percent were accidental shootings.

Source: U.S. Department of Health and Human Services, 2009.

BOX 8.6 VIOLENCE ACROSS THE LIFE SPAN

Homicide, Suicide, and Accidental Deaths of Older Teens

For adolescents age fifteen through nineteen years living in the United States, homicide is the second leading cause of death, followed by suicide. Of all deaths in this age group, 17 percent occurred from murder, 11 percent from suicide, and approximately 45 percent from accidental injuries. Automobile crashes cause 45 percent of accidental deaths in this age group. Approximately 11 percent of youth in this age group reported that they rarely or never use seat belts when riding in a car driven by another person.

Source: U.S. Department of Health and Human Services, 2009.

BOX 8.7 VIOLENCE ACROSS THE LIFE SPAN

School Violence

School violence is a problem in the United States. Bullying can take many forms, including verbal and nonverbal threats, physical attacks, and destruction of property. An especially insidious form of bullying that has become increasingly pervasive is cyberbullying. A cyberbully is someone who "repeatedly harasses, mistreats, or makes fun of another person online or while using cell phones or other electronic devices." In a recent survey of young people in the southern United States, about 20 percent of students disclosed that they had experienced cyberbullying. The most common types were posting nasty or hurtful comments or spreading rumors about classmates. Young women were more apt to cyberbully as well as to be the victims of cyberbullying by their peers.

Source: Hinduja & Patchin, 2010.

BOX 8.8 VIOLENCE ACROSS THE LIFE SPAN

Adolescent Violent Behavior: Risk and Protective Factors

More than 90,000 adolescents in grades 7 through 12 were surveyed between 1994 and 1995 in approximately eighty communities across the United States. The research concluded that several factors increase the risk for adolescent violent behavior. For both boys and girls, the first most predictive factor for violent behavior was having been previously involved in violence; the second predictor, a history of victimization. For boys, the third-ranked predictors included having repeated a grade in school, and having carried a weapon to school. For girls, the third-ranked predictors included having carried a weapon to school, having used alcohol, and having experienced emotional distress.

Several factors appear to help adolescents control aggressive impulses and avoid participation in violence. For boys, protective factors include positive parental school expectations, ability to discuss problems with parents, and positive relationships with adults. For girls, protective factors include school achievement, strong relationship or connectedness within their families, religious participation and beliefs, and feeling connected to their school.

Another survey of 250 rural students found that many high school students find applying these protective factors difficult. Sixty percent of the students reported a belief that no adult really understands teenagers; 42 percent believed that not being part of the right peer group prevented personal acceptance at school; and 34 percent reported knowing someone in school who was often lonely. Perhaps more worrisome is the fact that 29 percent of the students admitted that they often feel depressed, and 15 percent stated that they have thought about committing suicide. These responses demonstrate that many adolescents feel alone, cut off from meaningful dialogue with adults, and disconnected from peers and school.

Sources: Resnick, Ireland, & Borowsky, 2004; Schaeffer et al., 2006; Taylor, 2005.

roles and engage in new activities, such as work and intimate relationships, which dramatically alter how they perceive themselves and their relationships with others. This newfound independence can make discussing these important changes with parents difficult for many adolescents, thus making the role of mentors very important.

Parents are also experiencing a role transition from decision maker to facilitator, coach, and cheerleader. This transition is often difficult for parents, who naturally continue to feel responsible for their children's struggles, are not quite sure of their children's new competencies, and want to help their adolescents solve problems as quickly as possible. Although relationships with parents continue to be very important for most adolescents, conflicts with parents typically increase, especially during early adolescence. Family members' physical proximity and vested interest in an adolescent can cause them to overreact or become judgmental. Parents who have been the primary relationship in their children's lives may also experience difficulties as adolescents' peer relationships gain in importance.

Informal and formal mentors such as extended family members, teachers, coaches, church elders, and other community members have the advantage of standing outside of these family struggles. They can provide a safe haven for teens to air sensitive issues, while still transmitting adult values, advice, and perspectives. Unlike parental advice, which adolescents are often quick to dismiss, guidance and encouragement from a concerned adult noncaregiver is sometimes considered more seriously, particularly if the mentor has experience that the primary caregiver lacks. Peers, who also stand outside of the family, are often struggling with similar transitions, and lack the experience, knowledge, and intellectual sophistication to fully assist with complex issues. Mentors can fill a unique niche for adolescents, somewhere between their parents and peers (Rhodes, 2002).

The economic transitions of adolescence include the initiation of paid work. Work often provides affirmation that the educational system is not providing. Some adolescents contribute to the economic well-being of their family through working with their parents or other relatives, for example, as migrant workers and within family businesses. Such activities may have psychological as well as financial payoffs through increased self-esteem for their necessary contribution to their family. Too many hours of work, however, can interfere with school achievement.

Many adolescents also engage in some form of part-time, paid work that has the potential to increase their responsibility, teach skills, and provide adult role models. However, work in typical settings for adolescent workers (e.g., fast-food or other service jobs) does not necessarily teach skills that will be useful to the adolescent as an adult worker, or provide successful adult role models. Work in some settings may lead to cynicism and poor attitudes toward work. It may also lead to "premature affluence." In other words, because the youth's basic needs are still being provided for by the parents, the youth becomes accustomed to luxury items that she or he will not be able to afford as an independent young adult (Steinberg, 2011).

One way that many adolescents have of bridging the gap of school and work is through volunteer activities in work environments that they are drawn to as possible career paths. Some adolescents volunteer in hospitals, children's facilities, churches, and work projects such as Habitat for Humanity. As adolescents begin to explore how they might fit into the adult world of work and responsibilities, mentors function as role models exemplifying the knowledge, skills, and behavior that adolescents hope to someday acquire (Rhodes, 2002).

It is important to note that biological, psychological, social, and economic transitions interact within, and cannot be understood apart from, particular cultural and historical contexts. For example, the changes of puberty initiate a reorganization of the child's social life, including changes in the nature of interactions with peers, friends, and family members. In the contemporary United States, early maturation generally has positive effects on boys and negative effects on girls. A boy's body image typically remains positive throughout puberty. Furthermore, early-maturing boys tend to be leaders and to be viewed as socially and psychologically mature by adults and peers. In contrast, many early-maturing girls are embarrassed and dissatisfied with their bodies. They are more likely to enter into sexual relationships in midadolescence, and to experience a decline in academic performance and an increase in problem behaviors (Lightfoot, Cole, & Cole, 2009).

Sociocultural-Historical Factors

Cultural and historical contexts can exacerbate or ease the challenges inherent to adolescent development. Gender differences in children's responses to early versus late maturation may be related to cultural ideals for body types (Steinberg, 2011). Muscles and bulk are prized in males, so that boys' physiques become closer to the cultural ideal as they progress through puberty. In contrast, a pubescent body shape may be idealized for women, especially within middle-class, European-American communities. During puberty, the average girl gains a little over twenty-four pounds in body fat (Lightfoot, Cole, & Cole, 2009). Thus, as a girl proceeds through puberty, her body becomes less like the cultural ideal. Indeed, many girls worry about weight gain, and their body images decline.

Approximately half the girls in the United States are dissatisfied with their bodies by the age of thirteen, and many begin a pattern of weight obsession and dieting as early as eight or nine (Brumberg, 1997). Internationally, body dissatisfaction among girls age eleven to fifteen ranges from approximately 34 percent in the Netherlands, to 51 percent in the United States, to 62 percent in the Czech Republic (Sabbah et al., 2009). Poor body image is positively related to eating disorders, ineffective dieting, low self-esteem, depression, and high-risk behaviors among adolescent girls (see Liechty, 2010). There is, however, intracultural variation. Girls' responses to maturation are not uniform. For example, African-American girls are less likely than European-American and Asian girls to develop a negative body image, perhaps because a wider variation of female body types is appreciated in these communities (Steinberg, 2011).

Historical variation in girls' body images also are apparent. During the Victorian period, the consensus in middle-class and upper-class families was that adolescent girls deserved special attention and consideration because of their biology (Brumberg, 1997). A protective umbrella was created by female community members and spread over middle-class, adolescent girls from school to extracurricular activities. Between the 1880s and the 1920s, thousands of girls received mentoring by young women through Girl Scouts, the Camp Fire Girls, the Young Women's Christian Association, Bible study groups, literary societies, and other religious and secular organizations. In her analysis of the diaries of adolescent girls, Brumberg (1997) found that middle-class Victorian girls repeatedly wrote about the informal mentoring they received from their young women teachers and leaders. These women viewed the nurturing of all younger women, not only their biological kin, as their ethical responsibility. Through extracurricular activities, girls described enjoyable and meaningful interaction with their female mentors.

Many modern communities do not provide extended nurturance to adolescent girls as did the Victorian protective umbrella. Yet adolescent girls today are under more pressure and are at greater risk because of a unique combination of biological and cultural forces. Modern girls mature earlier physically, but there is no parallel increase in their emotional and intellectual development, creating greater vulnerability. Modern fashions and the media sexualize even prepubescent girls and focus on external appearance. In parallel with this trend, Brumberg (1997) documents a heightened concern with physical appearance in the diaries of modern girls. By contrast, in middle- and upper-class Victorian culture, girls' inner beauty—moral character, service to others, and spirituality—were prized (see Brumberg, 1997).

Clearly, there were many holes in the Victorians' protective umbrella. For example, it did not extend over girls from lower-income families, who were sent to be servants in the homes of the wealthy, sent out to work in sweatshops, or forced into prostitution because of poverty. In addition, young women today enjoy greater personal freedom, and can make more educational, professional, and social choices than their counterparts a century ago. A lesson that modern school social workers may learn from the Victorian model, however, is the protective value of personal attention and mentoring, experiences lacking in the lives of many young adolescents.

The vast majority of adolescents and their families successfully negotiate the complex physical, social, and economic transitions of adolescence. Some adolescents, however, will develop psychological problems, drop out of school, become homeless, or turn to substance misuse, which not only can curtail healthy social and emotional development, but also presents health risks (see box 8.9).

BOX 8.9 SUBSTANCE MISUSE ACROSS THE LIFE SPAN

Marijuana

In 2008, a major study found that approximately 14.5 percent of eighth-grade students and 30 percent of tenth-grade students reported having used marijuana. Approximately 25 percent of young people age eighteen through twenty-five have used the drug within the last year, and 16.5 percent used marijuana in the last thirty days. Young adult males use marijuana at almost twice the rate for females in the same age group.

For many people, the most hazardous effect of using marijuana is identical to the carcinogenic and respiratory dangers caused by tobacco. However, marijuana misuse and recreational use for individuals who are extremely sensitive to the drug can result in short-term memory loss, psychological dependence, cannabis intoxication delirium, cannabis-induced psychotic disorder, and cannabis-induced anxiety disorder.

Studies conducted on both people and animals suggest that marijuana misuse can cause physical dependence. A number of studies have shown an association between chronic marijuana use and increased rates of anxiety, depression, suicidal ideation, and schizophrenia. When trying to quit, long-term users report withdrawal symptoms that include irritability, sleeplessness, decreased appetite, anxiety, and drug craving, all of which make it difficult to quit.

Sources: Budney, Vandrey, Hughes, Thostenson, & Bursac, 2008; Moore, Zammit, et al., 2007; Substance Abuse and Mental Health Services Administration, 2009.

THE DEVELOPMENT OF MENTORING RELATIONSHIPS

Jean Rhodes, a leading expert on mentoring, once commented that mentoring is "strong medicine": appropriately administered it can be life saving, but administered incorrectly it can be ineffective or, worse, toxic. Research indicates that the positive impact of mentoring increases over time, but short-term relationships can actually be harmful to youth. It may take up to four months for some adolescents to lower their defenses and develop trust, and for mentors and youth to feel an emotional connection (see Morrow & Styles, 1995). In their analysis of data from a national Big Brothers–Big Sisters study, Grossman and Rhodes (2002) found that youth who were in relationships that lasted more than four months reported significantly higher levels of self-worth, social acceptance, and scholastic competence; and they reported that their relationships with their parents had improved, that school had become more rewarding, and that their drug and alcohol use had declined. Yet a significant number of mentors and young people did not sustain their relationships. Only 45 percent of relationships were sustained for one year or more. Furthermore, youth who were in matches that terminated within the first three months suffered significant drops in feelings of self-worth and perceived scholastic competence compared to youths without mentors. Because a personal relationship is the heart of mentoring, inconsistencies and terminations can touch the vulnerabilities of youth in ways that less personal youth programs do not (Rhodes, 2002). Generally, adolescence is a life stage during which issues of acceptance and rejection are paramount. Youth who have experienced unsatisfactory or rejecting parental relationships in the past may fear that others will not accept and support them. When adolescents sense that mentoring relationships are not going well, they may readily perceive intentional rejection (Rhodes, 2002).

Understanding the factors that lead to effective mentoring programs can help school social workers establish the best programs possible for adolescents. A major challenge to school social workers involved with mentoring programs is ensuring that matched adults and youth meet long enough and often enough to allow the possibility of establishing a relationship that could generate the life changes that mentoring programs seek to achieve. A developmental, ecological-systems analysis of biological, psychological, social, and cultural aspects of mentoring has a variety of implications for establishing school-based programs to maximize the potential of mentoring and minimize the potential risks.

Biological Factors

Clearly, the teenage years are a period of tremendous biological changes occurring within a social and cultural context. Indeed, the simple, biological fact of age is a consideration of successful mentoring. By middle adolescence, youth's romantic involvements and close friendships may increasingly compete with their relationships with adults. There is some evidence that preteens and young teens are more responsive to mentoring than are older adolescents. Indeed, mentoring relationships with older adolescents are at higher risk for early termination than those with younger adolescents (Rhodes, 2002). Mentors of older adolescents tend to experience their relationships as less close and supportive than do mentors of preteens. These observations suggest the value of establishing mentoring relationships relatively early in adolescence. They also suggest that mentors of younger versus older adolescents may need to be prepared for somewhat different roles.

Psychological Factors

Some adolescents struggle with issues of identity, relationships, and self-worth. Mentors can be strong allies and sources of support to youth. For many adolescents, simply sharing enjoyable activities with a caring adult—playing sports, games, eating out, talking, hanging out—can positively impact their sense of self-worth (see Morrow & Styles, 1995). Mentors also can be important sources of support for youth who are experiencing stress. For example, youth struggling with sexual identity may benefit from a safe, older mentor who has experienced similar struggles (Jucovy, 2000). Mentors may be able to assist adolescents in negotiating the special problems of transitioning to maturity in a society that is often intolerant of sexual identity struggles. Evidence suggests that mentoring programs are not as effective for youth experiencing severe psychological, social, or behavioral problems. For these youth, professional intervention is appropriate. At the other extreme, well-adjusted middle-class youth tend to derive relatively fewer benefits when compared to youth who are facing some degree of difficulty in their lives. Youth who fall in the middle of the continuum of psychological and social functioning appear most likely to benefit from mentoring interventions (Rhodes, 2002). These observations suggest that school social workers participating in mentoring programs must encourage careful screening and assessment not just of potential mentors, but also of potential adolescent participants.

Social Factors

The heart of mentoring is the formation of an interpersonal relationship between a young person and an adult. To be successful, mentors and youth must feel connected through mutual trust and a sense of being understood, liked, and respected (Rhodes, 2002). If an emotional bond does not develop, then the youth and mentor may disengage from the match before any positive change has occurred. When adolescents do form close relationships with mentors, their ability to connect with other adults, especially their parents, also improves (Grossman & Tierney, 1998). Interestingly, their relationships with peers may also improve, perhaps as a result of a changing sense of self-worth and improved social and leisure skills (Rhodes, Haight, & Briggs, 1999).

Although interpersonal relationships between the mentor and young person are central, they vary widely in their quality. Morrow and Styles (1995) examined eighty-two mentoring relationships over a nine-month period. They described two types of relationships: developmental and prescriptive. In **developmental relationships**, mentors' goals and expectations varied over time in relation to their perceptions of the adolescent's needs. In the beginning, these mentors devoted themselves to establishing a strong emotional connection with the young person and developing a reliable, trusting relationship. Mentors allowed youth to talk about anything without fear of judgment or reproach, reassuring youth of their availability when difficulties arose, and "just listening." These mentors possessed the ability to listen, understand, and accept the younger person. It was only after the relationship had solidified and strengthened and the youth's receptivity was established that developmental mentors expanded their focus to address other goals, such as helping the young person improve in school and be more responsible. Throughout their involvement with the young person, mentors kept the relationship enjoyable and were flexible in their plans, responding to the adolescent's ideas and preferences. In developmental relationships, mentors and young people demonstrated strong attachments to one another. At the end of the nine-month study, 90 percent of developmental relationships continued to meet regularly.

In contrast, **prescriptive relationships** are defined as those in which mentors prioritized their goals for the match, rather than the youth's, and set the goals and ground rules for the relationship. Mentors' primary purpose was to transform the young people, to guide them toward embracing values, attitudes, and behaviors that the mentors defined as positive. There were two subgroups of prescriptive relationships. In the first subgroup, mentors approached the match by setting goals (typically improving school performance) and focusing shared time on achieving these goals. In the second subgroup, the mentors required the youth to take equal responsibility for maintaining the relationship, a task beyond the capability of most young adolescents. Both subgroups of prescriptive volunteers resisted modifying their high expectations and ultimately felt frustrated. The youth were similarly frustrated, unsatisfied with the relationship, and less likely to share problems or regard their mentor as a source of consistent support. Over the nine-month period of study, the tension in these relationships grew. At the end of nine months, only 33 percent of prescriptive relationships continued to meet, and only 30 percent of those met regularly (Morrow & Styles, 1995).

Given the centrality of the interpersonal relationship to effective mentoring, the question arises as to whether mentoring is effective for adolescents who have experienced problematic relationships with caregivers. In light of their past experiences, adolescents living in foster care, for example, may find it relatively difficult to establish close, supportive relationships with mentors. Attachment theory and research suggest that expectations of self and others derived from early intimate relationships with parents can affect the development of subsequent close relationships (Bowlby, 1988). As a group, foster youth may enter mentoring programs with different relationship histories than youth not living in foster care. Indeed, because most children enter foster care today because of problems in parental functioning, including child abuse and neglect, some foster youth may find it relatively difficult to establish the close, supportive relationships with mentors that facilitate adolescents' development and well-being. Others, who have experienced close relationships with kin or unrelated foster caregivers, may welcome the relationship with a neutral adult outside the foster home.

Some evidence suggests that, as a group, foster youth can benefit from formal mentoring relationships. Rhodes, Haight, and Briggs (1999) examined the influence of a mentoring program (Big Brothers–Big Sisters) on the peer relationships of foster youth. Youth were randomly assigned to a mentoring group or a wait-list control group. As a group, foster adolescents appeared to have more difficulty establishing close relationships and trusting adults than youth not living in foster care. Despite the challenges, foster youth in the mentoring group were able to form, and in some cases benefit from, relationships with mentors. Overall, foster youth in the mentoring group reported slight improvement in the support they felt from their peers, while those foster youth in the wait-list control group reported slight declines.

Some recent research also suggests that natural mentors, those supportive, nonparent adults in the youth's existing social network, may also positively impact foster youth. Ahrens and colleagues (Ahrens, Du Bois, Richardson, Fan, & Lozano, 2008) found that foster youth who had mentors for at least two years in adolescence did better as adults on self-reports of overall health, educational attainment, physical aggression, suicide risk, and risk of sexually transmitted diseases than did foster youth without mentors. Munson and McMillen (2008) found that foster youth with a sustained mentoring relationship of more than one year reported lower levels of stress and were less likely to have been arrested by age nineteen than were foster youth without natural mentors.

These data suggest that school social workers and social workers in child welfare can enhance services for some children in foster care by helping them form a sustained, stable relationship with a caring mentor. Research also suggests that social workers recruit and educate mentors as to the centrality of the emotional relationship with the young person in the mentoring relationship. Exaggerated marketing campaigns to recruit mentors that encourage volunteers to be heroic in a short period of time may be counterproductive, especially to youth who already have experienced disappointing relationships with adults. Volunteers may enter these programs with unrealistic expectations, including fantasies of rescuing a child (Rhodes, 2002). Rather than rely on such heroic images, mentoring programs should recruit adults who value and are skillful at maintaining interpersonal relationships and have the capacity to sustain their involvement over the long term.

Sociocultural-Historical Factors

Biological, psychological, and social aspects of mentoring are embedded within, and cannot be understood apart from, a larger cultural and historical context. Jean Rhodes (2002) argued that within much of American culture there generally is a suspicion toward dependence and close relationships outside of the immediate family. Close relationships tend to be denigrated, and autonomy is viewed as the hallmark of emotional maturity. Trends to valorize independence as evidence of growth while minimizing interpersonal relationships can lead adolescents to devalue adult guidance and emotional support and lead to premature separation from adults.

Beliefs and practices within particular cultural communities in the larger American culture may also render certain youth more or less likely to respond to one-on-one mentoring. For example, youth from cultures that emphasize collectivism and a deep respect for their elders (e.g., Native Americans) may be uncomfortable in relationships with adults outside of their immediate communities. For these youths, more group-oriented approaches (Rhodes, 2002), or recruitment of natural mentors from within the community, may be preferable to other formal methods of matching mentors with young people.

Neighborhood and community factors also can impact mentoring relationships. For example, in urban communities with high crime or other dangerous conditions, children and adolescents may remain sequestered at home. They are safe, but their opportunities for contact with adults outside of home and school are greatly reduced. Furthermore, when schools, churches, and civic organizations disintegrate, adolescents often have no adults available to offer counsel as problems arise (Rhodes, 2002).

Family factors also can affect adolescents' mentoring relationships. For example, parental support of the mentor–young person relationship can be critical to establishing and maintaining relationships. Also, adolescents with more supportive parental relationships tend to have healthy relationships outside of the family, and to gravitate toward natural mentors. Parents who cultivate connections with well-meaning adults in their neighborhoods and channel their children to community-based recreational and social programs also greatly increase the likelihood that their children will form beneficial relationships with other supportive adults beyond their nuclear family (Rhodes, 2002).

These observations suggest that factors outside of the mentor–young person microsystem need to be addressed to establish effective, long-term matches. Contextual factors such as community norms for nonfamilial relationships, parental support, and opportunities for adolescents to form relationships with nonfamilial adults need to be considered by school social workers to develop effective mentoring programs for adolescents.

IMPLICATIONS FOR SCHOOL SOCIAL WORK WITH ADOLESCENTS

Mentoring is an example of a preventive intervention suited to the developmental needs of adolescents. Mentoring is not a cure-all for complex psychological problems, but can assist adolescents in transitioning into resilient adults. Poorly implemented programs, however, can have adverse effects on youth (Du Bois, Holloway, Valentine, & Cooper, 2002). Fortunately, there is an empirical literature to guide school social workers in developing effective mentoring programs.

1. *Focus on the quality of sustained interpersonal relationships.* For mentors to be effective agents of change, they must have the qualities necessary to develop and sustain any meaningful interpersonal relationship. Superficial pairings that do not achieve trust, respect, and closeness are unlikely to be of much value (Rhodes, 2002). Furthermore, the impact of mentoring grows as the relationship matures. Short-lived relationships are associated with negative outcomes for youth (Du Bois et al., 2002; Grossman & Rhodes, 2002). Mentoring can be harmful when mentors do not keep their promises to young people, especially to those with histories of problematic relationships (Rhodes, 2002).

2. *Screen, recruit, educate, and supervise mentors.* For the safety of the adolescent participants and the effectiveness of the program, it is important that programs carefully screen volunteers. For the best outcomes, it is important to engage and attract volunteers who are willing and able to make long-term commitments, and for program staff to educate, support, and supervise them (Sipe, 2002). Some mentors manage without training, but mentoring does not come easily to everyone, and

difficulties sometimes arise that overtax even the most skilled volunteers. Mentors who are offered continuing support and supervision are more likely to persist. Successful programs also include structured activities for mentors and youth, as well as expectations for frequency of contact, mechanisms for the involvement of parents, and monitoring of overall program implementation (Du Bois et al., 2002; Rhodes, 2002; Wheeler et al., 2010).

3. *Anticipate the challenges of school-based mentoring programs.* There are special challenges to school-based mentoring. Many relationships formed through school-based programs are described as less close than those formed in community-based programs. Perhaps this occurs because the school setting constrains the types of leisure activities that mentors and adolescents may engage in to build their relationships, as well as the time they spend together (see Rhodes, 2002). If school social workers anticipate the limitations of school-based programs, they could plan compensatory strategies, for example, supporting matches through planned events such as special school lunches or outings for mentors and adolescents.

4. *Recognize the limitations of mentoring.* Unfortunately, most interventions have focused on "fixing" at-risk children, while ignoring the ecological factors that contribute to their risk. Mentoring cannot make up for years of accumulated failure of the educational system and scars from other failures of family, community, and economy. Mentoring alone is not a magic wand. An array of other policies is essential (Rhodes, 2002; Wheeler et al., 2010).

Box 8.10 describes a mentoring program for public school children and adolescents.

BOX 8.10 MENTORING

TALKS is a mentoring program serving public school children and adolescents in Illinois and Indiana. TALKS' purpose is to enroll, educate, and facilitate interaction between adults and young people. Mentors are recruited to serve youth in the public schools and trained using the TALKS curriculum. The mentor commits to one hour per week during the school day for the entire school year. While some mentoring programs target only at-risk youth, the TALKS program serves all children. Children are placed in groups of three, incorporating students at academic levels from high to low functioning. Adult mentors provide ongoing support for at least a year to the students and facilitate the development of a supportive peer group to assist each other in school between group meetings.

Source: Davis, 2001.

SUMMARY

Adolescence is a complex time of biological, psychological, social, and economic transitions occurring within specific sociocultural-historical contexts. Social workers encounter adolescents in a variety of contexts, including the public schools. School social workers support the well-being and academic achievement of adolescents by providing services and advocacy. In recent years, mentoring has gained popularity as a prevention intervention especially suited to the developmental needs of adolescents. Mentoring relationships can result in the formation of mesosystems between microsystems in the family, school, and community, thus reinforcing and expanding adolescents' values, beliefs, and skills. Empirical evidence indicates that mentoring programs can be highly effective for supporting typically developing adolescents, including those experiencing considerable environmental stress. However, mentoring is not a substitute for adequate social resources and professional assistance for the many complex social, health, and mental health challenges facing adolescents. Furthermore, poorly implemented mentoring programs can be harmful to youth. A developmental, ecological-systems approach to mentoring can guide school social workers in developing and maintaining effective mentoring programs through consideration of biological, psychological, and social factors within a sociocultural-historical context. Box 8.11 presents the practice story and advice of a school social worker whose clients include mentally ill adolescents whose needs extend far beyond mentoring.

BOX 8.11 PRACTICE STORY AND ADVICE FROM THE FIELD

Brenda L., school social worker: "You really have to have a systems understanding."

Brenda L. is a school social worker with twenty years direct practice experience. Currently, she is a clinical assistant professor working with master's level social work students during their field placements in the schools. She has worked in a variety of schools, from public elementary schools to alternative high schools. She particularly enjoys the specialization of school social work because of the variety of children she serves, from well-functioning elementary children to adolescents with mental illness. She describes her experiences working in public schools with adolescents who have mental health needs, and offers advice for students considering school social work as a specialization.

Practice Story

Well, I think basically that these are kids [adolescents with mental illness] that need a lot of intensive help. They need flexibility and in a system things are very regimented—the bell rings, you can't go out in the hall unless you have a pass. You know if you have a bad day you can't go and tell someone to f——off and they're just going to lump it like they would do in a day treatment school, things like that. I had a girl—when I did her background report, she had been in so many psychiatric placements that I could not keep track. She was sixteen when I first met her . . . she had tried to kill herself a number of times and she had had a very tragic life. And so she had been in and out of residential placements for quite a while and was being stepped down into the community, and, eventually, the plan was that she was going to go home. So the semester before she was supposed to go home, she started transitioning back to a regular high school. And actually that went well. She came for a couple hours in the morning. And then, after a while, we tried her full time. And it went okay for probably the first six weeks, and then things fell apart. And I think what happened is that the nature of her illness, her mental health issues, is that she just kind of cycled in and out [of depression]. And when she ends up in a bad time, what she does is she says that she is going to kill herself. And usually, when she says it, she usually has some kind of a pretty good plan [for how to kill herself]. And one day she was upset about something and brought a knife to school. And you know the rules—zero tolerance. But it was a Swiss Army knife. None of the teachers were afraid that she was actually going to hurt them. But she was going to hurt herself and she wouldn't give it up, and she ended up having to be restrained. These are people that are not used to that on a regular basis, and the principal was just like, "We can't have this." We had to wait for the police and an ambulance. They had to shut off the area. They don't allow the kids to pass so the kids won't see all this going on and embarrass her even more—the whole set up was just not conducive to kids like that [with mental illness]. I call the principal just to let him know what's going on, and he says, "You tell her she's suspended for ten days pending expulsion because she brought a knife to school." And I tell her mom that, and her mom is like, "Don't those people understand that she has mental health problems?" So to me that was sort of a typical example of where the school system is just not equipped.

Advice

In school social work, you have to be really good in a lot of different areas. You have to be skilled at clinical issues—you have to be extremely skilled at diagnostic issues. You really have to know what is normal developmental behavior as opposed to abnormal behavior. You also have to be able to interact with people at a lot of different levels. So not only are you going to be doing prevention, you are going to be doing intervention, you are going to do consultation and collaboration where you work with teachers, helping them develop interventions for kids. You also are going to work with parents.

The other thing is that you have to really have a systems understanding. One of the things about school social work is you practice in a host setting. You really have to understand the politics of the organization because as a social worker you don't do what everybody else does there. You have to understand that even though you think your issues are important—and they are—they are not considered important by everybody else. So you have to really figure out how to work within the system. You have to understand the informal and formal politics. You have to be able to size up who the players are, and what their agendas are.

You also have to be flexible, especially when you deal with adolescents. We used to be able to have what was considered an office hour where we could catch up on our reports. And I normally didn't take mine—the one time that I did I probably wasn't in the door five minutes and someone said, you have an emergency back at your school and you've got to go. I went back, and they said, "We can't believe you weren't here!" A kid had taken an Exacto knife and had sliced his arm in a suicide gesture. And I mean, you can have this plan for the day, but you never know how things are going to work out.

The other thing, I think too, is that you have to be willing to do outreach as a school social worker. I like that, I like home visits. I like seeing people in their environments. But you do have to be comfortable going to places that you wouldn't normally go, and go into neighborhoods where you might—like for me, I am a white—I might be the only white person there. And they [residents] know either she is here for welfare or she is not here because she is visiting for no reason. So you have to be willing to do that. But I like that. I like the challenge of all that.

Study and Discussion Questions

1. How do modern developmental psychologists define adolescence? To what extent is it a period of "storm and stress" relative to other periods of the life cycle? What are some stereotypes about adolescents?

2. What are some biological, psychological, social, and economic transitions that adolescents experience? How might these transitions vary across the cultural communities in which you might practice as a social worker (e.g., urban versus rural communities)? How can such variability affect social work practice with adolescents?

3. What are the psychological consequences of early versus later maturation in adolescence? Why might the outcomes be different for boys versus girls?

4. Describe the goals and the development of mentoring relationships. Jean Rhodes describes mentoring as "strong medicine." How can we ensure that such strong medicine is healing and not toxic?

5. What is school social work? Who are some of the diverse clients served by school social workers? What are some of the diverse roles played by school social workers?

6. How can school-based health and mental health services support positive adolescent development?

7. What are some of the possible advantages and unique challenges of school-based mentoring programs? If you were to implement a school-based mentoring program, what are three program components you would view as essential?

8. Returning to our opening example, what is your position on the use of mentoring programs for vulnerable children in foster care such as Jeremy? Lydia and her husband plan to relocate to the West Coast to be with their children and grandchildren. How can Jeremy's relationship with Lydia be terminated? Should Jeremy's caseworker be giving more attention to obtaining formal mental health services for him?

Resources

Interested students may supplement this chapter through a number of excellent web-based resources.

The American Psychological Association provides an excellent overview of adolescent development. The article is designed to help professionals understand how teens develop socially, emotionally, cognitively, and behaviorally. Available at http://www.apa.org/pubs/info/brochures/develop.aspx.

The National Institute of Mental Health provides information for helping teens and children cope with violence and disasters. Available at http://nimh.nih.gov/health/topics/child-and-adolescent-mental-health/children-and-violence.shtml.

Indiana University's Center for Adolescent and Family Studies provides details about most mental, emotional, and behavioral problems experienced by teenagers. This website links to numerous authoritative reports and articles. Available at http://site.educ.indiana.edu/cafs/CAFSPublications/tabid/1608/Default.aspx.

The Centers for Disease Control and Prevention outlines the prevalence of adolescent and childhood obesity between 1963 and 2008 and provides additional research references. Available at http://www.cdc.gov/nchs/data/hestat/obesity_child_07_08/obesity_child_07_08.htm.

The use of antidepressant medications with adolescents and adults is discussed by the federal Food and Drug Administration (FDA) at http://www.fda.gov/cder/drug/antidepressants/default.htm. Manufacturers of all antidepressant drugs are requested by the FDA to include in their labeling an expanded warning about the increased risk of suicidality (suicidal thinking and behavior) in children and adolescents treated with these medications. Available at http://www.fda.gov/Drugs/DrugSafety/Informationby DrugClass/UCM096273.

The Academy of Child and Adolescent Psychiatry offers suggestions to help parents and clinicians respond to teens who self-injure. Available at http://www.aacap.org/galleries/FactsForFamilies/73_self_injury_in_ adolescents.pdf.

References

Ahrens, K., Du Bois, D., Richardson, L., Fan, M., & Lozano, P. (2008). Youth in foster care with adult mentors during adolescence have improved adult outcomes. *Pediatrics, 121*(2), 246–252.

Allen-Meares, P., Washington, R., & Welsh, B. (Eds.). (2000). *Social work services in schools* (3rd ed.). Boston: Allyn & Bacon.

Berenbaum, S. A., & Snyder, E. (1995). Early hormonal influence on childhood sex-type activity and playmate preferences: Implications for the development of sexual orientation. *Developmental Psychology, 31*, 31–42.

Boonstra, H. (2002) Teenage sexual and reproductive behavior. *Guttmacher Report on Public Policy, 5*(1), 1–9.

Bowlby, J. (1988). *A secure base: Parent-child attachment and healthy human development.* New York: Basic Books.

Brumberg, J. (1997). *The body project: An intimate history of American girls.* New York: Random House.

Budney, A. J., Vandrey, R. G., Hughes, J. R., Thostenson, J. D., & Bursac, Z. (2008). Comparison of cannabis and tobacco withdrawal: Severity and contribution to relapse. *Journal of Substance Abuse Treatment, 35*(4), 362–368.

Cole, S. A. (1993). *Peer education program.* Honolulu: Hawaii Department of Health, School Health Services Branch.

Curtis, T., & Hansen-Schwoebel, K. (1999). *Big Brothers Big Sisters school-based mentoring: Evaluation summary of five pilot programs.* Philadelphia: Big Brothers Big Sisters of America.

Davis, O. W. (2001). *Talks my mother never had with me: Mentor's guide.* Champaign, IL: KJAC Publishing.

Dewees, S. (2009). *The school-within-a-school model*. Educational Resource Information Center, U.S. Department of Education. Retrieved from http://www.education.com/reference/article/Ref_School_within_School/.

Dilley, J. (2009). *Research review: School-based health interventions and academic achievement*. Seattle: Washington State Board of Health, Washington State Office of Superintendent of Public Instruction, Washington State Department of Health.

Du Bois, D. L., Holloway, B. E., Valentine, J. C., & Cooper, H. (2002). Effectiveness of mentoring programs for youth: A meta-analytic review. *American Journal of Community Psychology, 30*(2), 157-197.

Erikson, E. (1968). *Identity: Youth and crisis*. New York: Norton.

Fisher, A. Q., & Rivas, M. (2001). *Finding fish: A memoir*. New York: W. Morrow.

Franklin, C., Harris, M. B., & Langan-Riordan, C. (2010). The delivery of school social work services. In P.A. Meares (Ed.), *Social work services in schools* (6th ed., pp. 256-276). Boston: Pearson.

Freedman, R. I. (1995). Developmental disabilities: Direct practice. In R. L. Edwards & J. G. Hopps (Eds.), *Encyclopedia of social work* (Vol. 1, pp. 721-728). Washington, DC: NASW Press.

Freud, S. (1922/1959). *Group psychology and the analysis of the ego*. New York: W. W. Norton.

Garmezy, N. (1985). Stress-resistant children: The search for protective factors. In *Journal of Child Psychology and Psychiatry, Book Supplement 4* (pp. 213-233). Oxford: Pergamon Press.

Germain, C. (1999). An ecological perspective on social work in the schools. In R. Constable, S. McDonald, & J. P. Flynn (Eds.), *School social work: Practice, policy, and research perspectives* (5th ed., pp. 25-35). Chicago: Lyceum Books.

Gladue, B.A. (1994). The biopsychology of sexual orientation. *Current Directions in Psychological Science, 3*, 150-154.

Graber, J.A., & Archibald, A. B. (2001). Psychosocial change at puberty and beyond: Understanding adolescent sexuality and sexual orientation. In A. R. D'Augelli & C. J. Patterson (Eds.), *Lesbian, gay, bisexual identities and youth* (pp. 3-6). New York: Oxford University Press.

Grossman, J. B., & Rhodes, J. E. (2002). The test of time: Predictors and effects of duration in youth mentoring relationships. *American Journal of Community Psychology, 30*(2), 199-219.

Grossman, J. B., & Tierney, J. P. (1998). Does mentoring work? An impact study of the Big Brothers Big Sisters program. *Evaluation Review, 22*(3), 403-426.

Grotevant, H. (1998). Adolescent development in family contexts. In W. Damon & R. M. Lerner (Eds.), *Handbook of child psychology: Vol. 3, Social, emotional, and personality development* (5th ed., pp. 1097-1150). New York: Wiley.

Haight, W., Carpenter, B., & Tata, L. (1999). Adult-supported social pretend-play: Strategies for facilitating young children's peer relationships. *School Social Work Journal, 24*(1), 15-28.

Hall, G. S. (1904). *Adolescence*. New York: Appleton.

Herrera, C. (1999). *School-based mentoring: A first look at its potential*. Philadelphia: Public/Private Ventures.

Hershberger, S. L., & D'Augelli, A. R. (2001). Issues in counseling lesbian, gay, and bisexual adolescents. In R. M. Perez, K.A. DeBord, & K. J. Bieschke (Eds.), *Handbook of counseling and psychotherapy with lesbian, gay and bisexual clients* (pp. 225-247). Washington, DC: American Psychological Association.

Hinduja, S., & Patchin, J. (2010, February). Cyberbullying Research Center. Retrieved from http://www.cyberbullying.us/research.php

Inhelder, B., & Piaget, J. (1958). *The growth of logical thinking from childhood to adolescence*. New York: Basic Books.

Isay, R. A. (1990). *Being homosexual: Gay men and their development*. New York: Avon Books.

Jucovy, L. (2000). *Mentoring sexual minority youth* (Technical Assistance Packet 2). Portland, OR: Northwest Regional Laboratory.

Kisker, E. E., & Brown, R. S. (1996). Do school-based health centers improve adolescents' access to health care, health status, and risk-taking behaviors? *Journal of Adolescent Health, 18*, 335–343.

Kost, K., Henshaw, S., & Carlin, L. (2010). *U.S. teenage pregnancies, births and abortions: National and state trends and trends by race and ethnicity*. Guttmacher Institute. Retrieved from http://www.guttmacher.org/pubs/USTPtrends.pdf

Ku, M. (2003). *Life stories of aboriginal juvenile prostitutes in Taiwan* (Unpublished doctoral dissertation). University of Illinois, Urbana-Champaign.

Kutash, K., Duchnowski, A. J., Robbins, V., & Keenan, S. (2008). School based mental health services in systems of care. In B.A. Stroul & G. M. Blau (Eds.), *The system of care handbook* (pp. 545–572). Baltimore: Paul H. Brookes.

Laird, J., Cataldi, E. F., Kewal Ramani, A., & Chapman, C. (2008). *Dropout and completion rates in the United States: 2006* (NCES 2008-053). Washington, DC: National Center for Education Statistics, Institute of Education Sciences, U.S. Department of Education. Retrieved from http://nces.ed.gov/pubs2008/2008053.pdf

Lefkowitz, B. (1986). *Tough change: Growing up on your own in America*. New York: Free Press.

LeVay, S. (1993). *The sexual brain*. Cambridge, MA: MIT Press.

Levine, A., & Nidiffer, J. (1996). *Beating the odds: How the poor get to college*. San Francisco: Jossey-Bass.

Liechty, J. (2010) Body image distortion and three types of weight loss behaviors among nonoverweight girls in the United States. *Journal of Adolescent Health, 47*(2), 176–182.

Lightfoot, C., Cole, M., & Cole, S. (2009). *The development of children* (6th ed.). New York: Worth Publishers.

Longres, J. F., & Etnyre, W. S. (2004). Social work practice with gay and lesbian children and adolescents. In P. Allen-Meares & M. W. Fraser (Eds.), *Interventions with children and adolescents: An interdisciplinary perspective* (pp. 80–105). Boston: Allyn & Bacon.

McLearn, K. T., Colasanto, D., & Schoen, C. (1998). *Mentoring makes a difference: Findings from The Commonwealth Fund 1998 Survey of Adults Mentoring Young People*. New York: Commonwealth Fund.

Monkman, M. M. (1999). The characteristic focus of the social worker in the schools. In R. Constable, S. McDonald, & J. P. Flynn (Eds.), *School social work: Practice, policy, and research perspectives* (4th ed., pp. 45–63). Chicago: Lyceum Books.

Moore, T. H., Zammit, S., Lingford-Hughes, A., Barnes, T. R. E., Jones, P. B., Burke, M., & Lewis, G. (2007). Cannabis use and risk of psychotic or affective mental health outcomes: A systematic review. *Lancet, 370*(9584), 319–328.

Morrow, K. V., & Styles, M. B. (1995). *Building relationships with youth in program settings: A study of Big Brother/Big Sister ventures*. Philadelphia: Public/Private Ventures.

Munson, M., & McMillen, J. (2008). Natural mentoring and psychosocial outcomes among older youth transitioning from foster care. *Children and Youth Services Review, 31*, 104–111.

National Center for Health Statistics. (2006). *Health, United States, 2006 with chartbook on trends in the health of Americans.* Hyattsville, MD: U.S. Department of Health and Human Services.

Portwood, S., Ayers, P., Kinnison, K., Waris, R., & Wise, D. (2005). YouthFriends: Outcomes from a school-based mentoring program. *Journal of Primary Prevention, 26*(2), 129–145.

Proctor, C. D., & Groze, V. K. (1994). Risk factors for suicide among gay, lesbian, and bisexual youths. *Social Work, 39*, 504–513.

Resnick, M., Ireland, M., & Borowsky, I. (2004). Youth violence perpetration: What protects? What predicts? Findings from the National Longitudinal Study of Adolescent Health. *Adolescent Health, 35*, 424–434.

Rhodes, J. E. (2002). *Stand by me.* Cambridge, MA: Harvard University Press.

Rhodes, J. E., Bogat, G. A., Roffman, J., Edelman, P., & Galasso, L. (2002). Youth mentoring in perspective: Introduction to the special issue. *American Journal of Community Psychology, 30*(2), 149–155.

Rhodes, J. E., Contreras, J., & Mangelsdorf, S. (1994). Natural mentor relationships among Latina adolescent mothers: Psychological adjustment, moderating processes, and the role of early parental acceptance. *American Journal of Community Psychology, 22*, 211–227.

Rhodes, J. E., & Davis, A. A. (1996). Supportive ties between nonparent adults and urban adolescent girls. In B. J. Leadbetter & N. Way (Eds.), *Urban girls: Resisting stereotypes, creating identities* (pp. 213–249). New York: New York University Press.

Rhodes, J. E., & Du Bois, D. (2006). Understanding and facilitating the youth mentoring movement. *Social Policy Report, 20*(3), 3–19.

Rhodes, J. E., Haight, W., & Briggs, E. (1999). The influence of mentoring relationships of foster youth in relative and nonrelative foster care. *Journal of Research on Adolescence, 9*(2), 185–201.

Rivers, I., & D'Augelli, A. (2001). The victimization of lesbian, gay, and bisexual youths. In A. D'Augelli & C. Patterson (Eds.), *Lesbian, gay, and bisexual identities and youth: Psychological perspectives* (pp. 199–223). New York: Oxford University Press.

Robins, L., & Rutter, M. (Eds.). (1990). *Straight and devious pathways from childhood to adulthood.* Cambridge: Cambridge University Press.

Sabbah, H., Vereecken, C., Elgar, F., Nansel, T., Aasvee, K., Abdeen, Z., . . . Maes, L. (2009). Body dissatisfaction and communication with parents among adolescents in 24 countries: International cross-sectional survey. *BioMed Central, 9*(52), 1–10.

Schaeffer, C. M., Ialongo, N., Hubbard, S., Petras, H., Masyn, K. E., Poduska, J., & Kellam, S. (2006). A comparison of girls' and boys' aggressive-disruptive behavior trajectories across elementary school: Prediction to young adult antisocial outcomes. *Journal of Consulting and Clinical Psychology, 74*(3), 500–510.

Schlegel, A., & Barry, H. (1991). *Adolescence: An anthropological inquiry.* New York: Free Press.

Sipe, C. L. (2002). Mentoring programs for adolescents: A research summary. *Journal of Adolescent Health, 31*, 251–260.

Steinberg, L. (2011). *Adolescence* (9th ed.). Boston: McGraw-Hill.

Substance Abuse and Mental Health Services Administration. (2009). *Results from the 2008 national survey on drug use and health: National findings* (Office of Applied Studies, NSDUH Series H-36, HHS Publication No. SMA 09-4434). Rockville, MD: U.S. Department of Health and Human Services. Retrieved from http://oas.samhsa.gov/nsduh/2k8nsduh/2k8Results.cfm#2.3

Tanner, J. M. (1962). *Growth in adolescence* (2nd ed.). Oxford: Blackwell Scientific.

Taylor, E. H. (2005). *A survey of violent perceptions and self-destructive thoughts in rural students.* Unpublished manuscript.

Tierney, J. P., Grossman, J. B., & Resch, N. L. (1995). *Making a difference: An impact study of Big Brothers/Big Sisters.* Philadelphia: Public/Private Ventures.

U.S. Department of Education. (2007). *Context of elementary and secondary education tables, school characteristics and climate, school year 2003-2004.* Retrieved from http://nces.edu.gov/programs/coe/2007/section4/table.asp?tableID=727

U.S. Department of Health and Human Services, Health Resources and Services Administration, Maternal and Child Health Bureau. (2009). *Child health USA 2008-2009.* Rockville, MD: U.S. Department of Health and Human Services. Retrieved from http://mchb.hrsa.gov/chusa08/pdfs/c08.pdf

Werner, E., & Smith, R. S. (1982). *Vulnerable but invincible: A longitudinal study of resilient children and youth.* New York: McGraw-Hill.

Wertsch, J. V. (Ed.). (1985). *Culture, communication, and cognition: Vygotskian perspectives.* New York: Cambridge University Press.

Wheeler, M. E., Keller, T. E., & Du Bois, D. L. (2010). Review of three recent randomized trials of school-based mentoring: Making sense of mixed findings. *Social Policy Report, 24*(3).

Zimmermann, M. A., Bingenheimer, J. B., & Notaro, P. (2002). Natural mentors and adolescent resiliency: A study with urban youth. *American Journal of Community Psychology, 30*(2), 221-243.

Zucker, J., Bradley, S. J., & Notaro, P. C. (2004). Gender identity and psychosexual disorders. In J. M. Wiener & M. K. Dulcan (Eds.), *The American Psychiatric Publishing textbook of child and adolescent psychiatry* (pp. 813-835). Washington, DC: American Psychiatric Publishing.

9

Social Work with Young Adults
Professional Development and Multicultural Education in Schools of Social Work

---

This chapter begins our discussion of development in adulthood. Clearly, development does not stop at the end of adolescence, but continues throughout the life span. In adulthood, the diversity of developmental pathways is even more apparent than in childhood and adolescence. All adults do not develop in the same way, in the same sequence, or at the same rate. Rather, individuals become increasingly diverse as they age. Contemporary theories of adult development do not assume universality, and the concept of developmental change, which does not assume an endpoint or goal toward which one moves, is favored over the concept of developmental progress.

The focal system of this chapter is the young adult, emphasizing the acquisition of an occupation and using the professional development of social work students as an exemplar. Just as it is important to consider the development of the client, so too is it important to consider the development of the social worker, who also is changing and adapting. As you read, consider biological, psychological, and social factors of young adult development as they interact within specific sociocultural and historical contexts. Consider especially the macrosystem of the social work profession. How do social work values and ethics relate to the professional development of social work students? How do the values of nondiscrimination relate to experiences students may have had in other cultural settings? What are the implications for multicultural education?

Social work with young adults (approximately twenty-two to thirty-five years old) is challenging and important. Young adults typically are at their peak physically and intellectually, ready to take on the many new responsibilities of adulthood. At the beginning of early adulthood, however, people are also relatively inexperienced. In the United States, few have supported themselves through full-time employment, negotiated the complexities of long-term intimate relationships, or held responsibility for the life of a child. Yet many young adults make decisions regarding an occupation or career, marriage, and establishing a family that can affect their lives for decades. By the end of early adulthood, many people have established a more stable niche within society through family, occupation, and community activities.

Forming lasting intimate relationships is a milestone of development in early adulthood. This young couple has been married for ten years, and they work together as artists and writers.

Others, suffering from unmet mental and physical health needs, substance misuse, poverty, and oppression, struggle to meet basic needs for food, shelter, friendship, and belonging (see box 9.1).

BOX 9.1 INTERNATIONAL PERSPECTIVES

HIV-AIDS Prevention Efforts in India

HIV-AIDS (human immunodeficiency virus/acquired immunodeficiency syndrome) has spread to nearly every nation on earth and is the cause of widespread fear and concern. According to estimates, around 31.3 million adults and 2.1 million children were living with HIV at the end of 2008. Sub-Saharan African countries have the highest prevalence rates, with some countries having as much as 28 percent of the countries' population infected with HIV or AIDS. To date, there is neither an effective cure nor a vaccine available for HIV-AIDS. Although new drugs called antiretroviral protease inhibitors prolong the lives of HIV-positive individuals, such medication is unaffordable to people in the developing world.

In 2007, 0.3 percent of India's population was infected with HIV. It is one of five countries (along with Russia, China, Nigeria, and Ethiopia) classified by the U.S. National Intelligence Council as representing the second wave of the HIV-AIDS epidemic. Second-wave countries have the most critical prevention and treatment challenges. In 2002, approximately 4 to 4.5 million Indians aged fifteen to forty-nine years were infected with HIV, with heterosexual contact being the primary mode of transmission.

The approximately 4 million Indian women engaged in prostitution are particularly vulnerable to contracting and spreading HIV-AIDS. Indeed, approximately 50 percent of these women already are HIV infected. Many of these women are undereducated and suffer from extreme economic impoverishment, as well as forced exploitation.

To combat the spread of HIV-AIDS, most major Indian cities now have HIV-AIDS prevention programs for women in prostitution. Lakshmi Tata, an Indian social worker, conducted an ethnographic study of prostitution in the red-light district of Poona, India, focusing on a peer-education program. This program employed former female prostitutes who provided education about HIV-AIDS and distributed condoms to prostitutes to encourage safer sex. Dr. Tata's research indicated that these peer educators were largely successful in transmitting information about HIV-AIDS to women, and in distributing condoms. She also found, however, that women's vulnerability and relative powerlessness was an impediment to their acting on this information to protect their health. Some male clients violently resisted the use of condoms. Others chose to take their business elsewhere. As one young prostitute, a mother, explained to Dr. Tata, when her male clients resisted the use of condoms, she could not turn them, and the income they provided, away. Her immediate need to feed her desperately hungry children took precedent over worries about her health in the future.

Sources: Tata, 2003; UNAIDS, 2008.

The assumption of a vocation or profession is an important milestone of development for those young adults who have the resources for an extended period of education, training, or apprenticeship. Transforming a novice into an expert is a complex process involving more than the acquisition of a technical knowledge base and a set of skills. It also involves the acquisition of a culture: a specialized language and way of understanding, norms of behavior, unique customs, rites of passage, and codes of conduct. Professions such as social work are characterized by a prolonged period of adult socialization that powerfully influences novices' knowledge, attitudes, behaviors, and identity. This intense process of learning and personal change transforms students into professional social workers.

The developmental processes of professional socialization may occur as a student is navigating the transitions of early adulthood. These processes may be experienced again (or for the first time) in midlife, for example, when adults return to schools of social work after working in social service or other fields. Consider how midlife adults might experience professional socialization in schools of social work. Their experiences illustrate the spiral nature of development as individuals revisit earlier challenges from distinctly different vantage points.

SOCIAL WORK EDUCATION WITH YOUNG ADULTS

Social work education with young adults occurs in a wide variety of contexts, including professional schools of social work in colleges and universities. Social work education developed at the end of the nineteenth century because members of charity organization societies were concerned about the quality and consistency of services for poor and dependent people. From their founding, charity societies provided in-service training for volunteers (Frumkin & Lloyd, 1995). Skills and knowledge, however, were acquired primarily through an informal apprenticeship system (Brieland, 1995). Over time, the complexity and potential malleability of human problems were recognized, and moralistic approaches were replaced with social science approaches for assisting those in need. By the end of the century, it was clear that formal education would be necessary to support the development of knowledge, ensure an effective level of services, and supply trained professionals. By the end of World War I, there were seventeen social work programs in the United States. Soon after, organizations were established to develop and monitor the delivery of an organized, high-quality curriculum. In 1946, the **Council on Social Work Education** (CSWE) was established. An important function of CSWE is accreditation, which involves monitoring the performance of social work educational programs in delivering a high-quality, standardized curriculum (Frumkin & Lloyd, 1995).

Currently, there are approximately 700 accredited social work graduate and undergraduate programs serving over 60,000 students in the United States (Council of Social Work Education, 2007; Group for the Advancement of Doctoral Education, n.d.). Many of the educators working in these programs have their doctorates as well as master's degrees in social work (MSWs), and have spent at least two years practicing social work before entering social work education. They contribute to the knowledge base of the profession by conducting research, and participate in administration in their schools and professional social work organizations. A primary function for most is educating a new generation of social work students to embark on careers as professional social workers.

When she was thirty years old, Lynn entered an MSW program at a large public university. She and her husband (Greg) and two-year-old son (Jeremy) had recently moved to the East Coast from their home and extended family on the West Coast, so that Greg could accept a professional position. It was an exciting time of positive change for Lynn, who had put off starting her own career to support Greg and begin their family. In her MSW program, Lynn felt that she had finally found her niche. She excelled in her classes, and her interests in social justice were reflected and supported by her classmates and teachers. She was eager to begin contributing to her community through meaningful work. At the same time, Lynn experienced considerable stress in her field placement at a child welfare agency. Although her middle-class, European-American background was very different from that of her primarily low-income, African-American and Hispanic clients, she quickly formed supportive relationships with the children. It was their parents with whom she struggled, especially during parenting classes. She viewed the parents as harsh and unloving, and they viewed her as naive and ignorant of the realities of their daily lives. Lynn also experienced anxiety about putting Jeremy in day care, stress within her marriage as she and Greg struggled to develop a new system of shared household chores, and loneliness because she was required to spend increasing amounts of time away from her family during her field placements. Over time, with the support of friends and one another, Lynn and her family adjusted to their new home and lifestyle, and Lynn developed a deeper understanding of working with others who lived in very different cultural worlds from her own.

SOME THEORIES OF DEVELOPMENT ACROSS THE LIFE SPAN

There are a variety of theories of life-span development that can deepen our understanding of the professional socialization of Lynn and her colleagues. In the 1960s and 1970s, a number of scholars made important contributions to understanding development in adulthood (see Hunter, 2008). As discussed in chapter 1, Erikson's (1963) theory of development was significant, in part, because he recognized and described developmental change throughout the life span. Indeed, three of his eight developmental stages occur in adulthood. As with earlier stages of development, at each stage of adult development, individuals confront a psychosocial crisis. The central conflict identified by Erikson for early adulthood is intimacy versus isolation. To resolve this conflict, one must develop the capacity to share with and care about others, without fear of losing one's own identity. Adaptive resolution of the conflict between intimacy and isolation results in an increased, mature capacity to love. A maladaptive resolution of this crisis results in loneliness and isolation.

In another influential developmental theory encompassing adulthood, Levinson (1978) conceptualized the life span as a sequence of eras lasting approximately twenty-five years (childhood and adolescence, early adulthood, middle adulthood, and late adulthood). During each era, individuals make key choices about the kind of life they want to live, set priorities, and pursue goals. Eventually, the choices come into question, setting up a transition period. The life structure is the underlying pattern of one's life at a given time. It entails choices, commitments, and related social roles and activities. Levinson considered the central elements of the life structure in adulthood to be marriage, family, and work.

Vaillant (1977) focused on psychological adaptation to challenges through defense mechanisms, that is, strategies used to deal with anxiety. Vaillant's theory is important, in part, because of its emphasis on developmental progress in adulthood without stages. Consistent with contemporary scholars, Vaillant recognized that adults do not progress through a universal, invariant sequence of qualitative shifts in development. He focused on a variety of defense mechanisms, including those he considered to be more mature: *Anticipation* involves experiencing emotions prior to the events and developing realistic alternative responses or solutions. *Affiliation* is seeking others for help or support and not blaming others for one's problems. *Altruism* is meeting the needs of others and feeling gratification from others' responses. *Self-assertion* is expressing feelings and thoughts without being manipulative or coercive. *Self-observation* involves reflecting on one's thoughts, feelings, and behavior, and responding accordingly. *Sublimation* is refocusing potentially maladaptive feelings or behaviors into socially acceptable behavior. *Suppression* is intentionally not thinking about disturbing problems, feelings, and experiences. The progression to more mature and effective defense mechanisms is gradual, and not everyone reaches the more mature levels.

The theories of Erikson, Levinson, and Valliant were influential in extending developmental thinking into adulthood. Clearly, individuals do not stop changing and adapting at the end of adolescence. Erikson also focused attention on the development of personal identity as embedded within a sociocultural context. Relative to more contemporary theories, however, early theories of adult development are limited in their perspectives on variation in adult development.

A number of developmental theories that emerged from the 1970s through the 1990s do not rely on the concept of stage. Instead they elaborate on the diversity of adult development. As discussed in chapter 1, Bronfenbrenner's (1979) ecological-systems theory is significant, in part, because of its analysis of context. The micro-, meso-, exo-, macro-, and macrochronological systems inhabited by adults are increasingly diverse, and this diversity is reflected in increasing individual variation in adult development. As in a number of other contemporary developmental theories, Bronfenbrenner viewed individuals as active interpreters of reality. How individuals perceive reality has very real consequences for their social emotional and behavioral responses. Furthermore, development is not only affected by the diversity of current contexts, but by diverse past environments.

Like Bronfenbrenner, Baltes (1987) recognized the diversity of adult lives. Instead of shared stages, Baltes emphasized that adults adapt to unique constellations of life experiences. Baltes's life-span theory recognizes development as a multidimensional, lifelong process that encompasses both gains and losses embedded within particular sociocultural and historical contexts. Baltes recognized the impact on development of normative, predictable, universally experienced events such as menopause; normative, history-graded events such as wars or technological advances; and nonnormative events or unique experiences such as losing a child or being elected to public office.

Elder's (1998) life-course theory also considers the interaction of biological and psychological aspects of development as embedded within specific sociocultural and historical contexts. Among the important concepts of life-course theory is role conflict, which can occur when one tries to fulfill the demands of two or more wholly or partially incompatible roles simultaneously, such as parenting an infant while holding down a full-time job. Role strain occurs when one's qualities or skills are a poor match for the demands of a role, for example, an introverted individual entering an occupation requiring high levels of social interaction. Life-course theory takes a long-term view of change over the course of a person's life trajectory. Transitions within the life trajectory can become turning points if they result in substantive changes, such as changes in one's perspective and behavior resulting from the birth of the first child. The impact of the transition also depends in its timing, for example, becoming a first-time parent at age twenty versus age forty.

HIGHLIGHTS OF DEVELOPMENT IN EARLY ADULTHOOD

Early adulthood forms the developmental context for some social work students. As suggested by our discussion of developmental theories, the beginning and ending of early adulthood are not defined by discrete biological, psychological, and social markers. Instead, early adulthood is marked by the acquisition of new roles, such as employee, spouse, and parent. For many people in the United States, early adulthood involves leaving home, completing an education, beginning full-time work, attaining economic independence, establishing a long-term sexually intimate relationship, and starting a family (Berk, 2009). The timing of these events varies greatly among individuals, much more so than childhood events or adolescence. Some women bear children in adolescence, while others wait until they are in midlife to begin families, or choose not to have children at all. Some individuals discontinue their formal education at sixteen, and others pursue advanced degrees into their thirties and beyond. In some cultural communities, young adults continue to live with their parents and other family members, whereas in others they are expected to live independently in late adolescence. The timing of development within early adulthood also is affected by the burdens of poverty, violence, and substance misuse (see boxes 9.2–9.5).

Development in early adulthood is supported by, and facilitates, a complex ensemble of biological and psychosocial changes within particular sociocultural and historical contexts.

BOX 9.2 POVERTY ACROSS THE LIFE SPAN

Household Incomes

In 2009, approximately 8.8 million American families (11 percent) lived in poverty, the highest poverty rate since 1994. Households headed by females with no husband present increased from 4.2 million (28.7 percent) in 2008 to 4.4 million (29.9 percent) in 2009. Poverty also increased for households headed by a single male with no female present. In 2008, there were 723,000 (13.8 percent) single-male households at or below the poverty line. By the end of 2009, 942,000 (16.9 percent) single-male households were living in poverty.

Source: DeNavas-Walt, Procter, & Mills, 2010.

BOX 9.3 VIOLENCE ACROSS THE LIFE SPAN

Violence and Alcohol

- Alcohol and illicit drugs increase the likelihood of suicidal ideation and suicidal attempts. One-third of suicides tested positive for alcohol.

- In the United States, 32 percent of all violent deaths involved the use of alcohol.

- Alcohol was involved in approximately 32 percent of all U.S. traffic fatalities in 2008.

- It is estimated that alcohol is responsible for 6.5 percent of deaths in Europe. In Russia, alcohol is responsible for 52 percent of deaths for individuals between the age of fifteen and fifty-four.

Sources: Centers for Disease Control and Prevention, n. d.; Karch et al., 2009; World Health Organization, 2009.

BOX 9.4 SUBSTANCE MISUSE ACROSS THE LIFE SPAN
The Cost of Alcohol

- Alcohol misuse costs Americans approximately $184.6 billion annually.
- In 2007, 23,199 deaths per year in the United States were related to alcohol.
- Alcoholism accounts for half of all deaths related to cirrhosis of the liver.
- In 2004, a study interviewed patients admitted to general hospitals. Approximately 40 percent of patients were diagnosed as having some problems related to alcohol use.

Sources: Harwood, Fountain, & Livermore, 1998; Smothers, Yahr, & Ruhl, 2004; Xu, Kochanek, Murphy, & Tejada-Vera, 2010.

BOX 9.5 SUBSTANCE MISUSE ACROSS THE LIFE SPAN
What We Have Learned from Animal Studies of Addiction

Our knowledge of addiction has been advanced by scientists' developing animal models that illustrate how changes in the brain's reward system and environmental learning interact to perpetuate substance misuse. Studies demonstrate that the behavior allowing an animal to gain access to a drug (by pressing a button) is learned and can be triggered by these events:

- signals from within a brain that has adapted and independently produces signals that the substance is needed
- environmental cues that have been paired with the drug experience (e.g., in humans, linking with certain peers, going to certain places, taking part in certain activities, or a combination of these factors)
- perceived stress

Animal studies have also shown that large individual differences influence the likelihood that drug use will be either initiated or inhibited. In both animal and human studies, drug use is highly influenced by stress (deprivation for animals) and a return to environments where a substance was previously consumed.

Source: Wise & Gardner, 2004.

Biological Factors

At the beginning of early adulthood (twenty to thirty years), young adults typically are at their peak physically. Toward the latter half of early adulthood (thirty to thirty-five or forty years), athletic skills, vision, hearing, and the skeletal system begin to decline gradually, hair begins to gray and thin, basal metabolic rate declines, and gradual weight gain begins. In women, fertility problems increase in the middle thirties. There are, however, vast individual differences in rates of aging, because of genetic and lifestyle differences. Some women conceive and bear healthy children into their early forties. As long as practice continues, athletic performance drops only slightly—about 2 percent per decade—into the sixties and seventies (Berk, 2009).

Psychological and Social Factors

A number of scholars have contributed to our understanding of cognitive, or intellectual, development in adulthood. K. Warner Schaie (1977/1978) observed that with entry into adulthood, individuals must use their reasoning abilities in increasingly diverse situations. The goals of mental activity shift from acquiring knowledge to applying it. Gisella Labouvie-Vief (1980, 1985) argued that in adulthood, reasoning moves from hypothetical thought characteristic of adolescence to pragmatic thought, as logic becomes a tool to solve real-world problems. As young adults settle on a specific career or vocation, their knowledge deepens and they develop expertise. Toward the end of early adulthood, as family and work lives expand, the cognitive capacity to simultaneously juggle many responsibilities improves, and creativity often peaks (Berk, 2009).

For many people, childbearing and child rearing occurs in the twenties and thirties. Becoming a parent is a major, life-changing event. In many families and cultural communities, having a baby is viewed as a joyous event. It can also be a time of stress within a relationship, and of vulnerability for young women (see box 9.6).

Having a baby also can trigger biological vulnerabilities: 50 to 85 percent of new mothers experience sadness, fear, anxiety, and loss of energy after the birth (Taylor, 2005). These mothers are experiencing what are known as "the baby blues." The loss of joy occurs almost immediately after delivery and has all the appearances of depression. This sudden change in emotions and loss of confidence most likely result from hormonal shifts and extreme fatigue triggered by the birth process. It may be exacerbated by a woman's failure to experience the expected feelings of joy and fulfillment in her baby. For most women the baby blues disappear spontaneously within a few days, although for some they may last from one to three weeks.

> **BOX 9.6 VIOLENCE ACROSS THE LIFE SPAN**
> **Intimate Partner Violence**
>
> Women as a whole are more likely than men to experience and sustain injuries from intimate partner violence, and pregnant women are particularly vulnerable to violence from their partners. A study by the World Health Organization examined intimate partner violence in ten countries and found that 15-71 percent of women experienced physical abuse, sexual abuse, or both at the hands of partners at some time in their lives. In the United States, more than 30 percent of women report physical or sexual abuse by husbands or boyfriends, with estimates of as many as 5 million women experiencing intimate partner violence each year.
>
> ---
>
> Sources: Bent-Goodley, 2009; Garcia-Moreno, Jansen, Ellsberg, Helse, & Watts, 2005; Próspero, 2007.

Once the baby blues are gone, the mother's normal affect, motivation, self-perceptions, and psychological outlook on motherhood return. The baby blues seldom prevent women from leaving the hospital or caring for their babies. Nonetheless, emotional support and assistance at home and with child-care tasks can be extremely meaningful to the new mother.

During the first twelve months after childbirth, up to 15 percent of mothers develop postpartum depression (Taylor, 2005). Unlike the baby blues, this can be a disabling, dangerous disorder that is less likely to disappear spontaneously. Women who develop severe postpartum depression are best treated with psychiatric medications and may require inpatient hospitalization. Box 9.7 describes facts about postpartum depression that are important for social workers.

> **BOX 9.7 POSTPARTUM DEPRESSION**
>
> In 2004 and 2005, approximately 10-15 percent of women reported feeling depressed within one year after giving birth. Social workers need to be aware of the following facts about postpartum depression:
>
> - Postpartum depression is real depression and not simply a state of sadness that can be willed away.
> - Mothers suffering from postpartum depression need mental health treatment as quickly as possible.
> - As the illness increases in severity, the mother may neglect, abandon, or physically abuse the baby.

- Mothers with postpartum depression often report doubting whether they can meet the child's needs, obsessively worrying about the baby's well-being, and having recurring fears that they are going to accidentally injure the baby.
- Some mothers report that they lost all interest in the baby or became upset when their child cried and could not be satisfied.
- Having had one or more children without a depressive episode does not assure that postpartum depression will not occur sometime during the first year after the next child is born.
- In addition to child-focused symptoms, mothers experiencing postpartum depression also report problems routinely seen in people with mood disorders, such as changes in sleeping and eating patterns, increased guilt, thoughts of hopelessness, and loss of interest in things that previously provided enjoyment or satisfaction.
- Having had an episode of depression, bipolar disorder, or other major mental disorder in the past places the mother at a higher risk for postpartum depression.
- Many mothers unknowingly have suffered from mild depression, anxiety, or other disorders and are also at a greater risk.

All prospective mothers and their families need preventive education and written information telling them how to identify and get professional help quickly for postpartum depression. Like other mood disorders, postpartum depression increases the risk for suicide. In rare cases, the depression can shift into a psychosis, causing the mother to lose sight of reality and to develop delusions and hallucinations. Postpartum psychosis occurs in only about one out of a thousand births, but it requires an immediate response from the helping communities.

Sources: Centers for Disease Control and Prevention, 2008; Taylor, 2005.

The many critical life choices and decisions surrounding careers, relationships, and families are complex even in the best of circumstances, let alone to adults facing challenges such as cognitive or physical disabilities, poor mental or physical health, poverty, or oppression. Marriage and children can bring great pleasures, but also great vulnerability, challenge, and responsibility. How does one meet a prospective mate and make the decision to marry? How does one raise healthy children within a racist society, or within divorced families? The answers to these and other questions are neither simple nor obvious.

Establishing families can be especially challenging for individuals in the sexual minority. By 2010, several U.S. states allowed same-sex marriage, and a few others recognized same-sex marriage on a limited basis (Lewis, 2011). The inability to marry legally in most states makes couples, children, and family units vulnerable to harassment and physical danger, unnecessary emotional stress, and economic hardships. Most gays and lesbians, like heterosexuals, desire long-term, caring, and lasting relationships (Flaks, Fischer, Masterpasqua, & Joseph, 1995; Patterson, 1992). The development of children raised by gay and lesbian parents does not differ from that of children raised by heterosexual parents (Flaks et al., 1995; Patterson, 1992). Young adults raised by gay or lesbian parents report high satisfaction with their family life, and close relationships with their parents (Garner, 2004; Patterson & Chan, 1997). When viewed as a whole, research findings discredit the logic of withholding civil liberties and penalizing homosexuals and their families.

In addition, the right to marry can be considered a basic human right. The United Nations defines a vulnerable group as a population that encounters discrimination and/or needs protection from possible exploitation. The groups listed under the banner of vulnerable groups include refugees, children, women, indigenous people, linguistic and ethnic minorities, persons with disabilities, persons with HIV-AIDS, and the elderly. The United Nations has not explicitly recognized members of the LGBT community as a "vulnerable group" despite clear evidence of discrimination against them (Reichert, 2006). Despite progress in protecting the civil rights of women and ethnic minorities, the United States has been slow in recognizing the rights of members of the LGBT community.

Yet collective action by the LGBT community and its allies has contributed to positive, if slow, change. Currently, the majority of U.S. citizens support civil unions, and there is growing support for gay and lesbian marriage (Avery, Chase, Johansson, Litvak, Montero, & Wydra, 2007; Schwartz, 2010). There remains much work to be done in securing the human rights of gays and lesbians. Social workers can join with the LGBT community as allies and advocates for human rights.

Sociocultural-Historical Factors

The biological, psychological, and social changes of young adulthood emerge and are shaped within specific sociocultural-historical contexts. These contexts may hasten or delay employment, financial independence, or establishment of intimate relationships, such as marriage and children. The gains in life expectancy in the twentieth century, for instance, allow for longer periods of education and the delay of marriage and childbearing. An American baby born in 1900 had a life expectancy of a little less than 50 years. In 1997, as a result of improved nutrition, medical treatment, sanitation, and safety, life expectancy rose to 76.5 years (Berk, 2009).

FACILITATING THE PROFESSIONAL DEVELOPMENT OF SOCIAL WORK STUDENTS

It is within the context of early adult development that many individuals begin their social work educations. As with any profession, becoming a social worker involves both the acquisition of a knowledge base and technical skills, and the acquisition of a set of values and ethics that inform practice. The knowledge base, type of skills, and depth of skills that social workers need are extensive. Social work draws upon various disciplines (e.g., biology, psychology, sociology, anthropology, political science, economics), professions (e.g., law, psychiatry, education), and contexts of practices (e.g., hospitals, schools, community mental health centers). Furthermore, social work is shaped in relation to the larger social and historical context, including fiscal constraints; increases in poverty, drug use, and violence; changes in family structure; demographic transitions, including the proportion of elderly people and people of color in the population (Hopps & Collins, 1995); health threats from HIV-AIDS; and fear of terrorist attacks.

Along with an extensive knowledge base and technical skills, social work students acquire a set of attitudes and beliefs. In his first-person account *Becoming a Doctor: A Journey of Initiation in Medical School*, Melvin Konner (1987) observed that student doctors acquire much more

Many critical life choices, including which occupation to pursue, are made in early adulthood. This young woman is visiting with a family as part of her preparation for a career in social work.

than a knowledge base and technical skills from their teachers. They carefully watch, and in some cases imitate, the attitudes and behaviors of their physician teachers toward patients and issues of illness, death, and dying. This socialization into the medical culture profoundly affects both the quality of patient care and students' ability to cope with the stress of becoming a physician, including students' ability to respond with empathy toward a dying patient and to recover emotionally from the experience of the patient's death.

Social work students, like student doctors, also learn through observations and participation in the culture of their profession. Students observe not only the content but the apparent attitudes and behaviors of their teachers and field instructors toward course material and clients. Are teachers comfortable discussing issues of child sexual abuse, or do they resort to inappropriate humor? Is the field instructor dismissive and condescending or respectful to parents involved with the child welfare system?

As in medicine, the scope and complexity of professional social work has led to specialization. As a consequence, the student specializing in child welfare will experience a somewhat different context and acquire a somewhat different knowledge base from the student specializing in medical social work. Furthermore, each practice setting will have its own set of skills, relationships, practices, and working conditions. Underlying this diversity, however, is a common culture: a set of values, ethics, and standards for professional conduct that distinguish and unify the social work profession.

Social work values include service, social justice, respect for the dignity and worth of each person, respect for diversity, and the importance of human relationships. Like other professions such as law, medicine, and engineering, social work has developed from its values ethical standards and guidelines for professional conduct. Ethical standards in social work appear in various forms, but the *NASW Code of Ethics* is the most visible compilation of the profession's standards (Reamer, 1995). The *Code of Ethics* begins by explicitly stating core social work values. According to the preamble, "The primary mission of the social work profession is to enhance human well-being and help meet the basic human needs of all people, with particular attention to the needs and empowerment of people who are vulnerable, oppressed, and living in poverty" (p. 1).

From the core values emerges a set of ethical principles. First, social workers' primary goal is to help people in need and to address social problems. Service to others is elevated above self-interest. Second, social workers challenge social injustice and pursue social change, particularly on behalf of vulnerable and oppressed individuals and groups of people. Third, social workers respect the inherent dignity and worth of each person. Social workers treat each person in a caring and respectful fashion, mindful of individual differences and cultural and ethnic diversity. Fourth, social workers recognize the central importance of human relationships and understand that relationships between and among people are an important vehicle for change. Fifth, social workers are continually aware of the profession's missions, values, ethical principles, and ethical standards, and practice in a manner consistent with them. Sixth, social workers practice within their areas of competence, develop and enhance their professional knowledge and skills, and strive to contribute to the knowledge base of the profession.

These ethical principles inform social work practice and guide social workers' conduct. The *NASW Code of Ethics* addresses social workers' responsibilities to clients and to other social work professionals: they are to perform the job the worker is hired to do, to enhance the well-being of society at large, and to support and promote the social work profession. Although the code provides a brief guide for dealing with ethical dilemmas in social work practice, it offers no set recipe. Simple answers are not available for many complex ethical issues involving, for example, confidentiality and conflicts of interest. Instead, the code offers a set of values, principles, and standards to guide decision making and professional conduct. It also is intended to educate members and to help socialize new members into the profession.

The culture of social work, with its distinct set of professional values, ethics, and standards for conduct, is transmitted to the social work student during the course of formal education, fieldwork, and early professional practice. An individual student's acquisition of the social work culture will be profoundly influenced by a variety of factors, including personal characteristics, level of development, support systems, and past experiences. Relatively little systematic research has explored the professional development of social work students. A developmental, ecological-systems analysis draws our attention to a variety of factors when we consider how best to support the professional development of social work students.

Biological Factors

Biological factors that can affect the social work student's professional development are nutrition, adequate rest, and stress management. Medical education provides a good illustration of the importance of attending to physical health during professional socialization. Critics of socialization practices in medical schools and patient advocates have long noted that poor eating habits, sleep deprivation, and intense stress experienced by student doctors can interfere with their technical competencies as well as their ability to empathize with and support patients (Black, 1993). Like student doctors, social work students experience stress during their professional development. For example, MSW students who have been academically successful as undergraduates may struggle to succeed on challenging exams and paper assignments. Students may also experience pressure during their field placements, where they encounter emotionally and professionally challenging cases involving child abuse, death, serious and persistent mental illness, or substance misuse. During their field placements, students may experience stresses endemic to the U.S. workplace, such as sexual harassment, discrimination, or other abuses of power.

In addition, students may be attempting to balance multiple responsibilities of adulthood, including work and family obligations, with social work education. Unlike the young adult population typically involved in medical education, many social work students are middle-aged adults in dual-career relationships, parents, single parents, and adults caring for aging parents. These students must attend to substantial components of their lives outside of social work school. The multiple stressors experienced by social work students can lead to inadequate rest and poor eating habits, which, in turn, can lead to illness and psychosocial problems.

Psychological Factors

Psychological factors that affect and are affected by professional development include the adequacy of the student's intellectual skills and preparation, and emotional readiness to succeed in school and the profession. Social work students and professionals must reflect on how their own psychological needs relate to their relationships with clients. For example, social workers avoid entering into **dual relationships** with clients. Dual relationships fulfill a psychological need of the professional, and hence shift the focus of the helping relationship from the client's needs. Such relationships can lead to an abuse of power that is harmful to the client, as when professionals have sexual relationships with clients. They can also lead to stress and possible burnout of the social worker.

Joshua Miller's (2001) reflections on his loneliness and need for family during his first professional social work job illustrate the complicated issues of dual relationships. After graduating with his MSW from the University of Washington, Mr. Miller moved to London to begin his first job. One of his first clients, Violet, came to him for help after leaving her abusive husband. Several weeks later, Violet's husband forced his way into her home and murdered her in front of their children. Far from family and friends, Mr. Miller threw himself into supporting Violet's traumatized children and their grandparents. Soon his life became intertwined with theirs, and he recognized that just as he was meeting their need for professional support during this traumatic period, they were meeting his own need for family. Questions soon arose: Was he the best professional to provide services to this family? How would they be affected by his eventual departure? Lacking professional supervision, Mr. Miller wrestled with these issues on his own. A young and inexperienced social worker, he did not know how to address complex personal issues related to his own **secondary trauma**: guilt, overwhelming emotions, rescue motifs, nightmares, social isolation, and persistent sadness.

From his current perspective as a social work educator more than twenty years later, Mr. Miller advises students in similar circumstances to get professional and personal help, think carefully about what they realistically can offer the family, and be cautious about dual relationships.

Social Factors

A student's professional development also affects and is affected by social factors. These factors include students' interpersonal relationships (microsystems) with family, friends, neighbors, employers, coworkers, other students, professors, field instructors, and clients. Relationships with family members can provide invaluable support to the student. On the other hand, relationships with partners and children can be harmed through neglect stemming from the pressing and sustained demands of professional training (Black, 1993). Balancing family with professional training is challenging, as one young medical student described: "When I'm involved in training, the house goes to hell, my husband complains that his needs are not being met, the kids complain. And the experience of tending to a lot of pressure at school, and then coming home and finding pressure there—I just feel like everywhere I turn I'm inadequate" (Broadhead, 1982, as cited in Black, 1993).

On the other hand, the student's professional success can provide security, status, and satisfaction to the entire family. Balancing the pressures of professional training with the needs of partners and children can be challenging. A university mental health counselor related: "At the clinic, many graduate students came to us when their marriages were falling apart, often around transition points like orals, preliminary exams, or graduation. The stresses in their relationship stay buried until these milestones come along that bring a couple to a crisis" (Scheinkman, 1988, as cited in Black, 1993).

Social factors beyond those of interpersonal relationships also impact students' professional development. Characteristics of university and field-placement mesosystems can be critical to a social work student's success. Annie Houston's (2001) reflections on ethical conflicts during her social work field placement at a women's jail illustrate the importance of the formation of strong relationships between universities and field placements. As a beginning graduate social work intern, Ms. Houston worked as an advocate for incarcerated women. Although the prison refused to supply safe-sex paraphernalia, widespread lesbian relationships raised serious concerns about the spread of sexually transmitted diseases, including HIV-AIDS. Houston found herself looking the other way as dams were illicitly passed to prisoners, raising complex ethical dilemmas. Was it ethical for a social work student to break the rules of the prison, thereby modeling the very same type of behavior that resulted in her clients' incarceration? Or was she obligated as a social worker to break unjust rules to help protect the physical well-being of her clients? There are no easy answers, but an important question raised by Janet Black (2001) is, Where was the faculty field liaison? Faculty field liaisons are employed by universities as liaisons between the field placement and the university. They serve as resources for students in creating a strong mesosystem between the university and field placement. As Black argues: "An interdependent relationship must exist between the university and the agency providing field education. The behaviors and interactions of each partner are related; one individual's disregard for the partnership may result in unsuccessful learning experiences and disruption of service and education" (p. 57).

Sociocultural-Historical Context

Students' professional development is embedded within and affected by the larger sociocultural-historical context, including the economic, political, and cultural characteristics of the larger society (macrosystem). The level of funding available for community mental health care can affect the type of interventions students may be exposed to during field placements. Chronic underfunding of community mental health as well as the social stigmatization of individuals with chronic mental illness can result in field placements that focus on case management and do not offer opportunities for supervision in diverse therapeutic approaches.

The sociocultural-historical context can critically impact students' field placements and first job experiences. Katherine van Wormer's (2001) narrative describing her first experiences as a social worker in Norway, where she served for two years as a treatment director at a private alcoholism treatment center, illustrates the impact of larger societal factors on social work practice. In Norway, alcoholism treatment usually is provided free of charge by the state. Because of the hostility toward privatization in Scandinavia with its strong socialist tradition, private centers such as the one described by van Wormer operated independently, without state regulation. The director-owner, a self-described "chief alcoholic," allowed questionable, corrupt, and flagrantly unethical practices. The director-owner pursued sexual relationships with former clients and staff members, individuals with as little as two months' sobriety were hired as staff, staff got reluctant individuals very drunk and then "kidnapped" them into treatment, and trainees were instructed to pretend that they were not working in order to qualify for sick-pay money from the state. Van Wormer went on to blow the whistle on this treatment center, bringing the unprofessional practices in private centers to the attention of the deeply shocked Norwegian social work organization and, ultimately, helping to change the system.

Subcultural Variation in Practice Contexts: Military Social Work

Sociocultural-historical contexts also affect social workers' experiences in the United States. As they begin their professional careers, new social workers can choose from a wide variety of contexts in which to practice, from solo practices to large government agencies. The military is one example that highlights unique subcultural characteristics of a specific practice context. Civilian and enlisted social workers provide services to military personnel and their families. They practice in settings that include military combat units, mental health facilities, substance misuse treatment programs, hospitals, prison and confinement facilities, community service agencies, research facilities, and major military headquarters. They are involved in humanitarian and multinational peace-keeping operations, child welfare, medical social work, program administration, and policy formulation (Harris & Pehrson, 2008).

Underlying the diversity of practice settings and services provided by military social workers, as well as various practice settings, is a common military subcultural context. The typical active-duty military social work career includes multiple and diverse professional assignments dictated by organizational need rather than by personal choice. Nearly all social work officers will serve in an isolated or overseas tour of duty at some point in their careers. Military personnel and their families have a unique lifestyle that includes mobility, periodic separations, overseas living, high-stress/high-risk jobs, and authoritarian management (Harris & Pehrson, 2008).

The unique subcultural context of the military can bring to the fore specific issues relevant to social work. Substance misuse and mental health disorders, for instance, have become an increasing source of concern to military leaders, soldiers, and their families. Military service, such as deployments to Iraq and Afghanistan, can be a significant source of strain. Military operations can include chronic exposure to noxious stimuli, including sustained combat, high-intensity guerrilla warfare, and ongoing threat of roadside bombs and improvised explosive devices. They also involve the removal of positively valued stimuli. Many soldiers experience repeated deployments away from their families and homes (Seal, Bertenthal, Miner, Sen, & Marmar, 2007). In addition, soldiers may be less likely to seek help and feel more alienated due to perceived or actual stigma regarding mental health conditions (National Institute on Drug Abuse, 2009; Riddle et al., 2007).

Research indicates that military service can be a significant source of strain. According to the National Institute on Drug Abuse, the operations in Iraq and Afghanistan have "placed tremendous strain on military personnel and their families." This strain is indicated by family disintegration, mental health disorders, and even suicide. From 25 to 30 percent of Iraq and Afghanistan war veterans have symptoms of a mental disorder or cognitive impairment (National Institute on Drug Abuse, 2009).

Of the soldiers returning from Iraq between 2003 and 2004, 19.1 percent reported mental health problems, as did 11.3 percent of those returning from Afghanistan and 8.5 percent of those returning from other locations. Mental health problems were associated with combat experiences.

The most common complaint was post-traumatic stress disorder (PTSD). PTSD also is strongly associated with substance misuse disorders and violence in relationships (Volkow, 2009). Returning soldiers also reported depression, suicidal ideation, and interpersonal conflicts (Hoge, Auchterlonie, & Milliken, 2006).

Of veterans separated from service in Iraq and Afghanistan between September 2001 and September 2005 and seen at Veterans Administration (VA) health-care facilities, 25 percent received mental health diagnoses, and 56 percent of these veterans had two or more distinct mental health diagnoses. PTSD was the most common diagnosis (13 percent; Seal et al., 2007). Box 9.8 describes substance misuse in the military as a maladaptive form of emotional coping.

BOX 9.8 SUBSTANCE MISUSE ACROSS THE LIFE SPAN

Substance Misuse as Emotional Coping in the Military

Substance misuse is one of the maladaptive ways in which soldiers cope with the strain of service, especially to reduce arousal due to post-traumatic stress disorder (PTSD). Problems with alcohol misuse in the military have a long history. Military personnel are significantly more likely than civilians to report engaging in heavy use of alcohol, as are combat-deployed veterans compared with veterans who were not deployed to combat. Military experts are concerned that the wars in Iraq and Afghanistan have led to an even greater problem of substance misuse among military personnel who have been deployed to these fronts.

Sources: Bray, Marsden & Peterson, 1991; Fiedler et al., 2006; Jacobsen et al., 2008; Riddle et al., 2007; Shipherd, Stafford & Tanner, 2005; Volkow, 2009.

IMPLICATIONS FOR SOCIAL WORK EDUCATION

For purposes of discussion, we have presented biological, psychological, social, and sociocultural-historical factors in professional development separately and at a single point in time. It is important to remember, however, that these factors interact in a complex fashion over time. The BSW, MSW, or PhD degree is only the beginning of a social worker's professional development. As the dean of a large social work school once commented, even the MSW is merely a "learner's permit." Ideally, development will continue throughout their professional careers as social workers learn through experience and continuing study. One of the contexts in which social work educators continue their professional development is through participation in the Counsel on Social Work Education (CSWE). Best known for its role in setting the standards for BSW and MSW programs through accreditation, CSWE also provides programs and resources to promote the professional development of social work educators. For nearly fifty years it has sponsored the Annual Program Meeting (APM), the largest national conference of undergraduate and graduate social work educators. This meeting offers more than 500 presentations, meetings, and receptions. CSWE also publishes *Journal of Social Work Education* to help educators develop their skills and curricula.

A developmental, ecological-systems framework has a number of general implications for enhancing social work education. First, adequate attention must be paid to biological factors. Some stress is inherent as students such as Lynn strive to achieve higher levels of competence. How a student responds to the challenges of professional development depends on a variety of complex contextual factors. It also depends, very simply, upon biological factors such as nutrition, adequate rest, and stress management.

Second, adequate attention must be paid to social and emotional factors. Forming and maintaining supportive relationships with others such as spouses can prove to be invaluable during the process of professional socialization. As Lynn testified, emotional support from family, friends, and peers can reduce stress and provide perspective. Professional supervision from experienced faculty and field supervisors can help the student reflect upon professional conduct and complex ethical issues in social work practice. The absence of such support can lead to difficult situations that present obstacles to professional development.

Social factors beyond the interpersonal also affect the socialization of social workers. A strong university and field-placement mesosystem can result in consistent guidance to students struggling to behave professionally in the ethically complex situations that are routine in social work practice. The absence of strong ties can lead to students' confused and unprofessional conduct, and risk to clients. When entering into field placements, students should consider the broader social context of their education. In particular, what is the quality of communication between the prospective field placement and their school of social work?

Third, attention must be paid to the sociocultural-historical context in which biological and social factors are embedded. Do women such as Lynn have adequate familial and societal support to develop their own skills and talents to the fullest? Is day care available? Do adult men participate in child care and household chores?

Finally, social workers continue to develop long after they receive their degrees. Some will enter into administrative roles, some in schools of social work. Box 9.9 addresses social work education and administration.

**BOX 9.9 PRACTICE STORY AND ADVICE
FROM THE FIELD**

**Dean W., "Our function in society starts fundamentally
from a moral paradigm."**

*Dean W. has worked in social work education for twenty-five
years and is currently the dean of a school of social work. She spoke
about her experiences as a woman in social work education, higher
education administration, and characteristics of successful social
work administrators.*

Practice Observations

Human service is moral work. I think this applies to educational
institutions as well. Our function in society is to socialize students into
certain professional roles. That is moral work . . . And because we are
the social work profession, there are things in our mission and how
we teach that differ from other units on campus. We are talking about
social and economic justice. I just photocopied an editorial from the
Journal of Social Work Education about access to higher education
that I am going to send around to the provost and chancellor because
I think it raises economic justice issues that are important in a university. That sort of moral work—and moral voice—is important to
how I see our particular unit in higher education.

Human service is gendered work . . . [in] higher education institutions, of course, . . . there are gender issues. I am constantly aware of
those in dynamics of various meetings I am in. And I think I have to
talk about race as well . . . This school, since 1980, has had two African-
American deans, including an African-American woman. I am not sure
if there have been many other members of the Council of Deans who
are African American. And that's still the case. You know, I look around
my peers, and I don't see a group that very much mirrors the diversity
that we have in society, and certainly that we hope to have on this
campus. And that's a concern of mine . . . there are many more women
in administrative roles on campus, but I still think that if you look at
the larger units, they all have men as deans: liberal arts, engineering,
business, the largest units on campus all have men as deans . . . that
makes for some interesting issues . . . when you have the issue of the
larger units, which tend to be more powerful, being led by men and
women in, by and large, smaller units, it's harder to get the issues
voiced that need to be voiced. Although the group has been pretty
good overall about listening and so on. But there is still this sort of
large-small split, and when you combine that with gender, it raises
some issues for me. I think it also combines with the social and economic justice issues . . . their graduates make a lot of money and so

they can raise tuition, so they are getting more money to run the different units . . .

Advice on Teaching in Higher Education

First about the teaching side . . . If you go out in the practice world and supervise [social work] interns, think about what it is in the internship situation that you are teaching, how you are drawing on what you learnt in social work education—theories, research—and be able to convey that in frameworks that help an intern . . . you have to start moving up a level in your thinking, so in other words you have to be reflective enough to be aware of the frameworks you are using so that you can teach about them . . . there is a whole knowledge base about how to teach, so one needs to begin to look at that knowledge base.

Advice on Administrative Careers in Higher Education

I think the thing that our [MSW] students don't realize is that within two years most of them will be in supervisory-level positions. They need to be paying attention to those aspects of theory and practice that relate to that, where there is role theory, organizational theory, etc., that will help them. And then there are administrative skills that apply across organizations. Yes, you need to know some things about higher education as opposed to service agency, but some of the things are the same. So you are learning about administration and organization and supervision all the way along, and you also need to learn just a little bit about what the issues are in administration.

Flexibility is key, both intellectually and emotionally . . . I can come in with a "to do list," with two or three things starred in my mind as the things that I would like to do today, and if somebody walks into my door and says that there is a problem . . . it has to be resolved now. Basically, for example, I had two to three weeks earlier this summer where we were negotiating with our major funders and everything else went off my plate for a little over two weeks . . . Your own life must have the flexibility you need . . . Shifting concentration from one thing to another instantly, but yet keeping everything moving forward.

. . . Information management is huge for all of us. E-mail will instantly triple, and triple is even an underestimation . . . On the other hand, getting the information you want can be difficult, so information retrieval skills are important, and not only for me but for my staff. For example my administrative assistant has to be a good administrative retrieval person and has to know some sets of university policies, my business manager has to know another set of university policies, so that they can support me in my role in carrying out the mission of the school.

Strategic and pragmatic thinking—you have to have a vision and you have to be able to convey that. What I must do is convey with enormous clarity my vision for the school ... Every time I am outside of this building interacting with anybody on campus, I have to be able to present the school.... whether I am on this campus, in the national social work scene, or in the accreditation meeting or deans and directors meeting, etc. I am the face of the school ... I need to be constantly presenting us in a way that makes sure everybody out there on campus or in the social work world knows that we are a top ten school, and this is why.

Working with the campus budget committee, or the campus commercial and tenure committee or the Council of Deans, we have to put forward a certain face. Yet you have to be yourself, you can't be anybody but other than who you are. And from the feedback I have received from people in committees like that is that I do an excellent job ... I do not pretend to be somebody other than who I am, and that's important to me.

IMPLICATIONS FOR MULTICULTURAL SOCIAL WORK EDUCATION

Understanding the complex interaction of biological, psychological, and social factors embedded within particular sociocultural-historical contexts over time has important implications for social work education. Nondiscrimination is a central social work value with which social work educators grapple. Social work students come from diverse cultural backgrounds. Many, like Lynn, are able-bodied, heterosexual, European-American, middle-class women from the suburbs. Others grew up in urban or rural communities; come from working-class homes; are black, Hispanic, or Asian; are challenged by disabilities; are gay or lesbian; or are male. However, given the nature of social work, as well as our increasingly pluralistic society, *all* will serve clients with experiences, values, and practices different from their own. How can educators facilitate students' understanding, empathy, and openness to others who are different from them because of age, gender, sexual orientation, ability/disability, ethnicity, or culture?

A developmental, ecological-systems approach to social work education suggests attention to a variety of factors. First, to learn, social work students must feel physically safe. A young, white, male, middle-class student initially made good strides in his understanding of children participating in an after-school program for inner-city, African-American children. During a misunderstanding with several adolescent boys in which he felt physically threatened, he regressed to racist thinking. As he wrote in his reflection journal,

They [older boys] were trying to act tough with me, so I wrestled with them for fun, but not enough to scare or hurt them. Suddenly one of them took a shot at my groin. I luckily dodged it and ended up with a bruise on my thigh. I did not feel comfortable with the boys' aggression that night. My personal reaction is that the African-American culture cannot be as aggressive and tough. If these boys' parents and culture are teaching them to always be tougher than someone else then there is no way they can learn to cooperate within their community in the United States. These kids have to stop their tough image because in this world it pays to be intelligent and not tough. No wonder there are so many African Americans and Hispanics in gangs. I think toughness and machismo might be part of their culture. (Haight, 2002, p. 189)

Clearly, in this context more professional supervision was needed. A supervisor might have asked the student to consider why these boys might feel threatened. Are they really being socialized to be tough? If so—why? Is being tough incompatible with being intelligent? Is it even appropriate for him to be wrestling with the boys, given his role? With closer supervision, the conflict between this student and the adolescent boys would not have escalated to the point that all participants were anxious for their physical safety, and racist beliefs were reinforced rather than challenged.

Second, successful professional development addresses complex psychological factors including students' feelings and values. In a study of European-American university students (Haight, 2002), the majority of students described intense and complex mixed emotional reactions to their work with African-American children in a computer club. One student expressed loving feelings toward a child, but antipathy toward the child's parent. Such intense emotional responses, including guilt and defensiveness in relation to issues of oppression (see Garcia & van Soest, 1997), can interfere with learning (see King, 1991; Tatum, 1992) through distortion of the "facts" and dampened motivation for continued multicultural learning. With adequate supervision, reflection, and interaction with peers, professors, and field supervisors, students will gain the perspectives necessary to function professionally with diverse clients in various settings.

Third, attention must be paid to social factors. Social work students, as members of particular communities, enter social work school with "social representations," "cultural models" (Goodnow, 1988), or "folk psychologies" (Bruner, 1990) of human behavior and diverse cultural communities. The cultural models of European-American students, for instance, may contain omissions and inaccuracies regarding people of color. Thus, students' initial frame of reference within which they interpret cross-race experiences, assess problems, and formulate goals and strategies may be inadequate, as well as discrepant with that of their future clients. Through exposure to the professional social work literature, as well as face-to-face interactions with diverse students, professors, field instructors, and clients, students will acquire information about a variety of cultural communities.

A developmental, ecological-systems approach also directs attention to the variety of contexts in which professional development occurs. Haight (2002) found that European-American, middle-class students' responses to multicultural education varied markedly with context. Students were relatively unchallenged by multicultural materials presented in books and lectures, but more challenged by face-to-face interactions with African-American adults. Some students were distressed and angered by the disciplinary practices (spanking) of some adults, which varied from their own preferred strategies (time-out). Fortunately, face-to-face interactions with members of culturally diverse communities are increasingly characteristic of field placements in social work. The challenge is to use such experiences, systematically, to enhance students' understanding and tolerance of emotionally difficult interactions. With adequate supervision, guided reflections, and planned debriefings, social work students can develop the perspective to function as effective professionals even within socially and emotionally complex contexts.

A developmental, ecological-systems approach also suggests attention to professional development as an active process that continues over time. The ways in which students actively interpret diversity relate to their own unique life experiences—including past and ongoing interactions with members of particular groups—and to their individual interests and strengths. Haight (2002) found marked changes over time in students' reported emotional reactions to their multicultural field placement, including increased comfort in interacting with African-American children and adults, and increased sadness at the plight of individual children living in poverty. In short, students' understanding, and hence the impact of the field placement on their development, changed over time.

SUMMARY

This chapter applied the developmental, ecological-systems approach to understand an important area of development in early adulthood, the acquisition of an occupation or career. In social work, a common denominator in professional development is the socialization and acquisition of a core set of social work values, and the ethical principles and standards of professional conduct that emerge from these values. Nondiscrimination is a central social work value with which social work students and educators grapple. Research on multicultural education suggests that the student's successful socialization into the professional social work culture requires an adequate knowledge base, attention to affect, and experiences that occur over time and in a variety of social contexts. A developmental, ecological-systems analysis of social work students' professional development suggests a variety of ways in which professional development may be enhanced. Although professional development may be most rapid during the initial years of education, it does not end with graduation. Social workers continue to develop as they take on new roles throughout their careers, and as practice and policy evolve over time.

Study and Discussion Questions

1. Early adulthood (roughly twenty-two to thirty-five or forty years) is a major life transition often involving the establishment of economic independence, a marriage, a family, and a career. What are some challenges that individuals may face in this transition, and how might social workers address these issues?

2. What is professional socialization, and what does it entail? How might becoming a professional social worker be similar or different from professional socialization in other professions such as medicine or law?

3. How might professional socialization into social work be experienced by individuals in early and middle adulthood? How might these similarities and differences reflect "spiral" developmental processes?

4. Describe the *NASW Code of Ethics* in terms of its content areas, goals, and guidelines.

5. How will you facilitate your own professional development while addressing the biological, psychological, social, and cultural factors discussed in this chapter?

6. What are some of the challenges to multicultural education? How might these challenges be successfully resolved?

7. Returning to our opening example, how might the multiple transitions of young adulthood experienced by Lynn impact one another (e.g., the transition into a profession, parenting, intimate relationships, and emotional and financial independence from family of origin)? How might socialization into the social work profession be experienced by an adult in midlife?

Resources

For students interested in learning more about development in early adulthood, Berk (2009) is an excellent place to begin. For the student interested in multicultural education, see Tatum (1992, 2007).

Interested students can also supplement this chapter through a number of excellent web-based resources.

The Alan Review addresses how young adults perceive, use, and understand spirituality. The electronic journal is sponsored by ALAN, an organization dedicated to a better understanding of late adolescents and young adults. Available at http://scholar.lib.vt.edu/ejournals/ALAN/spring96/mendt.html.

A discussion of Erikson's young adulthood stage of development is available at http://web.cortland.edu/andersmd/ERIK/stage6.html.

A National Institutes of Health news release documents that maintaining cardiorespiratory fitness in early adulthood significantly decreases the chance of developing high blood pressure and diabetes in middle age. Available at http://www.nih.gov/news/pr/dec2003/nhlbi-16.htm.

In 2005, the Annie E. Casey Foundation published a comprehensive report detailing the characteristics of individuals aged eighteen to twenty-four years and how they transition into adulthood. The complete report is located at http://www.aecf.org/upload/publicationfiles/da3622h1236.pdf.

The National Cancer Institute of Canada provides information about the epidemiology and treatment of young Canadian adults who develop cancer. Available at http://www.cancer.ca/~/media/CCS/Canada%20wide/Files%20List/English%20files%20heading/pdf%20not%20in%20publications%20section/Stats%202009E%20Special%20Topics.ashx.

The Rand Corporation compared smoking trends among four racial/ethnic groups. Researchers collected data from 6,259 individuals age thirteen through twenty-three years. Available at http://www.rand.org/publications/RP/RP1124/.

References

Avery, A., Chase, J., Johansson, L., Litvak, S., Montero, D., & Wydra, M. (2007, January). America's changing attitudes toward homosexuality, civil unions, and same-gender marriage: 1977-2004. *Social Work, 52*(1), 71-79.

Baltes, P. B. (1987). Theoretical propositions of life-span developmental psychology: On the dynamics of growth and decline. *Developmental Psychology, 23*, 611-626.

Bent-Goodley, T. B. (2009). A black experience-based approach to gender-based violence. *Social Work, 54*(3), 262-269.

Berk, L. E. (2009). *Development through the lifespan* (5th ed.). Boston: Allyn & Bacon.

Black, J. (2001). Between the agency and the university. In S. L. Abels (Ed.), *Ethics in social work practice: Narratives for professional helping* (pp. 57-60). Long Beach, CA: Love.

Black, J. E. (1993). In praise of families. In H. M. Swartz & D. L. Gotteil (Eds.), *Education of physician schools* (pp. 235-249). Rockville, MD: Beth Press.

Bray, R., Marsden, M., & Peterson, M. (1991). Standardized comparisons of the use of alcohol, drugs, and cigarettes among military personnel and civilians. *American Journal of Public Health, 81*(7), 865-869.

Brieland, D. (1995). Social work practice: History and evolution. In *Encyclopedia of social work* (19th ed., Vol. 3, pp. 2247-2254). Washington, DC: NASW Press.

Bronfenbrenner, U. (1979). *The ecology of human development*. Cambridge, MA: Harvard University Press.

Bruner, J. (1990). *Acts of meaning*. Cambridge, MA: Harvard University Press.

Centers for Disease Control and Prevention (CDC). (n.d.). *Impaired Driving Fact Sheet*. Retrieved from http://www.cdc.gov/MotorVehicleSafety/Impaired_ Driving/impaired-drv_factsheet.html

DeNavas-Walt, C., Proctor, B. D., & Mills, R. J. (2010). *Income, poverty, and health insurance coverage in the United States* (U.S. Census Bureau, Current Population Reports, Publication No. P60-238). Washington, DC: U.S. Government Printing Office. Retrieved from http://www.census.gov/prod/2010pubs/p60-238.pdf

Elder, G. H. (1998). The life course and human development. In W. Damon & R. M. Lerner (Eds.), *Handbook of child psychology* (5th ed., pp. 939-991). New York: Wiley.

Erikson, E. H. (1963). *Childhood and society*. New York: Norton.

Fiedler, N., Ozakinci, G., Hallman, W., Wartenberg, D., Brewer, N., Barrett, D., & Kipen, H. (2006). Military deployment to the Gulf War as a risk factor for psychiatric illness among US troops. *British Journal of Psychiatry, 188*, 453-459.

Flaks, D. K., Fischer, I., Masterpasqua, F., & Joseph, G. (1995). Lesbians choosing motherhood: A comparative study of lesbian and heterosexual parents and their children. *Developmental Psychology, 31*, 105-114.

Frumkin, M., & Lloyd, G. A. (1995). Social work education. In *Encyclopedia of social work* (19th ed., Vol. 3, pp. 2238-2247). Washington, DC: NASW Press.

Garcia, B., & van Soest, D. (1997). Changing the perceptions of diversity and oppression: MSW students discuss the effects of a required course. *Journal of Social Work Education, 33*, 119-130.

Garcia-Moreno, C., Jansen, H., Ellsberg, M., Helse, L., & Watts, C. (2005). *WHO multi-country study on women's health and domestic violence against women: Initial results on prevalence, health outcomes and women's responses*. Geneva: World Health Organization. Retrieved from http://www.who.int/gender/ violence/who_multicountry_study/en/

Garner, A. (2004). *Families like mine: Children of gay parents tell it like it is*. New York: Perennial Currents.

Goodnow, J. J. (1988). Parents' ideas, actions, and feelings: Models and method from developmental and social psychology. *Child Development, 59*, 286-320.

Group for the Advancement of Doctoral Education. (n.d.). Retrieved from http://www.gadephd.org

Haight, W. (2002). *African-American children at church: A sociocultural perspective*. New York: Cambridge University Press.

Harris, J., & Pehrson, K. (2008). Military social work. In T. Mizrahi & L. Davis (Eds.), *Encyclopedia of social work* (20th ed., Vol. 13, pp. 270-273). Washington, DC: NASW Press; New York: Oxford University Press.

Harwood H., Fountain D., & Livermore, G. (1998). *The economic costs of alcohol and drug abuse in the United States, 1992*. Washington, DC: National Institute on Drug Abuse and National Institute on Alcohol Abuse and Alcoholism.

Hoge, C., Auchterlonie, J., & Milliken, C. (2006). Mental health problems, use of mental health services, and attrition from military service after returning from deployment to Iraq or Afghanistan. *Journal of the American Medical Association, 295*(9), 1023-1032.

Hopps, J. G., & Collins, P. M. (1995). Social work profession overview. In *Encyclopedia of social work* (19th ed., Vol. 3, pp. 2266-2282). Washington, DC: NASW Press.

Houston, A. L. (2001). Do the right thing. In S. L. Abels (Ed.), *Ethics in social work practice: Narratives for professional helping* (pp. 27-33). Long Beach, CA: Love.

Hunter, S. (2008). Adults: Overview. In T. Mizrahi & L. Davis (Eds.), *Encyclopedia of social work* (20th ed., Vol. 1, pp. 48-56). Washington, DC: NASW Press; New York: Oxford University Press.

Jacobsen, I., Ryan, M., Hooper, T., Smith, T., Amoroso, P., Boyko, E., . . . Bell, N. (2008). Alcohol use and alcohol-related problems before and after military combat deployment. *Journal of the American Medical Association, 300*(6), 663-675.

Karch, D. L., Dahlberg, L. L., Patel, N., Davis, T. W., Logan, J. W., Hill, H. A., & Ortega, L. (2009). Surveillance for violent deaths: National violent death reporting system, 16 states, 2006. *Morbidity and Mortality Weekly Report (MMWR), 58*(SS01), 1-44. Retrieved from http://www.cdc.gov/mmwr/preview/mmwrhtml/ss5801a1.htm

King, J. (1991). Dysconscious racism: Ideology, identity, and the miseducation of teachers. *Journal of Negro Education, 60*, 133-146.

Konner, M. (1987). *Becoming a doctor: A journey of initiation in medical school.* New York: Penguin Books.

Labouvie-Vief, G. (1980). Beyond formal operations: Uses and limits of pure logic in life-span development. *Human Development, 23*, 141-160.

Labouvie-Vief, G. (1985). Logic and self-regulation fron youth to maturity: A model. In M. Commons, F. Richards, & C. Armon (Eds.), *Beyond formal operations: Late adolescent and adult cognitive development* (pp. 158-180). New York: Praeger.

Levinson, D. J. (1978). *The seasons of a man's life.* New York: Knopf.

Lewis, G. B. (2011). The friends and family plan: Contact with gays and support for gay rights. *Policy Studies Journal, 39*(2), 217-238.

Miller, J. (2001). Violet's seeds. In S. L. Abels (Ed.), *Ethics in social work practice: Narratives for professional helping* (pp. 111-129). Long Beach, CA: Love.

National Institute on Drug Abuse. (July, 2009). Substance abuse among military, veterans, and their families: A research update from the National Institute on Drug Abuse. *Topics in Brief.* Retrieved from http://www.drugabuse.gov/publications/topics-in-brief/substance-abuse-among-military-veterans-their-families

Patterson, C. J. (1992). Children of lesbian and gay parents. *Child Development, 63*, 1025-1042.

Patterson, C. J., & Chan, R. W. (1997). Gay fathers. In M. E. Lamb (Ed.), *The role of the father in child development* (pp. 245-260). New York: Wiley.

Próspero, M. (2007). Young adolescent boys and dating violence: The beginning of patriarchal terrorism? *Affilia: Journal of Women and Social Work, 22*(3), 271-280.

Reamer, F. (1995). Ethics and values. In *Encyclopedia of social work* (19th ed., Vol. 1, pp. 893-901). Washington, DC: NASW Press.

Reichert, E. (2006). *Understanding human rights: An exercise book.* Thousand Oaks, CA: Sage.

Riddle, J., Smith, T., Smith, B., Corbeil, T., Engel, C., Wells, T., . . . Blazer, D., for the Millennium Cohort Study Team. (2007). Millennium Cohort: The 2001-2003 baseline prevalence of mental disorders in the U.S. military. *Journal of Clinical Epidemiology, 60*, 192-201.

Schaie, K. W. (1977/1978). Toward a stage theory of adult cognitive development. *Aging and Human Development, 8,* 129-138.

Schwartz, J. (2010). Investigating differences in public support for gay rights issues. *Journal of Homosexuality, 57*(6), 748-759.

Seal, K., Bertenthal, D., Miner, C., Sen, S., & Marmar, C. (2007) Bringing the war back home: Mental health disorders among 103,788 veterans returning from Iraq and Afghanistan seen at Department of Veterans Affairs facilities. *Archives of Internal Medicine, 167,* 476-482.

Shipherd, J., Stafford, J., & Tanner, L. (2005). Predicting alcohol and drug abuse in Persian Gulf War veterans: What role do PTSD symptoms play? *Addictive Behaviors, 30,* 595-599.

Smothers, B. A., Yahr, H. T., & Ruhl, C. E. (2004). Detection of alcohol use disorders in general hospital admissions in the U.S. *Archives of Internal Medicine, 167,* 749-756.

Tata, L. (2003). *HIV-AIDS awareness among sex workers in Poona, India* (Unpublished dissertation). University of Illinois, Urbana-Champaign.

Tatum, B. D. (1992). Talking about race, learning about racism: The application of racial identity development theory in the classroom. *Harvard Educational Review, 62*(1), 1-24.

Tatum, B. D. (2007). *Can we talk about race? And other conversations in an era of school resegregation.* Boston: Beacon Press.

Taylor, E. H. (2005). *Atlas of bipolar disorders.* London: Taylor & Francis.

United Nations Programme on HIV/AIDS. (2008). *2008 report on the global AIDS epidemic.* Geneva, Switzerland: World Health Organization. Retrieved from http://www.unaids.org/en/KnowledgeCentre/HIVData/GlobalReport/2008/2008_Global_report.asp

Vaillant, G. E. (1977). *Adaptation to life.* Boston: Little, Brown.

van Wormer, K. (2001). Doing alcoholism treatment in Norway: A personal reminiscence. In S. L. Abels (Ed.), *Ethics in social work practice: Narratives for professional helping* (pp. 95-103). Long Beach, CA: Love.

Volkow, N. (2009). Substance abuse among troops, veterans, and their families. *NIDA Notes, 22*(5).

Wise, R. A., & Gardner, E. L. (2004). Animal models of addiction. In D. S. Charney & E. J. Nestler (Eds.), *Neurobiology of mental illness* (2nd ed., pp. 683-697). New York: Oxford University Press.

World Health Organization. (2009). *Handbook for action to reduce alcohol-related harm.* Copenhagen: Author. Retrieved from http://www.euro.who.int/__data/assets/pdf_file/0012/43320/E92820.pdf

Xu, J., Kochanek, K. D., Murphy, S. L., & Tejada-Vera, B. (2010). Deaths: Final data for 2007. *National Vital Statistics Reports, 58*(19), 1-136.

10

Race, Racism, and Resistance across the Life Span

Jane Marshall and Wendy L. Haight

Developing cultural sensitivity is a complex but key goal for students anticipating a successful social work career in the twenty-first century. This competence is congruent with a central theme infused throughout this text: human behavior and development cannot be understood apart from the complex sociocultural and historical contexts in which they are embedded. Within the diverse and fluid U.S. population, the concept of "race" is a central and continual problematic social construct for understanding human behavior throughout the life span. In this chapter, we consider concepts of race, ethnicity, racism, and white privilege. Then we consider how these larger sociocultural processes affect individuals and how individuals have affected them through discussions of racial identity development and resistance to racism. Native Americans, African Americans, Asian Americans, Latinos, and other people of color have endured a long history of oppression in the United States, and have developed strategies for resisting and effecting social change. Despite their contributions to U.S. society, as well as undeniable social progress, racism directed toward people of color remains a significant social problem, limiting the opportunities of individuals and societal progress. Social workers need to be aware of the social and psychological ramifications of race and ethnicity for their clients. They may also be involved in organized social and political movements to bring about a more just society.

In the United States, race is a complex concept wrought from a history of oppression and resistance. This history encompasses the genocide of Native Americans beginning in the fifteenth century, the approximately 300 years' enslavement of Africans and African-Americans until 1865, the military conquest of Mexico during the mid-nineteenth century, the internment of Japanese Americans during World War II, the injustices of racial segregation into the 1960s, the continued scourge of institutional and structural racism, and more. Not surprisingly, the process of learning about race in the United

In the United States, children, especially children of color, are at increased risk of living in poverty. These young children live in a migrant labor camp.

States is emotionally charged. The intense feelings that concepts of race evoke can often be traced back to our earliest experiences. Consider the following: While grocery shopping in Salt Lake City in 2005, Edith Hudley was approached by a young white child approximately four years old who openly inquired, "Why is your skin dirty?" Her young mother, obviously embarrassed, shushed the child. Edith smiled at the confused girl, introduced herself to the mother and child, explained to the child that she was African American, and allowed her to shake her hand. This little girl had just experienced one of her first lessons in "race" in the United States. In less skilled hands than Mrs. Hudley's, this little girl could have left the interaction confused and anxious. These are exactly the emotions reported by some European-American students in Beverly Tatum's course on the psychology of racism in relation to their earliest race-related memories. Students of color reported similar feelings in relation to early memories of name calling and other negative exchanges with children and even adults (Tatum, 1992). It is not surprising, then, that simply talking about race and learning about racism can be challenging for social work students.

Yet social work is a profession that deals increasingly with people from diverse racial backgrounds. To effectively serve our clients, it is essential that we overcome any of our own resistance to thinking and talking about race and racism. Within the U.S. population, approximately 66 percent are European American, 15 percent are Hispanic or Latino, 12 percent are African American, 4 percent are Asian American, 2 percent are bi- or multiracial, 1 percent are Native American, and 0.1 percent are Native Hawaiian or Pacific Islander. Further, the U.S. population is changing. It is estimated that by the year 2050, the percentage of the U.S. population that is European American will decrease to 46 percent, while the Hispanic/Latino and bi- or multiracial populations will double to 30 percent and 4 percent, respectively (U.S. Census Bureau, 2009b).

In addition, approximately 13 percent of the total U.S. population is foreign born, with about 28 percent of immigrants having entered the United States after 2000 (U.S. Census Bureau, 2009b). Since the 1970s, non-European immigration has accelerated. Middle Easterners, for example, from places as diverse as the Arabian Peninsula, North Africa, Iran, Iraq, and the Palestinian territories, established communities in the United States as far back as the late nineteenth century, but recently their numbers have been increasing dramatically. Many of these second-wave immigrants arrive from politically tumultuous Middle Eastern countries, seeking refuge in the United States. In 2008, there were approximately 3 million U.S. residents who reported Arab origins, and many more with other Middle Eastern heritages. The largest Middle Eastern population in the contemporary United States is Persian, from Iran. Although the majority of Middle Eastern Americans are Muslim, many are Christian and a smaller number are Jewish. These immigrants face many challenges, compounded by widespread misunderstanding of Middle Easterners, including stereotypes of them as terrorists (Conley, 2008).

This glance at the U.S. Census Bureau data might suggest that "race" is a rather straightforward construct. Although the U.S. population clearly is diverse, most individuals fit within one of the identified categories. Just beneath this surface, however, is a great deal of complexity.

"RACE" AS A SOCIALLY CONSTRUCTED CONCEPT

"Race" refers to a group of people who share physical characteristics and are thought to share a common bloodline (Conley, 2008). Yet contemporary scientists acknowledge that the concept of race has no "real," biogenetic basis. In the United States there is as much variation within as between these "races," groupings established more than one hundred years ago (Slaughter-Defoe, Johnson, & Spencer, 2009). In other words, racial groups do not reflect discrete biological categories, but are primarily social constructions. These social constructions, however, have very real consequences for the lives of all people in the United States. They reflect social and political divisions used primarily for the purpose of social, economic, and political subordination (Spencer, 2006).

That race is largely a socially constructed concept is illustrated by changes in racial categorization in relation to historical, sociopolitical, and economic shifts in social power (Kivel, 2002). Leeder (2004) argues that even the terms "minority" or "person of color" connote a way of seeing people who are not part of the dominant culture, minimizing their diversity and individuality, and comparing them with those in structurally dominant positions. She observed that until the abolition of apartheid in South Africa, there were distinctions among whites, blacks, and "coloreds," a distinction not made in the United States. In Brazil and other Latin American countries, people use the phrase "money lightens," which means that the more money one has, the more likely one is to be characterized as "white," regardless of actual skin color. In the United States, what it means to be "white" has changed over time (Kivel, 2002). At the turn of the twentieth century, Irish, Eastern Europeans, Jews, Greeks, and Italians were considered nonwhite (A. G. Johnson, 2006). They became "white" only after members of these groups became upwardly mobile and obtained social and economic power. When the Chinese were imported as cheap laborers during the nineteenth century, the California Supreme Court declared that they were not "white." Mexicans, however, many of whom owned large tracts of land in California, were considered to be "white." Today, Mexicans are no longer considered "white," while Asians increasingly are viewed as "white" (Kivel, 2002).

The concept of race is further complicated by **intersectionality**. Intersectionality refers to the multifaceted nature of our personal and social identities. Individuals differ not only along racial lines, but in age, gender, social class, sexual orientation, religion, and ability status, among other characteristics. There are diverse experiences of "race" related to these other important dimensions of our personal identities and social location. The importance given to these dimensions and how they intersect at different points in the life span can create disadvantages or advantages for an individual (Marsiglia & Kulis, 2009). Consideration of the multiple aspects of individuals' identities is necessary to adequately understand their experiences (Celious & Oyserman, 2001). For example, the racial experience of an African American who is upper middle-class, middle-aged, and lesbian varies in important ways from that of an African American who is adolescent, impoverished, male, and heterosexual. Understanding often-overlooked sources of within-group variation also is necessary for identifying and addressing social problems. For example, in discussions of issues relevant to African Americans, critical issues especially relevant to women may be neglected, such as single-parenting, domestic violence, and unequal status and pay in the workplace.

Furthermore, the concept of race should be distinguished from that of culture. Culture refers to the shared values, beliefs, behaviors, technology, and other resources such as language, literacy, and mathematics of a human group. Culture is transmitted and developed from one generation to the next. It is learned and can vary widely across and within racial and ethnic groups.

The concept of race should also be distinguished from **ethnicity**. Ethnicity refers to an individual's membership in a group that shares a common ancestral heritage, based on nationality and culture. It may have a biological component evident in the phenotype of group members. It may also include psychological attachment to the group, that is, ethnic identity. Ethnicity is largely voluntary, self-defined, and cultural (Conley, 2008). Until recently, groups who were not "white" were referred to as "ethnic." Yet whites also have ethnic-group memberships, and ethnicity does not necessarily capture the most salient, common experiences of groups who are not considered to be white. For this reason, the term "people of color" has become more accepted for referring to groups typically considered to be ethnic minorities: Native Americans, African Americans, Latinos, Native Hawaiian or Pacific Islanders, and Asian Americans. The histories of these groups are very different, but they share common experiences of exploitation and subordination by the European-American majority (Parke & Buriel, 2006).

To understand the impact of race and ethnicity on different groups, it is helpful to distinguish the concepts of **acculturation** and **assimilation** in U.S. society. Acculturation is a process of learning the language, values, and social competencies beneficial for functioning in the majority society. Assimilation is an outcome of acculturation, in which the ancestral culture is largely replaced with that of the host culture. European immigrants were able to acculturate and replace their cultures with that of the mainstream, U.S. culture, which has its roots in Anglo-Saxon Protestantism. They were accepted by the larger society and assimilated, typically by the second generation. This assimilation reflected their desire to become part of the dominant society, and to avoid discrimination directed against immigrants. The assimilation of European immigrants was facilitated by the physical appearance they shared with members of the majority group, who themselves were descendants of earlier European immigrants. Although ethnicity persists to some degree among some European Americans, it is optional and imposes little cost in everyday life (Parke & Buriel, 2006). For example, individuals may choose to acknowledge their English or German heritages without stigmatization, to keep them entirely private, or to ignore them altogether.

In contrast, people of color, who have been in contact with European Americans for centuries, have acculturated to varying degrees. But many have not assimilated, despite their desire to be part of the mainstream society, undeniable contributions to that society, and active attempts to eliminate racism. Their physical appearance and other group markers related to religion and social class, for example, communicate their race/ethnicity to others. For example, unlike most Americans of Irish descent, most Americans of African descent cannot choose to keep their ethnicity private. Others may see and associate their ethnicity with negative stereotypes (see Parke & Buriel, 2006).

In order to function within the larger society, including school and work, people of color may become bicultural. They may become fluent in majority (middle-class, European-American) culture. Yet they may rely on their cultures of origin within their families and communities, and to interpret racism in the larger society (Alvarez & Helms, 2001; Dinh, Castro, Tein, & Kim, 2009; Tugade & Frederickson, 2004). Bicultural fluency can be reflected in **code switching**, which occurs when individuals alter features of their language, including phonology, grammar, and pragmatics, in relation to social and cultural context. Code switching is used to navigate both mainstream, white-dominated America and ethnic America (DeBose, 1992). For example, African Americans may switch from an African-American to a European-American dialect when they interact in home and professional settings, respectively.

RACISM, WHITE PRIVILEGE, AND INSTITUTIONAL RACISM

Racism can be defined as a hierarchical system of advantages based on race (Tatum, 1992), which is reflected in our social institutions and individual attitudes and behaviors. The underlying perspective is that members of separate races possess different and unequal human traits (Conley, 2008). Racism in the United States persists despite significant progress. Progress is reflected in laws that prohibit race-based discrimination in institutional spheres, such as housing, education, and employment, a legacy of the civil rights movement of the 1950s and 1960s. Furthermore, in 2008, an African American, Barack Obama, was elected to what arguably is the most powerful position in the world, the U.S. presidency. There are many other examples of significant social progress toward a more just society.

Yet racism continues to take its toll. Our ongoing struggles with issues of race are reflected in many areas, including social service systems that disproportionately serve people of color. For example, African Americans are disproportionately represented across social service sectors, such as child welfare and juvenile and adult criminal justice systems (Halemba, Siegal, Lord, & Zawacki, 2004; Herz & Ryan, 2008; Puzzanchera, 2009; U.S. Department of Health and Human Services, 2010). African Americans make up 12 percent of the U.S. population, yet they make up 45 percent of prisoners and 49 percent of those living below the poverty line (Diller, 2007; U.S. Census Bureau, 2009b). Furthermore, the average life expectancy for African Americans is less than that of European Americans, with greater mortality rates at every age. Disease rates, such as strokes, hypertension, heart disease, asthma, and cancer, also are greater for African Americans (Centers for Disease Control and Prevention, 2004; Diller, 2007; National Heart, Lung, and Blood Institute, 2009).

To understand the impact of racism on individuals and society as well as its seeming intractability, it is important to distinguish it from **prejudice**. Prejudice is a preconceived judgment or opinion based on limited information and exposure to cultural stereotypes. Prejudicial attitudes, even positive ones such as "Asian Americans are good at math," are problematic because they deny a person's individuality. Prejudice by individuals of color in the United States, however, must be distinguished from that of whites because it is typically the attitudes of whites that carry social power inherent in the cultural reinforcement and institutionalization of racial prejudices. As Tatum argues (1992), distinguishing the prejudices of people of color from the racism of white individuals is not to say that either is acceptable; both are clearly problematic. This distinction is important because it identifies the power differential between members of dominant and subordinate groups.

One of the most pernicious means through which racism affects people of color is through **internalized racism**, that is, the individual inculcation of racist stereotypes, values, images, and ideologies perpetrated by the dominant society among members of racially subordinated groups. Internalized racism can lead to feelings of self-doubt, disgust, and disrespect for one's race or oneself (Pyke, 2010). Racist ideologies internalized and socialized by people of color have been described by a variety of authors as a particularly insidious form of oppression. As W. E. B. Du Bois wrote in his classic work *The Souls of Black Folks* (2008, p. 3), "It is a peculiar sensation, this double-consciousness, this sense of always looking at one's self through the eyes of others, or measuring one's soul by the tape of the world that looks on in contempt and pity." One example of internalized racism is skin-tone bias in communities of color. Virginia Harris (1994, p. 9) defines colorism as "prejudicial or preferential treatment of same-race people based solely on their color . . . [to] ascribe value and privilege to a same-race person based on lightness of skin." For example, while Edith Hudley was attending a segregated high school—an outwardly safe place for children of color—one of her African-American teachers explicitly favored light-skinned children and degraded Edith and other children because of their dark skin (Hudley, Haight, & Miller, 2003/2009). Virginia Harris (1994) describes the challenges to a child's self-esteem when racist ideologies are internalized and acted upon by family members and others closest to the child. Toni Morrison's classic novel *The Bluest Eye* (1972) portrays the devastating effects of pervasive European ideals of beauty on the psyche of a young black girl. France Davis (1997) describes how divisive colorism has been within African-American communities, including churches where dark- and light-skinned African Americans were once assigned to sit in separate sections.

Another example of internalized racism is defensive othering, in which individuals attempt to be like the dominant group or to distance themselves from stereotypes associated with their subordinated group. For example, some Mexican Americans denigrate newly immigrated Mexicans as "wetbacks," and some young adults from immigrant Korean and Vietnamese families use the term "FOB," an acronym for "fresh off the boat," to denigrate newly immigrated Asians (Pyke, 2010).

Pyke (2010) underscores that internalized racism is not the result of some weakness, gullibility, or other shortcoming of the oppressed. It is the result of complex, interlocking social processes. "All systems of oppression not thoroughly coerced through brute force and overt repression involved the dominant group's ability to win the consent of the oppressed . . . One need not experience discrete, identifiable instances of overt discrimination to internalize racial oppression. White racism can infiltrate the world view of the racially oppressed without their conscious consent . . . in a subtle process some refer to as 'indoctrination' and 'mental colonialization'" (p. 556).

Racism occurs not just at the level of individual beliefs and behaviors; it is part of our social and economic institutions. **Institutional racism** refers to social policies and institutional practices that place nonwhite racial and ethnic groups at a disadvantage. The evidence of institutional racism is unequivocal, and examples abound throughout history. Clear examples of institutional racism include the forceful removal of Native Americans from their ancestral homelands and relocation on reservations, and the military conquest of Latinos in the Southwest. The history of African Americans offers particularly vivid illustrations of institutional racism. Enslaved Africans were brought to the Americas from the sixteenth through the nineteenth century. During that time, efforts were made to strip enslaved Africans of their tribal or national traditions. Slavery remained a legal institution in the United States until the passage of the Thirteenth Amendment to the U.S. Constitution in 1865. Many Christian European Americans justified the slave trade and institution of slavery by claiming moral superiority over Africans (Franklin, 1980). During the Reconstruction period, Jim Crow laws instituted "separate but equal" practices. These laws further subjugated African Americans, as segregation resulted in inferior treatment and accommodations in economic, educational, and social arenas.

In the twenty-first century, African Americans have more economic, educational, and social access, opportunities, and power. Nevertheless, contemporary examples of institutional racism are profuse (Cunningham & Francois, 2009). The Personal Responsibility and Work Opportunity Reconciliation Act of 1996, for instance, resulted in states with higher percentages of African Americans and Hispanics adopting more stringent sanctions and caps related to Temporary Assistance for Needy Families (TANF), in particular, strict time limits and family caps (i.e., excluding from assistance children born to families already receiving public assistance; McLoyd, Hill, & Dodge, 2005; Soss, Schram, Vartanian, & O'Brien, 2004). Additionally, "restrictive TANF eligibility and policies are significantly more likely in states where electoral turnout is more biased toward high-income, as opposed to low-income residents" (Soss et al., 2004, p. 14).

Other twenty-first-century examples of institutional racism include restrictive housing contracts and bank lending policies, racial profiling by the police, use of stereotyped racial caricatures such as "Indian" sport mascots, the under- and misrepresentation of certain racial groups in the mass media, and race-based barriers to gainful employment and professional advancement. Cultural bias on standardized educational tests is another reflection of racism that occurs within educational institutions. On various standardized achievement and intelligence tests, African-American children tend to score lower than European-American and Asian-American children. Among the contributing factors is a significant amount of content on standardized tests that reflects European-American, middle-class experiences unfamiliar to some African-American children (Parke & Buriel, 2006).

A less obvious example of modern-day institutional racism may be found in the child welfare and juvenile justice systems. Available data reveal racial disparities at many different points of contact within these systems. In 2008, 78 percent of youth aged ten to seventeen years were white and 16 percent were black (Puzzanchera, 2009). Thus one would predict that approximately three-quarters of youth involved in the child welfare and criminal justice systems would be white, and less than one-fifth would be black. Yet black youth made up 22 percent of substantiated maltreatment reports (45 percent were white; U.S. Department of Health and Human Services, 2010), 32 percent of the foster-care population (40 percent were white; U.S. Department of Health and Human Services, 2009), 33 percent of juvenile property crimes (65 percent were white), and 52 percent of youth arrested for a violent crime (47 percent were white; Puzzanchera, 2009). Furthermore, once African-American youth become involved with child welfare or criminal justice systems, they have a higher risk of becoming entrenched in social service systems that can be punitive and unhelpful. Even when controlling for factors such as age, gender, neighborhood poverty, types of maltreatment, and types of criminal offense, African Americans experience deeper entrenchment in both the child welfare and juvenile justice systems (Needell, Brookhart, & Lee, 2003; Ryan, Herz, Hernandez, & Marshall, 2007). Compared to European Americans, African-American youth are less likely to be reunified with parents, more likely to be placed in congregate-care out-of-home placements, more likely to be adjudicated, and less likely to receive needed mental health services (Garland, Landsverk, & Lau, 2003; Needell et al., 2003; Ryan et al., 2007). This research points toward institutional racism not only in the child welfare and juvenile justice systems, but also in the political arena that guides the social service systems and the practice arena that treats families.

Clear examples of twenty-first-century institutional racism can also be found in contemporary educational systems. For example, in an apparent attempt to reduce ethnic conflict, Arizona's state legislature "banned the [Tucson] school district [which is 56 percent Latino] from offering any courses that are designed for students primarily of a certain race, as well as courses that 'advocate ethnic solidarity instead of the treatment of pupils as individuals'—at the risk of losing up to 10 percent of their funding. The state has also told schools statewide that teachers with 'heavy' or 'ungrammatical' accents are no longer allowed to teach English classes" (Kunichoff, 2010). In Texas, the State Board of Education has followed Arizona's lead. The board sought to move away from teachings pertaining to slavery and the civil rights movement. According to the board's directive, the "slave trade" would be renamed the "Atlantic triangular trade." This directive did not pass, but American "imperialism" was changed to "expansionism," and "capitalism" was changed to "free enterprise" (Paulson, 2010). Texas's color-blind and class-blind ideologies force classrooms to ignore a significant part of American history. By practicing the "we are all the same" approach, group differences and identities are denied, and the dominant, white, middle-class perspective is not only perpetuated, but legalized.

A corollary to racism is **white privilege**: the unearned advantages, entitlements, immunities, and dominance of individuals considered to be "white" at the expense of those who are not white (Du Bois, 1935; McIntosh, 1998; Wise, 2005). White college students have powerfully spoken to racial inequalities and their own unearned privileges: "[While growing up] I had a clear sense that they [Latinos] weren't supposed to be there" (Chesler, Peet, & Sevig, 2003, p. 222). Such feelings of entitlement may emerge through repeated exposure to multiple contexts of socialization, including primary and secondary school where classroom instruction on the United States' long history of oppression may be inadequate. In *Lies My Teacher Told Me* (2007), James Loewen documents and analyzes the invisibility both of content on racism and antiracism in U.S. high school history textbooks.

An important aspect of white privilege is that the behavior and values of the dominant group is seen as the norm. Beverly Tatum (2003) observed in her classes that students of color often described themselves by mentioning their race or ethnicity, while white students did not (Tatum, 2003). White privilege, then, includes a "luxury of obliviousness . . . Awareness requires effort and commitment. Being able to command the attention of lower-status individuals without having to give it in return is a key aspect of privilege. African Americans, for example, have to pay close attention to whites and white culture and get to know them well enough to avoid displeasing them, since whites control jobs, schools, government [the judicial system], the police, and most other resources and sources of power . . . To be white in America means not having to think about it" (A. G. Johnson, 2006, p. 22).

A second reason that racism and prejudice are difficult issues is that they conflict with closely held, European-American dominant cultural beliefs that with hard work and ability, anyone can pull him- or herself up by the bootstraps to succeed. Unfortunately, this prescription for success does not work equally well for everyone. **Meritocracy** is the myth that rewards are given based on hard work, achievement, and motivation, when in reality many rewards are also based on unearned privileges (Marsiglia & Kulis, 2009). Attending college in the United States, for example, is more determined by family socioeconomic status than by individual educational ability (Marsiglia & Kulis, 2009), and income is linked to race, with 25 percent of

African Americans versus 9 percent of European Americans living in poverty (U.S. Census Bureau, 2009a). Though disparities in educational achievement between European Americans and African Americans have narrowed somewhat since the 1960s, they still persist. In 1970, 31 percent of African Americans and 54 percent of European Americans graduated from high school, and 4 percent of African Americans and 11 percent of European Americans graduated from college. In 2008, 83 percent of blacks and 87 percent of whites graduated from high school, and 20 percent of blacks and 30 percent of whites graduated from college (U.S. Census Bureau, 2010).

To have public discourse about race within educational settings and elsewhere, people need to develop the important skills of critical consciousness and reflexive self-awareness. Critical consciousness is the perception of social, political, and economic contradictions and oppression. It also involves taking action against those injustices (Freire, 2005). Reflexive self-awareness is an ongoing process of becoming aware of personal biases and how we construct our own identity (Sisneros, Stakeman, Joyner, & Schmitz, 2008). To practice reflexive self-awareness, it is necessary to move beyond guilt, shame, or anger, and to understand how oppression manifests itself. "It's easy to have opinions, but it takes work to know what you're talking about . . . Unless you have the luxury of a personal teacher, you can't understand this issue without reading about it, because the discourse is lacking . . . in America. Many people assume they already know what they need to know because it's part of everyday life" (A. G. Johnson, 2006, p. 139).

The notions of meritocracy and white privilege undergird the foundation of color blindness, which some argue is the primary form of racism today. According to Neville (2009, pp. 117–133), color blindness legitimizes the dominant racial ideology (the core beliefs one holds about race and racism) and is used to

> camouflage racial inequalities in the United States and to justify [consciously or unconsciously] continued discriminatory practices . . . Cognitively, ideology serves as a filter of what one "sees" and responds to in the social world . . . One of the critical features of this definition [of color blindness] is the explicit connection between individual beliefs and dominant societal racial beliefs or ideas that are commonly understood and transmitted through a variety of civil society and structural mechanisms. The definition also underscores the function of racial ideology as a method in which individuals encode and interpret racial information and the values they attach to race(ism) . . . [T]he denial, distortion, or minimization of structural racism is the crux of color-blind racial ideology.

RACIAL IDENTITY DEVELOPMENT

Individuals' emerging understanding of their race in relation to the larger society is a complex and evolving lifelong process. As discussed in chapter 1, development consists of the processes of socialization (the display of patterned meanings for the novice) and acquisition (the novice's various responses to those messages). The complex social and physical ecologies within which these processes occur profoundly impact the rate and outcome of development. Adaptive socialization goals and practices vary to meet the demands of diverse ecological settings (Bronfenbrenner, 1989). For example, African-American parents need to socialize their children about the realities of life in racialized U.S. society. These racial socialization practices are based, in part, on parents' perceptions of how African-American children can be safe and successful within particular social and physical ecologies, as well as the individual responses of children to racist incidents and to socialization messages. Many children learn from caregivers and significant others how to cope with hostile racial environments while continuing to develop fully and to experience normal, rich lives. The racial socialization practices experienced by Edith Hudley as an African-American child growing up in the segregated South of the 1920s and 1930s evolved and were reshaped to fit the needs of her own adolescent sons growing up in Oakland, California, during the civil rights movement of the 1960s. Furthermore, Mrs. Hudley's socialization practices with her older, more compliant son also varied from those with her younger, "hard headed," risk-taking son (Hudley et al., 2003/2009).

In racialized societies such as the United States, racial-identity development begins early in life and may follow somewhat different trajectories for members of dominant and subordinate groups. In the United States, children generally are aware of race and hold racial attitudes from early childhood. By preschool age, most children distinguish skin colors, and then project certain attitudes toward race-related phenotypes such as skin color and hair texture. Between the ages of four and seven, children gradually learn that being a particular race has a social reality that adults and peers routinely acknowledge. By the age of approximately eight years, European-American children begin to verbalize their racial prejudices. By the age of approximately twelve, most have learned to quit doing so, while simultaneously becoming increasingly less democratic toward those who are perceptibly different (Allport, 1954; Swanson, Cunningham, Youngblood, & Spencer, 2009). Not surprisingly, more African-American and Latino children show early awareness of racism than do European-American children (Slaughter-Defoe et al., 2009).

Deeper and more sophisticated understandings of race and racism may develop for majority- and minority-group members during the later years of childhood and continue developing throughout adulthood (see Cokley & Chapman, 2009; Quintana, 2007; Scottham, Sellers, & Nguyên, 2005, 2008; Sellers, Smith, Shelton, Rowley, & Chavous, 1998; Slaughter-Defoe et al., 2009; Swanson et al., 2009). For example, people of color tend to explore their racial/ethnic identities and seek attachments to their in-group during adolescence (Quintana, 2007). This normative process is associated with the development of racial and ethnic group consciousness, and identity in general (Quintana, 2007).

Racial Identity Development in African Americans

A number of models of racial identity development focus primarily on young adulthood. One important contribution of racial identity development theories is to sensitize us to the various and changing reactions that individuals may have to issues of race. For example, Beverly Tatum (1992) used theories of racial identity development to describe various responses typical of her young adult college students to a course on the psychology of racism.

The Nigrescence Model. The Negro-to-black conversion experience, or the nigrescence model, is an early formulation of racial identity development for African Americans. This model, which has been revised since its inception in 1971, has four stages (Cross, 1971; Cross, 1991; Vandiver, Cross, Worrell, & Fhagen-Smith, 2002; see also Richardson, Bethea, Hayling, & Williamson-Taylor, 2010). In the pre-encounter stage, individuals have absorbed many of the beliefs and values of the dominant white culture, including racist beliefs that devalue African Americans relative to European Americans. Individuals may seek to assimilate and be accepted by European Americans, and distance themselves from other African Americans. There is a deemphasis on racial-group membership and emphasis on a belief in meritocracy. For example, one young woman in Beverly Tatum's class described a period in her life where she wanted to "be like and live like, and be accepted by" European Americans, even to the point of "hating" her own ethnic group (Tatum, 1992, p. 10).

Events such as rejection by European Americans force individuals to acknowledge the impact of racism on their own lives and precipitate movement into the encounter stage. Faced with the reality that they do not experience the same privileges as European Americans, African Americans are forced to acknowledge their identity as a member of a group targeted by racism. For example, one young woman in Tatum's class described her increasing awareness of racism through course readings and discussions, and realization that the racial comments she had previously ignored as a defense mechanism were, in fact, directed at her. She described her increasing irritation at racist comments, and willingness to confront others about such talk.

The immersion/emersion stage is characterized by involvement with blacks, and antiwhite sentiments. During this stage, there is an intense desire to surround oneself with visible symbols of one's racial identity, and actively avoid any symbols of whiteness. Individuals actively explore aspects of their own history and culture with peers from their own racial background. For example, some students in Tatum's class chose to work together to focus their final projects on African Americans. These projects reflected a deep concern with the well-being of African Americans and a desire to explore internalized racism. Toward the end of this phase, anger at whites dissipates, and security in a newly defined and affirmed sense of self emerges.

The internalization stage is characterized by black nationalism (e.g., a focus on black empowerment), biculturalism (e.g., seeing oneself as black and gay), and multiculturalism (e.g., a focus on three or more identities). Individuals maintain connections to African-American peers, but also begin to establish meaningful relationships with whites, and build coalitions with members of other oppressed groups.

Cross's model has also been applied to other people of color. In the following journal excerpt, for instance, a young, Korean-American woman in Tatum's class describes her racial identity development through the internalization stage:

> I have been aware for a long time that I am Korean. But through this class I am beginning to really become aware of my race. I am beginning to find out that White people can be accepting of me and at the same time accept me as a Korean. I grew up wanting to be accepted and ended up almost denying my race and culture. I don't think I did this consciously, but the denial did occur. As I grew older, I realized that I was different. I became for the first time, friends with other Koreans. I realized I had much in common with them. This was when I went through my "Korean friend" stage. I began to enjoy being friends with Koreans more than I did with Caucasians. Well, ultimately, through many years of growing up, I am pretty much in focus about who I am and who my friends are. I knew before I took this class that there were people not of color that were understanding of my differences. In our class, I feel that everyone is trying to sincerely find the answer of abolishing racism. I knew people like this existed, but it's nice to meet with them weekly. (Tatum, 1992, p. 12)

The nigrescence model has received significant scholarly attention and critique. Although it is seen as a model of developmental stages, they are not "stages" in the traditional sense of universal, invariant sequences. There is no one universal trajectory or sequence of racial identity development that all individuals follow (Cokley & Chapman, 2009). Racial identity development consists of numerous facets and possible trajectories (Cross & Cross, 2008). Furthermore, racial identity development is dynamic and may be nonlinear. For example, racial identity issues that one encounters early in life may be revisited as new issues and ecologies are encountered (Cokley & Chapman, 2009). Moreover, many African Americans raised in predominately black communities, including churches and schools, are socialized with positive messages about being black. Therefore, "it is possible for African Americans to never experience pre-encounter attitudes because negative messages about blacks were not a part of their reality" (Cokley & Chapman, 2009, p. 287). Note that Cross has revised his early model to respond to criticisms (Cross, 1991; Cross & Vandiver, 2001).

The Multidimensional Model of Racial Identity. Sellers's multidimensional model of racial identity (MMRI; Scottham et al., 2005, 2008; Sellers et al., 1998) is a theory of African-American racial identity development. This model is influenced by sociological theories on identity, which suggest one's identity is composed of many facets (Cokley & Chapman, 2009). It focuses on the diverse meanings of racial identity for African Americans, including how they feel about their racial group and self-concept at particular points in time and in particular contexts: How important is race to one's self-perception? What does it mean to be African American (Sellers et al., 1998)? The MMRI rests on the premise that there is no singular African-American racial identity, and individuals should be able to define what being African-American means for themselves without any value judgment placed on their perspectives (Scottham et al., 2008).

Sellers proposed four dimensions of black racial identity: salience, centrality, regard, and racial ideology. Salience refers to the extent to which race is relevant to the self-concept at a particular point in time and/or within a particular situation (Scottham et al., 2008, p. 297). Centrality refers to the extent to which race is a part of one's core identity. There are two aspects of regard: public regard refers to how one feels about others' perceptions toward one's racial group, and private regard refers to how positively or negatively one feels about one's racial group. There are four possible aspects of racial ideology. The nationalist ideology is characterized by the support of African-American organizations and preference for African-American social environments. The oppressed-minority ideology views African Americans in relation to other oppressed minority groups. The assimilationist ideology focuses on the similarities between African-American and mainstream American society. The humanist ideology views all humans as similar, regardless of race (Scottham et al., 2008).

Unlike the nigrescence model, which assumes that race is central to one's identity, the MMRI acknowledges that for some individuals at particular points in development, race may not be a central aspect of identity (Cokley & Chapman, 2009). Additionally, the MMRI stipulates that a person can be mentally healthy, but still have negative feelings about being African American or have low racial centrality. The nigrescence model, on the other hand, is seen as a continuum and suggests that mental health is positively associated with reaching higher stages, such as the internalization stage (Cokley & Chapman, 2009, p. 288).

Racial Identity Development in European Americans

Although recognition of racial identification may be central to the functioning of many individuals from minority groups, it is largely voluntary for members of the majority group. McKinney (2005) interviewed European-American college students and found that some felt envious of people of color because they perceived them to have a stronger bond with their cultural heritage. For example, some individuals of Irish descent said that they celebrate St. Patrick's Day only because of the media hype and its heavy advertisement by beer companies. Many felt that, in fact, they did not have a culture. Of course, European Americans have a complex and diverse cultural heritage. This heritage includes values and beliefs emerging from the European enlightenment, Anglican Protestantism, and Western colonialism, such as rationalism, individualism, personal responsibility, a strong work ethic, self-effacement, and mastery over nature (Perry, 2001).

In describing the responses of European-American college students to her class in psychology of racism, Beverly Tatum draws upon Helms's model of white racial identity development (Helms, 1990). This model focuses on the rejection of racism and the development of a nonracist white identity. It is subject to many of the same criticisms as the early nigrescence model: for example, the "stages" are not universal, invariant, or linear. Nonetheless, this model can sensitize us to possible responses that European-American students may have to issues of race as presented in college classrooms.

During the contact stage, students may show a naïve curiosity about or fear of people of color, based on stereotypes. Many students evincing these attitudes have lives structured so as to limit contact with people of color. Some may resist new race-related information that they find dissonant with their existing beliefs, for example, that negative cultural messages can impact the developing self-esteem of some African-American children, or they may attempt to withdraw from contact with people of color and the topic of racism.

The disintegration stage emerges if students have new experiences, for example, exposure to people of color or information on racism, which leads them to a new understanding of racism. At this phase, students may feel guilt, shame, and sometimes anger at the recognition of their own advantage and the role of whites in maintaining racism. Some students react to these feelings by entering a phase of reintegration in which the desire to be accepted by their racial group leads to the reshaping of their own belief systems to be more congruent with an acceptance of racism and belief in white superiority. For example, some students in Tatum's class expressed anger and resentment at people of color because, as one young woman articulated, "I didn't mean to be White . . . it's not our fault that society has deemed us 'superior' " (Tatum, 1992, p. 15).

Other students react to the discomfort of the disintegration stage with information seeking. During this pseudo-independent phase, students begin to abandon beliefs of white superiority, but may still behave in ways that unintentionally perpetuate the system. For example, education students learning about racism may continue to display lowered expectations for their African-American students. Looking to those targeted by racism, students in this phase may disavow their own whiteness through active affiliation with people of color. They experience alienation from whites who have not yet begun to examine their own racism, but may experience rejection from people of color who are suspicious of their motives.

As students enter the immersion/emersion phase, they seek to positively redefine what it means to be white through replacing racially related stereotypes with accurate information about what it means to be white in U.S. society. Learning about whites who have been antiracist allies to people of color and activists can be central to this process. White students in Tatum's class described feeling empowered by knowledge of how other whites have joined with people of color to resist racism.

The autonomy phase results as students internalize a newly defined sense of self as white, and let go of their racial privilege (Spanierman & Soble, 2009). The positive feelings that result from this development can energize students' efforts to confront racism and oppression in their daily lives, including forging alliances with people of color. We are all part of the system of privilege and oppression, and all play a role. White allies can act as positive agents of change to help identify and take actions that interrupt the cycle of oppression (A. G. Johnson, 2006; Tatum, 1992).

Biracial and Multiracial Identity Development

Bi- and multiracial individuals may experience different issues from those who are monoracial (Slaughter-Defoe et al., 2009). They may experience prejudice and discrimination based on **antimiscegenation** attitudes, that is, attitudes against the "mixing" of races. As children, they may be forced to entertain questions from peers who inquire, "What are you?" (Diller, 2007). As adolescents, they may straddle two or more social worlds without experiencing full acceptance in either. For example, their African-American peers may react negatively if they do not appear "black" enough, and their European-American peers if they do not appear "white" enough. Some children and adolescents may even be pressured to identify with one group over another, denying an important part of their sense of self and cultural heritage (Slaughter-Defoe et al., 2009). Despite the challenges they may face, as U.S. society becomes increasingly diverse, bi- and multiracial individuals who develop deep, multicultural understandings may emerge into adulthood with some distinct advantages over their monoracial peers.

Individuals of mixed racial heritage are among the fastest growing segments of the U.S. population. These twin girls are of African-American and Chinese heritage.

Of course, bi- and multiracial individuals may respond to these challenges in a variety of ways. Based on their empirical study of biracial individuals of African-American and European-American heritage, Rockquemore and Brunsma (2007) identified six stances toward racial identity. Individuals with a singular identity are of mixed racial heritage, but see themselves as either black or white. A border identity "lies between predefined social categories" (p. 43). Some individuals see themselves as biracial, yet others respond to them as either black or white. Other individuals are responded to as biracial, thus confirming their own self-understanding. Individuals assuming protean identity see themselves at times as black and at other times as white, and fluidly change their behavior depending on the particular ethnic group or situation they encounter. Individuals with a transcendent identity do not see themselves as racialized and "do not use race as a construct to understand the social world or their relative place in it" (Rockquemore & Brunsma, 2007, p. 71). Since individuals who take a transcendent stance do not identify with any racial group, they might be seen by racial identity theorists as living in denial, and therefore unhealthy. On the other hand, they may be refusing "to participate in the fallacy of race, whether in its mono-, multi- or biracial manifestations. From this perspective, the system of racial classification . . . and the hierarchical valuation of racial identities is damaging and fundamentally problematic" (Rockquemore & Brunsma, 2007, p. 116).

Racial Identity Development in Immigrants of Color

People of color in the United States include not just those who are native born, but those who were born and lived for various periods of time in other countries. These experiences clearly can shape how they come to think of themselves. For example, people of African heritage in the United States include not only those who are native born, but those from Africa, the Dominican Republic, Haiti, and Latin America, among other places. Although sharing some physical and cultural features, the cultures of origin of these individuals are diverse. Similarly, Latinos, now the largest "minority" group in the United States, consist of native-born individuals as well as immigrants from Mexico, Central and South America, Puerto Rico, and Cuba (Parke & Buriel, 2006).

Although diverse in their own right, first- and second-generation immigrants may be similarly affected by common social experiences in the United States. Rumbaut (1994) examined over 5,000 first- and second-generation adolescent immigrants from Asia, Latin America, and the Caribbean who resided in Miami or San Diego. He found that ethnic identity development for immigrants is related to common experiences they had in the United States. For example, those who had been discriminated against and attended public schools were more likely to identify with their native ethnicity. Moreover, as adolescents struggle to fit in with peer groups and mainstream white America, friction may emerge with their parents and other extended family members, who often prefer their children to maintain traditional ethnic and cultural ties. For example, an adolescent's exposure to U.S. society's emphasis on individual achievement, independence, and competition may conflict with the traditional Latino family values of respect for elders, loyalty, and contribution to the family, which they encounter at home (Tuan, 1998).

Our knowledge of racial identity development is evolving. More research is needed on this topic, however, especially for adults and for multicultural people. In addition, most research that examines racial identity development has been conducted on college students. This method of data collection has its flaws, because college students are often considered a privileged lot and are not necessarily representative of the general population.

RESPONSES TO OPPRESSION

Conley (2008) outlines several group responses to oppression. First, an oppressed group may withdraw. For example, the Jewish population largely left Poland after World War II, when 85 percent of the Jewish population had died and violence against Jews continued. During the Great Migration of the mid-twentieth century, large numbers of African Americans moved from the rural South in search of jobs, opportunities, and equality in the urban North and West. Second, an oppressed group may attempt to pass or blend in with the dominant group. For example, African Americans may attempt to look more like European Americans by chemically straightening their hair or chemically lightening their skin. Name change is a common way individuals have tried to pass. For example, large numbers of German Americans changed their last name during the world wars. Acceptance is a third response of oppressed groups. Oppressed individuals feign compliance and hide their true feelings of resentment. Examples of acceptance include African-American men who "played the fool" in the Jim Crow South. The fourth group response identified by Conley, and one on which we focus here, is resistance.

Just as racism has a long, entrenched history in U.S. society, so too does resistance to oppression at individual, group, and societal levels. From protective socialization practices within families and communities, to formal education and activism, progress is being made toward a more just society.

Protective Socialization Practices in Families and Communities

Some protective practices in families and communities are illustrated in African-American history and scholarship. Since their arrival on U.S. soil, individuals of African heritage have employed socialization strategies that allowed children not only to survive but to maintain their humanity, despite brutal treatment. The tradition of **fictive kin**, for example, emerged during slavery times and continues today. Fictive kin are individuals unrelated by birth or marriage with whom one has emotionally significant relationships and treats as family. Fictive kin included nonrelative adults within the slave community who reared children sold away from or otherwise separated from their parents (Guttman, 1976). Today, the tradition of fictive kin continues, through the practice of informal adoption and through mutual helping with the challenges of daily life (Stack, 1974).

In plantation areas, slaves organized underground churches and hidden religious meetings, which provided psychological refuge and coping skills, as well as practical help. As described in chapter 7, the African-American church has played a significant role throughout its history in providing concrete aid, as well as spiritual and social support, to individuals and families. In addition, this institution continues to underscore spiritually based beliefs that protect against racism, such as the equality of believers and the inherent worth of each individual as a child of God (see Haight, 2002).

Protective socialization practices continue today in families and communities. For example, Edith Hudley spoke eloquently of the importance of teaching African-American children not to internalize the racial hatred directed at them. Adults are responsible for clearly communicating and preparing children for these inevitable challenges of life within a racialized society. These skills include learning to recognize and evaluate race-based communications in the media, educational and work settings, and elsewhere (Hudley et al., 2003/2009).

The value of education and the importance of developing competencies also have deep roots within African-American communities, certainly dating back to times when blacks were prohibited from receiving an education, or received substandard educations in poorly funded, segregated schools. Direct education about their African heritage and the positive contributions of African Americans to the larger U.S. society also may serve as protective factors for children and youth. Indeed, children who are raised in households that encourage learning about racial history and values display a more positive self-concept than youth whose upbringing does not include such experiences (Carter-Black, 2005; Swanson et al., 2009).

Protective socialization practices can also be employed with children from the racial majority who face privilege. Such practices can occur through exposure to respectful attitudes toward diversity and appreciation of the contributions of men and women from various cultural communities (Dyson & Genishi, 1994; Ladson-Billings, 1992). It also can occur through formal education.

Formal Education

The formal education system can play a critical role in resistance to racism and privilege. Adequate understanding of the complexities of U.S. history and contemporary society for children and youth of all racial backgrounds requires attention to the contributions and struggles of diverse groups. Many schools integrate social diversity in their curricula, for example, by teaching about African-American leaders in the sciences or by talking about why many leaders in the sciences are European-American and male. African-American parents described teachers whom they felt were successful with their children as those who encouraged their children to "choose academic excellence . . . [and] maintain a positive identification with their own heritage and background" (Ladson-Billings, 1992, p. 382).

"Culturally relevant pedagogy," which "urges collective action grounded in cultural understandings, experiences, and ways of knowing the world," can be achieved in many ways, such as introducing students to children's literature whose main characters are people of color (Ladson-Billings, 1992, p. 383). It was not until 1920 that African Americans were featured in children's literature (V. J. Harris, 1986). *The Brownies Book* was a children's version of *The Crisis*, published by the National Association for the Advancement of Colored People (NAACP) and coedited by W. E. B. Du Bois. One of the objectives of this series was to make colored children realize that "being 'colored' is a normal, beautiful thing," and "to make them familiar with the history and achievements of the Negro race" (Du Bois & Dill, 1919, p. 285). Moreover, the series advocated that "to educate [children] in human hatred is more disastrous to them [who are] hated; to seek to raise them in ignorance of their racial identity and peculiar situation is inadvisable" (p. 285). It wasn't until 1963 that the first mainstream children's picture book featuring a black person, *The Snowy Day* by Ezra Jack Keats, was published. Exposing children to social and cultural diversity enables children of color to self-identify, while enabling European-American children to gain awareness and familiarity with people of color.

Progress also has been made within public schools for respecting and supporting the development and culture of children for whom English is not their native language. In one account of the importance of language, Rodriguez (1981) said that when he was five, his Spanish-speaking family began speaking English at home upon the recommendation of his Anglo-American teachers. Over time, his father became silent, regaining his spark only while speaking Spanish with others *outside of the home*, and his children's Spanish language skills were blunted. Intimacy in the home and playfulness were lost. Currently, there are many public school programs in which children's written and verbal development in their native languages as well as English is supported, and monolingual English speakers are introduced to a second language in elementary school. Although the first two-way immersion education programs in the United States were initiated almost forty years ago, with a French/English program in Massachusetts and a Spanish/English program in Florida, only recently have they gained more widespread popularity (Howard, Sugarman, & Christian, 2003). In the mid-1980s there were 30 documented two-way immersion programs (Lindholm, 1987), and by 2002 there were as many as 266 Spanish/English programs at the elementary level (Center for Applied Linguistics, 2002). Indeed, bilingualism increasingly is recognized as an important strength in our increasingly pluralistic U.S. society and global world.

Activism

Resistance to oppression also occurs at the level of political and legal systems. Gandhi, Martin Luther King Jr., Malcolm X, Robert Williams, Nelson Mandela, and many others have led resistance movements against racial oppression, using a variety of approaches. For example, King, inspired by Gandhi's teachings, advocated nonviolent resistance through peaceful sit-ins and protests, while Malcolm X advocated militant resistance. Williams, on the other hand, sought a dismantling of the American political and economic social systems (Twombly, 1971).

In the United States, organized resistance to racism has a very long, distinguished history, which has been richly detailed in numerous classic texts (e.g., Franklin, 1980; Twombly, 1971). Here we will give just a few highlights.

Early resistance to the dehumanizing effects of racism included the plantation churches of slavery times where, for example, spirituals contained hidden messages giving church members a secret way to communicate and, in some cases, to plan escape (e.g., Lincoln, 1974; Sobel, 1988). Post–Civil War resistance at the political level began in 1909 with the formation of the NAACP (Kirst-Ashman, 2010). The NAACP remains active today as one of the oldest and most influential civil rights organizations in the United States. Its mission is to ensure the political, educational, social, and economic equality of all people and to eliminate racial hatred and discrimination.

In 1947, President Harry Truman's Committee on Civil Rights "denounced racial discrimination, made many specific recommendations for legislation, and called for the elimination of segregation" (Twombly, 1971, p. 333). Shortly thereafter, Truman issued a public statement on civil rights, the first speech of its kind in presidential history. Moves were also made toward integration in the armed forces and requirements for fair employment in the federal government.

The civil rights movement gained momentum in the 1950s with help from the NAACP and its chief attorney, Thurgood Marshall. The NAACP was the litigation and legislation powerhouse against segregation, representing class-action suits and several key cases that went on to the Supreme Court. For example, Marshall defended Brown in *Brown v. Topeka Board of Education* in 1954. The Supreme Court ruled that state laws establishing separate public schools for black and white students denied black children equal educational opportunities and were unconstitutional. The bus boycott in Montgomery, Alabama, in 1955–1956 (two-thirds of the passengers were black) successfully challenged the city's policy of racial segregation on its public transportation system and gave momentum to peaceful protests. In 1957, Martin Luther King Jr. and sixty African-American ministers met at

Ebenezer Baptist Church, where they formed the Southern Christian Leadership Conference. This civil rights organization supported and organized nonviolent protests, and was central to the dismantling of segregation.

The Civil Rights Act of 1964, signed by President Lyndon B. Johnson, was a landmark piece of legislation that outlawed unequal application of voter registration requirements and racial segregation in the workplace, public facilities, and schools, which was still happening despite the 1954 ruling of *Brown v. Topeka Board of Education.*

The National Voting Rights Act of 1965, also signed by President Johnson, outlawed discriminatory voting practices, such as intimidation, violence, literacy testing, and poll taxes, responsible for the widespread disenfranchisement of African Americans.

In Mississippi, for example, at the end of the 1950s, 45 percent of the state's population was African American, but only 5 percent of that population was registered to vote (Civilrights.org, n.d.). Creative efforts, such as poll taxes and literacy testing, were made by some southern states to keep African Americans from voting. Only those whose father or grandfather had voted in a specific year prior to the abolition of slavery could vote without paying a poll tax. Literacy testing required otherwise qualified individuals to pass a literacy test before they could vote. Terrorism also was used to intimidate potential African-American voters through whippings, torture, and murder by the Ku Klux Klan, an organization with roots going back to Civil War times. This terrorist group has worked, unsuccessfully, to reassert the dominance of white Protestants (P. Johnson, 1997; Trelease, 1992).

In 1972, **affirmative action** first became an inflammatory public issue. Affirmative action refers to positive steps taken to increase representation of women and people of color in the areas of employment, education, and business. It is intended to give people who have been historically excluded a fair chance to engage in public institutions. When those steps involved preferential selection on the basis of race, ethnicity, or gender, they generated intense controversy. Recently, California joined the ranks of other states that have banned race-based affirmative action, arguing that affirmative action is unconstitutional and is actually reverse discrimination against white people (Elias, 2010). Yet as the ongoing debates continue, affirmative action is seen by many as responsible for the growth of the black middle class over the last forty years (Fletcher, 1998).

Thanks to the civil rights movement, African Americans have made gains in desegregation, voting rights, and the repeal of Jim Crow laws. Throughout the nation, contemporary progress in the form of resistance efforts, especially at the grassroots level, has taken hold post-civil rights. Despite much progress through the political system, eliminating racial injustice has been a long and difficult road, and the journey is not yet completed. In 2005, when Hurricane Katrina hit the Lower Ninth Ward of New Orleans, a neighborhood whose population was 98 percent African-American, the delivery of critical aid was delayed, compounding the loss of life (Greater

New Orleans Community Data Center, 2007). On Friday, August 26, 2005, the governor of Louisiana declared a state of emergency, and on Sunday the governor asked President Bush to respond with supplementary federal aid to "save lives, protect property, public health, and safety" (Office of the Governor of Louisiana cited in Thinkprogress.org). Food and water supplies dwindled, mass looting erupted, and people died. Despite the mandatory evacuation, many Lower Ninth Ward residents had no means of transportation and were stuck in their homes. Four and five days after the hurricane, people were still stuck in their attics, seeking refuge from five to ten feet of water below, with no rescue staff available. Neighbors mustered their own relief efforts, rescuing the disabled, elderly, and babies from their homes, and swimming them to taller buildings. Prison inmates were left to their own devices—locked in cells with no food, water, or medication, after prison guards left the premises for their own safety. Hospital patients died without electricity and staff. An estimated 25,000 people sought refuge in the Superdome (Treaster & Sontag, 2005). The conditions there were so dangerous and filthy, however, that many left to sleep on the highway. On Thursday, a desperate SOS was issued to the federal government. Finally on Friday, September 2, one week after the hurricane hit, the first federal funds were dedicated to relief aid.

SUMMARY

Cultural sensitivity is a professional goal toward which successful, contemporary social workers strive. Within the United States and many other societies around the world, the socially constructed concept of race remains a complex, problematic, and important part of personal identity development for many people. Native Americans, African Americans, Asian Americans, Latinos, and others have endured a long history of oppression in the United States. They have also developed important strategies for resistance, from protective factors within families and communities, to formal education, to political activism. Social workers need to be aware of the social and psychological ramifications of racism, resistance, white privilege, and institutional racism for their clients. They may also choose to be involved in organized social and political movements to bring about a more just society.

Study and Discussion Questions

1. Define and distinguish the concepts of race, culture, and ethnicity.
2. What is meant by *intersectionality*, and how is it relevant to understanding issues of race in contemporary U.S. society?
3. Distinguish between the concepts of acculturation and assimilation, and describe their relevance to understanding the experiences of immigrants of color.

4. Define *racism* and *white privilege*, and describe how these phenomena could impact you as a social worker.

5. What are the various ways in which prejudicial attitudes are problematic?

6. Describe internalized racism, and provide a hypothetical example of how this phenomenon might impact your social work clients.

7. Define *institutional racism*. Provide a contemporary example and steps you might take as a social worker to address this issue.

8. How might you, as an individual and a professional social worker, respond to oppression?

Resources

Interested students can supplement this chapter through a number of excellent web-based resources.

Expectations of cultural competence that guide social work practice are described at NASW's website: http://www.naswdc.org/practice/standards/NASWculturalstandards.pdf.

The NAACP is the nation's oldest and largest civil rights organization. The NAACP consists of lawyers, social workers, organizers, leaders, and many other professionals, who continue to fight for social justice for all Americans. Current social and economic justice efforts, as well as ways to get involved locally and federally, are described at http://www.naacp.org/content/main/.

The Child Welfare League of America is dedicated to informing research, practice, and policies on cultural diversity, competence, and sensitivity in work with children and families. Their website provides current evidence and efforts around such issues. Available at http://www.cwla.org/programs/culture/default.htm.

In 1968 the National Association of Black Social Workers (NABSW) was founded by African-American social workers who were disenchanted by the dominant Eurocentric practices of white American social workers of NASW. Today, NABSW continues to empower social workers and clients of African ancestry through advocacy, human services delivery, and research. NABSW's vision is guided by the seven principles, or Nguzo Saba, which are unity, self-determination, collective work and responsibility, cooperative economics, purpose, creativity, and faith; and the seven cardinal virtues of Ma'at, which are right, truth, justice, order, reciprocity, balance, and harmony. Publications related to NABSW's position on child welfare, families, and domestic violence are available at http://nabsw.org/mserver/.

The American Broadcasting Corporation (ABC) airs a series called *Primetime: What Would You Do?* Scenarios of social injustices, including racism and xenophobia, are staged by actors with props and hidden cameras. Nonactors and the actions such people take to counteract or participate in such injustices, are caught on film. Follow-up interviews with the nonactors as well as psychologists and sociologists are filmed to illustrate prejudicial or discriminatory decision-making processes. Available at http://abcnews.go.com/WhatWouldYouDo/.

A Class Divided is a documentary about an Iowa schoolteacher, Jane Elliot, who, the day after Martin Luther King Jr. was murdered in 1968, gave her third-grade students a first-hand experience in the meaning of discrimination. The story of what she taught the children, and the impact that lesson had on their lives, is available at http://www.pbs.org/wgbh/pages/frontline/shows/divided/etc/view.html.

Race: The Power of an Illusion is a PBS series on the social construction of race. The goal of the series is to clear away the "biological underbrush and leave starkly visible the underlying social, economic, and political conditions that disproportionately channel advantages and opportunities to white people." The series, reading material, and expert testimony are available at http://www.pbs.org/race/000_General/000_00-Home.htm.

References

Allport, G. W. (1954). *The nature of prejudice*. Reading, MA: Addison-Wesley.

Alvarez, A. N., & Helms, J. E. (2001). Radical identity and reflected appraisals as influences on Asian Americans' racial adjustment. *Cultural Diversity and Ethnic Minority Psychology, 7*, 217–231.

Bronfenbrenner, U. (1989). Ecological systems theory. In R. Vasta (Ed.), *Six theories of child development: Revised formulations and current issues* (pp. 187–249). Philadelphia: Jessica Kingsley.

Carter-Black, J. (2005). *Success oriented strategies employed by middle-class African American families: A focus on positive racial identity development and socialization* (Unpublished doctoral dissertation). University of Illinois, Urbana-Champaign.

Celious, A., & Oyserman, D. (2001). Race from the inside: An emerging heterogeneous race model. *Journal of Social Issues, 57*(1), 149–165.

Center for Applied Linguistics. (2002). *Directory of two-way bilingual immersion programs in the U.S.* Retrieved from http://www.cal.org/twi/directory/

Centers for Disease Control and Prevention. (2004). Asthma prevalence and control characteristics by race/ethnicity: US, 2002. *Morbidity and Mortality Weekly, 53*(7), 145–148.

Chesler, M. A., Peet, M., & Sevig, T. (2003). Blinded by whiteness: The development of white college students' racial awareness. In A. W. Doane & E. Bonilla-Silva (Eds.), *White out: The continuing significance of racism* (pp. 215–230). New York: Routledge.

Civilrights.org. (n.d.). Civil Rights 101: Leadership Conference on Civil Rights Education Fund/2001. Retrieved from http://www.civilrights.org/resources/civilrights101/voting.html

Cokley, K., & Chapman, C. (2009). Racial identity theory: Adults. In H. A. Neville, B. M. Tynes, & S. O. Utsey (Eds.), *Handbook of African American psychology* (pp. 283–297). Thousand Oaks, CA: Sage.

Conley, D. (2008). *You may ask yourself: An introduction to thinking like a sociologist*. New York: W.W. Norton.

Cross, W. E. (1971). The Negro-to-Black conversion experience: Toward a psychology of Black liberation. *Black World, 20*, 13–27.

Cross, W. E. (1991*)*. *Shades of Black: Diversity in African American identity*. Philadelphia: Temple University Press.

Cross, W. E., & Cross, T. B. (2008). Theory, research, and models. In S. M. Quintana & C. McKown (Eds.), *Handbook of race, racism, and the developing child* (pp. 154–181). Hoboken, NJ: Wiley.

Cross, W. E., Jr., & Vandiver, B. J. (2001). Nigrescence theory and measurement: Introducing the Cross Racial Identity Scale (CRIS). In J. G. Ponterotto, J. M. Casas, L. M. Suzuki, & C. M. Alexander (Eds.), *Handbook of multicultural counseling* (2nd ed., pp. 371–393). Thousand Oaks, CA: Sage Publications.

Cunningham, M., & Francois, S. (2009). African American children. In R. Shweder (Ed.), *The child: An encyclopedic companion* (pp. 41–43). Chicago: University of Chicago Press.

Davis, F. (1997). *Light in the midst of Zion: A history of Black Baptists in Utah*. Salt Lake City, UT: University Publishing.

DeBose, C. E. (1992). Standard English in the African-American linguistic repertoire. *Journal of Multilingual and Multicultural Development, 13*(1–2), 157–167.

Diller, J. V. (2007). *Cultural diversity: A primer for the human services*. Belmont, CA: Brooks/Cole.

Dinh, K. T., Castro, F. G., Tein, J., & Kim, S. (2009). Cultural predictors of physical and mental health status among Mexican American women: A mediation model. *American Journal of Community Psychology, 43*, 35–48.

Du Bois, W. E. B. (1935). *Black reconstruction in America*. New York: Free Press.

Du Bois, W. E. B. (2008). *The souls of black folks*. Rockville, MD: Arc Manor.

Du Bois, W. E. B., & Dill, A. G. (1919). The true Brownies. *Crisis, 18*(6), 285–286.

Dyson, A. H., & Genishi, C. (1994). Introduction: The need for story. In A. H. Dyson & C. Genishi (Eds.), *The need for story: Cultural diversity in classroom and community* (pp. 1–10). Urbana, IL: National Council of Teachers of English.

Elias, P. (2010, August 2). Affirmative action ban upheld by California Supreme Court (Web log post). Huffington Post. Retrieved from http://www.huffingtonpost.com/2010/08/02/affirmative-action-ban-up_n_667763.html

Fletcher, M. A. (1998, July 14). Affirmative action tops NAACP list. *Washington Post*. Retrieved from http://www.washingtonpost.com/wp-srv/politics/special/affirm/stories/naacp071498.htm

Franklin, J. H. (1980). *From slavery to freedom: A history of Negro America* (5th ed.). New York: Knopf.

Freire, P. (2005). *Education for critical consciousness*. New York: Continuum International Publishing Group.

Garland, A., Landsverk, J., & Lau, A. (2003). Racial/ethnic disparities in mental health service use among children in foster care. *Children and Youth Services Review, 25*(5–6), 491–507.

Greater New Orleans Community Data Center. (2007). Lower Ninth Ward neighborhood: People & household characteristics. Retrieved from http://www.gnocdc.org/orleans/8/22/people.html

Guttman, H. (1976). *Black family life in slavery and freedom*. New York: Pantheon Books.

Haight, W. (2002). *African-American children at church: A sociocultural perspective*. New York: Cambridge University Press.

Halemba, G. J., Siegel, G. C., Lord, R. D., & Zawacki, S. (2004). *Arizona dual jurisdiction study: Final report*. Pittsburgh, PA: National Center for Juvenile Justice.

Harris, V. J. (1986). *The Brownies' Book: Challenge to the selective tradition in children's literature* (Unpublished doctoral dissertation). University of Georgia.

Harris, V. R. (1994). Prison of color. In E. Featherston (Ed.), *Skin deep: Women writing on color, culture, and identity* (pp. 9–16). Freedom, CA: Crossing Press.

Helms, J. (1990). *Black and white racial identity: Theory, research and practice*. Westport, CT: Greenwood.

Herz, D., & Ryan, J. P. (2008). *Exploring the characteristics and outcomes of 241.1 youth crossing over from dependency to delinquency in Los Angeles County*. San Francisco: California Courts, Administrative Office of the Courts.

Howard, E. R., Sugarman, J., & Christian, D. (2003). *Trends in two-way immersion education: A review of the research* (Report 63). Johns Hopkins University.

Hudley, E., Haight, W., & Miller, P. (2003/2009). *Raise up a child: Human development in an African-American family*. Chicago: Lyceum Books.

Johnson, A. G. (2006). *Privilege, power and difference* (2nd ed.). New York: McGraw-Hill.

Johnson, P. (1997). *A history of the American people*. New York: Harper Perennial.

Kirst-Ashman, K. K. (2010). *Introduction to social work and social welfare: Critical thinking perspectives* (3rd ed.). Belmont, CA: Thomson Brooks/Cole.

Kivel, P. (2002). *Uprooting racism: How white people can work for racial justice*. Gabriola Island, BC: New Society.

Kunichoff, Y. (2010, May 15). New Arizona bills continue targeting of minority groups, critics say. *Truthout*. Retrieved from http://archive.truthout.org/new-arizona-bills-continue-targeting-minority-groups-critics-say59535?utm_source=feedburner&utm_medium=feed&utm_campaign=Feed%253A+TRUTHOUT+(t+r+u+t+h+o+u+t+%257C+News+Politics)

Ladson-Billings, G. (1992). Liberatory consequences of literacy: A case of culturally relevant instruction for African American students. *Journal of Negro Education, 61*(3), 378–391.

Leeder, E. (2004). *The family in global perspective: A gendered journey*. Thousand Oaks, CA: Sage.

Lincoln, C. E. (1974). *The black experience in religion*. Garden City, NY: Doubleday.

Lindholm, K. (1987). *Directory of bilingual immersion programs: Two-way bilingual education for language minority and language majority students* (Educational Report No. 8). Los Angeles: University of California, Los Angeles, Center for Language Education and Research.

Loewen, J. (2007). *Lies my teacher told me: Everything your American history textbook got wrong*. New York: Simon & Schuster.

Marsiglia, F. F., & Kulis, S. (2009). The intersectionality of race and ethnicity with other factors. In *Diversity, oppression and change* (pp. 42–54). Chicago: Lyceum Books.

McIntosh, P. (1998). White privilege: Unpacking the invisible knapsack. In E. Lee, D. Menkart, & M. Okazawa-Rey (Eds.), *Beyond heroes and holidays: A practical guide to K–12 anti-racist, multicultural education, and staff development* (pp. 79–82). Washington, DC: Network of Educators on the Americas.

McKinney, K. D. (2005). "Being born in the U.S. to White parents is almost boring": Whiteness as a meaningless identity. In *Being White: Stories of race and racism* (pp. 75-113). New York: Routledge.

McLoyd, V. C., Hill, N. E., & Dodge, K. A. (Eds.). (2005). *African American family life: Ecological cultural diversity*. New York: Guilford.

Morrison, T. (1972). *The bluest eye*. New York: Washington Square Press.

National Heart, Lung, and Blood Institute. (2009). *NHLBI Factbook, 2009*. Retrieved from http://www.nhlbi.nih.gov/about/FactBook2009_final.pdf

Needell, B., Brookhart, M., & Lee, S. (2003). Black children and foster care placement in California. *Children and Youth Services Review, 25*, 393-408.

Neville, H. A. (2009). Rationalizing the racial order: Racial color-blindness as a legitimizing ideology. In T. Koditschek, S. K. Cha-Jua, & H. A. Neville (Eds.), *Race struggles* (pp. 115-133). Champaign, IL: University of Illinois Press.

Parke, R., & Buriel, R. (2006). Socialization in the family: Ethnic and ecological perspectives. In W. Damon & R. Lerner (Eds.), *The handbook of child psychology* (6th ed., Vol. 3, pp. 429-504). Hoboken, NJ: Wiley.

Paulson, A. (2010, May 20). Texas textbook war: "Slavery" or Atlantic triangular trade"? *Truthout*. Retrieved from http://archive.truthout.org/new-arizona-bills-continue -targeting-minority-groups-critics-say59535?utm_source=feedburner&utm_ medium=feed&utm_campaign=Feed%253A+TRUTHOUT+(t+r+u+t+h+o+u+t+ %257C+News+Politics)

Perry, P. (2001). White means never having to say you're ethnic. *Journal of Contemporary Ethnography, 30*(1), 56-91.

Puzzanchera, C. (2009). *Juvenile arrests 2008*. Washington, DC: Office of Juvenile Justice and Delinquency Prevention.

Pyke, K. (2010). What is internalized racial oppression and why don't we study it? Acknowledging racism's hidden injuries. *Sociological Perspectives, 53*(4), 551-572.

Quintana, S. M. (2007). Racial and ethnic identity: Developmental perspectives and research. *Journal of Counseling Psychology, 54*(3), 259-270.

Richardson, T. Q., Bethea, A. R., Hayling, C. C., & Williamson-Taylor, C. (2010). African and Afro-Caribbean American identity development. In J. G. Ponterotto, J. M. Casas, L. A. Suzuki, & C. M. Alexander (Eds.), *Handbook of multicultural counseling* (3rd ed., pp. 27-239). Thousand Oaks, CA: Sage.

Rockquemore, K., & Brunsma, D. (2007). *Beyond black: Biracial identity in America* (2nd ed.). Lanham, MD: Rowman & Littlefield.

Rodriguez, R. (1981). A bilingual childhood. In D. Sattler, G. Kramer, V. Shabatay, & D. Bernstein (Eds.), *Lifespan development in context: Voices and perspectives* (pp. 76-80). New York: Houghton Mifflin.

Rumbaut, R. G. (1994). The crucible within: Ethnic identity, self-esteem, and segmented assimilation among children of immigrants. *International Migration Review, 28*(4), 748-794.

Ryan, J. P., Herz, D., Hernandez, P. M., & Marshall, J. M. (2007). Maltreatment and delinquency: Investigating child welfare bias in juvenile justice processing. *Children and Youth Services Review, 29*, 1035-1050.

Scottham, K., Sellers, R., & Nguyên, H. (2005). *The MIBI-T: A new measure of racial identity for use with African American adolescents*. Unpublished manuscript.

Scottham, K., Sellers, R., & Nguyên, H. (2008). A measure of racial identity in African American adolescents: The development of the Multidimensional Inventory of Black Identity—Teen. *Cultural Diversity and Ethnic Minority Psychology, 14*(4), 297–306.

Sellers, R. M., Smith, M. A., Shelton, J. N., Rowley, S. A. J., & Chavous, T. M. (1998). The Multidimensional Model of Racial Identity: A reconceptualization of African American racial identity. *Personality and Social Psychology Review, 2*, 18–39.

Sisneros, J., Stakeman, C., Joyner, M. C., & Schmitz, C. L. (2008). Self-awareness, critical reflectivity and identity. In *Critical multicultural social work* (pp. 20–37). Chicago: Lyceum Books.

Slaughter-Defoe, D. G., Johnson, D. J., & Spencer, M. B. (2009). Race and children's development. In R. Shweder (Ed.), *The child: An encyclopedic companion* (pp. 801–806). Chicago: University of Chicago Press.

Sobel, M. (1988). *Trabelin' on: The slave journey to an Afro-Baptist faith.* Princeton, NJ: Princeton University Press.

Soss, J. Schram, S. F., Vartanian, T. P, & O'Brien, E. (2004). Welfare policy choices in the states: Does the hard line follow the color line? *Focus, 23*(1), 9–15.

Spanierman, L. B., & Soble, J. R. (2009). Understanding Whiteness: Previous approaches and possible directions in the study of White racial attitudes and identity. In J. G. Ponterotto, J. M. Casas, L.A. Suzuki, & C. M. Alexander (Eds.), *Handbook of multicultural counseling* (3rd ed., pp. 283–299). Thousand Oaks, CA: Sage.

Spencer, M. B. (2006). Phenomenology and ecological systems theory: Development in diverse groups. In W. Damon & R. Lerner (Eds.), *The handbook of child psychology* (6th ed., Vol. 1, pp. 829–893). Hoboken, NJ: Wiley.

Stack, C. B. (1974). *All our kin: Strategies for survival in a black community.* New York: Harper & Row.

Swanson, D. P., Cunningham, M., Youngblood, J. II, & Spencer, M. B. (2009). Racial identity development during childhood. In H.A. Neville, B. M.Tynes, & S. O. Utsey (Eds.), *Handbook of African American psychology* (pp. 269–281). Thousand Oaks, CA: Sage.

Tatum, B. D. (1992). Talking about race, learning about racism: The application of racial identity development theory in the classroom. *Harvard Educational Review, 62*(1), 1–24.

Tatum, B. D. (2003). The complexity of identity: "Who am I?" In *"Why are all the black kids sitting together in the cafeteria?"* New York: Basic Books.

Treaster, J. B., & Sontag, D. (2005, September 2). Local officials criticize federal government over response. *New York Times.*

Trelease, A. (1992). Ku Klux Klan. In E. Foner & J. Garraty (Eds.), *The reader's companion to American history* (p. 625). Boston: Houghton Mifflin.

Tuan, M. (1998). *Forever foreigners or honorary Whites? The Asian ethnic experience today.* Piscataway, NJ: Rutgers University Press.

Tugade, M. M., & Frederickson, B. L. (2004). Resilient individuals use positive emotions to bounce back from negative emotional experiences. *Journal of Personality and Social Psychology, 86*, 320–333.

Twombly, R. C. (1971). *Blacks in white America since 1865.* New York: McKay.

U.S. Census Bureau. (2009a). *Income, poverty and health insurance in the United States: 2008.* Washington, DC: U.S. Government Printing Office. Retrieved from http://www.census.gov/prod/2009pubs/p60-236.pdf

U.S. Census Bureau. (2009b). *Statistical abstract of the US: 2009.* Washington, DC: U.S. Government Printing Office. Retrieved from http://www.census.gov/prod/2009pubs/10statab/pop.pdf

U.S. Census Bureau. (2010). *Educational attainment by race and Hispanic origin: 1970 to 2008.* Washington, DC: U.S. Government Printing Office. Retrieved from http://www.census.gov/compendia/statab/2010/tables/10s0224.pdf

U.S. Department of Health and Human Services, Administration on Children, Youth and Families. (2009). *Adoption and foster care analysis and reporting system (AFCARS): 2007.* Washington, DC: U.S. Government Printing Office. Retrieved from http://www.acf.hhs.gov/programs/cb/stats_research/afcars/tar/report 14.htm

U.S. Department of Health and Human Services, Administration for Children and Families, Administration on Children, Youth and Families, Children's Bureau. (2010). *Child maltreatment 2008.* Washington, DC: Author.

Vandiver, B. J., Cross, W. E., Worrell, F. C., & Fhagen-Smith, P. E. (2002). Validating the Cross Racial Identity Scale. *Journal of Multicultural Psychology, 49,* 71–85.

Wise, T. (2005). *White like me: Reflections on race from a privileged son* (2nd ed.). Berkeley: Soft Skull.

11

Social Work with Midlife Adults in Mental Health Contexts
Understanding and Treating Depression

The focal system of this chapter is the midlife adult, approximately thirty-five to sixty-five years old. For many individuals, midlife brings increased responsibilities, including rearing and launching children, caring for aging parents, taking on leadership roles at work, and preparing for retirement. These responsibilities can bring great joy, but also considerable stress. For many other individuals, midlife brings the accumulated stresses of a lifetime of poverty, violence, substance misuse, and unmet health and mental health needs. In vulnerable individuals, stress from positive and negative life changes can lead to mental health problems

In middle adulthood, many individuals reach the peaks of their careers. This social worker is a leader in supporting adults with major mental illnesses. The client was recently released from prison and is on probation, living in temporary housing. The client has been diagnosed as having schizophrenia, anxiety, depression, and alcohol abuse issues.

such as depression. As you read, consider how biological, psychological, and social factors interact within particular cultural and historical contexts to influence mental health in middle adulthood.

In the United States, most mental health services are provided by social workers in settings ranging from community mental health centers to private psychotherapy practices. As you read, consider how the normal blues can be distinguished from depression in midlife, and how effective intervention for depression triggered primarily by environmental stress is similar to or different from intervention for depression triggered primarily by genetic vulnerability. What unique roles do social workers play in a team of psychiatrists, psychologists, nurses, and others involved in care for those suffering from mental illness?

Social work with individuals in middle adulthood is as varied as the experience of midlife itself. In midlife, many individuals are functioning at their peak as they continue to enjoy good health and assume positions of responsibility at work and in their families (see Berk, 2009, for an excellent overview). Others are struggling with the burdens of decades of unemployment, poverty, and substance misuse (see boxes 11.1-11.3). Some adults in their early forties are new grandparents, as the children they produced in

BOX 11.1 POVERTY ACROSS THE LIFE SPAN
Median Income by Racial Group

From 2000 to 2010, gains in income were greatest for Asian-American and European-American households, and lowest for African-American and Hispanic households. The two-year average (2008–2009) median income was $32,584 for African-American households and $38,039 for Hispanic. For European-American and Asian-American households, it was $54,461 and $65,469, respectively.

Source: DeNavas-Walt, Proctor, & Mills, 2010.

BOX 11.2 POVERTY ACROSS THE LIFE SPAN
The Poor Get Poorer

Between 2000 and 2010, the poor got poorer at an increased rate. People in the lowest 20 percent of household earnings (20th national income percentile) saw their incomes decline 5.6 percent from 2008 to 2009, from a median income of $20,633 to $20,453. From 2002 to 2003, the lowest quintile of income earners saw a 1.9 percent decline. People in the top 20th percentile enjoyed a 0.8 percent increase of median income, from $90,860 to $100,001.

Source: DeNavas-Walt, Proctor, & Mills, 2010.

....

BOX 11.3 SUBSTANCE MISUSE ACROSS THE LIFE SPAN

Substance Dependence, Genetics, and Environment

Substance dependence results from a gene-environment interaction. The following environmental factors are believed to interact with genes and increase the probability for addiction:

- family dynamics, especially if addiction is part of the family system
- peer interactions
- individual temperament and social climate fit
- socioeconomic factors, such as low income and poor education
- cultural norms and beliefs

The risk for developing a drug disorder is eight times more likely for people with substance-misusing relatives, compared to individuals from families with no history of a substance disorder or mental illness. Twin studies indicate that the heritability for substance disorders ranges from 48 percent to 87 percent in males and 21 percent to 73 percent in females.

If a person is genetically predisposed to substance dependence but never uses that substance, an addiction cannot occur. Furthermore, a person who is not genetically predisposed for addiction can learn to misuse substances. In both misuse and addiction, environment plays a shifting and differential role. In the same person, environment can shift many times between having a major or minor influence. And once a person is addicted, the brain actually changes to create a need for the intake of that substance.

The close relationship between genes, brain adaptation, and environment has made it difficult to sort out genetic and environmental influences. This relationship may be clarified in the future as scientists learn to decode DNA.

Sources: Merikangas et al., 1998; Merikangas & Stipelman, 2004.

....

their late teens and early twenties begin their families, while other adults, who delayed having children until they established professional careers, are new parents. Some adults with careers in academia, law, or medicine, which require lengthy periods of formal education and apprenticeship, are just beginning to assume leadership roles in their forties. Those who entered the military in their late teens may be enjoying retirement or launching a new career in their forties. With this diversity of experience comes a wide range of challenges. Not surprisingly, social workers encounter midlife adults in a variety of contexts, including educational institutions, mental health centers, domestic-violence shelters, and medical settings. In this chapter, we consider social work in mental health contexts.

MENTAL HEALTH CARE WITH MIDLIFE ADULTS

Mental health care has been a special concern of social workers since the beginning of the twentieth century. In the late 1980s, social workers' commitment to serving those with mental illness gained momentum, clarity, and direction. Social workers began to understand mental illness primarily as a disease that affects and is affected by the individual's social and cultural context. Initiatives for improving social work interventions and research with those suffering from mental illness were sponsored by clinical treatment facilities, academia, NASW, and the National Institute of Mental Health (NIMH). In 1988, NIMH funded a planning committee to develop recommendations for increasing social workers' knowledge, involvement, and research with individuals suffering from mental illness. One result of this work was a series of federally sponsored training seminars and financial assistance for developing research centers within selected schools of social work (Taylor & Edwards, 1996).

Today, mental health is the single largest field of concentration for MSW students. Mental health social workers confront a wide range of issues with clients (see box 11.4 for a discussion of antisocial personality disorder). Individuals experiencing depression, psychosis, or anxiety may require a range of medical, psychotherapeutic, and social services to promote their well-being and to alleviate mental disorders. Social workers specializing in mental health have important roles on a team of medical professionals (psychiatrists, nurses) and social service and psychotherapy providers. Within this team, social workers can provide unique ecological perspectives: for example, how does the individual's living circumstances (housing, relationship with family members, etc.) upon discharge from the hospital affect long-term mental well-being? Social workers are also leaders in developing culturally competent mental health training and education: for example, they address how attitudes and beliefs about mental illness in the family and community affect compliance with psychotropic medication or participation in psychotherapy.

Currently, social work is second only to nursing as the largest occupational group on the staff of mental health facilities. Within the mental health field, social workers are nearly twice as prevalent as either psychiatrists or psychologists (Lin, 1995). In addition, mental illnesses affect most service sectors that are important to social workers. For example, mental illness is associated with poverty, is prevalent in prisons, and is common in families referred for child protective services. Thus, a basic understanding of mental

---

BOX 11.4 VIOLENCE ACROSS THE LIFE SPAN
Antisocial Personality Disorder

Professionals debate how antisocial personality disorder should be defined. Currently most mental health professionals use the definition and criteria provided by the American Psychiatric Association's text revision of *Diagnostic and Statistical Manual of Mental Disorders*. The disorder is described as starting in childhood or early adolescence and continuing into adulthood. Symptoms can generally be traced to the person's childhood. The diagnosis should not be made for a child, however, because not all children and adolescents who break social norms and fail to learn from experience will demonstrate antisocial behaviors as adults.

People with antisocial personality disorder have a long pattern of failing to conform with social norms, are extremely irresponsible, disregard the rights and concerns of others, violate the civil rights of others, and often are aggressive. It is not unusual for people with this disorder to get into physical fights, fail to learn from experience, and blame the victim rather than accept responsibility for their behaviors. Community studies show that about 3 percent of men and 1 percent of women meet the criteria for antisocial personality disorder diagnosis.

Psychotherapy and most rehabilitation efforts are not effective for people who fall into this diagnostic category. But with time, many improve. As the young adult approaches midlife, criminal and other antisocial behaviors decrease. No one is certain why this happens, but some researchers hypothesize that as the person ages, brain changes allow new insights and improved impulse control.

Sources: American Psychiatric Association, 2000, pp. 201–204; Black, 1999.

---

illness is important for all social workers (Greeno, 2008). This chapter elaborates on how a developmental, ecological-systems analysis can inform social work practice with depressed individuals in middle adulthood. Two cases illustrate the complexity of recognizing and appropriately intervening with individuals experiencing depression in midlife. As the cases illustrate, depression takes complex and various forms in midlife, and impacts not only the individual but also family and community.

> Joe is a fifty-six-year-old executive who has been married for thirty-three years. He and his wife have two successful adult children. Joe has a large, almost-paid-for suburban home; a secure, moderately high-paying job; money saved for retirement; manageable monthly bills; an ability to buy personal luxuries including short annual vacation trips; respect from peers; strong

religious faith and values; and routine invitations from friends to play golf. What Joe does not have is a sense of peace, of control over his destiny, and most of all, of happiness. Joe and his wife argue a lot and have sex only occasionally and in a perfunctory manner. The relationship problems started about six months ago and have increased over the last six weeks. For months, work has seemed mundane, and Joe's ability to concentrate has decreased. It seems hard to focus on or care about tasks. This is especially true at work but also occurs in almost every sphere of his life. Joe still performs all the necessary or required tasks, but with less interest, pride, and motivation. He often finds it difficult to get out of bed in the morning; he often feels numb and tired. He used to have no problem sleeping at night and getting up early. Now he goes to sleep at his regular time, but often awakens after a few hours and cannot get back to sleep. As a result, during the past few months, he has been using more and more sick leave. Unlike earlier in his career, he now says his work is just a job allowing him to limp toward retirement. Even his interest in golf has plummeted. He plays but tires more easily, loses more often, and gets into disputes with other golfers. In the past, he seldom argued or became upset when playing golf. Joe explains these difficulties away by telling people his life is in a rut that needs change.

More than anything, Joe blames his wife. He explains that she has changed and seems to have completely lost interest in their sex life. Joe realizes that at his age divorce would be costly to both him and his wife. He would lose at least 50 percent of the equity in their home, retirement, and savings accounts, and other community property. He also knows the idea of divorce would not be supported by his adult children or aging parents. There is no other person in his life, and he is not having any extramarital relationships. Life as presently arranged is just not working, and in Joe's mind there is no solution other than ending the marriage. As a result, Joe has an appointment with a lawyer, and he intends to start divorce proceedings immediately. Joe and others may see his situation as a midlife crisis. However, there may also be an alternative way for understanding his behavior and how he perceives his world.

Maria is a forty-seven-year-old Mexican-American woman who resides in a middle-class neighborhood. An internal medicine physician has placed Maria on an antidepressant and referred her for psychotherapy. Although she has no psychiatric history and does not consider herself an anxious or depressed person, she nonetheless has developed major depressive symptoms. Maria describes herself as a strong person who can take care of herself, her children, and other family members without help. Therefore, it is difficult for her to tell a stranger, especially a mental health social worker, that for the past three weeks she often cries, has problems sleeping, vacillates between having no appetite and gorging, and has little enjoyment, even from activities that used to be rewarding. At first Maria minimizes her difficulties, insisting that she simply has been emotional and came in to see the social worker because her doctor asked her to, but now has things under better control. However, after slowing the interview down, empathizing with

Maria, and winning a small degree of trust, the social worker listens as details of Maria's life unfold.

Maria has been a strong, productive person. She is the oldest of six children and grew up traveling rural America and harvesting crops with her migrant parents. She has many stories of the hardships involved in working the fields, caring for siblings, always living with inadequate medical care, and trying to piece together an education while on the move. Maria states she really never had a childhood. She was always either helping raise the younger children or helping harvest crops. As an older teenager, she worked part-time in the fields, attended school, helped care for her siblings, and worked on weekends at fast-food restaurants. In spite of these hardships, Maria excelled academically and won a scholarship to a small liberal arts college. After completing a bachelor's degree in accounting, she passed the CPA exam, joined a nationwide firm, married, and moved to suburbia. As an upwardly mobile person, she considered herself to have no major financial or emotional difficulties throughout her young adulthood. As she says, "I have passed every test life has given me, at least until now." Over the past nine months, Maria's life has had one major setback after another.

After working nineteen years for a nationwide firm, she lost her job three months ago when the company declared bankruptcy and laid everyone off. Although no criminal accusations were directed toward Maria, federal auditors have questioned the company's bookkeeping practices. As a result, she feels her trustworthiness and professional integrity have been questioned. She also strongly believes the company's bad publicity has played a major role in her inability to find new employment. Maria is presently without health insurance, and her doctor wants her to have a lump in her breast examined by a specialist. Along with these stressors, less than two months ago a flood destroyed Maria's aging parents' home. Everything was lost, and their homeowners' insurance did not cover floods.

Maria's parents, who have only a small Social Security income, are now living with her. In a moment of anxiety while arguing with Maria last week, her mother declared that the family's problems are occurring one after another because Maria no longer attends mass, is no longer religious, has forsaken her heritage, thinks she is better than everyone, and has caused someone with power to give her and the family the "evil eye." Maria is embarrassed to tell this part of the story. She feels certain that a social worker could not understand and that an educated person would not believe that her problems are caused by a mystic spell placed by a "witch." These were the beliefs and explanations she left in the strawberry and lettuce fields years ago. She is now forty-seven years old, and an uncertain financial future, worry about what the doctor will find and how to pay the bill, the fear of spirits, embarrassment for an uneducated family, and her mother's never-ending advice are all back! Every thought, anxiety, feeling, and person are once again crammed together in a house no longer financially affordable. Maria cries but expects no answers, no help. She just hopes that once again she can reach in and find the inner strength that used to be her hallmark, but at this point in time, Maria is not sure she has the ability to face the problems. Her energy, drive, and belief in herself are momentarily gone.

In the first case, Joe has been highly successful in his work, family, and social life. His current difficulties were not precipitated by any specific crisis or set of stressful events. They demonstrate behaviors that fit the popular-press stereotypes of midlife crisis. However, he also has behaviors that signal the onset of major clinical depression. According to the American Psychiatric Association's (2000) *Diagnostic and Statistical Manual of Mental Disorders (DSM-IV-TR),* **major depression** is a genetically determined biochemical disorder manifested by inability to experience pleasure and cope with everyday events. As Joe described his childhood, he identified symptoms of depression in his father and paternal grandfather. Joe, like his father and grandfather before him, is not only unhappy but seems to have lost interest in most or all of his activities and relationships. He performs only necessary tasks at work; golf is no longer enjoyable; he is upset with his spouse and finds it easier to give up part of his financial security than to resolve his marital issues. Solving these problems will require great energy, but Joe has difficulty even getting out of bed. Depression may be a cause of Joe's sleeping problem; it can cause people to routinely awaken after falling asleep and then be unable to return to sleep. Joe identifies his marital, work, and even golf problems as stemming from someone else. Furthermore, he is easily agitated in these environments and finds problem solving difficult. Depression often narrows people's perspectives and causes them to think in a very concrete manner.

Maria, like Joe, has experienced considerable success in her life but is currently experiencing symptoms of depression. Unlike Joe, Maria has no family history of depression, and her difficulties are clearly linked to stressful events. She is suffering from **reactive depression** occurring in response to adverse life events (loss of job, possible illness, family problems). Three important facts are illustrated by this case. First, environmentally triggered symptoms, emotions, and thought processes mirror the biologically triggered depression experienced by Joe. This occurs because Maria's neural chemical system is temporarily out of balance. She is not psychologically or unconsciously willing the depression; her brain has simply started to function in a depressed mode.

Second, Maria finds both strength and tribulation from her culture of origin. Her heritage can provide valuable hope and support, which are necessary to overcome the current crisis. It can also cause stress, as in her return to concerns about mystic evil powers and embarrassment about these concerns. Despite an individual's formal education or acculturation, cultural beliefs learned early within the family and home community can resurface during a crisis. Maria is caught in a mental struggle between beliefs, roles, and goals learned from two differing and sometimes conflicting cultures.

Third, Maria's story underscores that macrosystem policies and economic stability can change an individual's situation. Social workers must be prepared to identify when a person's problems are caused more by environmental factors than by internal psychological structures or brain disorder. As discussed in this chapter, the causes of depression have important implications for which combination of intervention strategies will be most effective.

HIGHLIGHTS OF DEVELOPMENT IN MIDDLE ADULTHOOD

Human development is shaped in relation to accumulating biological, psychological, and social factors operating within particular cultural and historical contexts. Common biological characteristics, such as changes associated with aging, may form a basis for common psychological and social characteristics. In addition, as individuals inch toward the senior years, their increasingly diverse developmental pathways lead to varied biological, psychological, and social characteristics.

Although considerable development does occur in midlife, there are wide individual differences. Levinson (Levinson, 1986; Levinson & Levinson, 1978, 1996) characterized midlife as the most difficult developmental era to describe in general terms. Midlife changes and tasks are shaped by each individual's culture, health, genetics, economics, politics, empowerment, and environmental opportunities. How biological aging in midlife affects individuals depends upon numerous social and cultural factors. Ashford, LeCroy, and Lortie (2001, p. 470) point out that "midlife is different from other developmental phases in that it is less affected by biological maturation. Indeed, adults are most affected by their own experiences."

Biological Factors

Biological changes, however, do occur as individuals age. Most adults in middle adulthood are healthy and energetic, but they may begin to notice gradual physical changes such as hair loss or graying, wrinkling of the skin, decreased sight and hearing, weight gain, and lessening of muscular strength and physical stamina. These changes are universal, but their timing and degree varies. This variability is related to a number of factors, including genetics, diet, health-care availability, health history, and risk taking.

Individuals in midlife also may develop troubles sleeping, due to biological changes, mental health problems, and environmental factors. Based on a cross-sectional survey of 1,506 adults, approximately 40 percent reported sleeping less than seven hours each night during the work week. Furthermore, 24 percent reported having only a few good nights of sleep each week, and 26 percent reported that they get a good night of sleep only a few evenings per month (National Sleep Foundation, 2005).

While a trend for less rest is reported by men and women, it appears to be more prevalent in middle-aged and younger women. This may result from physiological changes occurring from menstruation, pregnancy, and menopause. It may also occur because of mental health problems. About 20 percent of individuals reporting sleep difficulties suffer from depression, and up to one-third have some underlying mental disorder (Cummings & Mega, 2003; Hales & Hales, 1995). Unfortunately, the less individuals sleep, the more they "learn" not to sleep. An interaction can occur between bodily changes or pain that keeps a person awake and developing a habit, or learned response, of not sleeping. Approximately 15 percent of people seeking help for chronic insomnia have primarily learned not to sleep (Hales & Hales, 1995).

Environment can greatly affect sleeping patterns. Many of us have developed poor eating and exercise habits and consume substances like caffeine, nicotine, and alcohol that can induce insomnia. Work-related stress can also have a negative impact on a person's physical health and sleep patterns. Women working late shifts, for example, are at a higher risk for having irregular menstrual cycles, problems becoming pregnant, and a higher rate of miscarriages, premature births, and low-birth-weight babies (Hales & Hales, 1995; National Sleep Foundation, 2005). Because a wide range of physiological, psychological, neurological, and environmental factors can cause sleeping problems, social workers can best serve their clients by

- screening for sleeping problems;
- understanding that sleeping difficulties may stem from physical problems such as breathing difficulties while sleeping (sleep apnea), pain, and menstruation, as well as learned habits;
- knowing that some people, but not the majority, cannot sleep because of a mental disorder;
- recognizing that the inability to sleep may be a symptom of a more serious physical illness; and
- referring clients to appropriate sleep clinics and experts for a complete assessment.

Most social workers are not trained to independently assess and treat primary sleep disturbances. Once the diagnosis has been correctly made, under expert supervision social workers can assist some clients with relaxation to improve their sleeping environments and to overcome habits that interfere with gaining a restful night's sleep. Surveys indicate that as we age, quality sleep increases if one's lifestyle includes ongoing routine and trusting relationships, hopeful and positive attitudes, regular and appropriate exercise, and commitments for volunteer work or other organizational activities.

An important biological milestone for women in middle adulthood is **menopause**. Menopause is triggered by a decrease in ovarian function and consists of three stages. The first stage, premenopause, normally begins at about forty years of age, but may appear for some women in their early thirties. Throughout the first stage, the ovaries slowly decrease hormone production. The erratic ovarian functioning changes the woman's menstrual cycle and flow. Premenopausal hormone changes can also trigger weight gain and premenstrual breast tenderness and water retention. As a result, doctors often recommend that women restrict their salt intake and routinely exercise during the premenopause stage.

The second stage, menopause, begins a year after a woman has her last period and is no longer able to become pregnant. The average age at which women reach menopause is 51.4, and most women reach menopause between 45 and 55 years of age. Hot flashes and an inability to sleep through the night are common menopausal complaints that result from falling levels of estrogen. Hormonal depletion also causes fat to increase in the abdomen, breasts to be less firm, and skin to thin. Women and their spouses or partners also need to know menopause can cause breaks in the vaginal skin, dryness that makes sexual intercourse uncomfortable, urinary tract infections, and for some women unpleasant and embarrassing urinary leakage. More importantly, hormonal imbalance caused by menopause can affect women's hearts, bones, and brains. Without proper treatment the cardiovascular system is at risk for hardening of the arteries, bones lose calcium and become brittle, and the brain becomes vulnerable for memory loss, depression, and disrupted sleep patterns (Rapp et al., 2003; Seifert & Hoffnung, 2000; Shumaker et al., 2003). Many of these problem disappear as a woman enters postmenopause (third stage) and hormonal levels become more stable. However, periodic medical exams for loss of bone density and cardiovascular changes should continue throughout life.

Responses to the biological changes of menopause vary, depending on cultural context and women's individual expectations. In societies where a woman's role is largely reproductive, the inability to bear more children may result in a loss of status. In cultures where the wisdom and experience of older women is valued, menopause is seen as a more positive life event (Borysenko, 1997; Northrup, 1994). Margaret Lock (1993) studied menopause and the symptoms experienced by thousands of women age forty-five to fifty-five in Japan, the United States, and Canada. Lock hypothesized that Japan's history of war, poverty, and traditional societal rules and roles would cause Japanese women to experience more menopause symptoms than North American women. To the researcher's surprise, Japanese women reported significantly fewer symptoms than the U.S. and Canadian women. Shoulder stiffness (52 percent) and headaches (28 percent) were the leading Japanese complaints. In the North American sample, shoulder stiffness was hardly mentioned, but more than 33 percent of the Canadian sample and 37 percent of the U.S. women had experienced headaches. Only 10 percent of the Japanese women reported symptoms of depression, whereas 23 percent of the Canadian and almost 36 percent of the U.S. women indicated that menopause had caused them to feel blue or depressed. These findings suggest that culture plays a role, for example, through variations in diet and women's roles and status, in how individuals experience some of the body's biochemical changes. One wonders whether future generations of North American women will find changes in physical appearance caused by menopause to be an ever-increasing stressor. The popular print media and television document our continuing interest in antiaging creams, plastic surgery, and an endless search for the fountain of youth. Regardless of the cultural lens, menopause will continue to be a midlife event. The social worker's role is to provide education and support to help the woman, her spouse or partner, and her family to reduce psychological stressors and maintain positive interpersonal and intrafamily communications as women move through the menopausal stages.

Psychological and Social Factors

Individuals in midlife continue to experience psychological changes and development. Erikson characterized midlife as a period when thought and activities focus on moving from personal concerns to providing meaningful and creative care for others. A central challenge of midlife, according to Erikson, is generativity, a concern with improving or contributing to the well-being of future generations. Santrock (2002) documented that middle adulthood is a relatively productive and emotionally healthy period for women and men. Most people traverse midlife without developing major physical and mental health problems. Many middle-aged adults experience a period of feeling safe, secure, and settled. Perhaps with this sense of security comes a greater commitment and interest in nurturing the next generation, assumption of the role of carrier and transmitter of culture and knowledge, and a review of one's own past commitments (Lachman & James, 1997).

Less optimal psychological outcomes in midlife may include feelings of boredom and bitterness regarding forgone opportunities. Common psychological issues include an increased concern about future health, possibly a result of the inevitable physical changes associated with aging. Hooker and Kaus (1994) found that people in midlife are aware of their increased vulnerability for major illnesses, decreased motor skills, hearing loss, decreased vision, reduced sexuality, and other physical and psychological issues. Indeed, the prospect of developing heart disease or cancer, or having a stroke can be frightening (see box 11.5 for discussion of heart-attack warning signs).

> **BOX 11.5 HEART-ATTACK WARNING SIGNS**
>
> Although most individuals experience good health in middle adulthood, those with genetic vulnerabilities to illness and/or stressful lifestyles can experience ill health or the beginning of chronic disease. Heart attacks can be sudden and intense or start slowly and in the beginning cause only mild discomfort. More often the onset is slow and less dramatic, which can make a person uncertain about what is happening and about the need for immediate medical care. Here are common signs and warnings of a heart attack:
>
> - mild pain or discomfort in the center of the chest lasting more than a few minutes
> - chest pain that goes away and comes back, which can be described as pressure, squeezing, fullness, pain, or heartburn
> - mild pain or discomfort in other upper body regions such as one or both arms, the back, neck, jaw, or stomach
> - shortness of breath, which can occur before or simultaneous with chest pain/discomfort
> - cold sweat, nausea, and lightheadedness
>
> _____
> Sources: American Heart Association, 2003; Ashford, LeCroy, & Lortie, 2001; Seifert & Hoffnung, 2000.

Although a popular topic in the media, the phenomenon of a midlife crisis is not widespread. Research has generally failed to support the idea that by simply entering midlife, one becomes vulnerable to an emotional or identity crisis (Andreasen & Black, 2000; Lachman & James, 1997). The concept of midlife crisis is overly broad and highly influenced by culture, social class, and personal beliefs. Labeling a person as being in a midlife crisis does not inform the social worker how to treat the client.

Midlife takes on a different meaning for individuals who face a decreased life expectancy and an increased probability of developing a potentially fatal illness. Within the United States, life expectancy varies across ethnic groups. For example, American Indians and Alaska Natives die from tuberculosis at a rate 750 percent higher than the rest of the nation and from diabetes at a rate 420 percent higher. They also die from accidents and suicide at rates of 280 percent and 190 percent higher, respectively. Their deaths from alcoholism are 770 percent higher than that of the general population (U.S. Indian Health Service, 2002).

People in middle adulthood also experience social changes. They have been described as the "sandwich generation," caught between obligations to their partners, children, and aging parents. Nonetheless, many of these relationships continue to play an important supportive role in the lives of most individuals in middle adulthood. Many adults in midlife experience greater affection and love, especially in lasting partnerships. More people in midlife than in early adulthood report that their marriages are good or excellent. Furthermore, individuals who divorce during midlife have a less emotionally volatile relationship with former spouses than people who divorce at a younger age. Most parents in middle adulthood continue to feel close to their children and may regret not having spent more time with them. The experience of children leaving home, resulting in an empty nest, often increases rather than decreases life satisfaction; however, many children return home because of economic factors. Friendships are highly valued by most middle-aged people and can be a source of great joy and support. As during other periods of life, relationships with siblings vary widely; some middle-aged siblings grow closer while others drift farther apart (Santrock, 2002).

Sociocultural-Historical Factors

The meaning and purpose of middle adulthood vary across cultural and historical contexts. In Asian, African, and Native American societies, midlife is widely viewed as preparation to becoming a more powerful and respected elder. In U.S. and western European cultures, midlife is often viewed as a period of work and community productivity, consolidation of economic worth, and preparation for retirement. In terms of authority and power, midlife in America is what later adulthood is for people, particularly men, in Asian, African, and Native American communities. In general, within the United States, individuals are valued more during midlife as expert parents, workers, and community leaders than in later adulthood as retired senior citizens. In the United States, having adult status, expertise, and full-time employment is not only empowering, but is difficult to achieve before midlife, and even harder to maintain in later life. It is during midlife that one often achieves prestigious social titles, such as foreman, supervisor, chief, grandparent, and senior clinical social worker; gains practical knowledge and is at least partially sanctioned by society to give advice; gains increased assets; and is perceived as wiser than younger, less experienced adults.

There is, however, significant individual variation in how one understands and responds to middle adulthood. People live not only within the context of macrosystems, but also within particular communities and families. We develop our own "place in culture," or niche, that personalizes and reflects macro- and microsystems. Therefore, people may come from identical macrosystems, but because of their place in culture, experience personal and societal events differently. For some people, becoming a grandparent stirs warm emotions, a positive identity, parental validation, and a link to their historical culture, whereas others worry about aging, unwanted responsibilities, and economic concerns. Midlife attitudes and perspectives become individualized by health and physical changes, life experiences, beliefs, personality factors, genetics, and, for some, psychiatric disorders.

DEVELOPMENTAL, ECOLOGICAL-SYSTEMS ANALYSIS OF DEPRESSION IN MIDDLE ADULTHOOD

Depression is one of the most frequent psychiatric problems faced by individuals throughout the life span. Approximately 9 percent of North Americans suffer from depression, and it is estimated to be one of the most disabling and costly of mental disorders. By 2020, depression is predicted to be the leading cause of disability worldwide. Depression can cause or worsen disability in a variety of domains. It is associated with relationship problems and disruption of close relationships, lost work days and reduced job performance, and a variety of health-related disabilities (Greeno, 2008).

Depression occurs in both genders, but occurs more than twice as often in women as in men (American Psychiatric Association, 2000; hereafter *DSM-IV-TR*). African Americans and Hispanics are less likely to experience depression than non-Hispanic whites, and this lower risk is more pronounced among lower-income members of these groups (Greeno, 2008). Depression occurs at all ages, but the most vulnerable period for the onset of depression is between twenty and forty years of age (Stahl, 2000). Depression can limit people's ability to control not only their mood, but also energy, social perceptions, problem solving, information processing, motor coordination, and decision making. Depression is more than simple sadness, a lack of hunger, or an inability to sleep. While these are all possible symptoms of depression, the terms fail to convey an illness that captures, controls, and limits a person's mind, emotions, and range of possible behavioral responses (Taylor, 2005). Depression affects neurological, emotional, and body systems. The depressed individual may find it extremely difficult to understand abstractions, identify islands of hope, and develop alternative perspectives or solutions (Baldwin & Birtwistle, 2002; DePaulo, 2002; Taylor, 2003).

Symptoms of major, clinical depression usually develop over days or weeks. A major depressive episode involves depressed mood or the loss of interest or pleasure in nearly all activities, and four additional symptoms, including changes in appetite or weight, sleep, and psychomotor activity; decreased energy; feelings of worthlessness or guilt; difficulty thinking, concentrating, or making decisions; and recurrent thoughts of death or suicide (*DSM-IV-TR*). These symptoms persist for at least two weeks and are new or worse than before the episode. Depressed individuals may describe feeling down in the dumps, sad, hopeless, and discouraged. They may report a loss of interest in hobbies or work. Appetite may be reduced or increased with a craving for sweets and carbohydrates. Depressed individuals may suffer from insomnia, or oversleep. They may experience agitation or slowed speech, and have difficulty thinking, concentrating, and making decisions. Decreased energy, decreased libido, and fatigue are common, as are feelings of guilt and worthlessness. Frequently, they may think of death or suicide, and may attempt suicide. The degree of impairment in an episode of major depression varies, but there must be clinically significant distress, or interference with social, occupational, or other important areas of functioning.

Fortunately, depression is a treatable illness, and 75 to 80 percent of individuals who receive psychotherapy and/or medications experience substantial improvement within three to four months (Stahl, 2000). Left untreated, however, an episode of depression typically lasts for six months or longer before abating. Tragically, as many as 15 percent of all people who suffer from major depression will commit suicide (Stahl, 2000). In the United States, suicide is the eighth most frequent cause of death, and sixth in the United Kingdom. Among Americans age fifteen to forty-four years, suicide is the second leading cause of death (Baldwin & Birtwistle, 2002). Individuals with depression must be screened on a regular basis for suicidal thoughts and behavioral indicators. Social workers should not hesitate to ask a client if he or she has thoughts or plans for taking his or her life, when symptoms or signs of suicidal behavior are observed. Here is a list of some key risk factors for suicide that are often reported by clinicians and researchers (Taylor, 2005):

- a history of one or more suicidal attempts
- family history of suicide
- feelings of hopelessness
- statements about life not being worth living
- statements indicating that there are no solutions, or that the situation will not improve
- increased risk taking or impulsiveness
- written suicide notes, or obsessive writing, reading, or talking about death
- alcohol and substance misuse
- severe mental health symptoms, particularly hopelessness, sleep disturbance, anxiety, and agitation
- increased isolation
- recent or increased life stressor
- preparation for death (e.g., giving away personal items and money)
- poor response to psychotropic medications, or refusal to take medications

Some individuals experience episodes of depression associated with bipolar disorder (also known as manic-depressive disorder). During manic phases, individuals experience unusually high levels of exuberance, grandiosity, feelings of invulnerability, and extremely fast thinking. In this phase, an individual demonstrates poor judgment and decision making. The individual may vastly overspend his or her financial resources, exhibit hypersexuality, and engage in risk-taking behavior that can result in death (e.g., running across a highway, trying to dodge speeding cars). The individual may also display low tolerance and frustration that leads to arguments and physical fights (Taylor, 2005).

Biological Factors

Research indicates that major depression is a biologically based illness caused by structural and functional problems occurring in the brain (DePaulo, 2002; Goodwin & Jamison, 1990; Jamison 1999; Stahl, 2000; Taylor, 1997, 2005). Examination of identical twins separated at birth (i.e., individuals who share the same genetic code, but not the same environment) reveals strong associations between genetics and mental illness (Jones, Kent, & Craddock, 2002; Sadock & Sadock, 2003; Torrey, Bowler, Taylor, & Gottesman, 1994). Depression has a much higher probability of occurring in both identical twins, who share the same genes, than in both fraternal twins, who do not share the same genetic codes. In major depression, concurrent rates of depression for identical twins are twice that of fraternal twins (Jones, Kent, & Craddock, 2002; Kalidindi & McGuffin, 2003). Several brain chemicals, called **neurotransmitters**, play important roles in mood disorders such as depression. Neurotransmitters conduct communications between different brain cells. Neurotransmitters implicated in major depression include norepinephrine, serotonin, acetylcholine, and gamma-aminobutyric acid (*DSM-IV-TR*). Advances in technology provide further evidence of the biological basis of major depression. They include the ability to image neurological structures and measure the brain's metabolic rate and numerous differences in the brain's structure and function that occur between individuals with and without mental illness (Taylor, 2005).

The biological basis of depression is sensitive to, and interacts in complex ways with, psychological, social, and cultural factors. The stress caused by economic problems, interpersonal difficulties, and other hardships can trigger major depression in vulnerable individuals. In addition, severe hardships and trauma also can trigger the biological symptoms of depression in individuals who are not particularly genetically vulnerable (DePaulo, 2002; Taylor, 2003).

Psychological Factors

Major depression has profound psychological consequences that can block interpersonal development and positive growth (DePaulo, 2002;

Gotlib & Hammen, 2002). A major depressive episode can rob a person of hope, limit information-processing skills, slow and narrow cognitive abilities, distort social perceptions, cause paranoia, block empathy and social insights, and spark unexplainable agitation, anger, and social withdrawal (Gotlib & Hammen, 2002). Furthermore, individuals suffering with depression and other mood disorders may develop substance misuse disorders through their efforts to self-medicate and achieve temporary relief from their profound psychological pain (Mueser, Noordsy, Drake, & Fox 2003; Taylor, 2005). For individuals with bipolar disorder, the drug of choice is most often alcohol, but they may misuse street and prescription drugs during a depressive or manic episode. In the United States, 46 percent of individuals with a bipolar disorder, compared to 13 percent of the general population, either misuse or are addicted to alcohol. Additionally, 41 percent of people with bipolar disorders, compared to 6 percent of the general public, misuse street drugs (Taylor, 2005).

Temporary drops in psychological functioning caused by environmental factors may produce reactive symptoms. Changes in mental clarity may not stem from a neurobiological disorder like major depression, but rather from real and perceived environmental stressors. People become tired, grief stricken, anxious, or overwhelmed by obligations and events that appear to be beyond their control. Usually environmental and perceived problems decrease a person's mental wellness rather than cause a mental illness. The brain's physical structure has not been injured or changed, but the perceptual, emotional, and cognitive responses stimulated by upsetting environmental events have temporarily decreased the person's mental wellness. Another way of explaining this is that interactions with the environment temporarily restrict the brain from functioning to its fullest and healthiest potential. Even though personal problems may not stem from a brain disease or major mental disorder, decreased mental health can trigger hazardous behaviors, inappropriate affect, and reduced problem solving. An inability to cope with personal losses, high anxiety, or uncontrolled emotions can stimulate irrational thoughts or prevent a person from considering alternative solutions and problem-solving methods. As thinking is restricted, behaviors and decisions can be triggered that are extremely destructive for the individual, family, and community.

As social workers, we must always be mindful of temporary decreases in mental wellness, which, like neurobiological mental disorders, can cause internal pain, poor decisions, and behaviors resulting in economic hardships, family break-ups, physical abuse, and suicide. Therefore, it is extremely important to intervene therapeutically with people facing personal problems and decreased mental wellness. Such interventions, however, may emphasize environmental manipulation, support, case management, crisis intervention, and advocacy, rather than long-term psychotherapy or psychiatric medications. Severe symptoms resulting from grief, personal crisis, environmental factors, or other psychological issues may also require medication and psychotherapy. Before treatment can start, however, accurate assessment of the problem is required (see box 11.6).

BOX 11.6 THE ASSESSMENT PROCESS
Using the Developmental, Ecological-Systems Perspective

Assessment is a critical first step in the development and implementation of an appropriate, effective social work intervention. As used in this book, *assessment* refers to the systematic collection of information, guided by valid and appropriate theories of human development that are linked to empirical research findings. Social workers in all practice fields routinely assess the ever-changing challenges, skills, and resources of individuals, families, communities, and other social systems. The types of information we collect, as well as how we evaluate, interpret, and use this information, are guided by our theoretical and conceptual perspectives.

The first steps in the assessment process are to determine the relevant information to collect and how to go about collecting it. From our developmental, ecological-systems perspective, this information should include a description of biological, psychological, and social factors within cultural-historical contexts. The focus of this assessment is determined by the problem we hope to address through systematic interventions, for example, problems of living with major depression.

Once information has been collected, **clinical assumptions** are made: that is, certain facts are accepted with little or no challenge. It is a reality of social work that we will never have all of the relevant information. Budgets are tight, and we often rely on reports from clients and others that may or may not be accurate and complete. Making clinical assumptions is one of the most risky and potentially dangerous parts of the assessment. Bias, lack of experience and knowledge, and inability to see beyond the expected can lead us to accept incorrect or incomplete assumptions. If our assumptions are wrong, then we may misunderstand the person's behaviors and environments. Social workers must always question whether the "obvious" is camouflaging reality, and if our professional beliefs and assumptions are conceptually and empirically sound.

Given assessment information and clinical assumptions, the next steps in the assessment process are to form and then test clinical hypotheses. A **clinical hypothesis** explains an observed behavior, problem, or social interaction. The hypotheses we form and test, like the clinical assumptions we make, are guided by our theoretical perspectives. From our developmental, ecological-systems perspective, hypotheses typically include specific biological and social factors as contributing to the issues we hope to address through intervention.

The clinical hypothesis must always be tested and proven by multiple sources to be contextually valid. From a developmental, ecological-systems perspective, **contextual validity** means that the clinical hypotheses used for explaining observed behaviors are not only theoretically true, but apply the correct weight and meaning to reciprocal exchanges among environmental settings and the client. Contextual validity requires behavior to be assessed in concert with the environment, current and historical culture, and time and place. In isolation, behaviors have little meaning.

The assessment process of collecting information, making clinical assumptions, and forming and testing clinical hypotheses is continuous. Assessments are never final, because change can occur at any time from multiple interacting physical and social contexts. Thus, developmental, ecological-systems assessments are always tentative, and must be subjected to an ongoing analysis. The developmental, ecological-systems perspective provides an analytic framework, a heuristic, for approaching complex problems within social work, including assessment.

Social Factors

Psychological symptoms of depression have profound social consequences. The middle-aged person experiencing depression will find it difficult to hold a job, maintain family obligations, and sustain extended social networks. Problems of this nature create major problems at any age, but are particularly devastating in midlife. Losing a job may end realistic hopes for a secure retirement, force children to drop out of college, and jeopardize the long-term investment made in a home. Further, middle-aged people in mainstream U.S. culture are generally expected to reach out and care for others and to demonstrate mature behavior, knowledge, self-reliance, and civic responsibility. Depression makes these tasks practically impossible.

Individuals suffering from major depression often face family members, communities, and sometimes even mental health professionals who interpret their lack of activity as willful defiance and a considered decision to remain incapacitated. Depressive symptoms may be viewed as psychological choices, not biologically driven signs of illness. Unvoiced suicidal thoughts can be validated by social interactions that directly or indirectly (1) blame the individual for not improving; (2) provide little empathy for emotional pain; (3) deny that some family, social, or work tasks cannot be performed; and (4) fail to acknowledge that the accomplishment of any routine task requires deliberate physical energy and painfully difficult or slow cognitive processing (Bongar, 2002; Jamison, 1995, 1999; Taylor, 2005).

The National Alliance for the Mentally Ill (NAMI), founded in 1979, is an important grassroots support and advocacy group that helps combat the stigma of mental illness. NAMI comprises people with serious mental illnesses, their friends, and their family members. It works to achieve equitable services and treatment for individuals with mental illness and their families. Hundreds of thousands of volunteers participate in more than 1,000 local affiliates and fifty state organizations to provide education and support, combat stigma, support increased funding for research, and advocate adequate health insurance, housing, and jobs for people with mental illness.

Sociocultural-Historical Context

Throughout recorded history, scholars in science, philosophy, and religion have attempted to define and understand serious mental illness. Hippocrates described symptoms resembling schizophrenia and theorized that the illness was a form of organic dementia. As Western civilization struggled to develop, these early insights were lost or replaced by myths, religious hypotheses, and dehumanizing stigma. Not until the late 1800s, with the advent of European psychiatry, was the organic nature of serious mental illness again emphasized (DePaulo, 2002; Taylor, 2005).

Despite evidence of a biological basis for depression, the way in which depression and other mental illnesses are interpreted profoundly affects how they are personally experienced and responded to at the interpersonal and societal levels. For instance, numerous myths about depression persist in the United States. Symptoms of depression are often interpreted by others as anger, lack of motivation, poor personal choices, or immaturity. As a result, other people may not only reject and withdraw from the depressed person, but assigned roles and status normally given to a person who has reached full adulthood may be withheld or removed.

How one is positioned within the larger society also impacts the quality of care received. In the United States, there are treatment disparities, with African Americans, Native Americans, and Hispanics who suffer from mental illness less likely to receive care, and more likely to leave care prematurely, than non-Hispanic whites. Lower levels of service use by people of color is partially attributed to poverty and bias in the mental health system. In addition, when people of color do not receive treatment from someone from their own ethnic community, they may question the relevance of the help offered (Greeno, 2008).

As social workers, our responsibility is to help the depressed person obtain psychiatric treatment, to educate the community, to advocate for the family and client, and to help restore the person's place in society. Box 11.7 describes cultural components of social work with depressed clients.

··

BOX 11.7 PRACTICE STORY AND ADVICE
FROM THE FIELD

Susan C., mental health social worker: "This has never been just a job for me. It's been the living out of my spiritual values."

Susan C. has been involved in social justice issues since the 1960s, and has more than twenty years' experience as a social worker. She has practiced social work in a wide variety of cultural contexts, including Hawaii and the Marshall Islands. Currently, she is professor of social work at a large university, where she conducts research and teaches.

Practice Story

Many of the Vietnamese clients that I saw [at a mental health center in Hawaii] were dealing with depression that was the result of PTSD from the Vietnam war. This was at the time when the U.S. government was recognizing and allowing Vietnamese children of service men to come to the U.S. These children were outcast [in Vietnam] mainly because they were biracial. They couldn't walk on the street—it was very problematic. And many of them [parents] had experienced the loss of numerous children, spouses, parents, all of that. I worked with one mother over a period of time. As things were going along, she really wasn't feeling better, and even the meds she was receiving for depression were not working. Some of us because of our experiences have a great sadness. So I said, "What would you do in Vietnam?" She told me, "The women would get together and we would sit under a blanket and boil herbs. And we'd have a fire and we had certain herbs and it would be a process of helping us to put our sadness aside." So I said, "Why don't we do this?" And it was the first time that she laughed, and she said, "We can't do this in here!" I said, "I am willing to do that with you." And she said, "No, no, I don't think that's necessary." And I said, "Well let's talk about what would happen, during that ceremony," and then we went off of that, and we tried to deal with some of those issues. [The therapy did] validate something from her culture and brought it over here, and she could say, "I can do this in this way here." People were bombarded with "This is the way we do things here," and so they started to feel like nothing that was helpful there [Vietnam] could be helpful in the new culture. In therapy, clients realized, "Oh yeah, there may be things that I did before that I can use here, and how can I do that?" So it was the beginning of trying to integrate her past and her present in a positive way and to go on and not feel so isolated

··

and sad. You know, no matter how bad things are in the country of origin, they weren't like that 24/7. And it's still their family, and it's still their home.

Advice

I think we make the mistake of overgeneralizing. I am thinking about the number of Vietnamese clients that I have had. They fled along with U.S. troops because they had money. And their experience of Vietnamese culture was very different than [the experience of] this woman [client described above]. She was illiterate in her own language and had very limited resources in a lot of ways. Clients need to tell you what it means to be from their culture and what role that plays in their lives presently.

Often I worked with folks who were not very respected by some people. I always took a posture of respect for the person. That was very helpful for me. I felt my role was to help them see what those strengths were and how those allowed them to survive. I think that allowed me to be successful.

The other thing is that over the years, I realized that I was just one person in a lifetime of the person. What was there then, when I saw them, had been the result of many years. But I was optimistic because they could choose a different path.

Sometimes as a social worker, I had to go outside some of the established norms, not outside the ethical norms, and I think it made a difference. It made a difference when I was a student and one of the parents was seeing me after she came off a midnight shift. She was exhausted, and I brought in cookies for her, and that was a clincher. And that was only because I said, "Look, I made these for my family and for you. Have some cookies. You know you are really tired when you come in here, and it is hard to focus." And it shifted the relationship.

This has never been just a job for me. It's been the living out of my spiritual values. I was raised a Catholic. And so my being a pacifist and all of that is a result of really examining what it means to be committed to spiritual values. So I've struggled to make those consistencies in my life.

IMPLICATIONS FOR SOCIAL WORK

Although most people suffering from depression do not get treatment, depression is one of the most treatable mental health disorders. Treatment generally includes a combination of medication and talk therapy. Medical guidelines for treating depression are well established as effective, as are cognitive behavioral and interpersonal therapies (Greeno, 2008). In 2002, the Substance Abuse and Mental Health Services Administration of the U.S. Department of Health and Human Services released implementation kits to facilitate the adoption of six best practices for treating mental illness. Toolkit practices include standardized pharmacological treatment, illness management and recovery skills, supported employment, and family psychoeducation. Toolkit practices also include assertive community treatment, which helps clients stay out of the hospital, increase their skills with daily living, and decrease the need for their mental illness to be their primary daily struggle. Integrated dual disorders treatment also is important for clients who have co-occurring disorders, such as alcoholism and major depression (Dulmus & Roberts, 2008).

Social workers often work as part of a team to help individuals suffering from major depression. This team may include a psychiatrist, nurse, psychologist, and/or psychotherapist. In addition to providing therapy, social workers may contribute wellness techniques. Wellness techniques provide support, increase intact skills, and empower clients and their families. The goals and emphasis of wellness techniques vary depending on the origins, history, and severity of the depression. For individuals with long-standing major mental illness that originates in a brain disorder, interventions will be medically focused. However, for individuals who have stabilized on their medications, or whose depression stems primarily from stress and trauma, intervention might focus on wellness techniques in conjunction with psychotherapy or family therapy.

When working with depressed individuals, social workers need to remember that depression is a deadly illness. Depression is a significant risk factor for suicide. As stated earlier, approximately 15 percent of individuals with major depression commit suicide. Among people with bipolar disorder, 25 percent will make a serious suicide attempt, and at least 10 percent will succeed (Torrey & Knable, 2002). The probability that people will take their lives also increases if they have a history of previous suicide attempts; they misuse alcohol or other substances; the person is an aging, white male living alone; a family member committed suicide; or they have thoughts of suicide and develop an actual plan for killing themselves (Jamison, 1999). Therefore, it is important that medical and community social workers are well-trained for conducting suicide assessments. Social workers may feel awkward asking people if they have had thoughts about taking their own lives, but this discomfort will disappear with practice and knowledge about mental disorders and suicidal risks. It is helpful to understand that professionals and the public have, for far too long, incorrectly framed or spoken of suicide as a personal choice. Social workers should instead remember that when a person is depressed, suicide is not an existential choice, but can become an overwhelming obsession or drive produced by an ill brain (Taylor, 2005). As explained by Bongar (2002), depressed clients often are focused more on using suicide for stopping unbearable emotional pain rather than on the issue of death. However, depression can cause clients to obsess about death, and to experience unexplained impulses or urges to kill themselves (Taylor, 2005). We have an ethical and professional responsibility to help people live through depression, overcome suicidal thoughts, regain a personal direction over their lives, and reclaim the right of free choice. Depression is extremely treatable. Although medication, psychotherapy, support, and environmental manipulations may not cure depression, they can lessen symptoms, shorten the length of episodes, and delay or prevent future episodes (*DSM-IV-TR*; DePaulo, 2002, Taylor, 2003, 2005).

SUMMARY

Midlife, like all periods of life, has the potential for major life challenges. As a person ages, the probability increases for experiencing major health problems, family deaths, bodily changes, loss of peer relationships, and unreachable goals. However, the person also faces these challenges with increased life experiences, stronger self-efficacy, improved problem-solving skills, and an increased understanding of the environment and ability to make sense of difficulties that cannot be resolved. At midlife many individuals also face challenges with more power and status than they held as younger women and men. How midlife is lived and experienced depends on genetics, health, life experiences, economics, psychosocial support, beliefs, perceptions, culture, and macropolicies. Age represents only one factor in determining how the person develops and behaves.

Mental health settings are one context in which social workers encounter middle-aged adults. This chapter has applied the developmental, ecological-systems approach to understanding depression in middle adulthood. In middle adulthood, major depression can prevent an individual from taking leadership roles within the family, profession, and community. This lack of fit between individual functioning and social and cultural expectations can be demoralizing to the individual and devastating to the family, and can result in social stigma. Self-help and advocacy groups such as NAMI have played important roles in educating the public and advocating adequate interventions for individuals suffering from mental illness. With appropriate treatment, most individuals with major depression can experience significant relief from their symptoms and lead healthy, happy lives. Such treatment usually involves both medication and therapy. Untreated depression can have devastating consequences, including suicide.

Study and Discussion Questions

1. Ashford et al. (2001, p. 470) state that "midlife is different from other developmental phases in that it is less affected by biological maturation. Indeed, adults are most affected by their own experiences." To what extent do you agree or disagree? In responding, consider

developmental changes in biological, psychological, and social factors within cultural and historical context.

2. What is menopause? How might culture affect a woman's experience of menopause?

3. What is depression? In responding, consider diagnostic criteria, as well as discussion of biological, psychological, and social characteristics.

4. What are some of the consequences of major depression during midlife?

5. What are some of the roles of the mental health social worker in intervening with depressed clients?

6. To return to our opening examples, what are some options for intervention with Joe and Maria? What are some of the roles that social workers might assume?

Resources

Interested students can supplement this chapter with these web-based resources.

The John D. and Catherine T. MacArthur Foundation's Research Network on Successful Midlife Development offers readers authoritative information and suggestions for improved quality of life based on research findings. Available at http://midmac.med.harvard.edu/.

Planned Parenthood offers sound information for understanding and living with menopause. Their website also provides links to other web resources for women. Available at http://www.plannedparenthood.org/health-topics/womens-health/menopause-4807.htm.

The website Medscape offers articles on physical and mental health well-being by leading researchers and clinicians. Available at http://www.medscape.com/welcome/resource.

An excellent site for learning about women's health during midlife is the Melbourne Women's Midlife Health Project. This is a large sample study using an excellent research design for investigating women's health during midlife and menopause. The University of Melbourne initiated the study because of Australia's lack of adequate information about this important period of a woman's health. Available at http://www.nari.unimelb.edu.au/whap.

References

American Heart Association. (2003). *Heart attack, stroke & cardiac arrest warning signs*. Retrieved from http://www.heart.org/heartorg

American Psychiatric Association. (2000). *Diagnostic and statistical manual of mental disorders IV* (text revision). Washington, DC: Author.

Andreasen, N. C., & Black, D. W. (2000). *Introductory textbook of psychiatry*. Washington, DC: American Psychiatric Publishing.

Ashford, J., LeCroy, C. W., & Lortie, K. (2001). *Human behavior in the social environment: A multidimensional perspective* (2nd ed.). Belmont, CA: Wadsworth/ Thomson Learning.

Baldwin, D. S., & Birtwistle, J. (2002). *An atlas of depression*. London: Parthenon Publishing Group.

Berk, L. E. (2009). *Development through the lifespan* (5th ed.). Boston: Allyn & Bacon.

Black, D. W. (1999). *Bad boys, bad men: Confronting antisocial personality disorder*. New York: Oxford University Press.

Bongar, B. (2002). *The suicidal patient: Clinical and legal standards of care* (2nd ed.). Washington, DC: American Psychological Association.

Borysenko, J. (1997). *A woman's book of life*. New York: Penguin.

Cummings, J. L., & Mega, M. S. (2003). *Neuropsychiatry and behavioral neuroscience*. New York: Oxford University Press.

DeNavas-Walt, C., Proctor, B. D., & Mills, R. J. (2010). *Income, poverty, and health insurance coverage in the United States* (U.S. Census Bureau, Current Population Reports, Publication No. P60-238). Washington, DC: U.S. Government Printing Office. Retrieved from http://www.census.gov/prod/2010pubs/p60-238.pdf

DePaulo, J. R. (2002). *Understanding depression: What we know and what you can do about it*. New York: Wiley.

Dulmus, C., & Roberts, A. (2008). Mental illness: Adults. In T. Mizrahi & L. Davis (Eds.), *Encyclopedia of social work* (20th ed., Vol. 3, pp. 237–242). Washington, DC: NASW Press; New York: Oxford University Press.

Goodwin, F. K., & Jamison, K. R. (1990). *Manic depressive illness*. New York: Oxford University Press.

Gotlib, I. H., & Hammen, C. L. (Eds.). (2002). *Handbook of depression*. New York: Guilford.

Greeno, C. (2008). Mental health: Overview. In T. Mizrahi & L. Davis (Eds.), *Encyclopedia of social work* (20th ed., Vol. 3, pp. 221–232). Washington, DC: NASW Press; New York: Oxford University Press.

Hales, D., & Hales, R. (1995). *Caring for the mind: The comprehensive guide to mental health*. New York: Bantam Books.

Hooker, K., & Kaus, C. R. (1994). Health-related possible selves in young and middle adulthood. *Psychology of Aging, 9*(1), 126–133.

Jamison, K. R. (1995). *An unquiet mind*. New York: Vintage Books.

Jamison, K. R. (1999). *Night falls fast*. New York: Vintage Books.

Jones, I., Kent, L., & Craddock, N. (2002). Genetics of affective disorders. In P. McGuffin, M. Owen, & I. I. Gottesman (Eds.), *Psychiatric genetics and genomics* (pp. 211–246). New York: Oxford University Press.

Kalidindi, S., & McGuffin, P. (2003). The genetics of affective disorders: Present and future. In R. Plomin, I. W. DeFries, C. McGuffin, & P. McGuffin (Eds.), *Behavioral genetics in the postgenomic era* (pp. 481–502). Washington, DC: American Psychological Association.

Lachman, M. E., & James, J. B. (Eds.). (1997). *Multiple paths of midlife development*. Chicago: University of Chicago Press.

Levinson, D. J. (1986). A conception of adult development. *American Psychologist, 41*, 3–13.

Levinson, D. J., & Levinson, J. D. (1978). *The seasons of a man's life*. New York: Knopf.

Levinson, D. J., & Levinson, J. D. (1996). *The seasons of a woman's life*. New York: Knopf.

Lin, A. (1995). Mental health overview. In R. L. Edwards (Ed.), *Encyclopedia of social work* (Vol. 2, pp. 1705-1711). Washington, DC: NASW Press.

Lock, M. (1993). *Encounter with aging: Mythologies of menopause in Japan and North America.* Berkeley: University of California Press.

Merikangas, K. R., & Stipelman, B. (2004). Genetic epidemiology of substance use disorder. In D. S. Charney & E. J. Nestler (Eds.), *Neurobiology of mental illness* (2nd ed., pp. 710-719). New York: Oxford University Press.

Merikangas, K. R., Stolar, M., Stevens, D. E., Goulet, J., Preisig, M., Fenton, B., . . . Rounsaville, B. (1998). Familial transmission of substance use disorders. *Archives of General Psychiatry, 55*(11), 973-979.

Mueser, K. T., Noordsy, D. L., Drake, R. E., & Fox, L. (2003). *Integrated treatment for dual disorders: A guide to effective practice.* New York: Guilford.

National Sleep Foundation. (2005). *2005 Sleep in America poll.* Washington, DC: Author.

Northrup, C. (1994). *Women's bodies, women's wisdom.* New York: Bantam Books.

Rapp, S. R., Espeland, M. A., Shumaker, S. A., Henderson, V. W., Brunner, R. L., Manson, J. E., . . . Bowen, D. (2003). Effects of estrogen plus progestin on global cognitive function in postmenopausal women: The women's health initiative memory study: A randomized controlled trial. *Journal of the American Medical Association, 289*(20), 2663-2672.

Sadock, B. J., & Sadock, V. A. (2003). *Synopsis of psychiatry* (9th ed.). Philadelphia: Lippincott Williams, & Wilkins.

Santrock, J. W. (2002). *Life-span development.* Boston: McGraw-Hill.

Seifert, K. L., & Hoffnung, M. (2000). *Lifespan development* (2nd ed.). Boston: Houghton Mifflin.

Shumaker, S. A., Legault, C., Rapp, S. R., Thal, L., Wallace, R. B., Ockene, J. K., . . . Wactawski-Wende, J. (2003). Estrogen plus progestin and the incidence of dementia and mild cognitive impairment in postmenopausal women: The women's health initiative memory study: A randomized controlled trial. *Journal of the American Medical Association, 289*(20), 2651-2662.

Stahl, S. M. (2000). *Essential psychopharmacology of depression and bipolar disorder.* Cambridge: Cambridge University Press.

Taylor, E. H. (1997). Serious mental illness: A biopsychosocial perspective. In R. L. Edwards (Ed.), *Encyclopedia of social work* (Supplement, 19th ed., pp. 263-273). Washington, DC: NASW Press.

Taylor, E. H. (2003). Practice methods for working with children who have biologically based disorders: A bioecological model. *Families and Society, 84,* 39-50.

Taylor, E. H. (2005). *Atlas of bipolar disorders.* London: Taylor & Francis.

Taylor, E. H., & Edwards, R. L. (1996). The role of social work in psychiatry and mental health. In B. B. Wolman (Ed.), *The encyclopedia of psychology, psychiatry and psychoanalysis* (pp. 539-541). New York: Holt.

Torrey, E. F., Bowler, A. E., Taylor, E. H., & Gottesman, I. I. (1994). *Schizophrenia and manic depressive disorder: The biological roots of mental illness as revealed by the landmark study of identical twins.* New York: Basic Books.

Torrey, E. F., & Knable, M. B. (2002). *Surviving manic depression: A manual on bipolar disorder for patients, families, and providers.* New York: Basic Books.

U.S. Indian Health Service. (2002). *Facts on Indian health disparities.* Washington, DC: U.S. Indian Health Service, Office of the Director, Public Affairs Staff.

12

Medical Social Work with Older Adults
Alzheimer's Disease

The focal system of this chapter is older adults, age approximately sixty-five years until death. During the twentieth century, the number of people age sixty-five and older in the United States rose dramatically from 3 million in 1900 to 34 million in 1998. By the middle of the twenty-first century, older adults are expected to constitute 23 percent of the U.S. population (U.S. Department of Health and Human Services, 1999).

In later adulthood, everyone experiences the inevitable physical changes of aging, dying, and death. Most individuals in the United States also experience significant losses of loved ones, physical health, or prestige. As life expectancy increases, more individuals will live for extended periods with disabilities and chronic illness. Nevertheless, for many individuals, late adulthood brings a sense of fulfillment in life, continued curiosity about the world, engagement in meaningful social and individual activities, and a desire to leave a legacy. For others, the later adult years are marked by poverty, illness, loneliness, and despair.

As the number and proportion of elderly people worldwide accelerates in coming decades, societies will face greater challenges (Lutz, Sanderson, & Scherbov, 2008). Falling birthrates in countries like Japan and greater survival of the elderly combine to dramatically shift population demographics away from youth and toward the elderly (Japan Times, 2010). An aging population generally will be burdened with more illness, making health care more expensive.

Dementia is a set of medical disorders that occur almost entirely in late adulthood and is characterized by cognitive impairment sufficient to disrupt everyday activities. It rises sharply with age, affecting approximately 1 percent of people in their sixties, doubles in rate every five years, and stabilizes at 30 percent of individuals affected in their nineties (see Berk, 2001). Following an overview of development in late adulthood, this chapter elaborates a developmental, ecological-systems analysis of the most common form of dementia, Alzheimer's disease, which accounts for 50 to 60 percent of all cases of dementia and affects approximately 15 percent of those older than eighty. Alzheimer's disease is a leading cause of death in late adulthood, accounting for 100,000 deaths per year in the United States (see Berk, 2001).

This older woman living with Alzheimer's disease can become confused and disoriented even with her family in the context of her home.

Medical social workers assist older adults and families in the contexts of hospitals, assisted living and nursing homes, and community health and mental health centers. As Alzheimer's disease progresses, the medical social worker plays an important role in a team of physicians, nurses, caregivers, and others. As you read, consider how biological, psychological, and social factors interact within specific cultural and historical contexts to influence physical health in later adulthood. What is the unique role of the medical social worker in supporting individuals with Alzheimer's disease and their families?

At the age of eighty-two, Edith Hudley, a great-grandmother with a tenth-grade education, published her first book, a social work text (Hudley, Haight, & Miller, 2003/2009). At age seventy, former president Jimmy Carter climbed Japan's Mount Fuji (Carter, 2000). These two very different people illustrate a common but often forgotten fact: later adulthood need not signal an end to productivity, potential, or quality of life. The senior years do introduce never-before-experienced limitations that require adjustment, but they can also provide many new opportunities. Although President Carter was more strategic in planning his ascents than in his younger years, the retirement years allowed him the leisure time to pursue active hobbies. Although Mrs. Hudley's stamina for work was less than in her earlier years, she was able to pass down some of the wisdom she had gained over her lifetime for subsequent generations. Advancing age forces people to make sense and meaning of new challenges and limitations. Western societies often link aging with disabilities, inactivity, and the inevitability of death. For social workers, it is more helpful to think of aging as another period of a person's life in which developmental change creates new avenues for growth and rewards, as well as hazards and limitations. While passing through the life span, we build meaning, understanding, and satisfaction by living productively within our limitations. Healthy aging requires the same process and has the same potential of rewarding individuals with new self-knowledge, relationships, and achievements. As described in boxes 12.1 through 12.4, however, substance misuse, violence, and poverty can continue to threaten healthy development in later adulthood.

BOX 12.1 VIOLENCE ACROSS THE LIFE SPAN
Elder Abuse

The U.S. Administration on Aging states that elder abuse includes physical abuse, sexual abuse, emotional or psychological abuse, financial exploitation, neglect, and self-neglect (when an older person's life, health, or safety is jeopardized by personal behaviors). A committee for the National Academy of Sciences has developed the following broad criteria for researchers and clinicians to identify elder mistreatment/abuse. It occurs when (1) intentional behaviors and actions cause harm, (2) actions or behaviors place the person at risk of serious harm, (3) a caregiver fails to provide or satisfy basic care needs, or (4) an older adult is not protected from harm. The definition places violence by strangers in a separate category, but includes abuse, neglect, exploitation, and abandonment of aged individuals by others.

Elder mistreatment and abuse occurs in many contexts, including nursing homes and assisted-living residences; poorly managed housing for the elderly; their own homes and those of relatives and neighbors; and public places. As adults age, they may become more isolated, hiding instances of abuse or neglect from the public. The National Elder Abuse Incidence Study reports these data on elder abuse:

- In a one-year period, 472,813 people sixty-five years old and older throughout the nation experienced documented abuse, neglect, and/or self-neglect.
- Elder mistreatment and abuse is highly likely to go unreported. There may be as many as four times as many mistreated and abused older people as currently reported; estimates of the true rates of elder abuse and neglect range from 2 to 10 percent (1–2 million) of the elderly population. Financial exploitation is estimated at 5 million cases.
- Women are more likely than men to be abused as elders.

- Caregivers are often perpetrators of elder abuse. Alcoholic children and those who are financially dependent on their parents have higher risks of abusing their parents.

Identifying elder mistreatment and abuse is difficult and often overlooked by professionals. Older adults often fear disclosing abuse and have difficulty reporting family members and significant others. The process of identification is further complicated because few reliable and valid assessment instruments have been developed. As a result, social worker assessments most often depend on interviews with the client, family, and community members; review of medical and emergency-room reports; and expert consultation from medical personnel.

Here are some warning signs to look for.

- bruises, pressure marks, broken bones, abrasions, and burns
- bruises around the breasts or genital area from sexual abuse
- sudden changes in financial situations
- bedsores, unattended medical needs, poor hygiene, and unusual weight loss
- behavior such as belittling, threats, and other uses of power and control by spouses
- strained or tense relationships, and frequent arguments between the caregiver and elderly person
- unexplained withdrawal from normal activities, a sudden change in alertness, and unusual depression

Culture also plays a role in elder abuse. Cultural values, beliefs, and traditions influence family members' roles and responsibilities toward one another, how decisions are made within families, how resources are distributed, and how problems are defined. Culture further influences how families cope with stress and determines if and when families will seek help from outsiders. Understanding these factors can significantly increase professionals' effectiveness. Learning which questions to ask is an important first step.

- What role do seniors play in the family? In the community?
- Who in the family is expected to provide care to frail members? What happens when they fail to do so?
- What conduct is considered abusive? Is it considered abusive to use an elder's resources for the benefit of other family members? To ignore a family member?
- With immigrant seniors, when did they come to the United States and under what circumstances? Did they come alone or with family members? Did other family members sponsor them, and if so, what resources did those family members agree to provide? What is the immigrant seniors' legal status?

- What religious beliefs, past experiences, attitudes about social service agencies or law enforcement, or social stigmas may affect community members' decisions to accept or refuse help from outsiders?
- Under what circumstances will families seek help from outsiders? To whom will they turn for help (e.g., members of the extended family, respected members of the community, religious leaders, physicians)?
- What are the trusted sources of information in the community? What television and radio stations, shows, and personalities are considered reliable? What newspapers and magazines do people read?
- How do persons with limited English-speaking or -reading skills get their information about resources?

Sources: Fulmer, Guadagno, Dyer, & Connolly, 2004; Kosberg & Garcia, 1995; Lachs & Pillemer, 2004; National Center on Elder Abuse, 2003; National Committee for the Prevention of Elder Abuse, 2003; National Research Council Panel to Review Risk and Prevalence of Elder Abuse and Neglect, 2003; Nerenberg, 1995; Tatara, 1999; *Understanding and combating elder abuse*, 1997; U.S. Administration on Aging, 1998, 2005.

BOX 12.2 SUBSTANCE MISUSE ACROSS THE LIFE SPAN

Prescription and Over-the-Counter Drug Misuse by Older Adults

Elderly people account for one-third of the population who uses prescription drugs. Misuse of prescription medication occurs when one knowingly or unknowingly takes the drug in a manner that deviates from the prescribed dose, medical instructions, or purpose approved for the drug. It includes underuse as well as overuse of medication. Epidemiologists have estimated that anywhere from 3 percent to 33 percent of older adults overuse prescription drugs, with less than 1 percent for nonmedical purposes. Overuse of prescription drugs can result in addiction, medical crisis, and even death. Misusing benzodiazepines can increase an older adult's risk for falling, automobile accidents, and memory and cognitive problems. Underuse of prescription drugs can result in an acceleration of the disease process, or chronic pain. Problems resulting from the under- or overuse of prescription drugs are serious, can reduce the older adult's quality of life, and can drain economic resources.

The misuse of prescription drugs by the elderly can be framed, at least in part, as a failure of public policy. Consider the underuse of prescription drugs. When feeling better, some older adults will try to save money by forgoing one or two dosages in order to have the drug when more severe symptoms occur. Others underuse drugs to reduce or avoid drug-induced side effects. At first glance this appears to be an individual lapse of responsibility, but consider also how few public health nurses and other person-to-person information programs are available to the public, the amount of time that is actually spent with medical professionals during outpatient office visits, how quickly medical instructions and explanations are given, and short-term memory challenges of many older adults. Think about the difficulty some older adults have in getting to the doctor or paying for the services. The medical system, payment responsibility, transportation availability, and patient-teaching methods work against many older adults, and result in mismanaged geriatric medical care.

It is important for social workers to actively address the issue of prescription and over-the-counter drug misuse. Social workers can play important roles in helping to educate older clients about their medications, developing ways for them to remember to take medications, linking them with public health services, attending doctor appointments with them, and ensuring they receive their full medical insurance benefits. Social workers also can actively advocate for universal health coverage. When a nation fails to provide universal health and prescription drug insurance, and willingly allows older citizens to live below or at the poverty line, it is predictable that medications will be improperly used.

Sources: National Institute on Drug Abuse, 2005; Paterson, Lacro, & Jeste, 1999.

BOX 12.3 POVERTY ACROSS THE LIFE SPAN
Older Americans and Poverty

As one ages, poverty becomes a greater risk. In 2007, the poverty rate for people between sixty-five and seventy-four was 9 percent. This rate increased to 10 percent for people age seventy-five to eighty-four, and 13 percent for people older than eighty-five. Older women and people of color run the highest risk of living in poverty. In 1998, 26 percent of single African-American women age sixty-five to seventy-four lived in poverty.

In 2007, 27 percent of households headed by African-American women and 20 percent headed by Hispanic women age sixty-five and older had incomes below the poverty level. In contrast, 9 percent of households headed by white women and 5 percent of households headed by white men sixty-five years and older were below the poverty level. In 2006, 38 percent of older African Americans had trouble paying for prescription medications, and 68 percent were concerned they would have trouble affording medications in the next two years.

Sources: Federal Interagency Forum on Aging-Related Statistics, 2010; Kutner, 2007.

BOX 12.4 POVERTY ACROSS THE LIFE SPAN
Social Security

In 2010, the American Association of Retired People (AARP) reported that 27 percent of African Americans (up 8 percent since 2004) age sixty-five and older receive a private pension, and only 26 percent (down 3 percent since 2004) have personal assets providing all or part of their income. The largest provider of income for aging African Americans is Social Security. Approximately 84 percent of African Americans receive Social Security retirement payments. For one in four African Americans sixty-five and older, Social Security is their only source of income. Approximately 57 percent of older African-American women's income comes from Social Security retirement payments.

Sources: American Association of Retired People, 2010; Beedon & Wu, 2003; Fleck, 2010; U.S. Census Bureau, 2010.

As the nation and world ages (see box 12.5), social workers must become stronger advocates for older adults, for example, in securing and protecting retirement income, disability benefits, and health insurance for low-income people. Although many older adults continue to live active,

BOX 12.5 CHANGING DEMOGRAPHICS

U.S. and world demographics are changing, so that older adults constitute an increasingly large segment of the population. In 2008, it was estimated that 506 million people, or 7 percent of the world's population, were older than sixty-five. Based on current trends, this number will increase to 1.3 billion (an estimated 14 percent of the world's population) by 2040. Experts believe that global aging is occurring as a result of increased life expectancy, coupled with decreased international fertility rates. In industrialized nations, the twentieth century ushered in the largest life-expectancy gains for newborn infants ever recorded, as well as effective birth control. Since about 1950, life expectancy for citizens in emerging nations has also increased. Today, Americans and most other developed nations have a life expectancy of seventy-eight to eighty years. Japan has the highest proportion of older adults in the world (22 percent).

By 2030, the number of U.S. households with people who are sixty-five years of age or older will increase from 39 million (13 percent of the U.S. population) in 2008 to approximately 72 million (20 percent of the U.S. population). It is expected that people of color will increase from 20 percent in 2008 to 41 percent in 2050. Between 2008 and 2050, the number of African-American older adults is projected to increase from 9 percent to 12 percent. The number of older adults in almost all ethnic and majority populations is growing, but the distribution of males and females is expected to remain almost the same.

In the next twenty-five years, the world's developing countries will experience the largest increase of older adults. If migration patterns do not dramatically change, the number of people over sixty-five in the industrial developing nations will almost triple. The growing number of older people will be slowed only in the poorest parts of the world. Sub-Saharan Africa currently has, and is projected to continue to have, just over 4 percent of its population over the age of sixty-five. Rates of mortality caused by disease, poverty, poor sanitation, inadequate diets, unavailability of medical services, wars, and other problems are not projected to decrease.

An aging population has implications for human development, research, policies, and social work practice. Social workers need to be aware of the ways life-threatening illnesses have changed, the impact of illness on an older adult's quality of life, who in North America dies before reaching the national expected age, and the importance of advocating policies to increase and improve the lives of people living in the world's poorest nations. Moreover, as a result of wars, poverty, and other global factors, a growing number of aging political refugees and immigrants will find their way to North America and other industrialized countries. In addition, an unknown number of people illegally entering the United States to work will remain into their later adulthood. Specialized social work skills are required to help the undocumented aging person traverse ever-changing immigration regulations, health-care and mental health–care systems, and Social Security requirements; locate affordable housing and transportation; and meet other social welfare needs.

Source: Federal Interagency Forum on Aging-Related Statistics, 2010; Kinsella & He, 2009; U.S. Census Bureau International database, 2004.

productive lives, many people over the age of sixty-five experience health problems that limit their functioning. Epidemiological studies indicate that 80 percent of Americans sixty-five and older have at least one chronic medical disorder, and 50 percent suffer from two or more serious long-term illnesses. These illnesses are multifaceted and have reciprocal relationships: for example, those who are obese have more chronic pain, and those with chronic pain experience more depression and anxiety (McCarthy, Bigal, Katz, Derby, & Lipton, 2009). Obesity, dietary choices, and reduced exercise also contribute to the onset of diabetes in adulthood. Nearly one in five North Americans over sixty-five has diabetes, and this rate is expected to double by 2050 (Centers for Disease Control and Prevention, 2003). The increasing rate of diabetes is one example of the increasing illness burden for the elderly that likely will make health care more costly and bring associated complications, such as chronic pain, poor vision, heart disease, and strokes (Boyle, Thompson, Gregg, Barker, & Williamson, 2010).

As a result of the hardships of poverty and racism, older adults in our expanding communities of color generally experience more health problems, as well as more difficulties accessing medical services, than do older, middle-income whites. For example, American Indian and Alaskan Native people face death 4.4 years earlier than all other North American ethnic groups (Grim, 2002; U.S. Indian Health Service, 2001, 2002), signaling a need to attend to the health needs of these and other vulnerable older adults.

MEDICAL SOCIAL WORK WITH OLDER ADULTS

Given the increased vulnerability to disease, disability, and poverty of aging adults, it is not surprising that social workers encounter many aging adults in health-care settings such as hospitals, assisted-living facilities, and nursing homes. **Medical social work** (or health-care social work) is a subspecialization of social work that focuses on the impact of disease and disability on individuals of all ages, their families, and communities. It emerged in the beginning of the twentieth century when Richard Cabot and Ida Cannon introduced medical social services at Massachusetts General Hospital. There, professionally trained social workers helped patients and their families deal with personal and social factors that affect disease onset and recovery (Otis-Green, 2008). Today, much of what medical social workers do still involves helping patients and families cope with and adapt to changes brought about by illness, medical treatment, and disability. Hospitals remain a major context for medical social work. In addition, medical social workers practice in outpatient primary-care settings, home health care, long-term care facilities, public health departments, community health-care clinics, school-based health clinics, and associations focused on specific illnesses (e.g., HIV and AIDS consortia; see Berkman, 2011, for a historical overview).

To be successful in a medical setting, social workers must develop knowledge that is specific to diseases or populations at risk, including knowledge of various diseases, treatments, and their outcomes. It is equally important to understand the individual's and the family's perception of the disease, its causes and cures, and the family's resources for coping. How will the individual and family handle the stress of illness? How will the individual and family obtain necessary follow-up health care? Social workers use bio-psycho-social-spiritual assessments to understand how individuals adjust to illness and medical treatment, and to define what social health-care needs must be addressed. Services provided by medical social workers may be preventive, developmental, or remedial (e.g., social risk screening, discharge planning, psychosocial intervention, health education and referral, and advocacy).

In the following case, a medical social worker practicing in a city hospital tackles the complex task of assisting an elderly woman suffering from dementia, and her family.

Mrs. P., an eighty-five-year-old African American, was taken by ambulance to an emergency room in Missouri, following complaints of dizziness and difficulty staying awake. She was accompanied by a middle-aged friend with whom she was visiting. Mrs. P., who was visiting from her home in Texas, could not remember where she lived, which city or state she was in, how long she had been with her friend, the time or day of the week, or the season. She could not remember the name of her primary-care physician, or if she was on any medication. Mrs. P. was hospitalized for three days with dehydration and kidney failure. The friend reported that she had driven to Texas for Mrs. P. because Mrs. P. was deeply depressed and isolated, living alone with her husband of twenty years in a low-income, inner-city high-rise apartment. Her mood had improved greatly since coming to Missouri, and she did not wish to return to Texas. Her friend reported that Mrs. P. was taking no medication and provided the name and phone number of an adult son in Iowa and Mrs. P.'s husband. The social worker called the husband and learned that he, too, was ill and living with dementia. She then called the adult son, who reported that Mrs. P. had been diagnosed with dementia three years ago and, at that time, was placed on medications for high blood pressure and glaucoma. He had not visited her in the past three years and was unaware of the extent of her current dementia or his stepfather's illness. The social worker talked with Mrs. P.'s son regarding a long-term plan for her health care. He agreed to make arrangements for Mrs. P. and her husband to move into an assisted-living facility near his home where he could monitor their care. Prior to discharge, a medical social worker met with Mrs. P. and her friend to develop a plan for short-term care following release from the hospital. The friend agreed to take Mrs. P. to follow-up health-care appointments the following week, and to drive her to Iowa to meet her son.

Ten days later, the medical social worker received a call from Mrs. P.'s friend, who was very concerned. Although follow-up health care was uneventful, Mrs. P. had had an argument with her son and was refusing to go to Iowa. Instead, she wanted to return to her husband in Texas. It was clear, however, that Mrs. P. could not remember to take her medicine and was having difficulties with basic tasks of everyday living. The medical social worker arranged to meet with Mrs. P. and her friend that afternoon. She then researched services in Houston and contacted an agency providing home care and transportation services for seniors, as well as arranging volunteer opportunities to alleviate social isolation and depression. That afternoon, Mrs. P. resisted the need for services, expressing the opinion that "When I can no longer do for myself, God should just carry me away." The social worker spoke with her at length, and Mrs. P. agreed to allow a home-care provider into her home once a day to monitor her medicine, and to help her get to doctor's appointments. She expressed excitement about participating in volunteer opportunities with children. Unfortunately, Mrs. P. and her husband did not follow through with the referrals. At last contact, they were living alone in a low-income, inner-city apartment in Houston.

As this vignette illustrates, medical social workers can play an important role in the health care of older adults. Mrs. P. urgently needed to be stabilized, medically. During her hospital stay, however, it became clear that her dementia had become a barrier to independent living. An intelligent, independent, and strong-willed woman with a largely intact long-term memory, her short-term memory presented serious problems to everyday living, including taking necessary medications. The medical social worker assisted Mrs. P. and her family in developing a plan for her to maintain as much independence as possible for as long as possible while meeting her medical and safety needs. The reality, however, is that it ultimately is the decision of the client to accept or refuse services. Mrs. P., despite her emerging mental

Medical social workers help individuals adapt and cope with illness and treatment.

impairments, retained her power of attorney. Her life and sense of self had been built upon being a leader and teacher of younger generations, and at last contact, receiving assistance with daily living was not acceptable to her or her husband. The medical social worker, although unsuccessful in initiating services, did successfully alert Mrs. P.'s relatives to her deteriorating state as well as the availability of services when her needs become urgent.

OVERVIEW OF DEVELOPMENT IN LATER ADULTHOOD

Across the life span, developmental scientists study aspects of the human experience that may be universal and those that may reflect cultural and individual variation. Many stage theorists focus on universal aspects of human experience. Erikson describes a final stage of psychosocial development as occurring after the age of sixty-five. During this time, individuals confront the crisis of identity versus despair, as they look back and review their lives. This review may result in feeling at peace with oneself and the world, and an absence of regret or recrimination. Alternatively, the individual may experience feelings of wasted opportunities and regrets (Erikson, 1998).

Adults in their later years also confront a wide variety of other issues that reflect and contribute to cultural and individual variation in development. As life spans increase, the period of later adulthood can range from twenty to thirty years. During this time, much change and development can occur. Clearly, the healthy sixty-five-year-old working full-time to support grandchildren has very different needs from the frail, dependent eighty-five-year-old. To more clearly represent this diversity, some scholars argue that later adulthood should be divided into periods (e.g., Santrock, 2002). Individuals age sixty-five through seventy-four could be considered "young-old." They may be active within their community and with their families and friends. Many are employed part- or full-time. During this period, however, more and more individuals begin to experience chronic illness, and the phenomenon of women outliving their spouse emerges. Individuals between seventy-four and eighty-five could be considered "middle-old." They typically live more constricted lives; experience more physical impairments such as decreased hearing, vision, and response time; and have more chronic diseases, such as arthritis and cardiovascular disease. They also experience more stress due to loss of spouses, relatives, and friends. Some, however, continue to contribute to the arts, literature, science, and politics. The "old-old," age eighty-five and older, are the most dependent and frail, and experience more disabilities and chronic illnesses (see Ashford & LeCroy, 2010). They also are the most rapidly growing segment of the population. In 2008 they constituted 13 percent of the population, but by 2050, their numbers are projected to increase by 500 percent. The population of individuals age one hundred or older also will increase. By 2025, one in twenty-six Americans can expect to live to one hundred, compared with only one in two hundred in 2000 (Hooyman, 2008).

Another way to think about diversity in later adulthood is to consider functional rather than chronological age. Functional age refers to the ability to perform activities of daily living (ADLs), such as cooking, dressing, and bathing, which require cognitive and physical well-being. ADLs typically determine whether older adults can continue to live in their own homes, as most prefer (Hooyman, 2008). There is considerable variation in individuals' functional age during each period of later adulthood, because of genetics, environmental factors, diseases, nutrition, and availability of medical care. The aging process can be conceptualized as consisting of chronological, biological, psychological, and social age (Santrock, 2002). These components are not separate, but can be understood as a gestalt. A functional assessment of older adults will include attention to strengths, such as emotional control, problem-solving skills, memory, mobility, social network, economic stability, and physical health. For example, a socially isolated, depressed sixty-five-year-old suffering from several chronic medical conditions may be functionally older than a person who is eighty and is healthy and active in community and family. It is important to keep in mind, however, that all components of a functional assessment are not equal. An older adult may have a high level of emotional and cognitive functioning, and good economic stability, but be in the final stage of congestive heart failure. Unfortunately, the person's strengths—intact cognitive, emotional, and eco-

Many older adults continue to lead active, productive lives. This seventy-five-year-old man enjoys outdoor work with his eighteen-year-old grandson.

nomic systems—cannot compensate for an aged circulatory system. Social workers need to consider older adults' functional age to avoid making decisions from a stereotypical perspective of aging.

A variety of factors are related to diversity in functional age during later adulthood. For example, the consequences of racial and gender inequities, which limit opportunities from the beginning of life, intensify in later adulthood. They result in increased economic and health disparities for older women and people of color. In 1960, about 25 percent of older Americans lived in poverty; this number has declined to about 10 percent in recent decades (He, Sengupta, Velkoff, & DeBarros, 2005). This drop in overall poverty rate, however, masks growing rates of poverty within particular groups. Older women are almost twice as likely to live in poverty as are older men, and older African Americans and Latinos are approximately twice as likely to be poor as are whites. Older adults living in larger cities, the South, and rural communities also are more likely to be impoverished (Hooyman, 2008; Takamura, 2008). Low socioeconomic status is associated with poorer health outcomes across ethnic groups, but older people of color consistently have worse health outcomes than do older whites (Gardner & Gelman, 2008).

As discussed in chapter 10, cultural context also impacts aging. For example, in some cultural contexts the elderly are revered as wise, and in others a burden on their families (Sokolovsky, 2009). The changing demographics of aging in different countries also will impact older adults. Countries that are predicted to have larger youth populations in the coming decades, such as Angola and Afghanistan, will face very different issues than countries that are going gray, such as Japan and Sweden. A youth bulge can make a younger population restive if it leads to chronically high unemployment, while aging countries will need to import younger workers or utilize technology (e.g., robotics) to meet the needs of their elderly. International policy will need to address future conflicts over resources and migration as countries shift their demographics over the next few decades (Zelenev, 2006).

Biological Factors: Physical Aging, Death, and Dying

Physical aging begins early in adulthood. By the age of thirty, a person's bones have reached their maximum growth, and the process of slow deterioration toward brittleness has started. After thirty years of age, internal body organs lose their ability to function by approximately 1 percent per year, resulting in a 25 percent to 40 percent loss of peak organ functionality between thirty and eighty years of age. This slow, ongoing erosion places people at a higher risk for debilitating and life threatening diseases such as diabetes, heart disease, and arthritis (Smith, 2003). Box 12.6 lists a number of health problems that affect older adults.

> **BOX 12.6 PHYSICAL PROBLEMS WITH ADVANCING AGE**
>
> - Changes in cardiovascular and peripheral nervous systems cause older adults to have slower motor and sensory responses.
> - Circulatory and digestive systems change.
> - Skin wrinkles, and pigmentation is irregular.
> - Bones weaken and have less mass; osteoporosis can develop.
> - Muscle strength and speed decreases.
> - The respiratory system is less effective.
> - Sight and hearing decrease.
> - After seventy years of age, taste and smell sensitivity decreases.
> - Arthritis is a common chronic problem.
> - More than 58 percent of older adults die of heart disease, cancer, or stroke.
>
> _____
>
> Sources: Centers for Disease Control and Prevention, 2005; Smith & Gove, 2005.

Although physical aging is inevitable, good prevention efforts can enhance the quality of life in later adulthood. For many in the United States, aging is more difficult than necessary because illness prevention is not emphasized until people are between forty and sixty years of age. However, prevention for major physical disorders needs to begin no later than the age of thirty (Smith, 2003). The possibility of good health throughout the life span can be increased by routinely sleeping seven to eight hours; consistently eating a healthy breakfast; rarely snacking; keeping body weight within no more than over 20 percent or below 10 percent of what is medically recommended; routine, systematic, and safe exercise; no more than moderate use of alcohol; and no use of tobacco (Smith, 2003).

Despite the quality of prevention efforts, the final stage of physical development, of course, is death. There are several physical signs of the process of dying. Beginning one to three months before death, the person may sleep more and eat less. One or two weeks before death, the person may become disoriented, confused, or agitated; sleep more; and eat very little. The dying person may also experience increased perspiration, changes in skin color to pale yellow with bluish hands and feet, and irregular breathing and pulse. Days or hours before death, these signs intensify. The dying person may experience a surge in energy and be more alert, eat and socialize, and then slip into a coma. Hands, feet, and legs become blotchy and purplish, pulse is hard to find, and breathing becomes very irregular with long pauses between breaths. Eventually, the dying person becomes unresponsive, and breathing stops (Ashford & LeCroy, 2010).

Psychological and Social Factors: Coming to Terms with Death

The actual process of dying is a psychological and social process, as well as a physical process. Individuals, their families, and friends are confronted with and respond to mortality and loss. In her classic work *On Death and Dying*, Elisabeth Kübler-Ross (1969) describes the psychological aspects of dying, based upon years of interviewing and observing people dealing with their mortality.

- *Denial.* The person attempts to convince herself or himself that the situation is not hopeless, that death is not certain. Often denial results in an emotional explosion of energy in an attempt to prove that medical reports are incorrect or a search for alternative treatments.

- *Anger.* It is not unusual for people facing death to experience periods of anger. They may feel cheated, alone, and lacking understanding. They may be angry at people in general or specifically at family members, the medical profession, or God. Sometimes, the dying person is simply angry, unable to identify or label the subject of the anger.

- *Bargaining.* The person may try to bargain with God, promising that, if spared from death, they will live in service of the most needy. Others may try bargaining with medical personnel for experimental treatments or illegal medications believed to have curing powers. For others, the bargaining is in the form of requests and hopes to live long enough to see a special event, such as a birth, marriage, or graduation.

- *Depression.* When there is no hope, the person may experience an overwhelming sense of depression and hopelessness. The depressed person may think obsessively about past events, recalling and wishing things had been different, or focus on feeling embarrassed because self-care and personal dignity have slipped away. Depression can also appear as grieving for the lost future. Individuals may become sad and anxious that their dreams and relationships are ending. They may also worry about the future well-being and financial care of loved ones.

- *Acceptance.* The sting and fear of death primarily disappear. The person at a minimum acknowledges that death cannot be escaped, and often has made existential sense and meaning of the situation. Not all people reach this stage.

Originally, these stages were presented by Kübler-Ross as progressive. Today, most professionals recognize that they can occur in any order, they can be repeated numerous times, and some people never experience all the stages. Furthermore, certain stages may be more prominent at various phases in the life cycle (e.g., acceptance may be more difficult to achieve when death occurs at a younger age). Later adulthood seems to be a time when many individuals come to terms with their inevitable death. Compared to middle-aged adults, older adults generally have less fear of death. Perhaps this is because many older adults have experienced the death of friends and family members (Ashford & LeCroy, 2010), and their own death may be perceived as relatively normal and expected. An individual's psychological experience of death and dying may be profoundly affected by social relationships (e.g., a surviving spouse, child, or friend) and how significant others respond to the dying person and their own imminent loss.

When social workers support clients who are facing life's end, or their grieving families and friends, confirming and discovering each individual's unique emotions, rationalizations, fears, and beliefs related to death can be extremely important. To prepare for this role, it is helpful to reflect upon how our own beliefs about death and dying relate to those of our clients. Beliefs shape the very tone, goals, and motivations that direct our behavior and emotional responses. Beliefs can make us try to embrace or hide from death, to view it as a natural process or an enemy. Understanding how our own beliefs are similar to, or different from, those of our clients can minimize hurtful conflict and facilitate appropriate, effective support during what, for many, is an emotionally charged time of transition. The following observations and belief statements are provided to help social workers establish a framework and tone for guiding individuals who are in the process of dealing with death. These statements, while not comprehensive, provide basic boundaries and ideas for counseling and talking with clients about the end of life. While reading the statements, consider (1) the extent to which the statement matches your own observations and beliefs; (2) the emotions, anxieties, and thoughts each statement stirs; (3) whether you agree or disagree with these statements; and (4) which beliefs you would add, leave out, or change.

- Death is final, the end of dreams, plans, and personal and social development.
- People across all cultures deal with loss of life within both established social norms and their personal psyches, reflecting that death is universal yet markedly unique for each individual and family.
- The issues of spirituality, life after death, meaning of death, and use of religious and spiritual leaders and artifacts are highly charged beliefs and concepts that can cause pain and hardships if they are not addressed within the needs and belief systems of each client— if you do not understand the cultural or religious practice, do not fake it.

- It is the social worker's responsibility to identify the client's belief, and provide appropriate cultural and religious leaders, rather than trying to personally bridge all of the client's needs.

- The reality of death often changes how a person previously thought that she or he would respond when faced with death, and the new perceptions may change how the person chooses to use her or his fleeting time, and final wishes or directives.

- Cultural norms, expectations, and death-related ceremonies may or may not help an individual make sense and meaning of the loss and resolve grief.

- Grieving is linked to both culture and personal perceptions, beliefs, and realities.

- There are concrete legal, personal, financial, and emotional tasks that must be completed before death, at the time of death, and after the funeral is over.

- Unexpected death may or may not create a greater level of crisis and shock for the survivors than an expected death.

- It is the social worker's responsibility to provide as much or as little assistance, support, and crisis intervention as needed.

- Regardless of the available support, each person must individually explore, confront, and resolve the pain and void created by death.

- Death is emotionally painful. There are no words, symbols, beliefs, or interventions that erase the pain or reduce the magnitude of the event.

- Some mourners need attention for an extended period after the funeral, while others require respect, space, and time away from professionals.

- The person does not have to grieve or accept death the way others expect.

- Many, but not all, surviving family members would benefit from social work assessments repeated over months, and even years, to more quickly identify and prevent them from spiraling into poverty or a major mental disorder such as depression.

Clearly, counseling individuals facing their own death or the death of a loved one is a challenge. To be effective, professional social workers must understand themselves and know how to handle difficult interpersonal communications before intervening with clients about death. Spend a little time thinking about how you would handle requests that go against your own values or ethics. Let's say that you believe strongly that a person must believe in Jesus to reach heaven, and a Jewish client states that his suffering is done, today he is with God. Do you validate the grieving person, remain silent, or gently explain your beliefs? What do you do if you do not believe in God and prayer, and your client asks you to lead the family in a prayer for the dying person?

Research underscores the complexity of individuals' diverse responses to grief, and hence of grief counseling. There is no one correct way to grieve, and so no one correct strategy for counseling the bereaved. Some individuals openly express their emotional pain and benefit from talking. Traditional grief counseling assumes that this pathway—talking about, processing, and working through the grief—is necessary to a healthy recovery. Some researchers, however, question this generalization. Many people do not require formal grief work to overcome a loss, and insisting on processing grief actually may worsen symptoms, trigger rumination, and increase or induce depression in some people (Bonanno & Kaltman, 1999; Bonanno, Keltner, Holen, & Horowitz, 1995; Wortman & Silver, 1989). Bonanno and Kaltman (1999) present an alternative to traditional grief counseling in which the social worker helps the client

- evaluate or define how the death has created major life difficulties (i.e., help clients determine and examine life's realities created by the loss);
- regulate the conscious processing of and emotional reaction to the loss by employing relaxation methods, thought-stopping techniques, distraction, or other cognitive-behavioral methods;
- learn how an attachment and connection with the deceased can be continued rather than severed (e.g., through memories and rituals); and
- use laughter and positive emotions to break up extended periods of negative thoughts or feelings during the bereavement.

Lindstrøm (2002) concurs that grief counseling should not push people into an extended process, rumination, and long review of negative emotions. However, some people may expend considerable energy avoiding thoughts about the loss, and diverting or avoiding their feelings. Lindstrøm suggests that counselors need to take a middle-of-the-road perspective that validates sadness and distress but does not encourage clients to become overwhelmed or lost in negative emotions and behaviors.

Sociocultural-Historical Context: Caring for the Elderly and Dying

As with other developmental processes, sociocultural and historical contexts shape our interpretation and experience of aging and death. Western society generally places responsibility for adapting on the aging person;

that is, public opinion and professional assessments focus on the aging individual's physical health and psychological adjustment. Yet an individual's negative perceptions, motivation problems, and reduced activity may stem more from environmental than from psychological or neurological deficits. Within the community, work force, and family, the person can face age bias, stigma, and a lack of meaningful opportunities. Physiological changes occurring with age can come into conflict with cultural priorities and values (e.g., values emphasizing youthful appearance, energy, and productivity over wisdom and experience). When this occurs, older adults are tempted to deny the realities of their physical condition. Furthermore, when older adults are devalued by society, care for the elderly and dying may be compromised.

In contemporary Western society, the care of many elderly and dying people has become depersonalized. Before 1940, families in the United States generally cared for older adults at home (Kaplan, 1995). Today, 80 percent of all deaths in the United States take place in hospitals, nursing homes, or other institutions (DeSpelder & Strickland, 2002). Furthermore, because of our mobile society, key family members and friends often cannot be present when death occurs. Professionals also play a role in the depersonalization of death. Almost immediately after a person dies, medical, police, emergency-care providers, and others stop referring to the deceased by name. Bobby Jones becomes the "corpse," the "body," or a morgue identification number.

The way in which we experience our final days is affected not only by practices within a broader cultural and historical context, but by our particular position within that context and our interpersonal relationships. In her beautiful and moving portrayal of her mother's dying and death, Simone de Beauvoir (1965) draws our attention to the importance of personal care, and to the role of social class in the experience of dying. Beauvoir described the horror of her mother's final hours. Responding to Beauvoir's distress at her mother's suffering, a nurse commented, "But, Madam, I assure you it was a very easy death" (p. 88). Beauvoir goes on to reflect:

> For indeed, comparatively speaking, her death was an easy one. "Don't leave me in the power of brutes." I thought of all those who have no one to make that appeal to: what agony it must be to feel oneself a defenseless thing, utterly at the mercy of indifferent doctors and overworked nurses. No hand on the forehead when terror seizes them; no sedative as soon as pain begins to tear them; no lying prattle to fill the silence of the void . . . Even today—why?—there are horrible agonizing deaths. And then in the public wards, when the last hour is coming near, they put a screen round the dying man's bed: he has seen this screen round other beds that were empty the next day: he knows. I pictured Maman, blinded for hours by the black sun that no one can look at directly: the horror of her staring eyes with the dilated pupils. She had a very easy death; an upper-class death. (pp. 94–95)

Global Perspective on Death and Dying

Simone de Beauvoir's memoir draws our attention to political and societal factors that impact death and dying. If we expand our perspective, similar factors may operate at a global level. Demographers have documented that the leading causes of death for older people living in the industrialized world have shifted from infectious diseases and rapid onset severe illnesses to chronic and degenerative physical and mental disorders. In North America and Europe, death more often occurs from cardiovascular diseases and cancer, followed by respiratory diseases and injuries. In contrast, infectious and parasitic diseases cause the most deaths in Africa (Kinsella & Velkoff, 2001; World Health Organization, 2002). With the exception of HIV, which rages in many parts of Africa, existing medical science, manufacturing technology, sanitation knowledge, and modern distribution methods could erase much of the human suffering and premature deaths across the continent of Africa and other impoverished regions. In a global society, silence is not acceptable when people are dying from preventable illnesses like diarrhea, malaria, common childhood diseases, poor prenatal care, and treatable infections. For people in poor nations, the probability that life will be ended because of an acute, but treatable, illness is greatly increased. In industrialized nations, the odds are greater that individuals will reach an advanced age and be forced to learn to live for an extended period with chronic disorders, various levels of pain, and disabilities (Kinsella & Velkoff, 2001; World Health Organization, 2002).

ALZHEIMER'S DISEASE: DEVELOPMENTAL, ECOLOGICAL-SYSTEMS ANALYSIS

Among the various physical changes associated with aging, many people find changes in cognitive functioning most frightening, especially the possibility of developing dementia (National Council of the Aging, 2002). Therefore, it is important and comforting to note that a variety of intellectual functions remain intact or continue to develop into late adulthood. These intellectual functions include comprehension, vocabulary, verbal skills dependent on word knowledge, and verbal reasoning. There is no denying, however, that brain changes do occur with aging and that these changes do affect some aspects of cognitive functioning, particularly information-processing speed, accuracy, flexibility, memory, and verbal fluency (Raz, 2002).

Some older adults will develop a form of dementia, an umbrella term that covers a set of disorders that result in a progressive loss of intellectual functions. Common diagnoses of dementia include Alzheimer's, vascular, Huntington's, and AIDS dementia (Ropper & Samuels, 2009). Dementia is characterized by the diminishing of intellectual abilities such as short-term memory, judgment, and language. Personality changes also may occur: for example, a formerly outgoing person becomes withdrawn, a well-groomed person becomes disheveled, a sharp person becomes dull, or a socially sensitive person becomes moody and angry (Tobin, 1997). It is important that older adults experiencing what appear to be early signs of dementia receive a thorough medical exam to rule out a variety of other medical conditions that can result in confusion and various cognitive problems, but that can be resolved with proper medical care. For example, memory difficulties can be increased by poorly regulated blood sugar or reduced glucose tolerance (Convit, Wolf, Tarshish, & de Leon, 2003). Major depression commonly leads to low energy, poor memory and concentration, and irritability in the elderly, which clinicians sometimes call "pseudodementia" (Caine, 1981). Acute or chronic pain (Brown, 2009), hypothyroidism, and malnutrition (Fowler & Scadding, 2003) are other common and reversible causes of impaired cognition. Because the elderly are often on many medications, one of the first things to consider when they display altered mental states is medication side effects (e.g., Dunn, Adams, & Adams, 2008). Making a reliable diagnosis, and distinguishing between treatable and untreatable forms of cognitive impairment, is very important and usually requires an evaluation by a specialist in geriatrics, neurology, psychiatry, or neuropsychology.

Alzheimer's disease is the most common and well-known type of dementia. Behaviorally, Alzheimer's disease is characterized by a slow progression from "islets of confusion to total confusion" (Tobin, 1997, p. 17) and eventually results in death in anywhere from three to twenty years. Alzheimer's disease was identified in 1907 by Alois Alzheimer, a German neurologist. He described a case of a fifty-one-year-old woman whose intellectual functioning progressively deteriorated. Over a period of four years, she became bedridden, incontinent, and died. An autopsy showed that her brain tissue contained neurofibrillary tangles and amyloid plaques (described below), features recognized today as neuropathologic indicators of Alzheimer's disease (Tobin, 1997).

In the United States, Alzheimer's disease has become a major cause of disability among older adults (Tobin, 1997), and a leading cause of death in later adulthood (Berk, 2001). It almost always starts after the age of fifty, and most cases are genetically linked (Cummings & Mega, 2003). Only 2 to 3 percent of sixty-five-year-olds have Alzheimer's disease, but after age sixty-five the number of cases doubles every five years (Turner, 2003). In 1990 there were approximately 4 million people in the United States with the disease. In 2050, if life span and population growth continue to increase and effective medical interventions are not developed, social work and medical services will be needed for approximately 14 million North Americans living with Alzheimer's disease (Turner, 2003).

Biological Factors

Alzheimer's disease results from major structural and chemical changes in the brain. Many neurofibrillary tangles develop inside of neurons. These are bundles of collapsed and twisted neural structures. Outside of the neuron, amyloid plaques develop. These are deposits of material from dead neurons that are toxic to and destroy surrounding neurons and their communication networks. Although some neurofibrillary tangles and amyloid plaques are present in the brains of healthy middle-aged and older people, they are much less abundant and widely distributed. In addition to structural changes in the brain, Alzheimer's disease is characterized by chemical changes, specifically lowered levels of neurotransmitters necessary for communication between neurons. These brain changes progressively rob clients of memory, problem-solving skills, insight, control of moods, and, finally, life itself.

Psychological Factors

Alzheimer's disease advances in three behavioral stages, with each new stage marked by an increase in symptom severity and new problems. It may first appear as a personality change. The person may become indifferent and apathetic toward events, situations, and people that previously created a variety of emotions and behavioral responses. The person may become anxious and prone to angry outbursts. These personality changes are triggered by emerging cognitive deficits, which cause uncertainty and compromise social behavior.

Cognitive deficits in the early stages of Alzheimer's disease involve language, memory, visual spatial skills, abstract thinking, and calculations. Early language problems often appear as difficulties in naming known people and objects (**anomia**), and conversational speech that is empty of content. Memory problems first look more like carelessness or inattentiveness. Individuals may periodically forget to make appointments, complete tasks, or turn stove burners on or off. As the illness progresses, they forget well-rehearsed information. During the early stage of Alzheimer's disease, people may misplace their eye glasses and other items. As the disease progresses, they may completely forget they even need and use glasses. Calculation skills at first slow down, then partially disappear, and may deteriorate until even simple counting can no longer be mastered. As these changes progress, the person often is uncharacteristically indifferent to mounting personal, family, and social problems.

Depression may appear in the early stages of Alzheimer's disease. Depression may be part of the disease process, and it may also reflect the person's awareness of cognitive deterioration. Some people have articulated the devastation of loss of self, as illustrated by this quote from the diary of James Thomas: "Help me be strong and free until my self no longer exists . . . Most people expect to die some day, but who ever expected to lose their self first?" (as quoted in Tobin, 1997, p. 19). This experience of the dissolution of the self can be catastrophic for the person who is still aware and self-reflective.

In the second stage of Alzheimer's disease, symptoms become more severe and new problems appear. The neuromotor system becomes dysfunctional, causing people to experience extreme restlessness, and safety problems (e.g., roaming at night) may occur. The third stage is marked by increased severity of all symptoms and extreme problems with language, memory, abstraction, motor and visuospatial skills, and personality. Neurological deterioration results in **palilalia** (repeating over and over one's own words), **echolalia** (repeating over and over words spoken by someone else), or **mutism** (Cummings & Mega, 2003). Motor coordination difficulties, **myoclonus** (sudden uncontrolled contraction of muscles causing a jerking motion, often in the legs), seizures, and incontinence appear late in the disease (Kaufer & DeKosky, 2004). In the final stage, the person loses not only mental competency but also control over coordination, muscle groups, and flow of movement.

Social and Cultural Factors

Compared with caring for older adults with physical disabilities, caring for older adults with Alzheimer's disease requires substantially more time in caregiving tasks and results in more stress (see Berk, 2001). Education of caregivers about Alzheimer's disease (e.g., how to optimize communication with the person who has the disease) and social support are vital. Even with such education and support, caring for a loved one with Alzheimer's disease is stressful. The diary of Carol Swenson (2004) describes the profound impact that caring for her mother-in-law had on her, her husband (Dave), her family, and work. In a particularly moving passage, Swenson writes, "One night Mother became really upset, crying to Dave, 'Am I losing my mind?' He told me about it later; he was shattered. I remember my reaction the day she couldn't remember my sister-in-law's name. These things keep shocking us, no matter how 'prepared' we are" (p. 458).

Many caregivers and family members have found support and information through the Alzheimer's Association. This association has a nationwide network of eighty-one chapters. It provides a wealth of community programs and services, including help lines and telephone services to provide emotional support. It provides information on community resources such as home care, adult day care, assisted living, skilled nursing facilities, elder-care lawyers, and transportation. Chapters of the Alzheimer's Association also provide peer and professionally led support groups for caregivers and a wealth of educational materials on topics related to Alzheimer's disease (http://www.alz.org/Services/overview).

Intervention

As in all major disorders, there is no single treatment or intervention approach that fits all Alzheimer's clients and families. Treatment for Alzheimer's disease requires (1) specific medical supervision, (2) behavioral management and control of symptoms, (3) prevention of additional physical and emotional problems, and (4) family support (Cummings & Mega, 2003). Social workers provide a number of social services for Alzheimer's clients and their families. Most families need help developing a plan to prevent accidents and successfully maintain the Alzheimer's client at home as long as possible. Many families also expect professionals to help them limit or stop the client from driving a vehicle. In the first stage, some Alzheimer's clients are able to continue driving, but are usually limited to traveling on well-known, highly practiced routes on low-speed roads that are less congested and less hazardous. In an assessment of driving skills of twenty-one participants with very mild dementia and twenty-nine participants with early Alzheimer's disease, fourteen of the very mild dementia group and twelve of the early Alzheimer's disease group were scored as safe drivers (Duchek, Hunt, Roe, Xiong, Shah, & Morris, 2003). When Alzheimer's disease progresses from the first to the second stage, however, all driving must end.

As a general rule, discussions and education about driving and other lifestyle changes always include the Alzheimer's client and family. In order for clients to be successfully maintained at home, dangerous behavioral symptoms must be controlled through appropriate use of medications, humane techniques for **behavior modification**, cognitive training, social support, and environmental manipulations (Wise, Gray, & Seltzer, 1999). A standard treatment goal for social work interventions is to help clients maintain as much personal control, self-empowerment, and dignity as possible. Alzheimer's clients must not be treated as if they have no voice and no ability to comprehend information. In most cases cognitive skills dissipate slowly and unevenly, and existing competencies need to be used and practiced.

Eventually, Alzheimer's disease disrupts judgment, memory, motor skills, and the ability to learn from experience. Thus, safety decisions cannot be left solely to the client. Some families have difficulties recognizing and supporting the person's intact cognitive skills, while other families discover they cannot independently limit a loved one's freedom. At this stage, families may benefit from assistance in developing plans and methods for preventing falls, wandering, forgetting to eat, and hazardous behaviors such as leaving open flames and burners unattended, or going outdoors in extreme weather without appropriate clothing. As the client's memory and judgment fade, stepping outside, closing the door, and having neither a house key nor a coat is a real possibility. Some Alzheimer's clients may find it impossible to resolve such a problem, while others will neither look for a solution nor become emotionally distressed. For these individuals, Alzheimer's disease has destroyed awareness and knowledge about hazardous weather and ability to feel or notice when they are exposed to extremely hot and cold temperatures. They can become either hypo- or hypersensitive to pain and discomfort.

In order to prevent roaming and other dangerous acts, families are forced to install locks to stop the client from independently opening doors or having access to dangerous tools, kitchen knifes, and poisons. In some cases, families have to remove knobs for turning on stoves, food blenders, and other electrical devices. For many, restricting the freedom of a loved one creates sadness, self-doubt, and ambivalence, which, in turn, stops or slows them from taking appropriate action. When this occurs, family members need reassurance and specific information from professionals.

Alzheimer's disease and other neurodegenerative problems can also place clients at risk for victimization. Therefore, social workers must be prepared to screen and assess hidden and obvious signs of physical and mental neglect, physical and sexual assault, and financial theft. Forrest (1997) states that one indication of possible victimization is when an Alzheimer's client expresses stark fear that cannot be explained. Determining whether abuse has occurred can be extremely difficult because an individual with a deteriorating mind can believe that abuse is occurring when, in actuality, no victimization has taken place.

Alzheimer's disease can also cause individuals to develop behaviors in conflict with their moral values. Children who are unable to determine when and how to call for help or youth who are unable to defend themselves from molestation should not be left alone with a family member suffering from Alzheimer's disease (Forrest, 1997). Families can be helped to understand the importance of ensuring the entire family's safety through ongoing education and individual counseling. The probability that Alzheimer's disease will cause an individual to become a sexual predator is rather low, but it is a possibility that must be periodically examined by adult family members. Learning that Alzheimer's disease has the potential for causing sexual or violent behaviors totally uncharacteristic of the person's moral values and history can stir emotions, concerns, and questions for family members. To resolve highly charged issues, social workers may offer family members, in addition to education, individual counseling or the opportunity to meet other families who have experienced similar problems with a loved one with Alzheimer's disease and who have changed or redirected the disturbing behaviors in a satisfactory manner.

Factors such as anxiety, fear, grief, cognitive dysfunctions, false beliefs, depression, delusions, and hallucinations can cause a person with Alzheimer's disease to experience a severe psychological crisis (Sano & Weber, 2003; Wise, Gray, & Seltzer, 1999). When chaotic uncontrolled behaviors, emotions, or accusations stemming from delusions occur, it is helpful for social workers to quickly mobilize family members and service providers to develop an intervention plan and assess whether the client is at risk for suicide or violence to others.

Well-conceived, professionally presented activities may not improve functioning, but may help Alzheimer's clients pass time in a more pleasant and productive manner. Quality of life can be improved for Alzheimer's clients by ensuring that healthy activities remain accessible. Many pleasurable activities are lost with age-related changes in vision, hearing, taste, and mobility. Both depression and dementia severity are associated with low levels of pleasurable activities (Logsdon & Teri, 1997). At first it may seem demeaning to provide stuffed animals, baby dolls, chocolate, or beer to older adults with dementia, but at a practical level, these can make them happy, reduce agitation, and lower the amounts of medication needed (Belluck, 2010). Caregivers and family can improve the quality of sleep by using cognitive or behavioral techniques, which improve the quality of daytime alertness because less medication is necessary (McCurry, Logsdon, Teri, & Vitiello, 2007). Older adults with dementia may have lost their ability to self-organize exercise, but staff and families can adapt activities to physical and mental limitations. Physical activity can improve mood, reduce falls and injuries, promote good rest at night, and encourage socializing. This is a far different picture of caring for clients with dementia than in past decades, when medical sedation, physical restraints, and awful boredom characterized nursing homes (Logsdon, McCurry, Pike, & Teri, 2009).

Systematic social and cognitive interventions may assuage the family's feelings of grief and guilt even though they receive no relief from daily caretaking responsibilities. Psychosocial interventions for caregivers can significantly reduce psychological distress, increase knowledge, and improve coping skills, but do not decrease the burden of care (Brodaty, 2003). In addition, there is little doubt that in the early stages of Alzheimer's disease, difficult behavioral symptoms respond positively to psychotherapy, support, and cognitive reminders posted systematically in key locations (Sano & Weber, 2003). In addition, psychosocial interventions can delay the need for nursing home admission (Brodaty, 2003).

Each stage of Alzheimer's disease brings new challenges that affect caretakers differently. It is difficult to know when supports for a family or client will be most needed and effective. One critical period for families and clients is during the end stage of the disorder when death is nearing. By the final stage of Alzheimer's disease, the client's personality, behavior, and emotional reactions have changed drastically. The person known and loved by family and friends seems to have disappeared. This can frighten, upset, and trigger severe grief reactions from family members. The pain can be so great that they completely stop visiting the ill family member. Many times patients' reduced reasoning, abstraction, and memory skills prevent them from observing and understanding that they are being avoided. For others, however, islands of reality remain intact, and the person experiences feelings of emotional abandonment and chronic loneliness (Forrest, 1997).

Newer medications are successfully slowing the rate of neurodeterioration but currently cannot reverse or cure Alzheimer's disease. It is predictable that as treatment extends the early stages of this illness, clients and their families will benefit from social work case management that organizes home health services, transportation, adjustment to illness counseling, and family problem-solving therapies. In the later stages of Alzheimer's disease, cognitive disabilities force many patients into assisted living and nursing home facilities. Since the decision to move clients into a care facility almost always falls on family members, making this decision causes major emotional and economic costs for the client and family. Social workers can help ease the pain of placement by aiding the family in locating facilities that provide humane care and individual treatment plans, and incorporate the latest evidence-based medical and social interventions. It also becomes the social worker's job to help families remain focused on the realities of Alzheimer's disease and not be misled by false hopes, which can happen when activities designed to increase a client's quality of life are either inadvertently presented by the staff or perceived by the family as methods for healing. That is, movement, art, cognitive exercises, and other active interventions may reduce stress or depression and usher in short-term improvements in memory and other skills, but the onward destruction of Alzheimer's disease has not been arrested.

SUMMARY

In this chapter, we have focused on medical social work with older adults. Later adulthood is a developmental period that may be characterized by a sense of fulfillment, meaningful relationships, and continued curiosity about the world. It is also a period in which all individuals eventually will experience significant loss and death. Some older adults also will experience chronic and debilitating diseases, such as Alzheimer's disease. As the world's population continues to age, medical social workers increasingly will face clients and family members who need assistance in coping with this devastating disease. Medical social workers can function as part of a team of health-care professionals to provide support and education for individuals and families suffering from Alzheimer's disease. Box 12.7 contains a practice story and advice from an experienced medical social worker.

> ## BOX 12.7 PRACTICE STORY AND ADVICE FROM THE FIELD
>
> ## Tonya M., medical social worker: We're standing with the client on the shore, and a big wave is coming.
>
> *Tonya M. practiced as a medical social worker for twenty years in diverse settings including hospitals, nursing homes, and hospice care (palliative care for the terminally ill that focuses on providing physical and emotional comfort to the client and his or her loved ones). Perhaps her favorite setting is the hospital where she advocated for and supported clients and their families through the challenges of medical illness. For the past ten years, Tonya has worked as a clinical professor, passing along her wisdom and passion for the field to beginning medical social workers.*
>
> **Practice Story**
>
> When you work in a hospital, it's short term, four or five days, so you are referring. You are trying to equip that client with something to hold on to. And trying to keep them from being overwhelmed. I always visualize it like standing on the shore with a big wave coming and part of what medical social work does is have clients step back so that they can go ahead and deal with [their medical condition]. A lot of medical social work is dealing with the medical team. You are forever explaining clients to the doctors or to the nurses. They [members of the medical team] have a different mind-set. Not that social work has a better mind-set, just different. So you go to a hospital and a physician, they have in mind a medical model. A patient comes in with a medical problem. They want to fix it.
>
> I think probably the most difficult thing for a medical social worker is that they work in what I term a host environment. You don't go to a hospital to see a social worker—you go to get your medical problem fixed. So you are kind of an odd man out. So you have to be able to see many different viewpoints and respect those viewpoints. You have to be able to work in a team environment and to command respect—respect for your skills and your profession. And that does not always happen—if you can't think on your feet, if you can't be comfortable with people criticizing you, medical social work is not for you. A new social work intern talked about the physician who came in while she was sitting doing paper work and told her to get up. He told her that he was going to be charting. He wanted her to move. And I said, "Really? What did you do?" She said, "I got up, and felt bad about it ever since." So we role-played on how you can handle that a little differently. There is a hierarchy in a hospital, and you need to learn to smile and say, "There is an extra chair over there, Doc." This same intern was told that she needed to go clean up a mess—a patient had

vomited, and that she needed to go in and do that. At that point she did laugh and say, "You know, that's really not my job." But I was afraid when she started telling that story!

Advice

Cultivate flexibility. One of the exciting things about working in a hospital as a medical social worker is that you don't know what your day will be like. I used to walk in, as I was coming into work walking from the parking lot, I would turn on my beeper and be thinking about the things I would be doing that day, and it was all very logical in my mind. Generally speaking before I got to the hospital door, I was being paged, sometimes I was being paged overhead, to come to ICU stat. So there was no rhyme or reason to what the day might look like.

Become comfortable with strong emotion. When you are working in medical social work, you deal a lot with crisis. One of the things that I enjoyed most was working in trauma, but that is only one aspect of the crisis. You know there is always a crisis in people's lives when they are faced with loss. And that can be loss of life, it can be loss of function, it can be loss of role, but those losses are a turning point in the client's life and in their family's life. So you are forever working in a crisis situation . . .

Become comfortable—as comfortable as you can—with death. Death is symbolic as well as real, and when people see that indeed it is true that the person that they love is going to die and will be gone—then there is a lot of denial. Then the medical team can't understand why, when I have told [the patient's family that] their mother has less than six months to live, why they are asking about a lung transplant. For heaven's sake she has got lung cancer, what do they expect?

Be comfortable with emotion. The hospital is a place of high emotion. And you need to be comfortable with people who have not always expressed emotion. So you may be the brunt of anger. That's a very common thing, to be the brunt of someone's anger because you walked in the door. Or because you said that the doctor asked me to come and talk with you about when you are discharged from the hospital. That's very common.

Develop good communication skills. What you are doing then, so much of it is in promoting communication. When you are in a healthcare setting, they talk a different language. So many times a social worker will go in with the physician while they talk with the patient. And then they will go in and he will say, "Mrs. Smith, your results came back, it's malignant. I do not want you to be too upset about this. We're going to provide you with palliative care and I am sure the social worker here can explain things for you"—and he leaves. And the social worker learns to ask that person, "What do you understand that the doctor said?" And you discover that they have no idea what "palliative" means—it means comfort care. They are not sure what "malignant" means, because surely if it was cancer, the doctor would have said cancer. So you know the explanation comes many times from the social worker.

In turn, the social worker is working with that medical team, to help them understand, first of all, why you cannot send this patient home and expect the husband to give the injections. The husband is in early stage of dementia, and she is the caregiver for him, we have to get some more services in—you also are always explaining to physicians, although nurses can be bad on this too, why you have to go ahead and allow this person to make their own decisions, even if the decision is wrong, even if it's going to be a dangerous one. So you have frail elderly people, and the physician will say to send them to the nursing home. Your job is to go in there and find, first of all, what does that patient want, and then tell them the pros and cons of their decision. So if they say, "I want to go home. I am not going to nursing home. I want to go home." So you need to explain to them, "Okay, do you understand you have been falling, and you live alone. and you could fall, not be discovered, and die?" And if they understand, then you facilitate that decision.

Sometimes you are the only one that that patient can really talk to who understands what they are going through, and that's no exaggeration. Depends on what the problem is. Sometimes you will have families that come in, and they raise Cain with medical staff. "Mom isn't getting her medicine on time, I want more people in here, I don't believe the diagnosis." And then you are working with that family to find out exactly what's going on there. That's what I call the "daughter from California syndrome." She swoops in and says, "Hey, you are not going to send my mother to a nursing home. What's going on here? I don't care what the plans are, I demand this, this, and this." Which throws the medical team into a tizzy, but you find out that the daughter is kind of guilty that she has been away.

A medical social worker needs to be appropriately assertive and to learn how to spend their brownie points. You have to learn when to advocate and when to save your brownie points. You have to have good judgment. I have known social workers, a new social worker who stopped the vice president of the hospital in the corridor once and demanded that they be provided with more staff because they weren't getting the patients' needs met. She felt that it was a very appropriate thing [to do], and he thought that social workers are some kind of nut cases or something.

Be comfortable with being a token. You are a token, and as such you bear so much more responsibility than when there are a lot of you. Because the rest of the team will remember for years that strange social worker who did this strange thing. They will also remember for years where some social worker has been able to save the day. So you bear an extra responsibility because you are a token.

Learn medical terminology and ask questions. If I could tell students one thing to do before they go into medical social work, it would be to take a medical terminology course. Because they need to know the language to interpret for the client, and so they know what's going on. I relate to my students the first team meeting that I sat in on as a bachelor's [degree] intern. When they talked about the pulmonary function of the cardiac patient was such and such and the something or other was so and so—we needed to be sure and relate the situation to the family. I concentrated on keeping my face absolutely blank because I didn't know if it was good news or bad news. I'd no idea. When the nurse talked about that they put in a pig valve, I asked why they called it a pig valve. And she said, "Because it's from a pig!" "Really, a pig?" So there are a lot of things that you don't know, and if you take medical terminology, you know more, but you need to be comfortable about asking questions. We don't train, nor should we be training, medical social workers to understand all the procedures in medicine: that's not their job. But they do need to understand enough, and the only way to learn is when they get in the field, being comfortable with asking questions.

Be culturally sensitive. They need to be as culturally informed and sensitive as they can possibly be. And what they don't know, they need to be able to go and find out. So we don't equip students to walk out of here and be comfortable with all of the cultural values of African Americans, Hispanics, Hmongs, etc. It can't be done, it's impossible. But they will be the ones who will speak up for being culturally sensitive. And in the health-care setting, some 30 to 40 percent of the people now utilize alternative medicine. And particularly in some cultures this is very common, and can have a great impact on whatever the doctor's prescribing. They need to be able to talk with those clients, and hear in a nonjudgmental way that they are doing things like cupping, or that they have a faith healer. They need to be comfortable hearing that and not be judgmental. And find out how that can fit in with what Western medicine has prescribed, or how it can be explained to people of a different culture. Religion—you know you have certain religions that say no blood products, and [believers] are willing to literally put their lives on the line. It's very difficult for the health-care team to stand and watch a person die, because they are refusing blood products. So sometimes you end up being a counselor for the medical team. Sometimes you feel like an octopus, where people are tugging on all of your tentacles.

Study and Discussion Questions

1. What are some of the common physical, psychological, and social changes that occur during late adulthood?

2. Loss and related issues are major emotional challenges for older adults. Describe some common sources of loss in late adulthood.

3. What are some of the emotions and conflicts that a well spouse caring for an ill spouse may experience? What can a community do to support a person who has lost a spouse?

4. What are some of the physical and psychological characteristics of dying? How might the social and cultural context of dying affect the individual and his or her loved ones?

5. Those who work with older people need to be aware of the various types of dementia, including Alzheimer's disease. What are the causes of Alzheimer's disease, how is it manifested and treated, and what are the implications for families?

6. What are some implications of a developmental, ecological-systems model for social work intervention with individuals living with Alzheimer's disease and their families?

7. What might be some factors associated with more "successful" aging?

8. Ageism is discriminatory treatment based on age. How pervasive is it in our culture? Provide examples.

9. To return to our opening example, what are some of the possible strategies for engaging Mrs. P. and her husband in services as their dementia progresses? How might Mrs. P.'s adult son be involved?

Resources

Interested students can supplement this chapter with these web-based resources.

The Alzheimer's Association provides peer and professionally led support groups for caregivers and a wealth of educational materials on topics related to Alzheimer's disease. Available at http://www.alz.org/we_can_help.asp.

The U.S. government's Administration on Aging, in the Department of Health and Human Services, provides a wide range of practical information for helping older adults and their families make informed decisions and understand their rights. Available at http://www.aoa.gov.

Students interested in international issues of aging will find information at http://www.aoa.gov/AoARoot/AoA_Programs/Special_Projects/Global_Aging/index.aspx.

AARP provides an overview of resources for aging clients, including job, retirement, and health benefits. Available at http://www.aarp.org/research/internet_resources/.

The National Counsel on Aging provides information on how older adults can check on important benefits, including drug prescription assistance, and suggestions for help with rent, property taxes, heating bills, meals, and other needs. Available at http://www.benefitscheckup.org/.

The CDC's National Center for Health Statistics provides an overview of research findings about aging. Available at http://www.cdc.gov/nchs/nchs_for_you/older_americans.htm.

An important academic resource for students and clinicians is the American Psychological Association's journal, *Psychology and Aging.* Information about the journal and sample articles are available at http://www.apa.org/pubs/journals/pag/index.aspx.

References

American Association of Retired People. (2010, November 19). Social Security: Voices and values. *Surveys and Statistics.* Washington, DC. Retrieved from http://www.aarp.org/work/social-security/info-10-2010/social-security-values-voices-10.html

Ashford, J., & LeCroy, C. (2010). *Human behavior in the social environment: A multidimensional perspective.* Belmont, CA: Brooks/Cole.

Beauvoir, S. de. (1965). *A very easy death.* New York: G. P. Putnam's Sons.

Beedon, L., & Wu, K. B. (2003). *Social Security and African Americans: Some facts.* Washington, DC: AARP Public Policy Institute. Retrieved from http://www.aarp.org/work/social-security/info-2003/social_security_and_african_americans_some_facts.html

Belluck, P. (2010, December 31). The vanishing mind: Giving Alzheimer's patients their way, even chocolate. *New York Times.* Retrieved from http://www.nytimes.com/2011/01/01/health/01care.html?_r=1&pagewanted=all

Berk, L. (2001). *Development through the lifespan* (2nd ed.). Boston: Allyn & Bacon.

Berkman, B. (2011). Seizing interdisciplinary opportunities in the changing landscape of health and aging: A social work perspective. *Gerontologist, 51*(4), 433–440.

Bonanno, G.A., & Kaltman, K. (1999). Toward an integrative perspective on bereavement. *Psychological Bulletin, 125,* 760–776.

Bonanno, G. A., Keltner, D., Holen, A., & Horowitz, M. J. (1995). When avoiding unpleasant emotion might not be such a bad thing: Verbal-autonomic response dissociation and midlife conjugal bereavement. *Journal of Personality and Social Psychology, 46,* 975–989.

Boyle, J. P., Thompson, T. J., Gregg, E. W., Barker, L. E., & Williamson, D. F. (2010). Projection of the year 2050 burden of diabetes in the U.S. adult population: Dynamic modeling of incidence, mortality, and prediabetes prevalence. *Population Health Metrics, 8*(1), 29.

Brodaty, H. (2003). Meta-analysis of psychosocial interventions for caregivers of people with dementia. *Journal of American Geriatrics Society, 51*, 657-664.

Brown, C. (2009). Pain, aging and dementia: The crisis is looming, but are we ready? *British Journal of Occupational Therapy, 72*, 371-375.

Caine, E. D. (1981). Pseudodementia: Current concepts and future directions. *Archives of General Psychiatry, 38*(12), 1359-1369.

Carter, J. (2000). The virtues of aging. In D. Sattler, G. Kramer, V. Shabatay, & D. Bernstein (Eds.), *Lifespan development in context: Voices and perspectives* (pp. 187-190). New York: Houghton Mifflin.

Centers for Disease Control and Prevention. (2003). *Healthy aging: Preventing disease and improving quality of life among older Americans.* Atlanta: National Center for Chronic Disease Prevention. Retrieved from http://www.cdc.gov/nccdphp/aag_aging.htm

Centers for Disease Control and Prevention. (2005). *Causes of death among U.S. adults aged 65 or older, 2005.* National Center for Health Statistics, National Vital Statistics System. Retrieved from http://www.cdc.gov/chronicdisease/resources/publications/aag/aging_text.htm#1

Convit, A., Wolf, O.T., Tarshish, C., & de Leon, M. J. (2003). Reduced glucose tolerance is associated with poor memory performance and hippocampal atrophy among normal elderly. *Neuroscience, 100*, 2019-2022.

Cummings, J. L., & Mega, M. S. (2003). *Neuropsychiatry and behavioral neuroscience.* New York: Oxford University Press.

DeSpelder, L. A., & Strickland, A. L. (2002). *The last dance: Encountering death and dying* (6th ed.). Boston: McGraw-Hill.

Duchek, J. M., Hunt, L., Roe, C. M., Xiong, C., Shah, K., & Morris, J. C. (2003). Longitudinal driving performance in early-stage dementia of the Alzheimer type. *Journal of American Geriatrics Society, 10*, 1342-1347.

Dunn, W., Adams, S., & Adams, R. (2008). Iatrogenic delirium and coma: A "near miss." *Chest, 133*, 1217-1220.

Erikson, E. (1998). *The life cycle completed.* New York: Norton.

Federal Interagency Forum on Aging-Related Statistics. (2010). *Older Americans 2010: Key indicators of well-being.* Washington, DC: U.S. Government Printing Office. Retrieved from http://www.agingstats.gov/agingstatsdotnet/Main_Site/Data/2010_Documents/Docs/OA_2010.pdf

Fleck, C. (2010, November 1). Social Security protects many from poverty. *AARP Bulletin.* Retrieved from http://www.aarp.org/work/social-security/info-10-2010/social_security_barrier_to_poverty.html

Forrest, D. V. (1997). *Psychotherapy for patients with neuropsychiatric disorders.* In S. C. Yudofsky & R. E. Hales (Eds.), *The American Psychiatric Press textbook of neuropsychiatry* (3rd ed., pp. 983-1018). Washington, DC: American Psychiatric Press.

Fowler, T., & Scadding, J. (2003). *Clinical neurology* (3rd ed.). London: Hodden & Stoughton.

Fulmer, T., Guadagno, L., Dyer, C. B., & Connolly, M.T. (2004). Progress in elder screening and assessment instruments. *American Geriatrics Society, 52*, 297-304.

Gardner, D., & Gelman, C. (2008). Aging: Racial and ethnic groups. In T. Mizrahi & L. Davis (Eds.), *Encyclopedia of social work* (20th ed., Vol. 1, pp. 105-110). Washington, DC: NASW Press; New York: Oxford University Press.

Grim, C. W. (2002). *Elder health is family health.* Paper presented at the National Indian Council on Aging Conference, Albuquerque, NM.

He, W., Sengupta, M., Velkoff, V. A., & DeBarros, K. A. (2005). *65+ in the United States: 2005* (Current Population Reports, Series P23-209). Washington, DC: U.S. Government Printing Office.

Hooyman, N. (2008). Aging: Overview. In T. Mizrahi & L. Davis (Eds.), *Encyclopedia of social work* (20th ed., Vol. 1, pp. 88–96). Washington, DC: NASW Press; New York: Oxford University Press.

Hudley, E., Haight, W., & Miller, P. (2003/2009). *Raise up a child: Human development in an African-American family.* Chicago: Lyceum Books.

Japan Times Online. (2010). *Population shrank by record 183,000 in '09.* Retrieved from http://www.japantimes.co.jp/text/nn20100417a1.html

Kaplan, K. (1995). End-of-life decisions. In R. I. Edwards (Ed.), *Encyclopedia of social work* (19th ed., Vol. 2, pp. 856–868). Washington, DC: NASW Press.

Kaufer, D. I., & DeKosky, S. T. (2004). Diagnostic classifications: Relationship to the neurobiology of dementia. In D. S. Charney & E. J. Nestler (Eds.), *Neurobiology of mental illness* (2nd ed., pp. 771–782). New York: Oxford University Press.

Kinsella, K., & He, W. (2009). *An aging world: 2008* (U.S. Census Bureau, Publication No. P95/09-1). Washington, DC: U.S. Government Printing Office.

Kinsella, K., & Velkoff, V. (2001). *An aging world: 2001* (U.S. Census Bureau Publication No. P95/01-1). Washington, DC: U.S. Government Printing Office.

Kosberg, J. I., & Garcia, J. L. (Eds.). (1995). *Elder abuse: International and cross-cultural perspectives.* Binghamton, NY: Tayor & Francis/Haworth Press.

Kübler-Ross, E. (1969). *On death and dying.* New York: Macmillan.

Kutner, G. (2007). *AARP 2006 prescription drug study with Hispanics and African Americans.* AARP Knowledge Management: Surveys and Statistics. Retrieved from http://www.aarp.org/health/drugs-supplements/info-2007/hisp_aa_rx.html

Lachs, M. S., & Pillemer, K. (2004). Elder abuse. *Lancet, 364*, 1192–1263.

Lindstrøm, T. C. (2002). "It ain't necessarily so": Challenging mainstream thinking about bereavement. *Family Community Health, 25*, 11–21.

Logsdon, R., McCurry, S., Pike, K., & Teri, L. (2009). Making physical activity accessible to older adults with memory loss: A feasibility study. *Gerontologist, 49*, S94–S99.

Logsdon, R., & Teri, L. (1997). The Pleasant Events Schedule-AD: Psychometric properties and relationship to depression and cognition in Alzheimer's disease patients. *Gerontologist, 37*, 40–45.

Lutz, W., Sanderson, W., & Scherbov, S. (2008). The coming acceleration of global population ageing. *Nature, 451*, 716–719.

McCarthy, L. H., Bigal, M. E., Katz, M., Derby, C., & Lipton, R. B. (2009). Chronic pain and obesity in elderly people: Results from the Einstein Aging Study. *Journal of the American Geriatric Society, 57*, 115–119.

McCurry, S., Logsdon, R., Teri, L., & Vitiello, M. (2007). Evidence-based psychological treatments for insomnia in older adults. *Psychology and Aging, 22*, 18–27.

National Center on Elder Abuse. (2003). *A response to the abuse of vulnerable adults: The 2000 survey of state adult protective services.* Washington, DC: Author.

National Committee for the Prevention of Elder Abuse. (2003, March). *The role of culture in elder abuse.* Retrieved from http://www.preventelderabuse.org/issues/culture.html

National Council of the Aging. (2002). *American perceptions of aging in the 21st century: The NCOA's continuing study of the myths and realities of aging.* Washington, DC: Author.

National Institute on Drug Abuse. (2005). *Trends in prescription drug abuse* (Research Report Series, Prescription Drugs: Abuse and Addiction). Bethesda, MD: National Institutes of Health. Retrieved from http://www.nida.nih.gov/ResearchReports/Prescription/prescription5.html

National Research Council Panel to Review Risk and Prevalence of Elder Abuse and Neglect. (2003). *Elder mistreatment: Abuse, neglect and exploitation in an aging America.* Washington, DC. Author.

Nerenberg, L. (1995). *To reach beyond our grasp: A community outreach guide for professionals in the field of elder abuse.* New York: Goldman Institute on Aging.

Otis-Green, S. (2008). Health care social work. In T. Mizrahi & L. Davis (Eds.), *Encyclopedia of social work* (20th ed., Vol. 2, pp. 348–353). Washington, DC: NASW Press; New York: Oxford University Press.

Paterson, T. L., Lacro, J. P., & Jeste, D. V. (1999). Abuse and misuse of medications in the elderly. *Psychiatric Times, 16*(4). Retrieved from http://www.psychiatric times.com/p990454.html

Raz, N. (2002). Cognitive aging. In V. S. Ramachandran (Ed.), *Encyclopedia of the human brain* (Vol. 1, pp. 829–838). San Diego: Academic Press.

Ropper, A., & Samuels, M. (2009). *Adams and Victor's principles of neurology* (9th ed.). New York: McGraw-Hill.

Sano, M., & Weber, C. (2003). Psychological evaluation and nonpharmacologic treatment of Alzheimer's disease. In P. A. Lichtenberg, D. L. Murman, & A. M. Mellow (Eds.), *Handbook of dementia* (pp. 25–27). New York: Wiley.

Santrock, J. W. (2002). *Life-span development.* Boston: McGraw-Hill.

Smith, I. M. (2003). *Bodies begin to show wear and tear at 30.* University of Iowa Virtual Hospital. Retrieved from http://www.vh.org/adult/patieth/internal medicine/aba30/1992/aging.html

Smith, S., & Gove, J. E. (2005). *Physical changes of aging* (Fact Sheet FCS 2085). Department of Family, Youth and Community Sciences, Florida Cooperative Extension Service, Institute of Food and Agricultural Sciences, University of Florida. Retrieved from http://edis.ifas.ufl.edu/pdffiles/HE/HE01900.pdf

Sokolovsky, J. (Ed.). (2009). *The cultural context of aging: Worldwide perspectives.* Westport, CT: Praeger.

Swenson, C. R. (2004). Dementia diary: A personal and professional journal. *Social Work, 49*(3), 451–460.

Takamura, J. (2008). Aging: Public policy. In T. Mizrahi & L. Davis (Eds.), *Encyclopedia of social work* (20th ed., Vol. 1, pp. 100–105). Washington, DC: NASW Press; New York: Oxford University Press.

Tatara, T. (1999). *Understanding elder abuse in minority populations.* Philadelphia: Taylor & Francis.

Tobin, S. S. (1997). Aging: Alzheimer's disease and other disabilities. In R. Edwards (Ed.), *Encyclopedia of social work* (19th ed. Supplement, pp. 15–25). Washington, DC: NASW Press.

Turner, S. R. (2003). Neurologic aspects of Alzheimer's disease. In P. A. Lichtenberg, D. L. Murman, & A. M. Mellow (Eds.), *Handbook of dementia* (pp. 1–24). New York: Wiley.

Understanding and combating elder abuse in minority communities. (1997). Proceedings of a 1997 conference sponsored by the National Center on Elder Abuse.

U.S. Administration on Aging. (1998). *The national elder abuse incidence study.* Washington, DC: Department of Health and Human Services.

U.S. Administration on Aging. (2005). *What is elder abuse?* Retrieved from http://www.aoa.gov/AoARoot/AoA_Programs/Elder_Rights/EA_Prevention/whatIsEA .aspx

U.S. Census Bureau. (2010). Source of income in 2009: Number with income and mean income of specified type in 2009 of people 15 years old and over by age, race and Hispanic origin, and sex. In *Current population survey, 2010:Annual social and economic supplement.* Retrieved from http://www.census.gov/hhes/www/cpstables/032010/perinc/new09_006.htm

U.S. Census Bureau International database. (2004). *Midyear population, by age and sex* (Table 094). Retrieved from http://www.census.gov/population/www projects/natdet-D1A.html

U.S. Department of Health and Human Services. (1999). *Centenarians in the United States* (Current Population Reports P23-199RV). Washington, DC: U.S. Government Printing Office.

U.S. Indian Health Service. (2001). *Heritage and health.* Washington, DC: U.S. Indian Health Service. Retrieved from http://info.ihs.gov

U.S. Indian Health Service. (2002). *Facts on Indian health disparities.* Washington, DC: U.S. Indian Health Service, Office of the Director, Public Affairs Staff.

Wise, M., Gray, K., & Seltzer, B. (1999). Delirium, dementia and amnesic disorders. In R. E. Hales, S.Yudofsky, & J.A.Talbott (Eds.), *The American Psychiatric Press textbook of psychiatry* (3rd ed., pp. 317-362). Washington, DC: American Psychiatric Press.

World Health Organization. (2002). Deaths by cause, sex and mortality stratum in WHO regions, estimates for 2001. In *World Health Report 2002* (Annex Table 2, pp. 186-191). Geneva: Author.

Wortman, C. B., & Silver, R. C. (1989). The myths of coping with loss. *Journal of Consulting and Clinical Psychology, 57,* 349-357.

Zelenev, S. (2006). Towards a society for all ages: Meeting the challenge or missing the boat. *International Social Science Journal, 190,* 601-616.

13

Women and Gender across the Life Span

Kathleen Reutter and Wendy L. Haight

This chapter uses a developmental, ecological-systems framework to consider how gender profoundly shapes human development throughout the life span. Throughout history and across cultural contexts, women have been relatively more restricted than men, and vulnerable to gender-based oppression. Even after progress wrought from two long and arduous women's movements of the nineteenth and twentieth centuries, many women in the United States continue to struggle for equal pay for equal work, access to health care and child care, and protection from sexual assault and abusive partners. Around the world, women face a variety of threats to their safety and livelihood. Given the relatively greater vulnerability of women to gender-based oppression, it is not surprising that women's issues are central to social work. Social workers counsel domestic-violence survivors on rebuilding their lives, assist mothers whose children are in foster care, provide therapy for women with clinical depression, advocate for women living in poverty, and much more.

Gender, like race, is largely a social construct. What it means to be male or female varies in relation to cultural and historical contexts, as well as other features of social status. Becoming a socially competent social worker requires attending not only to specific issues of race, gender, sexuality, ability, and so forth, but to the ways in which they intersect. Throughout this chapter, we attempt to integrate the sociological theory of intersectionality to illustrate the ways in which oppressions of gender, race, class, and sexuality can interact on various levels and often in simultaneous ways to create systematic social inequality. Using this framework, we are reminded that women do not have one monolithic experience of gender-based discrimination. Instead, women's experiences are altered by their differing experiences of race, class, and sexuality, which intersect with their gender in multiple ways to contribute to pervasive systems of oppression. For women around the world, the experience of gender cannot be separated from the experience of race, class, and sexuality (Choo & Ferree, 2010).

We begin this chapter with a discussion of gender identity—that is, how individuals interpret what it means to be male or female—and describe how these perceptions change throughout the life span. We then discuss the process of gender identity development, focusing on the gendered messages individuals receive from their family, peers, the media, and so forth; the ways in which they respond to those messages; and how those responses, in turn, can influence gendered messages and social change. Finally, we discuss a variety of gender-related issues that individuals may experience at various points in the life span.

GENDER IDENTITY DEVELOPMENT

Gender identity—the perception that one is male or female or somewhere in between—is an essential part of how people come to understand themselves and the world around them, as well as how they perceive and respond to one another. Developmental research indicates that children are aware of gender remarkably early. Infants as young as three or four months can construct categories of male and female. Nine- to eleven-month-old babies are capable of differentiating the faces of men and women and associate these faces with male and female voices. Around age two, children begin to label their own gender ("I'm a boy!") and the gender of others ("Anna's a girl"; see Ruble, Martin, & Berenbaum, 2006).

Early childhood is a time of rapid gender identity development. At this age, children begin to associate each gender with certain toys, activities, tools, household items, professions, and games. Middle-class U.S. parents often notice that their preschool children become increasingly inflexible about what it means to be a boy or a girl. A preschooler may insist, for example, that all boys have short hair, play with trucks, and grow up to be construction workers while all girls wear pink, like dolls, and become homemakers. Preschoolers' activities reflect these newfound beliefs. Preschool girls, for example, may spend their school days in pairs engaged in pretend play involving home life. They are more likely to play with dolls, do artwork, and look at books than are boys, who tend to play in large groups, engage in pretend play involving superheroes and fantasy characters, build with blocks, chase each other, climb, and play-fight. By age four, children are much more likely to play exclusively with their own gender (Berk, 2009).

Early adolescence also is typically a time of gender intensification. The physical changes boys and girls undergo during adolescence make sex differences more visible, which may prompt family members and friends to think of adolescent boys and girls in more gendered terms and even encourage more gender-typed behaviors. For some young women, the transition from childhood to adolescence involves a decline in confidence and a heightened tendency to elevate others' needs above their own (Denner &

Dunbar, 2004). Increased concern with the perceptions of others may cause adolescents to focus on gender conformity (Berk, 2009). In the United States, many girls entering adolescence become increasingly focused on looking and acting in traditionally feminine ways. Adolescent girls may reduce their time engaging in sports and other forms of physical activity (Gordon-Larsen, Nelson, & Popkin, 2004), experiment with makeup, and focus on traditionally "feminine" subjects like language, art, and music in school, rather than the male-dominated fields of math and science. With peers, young adolescent girls may become more concerned about their appearance, making and keeping friends, and attracting romantic attention. Likewise, as teenagers start to date, they may augment their looks and behave in more gender-typed ways to attract partners.

As individuals grow into young adulthood, many become more flexible and less stereotypical in how they view gender. In one study of gender discriminatory behavior, for instance, adolescent and young adult males were given descriptions of average or outstanding male candidates behaving stereotypically or counterstereotypically, and were asked to indicate their personal election choice. Adolescents were more likely to choose the outstanding male candidate who was stereotypically masculine. In contrast, young adults rated both outstanding male candidates as equally deserving. This change between adolescence and early adulthood may be attributable to both cognitive maturation and the broadening social exposure that results from beginning college or joining the workforce (Lobel, Nov-Krispin, Schiller, Lobel, & Feldman, 2004). Older adults generally are more likely than younger adults to stereotype and exhibit gender-based prejudices. Yet when older adults are presented with evidence that contradicts their stereotypes, they are just as likely as younger adults to alter their initial beliefs. In addition, older adults are generally more concerned than younger adults with trying to avoid stereotypes. This suggests that older adults, while not always as successful at avoiding stereotypes, have both the desire and the potential to make significant strides toward egalitarianism (Radvansky, Lynchard, & von Hippel, 2009).

THE PROCESS OF GENDER IDENTITY DEVELOPMENT

Over time, young men and women become increasingly attuned to traditional gender roles, but they also respond in varied ways by embracing, rejecting, or creatively recasting the various gender-based messages they receive. Variation occurs not only across individuals but also across social and cultural contexts. For example, much research focuses on adolescent women's loss of voice and the entrenchment of traditional gender roles, but this is by no means a universal experience. In a study of eight adolescent women of Mexican descent living in government-subsidized housing in the United States, the young women rejected the notion that they were passive and prided themselves on their ability to speak up for themselves and others. Although they embraced traditional roles such as caretaker and peacekeeper in their families, schools, and communities, they also expressed the desire to be strong and capable of protecting themselves and their families (Denner & Dunbar, 2004).

Socialization

Individuals around the globe receive important lessons within their families, communities, schools, and society at large about what it means to be male or female. These lessons are powerful, in part, because of their redundancy: for example, the gender-role lessons children receive in their family may be similar to those they are exposed to in school and through the media. Yet variation also is apparent in the socialization messages children receive (e.g., some families practice more egalitarianism in gender roles), as well as in how children respond to these messages. Societal shifts in gender roles also occur over time; for example, gender roles in the United States became more egalitarian following the women's rights movements of the 1970s.

Families and Peers

Beginning in childhood, families and peers play an important part in gender-role socialization. Many parents communicate different perceptions and expectations of boys and girls, both directly through explicit instruction and indirectly through the ways in which they communicate, and the interests and activities that they encourage in their children. Beginning in infancy, parents sometimes consider their children's abilities along stereotypical lines. In one study, mothers of eleven-month-olds overestimated sons' motor skills and underestimated their daughters'. In actuality, there were no differences in motor abilities between the male and female infants (see Ruble, Martin, & Berenbaum, 2006). By the time their children are of preschool age, parents generally show some differences in how they interact with their sons and daughters. For example, mothers are more likely to label emotions with preschool daughters, encouraging girls to be aware of others' feelings, while they are more likely to explain emotions to boys and discuss causes and consequences, teaching boys the importance of controlling their emotions (Berk, 2009). In general, parents reinforce and encourage behavior that is gender stereotyped. For example, they tend to respond more when their children are engaged in same-sex play (see Ruble, Martin, & Berenbaum, 2006), and are more likely to purchase gender-specific toys such as guns and footballs for boys and tea sets and jump ropes for daughters (Berk, 2009). Parents may also help girls and boys develop different skills by providing them with different experiences. For example, parents generally provide more extensive science explanations in museums for boys than for girls, possibly encouraging boys to gain greater knowledge and interest in science (see Ruble, Martin, & Berenbaum, 2006). Boys generally experience more pressure to behave in gender-typical ways than girls. Parents, especially fathers, are generally less tolerant of sons who engage in behavior not typical of their gender. For example, parents tend to be much less alarmed if their daughter is called a tomboy than if their son is described as a sissy (Berk, 2009).

Other children also influence one another's gender-stereotypical behavior. For example, children without siblings tend to engage in less gender-typical behavior, suggesting that siblings may encourage some stereotyped behavior (see Ruble, Martin, & Berenbaum, 2006). Some research, however, indicates that other-sex siblings also can provide children with the opportunity to copy and engage in other-sex behavior and activities (Berk, 2009). Peers also play a role in children's gender socialization. For example, classmates and playmates can reinforce and police each other's gender conformity. By age three, peers encourage stereotyped behavior through praising, imitating, or taking part in the same activity when a classmate responds in a gender-typical way (Berk, 2009). When children engage in behavior not typical of their gender, however, peers are likely to express their disapproval. Boys are most involved in regulating the behaviors of each other. A boy who engages frequently in "girls'" activities is often ignored by other boys, even when he participates in traditionally masculine activities (Berk, 2009). Pressure from peers and family to choose same-sex friends is another important reason why children engage in sex segregation. Children who cross gender lines to make other-sex friends often endure teasing and taunting by their peers and their friendships may be discouraged, deliberately or inadvertently, by teachers and parents. In fact, children involved in other-sex friendships tend to be less popular with both same- and other-sex peers (Mehta & Strough, 2009). Many cross-gender friendships are enacted at home and in the neighborhood, but are hidden at school (see Ruble, Martin, & Berenbaum, 2006).

Although some process of gender socialization is present in every family, the phenomenon varies widely. Much of the research on how parents perceive and interact with their children is based on studies of white, middle-class U.S. families. The prevailing notion, born out of these studies, that parents view boys as strong and girls as fragile, foster more autonomy in boys, and expect boys to perform better in mathematics and the sciences, does not necessarily generalize across diverse families. Sharp and Ispa (2009), for instance, conducted a longitudinal study of nine African-American, low-income, single-mother families living in the inner city. While the mothers held different expectations for sons and daughters, these expectations were also different from the typical gendered expectations of white, middle-class parents. These African-American mothers focused on fostering strength, self-reliance, and independence in their daughters. Many added that they wanted their daughters to have goals in life and to be able to voice their thoughts. All five mothers with first-born daughters ranked leadership, being assertive, valuing oneself, or perseverance in their top three child-rearing goals. These expectations rested, at least in part, on the belief that men could not always be trusted and thus mothers needed to teach their daughters to be self-sufficient. Mothers were more pessimistic about their abilities to influence their sons' futures. Yet they expressed the desire that their sons be respectful toward women, be caring, and stay in school.

It is worth noting that the primary gender stereotypes at work among Sharp and Ispa's (2009) research participants—of the strong black woman and the endangered black man—while different than those observed in white, middle-class families, also reflect the belief that men and women are essentially different. The stereotype of the strong, invincible African-American woman, for example, arose during slavery in the United States and results in the belief that black women can withstand more hardships than other groups. Ultimately, these images can reinforce racist, classist, and sexist environments (Sharp & Ispa, 2009).

The intersections of race, class, and gender are also apparent in Hill's (2002) interviews with thirty-five African-American parents. Hill found that every parent supported gender equality to some degree regardless of the gender of the parent or child, or the family's socioeconomic class (2002). As one divorced mother of a nine-year-old son said: "I will definitely teach my son that men and women are equal; he is not the head of anybody. His wife will always have input and say-so in whatever is going on in their lives. And he needs to know that . . . when we were growing up, boys washed dishes, boys cooked; girls washed dishes, girls cooked. My mother taught us pretty equally to do everything, just in case you were on your own you wouldn't have to depend on somebody" (Hill, 2002, p. 497).

However, social class did play a role in the extent to which African-American parents supported gender equality. Parents who were "second-generation middle-class," that is, were raised themselves by middle-class parents, were most committed to gender equality, had the broadest definition of gender equality, and supported gender equality both in the workplace and at home. Middle-class parents who were reared in low-income homes expressed support for gender equality in the workforce, but were less likely to espouse this belief with regards to the home. Hill (2002) hypothesizes that these "first-generation middle-class" parents experienced more social-class anxiety than their second-generation counterparts and felt a need to distance themselves from the racial stereotype of the strong African-American mother. In this way, experiences of race and class interacted to produce different child-rearing beliefs relating to gender.

Families in which mothers are employed may provide less gender-typical home environments. Maternal employment is associated with fewer stereotyped beliefs in boys and girls and less stereotypical behavior and preferences in girls. This is probably due not only to the presence of a working mother as a role model, but also to less traditional ideas in the home and to access to more information outside of the home. Similarly, when fathers share equally in caregiving, their children tend to engage in less sex segregation and are more likely to consider less traditional occupations (see Ruble, Martin, & Berenbaum, 2006).

There is some evidence that lesbian mothers and gay fathers provide home environments that are less gender-typical than those created by heterosexual parents. Sutfin and colleagues (Sutfin, Fulcher, Bowles, & Patterson, 2008) found that children's bedrooms in homes headed by two-parent lesbian mothers were decorated in less gender-traditional ways than those headed by heterosexual couples. Lesbian mothers were also more likely to espouse liberal views, agreeing more often, for example, that it is as acceptable for boys to be shy as it is for girls. The children of lesbian mothers also had more liberal views about gender than the children of heterosexual parents (Sutfin et al., 2008). Bigner and Jacobsen (1989) found that gay fathers and heterosexual fathers were about equally involved with their children, but gay fathers tended to be more responsive to their child's needs, and more consistent in explaining reasons for appropriate behavior.

The gender socialization of children can be complex in immigrant families. The children of immigrants to the United States, for example, may encounter both socialization into the culture of their parents and socialization through schooling, peers, and the media into mainstream American culture. Because "being a woman" and "being a man" can vary widely across cultures, immigrant children may struggle with which norms of gendered behavior to conform. In Das Dasgupta's (1998) study of Indian immigrants to the United States, she found that first-generation mothers and their second-generation daughters were more likely to have liberal views on gender equality than their male counterparts, but that they also experienced more anxiety about these views than fathers and sons who held similar liberal beliefs. This suggests that the Indian immigrant women in the study may have experienced more pressure to hold traditional views than their male counterparts.

Educational Institutions

Schools also are important contexts for gender-role socialization. Although important strides have been made in equalizing the experiences of boys and girls, some gender stereotyping persists. The very structure of many schools models traditional gender roles. Men are more likely to hold positions of power, acting as principals or teaching high-prestige classes like physics, while women are generally overrepresented as teachers of younger children (see Ruble, Martin, & Berenbaum, 2006). In addition, many teachers interact differently with boys and girls. Preschool teachers, for example, tend to encourage children to engage in play associated with their gender and dissuade children from playing in non-gender-traditional ways. In the younger grades, girls tend to gather around the teacher and engage in directed activities, which may lead them to become compliant and to ask for help frequently. Boys, on the other hand, tend to play farther from the teacher, which allows them to engage more in creativity, leadership, and assertiveness (Berk, 2009). Seemingly benign school practices also help to encourage sex-differentiated behavior. For example, children may be separated by gender for relatively unimportant activities like standing in line (see Ruble, Martin, & Berenbaum, 2006).

Gender-role beliefs and practices can impact children's educational achievement. For example, consistent with a widespread belief that males are better at mathematics while females are superior at reading and verbal tasks, even very talented girls begin to turn away from mathematics as early as middle school. Although it is difficult to disentangle biological processes from sociocultural ones, research suggests any gender-based cognitive differences are much more nuanced. As summarized by Spelke (2005, p. 953), "Girls and women tend to excel on tests of verbal fluency, arithmetic calculation, and memory for the spatial locations of objects. Boys and men tend to excel on tests of verbal analogies, mathematical word problems, and memory for the geometric configuration of an environment."

These differences in cognition are small, however, with significant variation within both genders as well as overlap in male and female distributions. Researchers have concluded that men and women have equal capacities for math and science (Spelke, 2005).

There is an ongoing debate over whether teachers tend to provide more or different support for boys' and girls' learning. Some research indicates, for example, that throughout the grades, most teachers interact more with boys and interrupt them less than girls (see Ruble, Martin, & Berenbaum, 2006). In addition, evidence suggests that teachers praise boys more (Buchmann, DiPrete, & McDaniel, 2008). However, some research also suggests that schools may favor characteristics that girls tend to embody, such as sitting quietly, taking turns to speak, and so forth, which may place boys at a disadvantage. As in most other areas, it is difficult to determine what is biological and what is sociocultural (Okopny, 2008). Researchers recognize that a combination of both factors is most likely at work. For example, are boys more likely to move around and have trouble sitting still because of biological and developmental makeup, or because teachers more often chastise girls for poor classroom comportment while resigning themselves to the fact that "boys will be boys"? What is certain is that while girls tend to receive better grades in school, boys' achievement on standardized tests, such as the ACT and SAT, remains higher (Okopny, 2008; Wilson, 2007).

As societies advance and increasing levels of expertise are necessary to successfully compete, educational institutions play increasingly important roles in the lives of young adults. In wealthy countries, higher education is a robust reality for women. The current rate of women's enrollment in U.S. colleges and universities is ground-breaking, given that most were closed to women until the latter half of the twentieth century. According to recent estimates, about 58 percent of U.S. undergraduate students are women (Wilson, 2007). Women began surpassing men in college graduation rates as early as the beginning of the 1980s. In the United States, as well as in much of the industrialized world, more women attend college than men, and women get better grades (Buchmann et al., 2008; Mastekaasa & Smeby, 2008). Male undergraduates report that they spend more time playing video games, exercising, watching television, and partying and less time studying than female undergraduates (Wilson, 2007). How to help young men achieve academically is an important issue today for parents, educators, policy makers, and social workers in the United States.

The upward trend in women's educational achievement also exists with regards to graduate and professional degrees. In 1970, American women earned 40 percent of master's degrees and 14 percent of doctoral degrees. In 2008, women earned 59 percent of master's degrees and 49 percent of doctoral degrees. Similarly, in 1970, women earned 5 percent of law degrees, 8 percent of medical degrees, and 1 percent of dentistry degrees. In 2008, women earned 49 percent of law degrees, 47 percent of medical degrees, and 44 percent of dentistry degrees (Buchmann et al., 2008). The expansion of the community college system also opened up important educational opportunities for both men and women, particularly for those from marginalized groups. Although women are somewhat more likely than men to enroll in community colleges, this does not explain the higher rates at which women graduate from four-year colleges (Buchmann et al., 2008).

The same educators and policy makers who are concerned that boys are falling behind girls in primary and secondary school believe these trends signal a "boys' crisis" in university education as well. Some colleges are trying to attract more men by adding engineering programs and football teams, and making admissions brochures more appealing to men (Wilson, 2007). Other experts advise caution when focusing on gender differences in college enrollment. They note that most of the young men not attending college are from low-income and minority backgrounds, suggesting that the problem is related to the intersection of class, race, and gender. Indeed, the divide in educational achievement between black and white students is larger than between male and female students, and the gap between achievement of poor and wealthy students is even larger. The gender gap in educational achievement is largest for low-income students of all races but entirely disappears for students from the wealthiest families.

Although more women than men in the United States receive bachelor's degrees each year, significant differences remain in what men and women study in college. These differences explain in part why women and men remain segregated by occupation after college. Because fields traditionally dominated by women tend to earn less money than those traditionally dominated by men, these differences also partially account for the gender wage gap (Mastekaasa & Smeby, 2008), which is discussed at length later. Women are underrepresented in science and engineering fields while overrepresented in nursing and education programs. For example, in 2006, 57 percent of college graduates were women, but women made up only 25.1 percent of computer and information sciences majors, 21.4 percent of physics majors, and 20.5 percent of engineering majors (Fox, Sonnert, & Nikiforova, 2009). A ground-breaking report issued in 2007 by the National Academy of Sciences, the National Academy of Engineering, and the Institute of Medicine found that with every step up the academic ladder, the number of women in science and engineering falls significantly (National Academy of Sciences, 2007). In other words, as students transition from high school to college, more women than men who express an interest in science and engineering ultimately choose different majors. The same is true after college when more women than men with science and engineering degrees select alternative fields for further study. Likewise, fewer women than men with doctoral degrees in science and engineering apply for tenure-track positions at colleges and universities. Indeed, there are fewer women than men faculty members at colleges and universities, and an even smaller proportion are hired in science and engineering departments (Adamuti-Trache & Andres, 2008). Only 15.4 percent of full professors in the social and behavioral sciences and 14.8 percent of full professors in life sciences are women. The percentage of women in all other science and engineering fields is in the single digits (National Academy of Sciences, 2007).

Several reasons may account for the small number of women in science and engineering fields. The National Academies report found that women who do complete science and engineering degrees are "very likely" to face gender-based discrimination in their departments. Science and engineering departments tend—intentionally or inadvertently—to offer more support to men. In the face of colleagues who question their ability or commitment, women often feel that they have to continually "prove" themselves (National Academy of Sciences, 2007).

Family and peers also impact the educational choices of young people and may help socialize girls and boys into traditional fields. Notably, the belief that men are better at math and science persists, despite the fact that women receive better grades in math and science classes than men in elementary school, high school, and college (Buchmann et al., 2008; Mastekaasa & Smeby, 2008). Men also tend to overestimate their mathematical abilities, which may help explain why they are more likely to engage in activities that pave the way for entrance into science and engineering fields (Mastekaasa & Smeby, 2008).

Women's educational opportunities are associated with better outcomes not only for the women themselves, but also for their children. Around the world, increases in women's literacy are associated with better health outcomes for their children. For instance, children of mothers with higher rates of education and Arabic literacy were less malnourished, even when other socioeconomic factors were controlled (Glewwe, 1999). In Japan, education was linked with better nutrition among pregnant women, while occupation and income were not (Murakami et al., 2009). Maternal education is also linked with lower rates of childbearing. In a study of black South African women, each additional year of schooling was associated with 0.12 fewer children (Thomas, 1999). Research in rural and urban Mexico and Nepal and urban Zambia and Venezuela, conducted at Harvard University by the Project on Maternal Schooling, suggests that as women's school attendance increases, their literacy and comprehension skills grow, leading to improved understanding of health information (Schnell-Anzola, Rowe, & LeVine, 2005). The researchers hypothesize that better understanding of health information, in turn, leads women to better utilize health-care services, such as prenatal care, and more frequently use contraception and domestic health practices, which accounts for children's better health (Schnell-Anzola, Rowe, & LeVine, 2005). In all, it seems that greater rates of education for women—even small increases—translate to widespread gains.

Media

The media play an important role in our perceptions of men and women. Individuals of all ages receive daily messages about gender in television programming, movies, video games, music videos, the Internet, magazines, billboards, radio, and more. Many children spend much of their free time watching television, which offers an important way in which they learn about gendered stereotypes (see Ruble, Martin, & Berenbaum, 2006). One concern is the underrepresentation of women in television. In 1993, female characters made up about one-quarter to one-third of all roles in television programming. Children's television is particularly biased in favor of male characters. There are more men than women in children's programming, generally, and as many as four or five men to one woman in cartoons. The comparatively few female characters in contemporary television suggest that women are undervalued. Stereotypical portrayals of men and women in television are another concern. Although male and female characters are somewhat less stereotyped than in the past, men and women overwhelmingly maintain traditional roles in both adult and children's programming (see Ruble, Martin, & Berenbaum, 2006).This is of particular concern because research indicates that children are very susceptible to messages conveyed by the media (Baker & Raney, 2007). In 2006, there were more depictions of women possessing high-powered careers than in the past, but in most other arenas, women continued to be portrayed in highly stereotypical ways. For example, women are usually young, white, middle-class, slender, beautiful, and clad in revealing outfits (see Ruble, Martin, & Berenbaum, 2006).They tend to be emotional and take part in family and romantic situations (Berk, 2009). Men, on the other hand, while also typically white and middle-class, are generally older than female characters, muscular, and more likely to be dominant and powerful (see Berk, 2009; Ruble, Martin, & Berenbaum, 2006).

Children's books, although less stereotyped than in the past, continue to use gender stereotypes. Girls generally have limited roles and are depicted as more dependent and in need of help than boys.Although girls sometimes engage in less traditional behavior, boys are rarely depicted as feminine (see Ruble, Martin, & Berenbaum, 2006).

Similar concerns are found in music-oriented broadcasting, video games, and teen magazines. In radio broadcasting, music videos, and their accompanying advertisements, women are underrepresented, and are ten times more likely to be scantily clad than men. Many video games depict violent, gender-stereotyped scenarios and portray female characters as sex objects. Furthermore, magazines marketed for teenage girls make considerable use of gender stereotypes and focus on women's appearance and romantic desirability, while magazines marketed at boys provide entertainment and focus on hobbies and activities (see Ruble, Martin, & Berenbaum, 2006).

Children who watch television frequently hold more stereotypical notions about men and women than children who are occasional viewers. In fact, five-year-olds are aware of gender stereotypes on television and can predict whether men or women are most likely to play a particular role on television. Studies also indicate that adolescents who frequently encounter media with sexual content, such as soap operas or music videos, are more likely to think of sex in casual and stereotypical ways. One significant concern with studies such as these is determining the direction of influence. For example, does programming with sexual content influence adolescents' beliefs, or are adolescents who already view sex in these ways more likely to seek out media that confirm their beliefs? (see Ruble, Martin, & Berenbaum, 2006).

A fascinating study lends some support to the idea that the direction of causality goes from television programming to children. Children interviewed in Canadian towns without access to television held less stereotypical beliefs than comparison children. But two years after television was introduced, the stereotypical beliefs of these children increased (Williams,

1986).This study serves as a reminder that changes in access to media can influence attitudes and beliefs about gender.

Acquisition

Although individuals are influenced by their families, peers, schools, the media, and so forth, they are by no means passive recipients of gender-role socialization. Not all individuals or groups of individuals respond in similar ways to the gendered messages they receive. Some individuals and groups of individuals embrace traditional gender roles. Others resist traditional gender roles, not only in childhood, but through organized opposition to gender-based oppression as adults. Individuals' responses to gender-role socialization can impact subsequent socialization practices, so that the process of socialization and acquisition are mutually influencing.There is a long history of resistance to traditional roles and concomitant gender-based oppression. In the early nineteenth century, married European-American women had very few legal rights under English common law, and African-American women and Native American women had even fewer. After two women's movements at the end of the nineteenth and twentieth centuries, women's roles in U.S. society have broadened, and contemporary children and adolescents are presented with a comparatively wide array of options for their adult lives. Yet struggles for women's rights continue around the globe. In Pakistan, for example, women are involved in movements to change the legal definition of rape so that marital rape can be prosecuted. Israeli women, on the other hand, are struggling to end Orthodox Jewish laws that allow only husbands to seek divorce (Burn, 2005).

Gender Meaning-Making

That individuals actively interpret what it means to be male or female within their cultural context is apparent from early childhood. Indeed, children are active, creative, and intelligent participants in gender meaning-making. Consider the following example:

> Six-year-old Adam has a two-and-a-half-year-old sister named Amara. When Adam's six-year-old friend Jason comes over to play, Amara rushes to join in, calling herself a "baby boy."Adam and Jason become upset and report the incident to Adam's and Amara's mother.Their mother suggests that Amara is a "tomboy." Adam and Jason latch onto the word and teach Amara to say "I'm a baby tomboy." Once Amara's gender is reestablished, the three begin playing together.
>
> At age six,Adam and Jason are at the height of gender stereotyping.Two-and-a-half-year-old Amara, on the other hand, is in the process of learning her gender and the gender of others.When Amara labels herself a boy (perhaps because she hears her brother and his friend call themselves boys), the gendered roles of Adam's and Jason's world are violated. To feel comfortable

again, they teach Amara to call herself a "tomboy." Once she uses this word, the boys include her in their play. The boys' creative solution reinforces the male-female binary but also indicates some room for gender nonconformity within it.

Many children follow a developmental trajectory in which gender stereotyping peaks at age five or six and begins to wane at age seven or eight. Five- and six-year-olds often think in generalizations, not recognizing individual differences. Adam and Jason, for example, were unable to consider that Amara, a girl, might enjoy masculine activities like playing with boys. In a similar instance, five-year-old Jason told his family that "all doctors are boys," even though his mother is a doctor. He was aware of her profession but was not yet able to use this knowledge to revise his stereotyped belief. At age eight, however, Jason articulated that "some girls are doctors too." As his cognitive abilities increased, Jason's flexibility with gender stereotypes also increased. Interestingly, Trautner et al. (2005) found that children who saw the world in rigid gender stereotypes when they were young did not necessarily remain rigid as they grew older. In fact, the children who expressed rigidity at an earlier age were more flexible when they were older with regards to gender stereotypes than their counterparts were. In other words, these children were more likely as older children to say that a particular behavior or trait, such as doing the dishes, could be applied to both sexes, rather than just one. It is unclear why this might be the case, but one theory is that children gain flexibility at a steady rate from the peak of rigidity until age ten and if rigidity begins earlier there may be time for greater flexibility to set in (Trautner et al., 2005).

Children's Attitudes toward Their Own Gender

Individuals' ability to actively interpret the gendered messages to which they are exposed is also illustrated through their various responses toward their own gender. For example, few children in the Western world wish they were the opposite sex, but more girls do so than boys (Ruble, Martin, & Berenbaum, 2006). Gender-based oppression, including limited opportunities faced by girls, may help explain this discrepancy. Girls' desire to be male increases during adolescence, a time in which girls may become increasingly aware of unequal treatment of men and women and may experience more pressure to be conventionally attractive (Ruble, Martin, & Berenbaum, 2006). In the United States, girls' desire to be male decreased from the 1950s to the 1980s, a period in which U.S. women made gains in education and in the workforce, experienced growing sexual freedom, and drew attention and resources toward combating sexual assault and domestic violence. However, girls continue to show less satisfaction with their gender than boys. Egan and Perry (2001) found that more boys in fourth through eighth grade expressed gender contentedness than did their female peers (Egan & Perry, 2001).

Girls' dissatisfaction with their gender may relate to their negative perceptions of what it is to be a woman. According to one study, children older than ten recognize that women are less valued, and a recent study suggests that children as young as five or six are aware of gender discrimination. In addition, children pick up on stereotypes regarding men's and women's intelligence. Many five- to seven-year-old children consider men more competent overall. Similarly, girls and boys often do not share the same perceptions of their abilities (see Ruble, Martin, & Berenbaum, 2006). For example, when girls performed better than boys on achievement exams, their self-assessments were equal to boys'. As one researcher commented, "Girls did not credit themselves with being talented even when they performed better than boys" (Ruble, Martin, & Berenbaum, 2006, p. 872).

But boys by no means escape the binds of gender oppression. More than girls, boys who deviate from traditional gender behaviors endure teasing, taunting, and cruelty at the hands of their peers. This persecution may increase during junior high and high school, when children tend to identify more intensely with gender roles (Schope & Eliason, 2004). While women have made strides in equalizing their daughters' opportunities with those of men (like wearing pants, playing school sports, and attending college), boys who "act like girls" through their behaviors, interests, mannerisms, and appearance often have little support for their cross-gender behavior. Being or acting feminine retains tremendous negative associations. The stigma of male homosexuality is entwined with the policing of feminine boys. Schope and Eliason (2004) point out that lesbians tend to be less feared and that women who appear androgynous or "masculine" are generally not subjected to the same level of persecution as effeminate men.

The Gender Continuum

That individuals actively respond to gender-role socialization is illustrated by the fact that not all individuals engage in behaviors that are stereotypically matched to their sex. Some wear clothing and engage in activities associated with the opposite sex, and a small number identify strongly with the opposite sex. For some children, this is the beginning of their lives as transgender individuals—people whose gender identity is not the same as their sex at birth. Some children as young as three years old would like to be or believe they are the opposite sex (Lelchuk, 2006). In many non-Western cultures around the world, categories traditionally existed for individuals who identified as neither male nor female. Some researchers even suggest that it is a common feature of human societies for some individuals to live within a sex that is different from the sex into which they were born. In most of these cases, individuals who were considered neither male nor female were not intersex (possessing both biological male and female sex characteristics), but rather occupied a different gender classification because of social factors (Lang & Kuhnle, 2008). In the 1930s, anthropologist Willard W. Hill wrote about *nadleehe*, individuals who held high prestige as an in-between gender among the Navajo in the American Southwest. They performed both men's and women's jobs and served the important social function of mediating between men and women in arguments (Lang & Kuhnle, 2008).

The reciprocal nature of gender-role socialization and acquisition is illustrated by responses to children who do not conform to traditional gender roles; that is, children's acquisition of gender-role socialization messages impacts, in turn, their gender-role socialization. Today, an increasing number of mental health professionals, educators, pediatricians, and parents in the United States are adopting a stance of acceptance toward children who do not conform to traditional gender norms. In an earlier era in mainstream American culture, non-gender-conforming children would have undergone psychoanalysis and behavior modification, but now there is a growing belief that such children should be allowed to behave and dress as they choose. Park Day School, a private elementary and middle school in Oakland, California, for example, has taken steps to ensure that non-gender-conforming children are supported (Brown, 2006). Children are allowed to cross-dress and to be referred to by the pronoun of their choice, even if they are biologically the opposite sex. Teachers use gender-neutral language and line children up using shoe color, rather than gender. Children are given the freedom to find where they fall on the gender continuum—a term used by some gender identity activists to describe a range of feelings of femininity and masculinity (Brown, 2006). Finding a way to support such children is complicated by the extreme hostility and violence faced by many non-gender-conforming individuals. Many parents try to push their children toward conformity to protect them from harm. In 1993, a transgender man who called himself Brandon Teena was murdered in Lincoln, Nebraska, when friends discovered that he was biologically female. The 1999 feature film *Boys Don't Cry* was based on Teena's life (Sloop, 2000). In 2002, Gwen Araujo, a seventeen-year-old transgender woman, was assaulted and strangled to death in Newark, California, when her biological sex was discovered (Wright, 2003). As the gender identity rights movement gains momentum and the public becomes increasingly conscious of transgender concerns, there is sure to be growing discussion of this issue in social work circles.

SOME GENDER-SENSITIVE ISSUES

Gender-sensitive issues and experiences are those that only, or more frequently, affect one gender, such as pregnancy. Sexual assault is an example of a gender-sensitive experience; although it affects men as well as women, it more frequently affects women. Individuals may encounter a variety of gender-sensitive issues and experiences throughout the life span.

Certain issues may come to the fore at particular times of life, but others may resurface in different forms at various points in the life span. In this section, we discuss a few illustrative issues particularly relevant to social work practice with women. In adolescence, young women may be especially vulnerable to dating violence and sexual assault. In early adulthood, many women begin families, and issues around child-bearing may become salient. In midlife, as women work to support themselves and their families, gender discrimination in employment may be especially significant. In later adulthood, many older women struggle with issues of poverty. Of course, many of the issues described below can surface at many points in the life span and can impact men as well as women. In the final section, we discuss one such issue: body dissatisfaction as it emerges at different points in the life span and is inflected for women and men.

Adolescence: Dating Violence and Sexual Assault

Although intimate partner violence is a problem throughout the life span, adolescents are particularly vulnerable to dating violence—both as victims and as perpetrators. Research suggests that adolescent girls and younger women are more likely than older women to be in abusive relationships and, in particular, to experience sexual abuse at the hands of a partner (Próspero, 2007). Próspero conducted a study with young adolescents (median age 13.5) and adults (median age 23.8) and found that young adolescent boys were significantly more likely to respond aggressively to their partners than adult men, adult women, or adolescent girls. Researchers suggest that through their daily interactions with their families, peers, community members, and the media, some young adolescent boys learn to view themselves as superior to young adolescent girls and believe that they should control "their" female partners through violence. Adolescent boys who respond with violence may have witnessed role models and family members use violence against intimate partners and may have come to hold values and attitudes that condone intimate partner violence. Indeed, social institutions and families may teach boys that violence is an appropriate means of resolving conflict, and that within relationships boys should have control over partners and the use of violence is appropriate to maintain this control (Próspero, 2007).

Given their vulnerability to intimate partner violence, adolescents may be well served by violence-prevention programs, including those that help teenagers determine how to intervene on behalf of a friend experiencing intimate partner violence. Weisz and Black (2008) showed 202 urban, African-American seventh graders a video clip in which two adolescents confront a young man who is abusing his girlfriend. The students were then asked to respond in writing to several questions about how they would handle this situation. Most students responded that they would not get involved and that the violence was "only the couple's business." Some students expressed fear of getting hurt or making the situation worse, whereas others described sensible plans for intervention. Weisz and Black (2008) suggest the need for adolescent education about which situations warrant peer intervention and on how to intervene effectively and safely.

Although sexual assault is a crime that affects males and females of all ages, adolescent girls are particularly vulnerable. People of all ages can experience sexual victimization, but children and adolescents are most vulnerable. Indeed, approximately 22 percent of women and 48 percent of men who were victims of rape were younger than twelve when first victimized. In addition to being an act of violence that breaches an individual's human rights, rape is also a gendered crime. In the vast majority of cases, women and girls are raped by men. Approximately 32 percent of women victimized by rape were between age twelve and seventeen when first victimized (Tjaden & Thoennes, 2006).

In a nationwide survey conducted by the U.S. government, 17.6 percent of women and 3 percent of men interviewed had experienced an attempted or completed rape during their lifetime. In other words, about one in six women and one in thirty-three men are the survivors of rape or attempted rape. Although most women were first victimized as children or adolescents, many women experience subsequent rapes as adults. Because of fear that their attacker will seek reprisal, shame over the experience, or a belief that what happened to them was not a police matter, only about one in five women report their sexual assault to the police. In addition, only about 30 percent of women who were injured during their most recent sexual attack received medical treatment. Contrary to what was once thought, most rape victims know their attackers. The National Violence against Women Survey reported that only 16.7 percent of female victims and 22.8 percent of male victims were raped by a stranger. The majority of women were attacked by a current or former intimate partner, while most men were assaulted by an acquaintance, such as a friend, teacher, or coworker (Tjaden & Thoennes, 2006).

Although women of all backgrounds can experience sexual assault, some women are at heightened risk due to the intersecting oppressions of race and social class. Native American women are significantly more likely than white, African-American, or mixed-race women to experience rape (Tjaden & Thoennes, 2000). One in three Native American women will be raped during her lifetime. Indeed, Native women who live on tribal lands are more than twice as likely as white women to be raped (Duthu, 2008). Alaska is the state with the highest per capita incidence of rape in the United States. In Anchorage, Native American women are more than ten times as likely to be raped as non-Native women ("United States," 2007).

Although white and African-American women are usually raped by members of their own racial group, more than 80 percent of the rapes of Native American women are committed by non-Native men. The rapes of Native American women are often extremely violent. Weapons are used in the rapes of Native American women three times as often as in all other rapes (Duthu, 2008).

One significant barrier in the struggle to stop the sexual assault of Native American women is the difficulty of prosecuting their rapes. Many rapes of Native women are perpetrated by non-Native men. Yet federal law forbids tribal courts from trying non-Natives—even if the assault occurred on tribal lands—so rape survivors must take their cases to federal or state courts, which often fail to prosecute (Duthu, 2008; "United States," 2007). The lack of trained sexual-assault nurse examiners at Indian Health Service facilities to gather forensic and other evidence for trial is also a sizeable barrier to prosecution. Fortunately, in July 2008 Congress introduced the Tribal Law and Order Act with a section aimed at combating high sexual-assault rates of Native women by clarifying the role of federal, state, and tribal courts with regards to crimes committed on Native land, increasing communication between these courts, and ceding more power to tribal courts to prosecute these crimes (Amnesty International, 2008). Native activists, Amnesty International, and other advocacy groups, however, report few on-the-ground changes on tribal lands and urge the U.S. government to continue to take immediate action to address the sexual assault of Native American women (Amnesty International, 2008).

Like Native American women, African-American women have a horrific history of sexual abuse. During slavery, white plantation owners engaged in widespread sexual exploitation of black women. This sexual assault not only terrorized victims and their families and communities, but provided a brutal way for white masters to "breed" offspring to work their plantations. To justify the sexual assault of African-American women, stereotypes emerged that black women were overly sexual and therefore could not be raped. Throughout much of the twentieth century, employment barriers forced most African-American women to work as domestic servants in the homes of white families, a position that kept them highly vulnerable to sexual assault. Historically, successfully prosecuting a rape case was nearly impossible for black women, even when the perpetrator was black himself, further suggesting that African-American women were deemed "unrapeable." It was not until the late 1960s that a southern court made a conviction against a white man in a rape case filed by a black woman (McNair & Neville, 1996).

One contemporary example of law enforcement officers thwarting African-American women's efforts to prosecute rape was the allegedly deliberate misclassification of rape cases of thousands of low-income, African-American women in Philadelphia in the 1980s and 1990s (Irving,

2007; McCoy, 2003). In all, about 30 percent of rape cases were not investigated due to misclassification, and most of the victims in these cases were poor, black women (Irving, 2007). As an indication of how the unit viewed rape cases, the sex-crime unit's assigned investigator in 1995 nicknamed the sex crimes department "The Lying Bitches Unit" (McCoy, 2003). After an investigation by the *Philadelphia Inquirer* in 1999, the police department reopened those cases from the previous five years, the statute of limitations for rape charges, and some perpetrators were tried and convicted (McCoy, Fazlollah, & Matza, 2000).

When the law offers little protection, African-American women may be less likely to seek legal recourse. In fact, black women are less likely than white women to report rape (McNair & Neville, 1996). This may be due in part to the fact that African-American women are less likely than white women to be viewed as victims in sexual assault cases and are more often blamed for the attack (Donovan, 2007; McNair & Neville, 1996). Owing to the history of racial profiling and police brutality directed at African Americans, black women may also be wary of these institutions. If the perpetrator is black, African-American women may be reluctant to press charges because of the history of rape accusations leveled against black men. Their misgivings may also extend to other social service organizations, like rape crisis centers, which African-American rape survivors tend to underutilize (McNair & Neville, 1996).

Rape is a crime primarily motivated by abuse of power. According to some feminists, the threat of rape forms the foundation of men's power over women (Burn, 2005). Feminist scholars argue that much of the world lives in a rape culture in which societal practices condone and often encourage sexual violence (McMahon, 2007). The frequency with which individuals and the media objectify women's and men's bodies is one way in which societies perpetuate rape culture. The fact that rape laws around the world are weak and poorly enforced also indicates that governments do not take sexual violence seriously and even condone it through lack of protection (Burn, 2005).

Although women are the victims of rape most of the time, men can and are raped, almost exclusively by other men. The reporting rates of male victims are believed to be even lower than those of women. Only approximately 13 percent of men who had been raped since their eighteenth birthday reported the incident to the police (Tjaden & Thoennes, 2006). Shame, guilt, embarrassment, worry that they will not be believed, concern about confidentiality, and fear of being labeled gay are all reasons why men rarely report being raped (Sable, Danis, Mauzy, & Gallagher, 2006). Indeed, some of these worries are well-founded. In a study of U.K. medical students, male rape victims were viewed more negatively than female rape victims (Anderson & Quinn, 2009). In addition, some rape crisis centers do not offer services to men, and some are reported to be insensitive to male victims, factors that might also decrease rates of reporting rapes and seeking help (Tewksbury, 2007).

Early Adulthood: Childbearing

Starting a family is a significant event for many young adults. Access to high-quality prenatal, perinatal, and postpartum care is essential for the health of women and their children worldwide. But quality of maternity care varies widely across the globe, as does women's ability to procure it. In sub-Saharan Africa and South Asia, a significant number of women die from complications related to pregnancy and childbirth. Together, these regions account for 86 percent of the maternal deaths around the world. They are also the places where women have the least access to skilled health-care personnel, namely doctors, midwives, and nurses (World Health Organization [WHO], 2007). Some wealthier countries, with the United States featuring most prominently, also struggle in their mission to provide high-quality maternity care. In the United States, oppressions of race, class, and nationality intertwine to place certain women at greater risk (Kabakchieva, 2009). In addition, while women in sub-Saharan Africa and South Asia often lack access to maternity care, women in the United States may face over-intervention by medical professionals, which can also lead to complications for women and infants and can take away women's sense of agency over their reproductive lives (Althabe & Belizán, 2006; Goer, 1995).

Dying in childbirth is a true danger in sub-Saharan Africa. The risk of maternal death is highest in Niger, where the probability that a fifteen-year-old woman will die from pregnancy-related causes in her lifetime is one in seven (WHO, 2007). Hemorrhage, hypertensive conditions, and infections account for the majority of maternal deaths in sub-Saharan Africa—resulting in nearly 500 deaths per 100,000 births each year (Ronsmans & Graham, 2006). The risk of maternal death in sub-Saharan African stands in sharp contrast to many countries in the industrialized world, where better access to high-quality prenatal, delivery, and postpartum care; safe water; hygienic conditions; contraception; and education make childbirth considerably less dangerous. In the Netherlands, for example, the lifetime risk of maternal death is 1 in 10,200 (WHO, 2007). The difference in maternal mortality rates between developed and developing countries is considered by many to be the greatest discrepancy in all public health statistics (Ronsmans & Graham, 2006). Unfortunately, little improvement has been made in maternal mortality rates since 1990. Indeed, maternal mortality rates are falling by only a slight margin each year—less than 1 percent worldwide and about 0.1 percent in sub-Saharan Africa. WHO, which drafts extensive guidelines and recommendations to help countries safeguard women and infants, has made an urgent call for improved access to health care for women in childbirth. In particular, WHO recommends the use of midwives—specialists in normal birth—as the most appropriate providers of maternity care (Reibel, 2004).

Modern midwifery refers to a woman-centric model of care in which practitioners offer continuous support for laboring mothers. Midwives view childbirth as a normal, natural process that requires minimal intervention. Indeed, many midwives consider the experience of birth to be a source of empowerment for women (Hayden, 2004). This model differs from the approach typically taken by physicians, in which birth is considered to be a medical emergency often requiring medical intervention and regimented surveillance. While the focus of midwives' education is on watching over normal physiological births, doctors' education focuses on intervention, particularly surgical (Goer, 1995). In most of Europe, midwives attend the majority of births. In contrast, physicians attend 95 percent of births in the United States, 99 percent of which take place in hospitals (Hayden, 2004). In Africa, less than 50 percent of births are attended by a skilled health worker, be it a midwife, doctor, or nurse (WHO, 2007).

In the twenty-first-century United States, professional midwives receive extensive education. Certified nurse-midwives complete a nursing degree and a master's degree in nurse-midwifery and then pass a national certification examination. They usually train in hospitals and are licensed to practice everywhere in the United States. Direct-entry midwives gain expertise through an apprenticeship with another midwife and/or training in an accredited midwifery school. To gain certification, they pass a written examination and act as the primary midwife for a specified number of births, prenatal exams, newborn exams, and postpartum visits (North American Registry of Midwives, 2008).

Evidence suggests that midwife-supervised births are at least as safe as physician-supervised births for low-risk births, a classification that can be applied to the majority of births. In a review of eleven trials involving over 12,000 women, Hatem, Sandall, Devane, Soltani, and Gates (2008) found that midwife-led care in hospitals was linked with several benefits for mothers and infants, such as lower rates of certain forms of intervention, and had no adverse effects. Notably, women's satisfaction with various aspects of the birth experience was higher with midwife-led births. Hatem et al. (2008) concluded by recommending that most women be offered midwife care. However, women with significant medical problems were not included in the trial, so these results cannot necessarily be extended to all women. Research on planned home births has produced similar data. Johnson and Daviss (2005) found that, for women in the United States and Canada whose pregnancies were low risk, planned home births with certified direct-entry midwives were associated with similar safety outcomes and less intervention than low-risk hospital births.

The safety of midwifery is also suggested by maternal and infant mortality rates in countries where midwifery is widely practiced. In the Netherlands, at least 65 percent of women are attended by midwives during childbirth (Reibel, 2004). In addition, 30 percent of Dutch women give birth at home with midwives, a statistic that has remained stable for the past ten years (Amelink-Verburg et al., 2008; Reibel, 2004). The Netherlands has one of the lowest maternal mortality rates in the world, with 6 maternal deaths per 100,000 births (WHO, 2007) and one of the lowest infant mortality rates at 4.9 infant deaths per 1,000 births (MacDorman & Mathews, 2009).

Maternity care offered in the United States ranks far below the majority of industrialized nations in both maternal mortality and infant mortality (Keefe, 2003). Although substantially lower than in many developing countries, the reported maternal death rate in the United States is 11 maternal deaths per 100,000 births, more than twice the rate of many European countries (WHO, 2007). In fact, experts believe that the maternal mortality rate in the United States is considerably higher than current statistics report. In 1998, the Centers for Disease Control and Prevention (CDC) acknowledged that the U.S. maternal mortality rate may be as much as three times higher each year than reported, because of misclassifications. Too frequently, death certificates in the United States do not indicate the relationship between a woman's death and her recent pregnancy (I. A. Gaskin, 2008).

Several factors may explain the comparatively high maternal mortality rates in the United States. Oppressions of race and class play a large role. Chronic health conditions arising before pregnancy, often related to lack of health care or poor nutrition, which are in turn linked to pervasive social inequality, may put mothers at risk. Inadequate prenatal care further strains vulnerable groups during pregnancy and may contribute to complications during labor and delivery (Kabakchieva, 2009). African-American women, for example, are four times as likely as white women to die from pregnancy-related causes. This amounts to 35 deaths of African-American women per 100,000 births (I. A. Gaskin, 2008). Legal and undocumented immigrants in the United States are also at heightened risk as laws increasingly restrict their access to health care. Notably, many of the countries with lower maternal mortality rates, such as Sweden, where the maternal mortality rate is 3 deaths per 100,000 births (WHO, 2007), provide more accessible health care and social services throughout the life span (Högberg, 2004). In addition, Sweden's low maternal death rate has been attributed to midwifery's long-established role in maternity care and the strong alliance in Sweden between doctors and midwives (Högberg, 2004).

Another important factor contributing to the United States' maternal mortality rate is the relative lack of postpartum care. More than half of maternal deaths occur one to forty-two days after birth, but most women in the United States don't have a follow-up visit with a health-care provider until six weeks after birth (Kuznar, 2010). Many countries—including Australia, England, the Netherlands, New Zealand, Norway, Northern Ireland, Scotland, Sweden, and Wales (all of which have lower maternal mortality rates than the United States)—have implemented policies to reduce the risk and provide immediate treatment of the serious complications that can arise after birth. These complications include late postpartum hemorrhaging, uterine or perineal infection, and postpartum depression (I. A. Gaskin, 2008; WHO, 2007). These countries send nurses to women's homes for the ten days or so after birth to check for problems. In the United States, on the other hand, hospital policies are more likely to send women home—with no follow-up home visits—before certain postpartum complications can be detected. Women who have a home birth with a midwife in the United States receive postpartum care more on par with the countries just named, because midwives typically follow up with frequent home visits after delivery (I. A. Gaskin, 2008).

The U.S. infant mortality rate is also comparatively high. At 6.86 infant deaths per 1,000 live births, the infant mortality rate is almost 50 percent higher than the U.S. goal of 4.5 infant deaths per 1,000 births ("CDC," 2008; MacDorman & Mathews, 2009). Based on the data available from 2005, the United States ranks thirtieth in the world in infant mortality. A primary reason for the U.S. infant mortality rate is the high number of preterm babies born in the United States, who are at greater risk of death or disability than babies who are born after thirty-seven weeks or more (MacDorman & Mathews, 2009). In 2004, one in eight infants born in the United States was born preterm as compared to one in eighteen in Finland and Ireland (MacDorman & Mathews, 2009). Indeed, a recent study indicated that the highest rates of preterm birth occur in Africa and North America, with 11.9 percent and 10.6 percent, respectively, of infants born preterm (Beck et al., 2010). Although preterm birth is linked to many causes, African-American women and low-income women are particularly at risk for preterm births (Goldenberg, Culhane, Iams, & Romero, 2008), suggesting that social inequality plays a role in the U.S. infant mortality rate.

Medical overintervention may also contribute to the relatively high maternal and infant mortality rates in the United States. For example, the rate of cesarean sections—major abdominal surgery to deliver a fetus from the uterus—in the United States is 31 percent (Childbirth Connection 2008), substantially higher than the ideal rate of 10–15 percent recommended by WHO (Althabe et al., 2006). Although cesarean sections are necessary in a minority of births and can save women's and babies' lives, when too many cesarean sections are performed, rates of maternal and infant mortality go up (Althabe & Belizán, 2006). Indeed, the increase in the number of cesarean sections performed in the United States from approximately 6 percent of births in 1970 to 24 percent in 1986 did not improve birth outcomes (Althabe & Belizán, 2006). Complications arising from cesarean section are estimated to occur five to ten times as often as those associated with vaginal birth. Indeed, some studies indicate that the maternal mortality rate is four to five times higher with cesarean section than with vaginal birth (Goer, 1995). The overuse of other medical interventions, including induction, electronic fetal monitoring, the use of synthetic hormones to speed up labor, and the use of analgesics for pain relief, can lead to complications that increase maternal and fetal distress and can lead to unnecessary cesarean sections (Goer, 1995; Rausch, 2008). Some women also report being dissatisfied with or even traumatized by births that involve medical intervention. Soet, Brack, and DiIorio (2003) found that 34 percent of women who were interviewed late in pregnancy and again several weeks after birth described the childbirth experience as traumatic and, of those, 40 percent developed symptoms of post-traumatic stress disorder. Feelings of powerlessness and the experience of medical intervention, as well as cesarean section specifically, were associated with reported trauma postpartum. Lack of social support was also a significant predictor of trauma symptoms (Soet, Brack, & DiIorio, 2003).

Some midwives, activists, and researchers suggest that the physician model, which views birth as a medical emergency, contributes to a culture of fear and overintervention in the United States, which in turn lays the foundation for traumatic birth experiences (I. M. Gaskin, 2003; Goer, 1995). Indeed, women supported through drug-free childbirths have reported greater satisfaction (Declercq & Chalmers, 2008; I. M. Gaskin, 2003) and feelings of empowerment (I. M. Gaskin, 2003). Reibel (2004) suggests that the growing rate of intervention in the United States indicates that women's bodies are increasingly becoming the site of invasive procedures that medical research has not necessarily proven efficacious.

Although many experts believe that the majority of women worldwide are capable of giving birth naturally with no intervention (I. M. Gaskin, 2003; Goer, 1995), clearly there are important reasons for obstetric care provided by doctors. In countries where women lack maternity care, the shortage of medically necessary cesarean sections accounts, in part, for high rates of maternal and infant mortality. Placental abruption (when the placenta separates from the uterus before birth), placenta previa (when the placenta is below the baby and blocks its exit from the cervix), or a pinched or compressed umbilical cord (which cuts off oxygen to the baby) are some examples in which a cesarean section may be necessary (American Congress of Obstetricians and Gynecologists, 2005).

Because of medical research indicating the frequent incidence of overintervention in labor and delivery in the United States, some women are turning to midwives as their primary providers during pregnancy and birth. Although physicians continue to attend the vast majority of births in the United States, a movement is growing to relegitimate midwifery, a field that went out of favor in the mid-twentieth century (Rausch, 2008). In addition, an increasing number of women in the United States are turning to doulas for support during labor (Lantz, Low, Sanjani, & Watson, 2005). Doulas are trained labor assistants who provide continuous one-on-one emotional, physical, and informational support to women during labor and delivery. They are not medical professionals but use drug-free comfort measures (such as position changes, immersion in a hot bath, and massage), encouraging words, and their training in the physiologic process of birth to relieve pain, enhance a woman's confidence in her body's abilities, and facilitate the progression of labor (Simkin, 2008). A review of sixteen randomized controlled trials involving over 13,000 women found that women who had continuous one-on-one support during labor and delivery, such as that provided by doulas, had slightly shorter labors, were more likely to have spontaneous vaginal deliveries, were less likely to use analgesics such as epidurals, and reported less dissatisfaction with their childbirth experiences (Hodnett, Gates, Hofmeyr, & Sakala, 2007). In many regions in the United States, women can hire a private doula to accompany their birth, although a small number of hospitals offer volunteer doula services to laboring women.

Middle Adulthood: Employment

By middle adulthood, many women around the world are supporting their families, and work is a central part of their daily lives. Around the globe, 53 percent of women who are mothers are employed outside the home, and the employment rate for women without children is 63 percent (Burn, 2005). Some economists point to the increase in women in the workforce in wealthy countries as the reason behind global GDP growth in the first years of the twenty-first century. Include women's unpaid labor—taking care of children, cooking, doing laundry, and so forth—and women work more than men do. Indeed, men have one to seven more hours of free time per week than women (Burn, 2005). At the turn of the twenty-first century, the U.S. workforce is split nearly 50-50 between men and women, and economists estimate that women may surpass men in employment rates in the near future (Mulligan, 2009).

Despite their clear contributions to the global and national economies, women face numerous obstacles in employment. They continue to grapple with lower wages than men even when they work the same jobs (the **gender wage gap**), inability to gain promotions (the glass ceiling), and consignment to the lowest-paying jobs in the worst working conditions (the sticky floor). Women also struggle with sexual harassment on the job, lack of paid maternity leave, and lack of high-quality affordable child care (Burn, 2005).

Around the world, women earn two-thirds as much as men (Burn, 2005). In the United States, women make on average seventy-seven cents for every dollar men make. The wage gap is even more pronounced across race and class lines. White women's earnings are nearly 80 percent of white men's, while African-American women's earnings are roughly 69 percent of white men's, and Latinas' are about 61 percent (Hartmann, Hegewisch, Liepmann, & Williams, 2010). Although the wage gap affects women across the economic spectrum, it affects poorer women more. Indeed, if women in the United States earned the same amount of money as men, more than 50 percent of low-income households would rise above the poverty line (Barko, 2002).

The gender wage gap is attributed to several causes. One is **occupational segregation**. Men and women are concentrated in different occupations, and almost without exception "men's jobs" earn more money and are more prestigious than "women's jobs," even if they do not require more education or training, or have more intrinsic value to society. This is known as horizontal occupational segregation, and it is pervasive in the United States, where 41 percent of full-time employed women work at jobs of which at least three in four workers are female while 50 percent of men work jobs where at least three of four workers are male. In Iran and Pakistan, occupational segregation is the reality for most of the workforce, with 85 percent and 93 percent of the population, respectively, working in a field dominated by one gender. Thailand has one of the lowest rates of occupational segregation, with only 25 percent of the population working primarily among members of the same gender (Burn, 2005). Unfortunately, even when men and women work the same jobs, significant pay differences exist. For example, women who are secretaries and administrative assistants earn 83.4 percent of each dollar made by men holding the same positions. Another important reason for the gender wage gap is vertical occupational segregation. This refers to situations in which men and women work in the same field, but work different jobs within that field. For a given employer, women workers tend to have the lowest-paid, least prestigious jobs (Burn, 2005). For example, Levine (2009) found in a case study of occupational segregation in an American midwestern manufacturing plant that few women worked in the plant (horizontal occupational segregation) and those who did were relegated to the lowest-paying and least prestigious jobs in the plant (vertical occupational segregation). In fact, just over half of women worked in the four lowest-paying jobs, whereas only 6.7 percent of men worked these jobs (Levine, 2009). The proverbial glass ceiling keeps qualified women from advancing in careers, while the sticky floor keeps many "stuck" in the least desirable jobs offered by an employer. Only about 30 percent of women worldwide work in administrative and managerial positions. It is estimated that if women continue to gain advancement at the same slow pace, it will take centuries for men and women to share equally in upper-level positions (Burn, 2005).

Why do women and men often end up working different jobs, and why do women's jobs tend to be lower paid and less prestigious? Recruitment tactics aimed at one sex and not the other and obstacles to promotion and career development all result in excluding men and women from certain fields. Women, for example, are more likely to be denied employment in male-dominated fields, even when they are fully qualified (Burn, 2005). Gender stereotyping learned in childhood and reinforced throughout the life span also may help explain why men and women themselves often do not seek out jobs unconventional for their sex. For example, from a young age, many girls and boys come to believe that women are not construction workers, and men are not nurses. In college, women and men also tend to segregate when they choose fields of study, with men more often choosing math and science fields that make more money (Mastekaasa & Smeby, 2008). The possibility of social difficulties and sexual harassment in male-dominated fields or departments may also discourage women from attempting promotion (Levine, 2009). Other explanations for the gender wage gap include that women choose jobs that make parenting easier, such as those that offer more flexible hours, easier work, or agreeable work conditions, rather than jobs with larger paychecks (Burn, 2005; Glass & Camarigg, 1992). There is a scarcity of research, however, to support this idea. In fact, women's jobs often involve less flexibility and working conditions that are equivalent to or worse than men's. For example, women's jobs are more likely to involve working with difficult clients, lack of autonomy, and mindless repetition (Burn, 2005). Some scholars also suggest that lack of education and training accounts for the differences in men's and women's jobs. This is certainly an important factor in parts of the world where women receive less education than men. However, it does not fully explain the gender wage gap because, despite significant leaps in women's education worldwide, women continue to be paid less than men. In many wealthy countries, women attain equivalent or higher levels of education than men yet make less money and work less prestigious jobs (Burn, 2005).

Because the gender wage gap cannot be explained by the notion that women's jobs are easier or require less training, scholars have concluded that women are often paid less simply because they are women. There are three main reasons for paying women less because of their sex. First, jobs typically held by women are undervalued. There is an assumption throughout much of the world that if women do the work, it must not be as important—and should not be as highly paid—as the work men do. Second, employers justify paying women less because they assume, often incorrectly, that they are not the primary wage earners of their families. Men should be paid more, in other words, because "they have families to support." Lastly, women are paid less because employers can get away with paying them less and do so to increase their earnings (Burn, 2005).

Sexual harassment on the job is another important obstacle that working women encounter. In the United States two types of sexual harassment are legally recognized: **quid pro quo sexual harassment** and **hostile environment sexual harassment**. If an employee refuses unwanted sexual advances from supervisors and then experiences a tangible loss, such as being fired or passed up for a raise, this is quid pro quo sexual harassment. One example of quid pro quo sexual harassment involved Kimberly Ellerth, who worked from 1993 to 1994 as a merchandising assistant and later as sales representative for Burlington Industries in Chicago. During her tenure at the company, Ellerth's supervisor repeatedly made offensive comments about her body, insinuated that wearing shorter skirts would improve her performance on the job, and demanded sexual favors, with which Ellerth did not comply. When she was considered for a promotion, her supervisor expressed uncertainty because she was not "loose enough." Finding the harassment "unbearable," Ellerth quit, and then filed her lawsuit. She argued that her supervisor's actions made her fearful of retaliation and thus she did not complain of the harassment to those higher in the company until after she resigned. In *Ellerth v. Burlington Industries*, the U.S. Supreme Court decided in favor of Ellerth, agreeing that employers are accountable when supervisors create hostile work environments involving threats of job-related retaliation, even when these threats were not, in fact, carried out (Equal Rights, 2009).

The second form of harassment, hostile environment sexual harassment, refers to situations in which supervisors, coworkers, or clients repeatedly expose a worker to unwanted sexual behavior, but do not threaten them with job loss or demotion. One of the most famous hostile environment sexual harassment cases was *Jenson v. Eveleth Taconite Co.*, a class-action suit filed in 1988. The plaintiffs were some of the first women to work at the Eveleth iron mine after affirmative action forced the steel industry to hire more female workers. The women were subjected to offensive sexual language and derogatory remarks about women as well as unwelcome kissing, grabbing, and pinching. Their work areas were covered with pornography. Lois Jenson, the leading plaintiff, was also stalked by one of her supervisors, and her tires were slashed when she initially reported the harassment to the Minnesota Human Rights Department. In 1998, ten years after the case was filed, the plaintiffs and the Eveleth Taconite Company settled for $3.5 million. The 2005 film *North Country* is based on the case (Sexual Harassment Support, 2009).

Sexual harassment can lead to increased rates of absenteeism, job turnover, and requests for transfer, as well as reduced work productivity (Burn, 2005). Some women lose their jobs for not complying with sexual requests, and others quit in desperation. Women may also suffer psychological consequences (Burn, 2005). Jenson, for example, developed post-traumatic stress disorder while working at Eveleth (Sexual Harassment Support, 2009). Estimates indicate that as many as half of all employed women in the United States, Canada, and Europe experienced sexual harassment in the workplace in the 1990s (Burn, 2005).

In addition to facing sex discrimination on the job, many women who work struggle to meet their child-care needs. Most countries offer paid maternity leave. Women in India, Bangladesh, and Mexico, for example, receive twelve weeks of paid maternity leave. Sweden has one of the most comprehensive parental leave policies. Both parents' jobs are guaranteed for several years after the birth of a baby in case one or both wish to stay home. Parents may also receive 80 to 90 percent of their salaries for the first fourteen months (Burn, 2005). The United States is one of the few countries in the world that does not provide paid maternity leave on a national level. The opportunity to take twelve months of *unpaid* maternity leave is also only guaranteed to those working in companies with fifty or more employees. Finding affordable, high-quality child care is also a real concern for working parents. Sweden, again, has some of the best policies, offering a government-sponsored spot in day-care centers for children aged one to six and placement in a "leisure time" center for school-age children up to age twelve (Burn, 2005). In countries like the United States and the United Kingdom, where child care is the sole responsibility of parents, it poses particular difficulties to poor and single-parent families (Burn, 2005).

Another important factor in women's lives is domestic labor for which they receive no paycheck. Around the world, women spend more time than men engaged in unpaid household labor. This occurs in both industrialized countries and developing countries. Child care, cooking, laundry, shopping, and caring for aging family members are all examples of household tasks that are generally relegated to women. In developing countries, carrying water and growing food are time-consuming and labor-intensive tasks conducted by women. Most of these activities are vital to families; without them, basic needs are not met. This unpaid labor can also be translated into economic contributions. When a woman in the United States cuts out coupons to take with her to the grocery store or buys used clothes, she saves her family money. Similarly, in many countries women engage in countless hours of heavy labor to collect and transport dung, which is used as fuel, fertilizer, and building material. This labor contributes substantially to a family's ability to function and remain financially stable, but the time used and effort put forth are not recorded as work by governments, nor is the labor valued as work, despite its necessity (Burn, 2005). Child care is another important form of women's unpaid labor. Although exceptions exist, in most societies women are primarily responsible for child care. In fact, worldwide, men provide child care about one-third as often as women do (Burn, 2005).

Why is women's unpaid labor so often undervalued? One theory is that women's labor is viewed as "natural." Because only women can give birth and nurse infants, other activities seen as nurturing (e.g., child care, cooking, washing clothes) become associated with women's biological abilities and are viewed as "natural," as opposed to "work." In addition, feminist scholars suggest that because men have historically held the most power in societies, it is they who decide what labor is considered most valuable (Burn, 2005).

Later Adulthood: Poverty

Women are at particular risk for poverty as they age (Hartmann & English, 2009). Improved access to clean water, sanitation, basic medical care, and immunizations, as well as advances in medicine, all contribute to an increase in life expectancy worldwide (Wise, 1998). In Asia, the population age sixty-five and up is expected to more than quadruple in size by 2050, growing from 207 million in 2000 to 857 million (Goh, 2005). Because women outlive men, most of the aging adults around the world are, and increasingly will be, women. As the baby boom generation ages in the United States, it is estimated that the number of women age eighty-five and older will double between 2000 and 2030 and double again between 2030 and 2050 (Hartmann & English, 2009).

For a substantial proportion of men and women in the United States, growing older leads to growing financial difficulties. In the United States, 12 percent of women age sixty-five and older live in poverty, as compared to 6.6 percent of men (Hartmann & English, 2009). There are several reasons why elderly women are generally poorer than elderly men. Because women in the United States are on average paid less throughout their lives and work less at paid labor, they tend to accumulate fewer earnings and have lower pensions. In addition, women are more likely than men to be single as they age. Because women typically marry men a few years older and tend to live longer than men, they are likely to be widowed at some time in their adult life (Kinsella & Gist, 1998). Divorce is also on the rise for all age groups. Women who do not work or work little at paid labor during their adult lives—choosing to focus more on child rearing than employment, for example—may be especially hard hit financially at the death of a spouse or in a divorce. When a husband dies, Social Security benefits to his spouse decrease, and his pension decreases or may disappear. A divorced woman may have access to her ex-husband's Social Security or pension benefits, but these are less than when they were married. Widowed or single elderly women often live alone, generally have lower incomes than married couples, and are less likely to have a family member who can help out (Hartmann & English, 2009).

Finally, while elderly men suffer more from acute illnesses that result in death, elderly women are more likely to experience chronic illnesses that produce disability (Hartmann & English, 2009). Although about 95 percent of elderly men and women in the United States have health-care insurance through Medicare, out-of-pocket fees are high, and long-term care—especially necessary for women—is not guaranteed and can be very expensive (Hartmann & English, 2009).

Food insecurity, resulting in part from cuts in U.S. government assistance programs, is a significant problem among the aging, especially among elderly women (Klesges et al., 2001). Malnutrition is a significant concern for older adults. Nutritional deficiencies caused by lack of food have been linked to health problems, such as osteoporosis and iron-deficiency anemia, and may increase the risk of illness and death (Klesges et al., 2001). It is estimated that the health problems of one-third to one-half of older adults may be associated with malnutrition (Ryan & Bower, 1989). In a study of women age sixty-five and up who were moderately to severely disabled (but not severely cognitively impaired), 23.9 percent reported that they had financial difficulty acquiring food (Klesges et al., 2001). This difficulty was also associated with significantly higher rates of anemia when compared to elderly, disabled women who had enough food. Although rates of trouble procuring food were high among white women, they were significantly higher among women of color. About 13.4 percent of white women reported financial difficulty acquiring food as compared to 49.5 percent of women of color. Among women of color, a greater number of medical conditions were also associated with difficulty procuring food (Klesges et al., 2001). These statistics reveal the intersectional oppressions of gender, race, class, disability, and age that put elderly, disabled women of color at particular risk of inadequate food.

Old age poses difficulties in developing countries. Despite the idyllic belief that elderly individuals are more revered in developing countries and therefore have more positive experiences in old age, the reality can be quite different. One in five of the world's poorest people—those who make less than five dollars a day—are over age sixty (Van Dullemen, 2006). In many countries, the younger generation moves to urban centers to work while the elderly remain in rural villages struggling to make ends meet. In parts of the world ravaged by HIV-AIDS, the working generation has been massively reduced, and older people, who took care of dying family members, are left with most of the emotional, social, and financial duties (Van Dullemen, 2006). In much of Africa, elderly women continue to work, many up until their deaths, performing household duties, selling food and handicrafts in the marketplace, working in agricultural fields, and providing health care for family and community members (Van Dullemen, 2006). Many development programs that aim to reduce poverty, provide microloans, or prevent HIV infection, for example, do not provide for the elderly but focus instead on younger generations. Some changes may be occurring. The United Nations hosted a summit on aging and development in 2002, and the Tanzanian government recently included the elderly in their poverty-reduction strategy review. Similarly, the Ghana administration has added a program on aging. Caroline Van Dullemen, the founder of World Granny, a nongovernmental organization based in the Netherlands that works with and for elderly people in developing countries, recommends that policy makers view the elderly, particularly elderly women, as key players in their efforts (Van Dullemen, 2006).

Body Dissatisfaction across the Life Span

Although we've focused on gender-sensitive issues in relation to particular periods of development, clearly issues related to gender roles, sexual assault, caregiving, equity in employment, and poverty can emerge throughout the life span. In this final section, we examine the various forms that one issue may take at different points in the life span.

In the United States, body dissatisfaction or poor body image—negative appraisal of one's physical body—is commonplace throughout the life span and is of concern because of its links to depression, low self-esteem, and eating disorders in women (Glauert, Rhodes, Byrne, Fink, & Grammer, 2009). Although there is growing evidence that men struggle with body dissatisfaction, poor body image is much more common among women. This trend is seen as early as first grade in the United States. At age five, neither boys nor girls express dissatisfaction with their bodies, but between age six and eight, girls become more displeased with their bodies than boys, and many desire to be thin (Ruble, Martin, & Berenbaum, 2006). By age ten, even more girls are concerned with their weight. In one study, 81 percent of middle-class ten-year-olds reported that they were afraid of being fat (Mellin, Irwin, & Scully, 1992). But it is during adolescence that body dissatisfaction tends to peak, with rates as high as 80 percent among high school girls (Schooler, 2008). Eating disorders, which are often associated with body dissatisfaction, are particularly troubling. It is estimated that 1–3 percent of women struggle with eating disorders, and a much larger number engage in disordered eating (Feldman & Meyer, 2007; Schooler, 2008). **Anorexia nervosa**, in which individuals starve themselves, can be a fatal mental illness. Young women with anorexia are twelve times as likely to die as their counterparts who do not have the disorder (Schooler, 2008).

Body dissatisfaction is not limited to the young. Many middle-aged and elderly women experience body dissatisfaction. Researchers have suggested that the physical and psychological changes brought on by menopause may be similar to those experienced at the onset of puberty and menarche. Changes in bodily appearance, such as weight gain, and pressure from the media, sexual partners, and others to maintain their youthful appearance may intensify preexisting body dissatisfaction or create new feelings of poor body image. Eating disorders do occur in women in midlife and late adulthood and are most likely underdiagnosed in these populations. Health problems related to dieting and disordered eating are exacerbated among older adults. Osteoporosis and stress fractures, caused by nutritional deficits, are more likely to occur among these populations, and the risk of death associated with low weight is greater as women age (Lewis & Cachelin, 2001). Some studies suggest that body dissatisfaction exists through the life span but may increase when older women gain weight. In a study of body dissatisfaction in two age groups—women age fifty to sixty-five and women age sixty-six and up—the younger group showed slightly higher body dissatisfaction and more drive to alter appearance to meet appearance goals (Lewis & Cachelin, 2001). The older group, however, also experienced body dissatisfaction and exhibited a discrepancy between the figures they selected as looking like themselves and those that represented their ideal. Importantly, Lewis and Cachelin (2001) found a relationship between greater drive for thinness and heightened fear of aging.

Although body dissatisfaction is often thought of as a Western problem, data show a rise in other cultures as well. Jung and Forbes (2006) and Jung, Forbes, and Lee (2009) found that Korean women—both college students and middle school students—had higher rates of body dissatisfaction and engaged in more behaviors associated with disordered eating than their American counterparts. Jung, Forbes, and Lee (2009) hypothesize that as women gain more rights in Korea and reject traditional gender roles, their progress is undermined through increasingly restrictive beauty ideals. Researchers also suggest that globalization is transmitting Western beauty standards, creating a growing desire to be thin around the world (Lam et al., 2009). Adolescent girls in Hong Kong, for example, had high rates of body dissatisfaction, despite lack of pressure from their parents to be thin. Instead, media and peer pressure to lose weight accounted for the girls' poor body image and dieting. Many of their parents, in fact, might have preferred their daughters to be heavier, because of traditional Chinese beliefs that larger bodies connote prosperity and health (Lam et al., 2009).

Although a thin ideal may be gaining acceptance around the world, it is by no means the universal ideal. Beauty ideals vary widely across cultures. Tovee, Swami, Furnham, and Mangalparsad (2006), for example, found that men and women in the United Kingdom considered curvaceous female body types most attractive, while Zulus in South Africa preferred women who were less curvaceous. Zulu immigrants living in the United Kingdom, however, had preferences that matched those of the U.K. participants, further underscoring the sociocultural nature of beauty ideals. Even in countries in which body dissatisfaction and the desire for thinness are on the rise, cultural differences exist. In a study of upper-middle-class Mexican and

Spanish adolescent girls, Toro et al. (2006) found that the rate of eating disorders (6–7 percent) was similar for both sets of adolescents (and similar to the Western world), but the girls were dissatisfied with different parts of their bodies. Mexican girls wanted slender arms, shoulders, and backs, while Spanish girls wanted to decrease the size of their hips, buttocks, and legs, parts of the body that Mexican girls wanted to enlarge (Toro et al., 2006). In Mauritania, body fat is considered a sign of wealth, and women with very large bodies are deemed most attractive. Overfeeding and even forcefeeding girls in Mauritania to attain the cultural ideal has been common practice for years. Although government officials are currently trying to stem this practice, a 2001 government survey found that one in five women age fifteen to forty-eight had experienced deliberate overfeeding (LaFraniere, 2007).

The many images of idealized body types in the media are often cited as one cause for body dissatisfaction. Indeed, many boys and girls are exposed to idealized images on a daily basis. Children and adolescents in the West watch television in a given year more than they engage in any other activity, including sleeping (Hargreaves & Tiggemann, 2003). In addition, female adolescents read a remarkable number of magazines marketed to adolescent and adult women. The images of men and women in these magazines are overwhelmingly idealized, depicting very thin women and very muscular men in advertisements and article spreads (Jones, Vigfusdottir, & Lee, 2004).

The link between viewing idealized images of women's bodies and experiencing poor body image is strong. Frequent exposure to ideal body types is a problem in part because it can alter the viewer's perception of what a normal body looks like. In one recent study, when participants viewed images of thin women, their notion of a normal body and an ideal body became thinner, whereas when they viewed images of overweight women, the reverse was true (Glauert et al., 2009). In countries where extremely thin women make up the majority of women depicted in the media, it is possible that women come to see very thin bodies as normal and ideal and, in turn, find their own bodies lacking (Glauert et al., 2009). Feminist theorists argue that beauty ideals perpetuate gender inequality in two important ways. By focusing on women's appearance, beauty ideals undermine women's intelligence and capabilities. In short, beauty becomes the most important signifier of a woman's value and status in society. Second, the pressure to alter their looks to conform to these standards depletes women's financial resources and their feeling of self-worth (Jung, Forbes, & Lee, 2009).

The pressure to conform to beauty standards is exacerbated by the racialized nature of these standards. In the United States, the idealized woman is not only thin—she is also white. While white women may contend with pressure to lose weight, women of color experience a dual assault on their body image, both pressure to be thin and the impossible expectation of being white. This intersection of race and gender oppression is visible in the fact that white or European-American women most often undergo cosmetic surgery to modify the body, such as breast augmentation or liposuction, whereas Asian women tend to ask for "double-eyelid surgery," a procedure used to make the eyes look larger and their faces appear more "white" (Sengupta, 2006). Similarly, at a California high school, Hmong-American girls expressed the desire to be "Americanized," and some attempted to conform to American beauty standards by bleaching their hair and wearing colored contacts. Some also dieted to attain the extremely thin ideal, even though traditional culture in their families' native Laos idealized fuller bodies because of their association with fertility (Lee, 2007).

Although pressure from mainstream American culture to be thin affects many women regardless of race and ethnicity, there is also evidence that different groups within the United States maintain different cultural ideals. Some African-American women, for example, may experience less pressure to be thin and consider larger body types more acceptable. Most of the African-American adolescent ninth- and tenth-grade girls in one study judged images of thin women in the media as intended for white girls but not for themselves. Their sense of "otherness" in relation to these images, while likely reinforcing their experience of white supremacy, also enabled them to consider a broader range of body types as ideal (Milkie, 1999). In fact, television programming geared toward African-Americans uses a wider range of body types than mainstream television. Importantly, greater body satisfaction of African-American women and Latina adolescents has been associated with watching these programs. Like African-American women, Latinas in the United States must negotiate several beauty ideals. They encounter mainstream white body norms, the beauty standards of their own families and communities, and African-American ideals. Latina beauty ideals are hard to quantify, given the number and diversity of Latin American countries, but research suggests that these ideals tend to emphasize "buen cuerpo" or "thick" bodies, in which slender waists are coupled with large breasts, hips, and behinds. Because Latinas have a range of skin colors and may be perceived as black in the United States regardless of personal ethnic identity, African-American ideals also have resonance for some Latinas and may provide an important alternative to mainstream beauty standards (Schooler, 2008).

African-American women and Latinas, however, are not "protected" from unattainable beauty ideals. The majority of research on body dissatisfaction and eating disorders focuses on white, upper-middle-class college women, sometimes assuming that other groups do not struggle with body image. Recent research suggests that this is untrue. Gentile, Raghavan, Rajah, and Gates (2007), for example, found that among ethnically diverse, low-income urban college students, a higher percentage of Latin American, African-American, and Afro-Caribbean women met diagnoses for eating disorders than white women in the sample. More research is needed to illuminate the intersections of race, class, culture, nationality, and sexual orientation to pinpoint why women of all walks of life develop these illnesses.

Media representations of women also vary according to race and often play on demeaning racial stereotypes. In a study of depictions of white, black, and East Asian women in magazine advertisements, Sengupta (2006) found that white women were most often used to advertise beauty products, suggesting that beauty ideals are equated with whiteness. Black women, on the other hand, were overrepresented in clothing advertisements, which tend to objectify women's bodies, and East Asian women were overwhelmingly models for technology products, making use of the stereotype of East Asians as well-educated and experts at math and science (Sengupta, 2006).

Depictions of men in the media have also become increasingly objectified and increasingly unlike the bodies of average men. The idealized man is slender, but not thin, with very prominent muscles (Jung, Forbes, & Lee, 2009). There is evidence that rates of body dissatisfaction, eating disorders, and anabolic steroid misuse are on the rise among men (Jung, Forbes, & Lee, 2009). In addition to media depictions, American toy action figures have become increasingly—and impossibly—muscular over the last thirty years. Pope and Olivardia's (1999) study of the changing shape of action figures determined that they have become more muscular than the world's biggest bodybuilders. The term *muscle dysmorphia* was recently coined to refer to an obsession with attaining an abnormally muscular body, most commonly experienced by male bodybuilders. Individuals with muscle dysmorphia go to extreme lengths to build muscle, which may include excessive weight lifting, spending enormous amounts of money on ineffective supplements, and engaging in disordered eating and substance misuse (Mosley, 2009). Prolonged steroid use is particularly dangerous and is associated with raised cholesterol, prostate enlargement, male-pattern baldness, acne, enlarged breast tissue, and atrophy of the testes. Steroids are addictive, and withdrawal is linked with depression and even suicide. Some estimates suggest that 10 percent of bodybuilders experience muscle dysmorphia (Mosley, 2009). One man who suffered from this disorder misused steroids in high school and college. He experienced dramatic muscle gain, severe acne, and a heightened sex drive, and became very physically aggressive. He was eventually arrested for assault, an experience that led to his recovery (D.H., 2000). In the following passage, he describes how he felt in the midst of the disorder: "One of the main components of steroid addiction is how unsatisfied the user is with his overall appearance. Although I was massive and had dramatic muscular definition, I was never content with my body, despite frequent compliments. I was always changing types of steroids, places of injection, workouts, diets, etc. I always found myself saying, 'This one oughta do it' or 'I'll quit when I hit 230 pounds' " (p. 105).

In addition to muscle dysmorphia, a small number of men—about 0.5 percent—suffer from eating disorders (Feldman & Meyer, 2007). In one study of men with eating disorders, half wanted to lose weight and half wanted to increase weight and muscle mass, indicating that men experience pressure to be both lean and muscular (Gentile et al., 2007). Within clinical settings, 5 to 10 percent of individuals undergoing treatment for eating disorders are male. Although these numbers are small, they are rising, and many researchers believe that eating disorders in men are underdiagnosed and undertreated. Lack of awareness about eating disorders in men and other barriers, such as the paucity of research on eating disorders in men and few treatment centers devoted to men, likely contribute to inadequate diagnosis and treatment. Men are at risk for developing eating disorders if they are single, between the ages of twenty-five and forty-four, and underweight or overweight, or if they experience high levels of stress and/or exercise daily (Gadalla, 2009). The risk is particularly heightened for gay and bisexual men. While about 3 percent of men identify as gay or bisexual in the U.S. population, 14–42 percent of men with eating disorders in community and clinical settings identify this way (Feldman & Meyer, 2007). Researchers have suggested that in order to attract men, gay and bisexual men experience pressure similar to that of heterosexual women to conform to beauty standards. For example, gay and bisexual men may be more likely to view their bodies as sexual objects than heterosexual men, and this may lead to increased body dissatisfaction. Some researchers also suggest that gay communities place increased appearance pressure on men. Others, however, note that gay communities and institutions may protect men from developing eating disorders because they offer protection from a homophobic world and emphasize acceptance (Feldman & Meyer, 2007).

The focus on body conformity in many cultures can be devastating for individuals with physical differences. Writer and poet Lucy Grealy describes in *Autobiography of a Face* her childhood struggle with a rare and frequently fatal form of cancer, which resulted in the removal of a large part of her jaw. The real battle, she explains, was not the cancer but the pain and horror she suffered as a result of her facial disfigurement. Desperately wanting to be loved and believing that her face precluded the possibility of receiving love, Grealy underwent dozens of reconstructive surgeries to alter her face: "Beauty, as defined by society at large, seemed to be only about who was best at looking like everyone else . . . [E]ach time I was wheeled down to the surgical wing, high on the drugs, I'd think to myself, *Now, now*

I can start my life, just as soon as I wake up from this operation. And no matter how disappointed I felt when I woke up and looked in the mirror, I'd simply postpone happiness until the next operation. I knew there would always be another operation, another chance for my life to finally begin" (Grealy, 1994, 187).

Individuals with a range of disabilities may receive negative responses from others about their appearance, causing them to feel inferior, deformed, and, as Grealy describes, unlovable. The lack of portrayals of individuals with disabilities in the media leads many to feel invisible. The few portrayals that exist tend to romanticize or demonize disability or suggest that people with disabilities have superhuman strengths, contributing to the belief that they are qualitatively different from others. Individuals with disabilities may feel pressure to hide their bodies or to change them, sometimes through surgery, as in Grealy's experience. A study of Jewish Israeli women indicated that women with disabilities (mostly spinal cord and polio injuries) struggled more with poor body image than women without disabilities. Young adult women with disabilities, age twenty-one to thirty, struggled the most with body dissatisfaction (Moin, Duvdevany, & Mazor, 2009). Visible disfigurement has also been linked with psychosocial difficulties related to body dissatisfaction. Rumsey, Clarke, White, Wyn-Williams, and Garlick (2004) found that a high proportion of British outpatients with visible physical differences experienced psychosocial distress, particularly social anxiety with fears including interacting with others, revealing the disfigurement, and being the target of negative comments. Importantly, no relation was found between the severity of the disfigurement and outpatients' psychosocial problems. This suggests that other factors, such as social support, may be more important in determining psychological outcome.

Fortunately, some countries have taken measures to stop the media barrage of images of unattainable bodies. After the deaths of two fashion models in 2006 from anorexia nervosa (Uruguayan model Luisel Ramos and Brazilian model Ana Carolina Reston), Spain, followed by Italy, outlawed the use of underweight models in fashion shows. In 2008, France's National Assembly passed a ground-breaking bill that would ban media sources that encourage disordered eating. The bill mandated significant fines and possible jail time for magazines, websites, blogs, and so forth that distribute information valorizing eating disorders and offering how-to tips (Carvajal, 2008). Unfortunately, the bill stalled in France's senate.

Families, schools, and social workers can play a vital role in helping individuals navigate the media and feel better about their bodies. For example, education about how and why advertisers create images (e.g., the use of software to make models appear thinner) can help adolescents recognize that images are often unattainable and exploit women's and men's anxieties. Providing children and adolescents with alternative magazines, such as *New Moon* and *Teen Voices* (and *Bitch* and *Bust* for older children), can also help ensure that young women and men see a variety of body types and read publications that value internal characteristics, like creativity, compassion, and intelligence.

SUMMARY

Examining gender using a developmental, ecological-systems framework allows culturally competent social workers to understand gender-sensitive issues—rooted in social inequality—that have a major impact on individuals' lives. Beginning in infancy, individuals are socialized into what it means to be male or female. Families and peers, educational institutions, and the media work in tandem to teach messages about maleness and femaleness. Individuals are not passive recipients, however, nor are the messages universal. Significant variation exists across individuals—who may embrace, reject, and alter particular gender-based messages—and across social and cultural contexts. Although individuals' experiences of gender may vary, inequality based on gender is an all-too-common experience limiting the opportunities of women and men, as well as their contributions to the larger society. Men face discrimination and cruelty when they deviate from gender norms, while many women contend with their continued status as "second-class citizens" around the world. Issues of domestic violence and sexual assault, inadequate maternity care, discrimination in employment, poverty, and body dissatisfaction are salient in the lives of many women. Recognizing the ways in which gender oppression affects women, and some women in particular—namely those who are additionally oppressed by other forces, such as racism, economic inequality, and homophobia—is essential for social workers practicing in a variety of contexts.

Study and Discussion Questions

1. What does it mean that "gender" is a social construct?
2. Describe the significance of intersectionality in understanding our experience of gender.
3. Describe the process of gender identity development, including the role of various social contexts (e.g., the family, school, peers, the media). Provide one example of how your understanding of the process of gender identity development would be important to you as a social worker.
4. Describe individual variation in gender identity development. What is the significance of such individual variation?
5. Define what is meant by "gender-sensitive issues," and provide an example of such an issue that you might encounter in your social work practice.

6. Describe one gender-sensitive issue that might emerge in childhood, adolescence, early adulthood, middle adulthood, and later adulthood.

7. What is meant by "body dissatisfaction"? What are possible origins, manifestations, and consequences for males and females? What are several contexts in which body dissatisfaction might appear in social work practice?

Resources

Interested students can supplement this chapter through a number of web-based resources.

Women's Healthcare Topics provides information and online resources on doulas, midwifery, and pregnancy. Available at http://www.womens healthcaretopics.com/choosing_a_midwife_or_doula.htm.

Women around the world cope with domestic violence and abuse in a variety of ways, often depending on their culture. Middle Eastern women, some of whom are forced into marriage at a very young age and forced to endure abusive relationships not only with their husbands but also with their husband's family members, attempt suicide by setting themselves ablaze. With a lack of domestic-violence services and a culture that supports patriarchal practices, these women see no alternative to escaping domestic violence except through suicide. National Geographic's photojournalism provides insight into these women's lives. See http://ngm.national geographic.com/2010/12/afghan-women/rubin-text.

Suicide among Latinas is on the rise in the United States. The National Institute of Health's website has an article, "Suicidal Behavior in Latinas: Explanatory Cultural Factors and Implications for Intervention," by Zayas and Pilat (2008) that describes this phenomenon and offers a number of in-depth articles on suicide amongst Latinas. Available at http://www.ncbi.nlm .nih.gov/pmc/articles/PMC2662359/.

Zayas's expert testimony can also be found at National Public Radio's Latino USA website, hosted by Maria Hinojosa. This website also has an audio interview with Latinas and their families on the topic of Latina suicide. Available at http://www.latinousa.org/916-2/.

The media have a major impact on the way society views and treats men and women and boys and girls, and all who fall in between (e.g., transgender). The Media Awareness Network website provides educational resources for adults and children on the consequences of the media's treatment of gender roles and ways to reduce discrimination and stereotyping. Available at http://www.mediaawareness.ca/english/resources/educational/lessons/ secondary/gender_portrayl/gender_impact.cfm.

The Institute for Women's Policy Research website provides statistical and demographic information on gender disparities in a variety of social and economic sectors, including employment, health care, and immigration. Available at http://www.iwpr.org/.

The Center for Men and Masculinity at the Parent-Child Institute in Champaign, Illinois, provides treatment and educational resources for boys and men. The center's mission is to help males overcome society's expectations of the role they ought to play (i.e., stoic, stereotypical behavior and false power) and reteaches them coping, emotional, and communication skills beyond the narrow stereotypes of manhood or maleness. Specifically, the center believes that in order to be a parent, partner, and family and community member, men need a language of their own. Available at http://www.menandmasculinity.com/.

References

Adamuti-Trache, M., & Andres, L. (2008). Embarking on and persisting in scientific fields of study: Cultural capital, gender, and curriculum along the science pipeline. *International Journal of Science Education, 30*(12), 1557–1584.

Althabe, F., & Belizán, J. M. (2006). Caesarean section: The paradox. *Lancet, 368*(9546), 1472–1473.

Althabe, F., Sosa, C., Belizán, J. M., Gibbons, L., Jacquerioz, F., & Bergel, E. (2006). Cesarean section rates and maternal and neonatal mortality in low-, medium-, and high-income countries: An ecological study. *Birth: Issues in Perinatal Care, 33*(4), 270–277.

Amelink-Verburg, M. P., Verloove-Vanhorick, S. P., Hakkenberg, R. M. A., Veldhuijzen, I. M. E., Bennebroek Gravenhorst, J., & Buitendijk, S. E. (2008). Evaluation of 280 000 cases in Dutch midwifery practices: A descriptive study. *British Journal of Obstetrics and Gynaecology, 115*(5), 570–578.

American Congress of Obstetricians and Gynecologists. (2005). *Cesarean birth.* Retrieved from http://www.acog.org/publications/patient_education/bp006.cfm

Amnesty International. (2008). *Amnesty International applauds introduction of landmark legislation addressing jurisdictional maze that allows rape of Native women to go unpunished.* Retrieved from http://www.amnestyusa.org/document.php?lang=e&id=ENGUSA20080723004

Anderson, I., & Quinn, A. (2009). Gender differences in medical students' attitudes towards male and female rape victims. *Psychology, Health, & Medicine 14*(1), 105–110.

Baker, K., & Raney, A. A. (2007). Equally super? Gender-role stereotyping of superheroes in children's animated programs. *Mass Communication & Society, 10*(1), 25–41.

Barko, N. (2002, November 2). The other gender gap. *The American Prospect.* Retrieved from http://www.prospect.org/cs/articles?article=the_other_gender_gap

Beck, S., Wojdyla, D., Say, L., Betran, A. P., Merialdi, M., Requejo, J. H., . . . Van Look, P. F.A. (2010). The worldwide incidence of preterm birth: A systematic review of maternal mortality and morbidity. *Bulletin of the World Health Organization, 88*(1), 31–38.

Berk, L. E. (2009). *Development through the lifespan* (5th ed.). Boston: Allyn & Bacon.

Bigner, J. J., & Jacobsen, R. B. (1989). Parenting behaviors of homosexual and hetero-sexual fathers. *Journal of Homosexuality, 18*(1–2), 173–186.

Brown, P. L. (2006, December 2). Supporting boys or girls when the line isn't clear. *New York Times.* Retrieved from http://www.nytimes.com/2006/12/02/us/02 child.html

Buchmann, C., DiPrete, T. A., & McDaniel, A. (2008). Gender inequalities in education. *Annual Review of Sociology, 34*(1), 319–337.

Burn, M. S. (2005). *Women across cultures: A global perspective* (2nd ed.). New York: McGraw-Hill.

Carvajal, D. (2008, April 15). French legislators approve law against Web sites encour-aging anorexia and bulimia. *New York Times.* Retrieved from http://www.ny times.com/2008/04/15/world/europe/15iht-paris.4.12015888.html

CDC releases new infant mortality data. (2008). Retrieved from http://www.cdc .gov/media/pressrel/2008/r081015.htm?s_cid=mediarel_r081015

Childbirth Connection. (2008). *Report reveals serious problems in maternity care quality and value: Overuse of cesarean section and other interventions puts women and babies at risk, increases costs.* Retrieved from http://www.child birthconnection.org/pdfs/ebmc-press release.pdf

Choo, H. Y., & Ferree, M. M. (2010). Practicing intersectionality in sociological research: A critical analysis of inclusions, interactions, and institutions in the study of inequalities. *Sociological Theory, 28*(2), 129–149.

Dasgupta, S. D. (1998). Gender roles and cultural continuity in the Asian Indian immi-grant community in the U.S. *Sex Roles, 38*(11–12), 953–974.

Declercq, E., & Chalmers, B. (2008). Mothers' reports of their maternity experiences in the USA and Canada. *Journal of Reproductive & Infant Psychology, 26*(4), 295–308.

Denner, J., & Dunbar, N. (2004). Negotiating femininity: Power and strategies of Mexican American girls. *Sex Roles, 50*(5–6), 501–514.

D. H. (2000). Dying to be bigger. In D. Sattler, G. Kramer, V. Shabatay, & D. Bernstein (Eds.), *Lifespan development in context: Voices and perspectives* (pp. 102–105). Boston: Houghton Mifflin.

Donovan, R. A. (2007). To blame or not to blame. *Journal of Interpersonal Violence, 22*(6), 722–736.

Duthu, N. B. (2008, August 11). Broken justice in Indian country. *New York Times.* Retrieved from http://www.nytimes.com/2008/08/11/opinion/11duthu.html

Egan, S. K., & Perry, D. G. (2001). Gender identity: A multidimensional analysis with implications for psychosocial adjustment. *Developmental Psychology, 37*(4), 451–463.

Equal Rights. (2009). *Ellerth v. Burlington Industries.* Retrieved from http://www .equalrights.org/publications/reports/briefing/ellerth.asp

Feldman, M. B., & Meyer, I. H. (2007). Eating disorders in diverse lesbian, gay, and bi-sexual populations. *International Journal of Eating Disorders, 40*(3), 218–226.

Fox, M., Sonnert, G., & Nikiforova, I. (2009). Successful programs for undergraduate women in science and engineering: Adapting versus adopting the institutional environment. *Research in Higher Education, 50*(4), 333–353.

Gadalla, T. M. (2009). Eating disorders in men: A community-based study. *Interna-tional Journal of Men's Health, 8*(1), 72–81.

Gaskin, I. A. (2008, March–April). Masking maternal mortality. *Mothering Magazine, 147*. Retrieved from http://mothering.com/pregnancy-birth/masking-maternal -mortality

Gaskin, I. M. (2003). *Ina May's guide to childbirth*. New York: Bantam Books.

Gentile, K., Raghavan, C., Rajah, V., & Gates, K. (2007). It doesn't happen here: Eating disorders in an ethnically diverse sample of economically disadvantaged, urban college students. *Eating Disorders, 15*(5), 405–425.

Glass, J., & Camarigg, V. (1992). Gender, parenthood, and job-family compatibility. *American Journal of Sociology, 98*(1), 131–152.

Glauert, R., Rhodes, G., Byrne, S., Fink, B., & Grammer, K. (2009). Body dissatisfaction and the effects of perceptual exposure on body norms and ideals. *International Journal of Eating Disorders, 42*(5), 443–452.

Glewwe, P. (1999). Why does mother's schooling raise child health in developing countries? Evidence from Morocco. *Journal of Human Resources, 34*(1), 124–159.

Goer, H. (1995). *Obstetric myths versus research realities: A guide to the medical literature*. Santa Barbara, CA: Greenwood Publishing Group.

Goh, V. H. H. (2005). Aging in Asia: A cultural, socio-economical and historical perspective. *Aging Male, 8*(2), 90–96.

Goldenberg, R. L., Culhane, J. F., Iams, J. D., & Romero, R. (2008). Epidemiology and causes of preterm birth. *Lancet, 371*(9606), 75–84.

Gordon-Larsen, P., Nelson, M. C., & Popkin, B. M. (2004). Longitudinal physical activity and sedentary behavior trends: Adolescence to adulthood. *American Journal of Preventive Medicine, 27*(4), 277–283.

Grealy, L. (1994). *Autobiography of a face*. New York: Houghton Mifflin.

Hargreaves, D., & Tiggemann, M. (2003). The effect of "thin ideal" television commercials on body dissatisfaction and schema activation during early adolescence. *Journal of Youth & Adolescence, 32*(5), 367–374.

Hartmann, H., & English, A. (2009). Older women's retirement security: A primer. *Journal of Women, Politics, & Policy, 30*(2-3), 109–140.

Hartmann, H., Hegewisch, A., Liepmann, H., & Williams, C. (2010). *Institute for Women's Policy Research fact sheet: The gender wage gap: 2009*. Retrieved from http://www.in.gov/icw/files/IWPR_Wage_Gap_study.pdf

Hatem, M., Sandall, J., Devane, D., Soltani, H., & Gates, S. (2008). Midwife-led versus other models of care for childbearing women. *Cochrane Database of Systematic Reviews* (No. 4). doi: 10.1002/14651858.CD004667.pub2

Hayden, S. K. (2004). The business of birth: Obstacles facing low-income women in choosing midwifery care after the licensed midwifery practice act of 1993. *Berkeley Women's Law Journal, 19*, 257–269.

Hill, S. A. (2002). Teaching and doing gender in African American families. *Sex Roles, 47*(11-12), 493–506.

Hodnett, E. D., Gates, S., Hofmeyr, G. J., & Sakala, C. (2007). Continuous support for women during childbirth (review). *Cochrane Database of Systematic Reviews* (No. 3). Retrieved from http://childbirthconnection.org/pdf.asp?PDFDownload =continuous_support

Högberg, U. (2004). The decline in maternal mortality in Sweden: The role of community midwifery. *American Journal of Public Health, 94*(8), 1312–1320.

Irving, T. (2007). Borders of the body: Black women, sexual assault, and citizenship. *Women's Studies Quarterly, 35*(1–2), 67–92.

Johnson, K. C., & Daviss, B. (2005). Outcomes of planned home births with certified professional midwives: Large prospective study in North America. *British Medical Journal, 330*, 1416–1419.

Jones, D. C., Vigfusdottir, T. H., & Lee, Y. (2004). Body image and the appearance culture among adolescent girls and boys. *Journal of Adolescent Research, 19*(3), 323–339.

Jung, J., & Forbes, G. (2006). Multidimensional assessment of body dissatisfaction and disordered eating in Korean and U.S. college women: A comparative study. *Sex Roles, 55*(1–2), 39–50.

Jung, J., Forbes G., & Lee, Y. (2009). Body dissatisfaction and disordered eating among early adolescents from Korea and the US. *Sex Roles, 61*(1–2), 42–54.

Kabakchieva, V. (2009). Maternal morbidity and maternal mortality in the United States. *Journal of Children & Poverty, 15*(1), 63–69.

Keefe, C. (2003). Overview of maternity care in the U.S. *Citizens for Midwifery.* Retrieved from http://www.cfmidwifery.org/pdf/OverviewofMatCareApr2003.pdf

Kinsella, K., & Gist, Y. J. (1998). *International brief: Gender and aging mortality and health.* Retrieved from http://www.census.gov/population/international/files/ib98-2.pdf

Klesges, L. M., Pahor, M., Shorr, R. I., Wan, J. Y., Williamson, J. D., & Guralnik, J. M. (2001). Financial difficulty in acquiring food among elderly disabled women: Results from the women's health and aging study. *American Journal of Public Health, 91*(1), 68–75.

Kuznar, W. (2010). The maternal health care crisis in the United States. *American Journal of Nursing, 110*(7), 17.

LaFraniere, S. (2007, July 4). In Mauritania, seeking to end an overfed ideal. *New York Times.* Retrieved from http://www.nytimes.com/2007/07/04/world/africa/04mauritania.html

Lam, T. H., Lee, S. W., Fung, S., Ho, S. Y., Lee, P. W. H., & Stewart, S. M. (2009). Sociocultural influences on body dissatisfaction and dieting in Hong Kong girls. *European Eating Disorders Review, 17*(2), 152–160.

Lang, C., & Kuhnle, U. (2008). Intersexuality and alternative gender categories in non-Western cultures. *Hormone Research, 69*(4), 240–250.

Lantz, P. M., Low, L. K., Sanjani, V., & Watson, R. L.(2005). Doulas as childbirth paraprofessionals: Results from a national survey. *Women's Health Issues, 15*(3), 109–116.

Lee, S. J. (2007). The "good" news and the "bad" news: The "Americanization" of Hmong girls. In B. J. R. Leadbeater & N. Way (Eds.), *Urban girls revisited: Building strengths* (pp. 202–217). New York: New York University Press.

Lelchuk, I. (2006, August 27). When is it OK for boys to be girls, and girls to be boys? *San Francisco Chronicle.* Retrieved from http://www.sfgate.com/cgi-bin/article.cgi?f=/c/a/2006/08/27/MNGL2KQ8H41.DTL&ao=all

Levine, J. A. (2009). It's a man's job, or so they say: The maintenance of sex segregation in a manufacturing plant. *Sociological Quarterly, 50*(2), 257–282.

Lewis, D. M., & Cachelin, F. M. (2001). Body image, body dissatisfaction, and eating attitudes in midlife and elderly women. *Eating Disorders, 9*(1), 29–39.

Lobel, T. E., Nov-Krispin, N., Schiller, D., Lobel, O., & Feldman, A. (2004). Gender discriminatory behavior during adolescence and young adulthood: A developmental analysis. *Journal of Youth & Adolescence, 33*(6), 535–546.

MacDorman, M. F., & Mathews, T. J. (2009). *Behind international rankings of infant mortality: How the United States compares with Europe* (NCHS data brief, No. 23). Hyattsville, MD: National Center for Health Statistics. Retrieved from http://www.cdc.gov/nchs/data/databriefs/db23.htm#ranking

Mastekaasa, A., & Smeby, J. (2008). Educational choice and persistence in male- and female-dominated fields. *Higher Education, 55*(2), 189–202.

McCoy, C. R. (2003, June 23). From old report, 4 new charges. *Philadelphia Inquirer.* Retrieved from http://inquirer.philly.com/packages/crime/2003/062303inq main.asp

McCoy, C. R., Fazlollah, M., & Matza, M. (2000, April 16). Suspect charged in 1995 rape case. *Philadelphia Inquirer.* Retrieved from http://inquirer.philly.com/packages/crime/html/041600arrest.asp

McMahon, S. (2007). Understanding community specific rape myths: Exploring student-athlete culture. *Affilia: Journal of Women and Social Work, 22*(4), 357–370.

McNair, L. D., & Neville, H. A. (1996). African American women survivors of sexual assault: The intersection of race and class. *Women & Therapy, 18*(3–4), 107–119.

Mehta, C. M., & Strough, J. (2009). Sex segregation in friendships and normative contexts across the life span. *Developmental Review, 29*(3), 201–220.

Mellin, L. M., Irwin, C. E., & Scully, S. (1992). Disordered eating characteristics in girls: A survey of middle class children. *Journal of the American Dietetic Association, 92*, 851–853.

Milkie, M. A. (1999). Social comparisons, reflected appraisals, and mass media: The impact of pervasive beauty images on black and white girls' self-concepts. *Social Psychology Quarterly, 62*(2), 190–210.

Moin, V., Duvdevany, I., & Mazor, D. (2009). Sexual identity, body image and life satisfaction among women with and without physical disability. *Sexuality & Disability, 27*(2), 83–95.

Mosley, P. E. (2009). Bigorexia: Bodybuilding and muscle dysmorphia. *European Eating Disorders Review, 17*(3), 191–198.

Mulligan, C. A. (2009, January 14). A milestone for working women? *New York Times.* Retrieved from http://economix.blogs.nytimes.com/2009/01/14/a-milestone -for-women-workers/

Murakami, K., Miyake, Y., Sasaki, S., Tanaka, K., Ohya, Y., & Hirota, Y. (2009). Education, but not occupation or household income, is positively related to favorable dietary intake patterns in pregnant Japanese women: The Osaka Maternal and Child Health Study. *Nutrition Research, 29*(3), 164–172.

National Academy of Sciences, National Academy of Engineering, & Institute of Medicine of the National Academies. (2007). *Beyond bias and barriers: Fulfilling the potential of women in academic science and engineering.* Washington, DC: National Academies Press. Retrieved from http://www.nap.edu/catalog/11741.html

North American Registry of Midwives. (2008). *How to become a NARM certified professional midwife (CPM).* Retrieved from http://www.narm.org/htb.htm

Okopny, C. (2008). Why Jimmy isn't failing: The myth of the boy crisis. *Feminist Teacher, 18*(3), 216–228.

Pope, H. G., & Olivardia, R. (1999). Evolving ideals of male body image as seen through action toys. *International Journal of Eating Disorders, 26*(1), 65–72.

Próspero, M. (2007). Young adolescent boys and dating violence: The beginning of patriarchal terrorism? *Affilia: Journal of Women and Social Work, 22*(3), 271–280.

Radvansky, G. A., Lynchard, N. A., & von Hippel, W. (2009). Aging and stereotype suppression. *Aging, Neuropsychology, & Cognition, 16*(1), 22–32.

Rausch, C. (2008). The midwife and the forceps: The wild terrain of midwifery law in the United States and where North Dakota is heading in the birthing debate. *North Dakota Law Review, 84*, 219–255.

Reibel, T. (2004). Normal birth: A thing of the past or the new future for primary health care? *Primary Health Care Research & Development, 5*(4), 329–337.

Ronsmans, C., & Graham, W. J. (2006). Maternal mortality: Who, when, where, and why. *Lancet, 368*(9542), 1189–1200.

Ruble, D., Martin, C., & Berenbaum, S. (2006). Gender development. In W. Damon & R. M. Lerner (Eds.), *Handbook of child psychology:* Vol. 3, *Social, emotional and personality development* (pp. 858–932). Hoboken, NJ: Wiley.

Rumsey, N., Clarke, A., White, P., Wyn-Williams, M., & Garlick, W. (2004). Altered body image: Appearance-related concerns of people with visible disfigurement. *Journal of Advanced Nursing, 48*(5), 443–453.

Ryan, V. C., & Bower, M. E. (1989). Relationship of socioeconomic status and living arrangements to nutritional intake of the older person. *Journal of the American Dietetic Association, 89*, 1805–1807.

Sable, M. R., Danis, F., Mauzy, D. L., & Gallagher, S. K. (2006). Barriers to reporting sexual assault for women and men: Perspectives of college students. *Journal of American College Health, 55*(3), 157–162.

Schnell-Anzola, B., Rowe, M. L., & LeVine, R. A. (2005). Literacy as a pathway between schooling and health-related communication skills: A study of Venezuelan mothers. *International Journal of Educational Development, 25*(1), 19–37.

Schooler, D. (2008). Real women have curves: A longitudinal investigation of TV and the body image development of Latina adolescents. *Journal of Adolescent Research, 23*(2), 132–153.

Schope, R. D., & Eliason, M. J. (2004). Sissies and tomboys: Gender role behaviors and homophobia. *Journal of Gay & Lesbian Social Services, 16*(2), 73–97.

Sengupta, R. (2006). Reading representations of black, East Asian, and white women in magazines for adolescent girls. *Sex Roles, 54*(11–12), 799–808.

Sexual Harassment Support. (2009). *Jenson vs. Eveleth Mines.* Retrieved from http://www.sexualharassmentsupport.org/JensonVsEvelethMines.html

Sharp, E., & Ispa, J. (2009). Inner-city single black mothers' gender-related childrearing expectations and goals. *Sex Roles, 60*(9–10), 656–668.

Simkin, P. (2008). *The birth partner: A complete guide to childbirth for dads, doulas, and all other labor companions* (3rd ed.). Boston: Harvard Common Press.

Sloop, J. M. (2000). Disciplining the transgendered: Brandon Teena, public representation, and normativity. *Western Journal of Communication, 64*(2), 165–189.

Soet, J. E., Brack, G. A., & DiIorio, C. (2003). Prevalence and predictors of women's experience of psychological trauma during childbirth. *Birth: Issues in Perinatal Care, 30*(1), 36–46.

Spelke, E. S. (2005). Sex differences in intrinsic aptitude for mathematics and science? A critical review. *American Psychologist, 60*(9), 950–958.

Sutfin, E., Fulcher, M., Bowles, R., & Patterson, C. (2008). How lesbian and heterosexual parents convey attitudes about gender to their children: The role of gendered environments. *Sex Roles, 58*(7–8), 501–513.

Tewksbury, R. (2007). Effects of sexual assaults on men: Physical, mental and sexual consequences. *International Journal of Men's Health, 6*(1), 22–35.

Thomas, D. (1999). Fertility, education and resources in South Africa. In C. Bledsoe, J. B.Casterline, J. A. Johnson-Kuhn, & J. G. Haaga (Eds.), *Critical perspectives on schooling and fertility in the developing world* (pp. 138–180).Washington, DC: National Academy Press.

Tjaden, P., & Thoennes, N. (2000). *Full report of the prevalence, incidence, and consequences of violence against women: Findings from the National Violence against Women Survey.* Retrieved from http://www.ncjrs.gov/pdffiles1/nij/183781.pdf

Tjaden, P., & Thoennes, N. (2006). *Extent, nature, and consequences of rape victimization: Findings from the National Violence against Women Survey.* Retrieved from http://www.ncjrs.gov/pdffiles1/nij/210346.pdf

Toro, J., Gomez-Peresmitré, G., Sentis, J., Vallés, A., Casulà, V., Castro, J., . . . Rodriguez, R. (2006). Eating disorders and body image in Spanish and Mexican female adolescents. *Social Psychiatry & Psychiatric Epidemiology, 41*(7), 556–565.

Tovee, M. J., Swami, V., Furnham, A., & Mangalparsad, R. (2006). Changing perceptions of attractiveness as observers are exposed to a different culture. *Evolution & Human Behavior, 27*, 443–456.

Trautner, H. M., Ruble, D. N., Cyphers, L., Kirsten, B., Behrendt, R., & Hartmann, P. (2005). Rigidity and flexibility of gender stereotypes in childhood: Developmental or differential? *Infant & Child Development, 14*(4), 365–381.

United States: Crimes against Native women more frequent, less often prosecuted. (2007). *Off Our Backs, 37*(1), 5–6.

Van Dullemen, C. (2006). Older people in Africa: New engines to society? *National Women's Studies Association Journal, 18*(1), 99–105.

Weisz, A. N., & Black, B. M. (2008). Peer intervention in dating violence: Beliefs of African American middle school adolescents. *Journal of Ethnic & Cultural Diversity in Social Work, 17*(2), 177–196.

Williams, T. M. (Ed.). (1986). *The impact of television: A natural experiment in three communities.* Orlando, FL: Academic Press.

Wilson, R. (2007). The new gender divide. *Chronicle of Higher Education, 53*(21), A36–A39.

Wise, J. (1998). Global life expectancy rises. *British Medical Journal, 316*(7143), 1477.

World Health Organization (WHO). (2007). *Maternal mortality in 2005: Estimates developed by WHO, UNICEF, UNFPA, and the World Bank.* Geneva, Switzerland. Retrieved from http://whqlibdoc.who.int/publications/2007/9789241596213_eng.pdf

Wright, E. (2003). Guilty plea entered in murder of Gwen Araujo. *Lesbian News, 28*(9), 14.

14

Conclusion

Throughout this book, we have presented the perspectives of social workers interpreting social science research, or commenting upon and describing professional practice. We conclude with a narrative written by an adolescent who experienced social work practice as a client in the child welfare system. Before entering the child welfare system, Sarah spent her early childhood with her birth mother, who was alcoholic. Like many children of substance-misusing parents, Sarah cared for younger siblings, experienced maltreatment, and frequently did not have adequate food or shelter. She also felt love and loyalty toward her birth mother and siblings.

"At six years of age I went, along with my five brothers and sisters, into the foster-care system. I was partnered up with my little sister to go through the process. The previous night was terrifying because of a fight between my birth mother's drunken boyfriend and their friends. And now this total change of lifestyle was confusing and scary. My sister and I were put into a group home where we spent Christmas. I can remember there were a lot of boys and girls, and it felt like we were all shuffled around. It was strange and all so new to me, but I was glad that we had shelter and food.

"Out of everything that happened, I remember specifically the care of one social worker, Wanda, who impacted my life greatly. On one particular occasion she took my sister and me out [from the foster home where the girls were placed after their stay in the group home] to our favorite burger place for one of our regular visits. I had something to tell her, but I could not do it in front of my sister. On the way out the door to go out for lunch, my foster father had told me to watch what I said. At that moment I knew something was wrong. So I waited for my sister to go play in the playground. While sitting there I confided everything that pressed on my mind. My social worker made a difficult conversation easy by coming down to my level when I was trying so hard to reach hers.

"We never went back to that foster home. Wanda took us and drove for what seemed an eternity. I cried once. With the wind blowing in my face, I thought she would not notice, but somehow, I think she did. I was very scared about the new fate that lay before my sister and me. There was so much I did not know. What was going to happen to us now?

"I see now that my social worker was already coming up with a plan. She was thinking of a family that already had one of my little brothers. Within a short period of time, my little sister and I were in a family that would bring us up the way a family should. That is not all, though! Before we knew it, two more of my brothers were being adopted by this family.

"Mom and Dad took in six kids on top of their four. All six of us shared a common social worker who apparently had good judgment, character, and some love for us. I could have never dreamed up a more perfect family to be a part of."

As seventeen-year-old Sarah's story illustrates, social workers can play pivotal roles in the lives of their clients. Sarah's social worker helped place her on her current positive developmental trajectory: she listened when Sarah described problems in her foster home, took the psychological burden of care of her younger siblings from her, and eventually placed her and her five younger siblings with a stable, loving foster family who eventually adopted them all. In this book we have emphasized the characteristics of successful social workers. The outcome of any particular case, however, is also influenced by characteristics of the client and available resources. Despite her difficult early childhood, Sarah entered foster care as a bright, attractive child who was physically and mentally healthy. She had the stamina and inner strength to cope with her significant losses, trusted and confided in an adult, responded to the help offered, and adapted to a family very different from the one in which she had been reared. Despite the widespread shortage of quality foster homes, Sarah and her siblings were fortunate to be placed in a family with considerable emotional, spiritual, and social resources, and adequate physical resources to care for six additional children with many complex needs.

This story helps shift our focus from the perspective of social workers and social science researchers to social work clients. A continuing exercise and challenge faced by social workers is to imagine and then work from the perspective of the client. The clients with whom social workers practice are diverse and complex. Information about social science research is critical for social workers when requesting resources that are likely to be needed, and planning and developing programs. The consideration of client characteristics and context is also critical to evidence-based practice. A major challenge faced by social workers is to take research-based knowledge about a group and apply it to a specific individual within a specific setting. Sarah's very difficult early life put her at risk for various developmental and mental health challenges, and her social worker needed to be aware of those risks. These early experiences did not determine Sarah's developmental outcomes. In supporting Sarah, her social worker also was aware of Sarah's unique characteristics and strengths, for example, her intelligence, adaptability, and artistic talents. At seventeen, Sarah is now poised and talented, living a meaningful life, and prepared to make positive contributions to society. Ten years after entering foster care, Sarah has traveled to Africa with her church group to work and study, is finishing high school, works part-time,

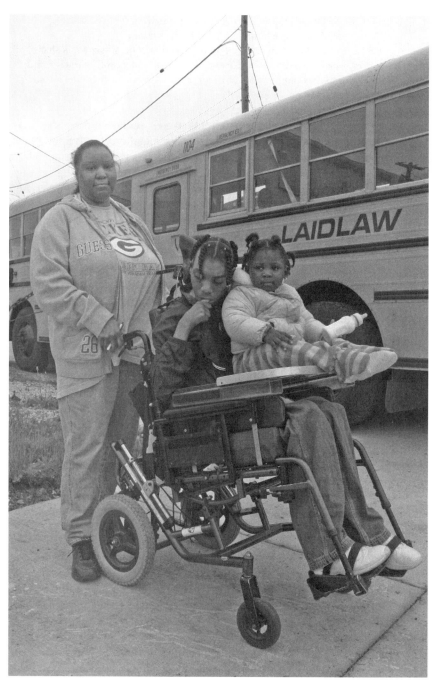

Social workers consider how the issues they confront affect entire families. This adolescent's physical and cognitive disabilities affect not only his life, but those of his mother and infant sister.

and plans to attend college. She has her struggles, but she dispels the stereotype of the victimized, at-risk child.

Sarah's story also illustrates the interaction of the social work issues presented in this book through boxes on violence, poverty, and substance misuse. Sarah's birth mother suffers from alcoholism, and is living in poverty and with violence. These multiple risk factors operate not independently, but together and over time to compound already-difficult circumstances. For example, impairment from substance misuse makes steady employment impossible, which, in turn, worsens poverty. Poverty may make it necessary to double-up, to live with friends and relatives who themselves may have substance misuse problems. When violence fueled by substance misuse erupts, Sarah's mother may believe that she has no alternative but to endure it. Finally, poverty, substance misuse, and violence profoundly affect not only adults, but their children and grandchildren as well. Witnessing violence between adults is a traumatic stress for children. In the absence of intervention, violence, substance misuse, and poverty may continue into future generations.

In concluding this book, we draw out several themes developed throughout that are relevant to understanding and intervening in the lives of clients such as Sarah.

A DEVELOPMENTAL, ECOLOGICAL-SYSTEMS FRAMEWORK GUIDES PROBLEM SOLVING IN SOCIAL WORK

A developmental, ecological-systems framework facilitates social work assessment and intervention in a range of practice settings such as schools, health, mental health, child welfare, and social work education. In this book we have presented a developmental, ecological-systems framework for understanding the complex lives of social workers and their clients. During human development, biological, psychological, and social factors interact over time in highly complex, mutually influential processes within particular cultural and historical contexts.

The developmental, ecological-systems framework draws upon and integrates empirical research from biological, psychological, social, and sociocultural-historical perspectives. Human beings are shaped both by nature and nurture: that is, they are shaped by biology within the sociocultural-historical contexts into which they are born. For example, girls reared in the Victorian and the twentieth-century United States integrated a new sexualized component of their self-concept when they reached puberty. Possibly because of changes in diet and health, Victorian girls entered puberty at later ages and were less exposed to sexualized images of young girls than U.S. girls are exposed to in the modern media. Furthermore, individual girls in the Victorian and the twentieth-century United States responded to puberty in various ways, for example, welcoming or resisting their change in status.

Thus, the experience and meaning of puberty has both universal and culturally variable aspects resulting from an interaction of biological and psychological factors within particular sociocultural-historical contexts.

The example of girls' responses to puberty also underscores that individuals are active in their own development. In chapter 1, we saw how Clara Brown, the nineteenth-century African-American pioneer, worked actively to use the resources presented to her in Central City and to avoid the risks associated with racism and sexism. She used nature and nurture to create a fit between her considerable strengths and her environment.

A developmental, ecological-systems framework views development as scaffolded by culture, which includes systems of language, mathematics, religion, music, and so forth, developed over centuries and interpreted and practiced by individuals living in specific communities. Individuals are not lone scientists out to discover the universe from scratch, nor are they unaided on this quest. Parents, teachers, social workers, peers, and family

Happy, well-functioning families come in diverse forms. This single mother is raising her biological and adopted children.

and community members support our emerging competencies. In the case of Sarah, her social worker and foster-adoptive parents helped her interpret her early experiences in a way that allowed for her positive development. This family drew upon Christian beliefs to find forgiveness, to accept the past, and to move into the future, secure in a belief in the inherent worth of each individual.

MODERN SOCIAL WORK IS EVIDENCE BASED

The developmental, ecological-systems framework stresses an evidence-based approach as necessary to professional social work practice and policy. The empirically based knowledge of modern social work is one of the most important features that distinguish it from the moralistic attempts at intervention that characterized nineteenth-century predecessors. It is our ethical responsibility as social workers to offer interventions that have been rigorously scrutinized and shown to be effective, and not to cause harm or waste scarce resources. Reliance on popular opinion and limited personal experience are simply unprofessional and unethical.

Our in-depth discussions in each chapter are based on systematic quantitative, qualitative, and mixed-method research. We encourage students to read critically, to ask themselves, Upon what is this claim or recommendation based: personal opinion, popular consensus, empirical research, practice experience? We also encourage students to practice the critical thinking modeled in empirical research to challenge existing practice and policy. We encourage students to ask, What are the alternative interpretations or explanations for the success (or lack thereof) of a given practice or policy? We remind ourselves that even the most effective intervention or policy is imperfect. To improve our profession, we must continuously access the limitations, as well as the strengths, of our practice, by holding them up to the most rigorous scrutiny.

We recognize the limitations of empirical research, and the important place of practice experience. First, empirical research is limited in scope. For many of the complex issues that social workers face every day, there are multiple valid perspectives and interpretations of human behavior. The child welfare worker, for instance, must consider the legitimate, but often conflicting, perspectives of the state, the parent, and the child. Such complexity of experience and perspective are not often adequately represented in empirical research. Second, objectivity in research is never perfect. Objectivity is a goal toward which we strive. Bias, however, enters into research at multiple levels, including the very questions asked and the projects that are funded. In research, some compelling questions, such as the role of religion in human development, have been inadequately addressed, although other questions less central to understanding human behavior in the social environment receive more attention and research dollars. Third, high-quality empirical research is time-consuming and expensive. The reality is that social workers urgently need answers to address emerging social problems, for example, the impact of parental methamphetamine misuse on rural children and the child welfare system. Funding and conducting the research necessary to address such complex and pressing social issues can take years. In teaching human behavior in the social environment, we constantly challenge our students to consider the following questions: What questions does this body of research leave unanswered or inadequately addressed? What are the limitations, as well as strengths, of this empirical evidence? Despite the limitations of empirical research, we are committed to empirical research as the best current strategy for fairly and rigorously examining the quality of social work practice and policy in order to enhance our effectiveness.

At the same time, social workers must balance knowledge of research with knowledge of individual clients and settings. Any empirical body of research must be applied to particular clients and settings. Social workers must use their professional knowledge and practice experience to apply research about a general population, or a specific community, to their own particular clients or community. We encourage students to ask, How might empirical research inform my practice with this individual client, or policy within this particular community? In the case of Sarah, her social worker was aware of research indicating the mental health risks of trauma experienced early in life. Sarah, however, was adjusting well within a family living in a remote, rural area. Rather than insist that the family travel long distances to seek treatment, the social worker educated Sarah's foster parents regarding children's response to trauma. Further, the family was provided with referrals for mental health care should Sarah require counseling in the future.

SOCIAL WORK ISSUES AFFECT MULTIPLE INTERACTING SYSTEMS

Throughout this book, we have concentrated on the individual as the focal system, but most social work issues affect multiple systems. Any given social work case is likely to involve many individuals at varying points in the life span, and many systems. Not only do these other individuals and systems have their own needs and resources, but also they may serve as important sources of support (or risk) for the social work client. The placement of a child in foster care affects not only the child but that child's parent, who may be struggling with issues in early or middle adulthood and who likely has complex needs of her own, perhaps for intervention with health, mental health, substance misuse, or domestic violence. Foster placement may also affect older siblings, such as adolescent siblings who are struggling to develop an identity apart from the family yet are still very dependent on and identified with that disrupted family unit. The placement of a child in foster care may also impact extended family, for example, grandparents who must deal with their own child's struggles, such as addiction, violence, poverty, and failure as a parent. Grandparents may also be called upon to help raise their grandchild at a time in life when they are anticipating retirement. The issue of an individual child placed in foster care also impacts multiple systems, including families, schools, and communities: the child may need to change schools in midyear, or go to live in another community.

In addition, any of the issues discussed in this book can affect an individual at varying levels of context. In the case of Sarah (the focal system), she was affected by her strong physical and mental health, the microsystem (e.g., her foster parents built a positive and supportive relationship with her), the mesosystem (e.g., her social worker and foster parents built relationships with one another to support Sarah), the exosystem (e.g., Sarah's foster father's employer encouraged him to take family time from work to help his new foster child adjust to her new home), and the macrosystem (e.g., social workers advocated policy changes to facilitate adequate health and mental health funding for foster children and substance misuse intervention for their biological parents).

SOCIAL WORK ISSUES AFFECT INDIVIDUALS ACROSS THE LIFE SPAN

For the purposes of analysis, we have presented in-depth discussions of specific social work issues at various phases of the life span. Many of these and other issues addressed by social workers, however, affect individuals throughout the life span. Adults organize attachment relationships with aging parents, partners, spouses, close friends, and children throughout their lives. Similarly, issues of spirituality, relationships with individuals further along in life (mentors), mental and physical illness, and even death can occur at any point in the life span.

The issues of poverty, substance misuse, and violence presented throughout the book in boxes illustrate how social work issues affect individuals and communities over time. Poverty affects individuals from conception to death. A pregnant woman's poverty can undermine her prenatal care. The location of prenatal clinics, availability of transportation, work requirements, and fear of losing a job for taking time off can prevent low-income mothers from using free or nearly free prenatal care. In infancy and early childhood, poverty can impact low-income mothers' access to health care and high-quality day care.

By middle childhood, poverty can impact schooling. School funding is often based on property taxes; therefore, middle-income districts can receive a greater amount of discretionary school funding than low-income districts. Some states and local governments do not support preschool or require kindergarten attendance. This may result in children from poorer neighborhoods entering first grade unprepared and unaware of how to fit into the classroom. Children growing up in poverty-stricken areas may have few role models who were successful in school, and parents may lack the experience and skills to teach children effective study skills. The interactions of poor school preparation, large chaotic classrooms, ineffective home study supervision, a need to earn money, and a neighborhood culture of academic underachievement can push all but the most exceptional children out of school.

Poverty also affects the development of adults. Young adults who have grown up in low-income families and failed to succeed in school may see little hope of working their way into the middle class and be more easily recruited into crime or use of street drugs and alcohol. Some young women from low-income families believe that marriage, especially a lasting marriage, may never be obtained. In order to maintain a sense of family and purpose, some young women who live in poverty choose to have children outside of traditional marriage. Children may be highly valued and represent a cultural and life goal that can be achieved.

Older low-income adults often lack critical medical care, proper nutrition, and social support. Without financial security, aging people can become isolated and forgotten. As illustrated in the chapter on older adults, far too many individuals, particularly people of color, are forced to continue working even though they are in poor health, or to survive on Social Security alone. Because of our Western idealization of youth, many older people have difficulty finding employment and experience a devaluation of their life experience. Illness for the aged person can be extremely frightening. Not only is death near, but inability to recover from illness may force the older adult into a nursing home. Because nursing homes are rarely fully funded by private or public health insurance, older adults fear that a lengthy nursing home stay will deplete their life savings.

A GLOBAL PERSPECTIVE IS NECESSARY TO SOCIAL WORK IN THE TWENTY-FIRST CENTURY

The main focus of this book has been on social work in the United States. As the world grows smaller, social workers and social agencies must become more globally minded and responsive—world poverty, for instance, can no longer be overlooked. Because the poorest nations are unable to compete in world markets, their governments and health organizations are unable to cope with epidemics of HIV-AIDS, tuberculosis, and other diseases. As social workers, we are concerned because a substantial number of human beings are living in substandard conditions and dying unnecessarily.

From a self-survival perspective, world poverty is a threat to industrialized nations. Revolutions, terrorism, and disease grow as desperation and hopelessness increase. The resettlement of refugees and increased illegal immigration expose citizens of industrialized nations to new and old communicable diseases. Simplistic policies such as closing borders or not aiding politically oppressed and impoverished immigrants are bound to fail. Unless world poverty is attacked in an organized global manner, Western nations will continue to experience an increase in illegal immigration and terrorist violence. Social workers must prepare to work more closely with relief organizations, refugee programs, and legal and illegal immigrants.

Glossary

Acculturation The process of learning the language, values, and social competencies that are beneficial for functioning in the mainstream society.

Acquisition The developmental process through which an individual actively interprets, responds to, and ultimately embraces, rejects, or elaborates upon the social patterns to which the individual is exposed.

Affirmative action Positive steps taken to increase representation of women and people of color in employment, education, and business.

Alzheimer's disease The most common and well-known type of dementia. It is characterized by progressive impairment of memory and cognitive function and may lead to a completely vegetative state and death after anywhere from three to twenty years.

Amygdala A part of the brain; involved in producing and controlling emotion.

Anomia Impaired comprehension in which the principal deficit is inability to name persons and objects seen, heard, or felt. It results from lesions in various portions of the language area of the brain.

Anorexia nervosa A mental illness in which individuals starve themselves. It can be fatal.

Antimiscegenation Prejudice against the "mixing" of the races.

Assimilation One outcome of acculturation, in which the ancestral culture is largely replaced with that of the host culture.

Attachment Close, enduring, affective bonds that develop throughout the life span, for example, between infants and their caregivers.

Attention deficit with hyperactivity disorder (ADHD) A behavioral syndrome consisting of short attention span, hyperkinetic physical behavior, and learning problems. Attention deficit disorder (ADD) presents without hyperkinetic physical behavior.

Attrition The problem of participants dropping out of studies. It may limit the confidence researchers have in the inferences they draw from their studies. It is a particular challenge to longitudinal research and research involving vulnerable populations.

Autism spectrum disorder Autism is a neurological disorder characterized by abnormal development of social skills and verbal and nonverbal communication. There is variation in the extent of individuals' impairments. Affected individuals may follow rigid rituals, have a narrow range of interests and activities, appear unable to understand others' feelings, and become upset with any changes in their environment.

Axon An elongated fiber that projects from the body of the neuron, typically, conducting electrical impulses away from the neuron.

Behavior modification The use of operant conditioning models (i.e., positive and negative reinforcement) to change behavior.

Behavior therapy The use of learning theory principles to modify behavior.

Bio-psycho-social-spiritual perspective An interdisciplinary framework embraced by social work that focuses on the well-being of the whole person physically, mentally, socially, and spiritually.

Bipolar disorder A psychiatric disorder characterized by episodes of mania, when individuals experience unusually high levels of exuberance, grandiosity, feelings of invulnerability, and extremely fast thinking; alternates with episodes of depression.

Cerebral cortex The folded, grooved, outer layer of the brain, sometimes referred to as the "gray matter."

Cerebral palsy A nonprogressive, noncontagious motor condition that causes physical disability in human development.

Chaos theory Field of mathematics characterizing the behavior of dynamic systems. It has broad applications, including biological and social systems.

Child welfare The government-organized, formal service-delivery system designed to assist children of all ages who have been abused or neglected, or whose well-being is at risk.

Classical conditioning The learning process by which an organism makes a connection between a neutral stimulus (such as a sound) when paired with an unconditioned stimulus (such as food) that results in an unconditioned response (such as salivation).

Clinical assumption Part of the assessment process in which certain facts are accepted with little or no challenge.

Clinical hypothesis Part of the assessment process that explains an observed behavior, problem, or social interaction.

Code of ethics The most visible compilation of the profession's ethical standards, for example the National Association of Social Workers' Code of Ethics.

Code switching A process by which individuals change features of their language, including phonology, grammar, and pragmatics, in relation to social and cultural context.

Cognitive development Intellectual growth.

Cohort effects Effects in research resulting from shared experiences of a group of individuals, for example, children born during the Great Depression.

Computerized axial tomography (CAT or CT scan). An imaging process that turns multiple X-ray images of a selected body area into high-contrast pictures. These scans provide sharper resolution of soft tissue than routine X-rays.

Constructivist theories of human development Developmental perspective that emphasizes the mutual impact of biological and psychological factors, as well as the individual's active role in shaping or constructing his or her own reality. This perspective is illustrated in the theory and research of Jean Piaget.

Contextual validity In the context of clinical assessments, the appropriateness of a clinical hypothesis drawn, in part, from theory, to the individual case under analysis. In the context of research, the appropriateness of the research methods to the sociocultural context under study.

Council on Social Work Education (CSWE) An organization established in 1946 for the purpose of accreditation, which involves monitoring the performance of social work educational programs to deliver high-quality standardized curriculum.

Crisis nursery services Provision of temporary emergency care for children.

Critical realism The philosopical perspective that there is an objective social world independent of our minds, but our biased perspectives limit our ability to perceive that reality.

Cross-sectional design A research design that makes inferences about change through examining individuals of varying ages or experiences at one point in time.

Culture The physical objects, activities, values, and patterns of living and meaning that are shaped by the experiences of earlier generations and elaborated by later generations.

Dementia An umbrella term that covers a group of diseases that affect the brain in middle to late adult life. It is characterized by a progressive loss of cognitive and intellectual functions, which includes the diminishing of short-term memory, judgment, and language.

Depression In psychiatry, a mood disorder in which the individual experiences persistent sadness that impairs functioning.

Developmental, ecological-systems theory The analytic perspective that examines biological, psychological, and social characteristics of the individual as they are shaped over time within sociocultural and historical contexts. It is related to the theory and research of Urie Bronfenbrenner.

Developmental relationship A relationship where a mentor's goals and expectations vary over time in relation to an adolescent's changing needs.

Disorganized attachment A type of attachment relationship in which children do not use caregivers as a secure base or employ any other coherent behavioral strategy to cope with stress. Rather, they show a range of responses to the "strange situation" procedure that are atypical of children in secure or insecure attachment relationships.

Dissociation An altered state of consciousness in which integration of psychological functioning is disrupted. It may be a response to anxiety or trauma.

Domestic violence Deliberate harming of a family member or intimate partner through physical, emotional, or sexual abuse.

Down syndrome A condition associated with cognitive impairment, short stature, and particular facial features due to the presence of an extra twenty-first chromosome.

Dual relationship Occurs when a professional has multiple roles in a client's life. Problematic if the focus of the helping relationship shifts from the client's to the professional's needs.

Echolalia A neurological disorder characterized by a person's involuntary, parrotlike repetition of words spoken by another person.

Ecology The branch of science that deals with the interrelations of organisms with their environment.

Ethnicity Membership in a group that shares a common ancestral heritage based on nationality and culture.

Ethnography The branch of anthropology that studies the beliefs, values, and practices of a specific social or cultural group within the cultural context. Ethnographic methods include interviews, direct observation, and review of records such as local newspapers and historical sources.

Evidence-based practice Using the best available empirical evidence in conjunction with the practitioner's knowledge of the context and client preferences in clinical decision making.

Exosystem From an ecological perspective, the level of context that consists of one or more settings that do not involve the person as an active participant, but in which events occur that do affect the person.

Experience-dependent developmental process A developmental process that makes adaptive use of experience that can be "expected" at a particular time and in adequate quality for nearly all juveniles of a species, for example, visual stimulation and social contact. Experiences that are impoverished or distorted can have lasting detrimental effects on brain development.

Experience-expectant developmental process A developmental process encompassing several forms of lifelong neural plasticity that allow for some modification of earlier brain development, for example, learning of particular vocabulary, spatial information, and social relationships. It occurs through new synaptic connections.

Experimental design A research design involving the deliberate manipulation of variables to observe their effects, that is, to establish causality. It includes random assignment of units (e.g., people) to one of at least two groups.

Fictive kin Individuals not related by birth or marriage with whom one has emotionally significant relationships and treats as family. This term emerged during slavery times and continues in use today.

Focal system The analytic vantage point of the ecological analysis, the perspective from which related systems are viewed (microsystems, mesosystems, exosystems, macrosystems).

Folk theory Informal understanding of human behavior and development. The theory includes values, beliefs, and explanations for how the social world works that are acquired within the family and community.

Frontal lobes A part of the brain; involved in planning, movement, and some memory.

Functional magnetic resonance imaging (fMRI) A process for studying brain (or other internal organ) functioning by measuring the response of hydrogen nuclei to changes in magnetic fields. It can produce a three-dimensional picture of any internal organ.

Gender identity One's self-perception as male, female, or in between.

Gender-sensitive issue An experience that only or more frequently affects one gender, for example, pregnancy and sexual assault.

Gender wage gap Payment of lower wages to women than men when they do the same or equivalent jobs.

Hippocampus A part of the brain; involved in memory and deciding which environmental events require immediate attention.

Hostile environment sexual harassment Harassment that occurs when an employee fears going to work because of the sexually offensive, intimidating, or oppressive atmosphere generated by the harasser. This activity is illegal in the United States.

Human development The sequence of changes that begins after conception and continues throughout life.

Individual education plan (IEP) A formal plan to address difficulties a student may be experiencing in school.

Information processing A computer metaphor used to explain how humans process, store, and retrieve information.

Informed consent An agreement to participate in research. It is based on voluntary participation, consent that may be withdrawn at any time, knowledge of any risks and benefits of participation, confidentiality of individual responses, and knowledge of what participation will entail.

Insecure/avoidant attachment A type of relationship reflected in the "strange situation" procedure in which infants remain more distant from their caregivers in times of stress than securely attached infants do.

Insecure/resistant attachment A type of relationship reflected in the "strange situation" procedure in which infants expend relatively more energy than do securely attached infants in monitoring the whereabouts of their caregivers, but are not readily comforted by their nearness.

Institutional racism Social policies and institutional practices that place nonwhite racial groups at a disadvantage.

Internalized racism Racist ideologies internalized and socialized by people of color.

Interpretive perspectives A philosophical position that there are multiple legitimate perspectives on the social world.

Intersectionality A sociological concept referring to the multifaceted nature of personal and social identities, for example, as black and female.

Learning disorder/disability/difference Neurologically based substandard cognitive functioning, which can challenge learning in certain contexts, especially school, for individuals with average to above-average intelligence.

Learning theory An explanation of behavioral changes as a result of experiencing the positive and negative consequences of behavior, as well as observing and imitating others. The theory is associated with the research of B. F. Skinner and John B. Watson.

Longitudinal design A design that follows the same individuals over time. It is associated with research in human development.

Macrochronological system From an ecological perspective, the level of context consisting of historical times and events.

Macrosystem From an ecological perspective, the level of context that consists of the cultural patterns of the larger society in which other systems are embedded. It includes widespread societal values such as individual freedom, major institutions such as government and education, and economic structures.

Magnetic resonance imaging (MRI) A medical imaging technique that uses a strong magnet to visualize in detail internal structures of the body, including the brain.

Major depression A biochemical mental disorder characterized by sustained depression of mood, sleep and appetite disturbances, and feelings of guilt, worthlessness, and hopelessness. Precipitating life events do not adequately account for the degree of depression. It may occur at any age, tends to recur throughout life, and is biologically based (family history). Major depression usually responds to antidepressants or electroconvulsive therapy.

Manic depression See bipolar disorder.

Medical social work A specialization that focuses on the impact of disease and disability on individuals of all ages, their families, and communities.

Menopause The permanent cessation of ovulation and menstruation. Because of a decrease in ovarian function, the menopausal woman has not experienced a period for at least one year and can no longer become pregnant.

Mentor An older, more experienced adult who has a relationship with an unrelated younger person in which the adult provides ongoing guidance, instruction, and encouragement.

Meritocracy The myth that rewards are based on hard work, achievement, and motivation. It does not recognize that rewards also are given for unearned privileges.

Mesosystem From an ecological perspective, the level of context that consists of the set of interrelationships between two or more microsystems.

Microsystem From an ecological perspective, the level of context that consists of the immediate social environment, the day-to-day reality of the focal system, which includes those settings in which people have face-to-face, sustained, and significant relationships with others, such as families, peer groups, schools, workplaces, and churches.

Mixed-method research Research combining quantitative and qualitative methods.

Mutism Organic or functional absence of the faculty of speech. It may indicate trauma or stress.

Myelinization A process where myelin, a fatty substance, sheathes axons. Myelin protects and assists electrical impulses in propagating rapidly along the axon.

Myoclonus Sudden, uncontrolled muscle contractions causing a jerking motion, often of the legs.

Neuron Nerve cell; the basic unit of the nervous system.

Neurotransmitter Any specific chemical agent present at synapses or neuromuscular junctions that is capable of transmitting an electrical impulse by binding to its cognate receptor, thus enabling communication between brain cells.

Nonprobability sampling Techniques for drawing a sample that do not reflect probability theory, for example, selecting key individuals because of their experience or perspective on a topic. This sampling technique is associated with qualitative research.

Observational research design A design that does not involve the active manipulation of variables. It is often used in descriptive and qualitative research.

Occipital lobes A part of the brain; primarily responsible for vision and visual associations.

Occupational segregation The concentration of men and women in different occupations. "Men's jobs" typically earn more money and prestige even if they do not require more education or have more intrinsic value.

Operant conditioning Changes in behavior shaped by the consequences of that behavior.

Oral history Historical information that is collected during interviews of individuals who have led significant lives.

Palilalia Neurological deterioration that results in a person's repeating over and over his or her own words.

Parietal lobes A part of the brain; controls language comprehension, spatial orientation and perception, and sense of touch.

Physical ecology Physical characteristics of the environment. They include climate, plant and animal life, and human artifacts.

Plasticity In neuroscience, brain changes resulting from social, educational, and treatment experiences.

Positron emission tomography (PET) A process for studying the brain by observing its activity. It produces computer images of metabolism of oxygen and glucose after the individual is injected with low dosage of radioactive substance.

Postpositivist Philosophical perspective that there is an objective social world existing independently of our minds.

Post-traumatic stress disorder (PTSD) A severe anxiety disorder that develops after exposure to a traumatic event such as war or a serious accident.

Prefrontal cortex The anterior portion of each cerebral hemisphere of the brain. Its functions include emotion, imagining, controlling attention, memory, forming explicit plans, and making decisions.

Prejudice Preconceived ideas based on limited information and stereotypes.

Prescriptive relationship A relationship between an adult and a young person, in which adults rather than the youth prioritize their goals for the mentoring relationship and set the goals and ground rules for the relationship.

Pretend play A form of play associated with early childhood, in which actions, objects, and persons are transformed or treated nonliterally.

Probability sampling A sampling method that takes a subset of units (e.g., people) from the larger population. It relies on random or chance selection of units each of which has a known probability of inclusion.

Puberty Biological changes during adolescence that result in sexual maturity and adult stature.

Punishment From the perspective of learning theory, the consequences of behavior that reduce the probability that the behavior will reoccur.

Purposive sampling A sampling technique by which key individuals are selected for a purpose, for example, to reflect a variety of experiences or because of their knowledge of the issues under study. It is associated with qualitative research.

Qualitative research A research tradition focused on understanding human meaning, beliefs, perspectives, and experiences.

Quasi-experimental design A design used to establish causality in the absence of random assignment to experimental and control groups. Design manipulations are intended to rule out plausible alternative explanations for any observed differences between groups.

Quid pro quo sexual harassment Harassment that results in a tangible loss because of an employee's refusal of unwanted sexual advances from those in positions of power, such as a supervisor. This activity is illegal in the United States.

Racism A hierarchical system of advantages based on race.

Reactive depression A "secondary" depression that occurs in response to real-life events, such as grief, illness, loss of job, and family problems. It is characterized by depression, anxiety, bodily complaints, tension, and guilt. It may disappear spontaneously or in response to a variety of ministrations.

Reinforcement (rewards) From the perspective of learning theory, the consequences of behavior that increase the probability that the behavior will reoccur.

Religion A system of symbols, beliefs, rituals, and texts shared by a community of believers. It provides a collective framework for expressing spirituality.

Religiosity Spiritual and/or religious involvement, for example, church attendance.

Representative sample A subset of units (e.g., people) drawn from a larger population that reflects the characteristics of that larger population.

Resilience The ability of people to find meaning in their lives even in the face of extraordinary hardship.

Schizophrenia A neuropsychiatric disorder characterized by abnormalities of perception, content of thought, and thought processes (hallucinations and delusions), and by extensive withdrawal of interest from other people and the outside world, with excessive focusing on one's own mental life.

School social work A social work specialization that blends the fields of social work and education to support the well-being and academic achievement of children and youth in schools.

Secondary trauma Guilt, overwhelming emotions, rescue motifs, nightmares, social isolation, and persistent sadness experienced from exposure to the trauma of others.

Securely attached A type of relationship assessed in the "strange situation" procedure in which children use caregivers as secure bases to which they may return in times of stress.

Self-report The systematic collection of individuals' reports of their own behavior or psychological processes.

Social developmental study A report by a school social worker that considers a child's developmental history in context, including prenatal and family history.

Social ecology The range of situations in which people interact, including the people with whom they interact, roles they play, what they do together, how they interact, and the dynamics of social groups.

Socialization The process by which experts structure the social environment and display patterned meanings for the novice; for example, parents teach children.

Social learning theory A framework designed to explain how learning occurs when we observe and imitate or model others. The theory is associated with the research of Albert Bandura.

Social science theory Formal, explicit framework designed to understand, explain, and predict the social world. Such a theory is developed through empirical research and logic.

Sociocultural-historical theories of human development The theoretical framework that views the cultural and historical context as a critical third factor in development through which biology and experience interact. This perspective is illustrated in the theory and research of Lev Vygotsky.

Spirituality The direct personal experience of the sacred; awareness of a higher power, a causal force beyond the material or rational, that operates in all aspects of existence.

Strange situation A procedure designed by Mary Ainsworth to evaluate young children's responses to a friendly female stranger in the company of their mothers, when they are left alone, and when they are reunited with their mothers. It allows observation of parent-child interaction during gradually escalating, low-level, relatively common, and nontraumatic stressors.

Strengths-based practice A perspective in social work that emphasizes the utilization of clients' strengths and resources in addressing problems.

Synapse The functional membrane-to-membrane contact of the nerve cell with another nerve cell; the connection between neurons.

Systematic observations of behavior A research method that involves the direct observation of the behavior of interest, for example, parenting practices, often through videotaping or audiotaping. The observations may occur in the real-world settings of participants' lives, or in more structured settings.

Systems theory An interdisciplinary study of the characteristics of interacting components of a whole unit, such as an individual, family, or society, as well as that unit with other units.

Temporal lobe A part of the brain; contains structures involved in the processing of auditory information, memory. and emotion.

Teratogen A drug or other external agent, for example, a chemical, virus, or ionizing radiation, that interrupts or alters the normal development of a fetus, with results that are evident at birth.

Transdisciplinary research team A team of scholars with specializations ranging from the biological to the social sciences, who work together to solve complex problems.

White privilege Unearned advantages, entitlements, immunities, and dominance of individuals considered to be "white" at the expense of people of color.

Working model In attachment theory, a mental representation of close relationships and their characteristics, meaning, and value.

Zone of proximal development The context in which individuals function at a higher level with the support of a more experienced individual than they could function independently. Central to the developmental theory of Lev Vygotsky.

Index

About the Authors

Wendy L. Haight (PhD, University of Chicago) is professor and Gamble-Skogmo Chair in Child Welfare and Youth Policy, University of Minnesota, Twin Cities Campus. Professor Haight's research focuses on vulnerable families involved with the public child welfare system. She is a leader in bringing diverse sociocultural perspectives to the study of children's lives so that social workers, policy makers, and others charged with improving child welfare can make use of this critically important information. She is known for her methodological versatility and sophistication. The overarching commitment across her career is building a more culture-inclusive understanding of diverse children's development and welfare. This has required engaging with a variety of perspectives and scrutinizing "mainstream" North American assumptions that undergird so much research in human development and child welfare. She is the author or coauthor of eight books and over fifty journal articles and chapters. Her books include: *Pretending at Home: Early Development in a Sociocultural Context, African American Children at Church, Raise Up a Child: Human Development in an African-American Family, Children of Methamphetamine-Involved Families: The Case of Rural Illinois,* and *Child Welfare and Development: A Japanese Case Study*.

Edward H. Taylor (MSW, University of Denver; PhD, University of Southern California, Los Angeles) is associate professor and director of the University of British Columbia–Okanagan School of Social Work. Previously he served as associate professor in the School of Social Work at the University of Minnesota, Twin Cities Campus; chief of social work for the Department of Psychiatry, University of North Carolina; and clinical social worker and researcher with the National Institute of Mental Health, Intramural Research Program. Throughout his career, Professor Taylor has specialized in assessing, treating, and researching children and young adults with severe mental disorders. He is coauthor of *Schizophrenia and Manic Depressive Disorder* and author of the *Atlas of Bipolar Disorders*.